Richard Wagner

Richard Wagner

The Last of the Titans

Joachim Köhler

Translated by Stewart Spencer

Yale University Press
New Haven and London

For information about this and other Yale University Press publications, please contact:
U.S. Office: sales.press@yale.edu   yalebooks.com
Europe Office: sales@yaleup.co.uk   www.yalebooks.co.uk

Set in Minion by Northern Phototypesetting Co. Ltd, Bolton, Lancs
Printed in the United Kingdom at the University Press, Cambridge

ISBN 0–300–10422–7

Library of Congress Catalog Control Number 2004110664

A catalogue record for this book is available from the British Library.

He cursed humanity for refusing to see that he was a Titan and that Titans should not be measured by ordinary standards

Marie von Wittgenstein

Contents

Illustrations

All illustrations courtesy of the author.

Preface

Few men can have cut as distinctive a figure as Wagner did when he set foot on the stage of history: a little man with a large head, as extravagantly dressed as the last of the tribunes and, like Rienzi, fired by an abiding belief in his mission to redeem the world – a little man with a theatrical streak and a need for attention that has been more than fully satisfied.

Who was this Wagner with his old-fashioned velvet beret, his hypnotic effect on others and his continuing ability, after more than one hundred and fifty years, to unsettle society – not just its musically susceptible members but non-musicians, too, raising their feelings to fever pitch and causing tormenting disquiet? A man like any other, driven by instincts only dimly perceived? A monstrous and misanthropic genius? A bringer of light chained to the rock of his own boundless imagination?

This is a question that was also asked by Wagner's friend and father-in-law Franz Liszt. Who was this 'incomprehensible' man, as he called him, a man who left no one who came into contact with him unchanged, penetrating deep into the soul of all for whom knowing Wagner was both a privilege and a curse?

Liszt's own answer was a wonderfully ambiguous image, comparing Wagner to a high mountain whose summit shone in the sunlight while it remained shrouded in impenetrable mists from the shoulders downwards. His alpine metaphor was not only intended to draw attention to the relative sizes of this diminutive man and the rest of humanity, it also describes Wagner's dubious relations with his fellow men and women: while his art cast its light far into the future, the ground all around him remained shrouded in darkness thanks to misfortunes that in Liszt's view were of his own making.

There was nothing more terrible, thought Liszt's eldest daughter Blandine, than to see such a genius locked in constant combat with the common obstacles of life. For her, Wagner – with whom she was in love – was like Gulliver enmeshed in the thousand and one little threads of the Lilliputians.[1] In short, he was like a bound giant, a Prometheus hoping all his life that he would be freed. But freed from what? If we may believe Liszt, the mountain had only itself to blame for veiling itself in mist: the Titan was caught in fetters of his own devising. The light that he brought was as inextricable a part of him as his perpetual debts and quarrels and scandals.

Blandine's husband was the French lawyer Émile Ollivier, and Ollivier, too, had looked this bundle of contradictions in the eye: Wagner's gaze, he reports, was deep and sombre, pensive and gentle, but it could also be piercing and spiteful. Above his eyes, his domed forehead betokened 'a vast ideality', whereas beneath them his lips were often enough contorted in a sarcastic grin. His pinched mouth was offset by a prominent chin that 'seemed to express the threat of a conquering will'. To Ollivier, the Saxon composer was a mixture of prophet and prankster.[2]

Another of Wagner's French champions formed an equally ambiguous impression: to keep looking at Wagner's head, wrote Édouard Schuré, was to see at one moment the full face of Faust and at the next the profile of Mephistopheles.[3] In short, the Master was capable, if need be, of performing the world drama on his own. And so he did. In his own theatre, Wagner played all the parts himself, both on and off the stage. When he turned to face reality, he seemed to be staring at himself as though in a mirror. His Janus-faced ambiguity was no secret to Wagner himself, of course: 'I am a mixture of Hamlet and Don Quixote,' he once confided to his second wife.[4] Both these characters were destroyed by their own inner contradictions, increasing Wagner's own chances of being destroyed in turn.

Even in death he insisted on being different. In accordance with his wishes he was buried in the garden behind his house. His contradictions were buried with him. While a heavy granite slab was placed over the truth, above it memory erected the effigy of the spotless idol of a religion of art. Where Wagner had once walked on earth, Bayreuth and its festival blossomed. The Master and the operatic enterprise of his final years were confidently declared a single entity. All that consorted ill with Bayreuth's corporate identity was ruthlessly erased, including those aspects of Wagner that refused to be annexed in this way.

True, he had dreamt of a festival along the lines of an Athenian tragedy and, with a tenacious instinct for power, forced his age to build him a theatre for it. But when the theatre finally stood there on Bayreuth's Green Hill, he no longer recognized his vision. Here the very kind of opera house that he had been at such pains to overcome was galvanized back into life. The old society that he hated basked in the radiance of his music. Even his life's work, the *Ring*, seemed unperformable and a failure. There were times when he wanted to burn down the theatre or, so that it would not all have been in vain, to sell it, together with his works, to the Jewish impresario Angelo Neumann.

It was Cosima who, in the face of Wagner's resistance, succeeded in saving Bayreuth. The property that had paralyzed her husband formed the basis of the family fortune, and the dramas in which he conjured up his vision of a new humanity now became the focus of a cult that she organized along the lines of a religious order, with herself as its self-appointed high priestess – never in his wildest dreams could Wagner himself have imagined that his wife would continue his life's work. But she replaced him so effectively that, to quote Felix Weingartner, it seemed 'as though he had never walked on earth in human form'.[5] His spirit, she claimed, had entered into her to such an extent that for years she did not even need to utter her husband's name.

This equation of Wagner with his legacy, assiduously promoted by Cosima, became the cornerstone of the Bayreuth enterprise. In turn, this led to a misunderstanding of both Wagner's personality and his works that continues virtually unnoticed to this day, with the last ten years of his life eclipsing and colouring our perception of the previous sixty. It was not the radical change that he himself had hoped for that formed the nucleus of this new world view but Cosima's religious needs. Bayreuth's long shadow plunged the iridescent kaleidoscope of his colourful existence into a uniform granite grey.

Did life exist before Cosima? The principal sources of Wagner's life – his memoirs and her diaries – were either dictated to or written by her, with the result that his life as a Hoffmannesque artist acquired a certain bourgeois stolidity. The biographical tradition that his wife summoned into existence was concerned not with the attempts to understand the world from a philosophical point of view with which Wagner had wrestled all his life but with establishing a canon of doctrinal beliefs. Brought up in Paris, Cosima promulgated her glad tidings with what Ernest Newman described as Jesuitical calculation, adopting the motto 'Cherchez le Juif'. In other words: 'The Jews are to blame for everything.' Historical truth was a matter of supreme indifference to her.

Long before scholars could gain access to them, the sources had twice been subjected to the censor's red pencil. Even Wagner himself had – not unsurprisingly – doctored his own reminiscences, glossing over embarrassing details and busily turning himself, quite literally, into a legend in his own lifetime. 'In view of the countless ways in which Wagner, in his campaign of mystification, manipulated the facts, it is sometimes tempting not to believe a single one of his remarks', sigh the editors of the new collected edition of his works.[6] Following in her husband's footsteps, Cosima continued the task of rewriting history, evincing a thoroughness that in other contexts would be considered commendable and purging Wagner's past of all that failed to reflect the sublime image of the Master that she was at such pains to promote. There were times when this process resembled an exorcism, so that the great love affairs to which he owed much of his inspiration were dismissed as fevered fantasies (a deception at which he himself connived), while his revolutionary activities were downgraded to the level of a daydreamer's idle imaginings. Documents that gave the lie to Cosima's fabrications were ruthlessly destroyed. By her own admission, she had no hesitation in burning 'almost all the letters from Wagner's friends and contemporaries', an act of barbarism to which she was more than happy to confess.[7]

Even Cosima's own correspondence with the Master fell prey to this auto-da-fé, presumably because, like the hundreds of incinerated letters from Heine, Baudelaire, Berlioz, Nietzsche, Mathilde Wesendonck, Semper, Gobineau and Hans von Bülow, it would have endangered the image of the canonized composer that Wahnfried was currently propagating. Long regarded as a self-sacrificial saint, Cosima was a genius at manipulation, and whereas her husband's final years had been overshadowed by illness and depression, in death she presented him to the German nation as a radiant redeemer and a beacon of light.

In this way an artist torn apart by inner contradictions became the nation's unifying saviour. And, just as Cosima usurped the dead composer for the purposes of her own private cult, so this private religion was effortlessly assimilated by the German national movement. Its leader could appeal to Wagner with a clear conscience: the Master had 'forged the sword' with which the NSDAP fought. But the idol that was worshipped by this Austrian Wagnerite, allowing him to turn himself into 'Wagner's Hitler',[8] was in fact Cosima's Wagner. It was Bayreuth's well-oiled publicity machine that transformed the composer's random ideas into a powerful ideology.

Even while he was still alive, a dedicated band of scholars had been formed with the aim of researching Wagner's life and works, cataloguing his activities with encyclopedic zeal and interpreting them in a spirit of public enterprise. Established by Cosima, this tradition can now look back on more than one hundred and thirty years of fruitful endeavour, extending as it does from Wagner's first official biographer, Carl Friedrich Glasenapp, to Houston Stewart Chamberlain, Curt von Westernhagen, Martin Gregor-Dellin and, among the current generation, Udo Bermbach and Dieter Borchmeyer. A whole host of tame authors could always be assured of Wahnfried's sympathetic ear, which in turn guaranteed them a widespread public impact.

As a branch of research, it is certainly unique, and there is no denying the debt that other scholars owe to it, but it is impossible to overlook its basic dilemma, which is that these researchers have all been writing about Wagner with the Wagners' blessing. Scholars who conduct their research in Bayreuth are dependent on the agreement of their hosts. They claim to be above all that is going on around them, while sensing that the Wagners are looking over their shoulder. In return for a fee and free tickets, these scholars publish their findings in the programme booklets that the festival uses to celebrate its own existence. Content with the material graciously made available to them, they say nothing about the documents to which they are denied access for whatever reason the festival cares to give. In much the same way, the festival continues even now to draw a veil of silence over the disappearance of the correspondence of Winifred, Wieland and Wolfgang Wagner with Hitler.

This 'prestabilized harmony'[9] between Bayreuth and its researchers means that both parties have flourished. When it was politically expedient for Bayreuth to highlight Wagner's pre-National Socialist thinking, scholars were ready to oblige. Following Hitler's downfall, when Bayreuth's very survival was at stake, they were just as vocal in denying that such ideas had ever existed. A number of writers have even managed to express both points of view with equal enthusiasm.

In this way, the voluminous literature on Wagner has continued to grow in a state of self-imposed dependency. It is only in recent decades that a number of individual scholars have begun to break free from Bayreuth's loving embrace. Independent researchers such as Robert Gutman, Michael Karbaum, John Deathridge, Barry Millington and Egon Voss have brought light to the mists of Bayreuth. The present author, too, has devoted two studies to suppressed aspects of Wagner: *Nietzsche and Wagner*, which appeared in English in 1998, throws light on Bayreuth's influence on Nietzsche and his 'will to power'; and *Wagner's Hitler*, first published in English in 2000, describes his influence on the world-view of the Third Reich.

Needless to say, this has not altered Bayreuth's special status, a status inextricably linked with the public family rows and scandals that have been its birthright since Cosima's day. Even now, Wagner continues to resemble the strangely deceptive mountain with which Franz Liszt once compared him, enshrouded in gloom, overshadowed by the distinctly dubious enterprise that bears his name, hidden beneath the voluntary self-restraint of researchers and forgotten by the music lovers who are content to bask in the summit's sun-drenched radiance.

My thanks go to Stewart Spencer for his translation and many improvements owing to his expertise on Wagner. Also an expert in this field, Barry Millington was generous enough to read through the translation and suggest a number of changes, for which I am grateful. Robert Baldock of Yale University Press has already earned my thanks by superintending the English-language editions of *Nietzsche and Wagner* and *Zarathustra's Secret*. I am further in his debt for commissioning the present translation.

1 Origins

Rosine and her Prince

Was there life before Wagner? For his mother, there certainly was, except that her past remained obscure. The events in question took place before her great son was born and even he, with all his genius for the theatre, suspected nothing, for all that her early life might have afforded him the material for a genuine German tragedy.

These events unfolded in the immediate vicinity of the Weimar court, where the poet in residence was none other than Johann Wolfgang von Goethe. The main role was taken by a prince who, as in the fairytale, freed his princess from the hands of a wicked stepmother. Or, according to an alternative reading, he merely seduced a young woman, then hid her away in a secret place where he could have his way with her whenever he wanted. The victim – little more than a child – pined away with longing, while her fairytale lover stayed away. This picaresque tragedy came to a premature end when the carefree princeling died and his mistress was left with no means to support herself, stranded in a large town and virtually abandoned in the gutter. The curtain came down on this tale of lost innocence even before the master of fully orchestrated tragedies had seen the light of the world.

The curtain was in fact the handiwork of the injured party herself, her concealment of the true facts of the matter proving so successful that not even her great son ever managed to see through its tissue of deception. Wagner's mother systematically removed all trace of the scandal that had uprooted her, even to the extent of falsifying her own name. She was called neither Perthes, as her children believed, nor Bertz, as Wagner's official biography claims. Nor were her parents mill owners but simple bakers, a fact not unknown in her home town of Weißenfels. Their real name was Pätz.

The daughter of the house, Johanna Rosine, was not born in 1778, as she herself claimed, but four years earlier – in the same year as that in which Goethe's *Die Leiden des jungen Werthers* was first published. Her mother died when she was fifteen and her father remarried. Daughter and stepmother evidently failed to get on, and within a year we find the former living under princely protection in the nearby city of Leipzig, where we then lose all trace of her for the next few years.

What had happened? A prince had appeared on the scene, or, rather, because this was Weißenfels, *the* prince – Constantin of Saxe-Weimar,[1] the brother of the reigning Duke Karl August and an officer in the nearby garrison town of Tiefurt. He had taken rooms in Weißenfels with the evident aim of deflouring the baker's daughter. Although he was sixteen years older than she was, he was still in good shape, had plenty of time on his hands and, like Rosine, clearly enjoyed the odd roll. Newly remarried, Rosine's father seems to have raised no objections to the prince's claims on his daughter. Perhaps the honest baker saw it as a great honour and may even have come to some small financial arrangement with her wealthy suitor. The bartered bride now severed for ever the bonds that had tied her to her family.

Needless to say, the prince never meant to marry a country wench like Johanna Rosine, who was intended merely to serve as his mistress. As she lacked everything that might have lent a certain spice to their relationship in the longer term, Constantin no doubt had her instructed in basic manners – always assuming that Frau Hesse, with whom she was lodged in the Brühl district of the city, was in any position to impart such knowledge. This, after all, was not an especially refined part of Leipzig, but was frequented by tradesmen, Jews and organ-grinders, who on the occasion of the city's regular fairs were joined by a large influx of visitors from the east. Frau Hesse, moreover, was the wife of a businessman teetering on the brink of bankruptcy and evidently hoped to earn a little on the side by keeping an open house. The absent Constantin was punctilious in paying her for the sixteen-year-old Johanna Rosine's board and education.

Her idol rarely appeared. He was not yet twenty when he embraced with open arms the career of an aristocratic philanderer in pursuit of perpetual variety. While briefly studying music and the theatre, he had devoted himself to a life of free love, fostering a meat-market economy by maintaining mistresses both at home and abroad. As a Saxon Don Juan, he professed openly to his weakness for the charms of the flesh, with no fewer than seven female friends in Tiefurt alone. In Weißenfels, too, Johanna Rosine was by no means the only working-class girl to grant the prince her favours. Local families clearly raised no objections when a real-life prince relieved them of the need to look after their own children. No doubt parents and children alike flattered themselves into thinking that they could hear the sound of wedding bells. The sufferings of the young girls do not seem to have come into it.

Prince Constantin died suddenly on a campaign in 1793, though not before Goethe had already joked that he was fit only to drag himself from whore to parade ground. He left behind him a far-flung harem of mistresses and an army of anonymous children. Johanna Rosine could make no claims on his family as she had no children to support. There followed a period of anxious waiting, at the end of which the ducal council, whose members included Goethe, granted her the sum of fifty thalers still due to her, with instructions that she be 'left to her fate'.

With her hopes now dashed, Johanna Rosine decided that, whatever fate may have had in store for her, she would put right past wrongs or, more simply, rewrite the past. Instead of pursuing her present course as Constantin's widowed favourite, thus adding insult to injury, she simply reinterpreted her relationship with the prince. The love nest under Frau Hesse's roof was transformed into a 'select seminary', while her late lover became a 'high-born fatherly friend' who, according to Wagner, was 'subsequently named as a Weimar prince'.

In this way, a new and fantastical perspective opened up. Unable to be her husband, the prince hovered over her second life as a secret father, allowing the little baker's daughter to move up in the world and become a prince's natural offspring. The play that had once been a tragedy now acquired a lighter touch, allowing Rosine's life to seem something of a success story. Although the truth was known in Weißenfels, all contact with the Pätzes had been broken off, allowing the legend to thrive for a whole century after Wagner's death.

Johanna Rosine's life as the prince's mistress ended in 1793. By the time she married a police registrar five years later she was already twenty-four and, to quote her son, 'no longer in the first flush of youth'. Presumably the man of her choice, the Leipzig-born Friedrich Wagner, believed the story of her blue blood and presumably he also assumed that she was younger than she was. Be that as it may, her education still proved embarrassingly deficient: she appeared to have heard of neither Goethe nor Schiller, leading her well-read husband to question the quality of the teaching at the 'seminary' that had proved so strangely hard to locate.

Yet he must have been attracted to her not only by her lively temperament and disarming quick-wittedness but more especially by the very mystery surrounding her background. They settled in the Brühl, not far from the school where she had boarded as a girl, and the marriage was soon blessed with children, eight of whom had already been born by the time the youngest, Richard, saw the light of the world in 1813. By now Johanna Rosine was thirty-eight. In a portrait painted by the Wagners' family friend, Ludwig Geyer, her youthful charms are still visible beneath her matron's bonnet, while her large eyes – inherited by her son – stare quizzically at the observer.[2]

The tragedy of rustic innocence betrayed and abandoned was not the only one to befall Wagner's mother, for a second one occurred shortly before his birth in 1813, no less dramatic than the first and, like its predecessor, no less shrouded in secrecy. Johanna Rosine loved not only her husband but, as her son was later to confirm, her husband's best friend, Ludwig Geyer. When Friedrich Wagner, emulating Prince Constantin, died suddenly at the age of only forty-three in November 1813, she lost little time in marrying the family friend, by whom she was in fact three months pregnant with Richard's younger sister by the time of the wedding.

This begs the question whether Wagner himself, born six months before Friedrich's death, was likewise the fruit of an adulterous union. Had Friedrich generously tolerated the liaison because, as his son once suggested, he had found a replacement elsewhere? Or – a more plausible explanation – had he simply been deceived by Johanna Rosine and his best friend? On Friedrich's death, Geyer stepped effortlessly into his predecessor's shoes, and it was not long before all memory of him had faded.

Who, then, was Wagner's father? Within two months of Richard's birth, his mother had left her husband and the rest of her children in order to travel to the Bohemian spa town of Teplitz, where Geyer was then staying and where the couple spent two weeks together at the same hotel. Did she have her youngest son with her? Did she urge her lover to acknowledge him as his own son? Whatever the answer, the child was not baptized until after her return to Leipzig: not quite three months after his birth he was christened Wilhelm Richard Wagner in the city's Thomaskirche. But no sooner had his official father died than the child was renamed Geyer, while the other members of the family retained their family name. Had the lovers agreed in Teplitz to pass Friedrich off as the child's father in order to spare his good name as police registrar, a deception that was no longer deemed necessary after his death?

Wagner himself spent his whole life puzzling the identity of his true father. His colleague and first biographer Carl Friedrich Glasenapp reports that he 'repeatedly expressed the possibility' that Geyer was his father.[3] It is no doubt out of mere piety that writers on Wagner have tended on the whole to resolve the paternity issue in favour of Friedrich Wagner, yet his oft-cited similarity to his eldest brother Albert, who was born long before Geyer appeared on the scene, must be set against the equally undeniable resemblance between Wagner and his younger sister Cäcilie, who was fathered after Friedrich's death.

It seems likely that Wagner was no more able to answer this question than Johanna Rosine herself, for it appears that she bestowed her favours on both men. Half a century later history repeated itself: when Wagner's lover Cosima brought a daughter into the world in 1865, her husband Hans von Bülow lay claim to the child. In 1914 Isolde took her mother to court in an attempt to prove that Wagner was her father, and it emerged in the course of the proceedings that Cosima had been on intimate terms with both men at this time, with the result that Bülow was confirmed as the father and Isolde definitively disinherited.

Just as Wagner was never able to ascertain who his father was, so he remained unsure about his mother's past. True, she had given him birth, but who exactly was she? Did she really hail from the house of Saxe-Weimar – a royal family of ancient pedigree? Or was there the suggestion that her cradle had stood in a country baker's parlour? Did Wagner ever ask his mother the question that Lohengrin forbids his bride to put to him? For Wagner, the question had unsettling implications.

At best – and Wagner always believed this about himself – it meant that he could claim to have blue blood in his veins. Perhaps he could even hope for a royal inheritance? Certainly he did not lack sovereign self-confidence when he assured King Ludwig II in 1866: 'I am an aristocrat.'[4] Invented by his mother and assiduously fostered by Wagner himself, the legend of his noble birth proved remarkably tenacious. Long after his death, Bayreuth continued to believe in the existence of an ancestral line that according to Houston Stewart Chamberlain could be traced back to Saint Elizabeth of Thuringia. 'The little secret that we find here', wrote Chamberlain, 'is no secret to initiates.'[5]

There remained the other – less flattering – alternative: did Wagner's mother perhaps have a dark secret to hide, a shady past that she wanted to keep to herself? And whom did she love when she was carrying her youngest son? The bureaucrat Friedrich Wagner or the artist Ludwig Geyer? Or both at once? Was his mother an adultress who wanted her husband dead in order to be able to marry her lover? The answer to this question was decisive in terms of Wagner's own self-perception, but it was one that his mother failed to provide. She kept her own counsel, while his stepfather was hardly the man to consult on a point of genealogy.

Like his father, Wagner's mother remained a lifelong puzzle. His autobiography glosses over virtually everything bound up with his origins, while maintaining a striking distance towards her. It is with some coldness that he describes her here as a 'remarkable' woman whose headaches obliged her to wear lace bonnets. The impression that she left on him was not that of a 'young and charming mother'. Never, he complained, had she shown him any tenderness, rarely the love for which he craved. His stepdaughter Natalie reported that even in his late adolescence his mother had treated him with 'harshness and indifference'.[6] There was always his stepfather and a whole host of other children to come between them. Already sickly by nature, Wagner soon turned into a bundle of nerves.

Johanna Rosine often sent the boy to stay with a family in the country, where he was tormented by feelings of homesickness. He felt abandoned and indulged in fantastical dreams of returning to his mother. Whenever she turned up, he thought of her as a creature from another world. She came and went like the mysterious Undine whose secret origins could never be questioned. Between that time and his death, the water sprite in Friedrich de la Motte Fouqué's fairy-tale was to be Wagner's favourite imaginary creature – perhaps also because she resembled his inscrutable mother on one essential point: 'Undine was no fisherman's daughter', wrote Fouqué, 'but in all likelihood was sprung from a mysterious house of high-born princes who hailed from foreign parts.' On the eve of his death in Venice in 1883, Wagner read Fouqué's tale aloud to his family.

As a child, Wagner loved his mother, for all that she concealed her erstwhile charms beneath lace bonnets and an austere exterior. And the more she withdrew from him, both in reality and in terms of her past, the more he loved her. She remained a stranger to him, a stranger sued in vain. Shortly before his death she too appeared to him in a dream, youthfully charming and elegant, 'just as he could recall her, at best, from her portrait'. The idealized portrait of her painted by Geyer showed the other aspect of this woman on whom such excessive demands were placed: a much-loved mother who smiled on her son whenever he was successful and who, adopting the tone of the Gospels, once whispered in his ear that he was well pleasing in her sight. 'My guardian angel', he called her in a birthday letter. But in the same letter he informed her that he would not be able to tell her much about his life in future, and he stuck to his word from that time until her death. He had long since distanced himself from her and now looked for love elsewhere.

Johanna Rosine died in January 1848, having survived the three men in her life. Shortly beforehand her thoughts seem to have returned to Prince Constantin, whom she imagined entering her room with a bouquet of roses as in the golden age of past pleasures. 'Ah, how beautiful!' she had exclaimed, 'how lovely, how divine! What have I done to deserve such kindness?'

Her son, who recorded these words in his memoirs, was profoundly upset by his mother's death. At her burial in Leipzig he was shocked by the sound of the clods of frozen earth falling onto the lid of her coffin, and it was with a feeling of 'total abandonment' that he set off on his journey back to Dresden.

The Fathers

However bright the light that researchers have shone on all the other figures who came into contact with Wagner, the man who has gone down in history as his father remains shadowy in the extreme. Not even his own son knew what he looked like. Although Geyer was a talented portrait painter, no picture of Friedrich Wagner has survived in the family. With his physical disappearance, all memory of him faded.

What did Wagner himself know about his dead father? Friedrich Wagner was born in 1770, the same year as Beethoven. The son of a Leipzig tax collector, he studied law, then found a job as a civil servant in the local municipal courts. At the age of twenty-eight he married Johanna Rosine Pätz, the woman with a past. History does not relate whether he met her in a professional capacity or, indulging his private passion, at the theatre.

The servant of the state spent his leisure time dabbling in amateur theatricals, preferring the company of actors and actresses and appearing with some success in Goethe's comedy *Die Mitschuldigen*. The performances took place in an ancient four-storey building on the Rathausplatz in Leipzig known as the Thomä House. In one of the rooms at the rear of this building was a magnificent hall with a painted ceiling depicting Olympus, its deities gazing down impassively on the municipal orchestra that shared the space with various troupes of actors. It was here that Friedrich Wagner performed whenever he stepped out of his uniform. And here, several years after his death, his scholarly brother Adolf was to rent rooms from a certain Jeannette Thomä, after whose father the property was named.

Friedrich Wagner even seems to have had some talent for the stage. According to the poet E. T. A. Hoffmann, who occasionally joined him for a drink, a liberal supply of rum would induce this 'exotic' individual to regale his audience with amusing parodies of well-known actors.[7] Wagner himself reports that his father's love of the theatre also entailed a 'gallant passion' for its more charming representatives.

Friedrich Wagner is said to have devoted particular attention to the actress Friederike Wilhelmine Hartwig. On stage she played tragic heroines so engagingly that her beau called two of his daughters after her finest Schillerian roles: Johanna Rosalie and Luise. If Friederike Hartwig was really Friedrich's lover, Wagner himself felt that Geyer might well have been tempted to repay the compliment: while Friedrich was spending his evenings away from home, soaking up the atmosphere of the theatre, 'the admirable actor' Ludwig Geyer 'generally took his place at the bosom of the family'. Thus Wagner, choosing his words very carefully, expresses it in his autobiography.

There remains the question whether this position in the bosom of the family was vacant at all and whether the painter and actor Ludwig Geyer could play his best friend's part with the agreement of all the parties concerned? Or was Wagner trying, with a nudge and a wink, to divert attention from a tragedy involving two friends? His father's frequent absences could, of course, be equally plausibly explained in terms of his job.

The linguistically gifted court official owed his successful career to Napoleon Bonaparte. King Friedrich August of Saxony had formed an alliance with the Corsican emperor in 1806 and introduced the Code Napoléon, with the result that French was now in demand as a foreign language within the ranks of the Saxon civil service. As a trained lawyer with a large library of classical texts, Friedrich Wagner was fluent in the language of Racine and Molière, and so found himself entrusted with the task of reorganizing the Leipzig police force.

When Napoleon's troops marched into Leipzig in 1813, it was Friedrich whom the local commandant, the infamous Marshal Davout, invited to head the newly formed police service designed to maintain civil order in the city. With war raging all around, Friedrich Wagner must have been kept fully occupied by his new position. He was, moreover, on the wrong side, a circumstance that both his son and the latter's biographers chose to ignore. Although invited into the city by the king of Saxony, the French represented an occupying army and were consequently hated. Prussia was at war with them, the populace rose up, and it was to prevent a similar uprising in Leipzig that Friedrich Wagner organized his forces. From the standpoint of the German nationalism that his son was later to espouse with such warmth, Friedrich Wagner was – to put it bluntly – a collaborator.

It was not only as a civil servant in the pay of the king of Saxony that Leipzig's chief of police remained on Napoleon's side to the bitter end. Many educated Leipzigers admired the Corsican general and supported him in his wars with the rest of Europe: the Romantic physiologist and landscape painter Carl Gustav Carus, for example, ran a French hospital. But a further reason for Friedrich Wagner's loyalty may well have lain in Napoleon's fondness for Freemasonry. Friedrich had long been a member of the Leipzig Lodge Balduin zur Linde, and his representative within the bosom of the Wagner family, Ludwig Geyer, was later to intercede with the Lodge on behalf of Friedrich's son Julius. That the civil servant welcomed the artist into his home and supported him over a period of many years was entirely in keeping with Masonic practice: 'Cultivate brotherly love', the Masonic constitution advises, 'for it is the foundation and capstone, the cement and glory of this ancient Fraternity.'

In November 1813, a month after the Battle of the Nations had been fought and lost near Leipzig, Friedrich Wagner succumbed to the typhoid epidemic that had broken out in the city. E. T. A. Hoffmann was in Dresden when the epidemic spread to that city and noted that its symptoms consisted of 'headache, dizziness, numbness, death, all within the space of a few hours!'[8] Wholly unprepared for her husband's death, Johanna Rosine placed an announcement in the *Leipziger Zeitung*, bewailing the fact that her husband had died 'as a victim of his profession . . . far too soon for me and my eight uneducated children'. She was especially grateful, she added, for the 'extremely tender care' of her late husband's friends.

With that, Friedrich Wagner sank into oblivion and disappeared virtually without trace. On the night of his death, the Leipzig town clerk noted only that a Prussian lieutenant had died at the Three Swans in the Brühl. Divested of his power, the chief of police no longer counted for anything.

From his father Wagner inherited only a dog-eared copy of the Code Napoléon, and so it was left to Friedrich's brother, Wagner's Uncle Adolf, to fill in the picture for him. Whenever Wagner thought of his father in later years, it was his uncle who came to mind. In the 1870s he set about reclaiming a portrait of Adolf Wagner that the latter had left to his servant girl in Leipzig: 'This is the race from which I stem,' he told Cosima with some pride. 'His beautiful, gentle way of speaking, the free and noble development of his mind, he was a true product of the school of Goethe.'[9]

A notable scholar who could turn his hand to poetry, Adolf Wagner lived a secluded life that could hardly have been more different from that of the extrovert Ludwig Geyer, his aim being not to offer a whole range of different distractions to an audience addicted to the pleasures of the moment, but to serve the truth, a truth embodied in the classical texts in his library. He read and wrote books and could not understand how anyone like Geyer could spend half his life wearing stage make-up and a costume. Cut off from the world and averse to all frivolous pleasures, he devoted himself to the affairs of the mind, which at this period in German thought meant the humanism of Weimar Classicism and the world-shaking visions of Hegelian philosophy.

In order to concentrate on his studies undisturbed, he had moved into a room in the Thomä House that was cut off from the rest of the building. Here he earned his living by accepting occasional commissions as a writer. Many of his favourite subjects, from Sophocles' *Oedipus Tyrannus* to Gozzi's *Il corvo* and Fouqué's *Undine*, were later to be found in his nephew's arsenal of myths. If E. T. A. Hoffmann had once said of his friend Friedrich Wagner that he belonged to 'the better school', this was even more true of his brother Adolf, for Hoffmann's 'dearest Alf', who bore a passing resemblance to the writer's Kapellmeister Kreisler, felt only contempt for decadent contemporary society. Geyer and his 'accomplice' Johanna Rosine were to feel the full force of his scorn.

Although Adolf Wagner had studied with Fichte and Schelling, his philosophical outlook was influenced above all by Hegel, for whom world history represented the revelation of the absolute spirit. To borrow Goethe's phrase from the end of *Faust*, all things transient were no more than a metaphor for Hegel. Behind each phenomenon lay concealed the eternal idea. It was mankind's task to comprehend reality as the expression of that creative spirit.

'Everything, first fleeing from the eternal', wrote Adolf Wagner in his Hegelian German, 'next strives to establish its own individuality and assert it in conflict with others, till lastly, taken up once more into the Idea from which it issued, it shines in perfect peace.'[10] This helps to explain why the entire world, from 'the lifeless inanimate rock to the deepest veins of the mind', seemed to Adolf Wagner to be uniquely 'aimed at reconciliation'. The true task of the human race could consist only in seeking to advance the reconciliation of the spirit that had become alienated in the course of world history, an aim that should be pursued through art, science and political action. All other activities, including such empty pastimes as acting, failed to encompass this divine mission.

From his Faustian study Adolf Wagner fired off missives fulminating against cultural decline. His favourite object of vilification was the theatre that had degenerated to the point where it was now 'the handmaid of rank luxuriance and a helpmeet in times of boredom'. Unable to reconcile himself to the present day, he had turned into an eccentric who cast an eerie spell on his nine-year-old nephew when the latter, for family reasons, needed a roof over his head. Generally it was only his uncle's pointed felt cap that the boy could see poking above the piles of dusty volumes in his study. Wagner remembered him as a 'thoroughly puzzling, baffling figure', while E. T. A. Hoffmann even expressed pity for the forsaken hermit who 'creeps through life in sombre surroundings and is inwardly so consumed'.[11]

Adolf's gloomy mood was undoubtedly caused in part by his late brother's family. He disapproved of Johanna's marriage to a painter-cum-actor not only on principle but probably also for reasons of jealousy, while Geyer's decision to put his daughters on the stage to earn their living seemed to him fatally flawed. He loathed the whole of the acting profession for replacing reality with an 'insipid and deceitful semblance of life' designed to obscure our true task in the world-historical process. Women in particular, Adolf warned, were 'torn apart and destroyed' by this world of deceit. He referred contemptuously to the theatre as 'Thalia's stables', claiming that his nieces could expect only to be abandoned by it, 'burnt out and hollowed out' like a Moloch.

For Adolf Wagner, the symbolic representative of this satanic world of the theatre was the writer of comedies August von Kotzebue. Kotzebue was additionally suspected of being a Russian spy and had been condemned by national fanatics as a mortal enemy of all that was German, even though his popular and sentimental plays were in the repertory of every theatre in the country. Adolf Wagner attacked the acclaimed playwright in coded diatribes: 'Such rabble', he wrote venomously, 'must necessarily perish in the ether of freedom' – in other words, in a free German republic – 'but it is better that slavery should die than that freedom should do so, and I hope that this will indeed happen as the axe has everywhere already been placed against the root.' Adolf's allegorically florid prediction was soon to come true, as in 1819 Kotzebue was assassinated by a German nationalist student by the name of Karl Ludwig Sand.

Adolf's hatred of the harmless playwright was not just politically inspired, it was also bound up with family jealousies, as Kotzebue seems to have been one of Geyer's favourite writers. As an actor, Johanna Rosine's second husband shone in Kotzebue's farces. Worse than that: the Wagner children also appeared in them in various walk-on roles, with even the four-year-old Wagner being pressed into service as an extra. The trivial subject matter of these plays clearly drew audiences like a magnet, encouraging Geyer to write his own comedies in the same style. The élitist Adolf must have looked on in impotent horror as Geyer, already anathematized as a painter and actor, now set out to become the new Kotzebue.

His stepson seems to have felt the same. In Bayreuth in 1878 he decided in a moment of misguided sentimentality to reread Geyer's play *Das Erntefest* but quickly laid it aside again. 'He doesn't care for the genre', Cosima noted drily in her diary. Her husband disliked the 'Dresden Kotzebue manner'.[12]

On Friedrich Wagner's death, Ludwig Geyer took over as the head of the household, becoming arguably the most influential person in his stepson's life. Geyer gave him his name, and so the young Wagner was bound to regard him as his father. Even when he discovered that this was not the case – perhaps it was his Uncle Adolf who told him – there remained the nagging, and abiding, suspicion that he was indeed Geyer's son.

Geyer stepped so effortlessly into his best friend's shoes as head of the household that it was impossible to be certain that he had not already played this role prior to Friedrich's death. And what a devastating indictment of his character this would have been. But if, by contrast, he had proved merely to be a selfless friend of the family, as family tradition had it, why was Wagner so afraid of him, a fear that tormented him all his life?

Few assessments of Geyer's true character have come down to us. One such account we owe to the composer of *Der Freischütz*, Carl Maria von Weber, under whose direction Geyer occasionally appeared as an operatic tenor at the Dresden Court Theatre. 'You're quite right about Geyer', he wrote to his wife in 1817, 'he's a man of reason.'[13] As a Romantic artist for whom feeling was everything, Weber had clearly seen through Geyer, dismissing as cool and calculating the singing jack-of-all-trades who acted, painted portraits and wrote farces.

The same could not be said of Friedrich Wagner. When Geyer's father died in 1799 and the twenty-year-old law student found himself in financial difficulties, Friedrich Wagner – his elder by nine years and already married – took him under his wing. As Geyer's 'truest friend', he even placed advertisements in the local papers, inviting readers to commission portraits from his young protégé. While completing a course at the Leipzig Academy of Art, Geyer eked out his living as a painter, specializing in 'portraits of elderly gentlemen and young ladies'. His surviving canvases include portraits of E. T. A. Hoffmann, Weber's librettist Friedrich Kind and various members of the Wagner family. A pastel painting of his patron, by contrast, is said to have been 'lost' while in the possession of his descendants,[14] a fate not dissimilar to their recollection of its subject.

Thanks to Friedrich, Geyer discovered a further talent that allowed him to earn some money: the theatre. The jurist introduced the painter to the amateur stage in the Thomä House, where Geyer was promptly bitten by the theatre bug and resolved to become an actor. By 1809 he was a member of Franz Seconda's well-known troupe in Dresden, with whom he returned as a successful actor to Leipzig, where the Wagners welcomed him with open arms. The company gave extended seasons in both cities, generally allowing Geyer to take advantage of his hosts' hospitality from Easter to the date of the Michaelmas Fair in October. Thus it was that in the autumn of 1812, when Friedrich Wagner's youngest son was conceived, Geyer was staying with the family in the Brühl – in the building known as the 'House of the Red and White Lion'.

As an actor, Geyer revealed astonishing versatility, playing the lover with the same accomplishment as he brought to the tragic hero, the hard-hearted king and the perfidious rogue, sometimes all in a single play. Writing in the *Zeitung für die elegante Welt* in 1810, an anonymous reviewer noted that in *Der Schauspieler wider Willen* Geyer had 'displayed an admirable versatility in the various disguises that occur here. Some of the characters could hardly have been more different from each other, while others differed only in nuance, yet in every case he revealed such variety in terms of posture, tone and language that several ordinary theatregoers actually questioned whether they were seeing the same person.'[15]

If Geyer was such an accomplished quick-change artist on stage, this was due not least to the fact that he was responsible for his own make-up and costumes. While his evenings were spent raising doubts in his audiences' minds about his true identity, he would use the daylight hours to paint portraits of the town's dignitaries and other members of the Seconda company. Both on stage and in his studio he gave notice of a talent to imitate others. But by the end of his life even Geyer himself seems to have doubted whether there was any substance behind the masquerade and whether he had an identity of his own that went beyond his talent for mimicking others.

The upheavals of war meant that, apart from a short season in Teplitz, the Seconda troupe remained in Dresden throughout the whole of 1813, with the result that on this occasion Geyer was denied the pleasure of the Wagners' hospitality. On 22 May, Johanna Rosine gave birth to a son whose christening was curiously delayed. The actor complained that he had 'never longed to see Leipzig as much as this summer'. There ensued the mysterious assignation at the hotel in Teplitz, after which the child was christened with the name by which the world later knew him. When Friedrich Wagner, officially attested as the child's father, died soon afterwards, Geyer immediately offered to help Johanna and invited her two eldest daughters to join him in Dresden. He himself assumed responsibility for the talented Rosalie, while her sister Luise was entrusted to the tragic actress Friederike Hartwig, in honour of whom she was named. Geyer and his late friend's lover may even have been living together.

The surviving correspondence between the actor and the newly widowed Johanna reveals little about their feelings, with Geyer's style in particular resembling nothing so much as a courteously restrained parlando designed to be read aloud. Both parties give the impression that they had come to terms as best they could with the death of the much-loved Friedrich, who had been buried for only a month when Geyer spoke openly about their mutual jealousy. At the same time he told Johanna how impatiently he had been waiting for the hour 'when I can talk to you candidly on the familiar sofa'. And he warned her to beware of Adolf, as though fearing a rival in him. 'I really don't like your brother-in-law's approaches', he complained. She should not allow Adolf to 'gain an insight' into her 'situation'.[16]

Once Johanna's fears about her rival in Dresden had been allayed and Geyer's mind had been set at rest about Adolf, she set off to visit him. The result of their (re)union was a child, who was born in February 1815, six months after the couple were married, and who was christened Cäcilie Geyer. Less than a year after Friedrich Wagner's death the family had a new home in Dresden, to say nothing of a new name.

Half a century later, Wagner's younger sister, who resembled him closely, sent her brother copies of the letters that Geyer had written to Johanna before they were married. Wagner professed himself deeply impressed by Geyer's selflessness in taking in the fatherless family. But then he looked more closely at the relationship. It was clear, he wrote, that Geyer was 'hoping to atone for some guilt in sacrificing himself for the whole family'.[17]

Later he told Cosima that although Geyer was not his father, his mother had 'loved him at the time – elective affinities'.[18]

Ghosts

At the time of Wagner's birth on 22 May 1813 a decisive battle of European import was brewing in the vicinity of Leipzig. His biographers are all of one mind that this was no accident: as befitted his nature, the Titan set foot in the world to the sound of rumbling cannons. But however symbolic the connection may seem, the course of world history left the child unmarked. When his father died as a result of the war, and the clandestine relationship between his mother and the family friend came out into the open, Wagner was still in his cradle. The influences that left their mark on him belonged not to the theatre of war but to the family environment in which he played his allotted role.

Many writers have none the less assumed that his place of birth left a lasting impression. The Leipzig Fair drew Polish Jews to the Brühl, where they sold their wares, their long fur coats and high fur caps, their strange faces, their pendent locks and their 'jumble of Hebrew and bad German' proving 'as eerie as Hoffmann's phantoms' – or so Wagner told his biographer Carl Friedrich

Glasenapp.[19] In fact, this observation dates not from the time of Wagner's earliest childhood but from the period when he returned to Leipzig from Dresden as a teenager. When he and his family left the Brühl he was barely eighteen months old and can have been no more aware of the Battle of the Nations than of the mix of nations engaged in trade. Only when he was living with Geyer in Dresden did he start to notice his surroundings.

In his autobiography, Wagner writes that his 'earliest memories are bound up with this stepfather and pass from him to the theatre'.[20] Geyer had not only assumed responsibility for his late friend's family, he also had control over them. From now on it was he who decided what was to happen to them and what role they were to play within the family business. As neither Johanna nor Geyer was possessed of any great fortune, their only chance of survival lay in their pooling their resources. In this way, the childhood of Wagner's elder siblings came to a premature end.

For each of them, their stepfather found a use. In spite of Adolf's disapproval of his brother-in-law and the scepticism of Geyer's new wife, who specifically warned her youngest son against pursuing a theatrical career, the children were groomed for a life on stage. As their stepfather knew, they could earn their living by singing, acting and playing the piano. And so their house in Dresden became a kind of cadet college devoted to the Muses. The tone, Wagner complained, was harsh, and sentimentality was not tolerated.

Wagner's four-year-old sister Maria Theresia died in January 1814, and there were fears for his own life, too. Sickly by nature, he fell ill in his 'tenderest infancy', and his health deteriorated so rapidly that, according to his own later account, he 'seemed beyond hope and my mother almost wanted me dead'. Presumably it was this disturbing memory that sparked a sarcastic poem that he dedicated to himself in the mid-1850s: ''Twas in the merry month of May / That Wagner saw the light of day. / How many people wish he'd stayed / Inside the egg the hen had laid.' Only his 'admirable stepfather' – or so his mother told him – refused to abandon hope. Needless to say, Geyer's position of preeminence was unassailable in his wife's eyes, and their children, too, were forced to get used to feeling grateful to him for everything in their lives. Had he not raised them up from the depths of financial misery following their father's death and, while they were still in their early adolescence, opened up the prospect of brilliant careers? Only praise befitted so upright and honest a man, and even in later life Wagner could see no reason to contradict this view.

Yet the view of his stepfather that Wagner promulgated in his official accounts of his life did not reflect his true feelings. He confided in his first wife

Minna that 'on the whole' he had 'had a miserable youth'.[21] In Geyer's empire children's games were frowned on, rivalry was encouraged, and only achievement counted for anything. According to Minna's daughter Natalie, Geyer even felt a 'great dislike' of the fidgety Richard.[22] Only later did this feeling turn to sympathy. In another birthday poem, penned in a similar spirit of self-irony, we read: 'Yes, yes, it was in May. / I too was there, they say. / They tweaked me by the ear, / So music's my career.' Tweaking Wagner's ear was not the only educational aid that he was later to recall.

Visitors to Geyer's apartment must have thought they had stumbled onto a rehearsal stage for the Dresden Court Theatre. Here the master of the house coached his five daughters Rosalie, Luise, Klara, Ottilie and Cäcilie, and since there were not enough existing roles for underage girls, he wrote plays especially for them in his 'Dresden Kotzebue style'. Luise was nine when she made her début in *Das Mädchen aus der Fremde*, while Rosalie was a blossoming fourteen-year-old – the delight of her father 'who loved her tenderly' – when she first appeared in *Das Erntefest*. The hero of this last-named piece is cast up on a foreign shore by an inclement fate. Here he recognizes the features of his lost wife in those of a fourteen-year-old girl. Both on stage and in real life, the girl was called Rosalie.

Wagner, too, was pressed into service in this way, albeit only as an extra. In Schiller's *Wilhelm Tell* he played one of the hero's sons alongside his sister Klara, while Geyer took the part of the villain Geßler. On another occasion the young lad was sewn into a flesh-coloured leotard as a little angel. He also appeared in Kotzebue's *Menschenhaß und Reue* ('Misanthropy and Remorse'), a title he misremembered – perhaps significantly – as *Menschen außer der Reihe* ('People out of Line').

There is no evidence to support the claim advanced by many of Wagner's biographers that Geyer's one ambition in life was to give the young boy a decent education. Wagner himself repeatedly insisted that from the very outset he was thrown back on his own resources. While the court actor devoted all his attention to his girls, who assiduously learnt their roles, sang Schubert songs or ran up costumes to his own instructions, their youngest brother, according to Cosima, 'was never really educated at all'.[23] As with his hero Siegfried, life 'in all its anarchy' forced him to be his own teacher.

In Geyer's hectic household, Wagner played a subsidiary role. It was hard for him to gain a hearing in the face of so many little prima donnas. Feeling neglected, he had to fight for his place by dint of his own achievements. Only when he shone with success was he rewarded with a smile, but unfortunately he could not compete with his talented sisters and so felt unwanted. And, as he later recalled, the 'poverty of his home did not allow his cheerful disposition to develop to its full extent'.[24]

Unlike his brother Albert, who trained as a singer, Wagner seemed to be unmusical. Instead of sending him for piano lessons with the other children, Geyer took him with him into his studio. It was above all the portrait gallery which, seeming to come alive, fired the boy's ambition. A lifesize portrait of King Friedrich August, who had returned from foreign captivity in 1815, inspired him to copy it. He planned it on the grandest scale, but the result, predictably, was little more than 'naïve daubing'. Geyer soon lost patience with his stepson and handed him on to a tedious cousin whose pedantic manner deterred the lad from continuing to perfect his technique. When Wagner threw in the towel, Geyer abandoned all attempts to give his stepson an artistic education. 'He wanted me to become a painter,' Wagner later wrote, 'but I was very bad at drawing.'[25]

As a result of this failure, which was bound up with Wagner's fear of his disciplinarian stepfather, paintings began to trigger traumatic reactions in him. In the presence of portraits in oils such as those that Geyer himself painted, he was assailed by the fear that they might come to life and haunt him. Although he was happy to look at flowers and fruit, he was unable to pick them up, much to his family's bemusement. Perhaps Geyer had simply told him not to touch his elaborate still-life arrangements.

Wagner later went out of his way to stress that in the case of his stepfather there could be no question of originality. He remembered Geyer simply as an imitator. When Minna expressed enthusiasm at his *Assumption of the Virgin*, Wagner simply shook his head, explaining that it was 'a mere copy. I'm very sorry to have to disillusion you.'[26] Decades later, when he saw a similar *Assumption* in Venice, he had 'reservations' about it since he was so disturbed by God the Father in it.

It is clear from his sisters' reminiscences that Wagner's ostensibly idyllic relationship with his stepfather was mere self-deception. The truth of the matter is that the boy was afraid of him. If Geyer kept his daughters in check by offering them the lure of theatrical fame, he found other ways of exerting his authority over their restless younger brother. In order to prevent him from secretly gaining access to the larder, he rigged up a large iron doll that gave him such a shock that he could still remember it sixty years later. On another occasion Wagner bought a whip with some stolen money, whereupon Geyer thrashed him with the corpus delicti, while his sisters cried outside the door.[27]

Wagner's fear of being punished seems to have been increased by Geyer's fondness for sombre roles. In this way his experiences in real life were intensified to the point where Geyer acquired the potential to pose a fantastical threat. On stage he could see his stepfather transformed into the blackest villains going about their bloody business every evening. The man who in his youth had specialized in heroic lovers now played classical malefactors such as Hamlet's fratricidal uncle, not even shying away from the characters in popular blood-and-thunder dramas such as *Die Waise und der Mörder* and *Die Teufelsmühle am Wienerberg*. Wagner never forgot the sheer terror he felt at these gruesome plays from Geyer's bag of tricks. When put to bed after performances like these, he repeatedly suffered from nightmares.

But even during daylight hours he soon found it hard to distinguish between real life and the world of his imagination. The stage that was his family's livelihood became a place of terror for him. He trembled at characters that he thought were real, yet was unable to resist their spell. Fear became fundamental to his existence, including the fear of punishment when he lied to his mother or stole money from his sister Rosalie's 'box'. Even a bell filled him with a real sense of panic when he looked into its 'jaws'. According to Cosima, 'he felt such terror that he burst into tears, nothing on earth would have persuaded him to cross the square'.[28] Life with so many brothers and sisters was already complicated enough without his having to contend with the additional problem of obsessive *idées fixes*.

His mood was not exactly brightened by Geyer's decision to send him away to stay with a village pastor. Clearly he was regarded as an intractable bundle of nerves whom a change of air would do the world of good. In the eyes of his sisters, he later recalled, he was 'a wild and abandoned creature who refused to conform'.[29] In 1820, then, he was sent to the village of Possendorf, where he felt he had been exiled and where he spent a year with the pastor Christian Wetzel, finding a fellow-sufferer in the figure of the castaway Robinson Crusoe and discovering in Homer's legendary characters the models for his earliest literary endeavours. He was tormented by feelings of homesickness.

He could barely wait for the holidays when he was finally allowed to return home. Precisely because he had known so little love in his life, his longing for his mother and sisters grew to be unbearable. The journey back to Dresden took him three hours on foot. When the time came for him to return to Possendorf, he would sink into a state of depression. These separations, with the prospect of a reunion no more than a dim and distant possibility, were among the 'most terrible things' to befall him during his childhood.[30]

Wagner's rustication was directly bound up with Geyer. A change had recently taken place in him, making him appear more irritable and intolerant. After a while he started to withdraw from his friends and seemed to sink into deep despondency. Whereas they had earlier been struck by the 'dual aspect of his character', causing him to veer between high spirits and melancholy, he was now in permanent thrall to depression. According to one of his friends, he was now so morbidly sensitive that everything was taken as a reproach, and 'even remarks made with the most honest of intentions were misinterpreted'. Whenever he was criticized as an artist, he felt that he was 'under attack and had been written off, so that he became gloomy and withdrawn'.[31]

Geyer dreamt of repairing to Italy's sunnier climes in order to paint but instead went to Leipzig and took rooms with Adolf Wagner. Quite why he should have moved into such gloomy quarters in the Thomä House, with its memories of his dead friend, remains a mystery. Here too he shut himself away from his old friends in order to spend his days working at his easel. He complained about the house's unhealthy ambience and also about a black poodle that annoyed him. He felt that the 'smoky figures' hanging on the walls of the guest room were staring at him.

He was plagued by 'a vague feeling of gloom'. Adolf Wagner, in whom Geyer refused to confide, spoke of 'terrible hypochondria'.[32] Sick in mind, Geyer lasted for a little over a month in Leipzig before returning to Dresden and arranging for his family to move to a larger apartment, which they did at Easter 1821. They were now living on the Jüdenhof, not far from the royal palace and opposite the old picture gallery. Geyer withdrew to his garden.

His final play in the style of Kotzebue was to prove a great success: in spite of its gruesome title, *Der bethlehemitische Kindermord* ('The Massacre of the Innocents') is a farce about artists, and following its successful performance in Dresden, it enjoyed a revival in Breslau that Geyer himself oversaw in the company of the now eighteen-year-old Rosalie. A month later he returned to Dresden, his health 'in ruins'. He was suffering from tuberculosis, which he travelled to Pillnitz to have treated, again with his favourite daughter at his side. His health now took an emphatic turn for the worse, and so he returned to the Jüdenhof where, racked by 'chest spasms', he was confined to his bed.

A messenger was despatched to Possendorf to fetch the young Wagner back to Dresden. When his mother asked him to play something on the piano to distract his dying stepfather, his keyboard skills were just good enough for him to pick his way through the hit of the year, the Bridesmaids' Chorus from *Der Freischütz*. According to Wagner's later recollections, the dying man asked his mother weakly: 'Could he perhaps be musically talented?' Misinterpreted by his biographers as a prophecy, this remark appears rather to have been meant to imply the opposite: although the family made music tirelessly, it does not seem to have occurred to anyone that the boy, now eight years old, might have been gifted in that direction. Only now that he was on his deathbed did Geyer pose this question, a question in which the overriding emotion would seem to have been one of bewilderment: whatever were they to do with their youngest son?

Neither Geyer's death nor his mother's tears left Wagner particularly moved. The sad events of September 1821 passed him by like so many dreamlike images. 'Anxious amazement' prevented him from crying. There was in any case little time for grieving as Pastor Wetzel arrived that very afternoon to take him back to Possendorf. If Wagner had hoped that he would soon be reunited with his mother, he was in for a disappointment. A week later, the dead man's brother, Karl Geyer, turned up in Possendorf to take his nephew to Eisleben, where he was to stay with Geyer and the latter's senile grandmother.

Wagner had been used to regular meals at the parsonage in Possendorf, where he had also enjoyed the run of the rector's library, and now he had to make do with a bachelor's dissolute lifestyle. Karl Geyer was a goldsmith and had already had an apprentice in the person of Wagner's brother Julius, the black sheep of the family. Perhaps it was hoped that this second black sheep would develop an interest in the same rewarding trade. Wagner, to whom the word obedience was unknown, preferred to spend his time catching robins for Grandma Geyer or practising tightrope walking, a skill he was inspired to take up by a troupe of visiting acrobats. He remained here for ten months, attending a school run by the local pastor (a man by the name of Alt) and taking his midday meals with a family of soap boilers. His uncle then took it into his head to get married, and Wagner was once again obliged to move on. This time it was the turn of his Uncle Adolf to take him in.

By now Wagner had grown used to the freedom of life in the country and found it difficult to settle with his learned uncle. In the faded splendour of the Thomä House, he was assailed by memories of his late stepfather, who had now been dead for barely a year. Until then, he had been distracted by his life of exile and appears to have suppressed all thoughts of his stepfather and the fear that he aroused in him. But the sight of the lifesize paintings on the walls revived the trauma that the portrait painter inspired in him.

Oddly enough, he was quartered in one of the guest rooms where his stepfather had previously felt a sense of unease and disquiet. Here his gaze fell on the smoke-stained portraits of figures from Saxon history. As soon as he was alone, they appeared to come to life and he was overcome by 'the greatest fear'. 'Sleeping alone in the presence of such eerie images', he later recalled, 'terrified me.' Not a night would pass without his being plagued by these ghostly apparitions and waking 'bathed in sweat'.[33]

Had his secret fear that the dead painter might return to haunt him been transformed into the appalling presentiment that these dead paintings might come to life? A few years before his death, Wagner relived his old fear of ghosts in Bayreuth and confided in the worried Cosima that, as a child, he had been terrified of 'inanimate objects suddenly coming to life. "I'd have been frightened of this syphon, of a chair, of anything."[34] Even ordinary pieces of furniture could induce a sense of terror in him when he was alone in a room and fixed his attention on them. In his panic-stricken fear that they might suddenly come to life, he would invariably scream for help.

But as he soon realized, this was not the case, and so his imagination came to the rescue and not a night would pass between that time and the end of his childhood without his 'waking up with a terrible scream from some dream about ghosts'. At his wits' end, his Uncle Adolf handed him back to his sister-in-law after only a few days, but the boy's fears remained as intense as before. He also saw ghosts at the Jüdenhof, where his stepfather had died, and every night he would scream aloud until his mother or sisters came running to comfort him.

He found it particularly difficult to climb the steep stairs leading to their apartment as an allegorical painting hung in the corridor. 'Nothing on earth would have persuaded me to go past that old nude figure', he later recalled.[35] This painting was not the only object that haunted him in the old house. He also felt a 'nervous fear' of the stone beer bottles that he could see on the kitchen shelves through the windows in the stairwell. According to his stepdaughter, their highly reflective surface left such an eerie impression on his excitable imagination that they seemed like 'grimacing devils', taunting and mocking him with their 'constantly changing shapes'.[36]

Was Wagner's phobia about beer bottles perhaps bound up with the fact that Geyer, well known for his mercurial ability to change shapes and assume new guises, was the only member of the family who had the right to drink beer? When the almost sixty-year-old composer brooded on the dubious character of thespians in his article *On Actors and Singers*, this archetypal image of the actor seems to emerge from between the lines much like a genie from a bottle. In the 'lowliest sphere of the actor's art', he wrote here, 'the mime', as soon as he set foot on stage, might 'imitate to perfection his landlord, the tapster and the police sergeant in order to avenge himself at night for the worries of his weary day'.[37] Was Wagner subconsciously recalling the beer-swilling Geyer, who mimicked his friend, the police registrar, in order to give some meaning to his empty existence as an actor? Only by means of such an 'exchange', wrote Wagner in his essay, could the actor acquire any dignity.

Just as the actor's ability to trigger a sense of fear could still inspire these metaphors in old age, so Wagner continued to have nightmares about his stepfather. Throughout his life the 'wicked father' was one of the principal characters who stalked the sombre scenes evoked in him by horror-struck memories of his childhood. Sometimes Geyer even appeared in the form of a vulture, his homonymous bird of prey. During one particularly 'bad night', the sixty-year-old Wagner saw his former lover Mathilde Wesendonck in a dream, showing him her newborn child. As she offered the child her breast, he was overcome by jealousy to discover that the child's head was covered with white hair and that it wore a curious bonnet. 'Then a great powerful vulture attacked both mother and child, R. tried to drive it off, but it swooped down on them again. Then he woke up.'[38]

Writers on Wagner have always agreed on Geyer's supreme importance in the composer's life, yet remains unclear which of his characteristics left their mark on his stepson – or was it his son? It has never been claimed that he introduced the boy to acting or painting, yet Wagner embarked on his musical career with no encouragement from Geyer, who on his deathbed had in fact expressed bemusement at the possibility of such a career. But which of his traits could have influenced the boy, whose education was for the most part entrusted to others? In short, how much Geyer really was there in Wagner?

According to one rumour, Geyer was Jewish, a possibility that Wagner's biographers have examined in wearisome detail. The claim advanced by the composer's apostate disciple Friedrich Nietzsche that Geyer was Wagner's real father and that 'a Geyer [vulture] is almost an Adler [eagle]'[38] – that is, a Jew – has given rise to lively debate. Is it conceivable that Wagner the notorious anti-Semite was himself of Jewish extraction? Is it possible that it was secret self-hatred that led him to make some of his more egregiously offensive remarks? Genealogists have left no stone unturned in their efforts to refute this hypothesis, and even in modern accounts of Wagner's life we still find writers asserting that Geyer's German ancestry can be traced back effortlessly to the seventeenth century. To claim otherwise is 'nonsense'.[40]

Although Wagner may have been in two minds as to whether or not Geyer was his true father, the question of Geyer's religious and racial affiliations seems never to have entered his head. The very fact that his stepfather hailed from Eisleben, the birthplace of one of the heroes of Wagner's childhood, Martin Luther, is in itself sufficient to render his suspicions unlikely. And Wagner was presumably familiar with the line from *Der bethlehemitische Kindermord*, 'the Jews have never brought us good luck'.[41] Although it was suggested to Geyer that he might consider converting to Catholicism when he was appointed court actor in Catholic Dresden, he turned down the idea and remained a Protestant, continuing to profess the faith of his ancestors until the end.

The question whether or not Geyer was Jewish played no part in Wagner's life. Strictly speaking, Geyer himself, who died prematurely when Wagner was only eight, played no part in it either. Yet his presence remained all-pervasive. Like the paintings that hounded Wagner, the dead man was a living force for him. In his imagination and in his nightmares, Geyer was a constant threat, becoming the living embodiment of everything that he feared. And so he came to hate him.

The emotionally vulnerable composer, so eager to be loved and consumed by a lifelong need for affection, was also capable of great hatred. But his stepfather was regarded as the 'saviour of the family', and so he had to find other outlets for his loathing. Whenever he was deprived of these, his subconscious provided him with the basis that he then rediscovered in real life. Glorifying 'father Geyer' in his recollections, he subconsciously transferred to other objects the terrible fear that Geyer triggered in him. He would then pursue them with all the bitterness that had been building up in him since childhood. In this way there developed a link between the man who threatened him but whom he was not allowed to hate and the nation that he was allowed to hate even though it posed no threat to him.

Geyer's great model, August von Kotzebue, attracted a similar degree of aggression. This second-rate poet was inextricably bound up in Wagner's imagination with his earliest impressions: the family would declaim his popular plays at home and memorize them for the stage, a process that left unintended traces on Wagner: from his farce *Männerlist größer als Frauenlist* to his comedy *Die Meistersinger*, the ghost of Kotzebue proved hard to exorcize. Indeed, Geyer held Kotzebue in such high regard that he even named Wagner's brother Julius 'Feldkümmel' after the playwright's Shrovetide farce, while Wagner himself was dubbed 'Amtmann Rührei', a reference to his propensity for bursting into tears. A number of Geyer's works, including his neo-medieval play *Die neue Delila*, were even printed in the *Kotzebuescher Almanach*. For Wagner, the name of the poet who was murdered in 1819 was for ever associated with that of his stepfather, who died two years later.

As a playwright, Kotzebue left Wagner feeling appalled. For him, his trivial verse plays epitomized the theatre's propensity for self-prostitution. During his own lifetime, Kotzebue had incurred the wrath of Adolf Wagner, and as late as 1867 he could still provoke his nephew into attacking him in print as a 'vain and evil-hearted man' who excited and gratified the public's curiosity with his lewdly lubricious fripperies. It was only logical, therefore, that Wagner should hail Karl Ludwig Sand, the murderer of this 'buffoon', as a German freedom fighter. Unfortunately, he concluded in this belated act of revenge, the Germans as a nation had learnt nothing from Sand's action and had even forgotten that the Jews had 'made merry' at the martyrdom of Kotzebue's assassin. It was thanks to them that the modern theatre was now firmly in the grip of 'Kotzebue's spiritual heirs'.[42]

This harmless writer of comedies, who had become the butt of the German nationalists' destructive rage, served merely as a scapegoat for Wagner, representing, as he did, the world of the theatre to which he had been introduced as a child by his stepfather. His hatred of the rundown theatre industry of his day was preceded by his early fear of the man who had brought that world into his reach: for Wagner, Geyer's demonic ability to assume new guises rubbed off on the scene of his crimes. From now on, the theatre was haunted by the ghosts of those villains in whose guise the father had taught his son the meaning of fear. The repressed fear of the man of the theatre was transformed into a horror of the theatre itself.

Wagner often used the emotive term 'horror' when speaking of the stage's world of appearances. It was a world that filled him with a dizzying feeling that something terrible could happen at any moment within a familiar environment, instilling a mixture of fascination and loathing from which he could never break free. The very idea of appearing in make-up before an audience filled the young Wagner with horror.[43] Later he wrote to an actor to say that he could imagine 'nothing more horrible' than a visit to a theatre dressing room. Made to look artificially young, the performers with their false wigs and seductively painted faces filled him with a very real sense of outrage.

Only when the music began did this 'whole infernal business' seem to end and were the ghosts laid to rest. At the time of *Parsifal* he uttered a similar sigh at the thought of 'all the costumes and make-up'. How much he would have liked to get rid of all the painted sets and costumed figures who cast their mendacious spell over audiences. In his invisible theatre there would have been space only for an invisible orchestra whose sounds would rise up from the mystic abyss.

This world of masks and costumes, of pots of make-up and painted backdrops, was Geyer's world. In condemning that world to destruction, Wagner was also trying to break free from his domineering stepfather. But it is clear from his dreams that these attempts were in vain: here his adversary appears now as a murderous male figure with instruments of torture, now as a bird 'that refused to leave my desk but kept clinging to it with its talons'.[44] Even his poetic imagination was fired by his memories of Geyer, who found his way into Wagner's works in a whole series of different guises.

On one occasion he even appeared as himself. On 1 September 1868 Wagner drafted a grotesque 'comedy' that contains all the ingredients of the third-rate theatres and opera houses on which he had long since declared war. Just as Wagner's pantophagy allowed him to digest all manner of ideas, including – when the mood took him – their opposite, so Kotzebue's mortal enemy appears here, surprisingly, as a latterday Kotzebue, with the inventor of the modern music drama putting his name to a mindless farce.[45] The prime cause was a bout of depression brought on by the unresolved nature of his relationship with Cosima. Once again he saw himself beset by rivals who, in the guise of her husband Hans von Bülow and her father Franz Liszt, seemed to contest his right to love her. The chance of slipping into the role of his hated enemy clearly brought Wagner relief from the feelings of jealousy that tormented him.

Donning his cap and bells, he turned back the clock half a century to the time when his family was still living in the Jüdenhof and gathered around the inveterate actor Ludwig Geyer. His consumptive stepfather, now at the end of his career as an actor, is given the risible role of the prompter Barnabas Kühlewind. Kühlewind is about to be dismissed from his post, and the opening scene depicts him asleep and tormented by nightmares. Just as groans were once heard to emerge from Geyer's sickroom, so Kühlewind's family listens anxiously, their depression deepening with each new groan. Life-threatening spasms convulse his frame, until the bed finally collapses beneath him at one particularly violent sneezing fit. Joining forces, his children carry him to the coffee table, where they brood on ways of averting the impending disaster.

A solution to the problem is provided by Wagner himself, who casts himself in the role of the 'dissolute' but linguistically gifted student Kaspar Schreiblich. Although Kühlewind points out that he has no talent as an actor, Schreiblich refuses to heed this 'evil prognosis' but insists that a magnificent future lies ahead. And his prophecy comes true when this sworn enemy of 'empty theatrical heroism' is offered a new appointment – not, it is true, on stage, but in Kühlewind's now vacant prompt box.

An active part in bringing about this happy ending is played by Kühlewind's daughter Hermine, who, as her consumptive father's nurse, recalls Wagner's sister Rosalie. As his guardian angel, she is surprisingly able to obtain a pension for her father, but all this excitement proves too much for the old man and, while they are drinking a toast to their 'tremendous success', he sneezes so violently that it kills him, leaving his heir Schreiblich to claim the hand of the doughty Hermine.

At the end of this fantasy à la Kotzebue, the fifty-five-year-old music drama-tist added a postscript: 'To ward off serious ill humour.'

The Angel

Wagner's childhood was influenced less by events than by people. Even when they later disappeared from his life, they remained a part of his own identity and, like all true archetypes, provided the models for his later experiences, as well as for the main characters in his stage works. Initially in his subconscious, but later in his conscious imagination, they developed into mythological char-acters who took on a life of their own in his music dramas, with art effortlessly imitating real life.

Reworked for the stage, these characters became larger-than-life personali-ties who in turn left their mark on Wagner's existence as independent realities. 'I'm fated to carry out in prose (in life) what I have already created in my work,' he told Cosima two years before his death.[46] Virtually all his experiences in life appear to repeat the events and relationships in which he first encountered these archetypes. Virtually all the people who played any role in his life appear in one or other of his works.

Wagner worked as a director not only in the theatre but in real life, too. With their changing fates, perspectives and moods, his life and his music dramas offered abiding scope for these archetypes to be resuscitated time and again. Both as real people and as the dramatis personae of his theatrical creations, they entered modernity's world of myth.

The male archetypes of the legendary prince, absent father and demonic Geyer are mirrored on the distaff side by the unpredictable mother and, as her total antithesis, the self-sacrificing sister. This last-named figure assumed the role of an 'angel' in Wagner's life and works, an evening star that lit his way out of the valley of death. Unlike Wagner's other sisters – Luise, Klara, Ottilie and Cäcilie – Rosalie, who was his senior by ten years, exerted a lasting influence. While the others competed with him for their parents' attention, she seemed to her brother, in need of love as he was, to be a surrogate mother. Johanna Rosalie gave him the affection that Johanna Rosine denied him.

Wagner's two elder brothers, Albert and Julius, were self-opinionated, unimaginative types of whom Wagner could expect nothing, so Rosalie was the only member of the family to whom he could turn whenever he needed help. She took an interest in him and it was not long before she was encouraging him in his attempts to become a musician. Whereas the others regarded him as a hopeless case, she actually believed in him. When she died in childbirth in 1837, he had the feeling that she had sacrificed herself in order to restore him to the straight and narrow.

Rosalie seems as though predestined for a role in Wagner's stage works. Even while she was still a child, a theatrical career was already mapped out for her by her father Friedrich. The first of her two Christian names, intended as a compliment to Friedrich's favourite actress, recalled Schiller's maid of Orléans. She herself was to play this role in the course of her brief life, appearing in it not only on stage but, in Wagner's eyes, in actual reality, too. Rosalie was one of Schiller's idealized characters, soulful and virtuous, the very embodiment of the noble stage heroine. That, at least, was how she had been brought up. She accepted this role and continued to perform it until her career as an actress came to an end and, with it, her life.

With her light brown hair and prepossessing appearance, she seems to have been the focal point of the family from the very beginning. In one of his poems, her stepfather describes her as a self-assured thirteen-year-old able to get her own way. She considered herself cleverer than the other members of the family, wrote Geyer, and held herself in 'tremendous esteem'. Everyone respected her.[47] When Wagner later claimed of his own heroine Adelaide that she was 'more domineering than her own mother', this was presumably true of Rosalie, too.

Geyer assumed personal responsibility for Rosalie's education. When she was fifteen, he wrote a play especially for her, and she duly made her professional début in her stepfather's *Das Erntefest*, prompting critics to praise her 'burgeoning loveliness' and thus to set the tone for the whole of her later career. The delicate-featured Rosalie delighted her audiences with her tender femininity and gentle charm.[48] There was talk of her grace and loveliness. All her heroines, from Goethe's Gretchen to Shakespeare's Cordelia and the distractedly lovesick Ophelia, bespoke the same charm, moving audiences by dint of their vulnerability.

In Geyer's thespian household, Rosalie was the undisputed star. It was not Wagner who was the apple of his stepfather's eye, as his biographers have claimed, but the lovely, feminine, delicate-featured Rosalie, whom her draughtsman stepfather captured for posterity in a positively erotic sketch: wearing only a nightdress and with her hair loose, she is depicted standing by the piano, where she seems to be listening to the strains of a dying chord. In his *Parzival* draft of almost fifty years later, Wagner was to imagine Klingsor's lascivious seductresses in the same 'clothing hastily thrown around them' and with the same 'dishevelled hair'.[49] Like Rosalie – the rose – they too would appear on stage as virginal flowers, beguiling observers with their transient charms.

Geyer called her his 'little spirit' and there is no doubt that he loved her dearly. No doubt she loved him in return, as a benefactor who, had anyone but known it, already preferred her to her mother. The hero of *Das Erntefest* certainly recognized the features of his lost wife in little Rosalie. And it was not Johanna Rosine who spent a month with him in Breslau but his lovely stepdaughter. When dying of tuberculosis, he also preferred Rosalie as his companion in Pillnitz, where he had gone in search of treatment. At a later date, the mysterious artist who was accompanied everywhere by his favourite daughter seems to have reminded Wagner of Goethe's Wilhelm Meister. When conversation turned to the figure of Mignon, whose fate affected him deeply, Wagner resisted the idea that the old harper was her father, but was convinced that some 'terrible crime' – perhaps child abuse – had been committed against the elfin child. Two months before his death, Cosima noted: 'He doesn't like the old harpist.'[50]

When Geyer died, it was Rosalie alone who retained her composure. Like Brünnhilde remonstrating with the 'children' who start to 'whine' when they hear of Siegfried's death, she assumed the mantle of sublime mourning and exhorted her family to remain calm and submit to the will of heaven. 'He was too good for us,' she said, 'and so God has taken him from us and raised him high above us.' Like a tragic actress, she raised her right hand and swore a solemn oath that she would 'carry out her filial duty to the departed', meaning that she would assume responsibility for them all. Only after her theatrical intervention did she secretly succumb to her grief, and 'because she had always loved her father so much, there were times when she freely expressed her deep anguish'.[51]

Rosalie's theatrical successes as a classical heroine and sentimental lover allowed her to keep her word and to become the head of the family and, in Wagner's own words, its 'principal support', her handsome salary helping to educate her brothers and sisters. As a result, she enjoyed certain privileges: in the common apartment, the quietest rooms were reserved for her; and choice dishes were provided by servants, while the rest of the family had to make do with 'lesser fare'. When she was engaged by the German Theatre in Prague in 1826, her mother and sisters accompanied her there, while Wagner was once again left behind on his own.

But Rosalie's career, which was entirely dependent on her youthful charm, was already drawing to an end, as she found it increasingly hard to appear convincing as an ingénue now that her youth was becoming a distant memory.

Finally there appeared at the theatre a 'genuine oriental beauty' who completely upstaged the blonde angel. Barely thirty, Rosalie was forced to relinquish her role as principal lover, and it was only in the familiar part of Gretchen that audiences accorded her what one sympathetic critic described as the 'acknowledgement that was her due'.

Having suffered the tragedy of lost youth, Rosalie was additionally unhappy in love – it was almost as though the role with which she was most closely associated had somehow left its mark on her private life, too. A late developer, she seems to have suffered her fate in secret. Even towards the end of his life, her youngest brother could still remember her 'pouring out her heart in anxious sighs and laments in her darkened room in the evening, when she thought that she was alone'. He told Cosima a comical anecdote according to which Rosalie's maidservant would burst into tears whenever she saw her mistress as Gretchen. When a neighbour tried to console her by pointing out that none of it was true, the servant had replied indignantly: 'Excuse me, I should know – I work for mademoiselle.'[52]

It was not long after this that Rosalie was struck down by a nervous disorder that brought her career to an end. In 1836 she married Oswald Marbach, a university lecturer who was her junior by seven years and who was a member of the Masonic Lodge Balduin zur Linde, to which her father had once belonged. She died a year later, following the birth of their first child, Rosalie. The cause of death was the same 'powerful rush of blood to the heart' that was to cause her brother's death.

Rosalie's death left Wagner deeply shaken: in his autobiography he describes it as a 'profoundly significant blow of fate'. Their relations had long been strained. She disapproved of his marriage to the actress Minna Planer, and Wagner responded by boycotting Rosalie's wedding. Following a family row, his mother told him that his sister had spent the whole day weeping at her brother's 'heartlessness'. But – his mother assured him – his sister's love for him was strong, and when some visitors called soon afterwards, Rosalie spoke of him and his talent 'with great cordiality'.[53] That Rosalie had remained true and never lost faith in him, in spite of every provocation, was something that he discovered only after her death.

'Rosalie was an angel who was too pure to go to a better world without first being reconciled with you', Wagner's mother wrote to him. Reconciliation was a word that left a deep impression on Wagner. And with the idea of reconciliation with the 'saintly Rosalie', as his mother called her, came the idea of sacrifice. 'It was for you all that poor Rosalie suffered,' Wagner later wrote admonishingly to his sister Cäcilie.[54] By now his angel had been raised to the level of an inexhaustible archetype who was to inspire him both in real life and in the world of his imagination.

And it was love that was behind all this. Unlike the mother who betrayed him and the sisters who abandoned him, Rosalie remained loyal. That, at least, is how he himself saw it, developing what almost amounted to an obsession with his older sibling. This encouragement on the part of his 'maternal sister' was something he received from no other member of his family, and he repaid it with an affection that assumed 'an element of tenderness, almost infatuation'. When the twenty-year-old youth sang her an aria from *Die Feen*, he hoped – as he later confessed – to provoke a kind of 'declaration of love' from her.

While working on this opera, he told her that he thought of her with almost every note he wrote. 'Good God,' he exclaimed like some pining lover, 'I'll soon be with you all – with you in particular!' He told her about his dreams in which he imagined his return as a 'constant climax'. His tribute ended with a word that he was to associate with her in death: 'But you – you remain my angel, my good, my only Rosalie! Remain so for ever!'[55]

It was not Geyer but Rosalie who awakened his interest in art. Although Wagner himself felt that she was not especially talented as an actress, her imagination and her appreciation of art and of the higher things of life were all the more keenly developed. 'It was from her that I heard the first amazing out-pourings about everything that later excited me too.' Long before Wagner himself, Rosalie was fired by a very real enthusiasm for Shakespeare and Goethe. Weber, too, was a source of profound inspiration, and she also sang Beethoven's Leonore to him, while accompanying herself at the piano.

The role of Leonore left a particularly deep mark on Wagner as Rosalie sang the part 'with both rapt enthusiasm and sadness at the fact that she had no voice'.[56] For her brother, she also sang Schubert's 'most beautiful' song, *Sei mir gegrüßt*. Even in old age this song still moved him to tears. 'That is German', he told Cosima, 'so pure and chaste and heartfelt.'[57] In *Tannhäuser* he was not only to erect a monument to his sister in the role of the pure, chaste, heartfelt Elisabeth, he also placed the words 'Sei mir gegrüßt' in her mouth in her very first scene.

It was presumably because he was introduced to the stage by his stepfather that Wagner developed such a strained relationship with the spoken theatre, whereas he felt the same affection for the musical theatre as the sister who embodied it for him. Even though he was later unconvinced by her abilities as both an actress and a singer, it was the link between them that impressed him. The kind of dramatic vocal art that brought her success was one that she held out to him as a serious professional possibility.

It was only because, as a famous artist, Rosalie put in a good word for her little brother at the Leipzig Theatre that Wagner received his earliest commissions. And it was only because of her connections that his early works were performed. It is quite possible that without her example, without her constant encouragement and financial support, he would not have had the perseverance to train as a musician. Later he rewrote this chapter of his past, as he wanted to present himself to the world as a Siegfried who, as the myth demanded, forged his own sword by himself. But it was Rosalie who offered him the space in which to try out his weapon.

Just as, in the world of Wagner's imagination, his mother Johanna and his stepfather Geyer came to embody the demonic in all its archetypal appallingness, so Rosalie represented that aspect of divine love that brings redemption through self-sacrifice. He discovered his own identity between these two extremes, forever unable to decide which side he belonged to.

He was the hero of the piece, a man who lived in the present but behind whom larger-than-life figures rose up out of the past, casting their shadows over everything he encountered and channelling into prescribed conduits all that he felt and thought and created.

The Wolf's Glen

For two years little Richard Geyer led the life of an exile. Only after serving time in Possendorf, Eisleben and the haunted house in Leipzig was he finally allowed to return to his family in Dresden in 1822. In December of that year the now nine-year-old youth enrolled at the city's Kreuzschule. Highly strung and easily distracted, he was smaller than the other boys in his class and so sought to make an impression through sheer noise and feverish activity, seeking to gratify his burning ambition to be the centre of attention through grandiose deeds.

His imagination found a new field of activity when he discovered a puppet theatre among his late stepfather's effects, its principal charm consisting in the sets that Geyer himself had painted. Writing in his autobiography, Wagner recalled wanting to surprise his family with a brilliant performance, and so he made some puppets, carving them himself, albeit 'with the greatest clumsiness'. Then, following his stepfather's example, he made suitable costumes for them, before finally sitting down and writing his first stage work. It was to be a 'Ritterstück', normally a neo-medieval piece about knights and deeds of chivalry, but in the light of his own experiences more likely to be a Gothic tale of love and death designed to inspire terror in its audience.

Wagner's model was Duke Bluebeard. At the age of only five he had seen Grétry's opera on the subject, a tale about the ruthless Raoul who punishes women's disobedience with death. One of Wagner's 'earliest childhood memories' was the surprise he instilled in his family when, following the performance, he regaled them with the monster's aria 'Ha! Du Falsche! Die Türe offen' ('Ha, false woman! The door is open!'). He performed it with great relish and with a paper helmet of his own devising on his head. As he later told Cosima, all that he lacked to complete the picture was 'Raoul's white plume'.[58]

Now the effect was to be reproduced on Geyer's miniature stage, but raised to a higher level by means of a play of Wagner's own composition. He had barely completed the opening scene when impatience got the better of him and he insisted on impressing his sisters with a sample of his skills, but instead of the horror he had hoped for, his performance elicited only 'immoderate laughter'. In particular, the line 'I hear the knightly footsteps falling', gasped by the bride when, mortally afraid, she is caught in flagrante delicto, was quoted back at him by his sisters who, to his intense annoyance, invested the words with exaggerated emotion.

Wagner's next attempt to follow in Geyer's footsteps was likewise dogged by misfortune. While staying at Loschwitz during the summer of 1822, he decided to perform his Gothic tragedy in the open air, with the result that theatre, sets, puppets and chairs had to be transported to the Burgberg, where the curtain rose on the afternoon performance of this gruesome piece in which the director himself operated all the puppets, mimicking Raoul's deep voice with the same impassioned enthusiasm as the desperate screams of his soon-to-be-butchered bride. The audience, which included Wagner's mother, unfortunately had little time to appreciate what was on offer as a storm gathered over the Burgberg, a perfect accompaniment to the play's Gothic subject matter. Gusts of wind overturned the stage and torrential rain poured down on the empty rows of seats. Wagner himself was left on his own, 'in the ruins of his own world', as Wotan was later to describe himself.

More fruitful was his encounter with a German example of Gothic horror that was to leave a lifelong impression on him. Carl Maria von Weber's *Der Freischütz* received its triumphant first performance in 1821 – the year of Geyer's death – and soon became a runaway success. It was no accident that Wagner had played its best-known tune to the dying Geyer. Nor was it long before Wagner himself attempted to stage the work in the family living room in Dresden, with school friends drafted in as his fellow performers. Once again he took personal responsibility for all the props, setting particular store by such details as Samiel's 'devilish whistle'.

He cast himself in the main demonic role of Caspar, whose drinking song 'Hier im ird'schen Jammertal' he is said to have carried off with incomparably 'devilish' expression in terms of both gesture and voice. Indeed, his enthusiasm for *Der Freischütz* went so far that at one performance he fell in love with the Aennchen, and he never forgot how, at the passage 'Blicke hin und Blicke her', she would coquettishly raise her apron and cover her face, while 'allowing her gaze to roam'.[59]

The model for his domestic performances of *Der Freischütz* – which were notable for their 'grotesquely painted' masks – was the Dresden production of 1822, which he often heard under the composer's own direction. Whenever he saw Weber passing his house after a rehearsal, he was overcome by a sense of reverential awe. The composer's delicate, haggard and 'spiritually transfigured appearance', he wrote in *My Life*, filled him with literally 'ecstatic concern'. The locals called him 'Limping Mary' on account of his hoppling gait, but to Wagner he seemed a being from another world. 'There goes the greatest man alive,' he would assure his sister Cäcilie. And whenever he saw Weber as an autocratic ruler in the orchestra pit, he would dream of taking his place: 'Neither emperor nor king, but to stand there and conduct like that!'[60]

Occasionally Wagner's idol would visit his widowed mother. When he enquired politely whether her youngest boy was thinking of becoming a musician, she replied that, although he was mad about *Der Freischütz*, there were no other signs of any 'musical talent'. Goaded by this insult, Wagner followed his sisters' example and tried to dazzle his listeners with a piano rendition of *Der Freischütz*, but lacking the requisite skills, he quickly gave up the attempt and decided to teach himself music.

Not meeting with much success, he persuaded his private tutor, a certain Herr Humann, to initiate him into the mysteries of piano playing. He had barely taken his first steps when he began to memorize the overture to the opera, initially without a score. The fruits of his efforts were presented to his family and proved 'extremely amateurish'. According to Wagner's own later account, 'my teacher heard it once and declared that nothing would ever become of me'.[61]

In practising *Der Freischütz* on his own, Wagner was clearly concerned not just to master the notes: there may well be another reason for the fact that he spent years grappling with this one particular opera – he wanted not only to master the piece but also to come to terms with the world that it represented for him. Only by learning and inwardly digesting *Der Freischütz* could he regain control of the feelings that the piece triggered in him. After all, it was very much the traumatic experiences of horror and the fear of ghosts that kept him awake at night and that were predictably revived here. The opera's 'eerie' subject matter was to exert a very real fascination on him for many years to come.[62]

It was almost as though the tune of the Bridesmaids' Chorus had become associated in Wagner's mind with the death of his stepfather, with the result that Geyer's demonic charisma now passed to *Der Freischütz*, just as it had once passed to the portrait gallery in the Thomä House in Leipzig. The sombre world that exerted such an oppressive influence on Wagner's imagination and also on his dreams was the opera's central theme. With all the means at its disposal, this alternative world was seeking to seize control. Its only aim, pursued with devilish ruthlessness, was the destruction of the innocent.

This dark world existed, then, and the proof was to be found in the music. The terror that seized hold of him at night acquired a tangible presence in Weber's harmonic writing. The very sound of the instruments tuning up instilled in him a sense of mystical agitation. 'I remember in particular that the open fifths on a violin seemed to me like a greeting from the spirit world.' Even before this, the sound of these fifths had recalled 'the sense of eeriness that had always excited me'. He could never walk past a certain town mansion near where an unseen violinist could be heard making these sounds, without feeling afraid. It was as though the music were being played by the stone putti that came to life as he approached – thus, at least, his trauma would have it. He later described these sustained pure fifths as 'the ghostly fundamental of my life'.[63]

The gates of the 'enchanted realm of horror' opened up to him each time he heard the swelling C of the *Freischütz* overture. Later, too, whenever he picked up a copy of the story on which the opera was based he would feel himself transported back to the threatening world of his childhood. 'In the evening R. reads me Apel's short story *Der Freischütz*', Cosima noted in her diary shortly before Wagner's fifty-sixth birthday. 'Much affected and excited by it. R. is afraid to put out the lights.'[64]

Wagner's reaction to this harmless tale is all the more astonishing in that it was very familiar ground here. By the time he learnt the story as a child, it had long been family lore. The family of its author, Johann August Apel, had lived in the Thomä House in Leipzig – the very house that was the scene of Wagner's darkest experiences. 'Gespenster-Apel', or 'Apel of the Ghosts', as he was known, had been friendly with both Adolf Wagner and his brother Friedrich, and there is even a possibility that he caricatured Wagner's father in his *Gespensterbuch* of 1810, which also includes *Der Freischütz*.

While E. T. A. Hoffmann had mentioned that Friedrich Wagner was not averse to the odd tipple of rum, Apel may well have immortalized him in the character of Actuarius Wermut – Registrar Absinth – who, every evening after he has 'dealt with his delinquents', turns up at the author's home to smoke his pipe and drink beer. In much the same way, the poet who turned Apel's tale into an opera libretto also makes an appearance in the Wagner family biography: Friedrich Kind had his portrait painted by Ludwig Geyer and was the author of *Der Weinberg an der Elbe*, in which the young Wagner appeared as a little angel.

It is difficult to find in Apel's naïve 'folktale' the potential for fear that it represented for Wagner. The poet tells a common-or-garden tale about devils in which, differently from the opera, evil ultimately triumphs. Two young lovers are allowed to marry only on condition that the bridegroom Wilhelm proves a crack shot. Only if he does so will he win both bride and the hereditary post of forester. But the devil, wanting to prevent this, casts a spell on Wilhelm's rifle, causing him in his despair to use magic bullets that a demonic figure with a wooden leg tells him how to make. When Wilhelm fires his trial short, the bullet strikes not the target but his own bride. Overcome by horror and feelings of guilt, he goes mad when confronted by her bier. Translated into Wagner's own private mythology, this must mean that, in order to deprive the hero of both his bride and his inheritance, his enemy persuades him to be untrue to himself. The result is devastating. Inwardly torn, the hero ultimately loses everything, including his reason.

That Wagner was able to rediscover in Apel's *Der Freischütz* the trauma associated with his own origins was due in no small measure to a number of details that seem almost to have been introduced into the narrative with Wagner himself in mind. The doleful hero, for example, is a registrar by profession – just like the police actuary Friedrich Wagner. The ancestral portrait that he inherits mysteriously falls from the wall at the very moment that Wilhelm confides in the one-legged man. The identity of this dark tempter becomes clear when Wilhelm shoots his first magic bullet: 'A great vulture [Geier] fell bleeding to earth.'

This conversation between the hero and his seemingly all-powerful adversary left such a deep impression on Wagner that decades later it recurs at a crucial point in the *Ring*. Just as the clerk, wanting to win his bride, is opposed by the devil himself, so Siegfried is detained by Wotan on his way to waken his bride. It is to Wotan that Siegfried owes the 'magic sword' that he wields, just as Wilhelm owes his magic bullets to the powers of evil.

In both scenes, the threatening father figure comes to remind his son of his dependency. While Wilhelm, with his bullets already in his pocket, brazenly retorts that 'what I need I've made myself', Siegfried makes it plain to the god that he has forged his sword on his own. Wotan's condescending reply, 'If only you knew me, bold scion,' echoes the words of Apel's devil, who asks the 'bold' freeshooter: 'Do you know me?' In both cases the sons inevitably fail to recognize the true nature of their disguised forebears, with the result that, following the exchange, the latter vanish without trace, while the heroes hurry away to certain ruin.

This archetypal relationship between the characters acquired yet greater poignancy in Kind's operatic reworking, in which the conflict between the two adversaries is elaborated with even more clarity, so that it was only in its operatic version that the story of *Der Freischütz* could serve as a mythological model that would explain Wagner's own past. The hero, who is now called Max, has become the hereditary forester's adopted son. As a young and aspiring huntsman, he duly falls in love with his adoptive father's daughter, Agathe, who thus becomes his 'bride and sister', their relationship acquiring an ambiguous aspect as something both fated and illicit.

Before the heroes can win their respective brides, both have to perform a task set them by their ancestors and achievable only with the help of evil. In the case of Kind, this power of evil was divided between the figures of the devil Samiel and his victim Caspar. Condemned to eternal wanderings like the Flying Dutchman, Caspar has to sacrifice a woman to his master at regular intervals. Once again his deadline is fast approaching, and the devil's factotum lures the naïve Max into his trap by mixing his drink with magic drops, just as the evil Hagen does with Siegfried. When the unsuspecting hero asks him to hand over the magic bullets, Caspar shouts at him: 'Are you in thrall to the vulture, comrade?'

He has long been in thrall to the vulture. So alienated is he from himself, the young huntsman now has to descend into the world of ghosts, a world which, like some demonic theatre, seems to hold out the prospect of a dream come true, whereas in fact he is to lose everything there: bride and inheritance, body and soul. Like the treacherous Hagen, Caspar too celebrates the hero's impending downfall as an act of 'revenge'. Admittedly, Kind and Weber avoided this denouement by having the magic bullet strike down the right man, but Wagner refused to accept this consolation: in the *Ring* – his own sequel to *Der Freischütz* – he was to give precedence to Apel's tragic variant.

From the outset, the spectacular scene in the Wolf's Glen seems to have been the opera's nucleus in Wagner's imagination. Here, at dead of night in the gloomy fairytale forest, decisive encounters take place: first, the devil meets his submissive instrument Caspar, after which Caspar himself awaits the hero, who unwittingly allows himself to be debased to the level of the instrument of an instrument. Scarcely has he arrived when spells are cast and a supernatural storm is conjured up, a storm that was later to shake the sets of the Nibelung theatre. It was in the Wolf's Glen scene that all hell first broke loose, a hell that Wagner would unleash on countless subsequent occasions.

When Wagner spoke of his fear of ghosts in the context of *Der Freischütz*, it will have been this scene, above all, that he had in mind, for his experience in the Thomä House in Leipzig, where dead objects had suddenly come to life, becomes a theatrical reality in the Wolf's Glen scene. The evil spirits are initially invisible, but the whole ravine soon starts to stir. 'The very stones are alive!' Max cries out in his dismay, as a branch tries to seize him like some mighty fist. As ghostly phantasms flit to and fro, the pit of hell opens up and Satan himself appears in the guise of Samiel in order to claim his fresh victim. The magic bullets are cast, and the Wild Hunt draws nigh in a storm cloud, while the earth appears to disgorge its very insides in a roaring inferno. Wagner's nocturnal hallucinations may have been out of his control, but here, at least, they were held in check by artistic means. And he recognized as the ruler over this world of sound the hunched figure who limped past his window at the end of each day's rehearsal.

In 1841, twenty years after the work's first performance, Wagner was asked to write an article on *Der Freischütz* for the benefit of Parisian audiences, and here he virtually equated the work as a whole with this one key scene. For him the nocturnal conjuration took place in a distant no-man's-land 'inaccessible to your steps' (to quote from Lohengrin's Grail Narration). Only a lonely huntsman, he fantasized, could reach this ravine by chance, so remote was it from the beaten tracks. He himself offered to act as a Virgilian guide through this Dantesque Inferno and indeed seemed intimately familiar with the place, with the result that his account of the Wolf's Glen scene contains far more detail than he knew from either Apel's story or Weber's opera. Clearly he allowed himself to be carried away while writing the article and reinvented the whole setting, reinstrumenting it along more elaborate lines. Fired by his own enthusiasm, he went far beyond the familiarly eerie world of the opera, perhaps only stopping short at the point where his nightmares had taken him in the wake of Geyer's death.

Even as the huntsman is still approaching the ravine, Wagner explained to his French readers, he hears a strange noise. Although there is no wind, a muffled moaning sways the branches of the ancient pines, which bow their dark heads to and fro unbidden. When he finally plucks up the courage to peer down into the abyss, he sees jagged reefs of rock towering upwards 'in the shape of human limbs and horribly distorted faces'. Beside them lie heaps of pitch-black stones in the form of 'giant toads and lizards'. Appalled, he sees these objects begin to move. What he thought were stones 'creep and roll in heavy, tangled masses'. Finally he realizes that everything that had crept along the ground and flown through the air, robbing him of his breath with its pestilential stench, is in fact dead: 'everything that seemed animated by a semblance of life in this bottomless chasm lay as though in a deathlike slumber, and all that had seemed to move merely moved in the mind of one plunged deep in dreams'.

Suddenly there are noises, filling him with 'horror'. But they too seem unreal, appearing, rather, to issue from a world of ghosts in which cause and effect are out of joint. 'A storm that stirs nothing and whose gusts he himself cannot feel', Wagner reports with the stunned immediacy of an eyewitness, 'howls over the ravine, then suddenly stops, as if listening to itself, before breaking out again with added fury.' Soon other sounds reach his ear, borne by the ghostly wind, terrible cries of grief, the screeches and groans of the damned that rend his heart with an anguish that he has never felt before. Then everything falls silent once again. 'All motion ceases; only in the depths does there seem to be a sluggish writhing.'

Although these experiences – as Wagner knew only too well – fill the huntsman with unspeakable fear, he none the less descends into the jaws of hell. Only here, in Weber's Wolf's Glen, can he cast the magic bullets that will win him both bride and inheritance. Boldly he enters the world of him who can conjure up hell. And hell obeys him: 'Everything awakens from its deathly slumber, everything comes to life and swirls and stretches; the howling turns to a roar, the groaning to the sound of raging fury; a thousand grimaces circle the magic ring.' His senses fail him, but the bullets have now been cast.[65]

Wagner's free retelling of the story of *Der Freischütz* was intended to whet his readers' appetite for the first French production of the work at the Académie Royale de Musique, but it actually describes the dynamics of Wagner's own creative response to it. Only he who exposes himself to the terrible visions of the subconscious can cast the magic bullets of music. From the bottomless pit of the early childhood terrors that he witnessed on stage as though in a mirror, the eerie world of the sounds of his later operas and music dramas would one day arise. In *Der fliegende Holländer*, *Lohengrin* and the *Ring*, he conjured up the demonic power that was to oppose his errant heroes in the guise of their fatal adversaries.

Weber himself had regarded his operas as a battleground between good and the powers of evil, allotting to the latter a world of sound that was as ghostly as could be and that was represented by instruments with eerie tone colours. 'I gave a great deal of thought to the question of what was the right principal colouring for this sinister element,' wrote the composer of *Der Freischütz*. 'Naturally it had to be a dark, gloomy colour – the lowest register of the violins, violas and basses, particularly the lowest register of the clarinet.'[66] Wagner learnt the art of tone painting from Weber, later telling Cosima that before

Weber no one had had 'any inkling of the ability of certain instruments (oboe, clarinet) to create a sense of horror'.[67]

And there is no doubt that since Wagner's day the music of the Wolf's Glen scene in *Der Freischütz* has sounded as though all the storms are brewing here that were later to be unleashed with their shrilly whistling fifths in *Der fliegende Holländer* and *Die Walküre*, while from the insidious flickering of the strings that herald the approach of Weber's witching hour there seem to rise the moonlit banks of the Rhine in Act Two of *Götterdämmerung*, where the Nibelungs Alberich and Hagen plot to kill Siegfried, like reincarnations of the black elves Caspar and Samiel. And, as the only genuine leitmotif in his opera, Weber gave his Satan the same diminished seventh as the one with which his successor was later to inspire such horror.

When the magic spell is cast in the Wolf's Glen scene, conjuring up the terrifying figures of the past, we hear a striking figure in the orchestra, flickering its way up and down the scale like some eerie will-o'-the-wisp. More than thirty years later, Wagner used a similar figure as the basis of his Forest Murmurs in *Siegfried*. In the soughing of the trees and the dancing beams of sunlight that fall through the trembling leaves, Siegfried feels an awakening longing to know who his true parents are. And at the same time he feels a mounting sense of anger at his adoptive father, to whom Wagner significantly gave the name 'Mime'.

As long as Siegfried can remember, the hypocritical ham actor has brought him up for his own selfish ends, until he has discovered at last that he is not his real father. For the reborn hero, the Forest Murmurs represent a promise that he can finally break free from the nightmarish Mime and begin to lead a life of his own. For Wagner, by contrast, it brought the certainty that he was the true heir of the composer who was the first to weave his mysterious spell in the forest. (Weber's name literally means 'weaver' in German.) 'I already know about the horrors that the hour of midnight weaves in the forest,' sings Max, the hero of *Der Freischütz*.

When in 1843 Wagner was appointed Weber's successor as court Kapellmeister in Dresden, he set himself the 'wonderful task' of continuing his predecessor's work, later even claiming that his Romantic forebear was his spiritual 'father'.[68] Weber was a Romantic who, as a painter in musical sounds, seemed to borrow those sounds from nature and who, in philosophizing about music, founded a school of 'German' opera. Even with his notorious claim that to be German meant 'doing something for its own sake alone', Wagner tacitly revealed himself as Weber's natural heir. After all, Weber himself had once said of the 'German artist' that he alone had the 'zeal silently to undertake something for its own sake alone'.[69]

Weber had been appointed Kapellmeister to the Royal Court of Saxony in 1816 with the brief to establish a German opera company in Dresden. By 1817 he had already invited the city's music lovers to forswear the 'sensual delights' of French and Italian opera and plunge uninhibitedly into the world of autochthonous music. German musicians alone could succeed in producing a 'self-contained work of art in which all the parts come together to form a beautiful, rounded whole'.[70] Until then the musical life of Dresden had been dominated by the likes of Francesco Morlacchi and Gaspare Spontini, but within five years Weber had routed them with the 'beautiful, rounded whole' of *Der Freischütz*, while dividing local audiences into two opposing camps: the German national patriots and the supporters of the Italian style that was favoured by the court.

In 1817, in a review of E. T. A. Hoffmann's opera *Undine*, Weber had defined his ideal of a national synthesis of the arts in which 'every element and every contribution on the part of the arts that have been used and pressed into service disappear by merging with each other and, as it were, vanish in order to form a new world.' Derived from the repertory of ideas associated with German idealism, this dialectical concept showed the way forward for the music drama of the future. That one first had to disappear – Weber uses the verb 'untergehen' – in order to be reborn on a higher level, both in life and in art, was later to become an essential article of Wagner's own faith.

Only months after Weber had formulated this forward-looking concept, the four-year-old Richard Geyer made his first appearance on stage, as a rose-coloured angel in *Der Weinberg an der Elbe*, for which the future composer of *Der Freischütz* had provided some of the music.

Richard Lionheart

At the age of thirteen, Richard Geyer suddenly found himself alone in the world again, when Carl Maria von Weber died unexpectedly in London in June 1826. His death, Wagner later recalled, filled his 'child's heart with horror'. It was shortly after this that his sister Rosalie, the family's breadwinner, who had done so much to encourage his own career, moved to Prague to take up an engagement with the German Theatre in the city. It was an engagement that was to lead to a lengthy separation from the brother who 'loved her tenderly'. Rosalie was accompanied to Bohemia by her mother and her three sisters Klara, Ottilie and Cäcilie, while Wagner himself found a pitiful refuge in Dresden with a family by the name of Böhme. It was presumably in an attempt to get over the loss of his sisters that he worked himself up into a state of what he called 'boyhood infatuation', first of all courting Malchen Lehmann, whose hair he was fond of stroking, and then falling for the aloof Leah David. The following year he met Marie Löw in Leipzig, who inspired in him feelings of ardent but unrequited love. Evidently it was Jewish girls who came closest to his early ideal in such matters.

No doubt, too, it was his own sisters who helped to fashion this ideal, now that they were no longer able to make his 'heart beat anxiously and violently' with the 'more delicate objects from their dressing rooms'. They were replaced by Böhme's grown-up daughters and the latters' female friends, who lent a certain lustre to the wretched confines of his new home. In order to help his awakening sensuality on its way, he pretended to be 'mindlessly sleepy in order to be put to bed by these girls with all the efforts that this state appeared to require'.[71] But as he was later happy to admit, he was not in fact sleepy at all. He had noticed to his surprise that these attentions brought him 'into direct contact with the female being', and from now on he was regularly overcome by tiredness in Dr Böhme's little parlour.

His desires were unexpectedly intensified when he paid a brief visit to Prague that winter and made some new acquaintances. Here his sister Ottilie introduced him to her friends Jenny and Auguste Raymann, who were regarded as the 'outstanding beauties' of the town. The fact that they were the illegitimate daughters of Count Johann Joseph von Pachta, who, as director of the Prague Conservatory, had been friendly with the young Ludwig Geyer, may have added to their charms in the eyes of the adolescent Wagner. At all events, he seems to have fallen for them on the spot. And following his return to a life of exile with the Böhmes, he thought only of throwing himself at their feet again as soon as he could.

His chance came during the 1827 spring holidays. Accompanied by one of Böhme's sons, he set off on the long march back to Prague, catching sunstroke on the way, so that Johanna Rosine had to treat him with a parsley poultice. We do not know whether the earlier romance was continued following his recovery, although his ardour seems not to have cooled as he arranged to meet the two beauties again many years later. As he was leaving Prague on the present occasion, he turned round, his bundle on his back, and casting a final glance at the city, fell to the ground, overcome by tears, in order to embrace his beloved Bohemian earth.

Not long after this, Wagner was confirmed, an occasion he later recalled 'with a shudder of emotion'. Now he wanted to become a poet. Having attracted attention at the Kreuzschule with his poetic reworkings of classical legends, he felt that the time had come to break free from 'the constraints of school and family'.[72] During the summer, his fondness for long journeys on foot took him back to Leipzig, where his Uncle Adolf had in the meantime broken free from his sister Friederike and her friend Jeannette Thomä. And at the age of fifty, he had tied the knot with a writer whose first name, oddly enough, was Adolfine.

As a result, Adolf had turned his back on the Thomä House in order to pursue his humanist studies elsewhere. With his felt hat on his greying skull, he continued to spend his days surrounded by ancient tomes, inhabiting a world of classical antiquity that had tempted his nephew into imitating it. From swift Achilles to nimble-witted Odysseus, Adolf could declaim Wagner's heroes in the original. He had translated Sophocles' tragedies and had even been commended by Goethe and Schiller. As before, he still waxed indignant at the decline of the German theatres that were being destroyed by foreign influences.

Uncle and nephew soon hit it off. Wagner regaled his uncle with his knowledge of classical antiquity, a knowledge all the more impressive for being so concentrated, encouraging Adolf to think that he was once again in the presence of his late brother Friedrich. This Nestor of the Wagnerian tradition now resolved on a significant gesture and took his nephew on one final visit to the Thomä House, where an old bookcase stood in the hallway. Adolf opened it and allowed his nephew's eyes to range over the 'fairly extensive library'. These, Adolf explained, had been his brother's books and were now to belong to Wagner. Whereas Geyer had left him only a puppet theatre, Friedrich Wagner had bequeathed him a veritable treasure in the form of books by classical writers in valuable complete editions. It was with 'delighted astonishment' that Wagner now claimed his inheritance. Could there still be any lingering doubts as to who his true father was?

Presumably this question was also a topic of conversation between uncle and nephew. From the outset, Adolf had objected to Geyer's intrusive presence in the family. He loathed the whole business of acting to which the family had remained committed even after Geyer's death. Now the moment seemed to have come to win back his promising nephew and reclaim him for the humanist Wagner tradition. Wagner's reaction to all this – the rediscovery of his true father and, with it, his emancipation from the hated Other – is clear from the fact that he now gave up Geyer's name and reverted to the one with which he had been christened. 'That he is not my father', his hero Siegfried was later to rejoice, 'how happy I feel at that!'

And Wagner drew the obvious conclusion from this, leaving Geyer's Dresden and the home of the widow of the court silver-washer where he had been renting rooms and settling definitively in his father's home town of Leipzig. At Christmas 1827 he moved in with his mother and sisters, who had in the meantime returned from Prague. And it was as Richard Wagner that he enrolled at the Nikolaischule in Leipzig at the beginning of 1828, where he immediately suffered a bitter blow, having to repeat a year to his own 'indescribable annoyance'.

There were evidently good reasons for this. During his final months in Dresden he had avoided doing any schoolwork and evaded the surveillance of the family with whom he was staying, preferring to seek refuge in an isolated attic and to conceive a stage play of Shakespearean dimensions. Already convinced that the piece was bound to be successful, he had neglected his studies and, to quote his own ironical comment, 'left far behind' him the 'paths of a regular academic schooling'. Rebelling, he soon turned the entire teaching staff against him and sought out his own path in life, a path by which he hoped to achieve his life's aim independently.

In this, he was not entirely alone, as his Uncle Adolf was there to support him. A 'truly free spirit', as Wagner described him, Adolf hated all forms of pedantry, especially those practised at the country's secondary schools, and he confirmed Wagner in his aversion to them by ridiculing blind obedience. When the director of the Kreuzschule complained to Wagner's famous uncle about his nephew's behaviour, Adolf effortlessly sided with Wagner, attempting to comfort him with the maxim that one's superiors are always right.

This may have been true for others, but Wagner reacted by withdrawing into himself. Every day the fifteen-year-old youth would accompany his uncle on his afternoon strolls round the city and discovered that a man who appeared to be an unworldly hermit was in fact a lively conversationalist who was a pleasure to be with. Sunk in 'profound and often animated discussions', the odd couple – Wagner later surmised – may well have provoked the amusement of passers-by, but the subjects that exercised them were none the less engrossing and wide-ranging.

Wagner heard his uncle hold forth on classical philology and German idealistic philosophy, on *Oedipus Tyrannus*, which Adolf had translated into German, and on Goethe, who had presented him with a silver goblet. They discussed *Faust*, although Adolf insisted that his nephew was still too young to understand it. And he also recited Shakespeare's plays, which he knew by heart and which he declaimed in a pleasingly resonant voice. Whereas 'the serious and the sublime' had hitherto been neglected in Wagner's education, his uncle now made up for lost time, Wagner commenting retrospectively that he was 'of considerable importance' for his 'idiosyncratic education'.

No doubt he also influenced Wagner's political views. Adolf Wagner believed in the German spirit that would one day triumph over decadent imported culture, just as the student Karl Ludwig Sand had put paid to the farceur August von Kotzebue. Taking his uncle as his lead, Wagner, too, felt 'drawn to all things German'. And while Adolf's worldly wisdom and the books bequeathed by his father may have struck him as tokens of this intellectual and spiritual superiority, he was soon to marvel at the student demonstrations on the streets of Leipzig, demonstrations that heralded German liberation.

By now Wagner had already embarked, in all secrecy, on his own course of liberation from the slavery of school and, at the same time, from his false family tradition. No longer would he belong to that painted species of man that liked to keep changing the mask it wore and enjoyed performing allotted roles without ever penetrating to their essence.

For Wagner, the essence was the work itself. The piece that he had begun in the garret of the widow of the man who had once washed the silver at the royal court in Dresden was now resumed in an attic overlooking the Leipzig Pichhof. Since 'falling out' with his school, he later explained, he had devoted himself exclusively to a work of art that claimed his whole attention for a considerable period of time. Needless to say, it was a 'great tragedy'.[73]

In fact, it was a *very* great tragedy, its four thousand lines bidding fair to equal Shakespeare's longest drama, *Hamlet*. And like the latter it would have lasted around six hours in performance. Wagner later claimed that it was Shakespeare who inspired him to create this monster. It was 'cobbled together from *Lear* and *Hamlet*', he recalled, to which may be added *Macbeth*, Goethe's *Götz von Berlichingen* and a number of tales of chivalry. It was in a spirit of irony that he reported on his attempt to emulate Shakespeare's tragedies, which he claimed to have interpreted in a 'demonically fantastical' light.[74] And he went on to assert that he had wanted to invest the whole with a 'hint of originality' by using a highly affected script. Thus, at least, he thought he remembered it. The manuscript, he added, had 'unfortunately gone missing'.

Wagner's much later claim that the play was 'essentially a variation of *Hamlet*' is not entirely true. Now that the manuscript has resurfaced, it is clear that its hero is in fact decisive in the extreme. Where Hamlet hesitates, Leubald blithely plunges in. And commentators have looked in vain for the 'forty-two people' who, according to Wagner's 'Autobiographical Sketch', died in the course of the piece, so that, as he drolly explained, they had to return as ghosts, otherwise he would have had no characters left for the final acts. A quick head count reveals that, including two murders that take place before the curtain rises, there are in fact only fourteen deaths. Moreover, the handwriting barely differs from the composer's usual calligraphy at this time. And his memory failed him even with regard to the title of his first work for the stage, which was not called *Leubald and Adelaide* but simply *Leubald: A Tragedy*.[75]

Wagner's unusual memory lapse is in fact understandable as the piece is at odds with his early reminiscences, in which he was invariably at pains to depict his own origins as serenely cheerful and idyllic. If as a writer of tragedies he portrayed human existence in all its inner discord, as his own biographer – especially in his dealings with Cosima – he wanted his childhood to appear in an idealized light. But the state of harmony that ostensibly reigned in the Geyer household was emphatically called into question by *Leubald*, whose eponymous hero succumbs to a fate very different from those suffered by Hamlet and all the other characters whom Wagner had previously encountered. Leubald became Wagner's own hero, his drama based on no direct model.

In his later works, from *Die Feen* to *Parsifal*, Wagner always borrowed from existing subjects, but in the case of his very first opus number he invented his only independent story line. And it was very much his own story – not the story that the memoirist dictated to his mistress to impress the king of Bavaria, but the events that the young Richard Geyer had experienced for himself and that he reinterpreted in the light of his own fantasies about his origins. *Leubald* was his first attempt to shed light on his mysterious family history. As a poet he was able to lighten the darkness that had beset him for years in the form of his fear of ghosts and nightmares. But this is something that the mature Wagner could no longer accept. Once he had tasted success, he preferred to reduce his origins to a series of harmless anecdotes.

For the young Wagner, the theatre had been bound up from the outset with the tormenting experience of horror. In *Leubald* he sought to confront the theatre on its own ground and to come to terms with horror by depicting it as such. If he locked himself away in his attic with this piece and, as he told his sister Cäcilie, 'neglected school because of it', it was because the figments of his imagination 'rose up before him out of the ground and assumed such vital forms that he himself was afraid of them'.[76]

And the piece certainly offered opportunity aplenty for horror. It creates the impression of a single sequence of monstrous crimes, most of them committed by the hero. That sorrow and grief are best overcome by being inflicted on others is Leubald's motto in life. In him, the author proudly painted his first self-portrait, calling him Leubald because he himself was born under the sign of the Red and White Lion in Leipzig – 'Leu' is a poetical word for a lion in German. Later he was to claim the 'dying lion' as his coat of arms.[77] Leubald's father, too, is likened to a brave lion who falls in battle to a feathered beast of prey.

At the beginning of this trail of horror, both summing it up and providing its starting point, is a clandestine act of fratricide. The hero's father Siegmer is insidiously poisoned by his best friend Roderich because – to quote Wagner's artificial verse – 'Bertha spurned Sir Roderich and gave herself to Siegmer'. Behind the figure of Bertha we may well suspect not only Shakespeare's Gertrude but also the poet's own mother, whose alleged maiden name, Perthes, sounds uncannily like Bertha when pronounced with a Dresden accent. And behind Roderich's mask the eyes of Wagner's stepfather Ludwig Geyer may clearly be seen to flash. Like a 'bird of prey' that 'circles over its prey ere it plunges down and snatches it away', the latter has poisoned his friend and taken possession of his wife. Siegmer's dispossessed son is left with no choice but to take his own life.

First, however, Siegmer's ghost extorts from him a vow to avenge his death – much as in Shakespeare's play. In this way he unleashes a breathtaking sequence of rapes, murders and sundry other crimes that are committed against the background of a play about cruel knights reminiscent of *Bluebeard* and couched in an earthy language teeming with the lewdest of metaphors. The neurotically anxious Prince of Denmark is effortlessly overshadowed by Leubald in both word and deed. Not only the hated usurper Roderich falls victim to his lionlike bloodlust, but his entire clan is wiped out. Only when 'his kin has atoned with his blood' can Leubald follow his hapless father and find his quietus in death. Perhaps similar thoughts assailed their author when, alone in his tiny attic, he again felt abandoned by his kin.

But unlike Wagner, who was forced to conceal his bitterness, Leubald is allowed to act. And all that he has planned is dutifully carried out and even repaid with interest: more horrifying scenes than the cold-blooded murders of Roderich, his wife and their sons can scarcely have been found even in plays as gory as *The Orphan and the Murderer*. Leubald and, with him, his fifteen-year-old author positively revel in overt sadism. When Roderich hears of his wife's murder, he is overwhelmed by a vision of cruelty: 'Is't so?' he screams. 'You saw her bleeding? Is't so? Her breast torn open, bared, so blood could flow unhemmed?' In Wagner's lurid imagination, the 'bloody wellspring' stains her 'bosom's swanwhite bed'.

Alongside this streak of cruelty, Wagner also indulged a particularly sophisticated fondness for sexual imagery, with lasciviousness, coupling and pregnancy occurring with striking frequency from the very first scene to the last, but always in their 'poisoned' variants of violence, adultery and incest. It is as though Wagner's insight into his own dubious origins had filled him with feelings of unease about the whole of the human race and forced him to speak with contempt and loathing about subjects which at that stage he can scarcely have known about from his own experience. Here, for the first time, he contrasted the 'sinful morass' of 'contemptible' sensuality with a tender love-death in which the gratification of desire is straightway expiated by death.

Even the opening scene of this schoolboy drama is unusually shocking. A homeless footpad by the name of Flamming boasts of having attacked a young couple who were riding through the forest in tender embrace. Having peremptorily despatched the young man, he throws himself on the bride. 'Hey, I say, we soon hit it off', the rapist brags, 'as soon as the cur had closed his eyes; – marry, that was the best of it! The forest floor was soft enough; – there'll be a round belly to follow that jape, or else I've lost my touch.' His companion retorts that 'it's an ill deed to kill a good knight and deceive his girl', thus providing the play with its moral right at the outset. And, indeed, *Leubald* revolves around this shameful act in all its variants. Above all, the consequences of his action – the 'round belly' that turns the covert crime into a public scandal – set the hero thinking.

On this point, too, Wagner went further than Shakespeare. Just as fratricide is associated with rape, so rape is associated with the creation of new life, hence Leubald's comparison of his father's murder with a pregnancy: the fatal poison that Roderich dispenses is likened to seminal fluid. 'The next time that you plan a poisoning / Take care none learns of it, nor any drop / Should fall to earth which, gravid with thy crime, / Bears fruit and so makes known the shameful deed!' A visit to a witch reveals the true nature of Roderich's shameful deed. 'The devil has betrayed my aged dam', she answers, speaking in riddles. 'He lied and lay with her – she's now with child!' The seducer had lied by disguising himself and wearing a mask. 'The eagle owl' – the witch proffers her sibylline prophecy – 'is the bastard father!'

In short, it was a nocturnal bird of prey. And who was the offspring of this secret and shameful coupling? The only possible answer is Leubald himself. Wagner's later retelling of the plot concentrates in the main on the murders committed by Leubald and on his 'burgeoning madness', with the result that these other aspects are not mentioned. But why does he start to go mad? And why does he keep mixing up his fathers? Only when the witch draws his attention to the 'mystery' – a mystery that mirrors the secret in the author's own family – does the play take a tragic turn.

The hero owes his own life to the shameful deed for which he thought he was atoning by means of his subsequent killing spree. And it is his own natural father and his half-brothers and half-sisters whom he unsuspectingly despatches to their deaths. As though aware of what he has done, he asks his father's ghost: 'Roderich? – Oh no! – Oh, did he then not know that I . . . Roder*ich*? O name, where is the man who yet may name the things thou bear'st within thee?' The little word 'ich' – 'I' – for example. For the youthful author, the link between the two names seems to have been so self-evident that he often wrote 'Leubald' instead of 'Roderich', on one occasion even addressing Roderich as 'my father'. The message that on this occasion can be read between the lines is later made abundantly plain by the chorus of spirits: 'Thy father hast thou murder'd; the whoreson hast thou drown'd; thy brother hast thou slain, thy mother hast thou poison'd.'

But the dramatist in Wagner was still far from finished: as if these tragic complications are not already enough, he has his autobiographical hero consumed with ardent love for Adelaide, who, as Roderich's daughter, is his own half-sister. When she admits to her dying father that she loves Leubald, he heaps the most blood-chilling curses on her head: her 'appalling love', he screams, was 'pimped by devilish cunning, given suck by a salamander bloated with venom, concealed beneath a dragon's rough scaly wings and, filled with poisonous vermin, her gravid body swelled by a scorpion's hideous brood'.

Such biblical hyperbole suggests that the relationship between Leubald and Adelaide has transgressed the bounds of normalcy. What an inspired idea on the part of the fifteen-year-old playwright to depict his Hamlet as the secret son of the fratricidal king of Denmark and have him love his own sister in the person of Ophelia! In this case, too, art was imitating life, for Wagner had already seen his stepfather play the fratricidal Claudius opposite his sister Rosalie in the role of Hamlet's lover.

In the flaxen-haired Adelaide, Wagner created an idealized portrait of his favourite sister. In the play, Adelaide tends her father Roderich as self-sacrificingly as Rosalie had once cared for the consumptive Geyer, prompting Roderich to declare her 'an angel of God'. But she feels genuine love only for Leubald. In thrall to her passion, she presses him to her breast in order to cradle him gently in her arms – thus Wagner dreamt of being cradled by his sister. 'Although my bosom heaves', she whispers to him, 'it rocks you deep inside my heart.' Leubald feels like a swan 'on the pond's billows', irresistibly approaching the goal of his longing. 'The grotto seems to refresh me', he sighs, 'soft the moss – rosy your mouth – and blissfully hot your kiss.' Decades later the hero Siegfried was to follow Leubald's example and plunge into the 'wondrously billowing wave' of Brünnhilde's embrace, with equally fatal results.

As with all the lovers in Wagner's great world theatre whose passion remains unrequited, Leubald and Adelaide die a love-death. First he wounds her with a mortal blow, then both sink down on the bed, 'wedded together' by death. His head falls loosely on her 'gently arched lap', and with a tender embrace their earthly lives are ended, while the morning sun rises over them in a gesture of reconciliation. The final words in the play sound as if they have wafted in on the wind from a distant nursery: 'Bring them to bed! – They're asleep!'

Wagner spent two years coming to terms with his family history through the medium of a verse tragedy, hoping that once it was successfully staged he would finally be free from all his dependencies. Initial readings from the piece, for which Ottilie was summoned to his attic, got off to a promising start, but initiation into his secret plan soon prompted 'fear and horror', and when a storm broke out during one of the 'most gruesome scenes', his terrified sister begged him to abandon so dangerous an exercise. Unfortunately, wrote Wagner later, 'far more ominous storm clouds soon gathered on my life's horizon'. Once it became known that he was neglecting his schoolwork, the deeper reason for his neglect could no longer be concealed, and so Wagner decided to surprise his family by telling them about his finished tragedy. He began by sending his groundbreaking work to his uncle, fully expecting the latter's 'sincere appreciation' of his talents as a poet.

'It turned out differently.' His family was aghast at this lapse, and Adolf Wagner hastened to apologize for the 'misfortune' that – as he feared – was laid at his door. Wagner was particularly pained to find his uncle reproaching himself for having driven his nephew 'to commit such eccentricities'. Meanwhile, his nearest and dearest left him 'literally stunned' with their complaints at this waste of his time. Had they in fact understood what had flowed from his pen? Adolf, at least, may have suspected something: according to Wagner, his uncle was filled with 'shock and astonishment'.

As for the play's author, it was another bitter blow to his self-esteem. Had he not written a tragedy which, in terms of its quality and length, far exceeded anything that could be expected of so youthful a poet? He was reproached for his alleged depravity. But had he not revealed a great sense of purpose by remaining true to his self-appointed task over a period of several years? Had he not thought up a story that could in large measure lay claim to originality? His critics failed to see this.

Not even Wagner himself could have foreseen that in writing this work he was laying the foundation stones for all the tragedies that lay ahead of him in real life as in the theatre. In spite of repeated setbacks, he continued to build on these foundations with dogged determination, as if these figures – these archetypes of his early consciousness – already had lives of their own. As he developed, so they too developed. And when the time was right, these figments of his imagination would spring from the ground fully armed.

Back in 1828, Wagner was humiliated in the eyes of his family and school, yet he was able to console himself in secret: after all, he knew that his work could be properly judged 'only if it was set to music, music I had decided to write myself'. That the spoken language was not to be his last word on the subject was already indicated by the name he had chosen for Leubald's bride, the sisterly 'angel' named after a song by Beethoven whose rapt refrain struck the young Wagner as 'a symbol of love's ultimate evocation'. It was Rosalie who had initiated him into the world of Beethoven's music, and so it was presumably she who first sang him the composer's well-known song.

But it was above all Beethoven's incidental music to *Egmont* which, indelibly imprinted on his mind, struck him as the ideal model on which to base the music for his own tragedy. In this way the 'various types of ghost' that peopled Wagner's spirit world would acquire their 'appropriate colouring' when accompanied by this kind of music. Among these 'various types of ghost' were, first and foremost, the two murdered fathers who had meddled in Leubald's love life to highly unfortunate effect. There was also an army of wild ghosts that swept through the air and that their inventor, already anticipating *Der fliegende Holländer*, wanted to accompany with 'thunder, lightning and whistling winds', although this would all have recalled the excesses of the Wolf's Glen scene rather than the noble grandeur of *Egmont*. In order to conjure up these elemental forces in sound, Wagner now had to immerse himself in a world that had so far been familiar to him only as a passive listener. In an attempt to assimilate this complex material, he copied out Beethoven's scores and, in the hope of understanding them better, borrowed Johann Bernhard Logier's new *System der Musik-Wissenschaft und der praktischen Komposition* from his local library, struggling to teach himself music in order to breathe life into his stillborn drama.

'I'm no composer,' he later declared, half in jest. 'I wanted to learn only enough to set *Leubald and Adelaide* to music.'[78]

Faust and Fenella

Wagner was one of those people who do not adapt to reality but force reality to adapt to them. As far as he could, he subjected political leaders to his will. He made artists respect him. He exploited publishers and took advantage of his patrons. He reduced self-sacrificing friends to humiliating subservience. His interlocutors were forced to listen to him. Since he was ultimately a librettist, director, conductor, intendant and, finally, theatre owner rolled into one, there was really only one person to deal with. Whenever an idea struck him, it required no roundabout means to realize it. As his admirer Heinrich von Stein once noted with amazement: 'Wagner enacts ideas.'

Convinced that 'the keynote of the true poetic element that distinguishes the present age is the way in which thought strives for realization',[79] Wagner lived his life accordingly, for ever striving to realize his ideas. He opened a new chapter in art, ushering in a new age that lay claim to historical universality. Nor did it end with his death: unhappy with the course that the world was taking, he put his spoke in the wheel of world history and, with Cosima's help, programmed the downfall of the gods.

It had been like this from the outset: *Leubald* had also staged a twilight of the gods in which world history, bloodstained and at its wits' end, held its breath. The lion from the Brühl in Leipzig had shown its claws. What the world demanded of the schoolboy at this time was something that he could not have offered it, even if he had wanted to. He withdrew, proposing as an alternative the end of the world in Leubald's castle. Within his own family, too, he seemed not to fit. They were disappointed that he had failed to meet the daily demands placed on him, while the challenges that he sought out for himself were not to his family's liking.

The megalomania and immoderation for which he was later to be criticized manifested themselves even now. Yet they concealed something else. What seemed to be a grim determination to add several cubits to his stature in order to compensate for his unhappiness at being undersized and of lowly origins sprang in fact from his realization that there was no place for him in the world as it then existed. Unable to accept this, he made up his mind to change it, and so he developed the strength of purpose that his enemies were to find so harsh and unyielding. Even as a child, Wagner was immoderate in his demands. He always wanted to play the lion. But the standards applied to him first by Geyer, then by his family and school, were not *his* standards, and so he had to create them for himself. The result was entirely predictable, and it was this that incurred the charge of immoderation.

It was his origins that were to blame for his inability to find his place in t he world. He did not know who his father was nor where his mother came from. He found himself surrounded by an army of brothers and sisters to whom he had to defer. He was passed from one uncle to another and had to get used to a different set of teachers and classmates every year. One place after another became his home until, at the age of fourteen, while his next of kin were out of the country, he found himself alone in an attic in Dresden, immured with his fantasies. No one who grew up in this chaos of changing points of reference could have found his footing, still less could he have known who he was.

And so he had to create this space, a space in which he could finally be himself. All his life he dreamt of a home where he would be supported by the world and no longer have to worry about his livelihood. In order to achieve this aim, he would first have to tell people loudly and clearly who he was. Nor did he have any choice in the matter, for the chaotic nature of his origins reduced him to a state of nervous uncertainty that found expression in his harried demeanour and a painful sense that he was being driven by forces beyond his control. And it also made him afraid. All the horrors and dread that plagued him, his whole fear of night and ghosts, were merely re-enactments of the same basic feeling that there was no firm ground for him to stand on. Yet at some point he must also have noticed that as soon as the old sense of chaos threatened to overwhelm him, his creative powers were rekindled.

As living proof of this severely shaken trust in reality there was the figure of Ludwig Geyer, who for Wagner embodied a world that defied comprehension: the constantly changing masks and costumes; the abrupt switch from the comic to the terrifying; the perpetual role-playing as actor, painter, puppeteer and, finally, as the dead man who awoke to cruel life in his puppets, masks and paintings – Geyer the ungraspable trying to grasp him and remaining ever-present in his changing shapes. In this way he became the Fiend, Wagner's lifelong adversary. And yet it was to Geyer's enchanted arts that Wagner owed the fact that the magic and infinite radiance of the theatre had opened up to him at all.

The past remained ever-present, above all when Wagner thought he had turned his back on it. For the past was part of his own world, the world that came into being when he reinterpreted reality according to his own particular yardstick and subjected to his will the people who could never make up their minds. Within this world he continued to find the archetypes of his early experiences, the perfidious actor and the treacherous mother, the royal forebear and the father robbed of both wife and inheritance. The maternal sister, too, kept reappearing, the sister who sacrificed herself because she was the only one who loved him.

However often he turned away from them, these figures from the past continued to steal a march on him. His life became a constant attempt to come to terms with them through the medium of his art as they forced him to keep correcting them at each new stage of his existence. In their midst he rediscovered himself as a hero having to assert his authority over them. But they were always one stage ahead of him, and so he could never win. At best he could perish with his sister in a love-death.

Wagner began his musical career under his own steam, digesting the setback he had suffered with *Leubald* and 'deciding to become a musician'.[80] He studied Logier's *System der Musik-Wissenschaft*, initially without his family's knowledge, and at the same time took harmony lessons with one of the members of the Gewandhaus orchestra, Christian Gottlieb Müller, who then passed him on to the violinist Robert Sipp. Sipp later described Wagner as his 'worst pupil'. Although Leubald remained silent, other works were written at this time: sonatas, overtures and a quartet, all of which are now lost. He also wrote an aria which, arranged for wind band by an eccentric called Flachs, was performed at one of the garden cafés in Leipzig.

There followed a pastoral opera based on Goethe, a piece designed along thoroughly fantastical lines but 'without the least understanding of how to write for instruments'. This too remained unfinished. When Heinrich Wolfram submitted his brother-in-law's collected works to an alcoholic music director in Magdeburg, they were dismissed as 'utter rubbish', causing Wolfram to burst out laughing, a reaction that the humiliated Wagner none the less found 'somewhat reassuring': this time he was prepared for defeat. Presumably he was under no illusions about his five-finger exercises either. Had he been a painter, he could have described these pieces as academy studies. Most received a single performance at best, before disappearing from the annals of music and leaving no trace behind them.

It was presumably not long before Wagner himself realized that this playing with notes, divorced from reality and obeying rules that had to be effortfully learnt, was not for him. Even so, he gritted his teeth, studied and composed, even if it was ultimately only to prove that he had an exceptional supply of willpower on which he could call. The inspiration and talent of which he dreamt could not be discerned in his works. Dry exercises 'disgusted' him, and so he resorted to free fantasies, yet these too bore as little fruit as the musical tribute that he planned to pay to the Greek War of Independence. Set as a chorus to Greek words and intended for the Nikolaischule, it was rejected by his music teacher as an 'act of shameless effrontery'.

The gulf between his own sense of mission and public recognition continued to grow. While his own ability to work himself into a state of 'musical ecstasy' increased, his family's sympathies shrank away to nothing. Forced back into his own private world, he found that music again acquired the mystical features that had once made it appear to him as some ghostly haunting. With delight he discovered in Beethoven's Ninth Symphony the open fifths that had earlier induced a sense of panic in him. Although this work was generally dismissed as the work of a madman, Wagner was convinced that it 'held the secret to all secrets' and for several nights in a row he sat up, copying it out. Once he thought he had seen a ghost and, with a scream, hid beneath the bedclothes, only to realize that it was merely the first light of dawn reflected off his bedroom wall.

It was Rosalie who finally helped to put an end to her brother's haunted visions and freed him from the blind alley of his self-inflicted isolation. She had returned from Prague to take up an appointment at the Court Theatre in her native Dresden and immediately used her influence to ensure that Wagner was given free admission to all performances. The 'fantastic inquisitiveness' that he had felt for the world of the theatre as a child could now be transformed into what he described in *My Life* as 'a more thorough, more conscious passion'. He now saw the plays of Shakespeare, Schiller and Goethe, together with Marschner's most recent successes, *Der Vampyr* and the no less dramatic tale of Gothic horror *Der Templer und die Jüdin*.

But there was one piece that Wagner thought he remembered filling him with even greater enthusiasm than all these other works, an opera that he had hitherto known only from Rosalie's rapt account: Beethoven's *Fidelio*, in which the new star in the German operatic firmament, Wilhelmine Schröder-Devrient, gave a sample of her skills in 1829. As a member of the audience, the young Wagner claimed that he was overwhelmed by a sense of ecstasy and felt an 'almost demonic fire' infuse his whole body. The blonde beauty was in Leipzig for only the briefest of visits, but Wagner insisted that he retained an impression of her naturalistic acting skills until his dying day. Wilhelmine Schröder-Devrient made no attempt to imitate reality but seemed to transport reality to a higher plane and invest it with a more intense form of life. The sixteen-year-old Wagner immediately wrote a spontaneous letter of homage to the singer, who was his senior by only eight years. Only with her present appearance on stage had his life acquired any meaning, he later claimed to have told her. It was she who had made him 'what I hereby swear to become'.

This was an exaggeration; indeed, if we may believe the latest research, it was actually untrue. It seems that it was not until five years later that the great soprano gave a series of guest performances in Leipzig, and it was not as Beethoven's Leonore but as Romeo in Bellini's *I Capuleti e i Montecchi*. Wagner's memory lapse, if such it was, is easily explained: clearly he wanted to minimize the importance of the role played by his sister at this critical juncture in his life, for there is no doubt that it is she who deserves the credit for the change of direction in his life that he ascribed to the fair Wilhelmine – whether in a momentary flood of emotion or as a conscious rewriting of history. It was Rosalie who gave meaning to his life at this period by paying for his music lessons and introducing him to the theatre and its fleshpots. It was she who was to make him what he was later to become.

The main theatrical event in Leipzig during the summer of 1829 was not *Fidelio* but the local première of *Faust*. And it was not Schröder-Devrient who provoked the storms of applause but Rosalie Wagner. The work was performed in the city to a packed house to mark Goethe's eightieth birthday, with Wagner's lovely sister playing the part of Gretchen so compellingly that critics were prompted to speak of her 'irresistibly gripping performance'. One of her admirers, Heinrich Laube, later claimed that he had 'never seen the role performed with such intensity of emotion. For the first time I felt my blood run cold when Gretchen goes insane'. For Rosalie spoke her lines in this scene 'in the same tone of voice that she had earlier used to utter her thoughts on love; it was this terrible contrast that achieved the greatest effect. I thought for a moment that this more than mortal anguish was no longer art and that if madness could be so movingly portrayed, poets should not be allowed to depict it'.[81]

It was this very art – art that broke the bounds of 'art' and became a part of real life – that was to become Wagner's own ideal. The experience that Laube owed to Rosalie's Gretchen was one that Wagner himself thought he owed to Schröder-Devrient's Leonore, an assumption that he finally heard in Leipzig in March 1834. When at one point in Beethoven's opera the soprano passed directly from song into speech, she created a 'tremendous impact' and her audience felt as though they had 'suddenly been wrenched from an ideal world and thrown back on the bare earth of terrible reality'. For Wagner, the apparent antithesis of art and reality was suspended in art.

There is nothing in Wagner's memoirs to suggest that he felt anything like this in the case of Rosalie's Gretchen, and even *Faust* is mentioned only in passing in a long list of plays that instilled in him a sense of 'excitement and enthusiasm', whereas the truth of the matter is that it was at precisely this time that he began to develop a deeper interest in the piece. At the Nikolaischule he even kept a copy hidden beneath his desk, taking it out whenever a suitable moment presented itself – or so a fellow pupil recalled. When the latter revealed that he wrote operas, Wagner immediately improvised a scenario to a piece that he proposed calling 'The Witches' Sabbath'.[82]

In this version of Wagner's, Faust's drama began in the 'wondrous kingdom' of horror, where the hero – rather like Max in the Wolf's Glen – suffers all manner of 'devilish seductions': old women, apes and cats are glimpsed, while beautiful women, damned to perdition, wander through the mystic half-darkness, their singing interrupted by a 'wailing cry from Hell'. At the end, Faust is reunited with Gretchen on a cloud bank, surrounded by 'wonderful choirs', while the devil Mephistopheles sinks through the ground 'with a crash'. This is exactly how the performance that was held to mark Goethe's eightieth birthday ended. In a radiant apotheosis and lit by a blue light, Rosalie's Gretchen had appeared with a hovering angel, while Mephistopheles' shattered body lay on the ground, 'lit by a fiery red light'.

For Wagner, Rosalie was always Gretchen, unhappy in love and prepared to redeem her lost lover through her own act of self-sacrifice. He recalled her in a love letter that he wrote in 1858 – years after his sister's death – to his lover in Zurich, Mathilde Wesendonck, who herself appears to have slipped into the archetypal role of a sister. In this letter, also known as his 'Morning Confession', Wagner admits to feeling a sense of raging jealousy at Mathilde's private tutor, who had appeared to Wagner in a dream as a threatening figure 'in whom I recognized what, for me, is the entire misery of the world'. Clearly Wagner had once again been tormented by a nightmarish vision of his father keeping him apart from his lover.

Scarcely roused from his nocturnal torment, Wagner praises Mathilde as his 'angel' to whom he 'fervently' prays. 'And this prayer', he writes, is his 'love, the wellspring of my redemption!' This leads him on to Faust, whose 'pitiful' behaviour he criticizes: it was unworthy of Faust to reject Gretchen's angelic love and hence 'salvation and redemption'. As a result, it is only in death that this 'grey-haired sinner', as Wagner calls him, is 'taken to this angel's breast and awoken to new life'.[83] Just as he was to do years later in Bayreuth, when he dreamt about a vulture, Wagner here associated the archetypal image of the wicked father with the child at its mother's breast, its face merged indistinguishably with that of the sisterly angel.

Within a year of the Leipzig première of Faust, the now seventeen-year-old Wagner had begun to apply his newly won skills as a composer to Goethe's tragedy. It was presumably Rosalie who inspired him to do so by providing the unknown musician with a commission, with the result that he set about writing some incidental music of the kind that he had already planned for Leubald. In the event, his efforts went no further than a number of choruses and songs, which he assembled in 1831 under the composite title Seven Compositions to Goethe's 'Faust'.

Two of them were dedicated to Rosalie and took the form of a song and a melodrama intended to show off her singing and speaking voice. Goethe's famous rhyme 'Ach neige, du Schmerzensreiche' must have sounded particularly delightful in her Leipzig accent. Wagner does not mention whether these pieces were ever sung by Rosalie, nor that they were inspired, in part, by Berlioz's *Huit scènes de Faust* of 1828–9.[84]

Rosalie again thought of her needy brother when in May 1830 she played the part of Beatrice in Schiller's *Die Braut von Messina* and encouraged him to write an overture and several additional numbers that may even have been performed. And it was also thanks to her efforts that in February 1832 an overture of Wagner's was used to launch the first performance of Ernst Raupach's new play *König Enzio*, even if, as a precautionary measure, his name was omitted from the playbill. The play proved a success. Set in the days of the Hohenstaufen Empire, its action unfolds against the background of the historically important wars between the German Ghibellines and the papal Guelphs and deals with the tragic end of Enzio, one of the sons of the Emperor Friedrich II. Once again Rosalie played the part of the angel who sacrifices herself to the hero whom she worships, voluntarily dying a love-death with Enzio in a subterranean prison. The atmospheric accompanying music was written by Wagner who, according to a playbill from one of the later performances, was also responsible for the grand finale.

In order to enable him to pursue a career in music, Rosalie introduced her truant brother to theatrical circles in Leipzig, acquainting him with local heroes such as Heinrich Laube, who exerted considerable influence both as a theatre critic and later as editor of the Leipzig *Zeitung für die elegante Welt*. She also introduced him to the conductor Heinrich Dorn who, presumably as a favour to her, agreed to perform Wagner's Overture in B flat major, with its unintentionally comical drumbeat. And she took him to see the composer of the moment, Heinrich Marschner, whose opera *Der Vampyr* was currently causing a stir.

According to Wagner's own later testimony, it was in the hope of 'forming an opinion about me' that Rosalie introduced her brother to Marschner, who was then lodged at the Golden Lute. Whereas Wagner could remember only that his famous colleague had proved 'not unfriendly', tradition has it that Marschner dismissed his C major Symphony as having been 'copied page after page from Beethoven's A major Symphony'. He advised Wagner's mother to 'ensure that the young man remains at school and receives a proper education'.[85] Yet Weber's successor was also to prove Wagner's precursor, with the ghosts from *Der Vampyr* and *Hans Heiling* returning decades later to haunt Wagner's own music dramas.

Rosalie's greatest theatrical success during these years was to leave an even deeper impression on her brother than her Gretchen. Yet this success, too, is passed over in silence by Wagner – and not simply because the character that she portrayed was, like Isolde, 'the mistress of silence'. A week after *Faust* had been staged in the city, Auber's grand opera *La muette de Portici* received its local première, with Rosalie as its famously silent heroine, Fenella. According to one contemporary eyewitness, she played the part with more passion 'than normally typified her predominantly tender nature'. Her mute expressions of love and anger elicited incessant bursts of thunderous applause of a kind that her brother could only dream of. If he later wrote that the impression made by Auber's opera 'left us all stunned', this was true above all of his sister's bravura performance – not that he ever acknowledged it with so much as a single word.

The story of the silent Fenella might have been written with Leipzig's Gretchen in mind: she too was abandoned by her lover and suffered all the torments of betrayal before finally sacrificing her life to his. If Wagner's later heroines, from Isabella and Elisabeth to Elsa of Brabant, make their greatest mark by means of their eloquent silences, this can ultimately be traced back to Rosalie's hushed-up triumph. When at the end of the opera Fenella's brother, the freedom fighter Masaniello, is murdered, she hurls herself to her death, just as her sisters Senta and Brünnhilde will subsequently do in their turn.

The final scene of *Götterdämmerung*, in which the whole world, including Siegfried's hallowed bride, is consumed by fire, is strikingly similar to the end of *La muette de Portici*: here Fenella throws herself to her death, after which the palace goes up in flames, there is a roll of thunder, and in the background Vesuvius spews forth molten lava, while the populace sinks to its knees in dismay.

Nor was the opera's political message lost on the young Wagner, for Fenella's faithless lover is the son of the viceroy, while betrayed innocence is the preserve of the simple people. And it is to free the populace that her brother takes up the selfless struggle, a struggle that proves his undoing. Decades later, Wagner recalled the revolutionary thrust of Auber's opera as though it were some force of nature that had just been unleashed: 'The recitatives rent the air like lightning flashes; from them we passed to the choral ensembles as though we were caught up in a tempest; and in the midst of this chaos of fury came energetic requests for calm reflection.' Each time that 'wild jubilation and murderous frenzy' broke out, Fenella's 'anxiously moving entreaty' restored a sense of calm.[86] Thanks to Rosalie's acting skills, to which her brother devoted not a word, *La muette de Portici* provoked a veritable storm of applause in Leipzig.

Crossing the footlights, the storm swept out into the world of political reality. After Lafayette had helped the 'citizen king' Louis-Philippe to sweep to power in Paris in the July Revolution of 1830, a performance of *La muette de Portici* in Brussels provided the signal to rise up in revolt. Student riots and workers' uprisings also broke out in Leipzig and Dresden in the September of that year. Rarely, wrote Wagner, had an 'artistic phenomenon been so closely bound up with an event of such universal import'. Whereas he had known from the time of *Der Freischütz* that the true nature of things is revealed by art alone, he now discovered that art was beginning to exert an influence on the very nature of things themselves. The world of the theatre, it seemed, took possession of reality. And so did Wagner.

The revolution that he had enthusiastically acclaimed on stage began in Leipzig with a student demonstration. Windows and streetlamps were broken, and cries of 'Long live Lafayette' were heard. Now a pupil at the city's Thomasschule and an eager sympathizer with the German national student cause, Wagner felt called upon to join in. 'The world of history', he later wrote, began for him with the events in Paris during the long hot summer of 1830, and now he 'became a fervent partisan of the revolution', throwing himself into the fray and gleefully participating in the violent demonstrations, when 'popular justice' was exacted.

No one, it is true, was strung up from a lamppost, but a certain establishment in the Klitschergasse, run by a Madame Schneider, was stormed on the grounds that it offended against revolutionary morality. In other houses, too, the 'most risible acts of wanton destruction' were perpetrated, and furniture and even the grand piano belonging to the registrar of police, Herr Jäger, was smashed to matchwood. When Wagner later admitted these misdemeanours to his friend the king of Bavaria, he recalled 'with horror the intoxicating effect of such a furious, incomprehensible action'. He claims to have woken up the next morning as though from a bad dream. All that remained of the previous night's excesses was a tattered scrap of red curtain.

It was not long, however, before a real revolution arrived in the form of rebellious workers, and now the students manned the city gates in order to protect the property of Leipzig's middle classes. It was a source of some pride to Wagner that his brother-in-law Friedrich Brockhaus assumed command of the Municipal Guard and restored order to a city that was seething with unrest. In the frenzy of this hard-won victory over the forces of chaos, Wagner saw in Brockhaus a 'Saxon Lafayette' and made haste to set down his impressions in music. Just as art had seized hold of reality, so reality was now to see itself reflected in the mirror of art.

The young composer drafted a 'political overture' in honour of the liberal King Friedrich August II of Saxony, who was appointed co-regent following the uprising. The work was based on a programme that reflected reality as Wagner himself had experienced it as a revolutionary. In this way, music became the medium for an ecstatic message that could only inadequately be expressed in words. The introduction would have depicted the 'dark oppression' that weighed upon the country, after which a theme would have 'made itself felt' that would have embodied the spirit of the uprising. In order to explain its meaning, Wagner labelled it 'Friedrich and Freedom'. As his first leitmotif, it was designed 'to be developed ever more grandly and gloriously before culminating in the most total triumph', thereby reflecting the struggle for freedom itself. 'I hoped', wrote the composer with more than a hint of self-irony, 'to see this triumph celebrated very soon at one of Leipzig's open-air concerts'.

But the Wagner who, gazing down from the heights of his career, recalled its beginnings with an Olympian smile was not the Wagner who spent this early period seeking his place in the world. At the time he could not have suspected that this was in fact the start of his career. The Wagner who desperately sought to obtain commissions to write for the Leipzig stage was not the Wagner over whom so many of Europe's theatres were to fight in later years. His self-irony, so often misconstrued as the wisdom of old age, was merely intended to entertain and to disguise the fact that the truth was far from entertaining, least of all for Wagner himself.

Once Wagner had mastered an art that set him apart his contemporaries, he was no longer so anxious to expose its true origins. He had no wish for an inquisitive public to see the cards he was holding. His own carefully cultivated image and political calculation now played a part – as did shame at all that had happened in secret and that he wanted to keep to himself. This was true not only of his fear of his stepfather but also of his secret love of his sister, who had encouraged him and who none the less aroused his envy.

But what business was this of others?

The Wedding

In Wagner's life there was one particular passion that, artistically speaking, was even older than his love of poetry and music, and that was his interest in classical antiquity. It was an enthusiasm that inspired nearly all his works either covertly or overtly. Even at school, the only subject to engage his attention had been classical antiquity. The only reason for learning ancient languages, he felt, was to gain access to what he really wanted to know: 'the subjects of Greek mythology.'

The Olympian world of heroes and gods from which had sprung such complex myths as the *Prometheia*, the *Oresteia* and the Trojan War fired his imagination. If Geyer's theatre and *Der Freischütz* had taught him the meaning of fear, he now followed in his Uncle Adolf's footsteps and entered a world of the beautiful and the sublime. Whereas he had earlier been confronted by the underworld forces of night and 'horror', he now discovered a radiant empyrean filled with ideals, an azure vault above which Phoebus Apollo drove his chariot of the sun.

'I do not believe that there can ever have been a boy who was more enthusiastic about classical antiquity than I myself at the time I attended the Kreuzschule in Dresden', Wagner wrote in 1872.[87] Encouraged by his favourite teacher, Magister Sillig, he chalked up his only known successes at school, throwing himself at the ancient texts with wild-eyed eagerness and hoping to wrest their secrets from them by translating them into German: among the passages that he rendered into German in this way was Hector's farewell to Andromache from the *Iliad*, a passage whose traces may later be found in the *Ring*. And he also tackled three books of the *Odyssey*, including the passage in which the homesick hero tears himself from Calypso's arms with words identical to those with which Tannhäuser bids farewell to the Venusberg.

Odysseus also provided the model for the hero of his first 'tragedy on Greek lines', a tragedy in which the hero is slain by his own son, whom he has fathered on Circe. Although by his own admission he made little progress with this work, the figure of Odysseus, condemned to a period of wandering, remained the prototype of his Flying Dutchman. True, his teachers at the Nikolaischule and Thomasschule in Leipzig managed briefly to destroy his love of myth, but the figures who peopled his feverish imagination refused to be banished entirely. Concealed by all manner of masks, they returned in his later works.

It was not, however, in the battling heroes and demigods of the Hellenic world theatre that Wagner discovered his ideal of 'the purest humanity', but in a woman. Like Hegel before him, he found in Antigone the epitome of Attic humanism.[88] The state of Thebes had turned unfeelingly against its own society. Here, according to Wagner, there was but a single 'sorrowing heart in which humanity had sought refuge – the heart of a sweet maid from whose soul there sprang into all-powerful beauty the flower of love'. Antigone's love was directed towards her brother who had fallen in battle with his own brother and whom the country's new ruler refused to allow her to bury. Although threatened with death, Antigone insisted on performing this labour of love because, in Wagner's words, she 'knew that she had to obey this unconscious and compelling need for self-annihilation'.

Antigone placed the law of her own heart above the law of the land. Her conscience meant more to her than life. By consciously sacrificing herself for her brother, she 'destroyed' the state with her love-death. For Wagner, she became 'the perfect human being' in whom 'love revealed itself in its greatest fullness and omnipotence'. Perhaps he also intended his hymn to Antigone as a way of apologizing to his own sister for past injuries. Almost as though he could see her before him as the maid of Orléans bearing the standard into battle, he ended his hymn with a passage that could hardly have been less Greek in tone: 'O holy Antigone! I call upon you! Let your flag flutter, that beneath it we may destroy and redeem!'

Neither the orgy of destruction that attended the revolution nor the student life of braggadocio to which he subsequently abandoned himself brought Wagner the redemption he desired, and so he resumed his studies in composition. In 1831 he registered as a music student at the University of Leipzig but made little use of the training on offer. To his own astonishment, he 'produced a respectable number of works' in spite of all the distractions afforded by drinking, gambling and even the odd challenge to a duel. At the same time he had been preparing a piano score of Beethoven's Ninth Symphony that he offered to Schott's in the hope of obtaining a fee, but to no avail. In an attempt to keep his head above water, he also wrote to various music publishers in Leipzig, offering to take on menial tasks such as proofreading and preparing piano arrangements.[89]

In the autumn of 1831 he had the good fortune to find a sympathetic music teacher in the city's Thomaskantor, Christian Theodor Weinlig, who evidently pitied Wagner's 'lack of musical training' and accepted the dissolute youth as his pupil, albeit on the discouraging condition that he renounced free composition for six months. Instead, Wagner learnt to write fugues, canons and other contrapuntal pieces under Weinlig's watchful eye, adding vocal lines to existing words, and also writing piano sonatas and fantasies, as well as orchestral overtures. There developed 'the most productive and loving relationship' between the two men, and it was not long before the pupil had outgrown his teacher. At the end of this intensive course in composition, Weinlig again gave proof of his generosity by declining to accept the agreed fee. His pupil later repaid the debt by dedicating his cantata *Das Liebesmahl der Apostel* to Weinlig's widow Charlotte Emilie.

Wagner was no infant prodigy, and so these works, in which he was testing his skills as a composer, are a reflection less of his own personality than of their models, which is what Weinlig had wanted. In some cases, the inspiration is Beethoven, in others Haydn, while Berlioz, Mozart's 'Jupiter' Symphony and even Bach's Chromatic Fantasy are also a haunting presence. But there is little that is recognizably Wagnerian. He himself had no illusions about these works and much later in life jokingly remarked that he had merely 'mimicked his favourite models'. He knew, of course, that this tendency to imitate others was simply the result of his own lack of musical imagination, but fortunately it was not long before he had learnt to overcome this weakness.

In itself, music meant nothing to him. When he wrote it, it left no impression. Only when it drew its strength from the dramatic situations that were at the basis of his imagination did he succeed in creating anything that he could call his own. Music had to give expression to a world of living ideas. Only then was it his language, only then did it seem to express the mystery of our origins, conjuring up the drama of the beginning and end of the world and, with it, the great silence that follows the tragedy of all existence.

These sounds belonged to another world and could only with difficulty be described as 'music'. The later Wagner was concerned in his art to express the true reality of ideas, a reality remote from blind and commonplace reason and attainable only through the combined efforts of poetry and music. 'With me', he told Cosima, 'the emphasis must be placed on the combination of poet and musician, as a mere musician I would be of no great significance.'[90] As long as his concern was no more than pure 'art' of the kind that he learnt during his studies with Weinlig, he succeeded in producing only artifice.

With his apprenticeship over, the now nineteen-year-old Wagner set off on tour, with his great C major Symphony in his luggage. Travelling via Dresden and Vienna, where he saw Hérold's operatic sensation of the season, *Zampa*, he returned to the scene of his early aspirations and dashed hopes, the castle of Pravonin near Prague, where, in the summer of 1832, he renewed contact with the sisters Jenny and Auguste Raymann, this time, he thought, as a self-made man. Presumably they had simply been waiting for him to return and resume his wooing. Certainly, he was received in the friendliest fashion and, thanks to Count Pachta, enjoyed 'the most stimulating hospitality'.

But however much he tried, he failed to make any impression where affairs of the heart were concerned, and not even his 'impressive growth of beard', about which his sister had written to forewarn the two ladies in her letter of introduction, succeeded in swaying their affections. Even so, the two beauties showed him their usual 'uninhibited and sisterly good nature', which Wagner, writing in his autobiography, claims to have seen as an invitation to fall in love with one or the other of them.

In fact, no such invitation was necessary, as Wagner had been in love with Jenny for years, and his latest visit to Prague was prompted by a desire to see neither the old count nor the old city. But it suited his narrative design to claim that these flirtatious young women had led him up the garden path only to torment him with their 'constant teasing'. Decades later, the Rhinedaughters, Wagner's teasing sisters of the watery deep, were to reduce the dwarf Alberich to a state of equally painful embarrassment, fuelling his sexual desires only to abandon him to them and in that way add to his torment.

Wagner seems to have regarded the behaviour of Count Pachta's illegitimate daughters in a not dissimilar light. They were being groomed for marriage to men of their own social standing and so could afford to make fun of the impoverished and unpropertied musician. To make matters worse, the sisters were regularly visited by serious suitors who struck Wagner as being no better than 'horse-breeding witless gallants'. Clearly he had no chance with the sisters and resorted to a kind of jealous indignation, chastising their suitors for their aristocratic presumption, while making pointed references to the French Revolution, thus earning the count's 'severe reprimands'.

In spite of all this, Wagner's infatuation put him in the mood for music, and one October evening, when he was sitting with Jenny at the piano, he was suddenly 'overcome' by emotion – or so he claimed in a letter to his friend Theodor Apel, the son of 'Apel of the Ghosts' mentioned above. In order to conceal his tears from her, he rushed outside. And 'ah, the evening star shone down on me'. The evening angelus was tolling, reminding Wagner of Apel's poem 'Die Entfernten' ('Glockentöne hör' ich klingen'), and so he returned to the castle to 'improvise' the piece on the piano.[91] For the present, the infatuated composer seems to have kept his passing inspiration to himself, but it was not long before he was able to celebrate another musical triumph when, thanks to Count Pachta's patronage, the symphony that he had brought with him from Leipzig was performed at the Prague Conservatory.

The summer romance ended even before it had started. Wagner, who had come to Prague as an original composer hoping to find a bride, saw that he had been deluding himself and that the sisters had taken him for a ride. The more they preferred their horse-loving suitors, the more he was plagued by 'feelings of genuine lovesickness', which he initially recognized by the 'strangely gnawing emotion of jealousy'. One evening, on his way to see the adorable Jenny, he was detained by her mother in the hallway and realized that other visitors had beaten him to it: her noble gallants were engaged in a lengthy tête-à-tête with both daughters, who were 'specially dressed for the occasion'.

With death in his heart, Wagner hurried away from the castle. Unable to see with his own eyes what was going on, he imagined the worst and suddenly thought that he understood the implications 'of certain satanic love affairs in Hoffmann's tales'. Was it not the case that certain acquisitive mothers had offered their innocent daughters as lovers to the devil or to other devilish suitors? This idea 'acquired a terrible reality' for Wagner, no doubt because it came perilously close to the truth. As he later discovered, the two sisters subsequently 'became the mistresses of Count Baar and Baron Bethmann'.[92]

This humiliating rebuttal came at a time when he had begun to gain in self-confidence, and it must have rekindled all his old complexes. Once again an evil calculating power had come between him and his lover, surrendering her to demonic seductions. Once again he had been robbed of his right to love, a right that the genuineness of his feelings seemed to authenticate. 'You'll be able to imagine all the wounds that ardent love can inflict,' he wrote to his friend Apel, 'but what it can kill is more terrible than anything!'

His jeremiad ended with the matter-of-fact remark that 'it was against this background that I drafted the poem to my opera'. Its text was complete even before he was back in Leipzig. He then left the letter lying on his desk for three weeks, before adding a postscript prior to sending it to Apel: 'I've rescinded the libretto and torn it up. You'll be hearing from me again soon. – Adieu, adieu! Yours, Richard Wagner.'[93]

From the outset, *Die Hochzeit* – as Wagner's first opera was to be called – was planned in secret: none of his friends was to know about it. In spite of the arctic temperatures, his room at the inn in Prague was unheated, and so he would spend the mornings at the apartment of an actor friend, working away at his libretto, while his friend was rehearsing at the theatre. Whenever the latter returned unexpectedly, Wagner 'quickly stuffed the manuscript down the back of the sofa'.

He had initially intended to write a short story in the style of the 'satanic' E. T. A. Hoffmann,[94] presumably in the hope of coming to terms with his experiences with the faithless Jenny at Pravonin. As summarised in *My Life*, the tale unfolds on the estate of an art lover, where a wedding is due to take place. But the bride – evidently modelled on Jenny – is distracted by an 'interesting, reserved and melancholy young man', whose arrival on the scene the ineffectual bridegroom can do nothing to resist. Indeed, the latter's situation becomes worse when a 'strange old organist' turns up, recalling the old harper in *Wilhelm Meister*. It at once becomes clear that a 'mystic relationship' exists between the mysterious musician, the bride and the interesting youth.

On the couple's wedding night, the strange celebrations turn to tragedy. The melancholic youth falls from a high tower and is laid to rest in an open coffin, at whose side – 'equally mysteriously' – we discover the dying bride, while the old man sits lifelessly at the organ, his stiff fingers picking out 'a triad that echoes endlessly'. Wagner's message seems to be that, after their 'father' has brought his 'children' together in a strange house and has realized that they will never find fulfilment in life, he gives them his musical blessing in the form of a love-death. If, as Wagner's autobiographical summary suggests, the old man is the 'strange guest' from *Wilhelm Meister*, the bride could be his daughter Mignon, whom Wagner later regarded as a victim of child abuse. And, just as Jenny from Bohemia may lie behind the bride, so Wagner's sister Rosalie may lie behind Jenny Raymann.

The short story could certainly be interpreted in this way, which would also explain why Wagner never wrote it. For in the libretto that he drafted in the home of his friend in Prague we look for the old man in vain. Rather, this libretto culminates in the dramatic disaster that was also to be the climax of the short story, with the melancholic youth Cadolt ascending to the chamber of his adored Ada and taking possession of her in place of her bridegroom. But 'in the struggle to defend her honour', the bride 'finds the strength' to thrust him through the window, thus killing her clandestine lover in this tragic conflict of emotions. Only beside his bier is she allowed to join him in death.

This impressive climax to his planned opera was taken from a volume published ten years earlier by Wagner's brother-in-law Friedrich Brockhaus, Johann Gustav Büsching's *Ritterzeit und Ritterwesen*. From Büsching's study of medieval chivalry, Wagner drew on three different episodes that are linked by a common feature: a tragic affair not between social equals, but between a noble knight and the wife of a simple burgher. Yet Wagner ignored this aspect of these episodes: it is almost as though he hoped to exorcize the ghost that reminded him of his rivals and of the origins of his mother. Like Leubald and Adelaide, his lovers were as close as brother and sister.

As other writers have pointed out, the scene in the bridal chamber may well be based on a similar one in Hérold's *Zampa*, which Wagner had seen earlier that summer in Vienna. But it was his own failed courtship that prompted him to set down his ideas on paper, a courtship that marked the end of a six-year infatuation. And its inner motivation stretched back even further in time: when

Wagner described the driving force of his drama as 'the mysterious power of passionate but unspoken emotions', what he meant – to borrow a modern expression – was the power of emotional repression.

The emotion that consumed both lovers, ultimately driving them to their common deaths, was their 'unspoken' passion. And like all repressed urges, it finally found violent expression. Their passion was repressed not only because the bride was already promised to another, but also because their love had an incestuous element to it. Just as Wagner used the 'organist' to suggest that the bride was in an illicit relationship with her father, so the latter's 'blessing' might indicate that the couple who loved in secret were brother and sister. In the summary in *My Life*, Wagner drew a veil over all this by referring merely to a 'mystical relationship'. In the opera, all that was to remain of this triangular relationship was the 'passionate but unspoken emotion' of the love between siblings.

In the event, Cadolt and Ada followed Leubald and Adelaide and disappeared from Wagner's mental rehearsal room without uttering so much as a single sound, and yet it was not long before they were reawoken to new life. The surviving fragment of *Die Hochzeit* reveals that a number of the phrases spoken by these early lovers were to be placed in the mouths of his later couples. Like Senta on seeing the Dutchman, Ada asks 'Who is the stranger?' when gazing into Cadolt's eyes. And the 'stranger' who turns up unbidden in Sieglinde's forest retreat in *Die Walküre* may well be descended from Leubald and Cadolt. She recognizes him as her brother by the same 'flashing' eyes that had typifed both his forebears. It is under his true name of Siegmund that he then abducts her from her husband.

The eye that shines with reciprocal joy was inherited from Wotan who, like the 'old organist', appears at his daughter's wedding as 'an old man dressed in grey', terrifying the wedding guests with the glint of his flashing eye and surreptitiously engineering the subsequent union between his twin son and daughter. This same flashing gaze, with its portent of marriage, had already been found in *Die Hochzeit*, where Cadolt gazes at Ada and a 'terrible passion' cuts through her heart.

As in *Leubald*, so in *Die Hochzeit* Wagner gave artistic expression to the 'unspoken' relationships that marked his early life. And just as had been the case four years earlier when he had immured himself in his attic in Leipzig, the act of expressing these experiences helped him to come to terms with the unbearable sense of his own abject failure. It was with a feeling of pride, then, that he could return to Leipzig at the end of 1832, with the libretto in his pocket and the score in his head. He lost little time in initiating Rosalie into this new large-scale project.

The result, as his letter to Apel makes clear, was annihilating. 'My sister did not like the libretto', he later remarked on the incident. 'I destroyed it without trace.'[95] Not entirely, as we now know. A septet, which Wagner's teacher Theodor Weinlig appears to have liked, has survived, as have the introduction and opening chorus. Equally open to doubt is Wagner's subsequent claim that he destroyed the work 'completely dispassionately'. After all, he had staked his whole life on it, and by an irony of artistic fate he had almost suffered the same destiny as his hero, whose amorous approach had been rewarded with an act of defenestration.

Long since famous in her own right, his favourite sister now dismissed him as a thing of insignificance, reducing him to the very state from which he was desperately trying to escape. Evidently she had some fundamental objection to his operatic début, an objection so basic that mere tinkering with the text could not rescue it. Was it – as Wagner thought he remembered – the lack of any 'embellishments' and of any 'relatively cheerful' scenes that had provoked Rosalie's 'annihilating' verdict?

But she herself specialized in heart-rending roles. The plays in which she had made her mark literally teemed with broken hearts, fits of madness and, in the case of *La muette de Portici*, the heroine's plunge to her death, to say nothing of the subterranean love-death of *König Enzio* and the illicit love between siblings in *Die Braut von Messina*. The role of the heroine of *Die Hochzeit* fitted his sister like a glove, conceived, as it was, in the spirit of the tragic parts that she herself preferred. What was it about this particular tragedy that so upset the tragic actress in her? Had Rosalie perhaps divined in its dark undercurrent the very thing that made it so irresistible in the eyes of her brother?

In short, Wagner's second attempt to make an impression as an artist had ended in a fiasco. He was now approaching twenty, still boyish in appearance and with the manners of a schoolchild. Within his impressive cranium he continued to brood on the course that his life might take, unable to meet its material demands either by completing his schooling in the ordinary way or through any other qualifications. Whatever musical talents he could throw into the scales in the hope of tipping the balance were still in the process of being tested. He had learnt to play the piano too late in life to become a virtuoso, and so only composition or conducting remained as viable alternatives. Yet even here it was clear that he had not been gifted with the gratifying talent needed to win both hearts and well-paid posts.

If any of his orchestral works were performed, it was simply because he enjoyed his sister's patronage and had bowed and scraped to intendants and conductors. If critics were well disposed towards him, it was impossible to avoid the suspicion that it was Rosalie's charms that had swayed them – this was certainly the case with her admirer Heinrich Laube. The compositional process, moreover, was attended by the same torments as his attempts to have his works performed. In each case he could be happy for them not to be greeted with open contempt, as had happened with his 'Drumbeat' Overture. His attempts to make himself useful by copying parts or proof-reading were turned down by the publishers that he approached. Even his grovelling offer to undertake the work 'at less than the usual price' had failed to awaken their interest.[96]

Genius – so indispensable if he was to enjoy a sensational success – was something that no one could discern in him, while his undeniable talent failed to produce the desired effect: far from being admired, he became a source of mounting concern, especially within his own family. It was feared that he would not progress beyond mere talent, and so he was advised to study something more practical. These were all severe trials for a proud but misprized composer. For Wagner knew very well where his future lay.

In most areas he had of necessity been his own master, and so he was free to set his own goals. And he set them correspondingly high. Hence his need to convince the world of who he was and what it owed him. He now began to exert his influence on a world that clearly thought it could manage without him. The world would see the error of its ways. He made sure that people sat up and noticed him, raising his voice until it cracked with excitement. And he kept showing them what he had learnt.

He had assimilated the art of composition with remarkable speed, at the same time learning how to instrument correctly, for the inner dramas that had pursued him since childhood demanded that they be depicted in music. Only a performance on the largest scale was appropriate in these circumstances. He should not have to worry about money and suchlike trifles any longer. And so he repeatedly ran up debts, feeling that the world owed him the little he required. And he also knew that what he had to offer the world in abundance in return could never be measured in terms of mere money.

Even in the course of his earliest tentative attempts to create his own independent works, he had learnt that the characters he bore within him also appeared in myth. The relationships in which humanity's experience of life had been stored from classical antiquity to the Middle Ages he rediscovered in his own subconscious. It was necessary only to understand their message for their doomed heroes and their demonic opponents, their self-sacrificing virgins and their satanic seducers, to begin to speak of their own volition.

And their language had long since been familiar to him. These remote figures rubbed shoulders with him every day. With each new subject he tackled, his personal experiences and traumas were transferred to the objective relationships that became the motivating force of his dramas. When Cadolt and Ada died, they returned as the Dutchman and Senta, with their roles little changed. They sprang back into life as the Volsungs and perished in the fire that destroys the whole world at the end of *Götterdämmerung*. Nothing new followed on from *Leubald*, save the creation of a world that had never existed before.

As the nineteen-year-old student sat brooding over his unfinished *Die Hochzeit*, there was as yet no intimation of this world nor of the role that he would play in it. Rather, he was bound to feel that he was a failure. The sad thing is that he was beginning to get used to this role. The sense of failure while all around him prospered remained with him all his life. Not even his successes changed this. He never overcame his fear of failure, just as he never forgot the hatred that he felt for what he regarded as the cause of his very first failure.

In 1876, the year that witnessed his greatest triumph with the opening of the Bayreuth Festival, the sixty-two-year-old composer, living in his own villa at Wahnfried and acclaimed throughout the whole of Europe, had a dream in which he found himself subjected to the bitterest humiliation. As recorded by Cosima, his dream ran as follows. He had arrived by train in a large city, where he was to conduct a performance of Beethoven's Ninth Symphony. Feeling hungry, he saw some frankfurters on display at the station buffet and ordered them. Although they must have been ready for some time, no one made any attempt to bring them to him. On going to fetch them, he saw that two men were already tucking into his order. He complained, but the buffet attendant shamelessly sent him packing and the manageress, bent on punishing him, refused to serve him not just the sausages but also the beer he had ordered.

He began by reacting angrily, but that did not help, and so he tried a more friendly approach, again to no avail. Cursing and swearing, he left the buffet and went to the concert hall where, hungry and thirsty, he was greeted with applause. He had already made his way through the orchestra when he noticed that he had to climb a steep slope, a task which, thanks to his agility, he managed to perform. But suddenly – and here the story ends – 'he comes to a place that is too steep and as he can't jump over it, he wakes up!'

After Cosima had noted down this nightmare on 6 January 1876, Wagner himself offered an explanation of it, one that suggests that decades before Freud he was already familiar with the workings of the unconscious: 'All one needs is bad experiences to stop the brain from carrying out the task for which it is intended, then demons of every description take control and produce nothing but hideous images!'[97]

2 Grand Opera

In the Enchanted Garden

In January 1833 Wagner experienced both the low point and the high point of his career to date. *Die Hochzeit* may have ended up in his recycling bin, but at least his C major Symphony was performed at one of Leipzig's prestigious Gewandhaus concerts. As a writer of operas he had failed spectacularly, yet as an orchestral composer he was showered with praise, not least in the columns of the *Zeitung für die elegante Welt*. And that very same month he received a letter from his brother that set him on the road to an international career.

He was invited to make a guest appearance in Würzburg, where the local music society wanted to hear one of his overtures under the young maestro's own direction. At the same time he was offered the post of a salaried répétiteur at the town's theatre for a season, a post that Wagner retrospectively upgraded to that of a chorus master. As the post also enabled him to avoid military service in Saxony, the new year seemed to have begun on a highly propitious note.

In fact, it soon turned out that the offer of help from the versatile Albert, who was employed at the Würzburg Theatre as singer, actor and stage director, was not entirely selfless, as he had planned his own series of guest appearances during the coming summer, when he and his wife would be absent in Strasbourg for a period of several months and would need someone to look after their three children, whom they would leave behind in Würzburg. The role seemed tailor-made for the young composer, who was known in his family as being 'good with children'. Unfortunately, Wagner underestimated the problems involved, and it was not long before the six-year-old Johanna and her two younger sisters Marie and Franziska began to show signs of neglect, including an infestation of head lice.

Abandoning his nieces to their fate often until late into the night, Wagner spent the summer in the company of hard-hitting and hard-drinking musicians, later reporting on a number of brief romances, including ones with Therese Ringelmann, the daughter of the local grave-digger, and Friederike Galvani, the fiancée of the orchestra's principal oboist. If his relationship with the 'barely educated' Therese progressed no further than a romantic friendship, the 'passionate advances' of Italian-born Friederike resulted in the now twenty-year-old Wagner's 'first youthful love affair'.

Musically, too, there was much for him to learn here. In addition to rehearsing such familiar pieces as *Der Freischütz, La muette de Portici* (always performed in German as *Die Stumme von Portici*) and *Fidelio*, he also had to work on Marschner's new magic opera *Hans Heiling*. And if Marschner had once accused him of plagiarism, Wagner now got his own back by accusing his fellow composer of 'a total lack of any overall effect'.[1] And the internationally celebrated Giacomo Meyerbeer now entered his professional life, when *Robert le diable*, already a runaway success in Paris and elsewhere, received its Würzburg première, with Wagner's brother as the tenor lead.

However disappointed Wagner may have been by the score of Meyerbeer's opera, he none the less made great use of it at a later date in his career. Meanwhile, he not only had to look after his brother's children, he also had to reinstrument a Bellini cavatina in order to lend greater brilliance to Albert's appearance on stage, and it was similarily at Albert's request that he wrote both the words and the music for a new Allegro section of an insertion aria for Marschner's *Der Vampyr*. 'My work', Wagner later declared, 'turned out to be demonic and effective', earning him the audience's applause.

Wagner's entertaining account of his year in Würzburg is drolly reminiscent of the writings of E. T. A. Hoffmann, but it obscures the fact that he was already fully aware of what he wanted. He had come to Würzburg not only as a fully trained musician whose collected works already filled a small suitcase, but with very clear ideas about the significance of these works. The fact that, in order to earn some money, he had to win the volatile goodwill of both audiences and intendants was of entirely secondary importance to him. For Wagner, the main thing was the music: in his view music was more important than anything else, in art as in life. Only in music did the essence of the whole find expression, a whole that German idealism had reclaimed for philosophy. Music alone expressed the truth.

While the constant bickerings that beset his attempts to have his music performed may be entertaining from a narrative point of view, the only thing that really mattered to the young Wagner was that the innermost secret of his art should reflect the innermost secret of the whole of existence. 'The essence of dramatic art', he wrote in 1834 when discussing operatic music, 'is certainly not based on particular subjects or points of view but on whether it succeeds in grasping and representing the inner essence of all human action and life: in other words, the Idea.'[2]

This sentence is so clearly expressed that one would think it had been for-mulated not by the upstart adventurer of Wagner's autobiography but by a writer on aesthetics of the Hegelian school, with the result that the authorship of the article has been called into question. But Wagner was always a philoso-pher even while he was a musician. Ever since he had peered down into the mystic abysses of German idealism in the company of his Uncle Adolf, reality had mattered to him only to the extent that it succeeded in representing the Idea in art. And for Wagner, this Idea – the building plan of the phenomenal world – reflected the archetypes of his life, archetypes whose basic relationships he rediscovered both in the myths of the ancients and on the modern stage. Art, in consequence, had a universal function, proclaiming the hidden truth of exis-tence by penetrating the mists of transient everyday life and shedding light on the sempiternal ideas.

Wagner spent his whole life developing these thoughts. In advancing them, he proved to be E. T. A. Hoffmann's best pupil, for Hoffmann was a philosopher of music whose ghost stories had been common currency in the Wagner house-hold from the time of the composer's childhood, a supremely gifted writer no less adept than Weber at conjuring up the terrors that we find in the music to the Wolf's Glen scene. Even towards the end of his life, when he was already living in Bayreuth, these terrors were still capable of inducing a very real sense of fear in Wagner.

Hoffmann's young admirer abandoned himself all too gladly to his prede-cessor's febrile imagination, discovering an enchanted fairy garden behind everyday reality. The mysterious creatures that inhabit this garden belong in part to this life, in part to that alternative existence, generally ensuring that they live in a state of confusion from which they need to be redeemed. But just as what seems to be the real world can suddenly turn into its magical opposite, so this alternative world can in turn be transformed into a living hell whose demonic accompanying phenomena cast their pall over both the enchanted garden and the earth, making them seem like a veritable vale of sorrow.

On his very first visit to the castle at Pravonin – later to be the scene of what he himself described as 'certain satanic love affairs' of a Hofmannesque stamp – Wagner had already been fascinated by this sinister world. Two years later, when he read Hoffmann's musico-philosophical tale about Christoph

Willibald Gluck, he found himself 'stirred by the wildest mysticism'[3] and imagined musical intervals as living creatures. He saw the world – fearsome, grotesque and ridiculous – through Hoffmann's glasses and at the same time began to resemble him as a writer.

After E. T. A. Hoffmann had recognized himself in his own sorcerer Lindhorst, Wagner, too, began to identify with him, and although this drolly demonic image refuses to be squared with his biographers' traditional picture of him, this seems not to have troubled Wagner himself. Wagner's friend in Dresden Wilhelm Fischer had also known Hoffmann, and when he pointed out the great similarity between the two men, Wagner declared that there could well be 'some truth' to his observation.[4]

It was in memory of Hoffmann that, while on his way to take up his new post in Würzburg in January 1833, Wagner broke his journey in Bamberg, where Hoffmann had written his famous *Fantasiestücke in Callots Manier*, a collection of tales that includes not only *Ritter Gluck* but also one of Wagner's particular favourites, *Der goldene Topf*. Here, too, Hoffmann had developed the world of ideas of his *Kreisleriana*, a world to which Wagner owed his basic views on the aesthetics of music. In 1814, Hoffmann had written that German opera could flourish only if it acquired a taste for Italian melody. In this the way forward had been shown by Mozart, 'in whose breast Italian singing burned brightly'. Twenty years later Wagner announced that German opera was too 'learned' to treat singing as Italian composers did. Only 'Mozart could do so; but it was the beauty of Italian song that he breathed into his human beings'.[5]

Like his friend Adolf Wagner, Hoffmann professed his faith in a Romantic religion of art in which the creation of great works was tantamount to a supreme act of divine worship. Art was sacred, the artist a godlike figure. The present day could not, of course, even begin to compete with the sublime works of the classical writers, and Hoffmann bewailed a dramatic decline in art, which, he argued, had been replaced by imitative histrionics. Operatic music, in particular, Hoffmann's Kapellmeister Kreisler believed, suffered from the 'perpetual demands on the part of impresarios' for empty 'effects', effects that desperate musicians sought to produce by means of increasingly blatant ideas. But their anxious attempts to create a 'so-called impression' ultimately led merely to vain 'imitation'.

Hoffmann's conviction that artificial effects produced by musicians were 'unmotivated' was summed up by Wagner when he famously referred to effects without causes. Hoffmann, too, hated the 'empty illusion' that typified modern music in its attempts to attract attention. This he contrasted with his vision of a true art in which eternal ideas were manifested. For him, true music was the product of our spiritualization. Its sounds expressed our 'presentiment of all that is highest and most sacred'. It was the medium for a 'spiritual power' that mere mortals could scarcely grasp.

In Hoffmann's view, it was only because the true tone poem sprang from deep within the composer, pouring forth unhindered from his breast through the agency of song, that it could penetrate deep inside the listener and fill him or her with the spirit of art: 'The spirit alone understands the language of the spirit.' And the spirit did not speak different languages that could be divided into the language of music and the language of the spoken word, depending on the different genres. It spoke only one: just as poet and musician were 'the most intimately related members of a single church', so the secret of words and music was one and the same. The true nature of opera would be revealed only when 'music emerges directly from the poem as a necessary product of the same'.

Hoffmann had scarcely expressed this idea in his dialogue 'The Poet and the Composer' when he advanced his ideal of a 'genuinely Romantic opera'. It alone would allow the poet to summon into existence the 'wondrous phenomena of the spirit world'. And he had already singled out a source for such a 'musical drama'. 'Think of the glorious Gozzi,' he urged his readers. 'In his dramatic fairytales he has provided exactly what I demand of a librettist, and it is incredible that this rich storehouse of outstanding operatic subjects has not been more fully exploited.'

Adolf Wagner had already set a good example as long ago as 1804, when he had translated Gozzi's *Il corvo*, and it was now up to his nephew to continue the family tradition. Wagner's choice fell not unnaturally on *La donna serpente* ('The Serpent Woman'), for here, as the title suggests, he was attracted by a character who belongs to two different worlds: as the child of a mortal father and a fairy mother, she hails from an enchanted realm whose privilege of immortality she enjoys until the time she falls in love with a mortal. Capable of changing her shape, the fairy Ada marries the unsuspecting Arindal and even bears his children. Her only condition is that Arindal shall never ask after her 'name and nature', as Wagner was to express the terms of this prohibition on another, later occasion. In this way, Ada appears not only as a precursor of Lohengrin but also as a successor of Melusine – for Wagner, an archetypal mother figure. Hoffmann himself had already adapted the Melusine story as the basis of an opera, taking as his source Fouqué's *Undine* – the very tale that Wagner was to read on the eve of his death.[6]

Thanks to Hoffmann's suggestion, the young Wagner was introduced to a new subject at the very moment that Rosalie tore from his trembling hand his earlier draft for *Die Hochzeit*. Moreover, Gozzi's *La donna serpente* seemed to satisfy his sister's demands on every point. Whereas the eponymous wedding between Ada and Arindal had degenerated into the blackest of tragedies, the marriage between the two main characters of his new work – Wagner defiantly retained their names from his earlier opera – was to prove its own worth after all manner of ordeals. In honour of Rosalie, marital love was glorified. The themes of madness, betrayal and death associated with the Wolf's Glen yielded to a light-hearted fairytale.

Mindful of his uncle's *Il corvo*, Wagner turned his heroine not into a snake but into stone, and so he was able to alter the original title to something less sombre: *Die Feen* ('The Fairies').[7] Instead of taking place in a gloomy castle, as his earlier opera had done, this new one is set in a delightful fairytale garden. And whereas *Leubald, Die Hochzeit* and Fouqué's *Undine* had all ended in a tragic love-death, Wagner's fairytale introduces us to a world of dreams ringing with the sounds of celestial harmonies.

Arindal is able to breathe life and love into his petrified wife by dint of the strains of his harp, a gift she repays by granting him happiness and immortality. Rosalie seemed satisfied. Wagner recalled that he was 'in a good mood' when he threw himself into the work in Würzburg, a state made possible by her 'loving concern'. During the summer break his income had shrunk to nothing, but with fairylike generosity she 'loyally' helped him out with 'enough pocket money' to keep him going.

Wagner repaid her by combining the ravishing fairy not only with the mysterious Melusine but also with his angel Rosalie, weaving into the work a whole series of older musical ideas that were more than familiar to his sister. He paid tribute to his Lady of the Sorrows, the Blessed Virgin Rosalie, with quotations from the Gretchen songs that were dedicated to her. The fact that these reminiscences are found only in connection with Ada suggests that Rosalie may have recognized in the heroine of the opera a flattering portrait of herself.[8]

In addition to the tried and tested ideas that Wagner took over into his new magic opera from existing works of his own, there were also three 'great' composers whom he was later prepared to name as sources of inspiration: Beethoven, Weber and Marschner. Yet he fails to mention his most important source, which was none of these three composers. The fairy kingdom's language of dreams, whose yearning magic is made clear to us from the opera's very first rising chords, was borrowed from one of Wagner's most famous colleagues.

It comes from Mendelssohn's Concert Overture no. 1, first heard in 1826 and better known as his overture to *A Midsummer Night's Dream*. Wagner took over not only the harmonic magic formula with which it begins but also the key of

E major, which he uses not only in the overture but at the end of the opera, too. In doing so, he lent the whole opera a Mendelssohnian touch that is by no means to its disadvantage. And is it possible that even at this early date he was also already familiar with Mendelssohn's Concert Overture no. 4 of 1833? Two decades later he was to use its magic formula to depict his playful water sprites in the opening scene of *Das Rheingold*. Although he fails to mention this work as a source of inspiration, Mendelssohn's dreamlike overture – *The Tale of the Fair Melusine* – was unquestionably familiar to him.

Yet for all that this may seem like mere plagiarism, it is by no means at odds with the idea of Wagner's originality. According to Hoffmann, the true nature of opera lay in allowing the music to emerge directly from the poem – in other words, from the ideas. In this way, a work's originality could no longer be measured by its 'novelty' but only by the appropriateness of its musical expression. If this expression had already been used by another composer, the composer's art consisted not in inventing it all over again but in learning to speak its language.

With *Die Feen*, Wagner began to express himself in the new language of ideas. Its basic concepts had already left their mark on him in the form of the 'open fifths' and the music heard in the incantations of the Wolf's Glen scene. Now he tried his hand at new settings such as a 'fairy palace' and 'subterranean ravines'. Even the barking of the pack of dogs in *Die Walküre* is heard for the first time here.

Wagner had finally struck out on his own. Yet no one listening to *Die Feen* could predict from these barren beginnings the course that his career was later to take. In January 1834, with the opera finished, he returned from Würzburg to Leipzig and won the acclaim of his family – no mean judge in such matters – being praised even by Rosalie. Now it was the turn of the Stadttheater to beckon, but in spite of his sister's persistent entreaties, the theatre proved tiresomely coy. Acceptance of the work was repeatedly delayed, and although a performance of the overture, with its magical chords, was scheduled, this too was subsequently abandoned. Wagner was simply being fobbed off.

Although he does not mention the fact, Wagner hurriedly revised the score that had been spurned in this way,[9] introducing into it the latest subtleties that he had picked up in March when he had heard Bellini's *I Capuleti e i Montecchi* for the first time. In the hope of obtaining the goodwill of the household gods of the Leipzig Theatre, he rewrote whole sections of the score and modernized others in an attempt to show willing. But, as he complained in a letter to the theatre's resident producer, the directors were evidently prejudiced against his 'whole trend'. Perhaps magic operas à la Hoffmann had simply passed their sell-by date. *Die Feen* remained obstinately silent.

Overcome by 'great depression', Wagner vented his aggression on one of his models, availing himself of the columns of Laube's journal to attack *Euryanthe*, the magic opera by his former idol Carl Maria von Weber.[10] Like Meyerbeer's *Robert le diable* and Marschner's *Hans Heiling*, this was a work that had substantially enriched his own musical language. But this was something he was no longer prepared to acknowledge.

The 'Young German'

If Wagner's first opera had been pulled even before it was completed, and if his second, though finished, remained unperformed, his third did at least make it to the stage. Yet *Das Liebesverbot* survived only a single performance, suffering a setback from which it was never to recover. Ill luck seemed to dog Wagner's every footstep.

The fact that even after the fiasco of *Die Hochzeit* and *Die Feen* the hapless composer was still prepared to try his hand at an opera says much for his determination to continue along the road on which he had set out. Moreover, the fact that he had three times changed his subject matter within the space of a mere eighteen months says much for his ability to adapt. The Gothic horror of his first tragic opera had been followed in a twinkling by a fairytale comedy, whereas he now struck a boldly modernist note in his hedonistic revolutionary opera *Das Liebesverbot*. This time his agenda involved neither a love-death nor marital love, but the free, uninhibited love of free, uninhibited men and women. This was the agenda of 'Young Germany'.

Consciously rejecting the 'old' Germany of subservient underlings and student associations, the Young German movement sought to give at least literary expression to the revolutionary ideals of July 1830. Whereas the Romantic poets had withdrawn into a state of noble seclusion and dreamt of enchanted gardens and minnesingers, the Young Germans threw themselves into the arms of reality and living human beings, rediscovering the power of language to bring them closer to the goals that the cannons of war were powerless to coerce.

A new style of writing arose, provocatively and implacably critical, using the rapier of ridicule to despatch not only the ancient spirit of feudalism, but also antiquated culture and petty German nationalism. The glorification of Prussian values, with their strait-laced moral strictness, was to be replaced by a free republic in which men and women were to be allowed to go about their professional lives and indulge their amorous desires in uninhibited freedom. It was called 'the emancipation of the flesh'. Heinrich Heine and Ludwig Börne contributed through their writings to this paper revolution, while Laube provided the young Wagner with the key concepts for his own emancipation.

Wagner himself later recalled that it was thanks to Laube's novel *Das junge Europa* that he succeeded in breaking free from 'abstract mysticism' and learnt to love the material world. 'Material beauty, wit and spirit were wonderful things to me', he wrote. 'As far as my music was concerned, I found both among the Italians and the French.'[11] Writing in the Young German *Zeitung für die elegante Welt*, he praised Bellini at Weber's expense and in the course of a summer visit to Teplitz gave practical expression to his newly acquired world-view.

In 1834, together with Theodor Apel, he repaired to the Bohemian spa that had played such a significant role in his family history, and here he generously allowed his well-to-do friend to support him. They travelled in their own coach, dined on trout, imbibed 'good Czernosek wine' and, in the gathering gloom of the summer evening, withdrew to their balcony room at the hotel the King of Prussia. Here they would sit up all night, discussing Hoffmann, Shakespeare and, above all, *Ardinghello und die glückseeligen Inseln* by the Utopian exponent of philosophical eroticism Wilhelm Heinse. They felt like 'young gods'.

When Wagner set off on his own to the Judenberg and breakfasted alone at the hotel on the Schlackenburg, he took his Shakespeare with him. Here in this idyllic ambience he set about rewriting the English dramatist's comedy of confusion *Measure for Measure* and turned it into a Young German opera for the future. In Palermo the austere Friedrich is raised by royal favour from a 'poor unknown' visitor to the king's own representative. As governor, he uses the king's absence to introduce the customs of his native Germany to the hedonistic town, with the death sentence as an instant penalty for all extra-marital affairs. The populace rises up in vain and is forced to look on in helpless dismay as Friedrich threatens to visit his draconian measures on Claudio for secretly impregnating Julia.

Fortunately Claudio has an angelic sister. A novice at the local nunnery, Isabella appears on the scene and begs the tyrant for mercy. Friedrich shows himself to be more than shaken by such a show of sisterly affection. Consumed by lust for the virginal nun, he not unnaturally suggests that she buys her brother's freedom by transgressing her own vow of chastity. Caught on the horns of a classic dilemma, the prudish Friedrich inevitably finds himself exposed as a lecherous hypocrite. Claudio regains his freedom and, with it, his lover. And even Isabella finds it hard to resist the temptations afforded by the emancipation of the flesh.

A revolution of love now breaks out in Wagner's imaginary Palermo – love, moreover, in its uninhibited Young German guise: 'Jetzt gibt's nicht Weib, noch Ehemann, tralalalalala! Es gibt nicht Vater und nicht Sohn, tralalalalala!' ('Now there's no wife or husband, tralalalalala!) There's no father and no son, tralalalalala!' With the carnival, the victory of the revolution is celebrated and, as in *Fidelio*, it coincides with the return of the benevolent king who, we may assume, will sanction the state of newly won libertinage.

With this 'bold glorification of "free sensuality"',[12] Wagner had, by his own admission, contributed to the Young German revolution in taste. True to his source, he found himself at odds with the authorities: according to his autobiography, the police took exception to the title of the opera when a production of the work was planned in Magdeburg in 1836. If the title had not been changed, he claimed, the 'Ban on Love' would itself have been banned. As later scholars have pointed out, there were absolutely no official objections to the harmless title at the time. In order to ensure that the performance went ahead during Holy Week, Wagner himself had on his own initiative adopted the more pious-sounding subtitle of 'The Novice of Palermo'.[13]

Nor was Wagner's sudden espousal of the Young German cause quite as precipitate or all-embracing as his memoirs would have us believe. Although the clattering castanets and tinkling triangle of the overture announce that, musically speaking, the composer had mastered two foreign languages in the form of Italian and French, the racy tone with which he hoped to make his breakthrough provides no more than the musical backdrop at best, for on closer inspection his 'grand comic opera', as he described *Das Liebesverbot*, is by no means as comic as Wagner appears to have thought. While remaining within the framework of contemporary Young German ideas, Wagner had returned to the world of tragedy.

Even his Shakespearean source had been 'very serious' in tone, and his interest as a librettist was presumably roused not by the original's amatory intrigues, which were of only secondary importance, but by a dramatic conflict that was long familiar to him. The Duke – the prototype of the 'good father' – has transferred his power to a representative who proceeds to abuse it. As the 'wicked father', he wants to punish his 'son' Claudio for loving Julia. As Claudio's sister Isabella is like a sister to Juliet, we once again find ourselves dealing with the archetypal situation of the disinherited prince who is threatened with death.

Once again the usurper has arrogated to himself the reins of power, depriving the legitimate heir of the woman who is in fact his sister, before taking his life as well. As a tragic consequence of this, Isabella has to sacrifice herself voluntarily to the devilish ruler in order to save Claudio's life. Urged to do so by her own brother, she raises the eloquent objection: 'Is't not a kind of incest to take life / From thine own sister's shame?' Only as a result of the intervention of the Duke, who has been listening to the conversation incognito, is disaster averted and justice – 'measure for measure' – restored.

There is little trace here of the feverish iconoclasm of the Young Germans. If Wagner had not driven the paternalistic Duke from the stage, there would have been virtually nothing left of their revolutionary reappraisal of love. And the king's return brings with it a conservative denouement. In place of a society that, having ousted its arrogant ruler, is freed from all dominion, only the false regent is dethroned, allowing the good king and his old imperial majesty to be reinstated.

If we focus on the struggle for power and the possession of women, *Das Liebesverbot* loses its outsider status in Wagner's overall output and takes its rightful place as the natural successor to the Gothic horror of *Leubald*, at the same time anticipating *Rienzi*, which likewise centres on a brother–sister relationship. Even at this date there could no longer be any question of a Young German revolution on the French model. If there is any revolution here for Wagner as an artist, then it is the 'German' variant of this revolution, a variant that finally reconciles the returning father with the son – or that ends in total destruction.

If this relationship is seen as central to Wagner's opera, then the figure of the sister willing to sacrifice herself becomes its principal character. And once again it was the noble Rosalie who served as the model, moving the populace with her 'mute gestures', as Fenella had done, and, like Gretchen, redeeming her fallen lover through her love. The pure angel who, as Saint Elisabeth, will later help the sinful Tannhäuser to find salvation, is discovered living in the Convent of Saint Elizabeth.

Here, in Isabella's sacred halls, Wagner introduces a motif which, against the background of the Mediterranean turmoil that typifies so much of the orchestral writing, sounds like a pre-echo of his later style. When the nuns launch into their *Salve regina* in praise of the Queen of Heaven, we hear the magical chord progression of the Dresden Amen, the sweetly ascending line of which symbolizes our ascent to divine mercy. Heaven's message of forgiveness was to ring forth not only for Claudio but, later, for Tannhäuser and, in Wagner's last work of all, for the knights of the Grail, whose community is in urgent need of redemption.

This is a motif to which Wagner was to remain loyal all his life and that he may have borrowed from Mendelssohn, although its pedigree is much older: the Dresden Amen dates back to the eighteenth century and was regularly heard in the city's churches,[14] including the Kreuzkirche, before Mendelssohn used it, to particularly memorable effect, in his 'Reformation' Symphony of 1830, a work that was first performed in Berlin in November 1832. Mendelssohn's secret imitator, who was a pupil at the Kreuzschule at this time, could have heard about the symphony from his friend Theodor Apel. Thanks to Apel's enthusiasm for Mendelssohn, Wagner knew all about the latter's career and in 1835 he even sent a number of his works to his successful rival, no doubt in the hope that Mendelssohn would help in having them performed. The following year, shortly after the first (and last) performance of *Das Liebesverbot*, he made Mendelssohn's acquaintance and soon after their meeting sent the admired conductor of the Gewandhaus concerts his C major Symphony, never to see it again.

Mendelssohn soon provided Wagner with a number of other ideas: in 1835, shortly after conducting a performance of his colleague's concert overture *Calm Sea and Prosperous Voyage*, Wagner used a number of elements of this tone-painterly water music in a related work of his own, a work for which Apel provided the starting point.[15] Like his father, Theodor Apel had literary ambitions. In the present case, the large-scale subject to which he turned his hand was the life of Christopher Columbus. History does not relate whether his source was Adolf Wagner's 1825 translation of a study of Columbus and his discoveries, but we do know that Apel consulted Wagner's uncle in his capacity as a Columbus specialist, evidently hoping to receive the expert's blessing for his own contribution to the subject. He then invited Wagner to write a musical prelude and postlude to his five-act drama, an invitation to which Wagner was all the keener to respond in that he was now in financial difficulties.

Wagner's enthusiasm for Apel's play knew no bounds, at least according to his letters to the author. Every page, he confessed, 'brought fresh tears of joy and emotion' to his eyes. Above all, he was delighted by the 'colourful, powerful brevity that strikes one everywhere'.[16] As with Meyerbeer at a slightly later date, Wagner was unstinting in his praise. But then he came to the point and revealed the true reason for his encomiastic tone: as a result of all manner of thoughtless actions, he had sunk into such a 'slough of debt' as to make his 'hair stand on end'. He later explained that it was 'the damned Jewish vermin' who was solely to blame for his plight. Only the 'golden boy' Apel could help him. And Apel duly helped with money and also with a gold signet ring. Presciently Apel noted in his diary: 'He's always complaining about his misfortunes, but he's mostly the one who's to blame for bringing them down on himself.'[17]

His monetary problems helping to concentrate his mind, Wagner lost no time in setting a chorus from Apel's drama expressing the sufferings of the Moors on their expulsion from Granada. This was followed by suitable closing music and finally by the overture, which Wagner claims to have written 'in the most exuberant haste'. Although tossed off in a hurry, this last piece impressed itself upon him to such an extent that he could still clearly recall it thirty years later: from the sea of notes available to him, the composer evoked the great ocean in all its seething turbulence, together with the ship that bore its hero towards an as yet uncertain future. Columbus's unshakeable desire to find a new way forward was represented by a 'powerful, passionately demanding and yearning motif'.

Soon, however, the theme that expressed the explorer's will was bound to give way to a new and completely unexpected motif: to the accompaniment of a 'twilight flickering in the highest register of the violins' there appeared, like some Fata Morgana, a six-part trumpet fanfare presaging the 'land towards which the hero's gaze is directed, a land whose existence he already dimly sensed'. But the vision then fades, as though wafted away by a spell, instilling a mood of anxious uncertainty, before 'rising up in the morning sky as a vast new world of the future'. The six trumpets then combine to create a sense of the most splendid jubilation, allowing the listener to forget that the fanfare had already been used in Mendelssohn's concert overture. In fact, it was not the fanfare itself that he borrowed, but the idea of a fanfare. Wagner had clearly found no better way to express the joy of discovery.

Apel's play *Columbus* opened in Magdeburg in February 1835 and closed the same month after a single performance, sinking beneath the waves so eloquently evoked by Wagner's score and thus sharing the same sad fate as *Das Liebesverbot*, which the following year was likewise to sink back down again beneath the musical horizon.

Wilhelmine

If Wagner's relationship with Wilhelmine ('Minna') Planer proved to be a disaster for his personal life, it was a stroke of luck for him as an artist. That it should have been in Bad Lauchstädt where they fell into each other's arms itself suggests the workings of fate, for it was here, just thirty years earlier, that a historic encounter took place between Wagner's parents and the two literary giants of Weimar, Goethe and Schiller. During the summer of 1803, the two parties passed each other in the street, Johanna Rosine confessing to her astonished husband that she had never even heard their names in all the time she had spent at her 'select seminary' in Leipzig.

Some thirty-one years later Bad Lauchstädt was one of several provincial German towns visited by the Magdeburg-based company of which Wagner – much to everyone's surprise, including his own – found himself music director. Here, too, he met his future wife. Now virtually a write-off as a composer, he made his début with the company on 2 August 1834, conducting Mozart's *Don Giovanni* – the choice seems somehow fated. The very next day saw a performance of Nestroy's magic farce *Der böse Geist Lumpacivagabundus*, in which Minna Planer, no less aptly, played the part of the fairy Amorosa. The conductor, by his own admission, was 'enthralled'. In the midst of this 'dust cloud of frivolity and vulgarity', the doll-like, mousey-haired actress seemed to him 'just like an actual fairy'.[18]

Anyone less like a fairy is hard to imagine, but the result of Wagner's perception was a double misunderstanding: just as the composer, inexperienced in matters of the heart, took the actress's playful coquetry for the real thing, so the older actress saw in Wagner not the youth in need of love but a conductor whose appointment held out the promise of financial security. Much buffeted by life's storms, Minna now craved a safe haven, while Wagner, his career in the doldrums, sought the open sea. She hoped for a respectable husband, he needed a sisterly Muse. From the outset, their love was at cross-purposes.

Buoyed up by their illusions, they drifted towards each other and by the time their true interests collided they could no longer break free from their relationship. Long before Wagner gave dramatic expression to the great conflicts between Elsa and Lohengrin, Wotan and Fricka, and Siegfried and Brünnhilde, he had already experienced these conflicts for himself in the theatre of his own home. It was a drama that struggled on for thirty long years before Minna died, wretched and abandoned, in 1866. From then on she tormented him only at night. Only a few weeks before his death, he dreamt that she had seen him crying and had 'gone mad' out of sheer delight.[19]

For Wagner, the relationship had likewise begun with tears and madness. Obsessed with the fair Wilhelmine – it was no accident that she played the 'leading lover' in the theatre – he thought that he could not live without her. By the time that his grand passion had degenerated into a Strindbergian marital war, it seemed impossible for him to live with her, but he could never really break free. Once they were separated, his obsessiveness returned as its polar opposite in the form of a feeling of persecution and permanent pangs of conscience. The position of superego that Minna occupied in his life was one she had to abandon only when Cosima laid her own irrefutable claim to it.

This position had already existed, of course, even before Wagner had got to know either Minna or Cosima. The feminine ideal that he looked for in them had long since been fashioned by two other women. As an actress, Minna was able to slip into both these roles, and so she represented both mother and sister in one. She was the angel who inspired him to perform great deeds and who selflessly sacrificed herself for him. And she was the mother who fed him and reduced him to childlike dependency.

But in keeping with the logic of this archetype, she did all this only so that she might all the more cruelly betray him and pursue him like one of the Furies. The tragic misunderstanding rested on the fact that this did not reflect the true situation but only Wagner's own private mythology. In this way there evolved within him a picture of womankind that led to one disaster after another for him and yet brought to his works an important new dimension. And it was in this that Wagner was so fortunate.

Christine Wilhelmine Planer was born in 1809 as the daughter of an unemployed military trumpeter. At the time of her marriage to Wagner, she gave her date of birth as 1814, and by the time she died she had knocked off another three years – at least according to the list of Dresden residents. As with Johanna Rosine, her impoverished adolescence had been briefly transfigured by an aristocratic Lohengrin in the person of a captain in the Royal Saxon Guards, one Ernst Rudolf von Einsiedel, who fathered on her a child she named Natalie, then vanished. In an attempt to ensure that the fifteen-year-old Minna at least had a chance of contracting an advantageous marriage, her mother agreed to pass the child off as her own. From then on, Natalie was believed to be Minna's younger sister.

By the time Wagner entered her life, Minna was already a celebrated actress and close to achieving her life's aim. A new Lohengrin had arrived on the scene in the guise of the young Herr von Otterstedt, who made her his mistress, presumably while promising to marry her. And thus she remained, even though he had in the meantime decided to marry another woman for reasons of social rank and convenience. But at least he left no child behind, merely a very fine oil painting in which she resembles Hoffmann's mechanical doll. Otterstedt painted this devotional portrait at a time when Wagner already thought of himself as engaged to Minna, and it left him feeling embittered when she gave it away to another of her aristocratic admirers who likewise had certain claims on her.

Just as Minna played the same parts as Rosalie on stage, so she seemed predestined for the role of elder sister in Wagner's life. He was unhappy as a member of a company of actors whose grotesque personnel included an alcoholic manager, his hip-shot nymphomaniac wife and a toothless theatrical dogsbody. Against the background of luminaries such as these, Minna stood out like a figure from a better world, seeming to extend roles such as Gretchen and Shakespeare's Juliet into real life and bringing the impetuous conductor a sense of spiritual nobility and astonished wellbeing. And so Rosalie's honorary title passed effortlessly to her successor, whom Wagner soon transfigured: 'Ah, my angel, redeem me', he wrote to her, 'otherwise I'll sink without trace.'[20]

Minna had everything necessary to help the young conductor on his way. Like Rosalie, she was spoilt by success and surrounded by admirers who placed their affluence at the service of their passion for the theatre. Wagner had no such material goods, much as he needed them to pursue his chosen lifestyle, and so he left Minna to act on his behalf. She tapped into sources of money for him, helped to fob off his creditors and, to the best of her abilities, furthered his musical career. Without realizing it, she offered him the expressions of affection that Wagner expected from a self-sacrificing sister. Rosalie had portrayed this type of woman to perfection in her performances in *La muette de Portici*, and it is no coincidence that this was the work that Wagner chose to conduct on the very eve of his wedding, allowing his fiancée to shine in the principal role.

Much later, Wagner claimed that he had married above all because he lacked a 'maternal home' to which he 'would like to have returned'.[21] Certainly, Wagner's passion, which appears to have been fired at their very first meeting, seems to have been triggered by Minna's 'maternal' demeanour. When his chronic erysipelas left his features 'terribly distorted', she sought him out in his sad lonely room, saw to his needs and even kissed him on his infected lips. Although she was not in love with him – or, as he wrote in his memoirs, only to the extent that she felt 'an affection bordering on passion' – she soon allowed him to sleep with her. And although there can be no question of any real desire on her part, she certainly did not respond to his own impetuosity with 'coldness', as he claimed in *My Life*. As the more experienced of the two, Minna allowed her lover to sense her advantage without letting him suspect that he was not the only man to profit from it.

Or did he suspect? As early as September 1834 he wrote to Theodor Apel, offering to share his new conquest. Filled with the pride of possession, he informed his friend that he too could 'have' Fräulein Planer. She had already 'transfigured' him 'sensually on a few occasions'. Although she was said not to love him or even be capable of loving him, she had allowed him to kiss her 'half dead'. Further reports of victory from the battlefield of love were to follow. The once 'so cold, unapproachable and indifferent creature', Wagner told Apel, had now been 'fired to the very marrow of her being, I've turned her into a tender-hearted, devoted woman'. She loved him 'to the point of sickness' and he had become her 'tyrant'. Wagner's stock had risen, and he had literally overwhelmed her with his sensuality. Having seen the extent to which he was held back by his 'pitiful bourgeois outlook', she knew only one wish – 'to be joined with me in marriage, an aim she would like to achieve whatever the sacrifice involved'. He himself, he told Apel, was secretly thinking of being unfaithful to her. With all the casualness of a Young German sensualist, he describes his intentions as 'a kind of knavery'.[22]

It was, rather, a kind of literary posturing, for behind Wagner's demonic bravado à la Don Juan lay the fear that he would lose his conquest as quickly as he had won it. Might Minna, whom he was already describing as a sexually compliant member of his harem, have already gone out of her way to fuel his suspicions? However much Wagner may retrospectively have blamed 'the stirrings of the sex drive' for their union, it seems to have been something else – something long familiar to him – that was the decisive factor here. He felt the 'cares and worries of lovesick jealousy'. From the day of their very first meeting, he was plagued by this sweet poison, and for good reason.

Minna's penchant for aristocratic lovers, lending her a hint of the kept diva, extended not only to her portraitist Herr von Otterstedt but also to a certain Herr von Bary, who is likewise believed to have asked for her hand in marriage. She would sometimes allow herself to be 'specially fêted' by a whole series of 'aristocratic gentlemen', who afterwards visited her at home. On realizing what was going on, Wagner felt all the old trauma of the earlier 'satanic affairs', and his memory of his 'sufferings in the Pachta house' filled him with a new sense of bitterness.

But worse was to come. It seems that in every town and city where she had appeared in the course of her career, Minna had acquired a reputation for responding to her suitors' attentions. In Dessau her lover heard all manner of rumours about her from some 'frivolous young people', rumours later confirmed by a privy commercial councillor called Moritz Cohn. News then reached him from Berlin that she had behaved there in a way that was 'unworthy' of him by 'mixing with the worst possible people and behaving extremely badly'. Finding himself by chance among a group of men, he was finally forced to listen to all manner of boastful tales about 'Fräulein Planer'.

The actress, he was told, had once been abducted and taken to a hotel in Meißen, where Wagner's informant claimed to have lost his way at night and, mixing up the doors, stumbled into her unlit room. Minna, in turn, had mixed up her visitors, and a 'highly interesting scene' had ensued, lasting some three-quarters of an hour. Like the rest of the group, Wagner was 'taken aback' and asked with some insistence whether his informant might perhaps have mixed up the names, a confusion to which the latter then readily confessed. 'He did everything', Wagner later told the poor maligned woman in a letter, 'to reassure me.'[23]

It was not long before Wagner had worked himself up into a veritable frenzy of love, threatening to take his own life and to stab Minna to the heart. Of course, she was pretty, perhaps even 'wonderfully pretty', as the painter Friedrich Pecht later claimed. But she was also 'beautiful and prosaic',[24] thereby adding a sober question mark to Wagner's effusive enthusiasm. She seems not to have shared his ardour and had only one ambition to offset his high-flown aims, and that was marriage. If we are to believe Wagner's own account in *My Life*, it was obvious to him from the outset that there was 'a very clear distinction' between the fairy Amorosa on stage and the woman who was looking for 'a respectable home'. Wagner claims that this was all that she had in mind from the very beginning. A 'respectable home', which, as music director, he had to provide, formed only a provisional stopping-off point in a not entirely respectable selection process among the men who were in a position to offer her such a home.

The feeling of jealousy that ought to have acted as a deterrent served rather to fascinate him, for, disconcerting as it was, it seemed all too familiar. Among the young Wagner's seminal experiences was the discovery that the women whom he loved dearly and longed for were not available because they had given themselves to others. His sense of embitterment was further increased by the fact that his renunciation of the affection that was his due was forced on him by a usurper who had insinuated himself into the position of his rightful father. Exactly the same thing had happened in the case of his first serious infatuation when he had been thwarted by the machinations of his aristocratic rivals. Now these same hated aristocrats had turned up again in the context of his first physically consummated relationship. Once again Wagner found himself caught in the toils of his own emotions.

A quarter of a century after his relationship with Minna began in Bad Lauchstädt, Wagner summed up its 'basic feature' and took stock of the situation.[25] In 1859 he wrote to his former lover, who was now his wife, albeit separated from him, claiming that the nub of any 'fleeting infatuation' is regularly to be found in the most 'tremendous jealousy'. This jealousy constitutes 'almost the greater part' of a person's passion and is intended to safeguard the individual's right 'to keep others away from the coveted object'. We do this, Wagner generalized, without regard for the fact that, in asserting our own 'selfish desires', we may be jeopardizing our partner's happiness. Wagner leaves us in no doubt that he is referring to himself here. If his wife was ever asked about the origins of their misalliance, she should reply quite candidly: 'After leading me such a pretty dance with his jealousy, he was so mad that he insisted on marriage just to stop anyone else from coming near me.'

Even his friend Apel was exposed to Wagner's jealousy, and this was now joined, as an aggravating circumstance, by the feeling of betrayal. Following their engagement in January 1835, the couple lived in a permanent state of attraction and repulsion, with neither informing the other when or even whether they intended to tie the knot. In the end, Minna appears to have lost the will to do so and to have informed Wagner that she planned to leave on the next available mailcoach. In open breach of her Magdeburg contract, she intended to take up a new engagement in Berlin after the one in Königsberg. One morning in November 1835 she duly abandoned her fiancé, leaving him in tears and a state of madness reminiscent of the young Werther.

Nine letters, dashed off in the space of a week, attest to his breakdown, which reduced him emotionally to the state of an abandoned child. His heart was broken, he complained, he was almost out of his mind. He was crying and sobbing like an infant. With a sigh, he described the trauma that had hounded him since his first experience of rejection: 'It suddenly seemed terribly certain that this carriage was tearing you away from me for ever.' With the perceptiveness of despair, he saw that he could not live without her: they would have to get married as soon as possible.

Within days, he became aware not only of the betrayal of her departure but of a further act of treachery that weighed even more heavily on his already distraught mind. Were the reasons that she had given for her departure perhaps no more than a pretext? Why could she not come back to Magdeburg? 'What crime have you committed against me in this way?' he asked, adopting the tone of a public prosecutor. 'At all events, you've gone behind my back and tricked me.' What he meant was clear from her undeclared affairs of the heart: Minna, he suspected, had been carrying on an affair with one of the furtive usurpers. And he ended his outpouring of emotion with a scarcely veiled threat that if she continued to spurn his offer of marriage, he would 'find other ways' of showing her the force of his love. The next day he made it abundantly plain that a young woman whose heart remained impervious to such an entreaty could presumably be made to see reason only with the help of a 'sharp knife'.

She returned. After Wagner had consulted her family and agreed on the details of their future life together, he took back his fugitive fiancée. In the course of a routine examination of her correspondence, he discovered that his suspicions had been all too justified. Minna's precipitate departure for Berlin was clearly bound up with a Jewish businessman by the name of Schwabe, who throughout her stay in the city had earned her gratitude for the affluent conditions she had enjoyed there.[26] Schwabe had presented himself to Wagner in Berlin as a sympathetic friend, only now to turn out to be a secret rival for Minna's favours. 'All the jealousy that had been building up in me', wrote Wagner, 'all the profound doubts in Minna's character found expression in the rapid decision to abandon the girl without delay.'

Wagner and Minna were married in Königsberg on 24 November 1836, exactly a month after Rosalie's marriage. The previous day at the vicarage they had had a row over what she should wear at the gala performance of *La muette de Portici*. The unemployed Kapellmeister had already taken on the task of designing his wife's wedding dress and presumably also wanted a say in his heroine's costume. As we shall see in due course, women's clothes were his secret passion. It was with mixed feelings that they stood before the altar together in the Tragheim Church at Königsberg. Failing to follow the minister's words, the nervous bridegroom, his mind elsewhere, forgot to place his ring on the prayerbook proffered to him by the parson.

At this instant he was struck by a vision of his life as a river. Made up of two cross-currents, one on top of the other, it forced him in two directions at once. While the upper current, facing the sun, bore him towards the future as though in a dream, the darker undercurrent held him bound to the past 'in deep and inexplicable anxiety'.

He had a similar vision on a visit to Italy in 1853. After a feverish night, he sank into a kind of 'somnambulistic state' – possibly drug-induced – and was suddenly overcome by the feeling that he was 'sinking into fast-flowing water'. The rushing sound of this inner river was transformed into a state of musical harmony that 'surged along unstoppably in a figured arpeggiation'. It was with a sense of 'sudden terror' that he woke up, feeling as though the waves were breaking over his head.[27]

Wagner later expressed these musical hallucinations in the form of a surging E flat major chord: from the dark sounds of the depths that held him fast in anxious immobility, as though in his wedding-day vision, the brighter sonorities broke free in increasingly rapid figurations, before rising towards the sunlight.

This chord, in which his own contradictory nature found expression, formed the primal sound from which his great vision of the world in *Der Ring des Nibelungen* was later to emerge.

The Other Wilhelmine

With the exception of his spectacular lack of success, the picture of Wagner that emerges from his period in Magdeburg is very much the one that posterity painted of him. He worked away at *Das Liebesverbot* and the incidental music to *Columbus* like a man possessed, while at the same time rehearsing the municipal orchestra in a repertory ranging from *Zampa* to *Il barbiere di Siviglia*, conducting these works every evening with characteristic ardour and a breathtaking final accelerando. Wagner lived and breathed music. He wrote it, he performed it and, in Laube's and Schumann's journals, he even wrote about it. But what exactly was it about music that fascinated him – apart, that is, from the opportunity it gave him to earn his living?

He had discovered at a very early date that something was revealed in music that did not belong to the world of musical sounds. In the tuning up of the orchestra he thought he could hear a greeting from the spirit world; and when he heard open fifths, inanimate matter seemed to come alive and the storm winds whistled threateningly. For Wagner, music always expressed ideas that went beyond the world of actual sound. From the notes the instruments played there arose a world that already existed in the magical realm of poetry.

The terrors of the Wolf's Glen, the enchantment of the fairies' garden and the glittering charm of the water nixies could all, of course, be depicted by means of notes, tone colours and rhythms. But in order for them to be properly understood, words were needed, the expression that denoted the Idea. It alone could invest the fleeting musical shape with permanence and tie it down to a specific meaning. For Wagner, the world of sound ruled over by the musician was always based on another world that the poet alone could conjure into existence. This was the realm of ideas, a realm that found objective expression in language. Music lacking this higher meaning meant nothing to him.

It was no accident that Wagner broke off his second attempt at a classical symphony in the summer of 1834 and that he never again wrote such a multi-movement piece. Instead of composing pure music whose meaning, by its very nature, was bound to remain vague, he became an ardent champion of song, as based on the poetic word. In several programmatical articles he described operatic singing, in which melody and poetry were combined, as the true 'voice of the people'.[28] Only when depicted on stage did the living reality of existence find expression, only in song could music say what it really meant.

For Wagner, song was 'the language in which man is intended to communicate through music'. But the language in which song communicated itself was first and foremost the language of words. After all, it was not notes that the singer sang, but words. Moreover, ever since he had read his E. T. A. Hoffmann, Wagner had known that music was not imposed on words from outside but that it had to issue from the very heart of those words. Only when the singer made the language sing could the music that lay hidden in the words awaken into life. It was then that the melody lent language its true meaning, a meaning that blossomed into full and refulgent life when the melody was additionally harmonized.

During the spring of 1834 Wagner first encountered on the Leipzig stage a singer who, more than any other, made language sing. She breathed the 'warm, true life' of the Idea into each and every note, a life that he had hitherto sought in vain in opera. This singer was Wilhelmine Schröder-Devrient. As he recalled in his autobiography, he managed to talk her into giving two performances in Magdeburg, which he himself conducted. She sang for him in Rossini's *Otello* and Bellini's *I Capuleti e i Montecchi*, and also – and this seems to have slipped his mind – in his two favourite operas, *Der Freischütz* and *Fidelio*. Her appearances were the 'main event of the season'. Wagner, who claimed to have admired her since his youth, recalled being filled all over again with 'fire and warmth'.

Wilhelmine Schröder-Devrient regarded herself as both an actress and a singer. Her listeners were no longer aware of the difference between the sung and the spoken word and hence between art and reality. Under the impression left by the appearances of a performer who knew how to speak through her singing, Wagner demanded that 'dramatic singing' should do the same: it should be able to depict a highly charged situation not only by imitating real life as closely as possible – with what Wagner calls the 'last drop of the singer's heart's blood' – but it should always retain a clear awareness of the fact that it is producing an 'artistic form'. This 'supreme triumph of artistic execution', he wrote in one of his early articles, was something that he had experienced only with Wilhelmine Schröder-Devrient, 'the greatest living German dramatic singer'.[29]

Behind this 'youthful model'[30] of Wagner's there once again lay the figure of Rosalie. Even before he first saw Schröder-Devrient, his sister had played the same roles and given her brother his first inkling of 'impassioned singing' and 'eloquent' acting. Like her famous rival, Rosalie suffered from a relatively weak singing voice, for which she sought to compensate by means of her diction and acting. When Wagner was once asked whether Schröder-Devrient's voice had really been so very 'significant', he couched his reply in the guise of a witticism: 'No, she had absolutely no "voice"; but she had such superb breath control and was able to pour out her truly feminine soul in such wonderful sounds that listeners thought neither of singing nor of speaking when they heard her.'[31]

With this ideal state in mind, Wagner could no longer be satisfied with traditional opera, which was concerned almost entirely with singing and the voice. At the same time, it is clear from his contemporary opera, *Das Liebesverbot*, that he did not yet have the artistic means needed to depict this new world of authentic expression himself. His dream of creating an 'incomparable work of art', each of whose parts would be worthy of the 'interpretative talent of such an artist', was to remain unrealized for some time to come.

His view of Rosalie as an artist faded before the sheer force of Wilhelmine Schröder-Devrient. Unlike the diminutive Wagners, she was tall and voluptuous, fond of tossing back her hair – described by some writers as blond and by others as chestnut-brown – and laughing provocatively. As a thoroughbred entirely to the taste of the Young German movement, she ensured that every performance revolved around her, thanks to her gift for bringing more life to it than any other artist. Nor was she afraid to shout, sigh and wail whenever she needed to express her true emotions. When she later appeared as the somnambulist Senta in *Der fliegende Holländer*, Berlioz felt called upon to complain about 'the spoken phrases that she finds it necessary to interject throughout the role'. She had succumbed, he went on, to the 'demon of personality', seeing herself as 'the focus of the drama, the only character with whom the audience need concern itself.'[32] Wagner was bound to take this personally.

When she appeared in Magdeburg in 1835, it was again her Romeo that 'enchanted' the young conductor. Even in old age he could still recall her appearance and the way in which she had dispensed with the usual helmet and armour, preferring instead to rush out onto the stage with her blond hair flowing and wearing only a tabard. Her Romeo was first and foremost a hero who, as the emissary of the Ghibellines, resolutely faced the enemy, initially offering them peace and then, following the rejection of his offer, challenging them to battle.[33] As in *König Enzio*, in which Rosalie played the main part, so in Bellini's opera Wagner witnessed the effects of that mythic final battle fought out between 'German' Ghibellines and papist Guelphs.

The ardour that Schröder-Devrient breathed into the role of the hero also affected her portrayal of Romeo as a lover. As a woman, she could abandon herself to Romeo's exchange with Juliet with all the necessary uninhibitedness and none of the usual awkwardness. Such candour was unusual at this time, and Wagner seems to have been struck by it. Even in Bayreuth, he thought that only a passionate woman like Schröder-Devrient – and certainly not 'a runt of a tenor' – could portray 'the beauty of those wild embraces'. The 'effusive ecstasies' of the second act of his own *Tristan und Isolde* would have been impossible without the example of Schröder-Devrient's wild-eyed Romeo. Erotic scenes of this nature, he concluded, should be played by 'a brother and sister, specially trained for it by their father'.[34]

Fired by the 'ravishing beauty' of her Romeo, Wagner devised a plan intended to ensure his future both artistically and financially. He had accepted the post in Magdeburg in the hope of finding a steady income, but instead the town had become a hotbed of creditors. In order to be able to offer his adored Minna even a fraction of the gifts that her aristocratic admirers laid at her feet every day, he had run up debts far in excess of anything that he could ever pay back from his modest income as a conductor. Add to this his own independent and scarcely less expensive requirements in terms of velvet-upholstered furniture, a silkily soft wardrobe and a well-stocked cellar of wine, and it is easy to understand that he was already deep in debt. The liabilities that he had incurred with Apel and his own brothers-in-law seemed a mere trifle by comparison.

His plan was to combine business with pleasure by persuading the soprano to give a concert for his own benefit – or, as he later claimed, to allow the singer to talk him into giving a benefit performance on his behalf. He cheerfully consoled his creditors with the promise of the 'fabulous receipts' with which he would be able to satisfy all their demands as soon as the concert was over. So confident was he of the outcome that he invited them all to appear at his hotel on the morning after the concert.

Fully expecting that the receipts would be correspondingly high, Wagner spared no expense but offered his audience every conceivable 'musical luxury', engaging a particularly large orchestra, scheduling a sizeable number of rehearsals and commissioning several 'expensive machines' that were specially designed to imitate the sound of shelling and gunfire, for the programme included not only the overture to Theodor Apel's *Columbus* and Beethoven's *Adelaide* but also, as the high point of the evening, the same composer's 'Battle' Symphony.

The concert took place on the evening of 2 May 1835 and was intended to bring Wagner both artistic success and financial release from his crippling burden of debt. Instead, it turned into one of the greatest débâcles of his life. The hall, which he had leased in the Hotel zur Stadt London, was almost empty – only the orchestra pit was packed to overflowing. Clearly, he concluded, the good people of Magdeburg had assumed that his announcement that the great Wilhelmine Schröder-Devrient would return specially to the town for his own benefit performance was no more than a 'deceitful manoeuvre', while the few who turned up for the concert were soon intimidated by the sheer volume of sound, which the hall's acoustics were unable to accommodate.

Wagner later recalled the succession of terrors that he unleashed on his audience. First, the victory trumpets in his *Columbus* Overture instilled a sense of sheer horror, after which Beethoven's panoramic picture of war created an ear-splitting impression that literally emptied the hall. 'There now began a battle of such ferocity', he reminisced, 'as has seldom been fought in a concert hall.' The hall shook with the echo of the naturalistic explosions, during which the last remaining listeners fled the building, with even the singing actress herself, who until then had remained in her seat, displaying commendable bravery and a sense of true friendship, 'wringing her hands' and rushing outside. By the time they began the final movement of the work, with its depiction of Wellington's victory over the French, only Wagner and his players were left in the hall.[35]

When Wagner returned to his room the next morning, he found a long queue of men and women, two abreast, standing in the hallway: they were his Magdeburg creditors anxious to press home their claims. That he managed to escape unharmed, in spite of his penurious state, he owed to a 'trustworthy Jewess', as he candidly calls her in his autobiography, a certain Frau Gottschalk, who assured his complaining creditors that he had wealthy relatives in Leipzig and who in that way managed to appease them. Perhaps pity also played a part here.

Frau Gottschalk was destined to reappear in Wagner's life, this time at the benefit performance of *Das Liebesverbot* that he organized in the wake of the work's inglorious première in March 1836. He pinned the same sort of hopes on this performance as he had done with the memorable benefit concert the previous year, and once again he was greeted by the spectacle of an almost empty house, the only exceptions being Frau Gottschalk, who had taken her seat in the orchestra stalls, together with her husband and a 'Polish Jew in full regalia'. Wagner does not say whether her attendance was due to her trust in him as an artist or in his ability to repay her at some later date.

He was forced to disappoint her on both counts. The performance of *Das Liebesverbot* was prevented from going ahead when the principal performers, goaded by real-life jealousies, came to blows even before the curtain had risen: blood flowed freely, with the leading soprano's husband laying into his wife's lover, while the lady herself went into convulsions. The sounds of this second débâcle wafted down into the auditorium, reaching the ears of Frau Gottschalk and her two male companions and marking the end of Wagner's 'highly promising career as a conductor and composer in Magdeburg, a career that had begun with relatively large sacrifices on his part'.

Wagner lost no time in firing off an envenomed barb against the town that had humiliated him in these various ways, commenting anonymously in Schumann's *Neue Zeitschrift für Musik* that the townsfolk could be induced to attend concerts only if food was available on the premises after the performance. Even during the slow movement of a symphony, he claimed with some malice, one could already hear the clattering of plates in the adjoining room.

As the Magdeburgers understood so little about music, he ended his anonymous musings by wondering what could have induced the composer Richard Wagner to stage a splendid new work like *Das Liebesverbot* in such a town.[36]

The High-Born Bride

The sacrifices had already begun, and the failures, too, continued to dog Wagner's career. In May 1836, Minna hurried on ahead of him to Königsberg to take up her new engagement at the local theatre, leaving her impoverished husband to evade his Magdeburg creditors and make his way to Berlin. Here, in keeping with his status, he took rooms at the Hotel zum Kronprinz in the Königsstraße – the very hotel where, six months earlier and unbeknown to him, Minna had met her admirer Herr Schwabe, who, loyal to her memory, still had the same room.

Short of money as he was, Wagner decided to test the lie of the land. He was directed to the Königsstädter Theater, where operas were occasionally performed and where he entered into negotiations with the manager, a former horse dealer called Hirsch, who, now a 'commission councillor', had changed his name to Cerf and who held out the promise of a production of *Das Liebesverbot*. In the shorter term, Wagner was to make himself useful as a conductor. Unfortunately, these promises turned out to be hollow, and Wagner was forced to admit that the patronizing Cerf had 'played an almost malicious trick' on him, deceiving him 'purely out of pleasure'. But perhaps it was not just out of pleasure: on 1 July 1836 Cerf had to close his theatre as he was unable to pay his creditors.

Wagner's resentment at the Jewish Cerf was combined with his anger at the Jewish businessman Schwabe. As Minna's former lover, Schwabe had insinuated himself into her guileless fiancé's confidence. Fiancé and lover attended a performance of *Fidelio*, Beethoven's song of songs to marital fidelity, during which Wagner had 'wept hot tears' of longing in his desire to be reunited with Minna. He even reported with some pride that Schwabe wanted to set aside 'the finest and heaviest white satin' for Minna's wedding dress. Only later did Wagner discover that the man who had cuckolded him had also led him by the nose.

Meanwhile Wagner had also fallen out with the once so good-natured Madame Gottschalk. Although he had decamped from Magdeburg with the firm intention of settling his old debts once he was in Berlin, this hope proved unduly sanguine, with the result that from now on the Gottschalks pursued him relentlessly. When Schwabe informed him that his former benefactress was dead, the news left him cold. Wagner remembered only that she had always looked miserable, 'and a wicked person she was, too'.

In the hope of avenging himself, if only in part, for the adversities he had suffered in Berlin, Wagner sent Schumann an article that was bitterly critical of the doyen of local critics, Ludwig Rellstab, for safety's sake demanding that the piece appear under the pseudonym William Drach.[37] In the event, Schumann did not publish the attack, but Rellstab got wind of the affair, ensuring that Wagner now had a lifelong enemy in the Prussian capital.

A week after Cerf was declared bankrupt, Wagner left Berlin in a horse-drawn carriage, his travelling expenses paid for by Laube's Young German friends. Schwabe, too, will have contributed generously, in addition to sending his warmest good wishes to faraway Königsberg. The journey through the 'desolation of the Brandenburg marches' was difficult in the extreme, at the end of it an uncertain future for Wagner: although Minna was waiting in Königsberg, there was no job for him. She was living in one of the poorest quarters of the town, in a run-down house with a view of an alleyway like a scene from village life. Russia was not far away.

But envy, too, awaited Wagner, the envy of colleagues who turned his difficult wait for work into a 'living hell'. When Minna's theatre company set off in August for a summer season in Memel on the Lithuanian border, her melancholy fiancé followed by sailing ship, plagued by an ill wind and bad weather. On passing an old castle where one of E. T. A. Hoffmann's most bloodcurdling tales is set, he was reminded of the 'fantastical impressions' of his youth. With the fear of bygone nights to torment him and his 'most anxious situation' ahead of him, he suddenly felt creative again after a long period of inactivity.

It was *Die hohe Braut* ('The High-Born Bride') that had fired his imagination. Set at the time of the French Revolutionary Wars, Heinrich Koenig's Young German novel is in many ways related to Auber's *La muette de Portici*. In both cases, destiny destroys the work's leading characters against the background of revolutionary changes in world history, and in both cases these characters go to their deaths transfigured by the rays of the rising sun of freedom and liberty. Koenig's 'admirable novel' was brought to Wagner's attention by Heinrich Laube. Wagner prepared a prose draft based on the novel, but instead of working it up into a libretto himself, he had it translated into French and offered it to the librettist of *La muette de Portici*, Eugène Scribe. Scribe, he wrote in a covering letter, could versify the draft and dispose as he liked of the income that would accrue to him once Wagner had set the libretto to music.

This appeal to Scribe's generosity echoed Wagner's own generous treatment of Koenig's intellectual property, and it was one that went unanswered. The famous librettist never received the parcel from his unknown correspondent in Königsberg – or perhaps he declined to accept it, as Wagner was in the habit of sending his mail unfranked. This further attempt to write operatic history having proved no more successful than his earlier ones, Wagner spent the following years offering the text to a series of other composers, and in the end it was the director of the Prague Conservatory, Jan Bedřich Kittl, who set the work to music in 1848 on payment of the sum of two hundred florins. By now the high-born bride was already somewhat long in the tooth.

It was, of course, financial necessity that was the mother of invention. With a brazen attempt to force open the door of the Paris Opéra, Wagner had hoped to remedy his desperate situation once and for all. Writing to the acclaimed librettist was tantamount to staking everything on a single card. In taking this step, Wagner had nothing to lose, but unfortunately – and this he could not have known – he had nothing to win either. If the subject matter had been politically relevant in 1833, it was already hopelessly outdated by 1836. With the increasingly reactionary thrust of the July Monarchy, the enthusiastic élan of the revolution and its love of liberty had given way to growing pessimism. The *Marseillaise*, which Wagner had planned to include in a rousing final tableau, would have been a dangerous faux pas in the Paris of 1836. But time was on Wagner's side: by the time he offered the libretto to his friend in Prague in the late 1840s, revolution was again on everyone's lips.

Writers on Wagner have generally viewed *Die hohe Braut* as an attempt to 'celebrate' the French Revolution 'by theatrical means' – not just the Great Revolution of 1789 but also Lafayette's uprising of July 1830. According to this reading, the piece deals with 'the oppression of the populace by their "superiors"'[38] and would therefore have been the first step on Wagner's route to active revolt in 1849. Stagnating in faraway Memel, he dreamt of the overthrow of existing conditions and, taking little trouble to encode his message, incorporated it into his plot. But the opposite could just as well be true, for the relationships underpinning the drama and motivating the action were familiar to Wagner long before revolution played any part in his life.

As so often when Wagner's Muse beckoned, it was the trauma of frustrated love between siblings that formed the theme of *Die hohe Braut* – a love that had been rekindled at this time to particularly painful effect. Minna, 'bride and sister' in one, had to be shared with others. Königsberg's theatregoers swarmed around her, and, as before, elderly beaux were waiting with their patents of nobility and family fortune. And as in Magdeburg, she was able to oblige with public successes, a regular income and social prestige, leaving her husband with only the pitiful life of a misprized genius. 'I'm a loathsome person', he wrote to Minna contritely in the summer of 1836, 'a grey and black page in your book of life, a bird of ill omen. ... Have pity on me, have pity, my angel.'[39]

His new scenario reflected his mood: Bianca, the angel, and Giuseppe, a huntsman, are in love. As the daughter of a marchese, Bianca seems socially far above her lover, but both had been suckled by the same foster mother, 'drinking in the mother's milk of universal brotherhood at one and the selfsame breast'. Their happiness would have been complete if the marchese had not already promised his daughter to another member of the nobility, the sombre-miened Count Rivoli. Like Siegmund in years to come, Giuseppe longs to break down the barriers that still separate him from his lover. But his sister comes to the resigned conclusion that 'paternal rights are an invincibly rigorous power, even though they defy nature'. Anyone who tried to resist them would be destroyed.

Like the novice of Palermo, Bianca offers herself as a sacrifice to the fiancé she does not love in order to save her foster brother, whose very life is threatened. Another unhappy sister appears at this point: Brigitta is driven to kill herself by her brother, Count Rivoli, for marrying Sormano, who is from a lower social class. Sormano and Giuseppe swear to avenge his shame. At the end, Brigitta is borne on stage to the strains of a pilgrims' chorus, anticipating Elisabeth in *Tannhäuser*. Beside her corpse lie those of the Count, struck down by Giuseppe, and the 'high-born bride' herself, who has poisoned herself in an overhasty attempt to avoid dishonour.

This terrible catastrophe, Wagner impressed on his friend Kittl, could be followed only by 'the unique and terrible sense of sublimity inspired by the inevitable progress of a great world-destiny, personified here in the French Revolutionary Army, which marches in, in dreadful splendour, over the ruins of old (family) relationships',[40] while the tricolour wafts high above them and the *Marseillaise* rings forth on their lips. This, however, was not a part of the actual story. The boots that trample over the ruins of old family relationships cannot awaken love. The sibling tragedy ends before politics can celebrate its arrival upon the world stage.

The revolution provides only a historical backdrop for Wagner's inner drama, a drama which, conversely, explains why he was always so fascinated by the 'dreadful splendour of the coup d'état'. Only radical surgery, he realized, could help to break the 'invincibly austere power' of the wicked father. But a new beginning would be possible only following the supersession of those family relationships whose lovelessness had allowed the father to obtain power in the first place. Only then could the true ruler return and restore the world's lost state of harmony. Just before Giuseppe is felled by a French bullet, his last words are directed at the old regime that is already long forgotten: 'My liege's flag once more / I ruefully enclasp / And seek, imbrued with gore, / The welcome of death's grasp.'[41]

Not only did Wagner receive no response from Scribe, but there were delays to his hoped-for appointment as music director in Königsberg, leaving him only with his unhappy lot as the husband of a popular actress famous for breaking men's hearts. To add to his misfortunes, her charisma was not limited to the theatre, and in Königsberg as elsewhere Wagner was forced to admit to himself that Minna was not exactly suited to the role of the ideal sister. Quite the opposite: she showed no inclination to sacrifice herself for her husband. Unlike Bianca in *Die hohe Braut*, she took no poison when Königsberg's Rivolis threatened her with dishonour. Indeed, as Wagner later wrote, she even allowed herself to be misled into committing certain 'acts of condescension in order to maintain her affluence'. Wagner was presumably in no doubt as to the true nature of these acts.

This 'deeply worrying point' – his fear, namely, that he would be betrayed and sold by his lover – gave rise to violent arguments between the two of them. Wagner himself described them as 'repugnant'. Decades later, his stepdaughter Natalie, who was still being passed off as his sister-in-law at this time, recalled with horror the way the jealous husband would rant and rave all night, committing acts of domestic violence so serious that Minna 'lay there in convulsions for hours on end'.

Overcome by remorse, he would then throw himself at her feet and, weeping, 'beg for forgiveness like a child'.[42] The couple seemed ideally matched: time and again she manoeuvered herself compulsively into situations in which she could be seduced and to which she owed her unhappiness, while he mistreated her until she betrayed him, a betrayal that was hell on earth for him. In this way they played into each other's hands, with each attempt to break out of the situation leading to a renewal of their old familiar torments.

As Wagner fled from his creditors, so Minna fled from her husband. The well-to-do Schwabe was replaced by a no less wealthy businessman by the name of Dietrich, who invited the ladies of the Königsberg Theatre to lavish dinners, giving Minna to understand that these occasions were merely a foretaste of all that he wanted to lay at her feet. Wagner described him as affected and repulsive of aspect, but on Minna he seems to have had the opposite effect, assuring her in his charming way that his concern for her fate was motivated only by Wagner's 'hurtful excesses' and promising to take good care of her.[43] Once again she gave in.

On 1 April 1837, Wagner was appointed musical director of the Königsberg Theatre. By May his income was already drying up again, when Minna decamped with Dietrich, taking with her all her goods and chattels, including Natalie. Wagner returned home one day from a morning rehearsal to find a half-empty apartment in which an unlaid table awaited him. With death in his heart, he rushed to see his friend Abraham Möller.

Möller was a philanthropist and a regular theatregoer who, in Wagner's own words, was 'Dietrich's personal enemy', so that Minna's abduction affected him as much as it did Wagner himself. He also knew Minna very well, having approached her soon after her arrival in Königsberg in order to commend himself to her – as he did to Wagner on his arrival – as someone to whom they could turn whenever they needed help. Möller had a weakness for actors and actresses, and it was not long before he became friendly with Wagner, who normally nurtured only suspicion towards his wife's many admirers.

This friend of the Muses proved surprisingly keen to see the young couple married, even offering them financial inducements to walk down the aisle together. His apparently wholly disinterested pleasure in Minna's company ensured that he enjoyed Wagner's boundless trust. As Möller knew exactly with whom, when and whither Minna had disappeared, her abandoned husband was able to pursue her to Berlin and thence to Dresden, where he found her living with her own family and in a state of desperation. Of her abductor there was no sign.

The two were reconciled and spent some days together in Blasewitz, recovering from their ordeal. Here Wagner read Bulwer-Lytton's best-selling novel *Rienzi, the Last of the Roman Tribunes*. Meanwhile Minna had prevailed on him to sign an affidavit with the Dresden District Court enabling her to claim maintenance from her former seducer Count Einsiedel.[44] Their visit to the authorities over, she again absented herself under some risible pretext or other, and while her husband waited for her patiently, she betook herself to Herr Dietrich, who was lying low at a local hotel. Together the lovers made good their escape.

Once again it was to Möller that Wagner turned for help. On hearing where Minna was staying, the cuckolded composer armed himself with a whip and a pistol and made his way to the hotel, intending to thrash Dietrich and challenge him to a duel.[45] Unfortunately he arrived too late. With some justification he asked his Norns why he was 'fated to suffer so terrible an experience at so tender an age, an experience that bade fair to poison' the whole of the rest of his life. Not even at a later date does he seem to have asked himself exactly what role the surprisingly sympathetic Möller had played in all this.

He then discovered that Minna was staying with her gallant at a hotel in Hamburg and, again with Möller's help, he lost no time in 'taking the necessary steps for a divorce'. He found it all the easier to renounce his wife in that, during a brief visit to Berlin, he had renewed acquaintance with Minna's younger sister, the singer Amalie Planer, whose voice he particularly admired – so much so that in Magdeburg he had worked through the role of Bellini's Romeo with her. They got on so well that they attended a performance of *Fidelio* together, just as Wagner had done with Schwabe the previous year. Again he burst into 'tears and sobs', with Amalie joining in. In general they seem to have wept a great deal together.

Consolation came in the form of a new contract appointing Wagner conductor in Riga, where he arrived after a four-day sea voyage in August 1837. When it turned out that the company lacked a good singer, he suggested Amalie and set aside rooms for her under his own roof. Not entirely unexpectedly, Minna then wrote him a rueful letter apologizing for her behaviour, and all talk of a divorce was abandoned.

As he had hoped, the couple became a threesome at the end of October, with Wagner's happiness increased by the fact that, shortly after her arrival, Amalie was able to make her début as Romeo. As a result of this felicitous turn of events, Wagner later recalled, 'the three of us felt cheerful and comfortable together in the far North'. They planned to begin a new life in the Russia of Nicholas Pavlovich I. The revolutionary of 1830 made a start by writing a hymn to celebrate the tsar's accession.

The Last of the Tribunes

After Magdeburg and Königsberg, it was arguable whether things could get any worse for the ambitious conductor, but it was a question Wagner himself had no hesitation in answering in the affirmative. In every way, Riga brought an increase in his burden of unhappiness. When, after barely two years, he fled to escape from the whole sorry mess, it was no ordinary attempt to slip away from his creditors and the usual inconveniences but a full-scale flight from himself.

Everything about Riga struck him as part of an all too familiar pattern: it was as if nothing at all had changed. Here, once again, was all the old theatrical routine that had filled him with loathing since Geyer's day, with even the company's director, Karl von Holtei, stepping effortlessly into his late stepfather's shoes. If Minna had changed from the ideal sister to the wicked mother who betrays her own son, so Holtei took over the role of the usurper who wins the wife by destroying her lover. It was Wagner himself who first raised the possibility of this archetypal relationship in his memoirs and, at least as far as Holtei is concerned, triggered a certain scholarly scepticism.

This sociable and universally popular individual, to whom Wagner owed the lifeline of his appointment, had already made a name for himself in the German theatre. It was to Holtei's undying credit, for example, that the French vaudeville had found a home on the German stage, where it had been combined with elements of the autochthonous farce and the Singspiel. This in itself was enough to make him suspect in the eyes of a man like Wagner. In everything that Holtei did in his attempts to boost audiences, he resembled Kotzebue and – not least in his confusing versatility – Wagner's stepfather Ludwig Geyer.

From the outset, Holtei used his young protégé for demeaning tasks, beginning by asking him to set the words of an aria that he had written for the comic opera *Mary, Max und Michel* and following this with a request for a 'prayerlike' addition for Joseph Weigl's popular lyric opera *Die Schweizerfamilie*. In the case of the commission for a tsarist anthem, he could hardly have known that Wagner had only recently performed his own *Polonia* Overture in Königsberg, a work that glorifies the anti-tsarist war of independence waged by the Polish nation. In the circumstances it was inevitable that a man who was as fond of operettas as Holtei should insist on Wagner's writing his own Singspiel in the style of a vaudeville.

But even worse was in store for Wagner, who already resented what he regarded as a betrayal of his own theatrical dignity, for it seems that the farceur had designs on his life. In the middle of winter – or so Wagner indignantly recalled – Holtei forced him from his sickbed and, in spite of a high temperature, packed him off to the remote town of Mitau where, in an arctic auditorium, he had to conduct a guest performance that exposed him to 'the most dangerous exacerbation' of his ailment. As a result, Wagner succumbed to typhus, the very illness from which his father had died. Holtei ventured the cynical prognosis that he was already 'bent on leaving'. When his long-suffering conductor had recovered, the perfidious mountebank tried to make amends by offering his post to another conductor, who turned out to be none other than Wagner's old acquaintance from Leipzig, Heinrich Dorn.

Wagner's picaresque account of this period contains a further surprise: while he himself was rehearsing, Holtei was allegedly importuning the unoccupied Minna and 'openly courting her affection'. When his blandishments failed to bear fruit, Holtei attempted to pair her off with a 'handsome and at the same time very wealthy young man' whom Wagner describes as a businessman by the name of Brandenburg.

The attempt miscarried, but by no means to Holtei's disadvantage, for behind these machinations, Wagner claimed, lay the wish to divert attention from his 'depraved goings-on'. It was Holtei's 'fear of extremely harmful revelations' that finally forced him to flee from Riga. Thus Wagner's own idiosyncratic perspective on his superior. The insinuation that Holtei was homosexual was regarded even by a hagiographical writer like Gregor-Dellin as a 'groundless and shocking accusation'.[46]

Even if there was no truth in Wagner's perception of the situation, he himself presumably believed that there was. After all, he was conditioned to think that every benefactor, however well-meaning, must at some point allow the mask of deception to fall and reveal himself as his mortal enemy. Traits similar to Holtei's – his 'genius as an actor' and his criminal 'courtship' – had long since left him scarred for life, and so it suited the old familiar picture that he felt persecuted and abused. The future international genius had to waste his time and effort on Dorn's historico-comic opera *Der Schöffe von Paris*, while Holtei is said to have felt only 'genuine contempt' for Wagner's love of full-scale opera, a passion he 'maliciously dismissed out of hand'.

Yet if we take a closer look at the actual repertory of this allegedly tiny theatre, we find that in Wagner's first season there were fifteen operas and no fewer than twenty-four in his second. Among the works performed were not only *Don Giovanni*, *Il barbiere di Siviglia*, *Fidelio* and *Der Freischütz*, but also *I Capuleti e i Montecchi*, *La muette de Portici* and even *Die Zauberflöte*, all of them rehearsed and performed by the company's hard-working conductor Richard Wagner. Later he even boasted that the 'barn' in Riga, with its amphitheatrical seating, darkened auditorium and sunken orchestra pit, gave him the idea for his theatre in Bayreuth.

Everything in Riga seemed to conspire against him. His servant girl stole from him; his surrogate sister Amalie became engaged to an aristocrat, one Captain Carl von Meck of the Russian cavalry; and Holtei found fault with everything he did. That Wagner soon felt that he was a lonely rebel was also due to the subject that had taken possession of him since he had first become acquainted with it during his brief stay in Blasewitz during the summer of 1837. Like Wagner himself, the hero of Bulwer-Lytton's novel was an idealist weighed down by the human and cultural decline of the world around him. On rising up against these conditions, Rienzi unleashes the most violent resistance on the part of the powers that be, who harbour designs on his sister's honour and seek to destroy Rienzi himself.

While Wagner was recasting Bulwer-Lytton's best-selling novel in his imagination and turning it into a suitable draft for an opera, life was imitating art in Riga, as Wagner transformed his Kapellmeister's existence into a tale of suffering that resembled the story of his hero. He hoped that with his grand opera *Rienzi*, he would finally be able to leave Livonia's cultural wasteland in triumph.

The real-life figure of the Roman tribune Cola di Rienzo was one of history's great outsiders. Emerging from nowhere, these outsiders regularly incite the populace to revolution, then, after briefly enjoying the heady joys of success, sink back into oblivion once more. Rebelling against the ruling classes, Rienzi suffered a martyr's death and became a role model for the Young Germans. It is no accident that it was his friends Heinrich Laube and Theodor Apel who drew Wagner's attention to the subject's political explosiveness, an aspect that would never have occurred to Baron Lytton's average reader.

From the outset Wagner must have been struck by the parallels with his own life: born exactly five hundred years earlier, Cola Rienzi was the son of an innkeeper who found himself at war with the *nobili* – the aristocrats who had not only murdered his brother but seized unlawful control of his home city of Rome, robbing its citizens of their inheritance and destroying its glorious tradition. Roma, the sacred mother, had been violated. Rienzi called on its citizens to rise up against their aristocratic usurpers. In this he was inspired – as was Wagner himself when he read Bulwer-Lytton's novel in Blasewitz – by the secret belief that blue blood pulsed through his veins.

Rienzi regarded himself as the natural son of Heinrich VII, thus entitling him to think of himself as Barbarossa's legitimate heir. In consequence, his uprising was merely a continuation of the old conflict between the Ghibellines and the Guelphs that had been familiar to Wagner for many years. Sustained by his ardent sense of mission, Rienzi mobilized the masses and defeated the *nobili*, but his career as the people's tribune came to an abrupt end when he was betrayed by the combined forces of the Church, the aristocracy and the populace and brutally stabbed to death.

Wagner must have recognized himself in this 'visionary dreamer who appears like some beacon of light among a depraved and degenerate nation'.[47] But he had less luck with the other members of Rienzi's family. Bulwer-Lytton's tribune was married, and his sister Irene had no intention of sacrificing herself for her doomed brother, and so Wagner made a number of changes to his source that reflected not only his own family relationships but his present situation in life.

To begin with, he did away with Rienzi's wife – his recent experiences with Minna must have suggested this change to him – and replaced her with his sister. In order for the latter to resemble his archetype, he invested her with features that one looks for in vain in Bulwer-Lytton's novel. Irene became the self-assured heroine and, in succession to the idealized Rosalie, the self-sacrificing lover. And because Wagner wanted to spare his hero a contemptible death at the hands of a dagger-wielding assassin, brother and sister were permitted to suffer a common love-death in the flames of the burning Capitol.

Even more far-reaching was the change that Wagner made in his desire to expose the true nature of the *nobili*. Following the disastrous experiences that he had had with certain 'satanic' seducers, his enemies now bear the unmistakable imprint of rapists. Two different passages in the opera that were not present in his source express what he was thinking in barely coded form.

The very first scene includes a graphic account of the *nobili* breaking into Rienzi's house at night and dragging the plebeian Irene through the window 'with rough tenderness' in order to have their communal way with her. 'As long as she submits', they add scornfully, 'she'll suffer no disgrace.'[48] Only at the very last minute is she rescued by a group of rival *nobili*, who renounce their prey only when another member of the aristocracy offers her his protection.

This attempted rape is no mere operatic adjunct but constitutes the nub of the entire drama, as Wagner made clear by means of a mimed scene that he interpolated at a central point in the opera. This exceptional scene, its author explained, was 'no simple festive entertainment' but should be entrusted to real actors in order for its 'genuinely tragic meaning' to be brought out in full. When the authorities in Dresden thought of cutting part of it, he insisted on its retention: it 'absolutely had to be shown' on stage.[49] Unsurprisingly for a work set in Rome, it revolves around the classical motif of the rape of Lucretia, in which Collatinus's wife, raped by Prince Tarquinius, kills herself and thereby gives the signal to rise up and overthrow the usurper.

In including this obvious allegory, Wagner may well have been inspired by Marschner's opera *Lucretia*, completed in Dresden in 1826. No doubt he was also familiar with Shakespeare's version of the legend, in which Lucrece's 'sad behaviour' feeds the rapist's 'vulture folly'. Here the victim's reaction is ambivalent in the extreme: although Tarquin forces her into sexual submission, he provokes an unintended response in the resistant Lucrece, so that her suicide acquires a totally different motivation, Shakespeare's Lucrece killing herself not merely out of a sense of offended honour but also on account of the tragic conflict that stems from her involuntary acquiescence in the rape. In this her case resembles that of the abducted Minna who, in spite of her love of Wagner, allowed herself to be misled into committing 'acts of condescension'. Once again we see the wicked mother in the background, betraying her own husband in order to marry the usurper.

Like the play within a play in *Hamlet*, Wagner's dumb show presents his audience with the silent spectacle of an offence that is no less rank. The act of violence of the *nobili* towards the 'holy mother' of Rome is depicted in a contest whose painful details look back to the excesses of *Leubald* and forward to the scene in which Siegfried violates Brünnhilde. It is very much the sheer speechlessness of this scene, rising up like an island from the deafening bombast of the orchestra, that invests Lucretia's attempt to resist her unknown assailant and her own weakness with an oppressive, almost obscene realism. And it provides the actual logic behind the drama as a whole. Only the attempted rape of Rienzi's sister and then the actual rape of Lucretia in her guise as Mother Rome spark the 'dazzling ray of light' that allows Rienzi to lead the Roman people into his 'holy war'.

But the city that the hero worships as a 'high-born bride' has no word of thanks for his act of liberation. Its inhabitants prove fickle and inconstant: no sooner have they acclaimed him than they are already planning an act of the blackest betrayal. The naked horror that dominates both the opening of the opera and the rape scene returns at the end of the work, where Rienzi is beset by a raging mob, and burning torches rain down on him as though on the maid of Orléans. His final refuge, the Capitol, goes up in flames.

But the opera's message has nothing to do with mob rule and lynchings. In the midst of the inferno in which evil seems to triumph, the 'angel' Irene appears. Brother and sister 'embrace' and above the pitiful picture there rises the radiant symbol of their love-death. The betrayal of the mother – thus Wagner signals his message with his operatic apotheosis – is cancelled out by the sister's act of self-sacrifice.

At its most superficial level, Wagner's self-styled 'grand tragic opera in five acts' is a historical piece modelled on Spontini's *Fernand Cortez*, which Wagner had seen in Berlin in May 1836 after Minna had left for Königsberg. Under the combined influence of Spontini's grandiose costume drama and his reading of Bulwer-Lytton's novel, he decided to make his own *Rienzi* no less grand 'in terms of its conception and formal execution'.[50] As a result, triumphal marches, dramatic confrontations and standard-bearing massed choruses found their way into Wagner's armoury of operatic devices, prior to crossing the footlights a century later and entering the real-life world of German history.

As a result, the freedom fighter's meteoric career eclipsed the actual drama surrounding brother and sister and the silent Lucretia. Wagner had not yet mastered the compositional resources necessary to shape his principal characters' inner lives, and so he took his cue from Spontini, Halévy and Meyerbeer: in the grand operas with which he was familiar, success was attainable only through ostentation on the grandest scale.

The militaristic splendour, keenly accented rhythms and enthusiastic revolutionary hymns meant that the political conflict overshadowed all other considerations. Although Wagner was by no means blind to Rienzi's 'dark and demonic depths', he turned him into the radiant figure of a modern freedom fighter, while his enemies function as representatives of a satanic, repressive regime. In order to secure their rule they butcher fathers and sons in cold blood, violate wives and daughters and finally destroy the Holy Roman Empire. Mother Rome, Rienzi accuses his enemies, has been humiliated, abused, reviled, dishonoured, defiled, derided and changed beyond all recognition by them.

Once again, Wagner's archetypal adversary provided all that was needed for this egregious list of atrocities.

A Happy Family of Bears

Throughout the summer of 1838 Wagner could be seen in the first-floor flat of a Russian merchant's house in the Riga suburb of Saint Petersburg, a pipe clenched firmly between his teeth and a Turkish fez on his head. From his new corner salon he would gaze down, amused, at life in the street below him. His rooms were lavishly furnished, and in his study stood a splendid grand piano on which lay the earliest sketches of *Rienzi*. Whenever he felt tired, he could rest on a comfortable divan. As usual, Wagner had made the room snug with a profusion of silks and satins, and even the rooms of the two women, two of which were occupied by Amalie, were furnished with an eye to fashion.

Unfortunately, the relationship between Amalie and her sister had worsened considerably since her engagement with Captain von Meck. At first, they had argued on a daily basis, paying little heed to the composer, but now they had lapsed into a frosty silence. The situation was exacerbated by the fact that the

Lucullan splendour of the Wagner household was merely borrowed. The furniture still had to be paid for, and the local salmon, fresh caviar and champagne were invariably bought on tick. Wagner's old debts from Magdeburg and Königsberg were now compounded by new ones that he could never have paid off from his modest salary and from which he could not escape by fleeing: Wagner had no passport, and so he was stuck in Russia.

Of necessity, he broke off work on *Rienzi*, on which he could not expect any return until some point in the distant future, and condescended to subscribe to Holtei's theory of art. Vaudevilles were the flavour of the month, and so he wrote a piece of his own to set alongside two works that were hits with local audiences, Ignaz von Seyfried's *Ochsenmenuette* and Matthäus Stegmayer's *Rochus Pumpernickel*. His own piece rejoiced under the cumbersome title of *Männerlist größer als Frauenlist, oder Die glückliche Bärenfamilie* ('Men's Cunning Greater Than Women's, or The Happy Family of Bears'). It was a work that he preferred to forget, and in an attempt to avoid the suspicion that he had given in to Holtei, whose 'intervention' in his life he regarded as 'uniquely repellent',[51] he claimed that he had written it a year earlier than was in fact the case.

At the same time he enhanced its status, turning what had been conceived as a musical farce or, at best, an operetta into a 'comic opera'. He completed two numbers by way of an experiment, but was later unable to recall whether the music owed more to Auber or to Adam.[52] He then lost all interest in the work and thrust it aside with a gesture of disgust, leaving his assistant, the local music director Franz Löbmann, to set the remainder of the text.

The red fez that Wagner wore in Riga certainly suited the subject matter. On reading the *Arabian Nights*, which Meyerbeer had already mined as a source,[53] he had stumbled upon a tale that is a variant of the archetypal story of the mistaken bride: a distinguished merchant is tricked into spending his wedding night with a repulsively ugly woman instead of the bride he has been expecting but exposes the misalliance by revealing that he has merely feigned his noble provenance and is in reality the son of itinerant musicians. In choosing this subject, Wagner could not only pillory Holtei, with his predilection for 'dissolute' actors, he could also – to quote Ernest Newman – turn 'a humorous eye, in Geyer fashion, on the Wagner family circle'.[54] It presumably escaped the composer's attention that it was the ghost of Kotzebue who guided his pen in all this.

In order to adapt the Arabian subject to his own particular needs, Wagner transferred the action from Baghdad to a large German city that could easily be Dresden or Leipzig, and the main character was changed from a nameless merchant to a goldsmith by the name of Julius Wander – an obvious reference to

Wagner's own brother who, at the end of his apprenticeship as a goldsmith in Eisleben, had embarked on a peripatetic life much like that of his younger brother Richard. At least on stage, the composer was now to be rewarded with the success that was denied him in real life.

Before the curtain rises, it transpires that Julius has been separated from his father and brother and adopted by a wealthy jeweller whose inheritance he succeeds in securing for himself in spite of his stepmother's intrigues. This entitles him to claim that 'men's cunning is greater than women's' and to use this boast on his shop's hoarding, thereby provoking a young beauty into deciding to teach him a lesson. She complains that her miserly father keeps her locked up and that, in an attempt to ward off suitors, he has put it about that she is a hideous monster. Overcome by love, Julius decides to woo her.

But the man whose name she gives to the credulous Julius is not her father. Nor is he a judge, as he was in Wagner's source. Rather he belongs to a completely different world, a world whose language and whole demeanour are depicted in such a way that there can be no question as to his true nature: this is the hostile world that Wagner had equated with the Roman *nobili* in his earlier tragedy and that he now equates with the German-speaking nobility in this latest comedy of his.

Julius's antagonist calls himself Baron von Abendthau and is possessed of three characteristics that mark him out as the archenemy of all Wagner's heroes: he is aristocratic, wealthy and, as his name makes plain, Jewish. Whereas Rienzi's adversaries had arrogated to themselves the inheritance of the Roman people, Abendthau seeks to propagate his own inheritance with the help of others, launching into a series of jeremiads reminiscent of Shylock in expressing his belief that his race – this 'tribe of all tribes' – may die out because 'everyone has conspired against this glorious line'. He himself – 'the unhappiest of my inconceivably ancient race' – has only one aim in life, which is to see his daughter Aurora married, if possible to a scion of the ancient nobility. Unfortunately, his daughter lacks the attractiveness necessary to lure any suitable candidates.

Almost thirty years later, when Wagner retold this story for the benefit of King Ludwig, he concealed Abendthau's name, even claiming that he belonged to a group of French aristocrats who had fled to Germany to escape from the Terror, although this hardly explains why he gave them such obviously German Jewish names as Abendthau and Perlmutter. By the same token, the desire to be assimilated into society by marrying into the German aristocracy is a feature that makes far more sense in the context of the stereotype of the German Jew: only by cunningly intermarrying, ran the anti-Semitic cliché, could the Jewish tribe, which was otherwise fated to die out, have any hope of survival.

In his anger at actors and well-to-do rivals, Wagner sank to new depths of tastelessness: the object of his desire, for whose hand Julius credulously sues, turns out to be a Hoffmannesque freak from Hell. As ugly as sin, Aurora von Abendthau is notable above all for the size of her nose – the very feature for which the other members of her race are said to be renowned. For her appalled fiancé Julius, it seems big enough for him to hang himself on it. Moreover, Wagner insists that Aurora's hideous appearance is not to be construed as merely a personal shortcoming: this 'degenerate' creature bears the burden of 'every form of ugliness inherited from her forebears'.

The idea that a large dowry was enough for a Jew to be able to marry off his elderly ugly daughter to a German son-in-law was also part of the anti-Semitic currency of the time and is the subject of a contemporary poem by Heinrich Heine: in 'Erlauschtes', the poet mockingly claims that Jekef's 'little daughter' cost her father sixty thousand marks because she was 'a little rusty' and 'pert'. For exactly the same reason, Baron von Abendthau finds it difficult to avert the natural downfall of his race by means of an infusion of new German blood.

It is to help him out of this dilemma that Julius's beautiful female visitor sends our hero to her uncle Baron von Abendthau. Suspecting nothing, Julius courts this 'monster of ugliness' who, as Wagner makes all too plain, cannot be married off in spite of attempts to disguise her with 'elegance, tincture and plasters against prejudice'. Once the duped Julius has drawn his future father-in-law's attention to his aristocratic pedigree, nothing stands in the way of his marriage with the latter's as yet unseen daughter. But when, instead of the expected beauty, Julius is faced with the hideous Aurora, he almost faints. 'What a terrible dream', he groans, 'it's an absolute nightmare.' At this juncture, two surprise visitors put an end to his nightmare: one is the bearkeeper Gregor, in whom Julius recognizes his lost father and in whom later scholars have seen Wagner's stepfather Geyer.[55] The second visitor, dressed in the skin of a dancing bear, is the goldsmith's long-lost brother Richard, whose skills have been exploited by Gregor as a source of income and livelihood.

Accompanied by capering apes, the troupe of travelling entertainers turns up for the engagement party, allowing Julius, beaming with delight, to welcome them as members of his own family. Baron von Abendthau seems almost to 'turn to stone' at this unmasking of the alleged aristocrat and immediately annuls his daughter's marriage with 'the brother of a bear'. The moral of the piece is that 'men's cunning' is, after all, superior to that of women and that Wagner, having had to dance in disguise to the tune of others, is finally able to triumph over his enemies.

Among these enemies he reckoned everyone of whom he was afraid. In his childhood, his fear was directed at the figure of his stepfather, whereas the latter's qualities were now transferred to those who taught him fear. In particular, it was the element of hypocrisy that became his enemies' main distinguishing feature. During the recent past, he believed that he had been tricked by Frau Gottschalk, by the businessman Herr Schwabe and by the theatre manager Karl Friedrich Cerf. In exactly the same way, his hero Julius is the victim of an act of duplicity that comes close to destroying him completely. Rienzi, too, is betrayed by the very *nobili* whom he magnanimously pardons, much though they deserve to die. The camp of evil, which was integral to all his works, was assuming increasingly clear-cut outlines in Wagner's imagination. From the time of *Die glückliche Bärenfamilie*, it bore decidedly Jewish features.

But why did such a highly gifted all-round artist like Wagner need a construct of a kind normally found only among religious fanatics? The archetype of evil grew within him, as did the fear that he felt for it. Later it helped him to explain why he was one of those disadvantaged individuals who always drew the short straw – 'short' being the operative word. The enemy stopped him from developing. As soon as he wrote independent works and hoped for recognition, he encountered rejection upon rejection. Whatever he did seemed to go wrong. Every work that he forced from himself met with scorn and disapproval. All his serious attempts to make a name for himself as a poet or composer proved spectacular failures. From *Leubald* to his latest farce, his works had all faded back into oblivion.

But not his own oblivion, for every defeat that he suffered was bound up with a sense of humiliation, with failed illusions and with a gnawing feeling of inadequacy that was to pursue him until the very end. Why was he forced to suffer the same self-inflicted fate as his tragic heroes? Why did failure dog him as surely as it dogged his hero Siegmund, for whom everything turns to 'ill fate' until he dies at the hands of his own father? The answer to these questions was provided by his own works, whether musical, poetic or reflective. It was a metaphysical answer that seemed to lay claim to universal validity and yet was of universal validity only for Wagner himself.

The farce about the hideous Jewish fiancée and the happy family of bears was not so much one of Wagner's creative works as one of those with which he avenged himself for having been prevented from writing creative works. In later years, too, he used the tools of his trade to wreak vengeance on all who got in his way. His linguistic gifts provided him with the wherewithal to avenge the suppression of his genius and seek reprisals by journalistic means. His ability to use language as a fatal duelling weapon is something that he learnt from the Young Germans.

And so he dipped his pen in vitriol and attacked the 'evil' that stopped him from working creatively. From his anonymous assault on Rellstab to his anti-Semitic operetta and his pseudonymous 'Jews in Music' he persecuted those who he thought were persecuting him. The tragedy lay in the fact that these persecutors were just as much a figment of his imagination as the evil that he imputed to them. Yet his extraordinary imagination, coupled with his brilliant ability to express himself, allowed him to place the stamp of universality not only on his world of entirely personal ideas but also on the evil against which that world was ostensibly meant to assert itself.

Wagner himself used the word 'demon' to describe this enemy. And because he felt its effects, he believed in it. Sometimes its fictional reality assumed a physical identity. Just as the horribly lifelike nature of the theatre had convinced him of the existence of the demonic when he was still a child, so he quickly discovered signs of it in his own later life. It inhibited his success, undermined his relationships and destroyed his happiness.

It is for this reason, he once wrote, that he developed such 'a powerful belief in an evil star that is directed quite specifically at me'.[56] This misfortune followed him everywhere, and it did so, moreover, with logical consistency as it sprang not from chance but from a particular quirk of fate. As was clear from Apel's *Der Freischütz*, it was the more powerful force, a power which, at least on earth, destroyed what was good. The 'beauty' that Wagner wrested from his evil star had to be 'paid to the demon', as he noted in 1865.[57] What seemed at the time like good fortune was invariably followed by disaster.

But in many respects the beauty that was wrested from this alternative world bore the features of that world. Wagner depicted all that troubled him and did so with troubling accuracy. Whatever prevented him from working fired his imagination – this was certainly the case with the smith in Zurich whose enervating hammering was to find its way into the smithy of the demonic Nibelungs. For his friends, who assumed that all artistic work was bound up with smiling Muses and a Goethean delight in creative endeavour, this connection made little sense.

'It seems', he once wrote imploringly, 'that none of you understands how unhappy it makes me that my art comes only from my own unhappiness.'[58] He often confirmed that it was threatened by misfortune, too: throughout his life he was tormented by the idea that illness or death might prevent him from completing a work and was afraid that his demon might thwart his plans at the very last minute. While he was composing, he was often overcome by a strange feeling that the devil was standing behind him and trying to stop him from completing whatever he was working on. The closer he drew to death, the more this anxiety grew. Once he had managed to complete a work, he felt as if he had 'sweated some tremendous anxiety' out of his body.[59]

Wagner was entirely serious when discussing his demon. It was no poetic metaphor, still less did his fear of it strike him as childish. For him, everything that affected him and his life was real. In turn, this mysteriously active nucleus to his existence could be grasped and described in the language of art. In the words of *Der Freischütz*, it involved an act of conjuration.

For Wagner, the theatre became a place where the different forms of reality that eluded our everyday understanding could be summoned into existence. They appeared as myths not because they could not stand up to rational scrutiny but, conversely, because reason inevitably foundered on their superior force. For Wagner, the theatre was neither an educational institution à la Schiller nor a place of entertainment à la Holtei but a 'demonic abyss containing within it the potential for all that is most base and most sublime'.[60]

The demon that in the theatre would respond to a wave of his baton, just as the archetypal earth goddess Erda rises up from the depths, could never be brought under control in real life. Perhaps the sheer violence of his counterattacks on those he regarded as the physical embodiments of his demon can be explained only in terms of the desperate helplessness that he felt in the face of that demon.

'Everyone has his own demon', he told a French admirer in 1865, 'and mine is a terrible monster. Whenever it stalks me, disaster hangs in the air. The only time I was ever at sea I was almost shipwrecked; and if ever I were to go to America, I'm sure the Atlantic could receive me with a hurricane.'[61]

Wagner's disastrous sea voyage in the summer of 1839 marked the climax and culmination of his foray into the east and did indeed seem to be attended by a 'curse'. One of his most masterly pieces of prose writing, reminiscent of Edgar Allan Poe, describes his flight from Livonia, but it scrupulously avoids all mention of the one incident that most clearly reveals the fatal workings of that curse.

This new flight was the result of Wagner's decision to defy the adverse conditions that made life impossible for him in Riga. 'I won't allow people simply to kill me off with my hopes and plans,' he wrote at this time. His desire to quit this 'Siberia' and make for France was by now irresistible, although, truth to tell, he had no choice in the matter: once he had lost his job, there could no longer be any question of his paying off his manifold debts. Even the few luxuries in life to which he had grown accustomed were no longer within his reach. But it was not only a lack of money that prevented him from undertaking an expensive journey: his perpetually mistrustful creditors had had his passport impounded.

Wagner secretly sold his furniture, some of which he had not yet paid for, and organized a benefit concert for himself, allowing Minna to display her faded charms as an actress one last time. The proceeds were just enough to pay their travelling expenses. According to his later account, he would have used the money to pay his creditors, if his friend Abraham Möller had not suggested using it to repair to Paris and dealing with their demands from there. Needless to say, this was a lie intended to cover his tracks. Once Wagner had made up his mind to do something, he did not vacillate for long. Whatever else Paris might have to offer, he would at least be safe from his creditors.

Their flight was not without its dangers. First, they lacked the necessary papers and so had to cross the frontier illegally, and this in turn meant slipping past the Cossack border guards, who were armed with rifles. Secondly, if Wagner were to use the mailcoach after crossing the border, he ran the risk of being arrested each time the coach stopped: not only had he crossed the border illegally, but he was also guilty of trying to evade his creditors. As a result, he chose the more elaborate option of escaping by sea, even if he later claimed that he did so out of consideration for his Newfoundland dog Robber.

In order to avoid attracting attention in Riga, they fled in secret from Mitau on 9 July 1839 – the theatre was holding its regular summer season here. The couple survived all manner of passing anxieties and reached the Prussian border unharmed, but in skirting the city of Königsberg they suffered an accident that was to have serious repercussions, when the carriage in which they were travelling to the port of Pillau overturned, throwing Wagner into a slurry pit and leaving Minna so badly shaken that while her husband went to change his clothes in a nearby farmhouse, she suffered a miscarriage. Natalie, to whom we owe this information, claimed that Minna was unable to have children after this.

They slipped past the Prussian harbour police at dead of night and crept aboard a schooner, the *Thetis*, where they were concealed in a cramped storeroom as illegal passengers until the vessel was out at sea. They reached Copenhagen a week later, and on passing the castle at Elsinore, Wagner was reminded of his youthful passion for *Hamlet*. A calm sea and prosperous voyage seemed to be in the offing.

And then the storm broke. For a whole day the elements raged. Cooped up in the captain's cabin, Wagner and Minna suffered a combination of mortal anguish and *mal de mer*. The whistling of the wind in the rigging, Wagner later recalled, left a 'curiously demonic impression' on him. The howling wind penetrated his very being, 'sounding like the purest music', when suddenly a ship rose up before them, only to disappear again just as quickly into the surrounding gloom. He was 'at once struck by the thought of the Flying Dutchman', Wagner later reminisced.[62]

On 29 July Captain Wulff abandoned his struggle with the wild west wind and sought shelter on the Norwegian coast. Here Wagner, exhausted by the exertions of the journey, experienced 'one of the most wonderful and most beautiful impressions' of his life: individual cliffs rose up eerily out of the water, and then they formed themselves into groups until they enclosed the ship on both sides like some bewildering labyrinth. The wind died down, the sea grew calmer, and before them there opened up the rocky valley of a fjord. In the midst of the deep silence, the crew's rough cries rang out: less than two years later, its echo, thrown back by the huge granite walls, was to reverberate in Wagner's next opera.

Wagner later discussed with his fellow composer Hector Berlioz this link between personal experience and creativity, and they spoke about 'the mystery of "artistic conception"'.[63] Certain 'experiences in life', Wagner declared, had a literally enthralling effect on the human mind, but this effect did not necessarily find immediate expression in art. Rather, these impressions tended first to stir 'mental forms' – 'Seelenformen' – into life, forms that slumbered within the individual. It was the artist's function to raise these into the light and give them artistic shape.

In Wagner's view, then, the work of art was no mere reflection of some impression that the artist receives. Rather, this impression simply inspires the artist to embark on a creative process whose aim is to 'develop his innermost mental forms'. In short, external impressions were merely trigger mechanisms from which the artist had to break totally free in the course of the creative process. Like so many others, this idea, which Wagner developed in his conversation with Berlioz, derives from E. T. A. Hoffmann's conceptual world, a world that had long been part of the forms that made up Wagner's mental and emotional universe.

By the time Wagner had assimilated the rhythmic cry of the sailors and the echo of the granite walls, the *Thetis* had put to sea again. Unfortunately, the vessel scraped the side of a reef, and it was not until the following day that they were able to resume their voyage to London. After four days of deceptive calm, the storm returned, battering the boat with such 'unprecedented fury' that crew and passengers feared for their lives. The schooner was tossed aimlessly to and fro, plunging down into the deepest troughs before being drawn up again to the crests of the mountainous waves.

During the first storm, the breakers had shattered the attractive figurehead at the prow of the vessel, and this time it was the turn of Minna's trunk, which was washed overboard, together with all the silverware they had managed to salvage in Riga. To make matters worse, the captain lost his bearings, leading the superstitious sailors to cast threatening glances in the direction of the two passengers whom they held responsible for their present misfortunes. In the event, the feared disaster struck only some years later, when the tiny schooner, unsuited to the open seas, sank with all hands in a similar storm.

On this occasion, crew and passengers survived, sighting the English coast on 10 August and making their way between dangerous sandbanks, while the storms continued unabated. They reached the Thames Estuary on 12 August and, in order to hasten their journey, the Wagners, together with their New-foundland dog, switched to a modern steamer. Instead of a week, the journey had taken a month. They disembarked in a city that was not on their direct route to Paris and, forced to endure a few days here, spent a not inconsiderable part of their savings. Even so, they managed to find suitably cheap accommo-dation, thanks to a 'little hunchbacked Jew' from Hamburg.

Fate willed it that, in the course of their crossing to France, they met a Mrs Manson, a Jewess friendly with the great Giacomo Meyerbeer. Armed with a letter of recommendation and Meyerbeer's address, Wagner set out for Boulogne-sur-Mer, intending to pay his respects to the man who ruled over the fabulous world of the Paris Opéra in plenipotentiary splendour.

Hitherto dogged by ill fortune, Wagner was finally in luck: Meyerbeer was at home.

The 'ne plus ultra of art'

It was not just good luck that seemed to be smiling on Wagner, but Providence itself. Wagner was able to meet the acclaimed composer in a seaside resort that happened to lie on his journey. Like Columbus, he had set out to discover a new world without having the least idea of what to expect. However concrete the threat from which he was fleeing, the goal to which he was drawn was fantas-mal in the extreme. The Paris Opéra was a myth like the Castle of the Grail, its shimmering aureole rising high above the metropolis's sea of houses. At its inaccessible heart Meyerbeer held sway like some high priest, celebrating the solemn Mass of his art. Wagner had set out in search of a dream and seemed to have come straight to El Dorado.

For the first time in his life the notoriously indigent Wagner found himself in a chic coastal resort where high society held court and every visitor was accompanied by a liveried servant sporting a parasol. In the midst of such cosmopolitan elegance that glided past him in high-wheeled carriages, he was permitted to call on the famous composer and abandon himself to the heady feeling that he was Meyerbeer's equal as an artist. A rose-coloured world of satin and silk smiled benignly upon him.

The good-natured Meyerbeer, who had once been a close friend of Carl Maria von Weber, even summoned up the patience to listen to parts of *Rienzi*. He invited Wagner to supper and also to private parties with the celebrated pianist Marie Leopoldine Blahetka and the famous composer Ignaz Moscheles, who eleven years later was to defend Meyerbeer against the vicious attacks of his guest.[64] The young Saxon composer felt in his element. When Meyerbeer, who had a soft spot for impoverished colleagues, gave him letters of recommendation for the Opéra's director Charles Duponchel and its principal conductor François Habeneck, he felt that he had finally turned the corner. Success was at hand. Wagner needed only to travel to Paris and garner his due rewards.

Misfortune struck as soon as he arrived and continued to blight his existence throughout much of the next three years. And in spite of his subsequent claims to the contrary, he owed this misfortune not to his host in Boulogne but simply to his own inexperience. He wanted to be a success in a city that he did not know and to conquer the Paris Opéra without knowing how. He did not even know how the Opéra functioned as an institution.

Ever since *La muette de Portici* had opened in 1828, the Paris Opéra had been a social institution in which the parvenu society of the July Monarchy held up a flattering mirror to itself. The art form that triumphed on the operatic stage was one of that society's preferred ways of spending the newly abundant resources at its disposal. Anyone who, like Meyerbeer following the international success of *Robert le diable* in 1831, was at the heart of this cult could pocket his share in the proceeds and do so, moreover, with a clear conscience. While in Germany art continued to be synonymous with penury, in Paris it meant affluence and prestige, at least for Meyerbeer and his librettist Eugène Scribe. Wagner had already corresponded with both these men and drawn their attention to his talent. Now that he found himself standing at the gates, he asked them politely whether he might perhaps be allowed to join them.

His disillusionment began as soon as he set foot in the city. There was no longer any sign here of the brilliance of the coastal resort, none of the brightly lit salons bustling with servants, no curtains wafted by the breeze, no potted palms or champagne buckets. Everything was just as it had been in Magdeburg and Riga. Originally he had planned to make do with a single room with an alcove in which Minna was to keep house, but in the expectation of imminent affluence they had moved to a *hôtel garni*, furnishing its fourth-floor rooms with Livonian chandeliers. Although they ate out in expensive restaurants, they felt 'degraded' by this, and Wagner sensed a 'growing anxiety'.

All too predictably, their cash soon ran out, and Wagner turned to relatives and friends for the support that the world owed his genius. Among the skills he picked up at this period was an epistolary style that proved utterly irresistible: Wagner became a virtuoso at raking in money, and as in his art he was not afraid of using extreme means, the excuses that he offered ranging from an urgent need for medical supplies to the threat of imprisonment for debt, a threat that on one occasion he even claimed had been realized.[65] He also adapted the tone of his lamentations to suit his addressee, demanding active sympathy from one, brotherly solidarity from another and, from a third, a legitimate advance on future profits.

It almost always worked. He later was criticized for ingratitude towards his countless almsgivers. In this his critics have overlooked the fact that the money was invariably hard earned: whether he was preparing a vocal score of a Donizetti opera (as he was unfortunately soon required to do), composing an extra number for a comic vaudeville or drafting a begging letter to his friend Theodor Apel, the exercise was labour-intensive. Everything demanded time, understanding and patience, together with a fair amount of cheek and the sort of histrionics of which he was said to be innocent as an artist.

Soon he even began to believe in the picture of wretchedness that he painted for his potential benefactors, with the result that his years in Paris feature in his autobiography as a time of hunger, misery and national degradation. His return to Germany in 1842 assumed the status of an act of redemption and liberation. In accepting this picture, writers have overlooked the fact that it was a part of his myth of himself as a survivor, a myth that he exploited in his attempts to collect money for his own good cause. The truth of the matter is that he simply had to face up to the consequences of his own actions.

Wagner had not been invited to Paris but had literally forced himself on the city. When he was not offered immediate access to the gold mine of the Paris Opéra, he felt that others were to blame for his misfortune. But on closer inspection, this misfortune turns out to be a consequence not of French insensitivity and intrigue but of his own lifestyle. Indeed, it is tempting to think that he manoeuvered himself into a position of wretchedness so that, abandoned by the whole world, he could objectivize his 'innermost mental forms' and turn them into a work of art. It was, after all, in this self-induced predicament that he came up with the idea of *Der fliegende Holländer*, a work which, like some terrifying ghost ship, was to outstrip everything previously known in the world of opera.

It was not long before he was introduced to a number of ex-patriot Germans, all of them companions in misfortune who had sought their fortune in the French capital and failed to find it. He met the Beethoven expert Gottfried Anders, who worked at the Bibliothèque Royale and who drew his attention to the *Gazette musicale*. Anders's friend the Jewish scholar Samuel Lehrs must have struck the young musician as a reincarnation of his bibliophile Uncle Adolf. Lehrs introduced Wagner to medieval poetry and its heroic legends, while also drawing his attention to the history of the Hohenstaufen emperors that was to prove so fertile a field of artistic inspiration. Most of all, Wagner felt drawn to the painter Ernst Benedikt Kietz, who, like the others, gave him financial support and who immortalized him in an important portrait of him as a beau of the bourgeois monarchy. In his memoirs, Wagner acknowledged his debt to all three of these stranded souls, while finding only words of contempt for the artistic establishment to which he was forced to kowtow.

He began with Charles Duponchel, the monocle-wearing director of the Opéra, who gave Meyerbeer's letter of recommendation only the most cursory of glances, suggesting that countless ones like it had already passed through his hands. Wagner, who had expected Duponchel to show him the way forward, heard no more from him. When Habeneck asked for a piece of Wagner's handiwork for him to assess, the composer produced his old *Columbus* Overture from his days in Magdeburg. The excellent Conservatoire Orchestra played through the second-rate piece at one of its rehearsals and left it at that.

In addition to the *Columbus* Overture, with its unmistakable echoes of Mendelssohn, Wagner had also brought with him his ill-starred opera *Das Liebesverbot*, clearly convinced that Paris's metropolitan audiences would accord it the acclaim denied it at home in Germany. He evidently harboured illusions about the quality of these pieces that were not shared by his sceptical listeners. In 1841, in spite of Habeneck's paternalistic advice to the contrary, he forced through a public performance of the *Columbus* Overture, only for this to prove a spectacular failure. On Meyerbeer's recommendation, *Das Liebesverbot* went into rehearsal, whereupon the theatre promptly went bankrupt, a state of affairs that a production of this no less old-fashioned work would presumably not have averted.

Wagner's run of bad luck had nothing to do with the envy of rivals, still less with ingrained prejudices on the part of Parisian audiences, being due rather to the weakness of the pieces themselves. He could have spared himself these problems if only he had been a little more patient. Although he knew that he had outgrown the world of Kapellmeister music to which they owed their origins, he had nothing to show for his later developments and could offer no examples of the world of music that he now inhabited, a world of tone-painting and ideas. And so he failed to make any impression with works in which he himself no longer believed, but had to keep to himself the new works with which he might conceivably have won over Parisian audiences.

The works that are bound up with his years in Paris belong to three different stages in his development. In addition to the unfortunate specimens he had brought with him, there was also *Rienzi*, now nearly complete, a piece that could stand comparison with anything currently on show at the Paris Opéra. Finally, towards the end of his stay he wrote the words and music of *Der fliegende Holländer*, a work that looked beyond anything currently being written by even such an avant-garde composer as Berlioz, revealing Wagner to be in total command of a universal musical language. But Parisians knew none of all this and, on the strength of the pitiful samples of his work to which they were exposed, concluded that his *Columbus* would never help them to discover the new world of music.

For his own part, Wagner discovered the world of the Paris Opéra. With its lavishly resplendent resources, which were used 'for an inspired artistic aim', this institution struck him as the 'ne plus ultra of art'.[66] Overwhelmed by a feeling of 'sensually flattering warmth', he became increasingly convinced that he would triumph here one day. Unfortunately, the gates of Paradise continued to remain locked and bolted for the foreseeable future.

As a result, Wagner had to make do with more menial activities, later feeling so ashamed at what he had done that he even confused their chronology. From the very beginning he started to look round for ways of earning some extra money, rather than only at a much later date, when forced by hardship to do so, as he claims in his autobiography. The man who wanted to conquer Paris kept his head above water by temping.

In his autobiography, Wagner also claimed that it was not until the winter of 1839–40 that he wrote an insertion aria for the famous bass Luigi Lablache to sing in *Norma*, whereas it was in fact written soon after his arrival in Paris. Conversely, a carnival chorus for the vaudeville *La descente de la courtille* was not performed at the Théâtre des Variétés until January 1841, rather than during the early months of his time in Paris. We also know that he began working for Meyerbeer's publisher, Maurice Schlesinger, soon after his arrival in the city, and that a lucrative business relationship developed between the two men, with Wagner correcting proofs and preparing various arrangements.

He proved a skilful arranger, providing Schlesinger with highlights and pot-pourris from popular operas by Donizetti, Halévy and Auber and also arranging these scores for the most disparate instruments, including piano, strings, flute and even the *cornet à pistons*, even though he understood nothing about this last instrument. Evidently finding this work relatively congenial, he offered his services to other publishers and earned enough by this means to survive.[67]

Wagner's own account of this period flatly contradicts what we now know to be the truth of the matter. In *My Life*, he claims that, Meyerbeer's recommen-dations having proved worthless, he had suddenly found himself without any income. As a result, Meyerbeer had suggested that he should 'look round for some modest employment' and to this end introduced him to his publisher Maurice Schlesinger, an acquaintance that Wagner describes as 'monstrous'. Only because he was forced to do so by extreme necessity had he agreed to this act of self-abasement. Schlesinger, a converted Jew, had been the one to bene-fit.

This appealing picture of the innocent abroad reduced to abject slavery by two calculating Jews found its way into the Wagner legend. But the truth of the matter was rather different. It was only because Wagner had got into difficul-ties of his own making that he was forced to hire out his services. He carried out the commissions promptly, and so he was offered new ones. Of course, this mundane reality consorted ill with the picture of the brilliant composer of *Rienzi* that Wagner became each time he had delivered his latest batch of arrangements. But the contradiction that his biographers have failed to notice was part and parcel of Wagner himself. It was very much his ability to change his persona at random that enabled him to achieve his various goals in life even under the most adverse conditions. His work, it is true, varied widely in qual-ity, but this was simply because the Wagnerian scale was open at both ends.

The decisive musical experience of this period was provided not by the Paris Opéra but by Hector Berlioz. Under the direction of the composer, Wagner heard his *symphonie dramatique, Roméo et Juliette*, in either late November or early December 1839, and so powerful was the performance that it had a 'liter-ally stunning' effect on him. An outsider on the Parisian musical scene, Berlioz had mastered the language of musical ideas in a way that none of his predeces-sors had succeeded in doing. At the same time, he extended the expressive potential of the instruments of the orchestra, investing them with a range never previously known. This impression produced in Wagner the 'artistic conception' that he was to describe to Berlioz years later. What he heard in Berlioz's work struck a chord in him.

As a tone-painting, *Roméo et Juliette* was unique and, as such, Wagner admitted, it 'overawed' his 'own musico-poetic sensibility' with such 'ruthless violence' as to drive it back into his 'innermost being'. Here, in keeping with his own theory, it awoke the 'mental forms' that were slumbering there. After listening to other works by Berlioz, including *Harold en Italie*, the *Symphonie fantastique* and the *Grande symphonie funèbre et triomphale* that Berlioz had written for the victims of the July Revolution, Wagner felt 'a mere schoolboy', a feeling he had not previously known in relation to any living composer. But his pride was greater than his admiration, and so he denied that Berlioz's *symphonie dramatique* had any influence on the initial version of his *Faust* Overture that dates from this same winter of 1839–40. Instead, he claimed that honour for Beethoven's Ninth Symphony, a performance of which he brought forward in his memory by the space of several weeks.[68]

That Wagner suffered occasional hardship at this time is beyond doubt. Fully expecting that *Das Liebesverbot* would be a success, the Wagners had moved into a larger apartment in April 1840 and furnished it on tick. When the theatre went into liquidation, they were forced to sublet the accommodation to tourists from Leipzig and to a travelling salesman called Brix who also played the flute. Minna prepared breakfast for them, washed the dishes and cleaned their boots. As she had Wagner to thank for this 'humiliation', she showered him with endless reproaches and grumbled continuously. This in turn must have added to the 'hardships' about which he so often complained.

His complaints did not go unheard. Back in Leipzig, Heinrich Laube mobilized a number of patrons of the arts, including a Jewish businessman by the name of Axenfeld. Together they came to the rescue of the 'Young German' artist who was starving in Paris. Even Theodor Apel, who had gone blind following a riding accident in 1836, yielded to Wagner's entreaties. The latter began his assault on Apel's emotions by pretending that he had 'not earned a single groschen' for a whole year, and when this failed to do the trick, he claimed to have been thrown into prison for non-payment of his debts. The possibility that their idol might actually have served a term of imprisonment has generally been dismissed by Wagner's biographers, who evidently find it easier to accept the idea that he exerted moral blackmail on an ailing friend whom he had long since written off.

Help also came from the 'monstrous' Schlesinger, even if that help was offered unwillingly, as Wagner claimed in *My Life*. During the winter of 1839–40 Wagner set Heine's poem 'Die beiden Grenadiere' and, fully expecting a large turnover, asked Schlesinger to print it at his own expense. He even included the *Marseillaise* at the end, convinced as he was that this would add to the work's marketability, but in the event not a single copy was sold. Schlesinger insisted on being repaid the sum of fifty francs, and it was at this juncture – or so Wagner explains in *My Life* – that the publisher suggested he should write for his periodical, the *Gazette musicale*. The fee was derisory, yet even this sum had to be shared with a translator.

In his earlier reminiscences, by contrast, Wagner conceded that it was Schlesinger who encouraged him to write in order to earn some extra money. He himself, he added, regarded this journalistic activity as an opportunity to introduce a note of poetic justice into his unfortunate situation: in 1851 he claimed that he felt his work on these trivial opera arrangements to be a form of the 'deepest humiliation' and that he became a music journalist in order to 'avenge' himself for this 'humiliation'.[69]

His very first short story, 'A Pilgrimage to Beethoven', caused something of a sensation. With its sequel, 'The End of a Musician in Paris', its author took explicit 'revenge for all the shame' he had suffered, striking a sarcastic note that was even praised by both Heine and Berlioz. Although Wagner claimed to have written these texts with a knife to his throat, they proved so brilliantly successful that one might think they were the joint work of Heine and E. T. A. Hoffmann. It is tempting to believe that, as an outstanding journalist, Wagner exaggerated a little in order to blacken Schlesinger's name. Perhaps the publisher had noticed that, in matters of creativity, Wagner needed to be placed under pressure.

During his two and a half years in Paris, Wagner not only worked on his own and other composers' scores, he also wrote three short stories and seven articles for the *Gazette musicale*. But his exceptional workload additionally included numerous articles for the Dresden *Abend-Zeitung*, August Lewald's *Europa* and Schumann's *Neue Zeitschrift für Musik*. The pressure on him must have been enormous. Given their literary quality – a quality generally absent from his later writings – one might almost wish that other editors had wielded a whip over him as Schlesinger did.

Meyerbeer, too, did what he could to help. It soon became clear to him during one of his visits to Paris that his protégé was getting nowhere on his own, and so he introduced him to the new director of the Opéra, Léon Pillet. Together, the two men considered ways of obtaining work for Wagner, including writing a ballet, a suggestion that Wagner rejected as an example of barefaced effrontery. He also took it as a personal affront that his great benefactor spent so little time in his – Wagner's – new adoptive homeland.

'I am sure', Wagner complained ironically, 'that I should soon have achieved my goal had it not been my misfortune that throughout my stay in Paris Meyerbeer was away most of the time.'[70]

Meyerbeer

Meyerbeer had been born in 1791, a whole generation before Wagner – and at the opposite end of the ladder of social success. As Karl von Holtei later recalled, Meyerbeer's parents kept open house in Berlin, entertaining 'all the most brilliant names not only at court but from life and from science and the arts in general'. He was born Jakob Liebmann Meyer Beer, but at the age of twenty conflated his unusual given name 'Meyer' with his surname 'Beer' and added the Italian Giacomo, presumably in an attempt to reduce its Jewish associations.

The Berlin in which he grew up was an enlightened and tolerant city, and the family was fully assimilated into the local community, but the musical prodigy still felt traumatized by his origins. 'Not even the bath of baptism', he told the baptized Jew Heinrich Heine in 1839, 'can make the little piece of foreskin grow again.' The man who had not already bled to death when circumcised 'will bleed his whole life long, even after death'.[71]

Meyerbeer not only inherited a fortune, he was also talented, two qualities that from the outset ensured that he was reviled by German critics, whose hostility was further fuelled by the undeniable successes he enjoyed abroad. He very soon found himself labelled a Jewish traitor. When his opera *Emma di Resburgo*, which had already been hugely successful in Italy, was performed in his native Berlin in 1820, a group of 'enthusiastic Jew-haters' ensured that it was a failure.[72] But Meyerbeer's rejection in Germany did not prevent him from becoming the most famous opera composer of his day in Italy.

Composed to a libretto by Scribe and first staged in Paris in 1831, Meyerbeer's five-act opera *Robert le diable* not only conquered the Opéra, it also proved one of the greatest operatic successes of the century, yet while German audiences were unable to resist the appeal of so novel a work, the country's critics continued to maintain a common front against the intruder. A Jew himself, Mendelssohn compared the opera to 'scene-painting' and complained that it was cold and heartless: although it was 'effective, when you look at it carefully you see that it's been painted with the feet'.[73] Rellstab, too, found fault with it, objecting to its 'accumulation of effects' and lack of originality. Instead of creating something he could call his own, Meyerbeer was evidently happy to 'follow the well-worn paths of Rossini, Auber, Hérold and others'. Rellstab could account for Meyerbeer's considerable reputation only by supposing that 'French critics are either venal or blind'.[74]

Rellstab's arguments reflect the current resentment against a composer as successful as Meyerbeer. When Germany finally succumbed to the Meyerbeer mania that swept across the whole of Europe, these ideas were repeated in an even more virulent form in the pages of Schumann's influential *Neue Zeitschrift für Musik*. In 1838 Meyerbeer himself was sent a copy of an anonymous article 'in which the most hateful and vulgar passages were marked in ink'. He felt a resurgence of all his old anxieties, anxieties which, as he told his wife, sucked the very marrow from his bones: 'To be so hated is a feeling that almost literally kills me.'[75]

The article in question was an open letter to Heine and was written pseudonymously by Anton Wilhelm Florentin von Zuccalmaglio, better known as a collector of folksongs, who accused Meyerbeer of stealing the intellectual property of others and of hankering after empty effects, ending by ascribing the composer's 'European reputation' to the fact that he had 'bought up all the pens that money could buy'.

This rumour had been put into circulation by Heine after he himself had taken steps to ensure that it was true by blackmailing Meyerbeer into paying him protection money. Intimidated by the Young German poet's dangerous eloquence, Meyerbeer paid up and said nothing. As Laube noted, his anxiety and wariness were increased by his suspicion that 'emancipation would not really last'. As a result, he crept away 'like a badger to its sett', enjoying his triumphs in secrecy and waiting to see what sort of punishment fate would inflict on him for doing so.

Meyerbeer had entered Wagner's life in spectacular fashion in early 1833, when the Würzburg Theatre had staged *Robert le diable* as the operatic event of the year. Albert Wagner had sung the title role, while the massed choruses were rehearsed by his little brother Richard. This vast work could hardly have failed to make an impression on him. In Riga, too, he staged the piece and even chose it for his benefit performance in November 1838, when he provided his own string transcription of the harp part in Isabelle's fourth-act cavatina.

In Magdeburg, Wagner had already dreamt of emulating Meyerbeer and writing Italian operas for the Italians and French operas for the French.[76] In Riga in 1837 he had appealed to Meyerbeer directly and poured out his heart to him. Confessing that he had been set on the right course by dint of his decision to merge the French and Italian schools, he asked his colleague to extend the hand of friendship and fulfil his 'most ardent wish to be able to come to Paris'. Wagner's epistolary style was almost familiar in its tone and was bound to have an alienating effect on its circumspect addressee. With the barely concealed importunacy of a fanatical admirer, he thrust himself on Meyerbeer as a young artist in need of his help.

Wagner forced Meyerbeer to play the role of a father, whether he wanted to or not. The younger composer's admiration was genuine, and – for once – it was not mere opportunism that motivated him. He was clearly impressed by *Robert le diable*, which Heine, too, had praised as a 'magical piece full of devilish delight and love'. One reason for Wagner's enthusiasm was no doubt his feeling that in this work Meyerbeer emerged as a kindred spirit. While the opera as a whole recalled his own early tales of chivalry now seemingly transferred from the puppet theatre to the large stage, the homeless and rootless composer could also recognize himself in the hero of the opera.

Duke Robert is sprung from the union of a prince's daughter with the devil. He is accompanied everywhere by his father, whom he does not recognise in the guise of the sombre Bertram and who will deliver him to Hell as soon as his time is up. Urged on by this paternal Mephistopheles, Robert develops into a Faustian seducer, so that, driven from his homeland by his crimes, he seeks refuge in flight, ending up in Palermo, which is where the opera is set.

Here he meets Princess Isabelle and immediately falls in love with her, a love that she returns. When Bertram sees his plans frustrated, he uses his devilish wiles to force the couple apart, advising the hapless Robert to win back his lover by means of magic. In order to do so, he has to enter the abandoned Convent of Saint Rosalie and break a cypress branch from her grave. Urged on by a ghostly ballet of nuns, he lets himself be seduced by the vampiric Mother Superior and violates Rosalie's grave, in the course of which he recognizes his mother in Rosalie's features. But instead of taking possession of his lover with the devil's help, he is persuaded to change his mind by Isabelle's prayer for his soul's salvation, and so he breaks the enchanted branch, wins his bride and despatches the demonic Bertram to Hell after the latter has revealed himself as his father.

It is inconceivable that Wagner did not recognize in this plot his family's own archetypal situation: on the one hand, there is the satanic father who disinherits his son and condemns him to endless flight and, on the other, Rosalie, the holy sister. The hero is even united with her in the end in the redemptive figure of Isabelle. It is no accident that when writing *Das Liebesverbot*, Wagner had shifted the setting from Shakespeare's Vienna to Meyerbeer's Palermo. In the same way, Meyerbeer's resolute princess resembles the novice Isabella, just as the restless Robert resembles Wagner's heroes in their search for ultimate peace.

And the dead nuns, stirred into lustful life by the devil, will return in Wagner's last work as a corps de ballet of enchanted flowers that tempt the hero Parsifal into their fairytale garden.

Even the musical language that Meyerbeer invented for his opera on the theme of redemption returns in Wagner's works: although *Robert le diable* remains indebted to the French and Italian operatic tradition, Meyerbeer was keen to explore a new world of expression, which he did by means of the careful use of instrumental colour. In this way he produced unfamiliar mixtures that Berlioz took over into his *Treatise on Instrumentation*, a work that Wagner is known to have studied in detail.

For the power of evil, in particular, Meyerbeer used sounds that came very close to Wagner's concept of the uncanny. His chorus of infernal demons produces exactly the same sense of horror as the dead sailors in *Der fliegende Holländer*, while his insidiously flickering violins help to fan flames that will one day encircle Brünnhilde's rock, instilling fear in all who draw near. With its magic orchestral fire, Saint Rosalie's cemetery is the link between Weber's Wolf's Glen and Wagner's Nibelheim.

By the time Wagner dictated his autobiography, he was keen to deny such a link, claiming that with the single exception of a 'subterranean keyed trumpet as the voice of the mother's ghost' the score had left him cold even in Würzburg and that the work as a whole had 'disgusted' him. This, too, was one of his compulsive retouchings, as he was still claiming in Paris in 1841 that there was 'something strange and almost eerie' about this 'imperishable' piece.[77]

Twenty years later he was to prove this point himself. While out walking with the composer Wendelin Weißheimer, Wagner began humming a striking motif to himself, and when Weißheimer asked 'what the grim Robert the Devil had done to him that he wouldn't let him go', Wagner showed incomprehension, prompting Weißheimer to remind him of the opening bars of the timpani solo from Meyerbeer's opera. But Wagner had not been thinking of *Robert le diable* at all. Laughing, he admitted that the motif he had been humming was the opening of the recently completed prelude to his own *Die Meistersinger*.[78]

As late as 1840 in Paris, Wagner had told Heinrich Laube that Meyerbeer was his 'model'. Indeed, he was far more than that, something none of Wagner's friends could have known: having discovered their spiritual affinity, Wagner now expected to be treated as a relative. Having confided in Meyerbeer like a son, he hoped that Meyerbeer would behave towards him like a father. In countless begging letters whose obsequious flatteries seem almost a parody, the younger composer made it clear that he saw his fate as inextricably linked to Meyerbeer's.

Wagner's missives border on self-revelation, their writer sounding like a prodigal son beating at the door of his father's house and, finding that he is not being heard, finally beginning to shout in a strident attempt to make his point. Virtually everything he wrote went beyond the bounds of civility and even good taste. Subliminally, however, he was convinced that, as a kindred spirit, he could allow himself to do so.

Wagner seems to have set out from the idea of a tacit agreement that would allow him to write down whatever passed through his mind. In order to support him, the 'revered commander of sounds' should not even shy away from 'terrorism' as a means to this end.[79] And in the same breath he went on to confess, in an unmistakably religious undertone, that no salvation could be expected in this world save that which came from his benefactor. On another occasion, he signed himself his correspondent's 'vassal, eternally indebted in heart and blood', and promised to 'pursue him with stammered thanks from eon unto eon. I can assure you that even in Hell I shall continue to stammer my thanks.'

To Meyerbeer, this must have sounded like Heine at his most contemptuous, a petitioner avenging himself for being a petitioner, yet it was in fact more like the desperation of a child attempting to gain its parents' attention. In a further letter Wagner openly conceded: 'I see that I must be your slave, body and soul. . . . I shall be a loyal and honest slave – I freely admit that I'm a slave by nature; it feels infinitely good when I can give myself unconditionally.' It was only logical, therefore, that this act of voluntary self-denial should culminate in the offer 'Buy me, dear Sir, you will be making a not unworthy purchase!'[80]

It is, of course, tempting to think that a consummate actor was trying to fool a wealthy idiot. But Meyerbeer was not sufficiently naïve as to take such flattery at face value, nor could Wagner seriously assume that he could coax Meyerbeer into giving him the help he wanted. The old badger in his sett was bound to suspect the reason for this bait. Did Wagner himself know? Was he aware that his obsessive, almost grotesque subservience was designed to obtain far more than mere cash and letters of recommendation?

In June 1840 he wrote to Meyerbeer again – the older composer was once again absent from Paris – and noted that he was now 'tired of a living death', adding that, if there were no other opportunities in Paris, he would abandon his music and support himself by engaging in some trade or other. This sounds all too similar to his later admission that, like his brother Julius, he should have learnt a proper profession with his Uncle Karl in Eisleben. Meanwhile he was awaiting Meyerbeer's return and 'languishing like a lover'.

Meyerbeer's heart melted. On receiving this latest confidence, he wrote to his secretary, explaining that he had received a 'most touching letter' from Wagner, on whom 'fortune has not smiled', and asking his secretary to send him the money he had asked for.[81] Although he was unable to warm to the role of the patron saint that Wagner had proposed for him, he none the less did what he could to support his stranded fellow countryman. The help he gave Wagner was entirely in keeping with the pragmatism and willingness to assist others that Alexander von Humboldt noted as one of Meyerbeer's most salient characteristics, when he wrote that the composer was 'not simply a noble and selfless individual, but also well versed in the ways of the world, and modest and practical to boot'.[82]

Meyerbeer helped Wagner by giving him money, and he also helped him to help himself by introducing him to men like Schlesinger and Pillet. In the three months following Wagner's unexpected arrival in Paris, he was actively involved in helping Wagner on no fewer than seventeen separate occasions, inviting him to dinner, introducing him to various people, advising him in his negotiations, writing letters of recommendation and attending a rehearsal of the *Columbus* Overture. Even Wagner's intense activity as Paris correspondent of the Dresden *Abend-Zeitung* was almost certainly due to Meyerbeer's influence: the paper's editor, Theodor Winkler, was not only the guardian of Carl Maria von Weber's children, he was also friendly with Meyerbeer and had translated *Robert le diable* into German. 'Without Meyerbeer', Wagner admitted to his admirer Eduard Hanslick in 1846, 'my wife and I would have starved in Paris.'[83]

Just as Meyerbeer helped Wagner to survive in Paris, so he helped him in his subsequent career in Germany. As early as 1840 he recommended *Rienzi* to the Dresden intendant August von Lüttichau, and the following year it was the turn of *Der fliegende Holländer*, which he commended to the general intendant in Berlin, Count Friedrich Wilhelm von Redern. Without his personal endorsement, it is unlikely that either opera would have been accepted as soon as it was. Even as late as 1845, we find Meyerbeer writing to the king of Prussia in his capacity as general music director and petitioning Friedrich Wilhelm directly to give his particular backing to operas by German composers such as Wagner. Presumably the beneficiary of these manoeuvres was aware of all that was going on: in 1872, for example, he dreamt that he was walking 'arm in arm with Meyerbeer in Paris' and that the latter had 'smoothed the pathway to fame' for him.[84]

We can only speculate as to the reasons why a composer as successful as Meyerbeer should ultimately have been persuaded to help a potential rival until the latter could proclaim on a note of triumph that he had finally overshadowed Meyerbeer. Equally uncertain is the cause of Wagner's sudden and total change of heart. The only thing that is certain is that Wagner changed almost overnight from a grateful son to a spiteful enemy. In January 1842 he was still thanking Meyerbeer for the 'renewed demonstrations' of his 'friendship'. Within days, he was writing to Schumann – a self-confessed foe of Meyerbeer – to say that the latter, although his 'protector' and 'an amiable individual', was none the less an 'intentionally cunning trickster'.[85]

It seems that in its tempestuous voyage out into the open sea Wagner's ship was always bound to founder on the same reef. As with Minna, so with Meyerbeer he had thought he had found the ideal figure that life had withheld from him until then. Instead, he once again discovered that, as with his dearly beloved angel, a different reality lay behind the attractive façade: the old suspicion returned, bringing with it the fear of dispossession and treachery, betrayal and attempted murder. The image of the 'good father' became that of its 'evil' antithesis.

Whatever efforts Meyerbeer might make on Wagner's behalf, there was nothing he could do to counter the 'inner mental form' that was beginning to stir in Wagner. From the flattering view that Wagner had formed of his benefactor, there now emerged the old familiar image of horror that the actor, imitative portraitist and second-generation Kotzebue had imprinted upon him. The archetypal fear that Geyer triggered in him was mirrored by the implacable hatred with which Wagner was now to pursue his reincarnation.

The qualities that Wagner had ascribed to his villain over the years had coalesced in the literary figure of the Jewish Baron von Abendthau, but now he was finally able to attribute them to a living person. Like Geyer, Meyerbeer was not an authentic artist but a mere imitator who used the western musical tradition like a quarry, exploiting every existing style by 'necessarily twisting and distorting it'. What he was seeking to achieve was not true art, which was concerned only with the inner truth, but 'superficial effectiveness', which led to a 'denial of interiority'.[86] In an attempt to achieve his cheap theatrical effects, he misused the achievements of genuine composers and 'sold the inalienable secrets of creative art',[87] a charge identical to the one levelled by Adolf Wagner at Geyer.

The result was painfully similar to one of Kotzebue's barnstorming plays, a 'monstrously variegated, historico-romantic, diabolico-religious, fanatico-libidinous, sacro-frivolous, mysterio-brazen, autolyco-sentimental dramatic hotchpotch' well suited to the tastes of modern audiences.[88] This cunningly calculating puppeteer took everything currently on offer and mixed it all up to produce a 'monstrously colourfully mixed phrase' in which art was sold short and great geniuses were cast down into the abyss by the 'grim devil Robert', as Wagner later called him in *Opera and Drama*.

Just as the Geyer of myth had once betrayed his friend Friedrich Wagner, so – according to *Opera and Drama* – Meyerbeer had 'betrayed his friend' Carl Maria von Weber, abandoning Weber's 'wealth of melodic life' in order to follow 'Rossini's siren song' and turning his back on his homeland. The wrong that he did Weber was to be perpetuated in his dealings with Weber's legitimate heir, Wagner. If Geyer had feigned friendship with Wagner in order to leave him to waste away, Meyerbeer, too, had initially shown him a degree of benevolence that ultimately and self-evidently concealed the 'selfless joviality' of Caspar in *Der Freischütz.*

As always, it was all sheer hypocrisy. This 'perpetually kind and obliging man', Wagner confessed to Liszt years later, had merely 'given the impression' of supporting him. He now realized that Meyerbeer had 'made a fool of him', although this did not particularly trouble him as he had never been 'at all fond' of the older man. Neither of them had been serious and each had used the other only as long as it was 'advantageous' to do so.[89]

Even Meyerbeer's letters of recommendation were later said to be mere attempts to deceive, with Wagner's biographer Carl Friedrich Glasenapp, for example, retailing the legend that Meyerbeer always wrote two letters: 'In the one he gave Wagner to take away with him, he would describe his young protégé as exceptionally gifted, while in another letter, already in his correspondent's hands, he would warn the latter in advance that Wagner was an incompetent individual' whom he was anxious to get rid of.[90] Needless to say, Wagner himself believed this version of events, as he was reluctant to admit to himself that it was to his enemy that he owed the first productions of two of his early operas. The idea of Meyerbeer's 'Uriah letters' later went the rounds in Bayreuth – a reference to the letter that David, the king of the Jews, wrote in order to dispose of his rival.

When Schumann heard *Der fliegende Holländer* in 1843 and spoke of its unmistakable echoes of Meyerbeer, Wagner reacted with 'bitterness': he could never – he assured Schumann – draw his inspiration from that particular source, 'the merest smell of which, wafting in from afar, is sufficient to turn my stomach' and to sound 'the death knell of my creative powers'.[91] And in 1851 he wrote to Liszt to say that, as Meyerbeer's total antithesis, he was driven to distraction by the claim that he had anything in common with his rival. Time and again he seems to have been anxious to prove that he was not the son of Ludwig Geyer. His own development depended on his ability to break free from this spectre, which now bore the name of Meyerbeer.

'In view of all that I want and feel,' Wagner continued in his confession to Liszt, 'I cannot appear before any of my friends with the requisite pureness and clarity until such time as I distance myself completely from this vague image with which so many people still associate me.' Only by forcibly breaking free from Meyerbeer, whose living image had dissolved in his own imagination into eerily vague outlines, could he undertake this act, which was necessary 'if my mature self is to be fully born'.[92]

It has long remained unclear what triggered this change of heart, transforming Wagner's erstwhile patron into a common cheat. Meyerbeer himself seems to have given him no immediate reason to change his mind, a change which, derived from his fear-fed imagination, continues to puzzle his biographers.

Just as it points back to his childhood fixation, so it also anticipates that other great mystery in Wagner's life, a mystery bound up with his anti-Meyerbeerian essay 'Jews in Music'. Yet this riddle, too, can be solved. For Wagner discovered in Paris the genius who would inspire his hatred of Meyerbeer.

Henri Heine

Heinrich Heine was the second of the two mythical figures from his youth whom Wagner was destined to meet in Paris. Like Meyerbeer, Heine had become an international celebrity while living abroad, and each in his own way had contributed to the splendour of a city whose population in 1841 was not far short of one million. In comparison with them, Wagner was bound to think of himself as a non-entity. Yet unlike the veritable armies of German émigrés who thronged the capital, he enjoyed the undeserved advantage of their company and goodwill.

It was Wagner's friend from Leipzig Heinrich Laube who introduced him to the great Heine, this idol of the Young Germans who was at the same time the most outspoken and irresistible critic of Germany and the most brilliant stylist since Goethe. That the great classicist was to make fun of the young iconoclast was something that the latter later held against him. But when he sat opposite him in Laube's Paris salon in 1840, he was still able to laugh heartily with him.

Like Meyerbeer, Heine – who was friendly with the Beer family – altered his name in order to ingratiate himself with his Christian readers. Born Harry Heine in 1797, he took the fine old German name of Heinrich when he was baptized in 1825, and by the time Wagner met him he was known to the world of Parisian society as Henri. Having no private fortune of his own, he had to write to earn his living. What he lacked to indulge the lifestyle he wanted to enjoy in Paris he begged from his more fortunate contemporaries. Wagner was by no means the first artist with a gift for extorting money from other people.

In obtaining money from others, Heine was helped by his sharp pen. The journals and newspapers were open to him, allowing him to guide the all-powerful press in whatever direction he chose. And so he used it to help his acquaintances or to harm them, depending on how he felt about them and how much he had received from them. His malice was feared as he destroyed no one without previously having made them look ridiculous. He first began to attract attention as a critic of the Paris Opéra at the very time that Meyerbeer's golden age was dawning in the French capital. As Meyerbeer had no desire to attract attention as the butt of Heine's criticism, he assumed the role of the latter's benefactor and, at least at first, played the part very well.

Heine, too, was one of Wagner's models – Heine who, in the face of the latter's naïvety on his arrival in Paris, is said to have 'clasped his hands in prayer'.[93] Wagner had been devouring Heine's writings since 1830 and had assimilated the 'frivolous elegance' of his style, as is clear from his articles for both the *Gazette musicale* and Winkler's *Abend-Zeitung*. In his search for new subjects he had even found one in Heine's writings in 1838, discovering the legend of the Flying Dutchman in his *Memoiren des Herren von Schnabelewopski*, which he was then able to discuss with the author in person in Paris. Like Meyerbeer, Heine, with his legendary linguistic virtuosity, seems to have felt drawn to his loquacious visitor from an early date.

By December 1839 Heine had already accepted the young German artist into his circle of friends,[94] and it was presumably to thank him for his help that Wagner set a French translation of his sentimental and nationalistic poem 'Die beiden Grenadiere', which he incautiously had printed at his own expense. The short stories that Wagner wrote for Schlesinger's *Gazette musicale* – ostensibly to pay off the debts incurred in publishing *Les deux grenadiers* – were submitted to his new benefactor, who is said to have praised them, claiming that not even E. T. A. Hoffmann could have written anything comparable to 'The End of a Musician in Paris'. In order to prevent the poor short story writer from suffering a fate similar to that of his hero, Heine even allowed himself to be talked into giving Wagner financial assistance in 1841: it seems that he offered him both cash and a loan – an indication of how skilful or (according to Wagner's own reading of the situation) how indigent the composer was at this time.

It was not only as a composer that Wagner showed his gratitude to his patron. When it was rumoured in 1841 that Heine had been punched in the street, Wagner entered the lists on his behalf in his capacity as a journalist and, as though wanting to vent his indignation at his own fate, reminded his fellow Germans of the generous folk they were. They had set the police on a man who had roused their youth from a state of lethargy and had driven from their country a poet who had inspired them to imitate him. They had allowed a talented artist to be 'disfigured' by exile, an artist who would otherwise have ranked among 'the greatest names in German literature'. Now they applauded the fact that he appeared to have been publicly humiliated. Wagner ended his impassioned indictment by making a surprising point, claiming that it would never have occurred to the French to 'slander' one of their own poets in this way. 'I have no reason to feel passionate about the French,' he confessed, 'but here I take them as my model.'[95]

Leaving aside the fact that Heine was himself one of the most gifted of slanderers and that Wagner was his worthy pupil in this regard as in others, the latter was entirely serious. If he allowed himself to be influenced by Heine, it was not simply out of gratitude for his undoubted kindness. They also had a number of points in common with regard to matters Meyerbeerian. Heine had long since commended himself to Meyerbeer's generosity and when necessary given it a helping hand. He too had been reduced to a state of painful dependency by secretly forging a link between Meyerbeer's financial contributions to his cause and his own published opinion of him. Long before Wagner, Heine was fixated on the composer and found a number of ingenious ways of making him atone for being so wealthy.

Liszt's friends were fond of telling the anecdote that following one particular article Heine had written in support of Meyerbeer, the poet received two thousand francs from the composer, but returned the sum, indignantly insisting that what he had written was based on conviction. Shortly afterwards, however, Heine sent Meyerbeer a note asking him for twenty thousand francs to cover a debt of honour.[96] In this way fulsome praise led to more and more gifts, and if Meyerbeer failed to oblige, the poet would play on his anxieties. In 1835 he warned his 'maestro divino' and 'triumphant hero with a laurel wreath' that German journalists were planning 'a campaign of conscious vilification' and that this could be averted only if he handed over some money. In consequence, Meyerbeer was invited to 'place the sum of 500 (five hundred) francs' at his disposal 'without delay'.[97]

The anxious composer was left with no choice but to comply with his brilliant embezzler's wishes. It emerges from Meyerbeer's diary that on one occasion he summoned up the courage to refuse the requested sum on the grounds that 'I have already lent him so many thousands in my life, not a penny of which he has repaid, of course'. Heine immediately responded by 'bluntly' informing him that he would now direct his pen against him.[98] Even when Heine was dead, Meyerbeer continued to fear his 'lies and calumnies', allowing the poet's widow to extort three thousand francs from him on condition that she suppressed a number of offensive passages in her late husband's unpublished papers: 'I'm weak enough to agree to this.' And he paid a further four and a half thousand francs to ensure that four additional poems, all of which made him look ridiculous, did not appear in print until after his death.

In short, Meyerbeer paid Heine to keep quiet. But he never paid enough, and so Heine soon knew too much to remain silent. In the circumstances it was inevitable that a newcomer like Wagner, who was sailing under Meyerbeer's flag of convenience, should be initiated into Heine's intimate secrets. If Heine made fun of Wagner, it was no doubt in part the latter's credulity that excited his ridicule. 'Meyerbeer recommends him,' he wrote on one occasion, 'which proves that he has no talent.'[99] On another occasion, he thought that Wagner's talent was 'suspect precisely because Meyerbeer supports him'.[100]

Heine was not merely a brilliant satirist when it came to pillorying his victim. He also wrote for more general amusement, and always at Meyerbeer's expense. In 1846, for example, he compared the object of his wit to a bear that had 'to be made to dance' and on another occasion to a sly fox that he planned 'to skin' himself. Mockingly he referred to him as the 'Musikverderber Beeren-Meyer' – the 'Berry man who ruins music'.[101] His operas, he claimed, were 'thin and prosaic', their effects achieved by means of 'banal calculations'. His fame, he insisted in an article published anonymously in 1847, he owed to an 'artificial and expensive machine' of corrupt hack writers. For a composer of such 'colossal egoism', other people were of interest only to the extent that he was able to 'exploit them'.

Heine developed a regular paranoia towards Meyerbeer, so that the more the composer resisted his attempts to extort money from him, the more implacably malicious he became, while at the same time growing increasingly terrified that Meyerbeer would take reprisals against him. During the years leading up to his death in 1856, Heine became more and more convinced that his adversary was using 'the basest creatures' to attack him 'indirectly'. No less grotesque was Heine's claim that Meyerbeer had 'a pack of bandits in his pay', one on every newspaper, 'not letting through anything against him and everywhere actively working on his behalf'.[102] For Heine, Meyerbeer was 'the soul of all intrigues', ultimately turning into a kind of musical louse that he called 'Wanzerich' (from the German 'Wanze' meaning 'bug') and that could not even be crushed underfoot without filling the air with a noxious stench and dirtying the soles of one's shoes.[103]

In his dealings with Meyerbeer, Wagner learnt a lot from the witty and libellous poet, eagerly espousing the latter's views and even giving his rival the nonsensical name 'Bärenmaier',[104] while in his assessments of other composers such as Donizetti, Auber and Halévy, we find him repeating opinions strikingly similar to those already advanced by Heine. In his articles for the Dresden *Abend-Zeitung*, he even adopted 'Heine's piquant manner', as he later admitted in *My Life*.

Even more important was Heine's influence on Wagner's librettos. Virtually all the mythological themes that were later to be associated with Wagner's name were already touched on in Heine's *Die romantische Schule* and *Elementargeister*: here Heine had already drawn attention to the cycle of legends surrounding the Holy Grail, including Parzival and Lohengrin; here too he had written about Tristan and Isolde, as well as the famous water sprites that demanded silence of their lovers; he had also recounted the tales of Wieland the Smith and the ill-starred lovers Siegmund and Sieglinde; he had told of the Valkyries exultantly cleaving the skies on their air-borne steeds; and he had described poor Tannhäuser's journey to the Venusberg, where the sweet strains of a harp bid him welcome.

In Heine's mind, memories of a mythic past were bound up with hopes of a liberated Germany. It was not the voice of reason, he prophesied, that would stir the nation into revolutionary activity but simply 'the man whom the German folk expects, the man who will finally give them life and happiness'. This man, whom the younger generation longed for so impatiently and 'who bears the godly sceptre of freedom and the crossless imperial crown', would be none other than the revenant 'Emperor Frederick, the ancient Barbarossa'. He himself, the poet concluded his account, had once stood outside the Kyffhäuser and called out: 'Come, Barbarossa, come!' and 'my heart burnt like fire in my breast, and tears ran down my cheeks'.[105]

Presumably Wagner was also familiar with two of Heine's poems in which the poet's feelings of patriotism were directly linked with the Nibelung skein of legends. His *Buch der Lieder* of 1827, which Wagner had read while still in Leipzig, contains a poem in which the power of evil rebels against God's creation. From the 'dark abysses' of night, black dwarfs rise up against heaven's citadel, where they snatch the crown from the head of the 'pallid god' and set his kingdom on fire.

This act of despoliation culminates in the rape of a blond-haired angel by a 'hideously ugly black goblin'. 'And piercingly a scream resounds throughout the universe,' the apocalyptic Heine wrote, 'the pillars break, the earth and heavens sink down with a crash, and ancient night resumes her sway.' Heine's sombre vision bore the ominous title 'Götterdämmerung'.

During the summer of 1840 – at a time when Wagner was in regular contact with him – Heine wrote a poem that seems like a response to the threat posed by the twilight of the gods. In it Heine compares Germany to the young Siegfried, who begins as a 'clumsy little giant', before becoming a dangerous hero and killing the 'hideous dragon' with a sword of his own making. Only when the world-threatening power of evil is removed will he 'gain the hoard', and Barbarossa's 'golden crown' will glint on his head. This prophetic poem was called 'Deutschland'.[106]

The Flying Dutchman

Even while he was still in Paris, Wagner's borrowings from the world of Heine's ideas were already bearing fruit. He remained in contact with the poet while working on *Der fliegende Holländer* and even admitted to Cosima that he had submitted his French prose draft to Heine for his approval.[107] But it was not long before he was devising imaginative ways of playing down Heine's contribution to his opera. Writing in 1843, in his 'Autobiographical Sketch', he suggested that his 'inner familiarity' with this demon of the oceans predated his reading of Heine's tale in Riga, but at this date he was still willing to concede that it was Heine who had 'invented' the ending of the story, with its dramatic account of the hero's redemption.

When republishing this 'Sketch' in 1871, he replaced this with the claim that the poet had not devised the subject of the Flying Dutchman himself but had 'taken it from a Dutch stage play of the same title'. But this was in fact one of Heine's own literary attempts to surround his works with a certain mystique, an attempt that Wagner took at face value. In his *Communication to My Friends* of 1851 Wagner insisted that the subject derived from the 'morasses and floodwaters' of his life, while in *My Life* he speaks only of 'my' Dutchman. Glasenapp's Wagner-inspired biography, finally, refers simply to 'superficial contact' with Heine: Wagner had absolutely no time in Paris to 'indulge in the sort of superficial distractions' that Heine's circle had to offer.[108]

But there was no need for Wagner to falsify the facts in this way, as Heine's comically misogynistic tale was merely the starting point for his own Romantic opera about a wandering seafarer, acting as a trigger mechanism in keeping with his theory of artistic conception. It evolved within him, the intellectual form that he gave to it being so much a part of himself that it would qualify him as one of the few original masters of the genre, even if he had composed no other operas. The sort of work that was currently causing a furore at the Paris Opéra, whether by Meyerbeer, Auber, Adam or Halévy, seemed outdated and fustian when set beside this powerful psychological drama.

Here, there is no longer any sense of the different aspects of art, from theatrical pomp to coloratura singing, vying for the audience's favour: everything in *Der fliegende Holländer* is part of a unified whole, everything speaks the same language of tragedy, unfolding within the narrowest possible confines and moving irresistibly towards a tragic denouement. Everything speaks the same language, and all who hear it can understand it.

The work is not a succession of climaxes, succeeding one another in a series of self-contained numbers. Rather, it depicts a single concept developing and moving implacably towards its natural conclusion, with the basic dramatic idea emerging from the interplay between contradictory archetypes, an interplay reflected in turn in the confrontation between the leitmotifs that make up the work. *Der fliegende Holländer* was Wagner's French Revolution, although no one noticed it at the time.

But Wagner had first tried his hand at a symphonic work, once again working away from the public gaze. He wanted to depict the drama of a great individual who, despairing of the world, longs for his end and finds redemption through a loving being. During his early months in Paris, Wagner still nurtured certain hopes, and it was against this sanguine background that he drafted a symphony dealing with the tragic fate of a superman. His lack of success and increasing shortage of money meant that he had no difficulty in identifying with this character.

According to his own account in *My Life*, his work on this new piece was triggered by his renewed acquaintance with Beethoven's Ninth Symphony, the 'stream of inexhaustible melody' of which 'gripped' his heart 'with ineffable power'. Only Beethoven's work, as performed by Habeneck's Conservatoire Orchestra, could inspire in him the desire to create something similar.

In fact, Wagner's claim is based on a lapse of memory. Long before he could have heard Beethoven's work in Paris, he had attended a performance of Berlioz's *Roméo et Juliette*. Under the heady spell of this new experience, which had given him a clear idea of the possibilities of modern tone-painting and the art of instrumentation, he planned a counterpart piece of his own, finding his tragic hero in the old familiar figure of Doctor Faust. Berlioz's *Huit scènes de Faust* had already inspired him to explore the Faust legend in 1831 in a set of seven vocal works dedicated to his sister Rosalie, and now he attempted to combine its dramatic sound world with Beethoven's demonic 'open fifths'.

But his plan to write a four-movement *Faust* Symphony foundered, and only its opening movement was finished. Following the example of Berlioz, who had headed one of the movements of his own symphony 'Roméo alone', Wagner called this movement 'Faust in solitude'. Although he helped himself liberally to the contents of his French colleague's pot of paint, his work seems feeble, its self-regarding motifs suddenly springing up from nowhere but never really developing. Above all, the listener is acutely aware of the absence of Gretchen's alternative sound world that Wagner had reserved for the following movement. He renamed the fragment an 'overture'.

In writing the work, Wagner fell far short of his model Berlioz. But the most depressing part of the whole affair was the fact that he failed to do justice to his own idea of what a musical drama should be like. Although Faust provided him with the best possible dramatic basis, he tried to portray this drama by using symphonic resources when he should have depicted the drama itself: in other words, what he should have presented on stage was not a reflection of reality, but reality itself. The essence of his heroes should not be expressed by musical themes. Rather, they ought to be able to express themselves in the language used by living human beings. The music would then follow as a matter of course.

With his main character, Wagner aimed to depict a man for whom womankind is a 'vague and formless object of yearning'. As soon as Faust realizes that this is unattainable, he falls into a state of despair, cursing 'the tormenting idea of the beautiful' and 'plunging headlong into a bewitched world of insane anguish'.[109] Faust suffers the hellish torment of not being allowed to love. Wagner later prefaced the work with a quotation from Goethe's play, including Faust's despairing lines 'Thus life has taught me, with its weary weight, / To long for death, and the dear light to hate.'

As long as Wagner was content to depict his Faust with no more than a few lines of verse and random musical ideas, the character was bound to remain pallid. The hero, Wagner realized, needed to be able to express in his own words his sense of yearning and his disgust with life. While working on the second movement, which was intended to depict 'the phenomenon of womankind', Wagner 'abandoned the whole exercise and, true to my nature, turned to the "Flying Dutchman", breaking free from the mists of instrumental music and finding a solution to the problem that confronted me in the specificity of the drama'.

This is a remarkable sentence. It comes from a letter that Wagner wrote to his friend Theodor Uhlig in 1852 and signals the great leap forward that he had taken during his time in Paris: from the vagueness of his emotions (a vagueness that found expression in the indistinct characterization of his hero), he moved towards the specificity of the Idea that was expressed in both verse and music. He brought the contrasts into conflict with each other, developing them from the contradictions between them.

This conflict, which he conceived in Hegelian terms, demanded a solution: the contradictions needed to be resolved on a higher plane. This alone could bring clarity to the subject and, in the language of the Romantics, provide a sense of 'transfiguration'. And it was this that now became his object as a dramatist, remaining so from the Dutchman's opening monologue to the final words of *Parsifal*.

Just as Wagner's silent Faust gave way to the poetically eloquent Dutchman, rising to tragic heights on the wings of his mournful melodies, so the captain's daughter Senta emerges from the undeveloped figure of Gretchen, appearing before the Dutchman's eyes not just musically but physically, too. In one particular sketch, the Gretchen themes from the *Faust* Symphony appear, in fact, intertwined with those that were to characterize Wagner's later heroine.[110]

Only on a formal level may Wagner's musical drama be said to derive from a Classical 'number opera'. Its real origins lay rather in the sort of symphony that sought to depict an 'Idea'. But the symphony was bound to fail in its task as soon as it elected to depict the drama of real people, and so Wagner inevitably found himself forced to take the step towards opera: real people could not be defined by music – they defined themselves by dint of their voices, acquiring a real existence not through the art of orchestral characterization but through their actual presence, their words and their singing. But they were not merely accompanied by the music, as they were in opera: in the drama that Wagner envisaged, the music would emerge directly from their words. For the first time in the history of opera, this was *their* music. The symphonic writing brought alive the atmosphere and mood, creating, as it were, the general weather situation on the world's stage, while leaving the human characters to take care of the drama themselves.

It was probably in Leipzig in 1831 that Wagner first encountered his new hero: in Heine's *Reisebilder* he was able to read about the ghost from the past whose life impinges on the present and whom observers 'see sailing past in the storm with sails unfurled'. The fact that in the very paragraph in which he mentions the legend of the Flying Dutchman Heine also refers to a 'miracle-working child' by the name of Felix Mendelssohn Bartholdy who delighted his fellow men with the 'sea sprites' nocturnal round' may also have left its mark on the eighteen-year-old Wagner. Seven years later in Riga, Wagner then discovered a much fuller account of the life of the hapless mariner in Heine's *Memoiren des Herren von Schnabelewopski*.

Since time immemorial – thus Heine's version runs – a Dutch captain has been condemned to sail the seven seas: he once swore by the devil that he would round a certain cape even if it were to take him till the Day of Judgement. The devil took him at his word but offered to remit his punishment if he were 'redeemed by a woman's loyalty', a condition held out as highly implausible, for all that the Dutchman is allowed to set foot on land once every seven years in an attempt to prove him wrong. Heine's devil simply meant a wife who would not be unfaithful. In keeping with the main character's nationality, the author claimed to have seen the legend staged in an Amsterdam theatre.

Heine states that he saw the poor Dutchman buying a Scottish merchant's daughter in return for a fistful of diamonds and that the said daughter would keep gazing wistfully at an old painting that depicted the Dutchman. She is told that people must beware of the seafarer who is forever breaking women's hearts. When her father brings the Dutchman home, the latter gives her a graphic account of the sitter's sufferings, explaining that he can neither live nor die, with the result that he is known as 'the Wandering Jew of the oceans'. At the same time, he attempts to allay her suspicions that he is in fact the man depicted in the picture and extracts a vow of fidelity from her. But such is his love for her that he finally resolves to spare her the fate of becoming 'Mrs Flying Dutchman' and hurries back to his ship. In turn, she resolves to spare him the fate of ever being betrayed by her and ensures this by leaping into the sea from a high cliff. Heine claims to have seen all this in the theatre at a performance that was only a part of his own retelling of the tale. Its moral, he concludes, striking a note of mockery, is that women should be wary of such men, just as the latter should avoid the sort of women who 'at best' will be their ruin.[111]

In 1840, Wagner prepared a prose draft based on the play described by Heine, while at the same time giving his heroine a lover. He then translated it into French and sent this translation to Scribe, hoping that the latter would work it up into a libretto for the Paris Opéra. As with *Die hohe Braut*, the librettist failed to rise to the bait, and so Wagner approached the new director of the Opéra, Léon Pillet, and tried to interest him in it. If we are to believe the account contained in his 'Autobiographical Sketch', Wagner allowed himself to be black-mailed into parting with the draft. According to *My Life*, he received five hundred francs for it, but according to other sources it might have been less.

Scarcely had Wagner pocketed the money he had been paid for renouncing his rights to the opera when he set to work on his own version of the piece, thereby carrying off the proverbial trick of having his cake and eating it. He spent the summer months of 1841 composing *Der fliegende Holländer*, which, as in Heine's version, was originally set in Scotland. And he certainly displayed impressive speed in his attempt to beat his rivals to the finishing line. Moreover, he achieved his goal: first staged in Paris in November 1842, the French version of the piece had already sunk without trace by the time his own opera received its first performance in Dresden in January 1843.

And it was, indeed, *his* version. Although the story itself may have been Heine's and although, as Heine himself stressed, it was 'designed almost entirely with the stage in mind',[112] Wagner had changed it in one important respect, replacing the irony of the original with a note of overriding seriousness, with Heine's witty metaphor of the 'Wandering Jew of the oceans' triggering completely different associations in him, not least as the Dutchman is depicted as a demonic seducer. In much the same way, the concept of 'redemption', with which his source had teasingly toyed, has a positively metaphysical significance for Wagner. In the composer's hands, the frivolous tale that cocked a snook not only at the accursed seafarer but also at the whole idea of 'eternal fidelity' became a fatal drama acted out between two lovers with an altogether surprising conclusion.

And Wagner was able to do this by dint of a single sleight of hand. In the figure of the ghost from the past that the present found so unsettling Wagner discovered his own spectral past, a spectre that could not be laid to rest. Now fully in command of the language required to exorcize ghosts, he had no difficulty in staging this drama and confronting his past. The world of musical sounds that for him began with Beethoven's late period and that found its most eloquent expression in Berlioz mirrored the conceptual language that was available to him as a poet. The ideas that seethed within him could acquire independent existence in the material world now that the archetypes of his subconscious had begun to speak for themselves, rising up from the 'morasses and floodwaters' of his life and, having once been depicted in his art, never again sinking back beneath the surface.

And they had risen to the surface accompanied by the sounds of the spirit world that ever since his childhood had been associated with open fifths. Even the very first notes of the overture leave us in no doubt that all is not right: something terrible is about to happen, and Wagner has no qualms about making this penetratingly clear to his listeners. With the strident fifths familiar to him from the stone figures in Dresden, from the Wolf's Glen scene and from Beethoven's Ninth, he conjures up a howling gale that goes far beyond anything previously known. Listeners were shocked when it burst out of nowhere without any warning – just as Wagner intended.

This was the familiar world of ghosts which, as a source of long-standing fear for him, he now unleashed on his listeners. While the storm increases in intensity, raging, whistling and whipping up the elements into a state of chaotic confusion, Wagner deploys his art of reining in the horror and subjecting it to his will. The otherworldly power that seems to belong to the kingdom of the dead and hell brings fear and terror to the petty, transient world of humankind. The menace posed by this other world remains omnipresent throughout the whole opera. It is against this sombre background that Heine's tale is acted out.

In the opening scene we discover Daland seeking refuge from the raging storm in a rocky inlet and thus unwittingly falling under the spell of the man who unleashed the storm in the first place. Once he has concluded the deal that the Dutchman so desires, the wind veers round and guides the Dutchman to Daland's house. Everything in this piece obeys the power of the demon who, in order to conceal his true nature, disguises himself whenever he goes ashore. In Heine's version the Dutchman wore 'the costume of the Spanish Netherlands', a type of dress that must have stirred Wagner's memory of his stepfather, who, towards the end of his career, had appeared, dressed in black, as King Philip in Schiller's *Don Carlos*. Like him, Wagner's Dutchman wears a 'black Spanish costume'.

Before meeting Daland, the demon reveals himself as a man accursed. Condemned to eternal wanderings upon the seven seas, he longs for death but cannot find it. Half vampire, half human being, he is allowed to seduce a woman once every seven years in order to test her fidelity. But it has always proved impossible to find a woman who will be faithful to him till death, and so he now waits impatiently for the end of the world, praying for it to happen. Nor is he alone in this: when, in the final lines of his monologue, he invokes the end of all things and, with it, the end of his sufferings, a chorus of ghosts replies from the coffin-like hold: 'Eternal oblivion, make us yours!'

Now the Dutchman makes one final attempt to find salvation, skilfully passing himself off as a worthy seafarer and buying the covetous Daland's daughter. Following in Daland's wake, he sets sail to see his new bride and, like Bluebeard, puts her to the test. But before he arrives, Wagner introduces us to the young woman herself, presumably falling back on Gretchen's unused themes from his *Faust* Symphony. Senta, whose name he coined for the opera, is discovered sitting with other young women in the spinning room in Daland's house, sunk in her own sombre thoughts, for the demonic Dutchman has already entered her idyllic existence. His lifesize portrait hangs on the wall.

Senta stares at the lifeless canvas with its portrait of a man in an ancient Spanish costume, seemingly trying to entice him down from his frame. Ever since the nights he spent at the Thomä House in Leipzig, Wagner had known that old paintings could exert an eerie force, capable of coming to life at any moment and calling the observer to account. Pictures were a source of anxiety inasmuch as they could bring the past back to life. But they could also waken an insatiable longing if they depicted the object of one's desire, an object no longer attainable.

Nor is there any doubt that the young woman is in love with the portrait. The other women have been singing a harmless spinning chorus, but as soon as they stop, Senta invokes her distant beloved. Her 'Ballad' – which is in fact more of an ecstatic incantation – tells of the 'pallid man' who is condemned to a life of eternal wandering from which only a woman's true love can release him. Senta sings with such fervour that her song conjures up the mariner's magical presence, so that the spell cast by the demon in order to ensnare her father and gain possession of a wife is now countered by the spell of love that summons from a different dimension the man for whom she longs. Already she sees him standing before her, prompting her to ask, as though in a deep dream: 'Father, say! Who is the stranger?'

This was a familiar dream. In 1832, in the draft for *Die Hochzeit*, Ada had asked the very same question when the sombre figure of Cadolt had suddenly appeared in her presence. After hurling him from her tower window, Ada joins her secret lover in a typically Wagnerian love-death. It was presumably his own sister Rosalie who provided Wagner with the model for the self-sacrificing fiancée and whose stage persona as Gretchen likewise left its mark on her character. Although Wagner later claimed that in writing Senta's Ballad he 'unconsciously planted the thematic seed of all the music in the opera',[113] this was not in fact true of the actual score, but it may well apply to his 'unconscious' conception of the role of Senta herself.

Senta is a further embodiment of the archetype of the self-sacrificing sister. A further detail – the fact that Daland's daughter is discovered waiting for her distant beloved in a spinning room – also seems to recall Rosalie: in 1827 she had appeared as Marguerite in Boieldieu's *La dame blanche*, sitting at a spinning wheel and singing her famous Romance, 'Fuseaux légers, tournez' – 'Agile spindles, turn'. With its lifesize family portrait on the wall, this scene already anticipates the second-act setting of *Der fliegende Holländer*.

The following year saw the Leipzig première of Marschner's *Der Vampyr*, in which Doris Devrient, who was related by marriage to Wilhelmine Schröder-Devrient, sang the heroine Emmy, conjuring up the image of a seductive demon in words similar to those used by Senta: 'Behold, mother, the pallid man,' she groans in a hypnotic trance, whereupon the spectral stranger promptly enters her chamber in search of yet another young victim whose bloodless corpse he will deliver up to hell.

Wagner's *Der fliegende Holländer* is an opera in which extremes meet. Bent on offering a stranger his hospitality, the hearty captain ends up selling him his own daughter. In the petty bourgeois spinning room in which we have just heard a chorus of well-mannered young ladies, the daughter of the house reveals herself to be a somnambulist with a penchant for conjuring up ghosts, while the demon whom she summons into life appears wearing an old-fashioned costume and singing a sentimental aria. Nothing is what it seems to be when a painted piece of lifeless canvas can suddenly become the most terrifying reality. True, the Dutchman arrives as a well-bred bridegroom, but the audience knows what lies behind his costume: a man neither alive nor dead who seeks out his victims once every seven years.

Whereas Heine described his Dutchman as the Wandering Jew of the oceans, Wagner called him 'the Ahasuerus of the oceans',[114] thereby projecting onto the figure of the Dutchman a mythological dimension that it did not really have. As a result, the curse that drives him on has very different causes, deriving not from a chance wager with the devil but from an act of a far more damnable kind.

According to anti-Semitic legend, Ahasuerus was a Jew who mocked the suffering Redeemer and so was condemned to wander the world in search of salvation and never find the peace of death. 'Ahasveros', wrote the German revolutionary and Romantic apologist Joseph Görres, 'is Death and the Devil, the desire to die and, at the same time, the inability to die, the Jewish ghost that bestrides the universe.' This is exactly what Heine, too, had in mind, and as such it was taken over by Wagner. His Dutchman is one of the undead, condemned to restless wandering and to destroying the innocent in the process.

This 'Ahasuerus of the oceans' had other qualities, too, that Wagner ascribed to his enemy. In 1853 the composer revealed that the Dutchman was condemned 'to sail the ocean waste for all eternity in search of treasures'[115] – just like the acquisitive Nibelung Alberich. His crew called him the 'black captain', in which guise he terrified people, reducing them to mute fear and precipitate flight. On hearing the ghostly singing of his undead crew, Christian sailors would be 'overcome by terror' and beat a retreat. If, in the course of their flight, they made the sign of the Cross, then, according to Wagner, the ghostly crew would break into 'stridently mocking laughter'. Yet all the Dutchman's destructive features can ultimately be traced back to one: his inability to love. He has turned his back on humankind and, like the night-elf Alberich, forsworn love, hence Wagner's description of him as a 'fallen angel'.[116]

But unlike Ahasuerus and all the other 'fallen angels', the Dutchman can still be helped, for within him is to be found not only the demon who refuses to love but the demon's victim, who is not allowed to love. In this way he is not only Geyer the usurper, but also the son who has been driven from home. Within the figure of the Dutchman we find not only Richard and Leubald but also Sieg-mund and all the other heroes who have been cut off from the possibility of experiencing love. This explains why the Dutchman is able to 'find the redemp-tion still denied the Wandering Jew'. The Dutchman longs for the love that is denied him, and so he can be redeemed by the woman 'who sacrifices herself to him out of love'.

In this ambivalence lies the Dutchman's secret. If he had played only the role of the villain, both punishment and reprieve would have remained superficial. Only because he bears this contradiction within him can he find the redemp-tion that comes from within. Only because he is both culprit and victim can he reconcile them at the moment of his death. His ambivalent nature is already clear from Senta's Ballad, where she says of him: 'He wooed every seven years . . . yet never has he found a faithful wife!' When applied to the seducer who wins women over with his gold, this is as much as to say that any woman can be tempted into being unfaithful – and tempted, moreover, by the Dutchman himself. In short, there can never be any question of love, but only of a living death. But if Senta's remark is applied to the outcast son, it could then mean that the only woman whom the Dutchman truly loves and whom he now seeks in all other women is untrue to him and will always remain so.

This unhappy man is destroyed by life as surely as his evil alter ego. But he is unable to die, so potent is his longing for the love that is denied him. He yearns for the 'angel of God' who will save him. While he himself, in his homeless wan-derings, resembles Wagner, Senta bears the features of 'Saint Rosalie'. Like brother and sister, Senta and the Dutchman bear each other's image within their hearts. Both have given their love to a being whose existence they can only suspect. When they are first ushered into each other's presence, their eyes remain locked on each other for a very long time. 'As though from distant ages past', sings the seafarer, 'this young girl's image speaks to me; just as I dreamt for anxious eons, I see it here before my eyes.'

Senta, too, has fallen hopelessly in love with a picture and now, after a long night of uncertainty, feels that 'the day of awakening' has dawned. Like the twins Siegmund and Sieglinde, they recognize each other and are united with one another even before the first word has been spoken. Like a light – thus Wagner explains this miracle – Senta's gaze penetrates the Dutchman's night and 'a flash of lightning' seems to cleave 'his tortured soul'.[117] Exactly the same will happen to Siegmund when he sees his sister's eye flash brightly in the dark-ness of Hunding's hut. It is the light of love as it recognizes its like in the chaos of existence and in the waves of the world-embracing ocean.

This moment of rediscovery contains within it the whole act of redemption inasmuch as it allows all the contradictions to be resolved. And Wagner himself later discovered in it the nature of music itself: writing from the vantage point of 1851, he claimed that it was only because of this discovery that he was able to write the music of *Der fliegende Holländer* in Paris as the music had approached him in the guise of an angel, just as Senta had approached the wandering seafarer. 'In the blood-warm night of my violently longing heart', it lent him the 'life-giving strength' to depict the images within him and present them 'to the world of day outside. Only in love can I conceive the spirit of music', he concluded.[118]

When Wagner claimed that the magical invocation of the distant beloved was the germ cell of the opera, this was true in a different sense, too: just as the lifeless image of the demon is stirred into terrible life in order to disseminate fear and death, so the same image, stirred into life by the song of yearning, could be transformed into the living, loving present. This was exactly how Wagner regarded music when it filled the 'dead' concept – the words of the libretto – with canorous life. Although this life was stirred from without, it none the less sprang from within him.[119]

Fate still has one further ordeal in store for the lovers before they are transfigured by their love. Senta's fiancé, Erik the huntsman, appears on the scene, hoping, like Max in *Der Freischütz*, to save his Agathe from the power of the black-hearted Caspar. Needless to say, his warning that 'Satan has ensnared you' goes unheard as Senta knows better. At the same time, however, Erik is right: when seen from his own standpoint, the stranger has intruded upon their love like some usurper. The Dutchman has 'bewitched' the young woman and thrown his wealth into the scales in order to win over Daland. Erik feels that he is a lover whom Satan has robbed of his bride.

What seems like a dramaturgical trick designed to force Senta to make up her mind is in fact intended to demonstrate the Dutchman's original sin – namely, the compulsive destruction of love. In this case, too, his curse seems to show that he will 'never find a true wife', because in order to follow the Dutchman, Senta has to break faith with her desperate lover. In this way she loses her angelic purity but in the process gains something far more important: out of her love for the Dutchman, she destroys the final distinction between them. Only by taking his sin upon her is she finally united with him.

In keeping with a dramatic finale, events now come thick and fast: the Dutchman, misunderstanding the confrontation between the engaged couple, believes that Senta is untrue to him and tears himself away in the hope of saving her from damnation, so much does he love her. But Senta proves that in her 'disloyalty' she is actually loyal to him by following him into damnation as he weighs anchor and sails away. Like Fenella in *La muette de Portici*, she leaps from a cliff to her death.

Scarcely has she sunk beneath the waves when she rises again, united with the Dutchman in death. Only a woman prepared to follow her lover to hell – thus the opera's message – can ascend to the heaven of love with him. According to Wagner's own stage direction, 'The Dutchman and Senta, both in transfigured form, rise out of the sea; he holds her in his embrace.' The music leaves us in no doubt that both of them perish as individuals in order to be reborn transfigured, now that they finally understand their true nature. The shrill dissonances of the spirit world slip gently into the sounds of redemption that betoken their refound humanity.

On Meyerbeer's recommendation, Wagner sent the completed score to the general intendant of the Berlin Court Theatre, Count Friedrich Wilhelm von Redern, who wrote back in March 1842 to announce that the work had been accepted for performance in the city. On 7 April, Wagner and Minna boarded the mailcoach that was to take them back to their homeland. Tears flowed in abundance as they bade farewell to Paris, and more tears flowed when they reached the Rhine and Wagner swore 'eternal fidelity' to his homeland. 'At last', he recalled, 'the hour of redemption had struck.'

Only Heine's mocking voice was heard calling after them, deriding Wagner for 'heeding the voice of reason and a full stomach and thus abandoning the dangerous project of the Paris Opéra in order to flutter away back to the German potato-land'.[120]

3 Revolution

Down the Mines

Wagner's return to Germany proved to be something of a trip down memory lane. Having fled the country in pursuit of success and having failed to find it in Paris, he now found himself back in a world he thought he had left behind him. The fame he now encountered for the first time in his life had nothing to do with the present but was due to *Rienzi*, his much earlier tribute to the Paris Opéra.

Just as a bygone world finally helped him to advance his career, so an even earlier world continued to torment him, with creditors from distant ages past arriving from all four points of the compass, keen to press for repayment of the debts he had run up in Magdeburg, Königsberg, Riga and Paris. The ghost of the past returned to haunt him and to remind him that he had incurred a burden of guilt. After paying off his old debts, he lost no time in running up new ones, greater than ever before, so that his life came to resemble one long Magdeburg hotel corridor lined with his creditors and stretching out into infinity.

Another old enemy likewise reported for duty, appearing at exactly the same time as the successful production of *Rienzi* in the form of critics who had evidently just been waiting for his return in order to sour his good fortune as an artist, his traditional *Rienzi* proving as much of a challenge to them as his revolutionary *Holländer*. His dismay at this state of affairs was such that he forgot that as a writer for the arts pages of French and German newspapers he himself had struck the superior tone that now left him mortally wounded. His violent reaction, expressed in a whole series of public statements, ensured that with the passage of time he had to contend with a veritable army of critics in whose distorting mirror he could dimly discern himself as the artistic non-entity from whom he had fled to Paris. 'I've no further wish to live in this world,' Wagner later told his second wife in connection with this curse-like mechanism for attracting misfortune, 'for wherever one stirs, ghosts rise up. The Flying Dutchman is nothing compared to me.'[1]

But the past also exercised him in the form of legends. Even while he was still in Paris, he had busied himself with the history of the Hohenstaufen emperors and, probably thanks to Heinrich Heine, had stumbled upon the old poems about Tannhäuser and the Wartburg Song Contest. Now he began to discover in the Middle Ages a reflection of his own essential nature: 'A whole new world', he later wrote, 'opened up to me in this way.' During these few brief years in Dresden, Wagner discovered the subject matter of the music dramas that were to occupy him throughout the rest of his life.

Infected by the inquiring spirit of the Brothers Grimm, whose *Deutsche Sagen* and *Deutsche Mythologie* he studied in detail, he unearthed a hidden level to existence beneath the surface of everyday life, entering a whole new world full of meaningfully mythical creatures over which towered supermen like Lohengrin and Parzival. He dug even deeper until he reached the Nibelung legend and its Old Norse variants, where he made the acquaintance of several new monsters as well as heroes like Siegmund and Siegfried. And finally he came to the deepest level of all, a level he recognized from his earliest schooldays. This was the world of Greek drama, the world of Titanic struggles and never-ending family tragedies.

Wagner lived in a permanent state of regression, a state that resembled a descent into an abandoned mine, its tunnels extending not only as far as the forgotten legacy of the 'German folk' but also to the legacy of his own particular past. The incalculable treasures he had always dreamt about lay ready for him to gather up, for the place where his origins were to be found was also the wellspring of his own creativity. The fact that, like his own Dutchman, he had to start all over again after a period of seven years was due to his own impatience. He sought to take a decision that would ensure his status once and for all and free him from all his enemies, and he lost. Just as he appeared from nowhere in 1842 as the great white hope of the German operatic scene, so he was forced to admit defeat in 1849 and go into hiding as a traitor, but at least he was now in possession of his rightful inheritance.

Wagner returned to his native Germany in April 1842 in the full expectation that his two Paris operas, *Rienzi* and *Der fliegende Holländer*, would shortly be staged in his homeland. From his carriage window he saw the Wartburg glide past him, together with what he took to be Venus's Hörselberg. For the first time in six years, he was able to embrace his mother and sisters and even his brother Julius, the 'unsuccessful goldsmith'. Only Rosalie was missing: she had died in 1837.

As so often in Wagner's life, happiness always seemed to lie elsewhere. He now wept bitter tears whenever he thought of the glamour of Paris and of the friends whom he had left there. If Minna had had any say in the matter, they would have returned there without delay. Their sense of nostalgia increased when they discovered that Count Redern's promise to stage *Der fliegende Holländer* in Berlin was hollow, having been made, as it was, at the very moment that he was on the point of relinquishing his post.

Wagner immediately travelled to Berlin in the hope of importuning Meyerbeer, but his colleague was again 'away on business'. Only the intendant in Dresden, August von Lüttichau, proved as good as his word and staged *Rienzi* at the Court Theatre at the time they had agreed on. Otherwise, Wagner was forced to admit with a certain resignation that they had not exactly been waiting for him. He could just as well have stayed in Paris, satisfying Schlesinger's need for operatic arrangements.

As a safeguard he had in fact brought some work with him from Paris: in his suitcase was Halévy's latest success, *La reine de Chypre*, of which Wagner was to produce various arrangements for his French publisher.[2] But he also had with him drafts of two music dramas of his own: the historical drama *Die Sarazenin*, set in the imaginary and ill-starred world of the Hohenstaufens, and an adaptation of E. T. A. Hoffmann's short story *Die Bergwerke zu Falun*. He later sold this second draft to the Jewish composer Josef Dessauer for two hundred francs, although in the event Dessauer made no use of it. Unlike Dessauer, who fell within Schlesinger's catchment area, Wagner knew very well what potential the draft contained. He subsequently donated it to his friend August Röckel in Dresden, but Röckel, too, declined to set the tragedy, perhaps because he felt the ending to be too sombre.

Hoffmann's *Serapionsbrüder*, from which *Die Bergwerke zu Falun* was taken, had long been one of Wagner's favourite books. Here the ending of the tale constitutes its climax, with the discovery of the body of a young man that has been preserved from decay by vitriol. His features still bear all the signs of life, and in them an old woman recognizes her fiancé Elis who had disappeared fifty years earlier on their wedding day. Overwhelmed by her former feelings, she throws herself upon her lost lover, breathing her last in a final embrace as his body turns to dust.

Wagner must have recognized in this a variant of the love-death that allows his Dutchman to be freed from his fate of not being able to die. Even the curse that affects him recurs in Hoffmann's short story, in which Elis, a sailor, goes ashore and is directed by a demonic old man to a subterranean world of magic that seems familiar to him from his boyhood. In a dream he wanders through the crystalline depths and in the midst of a magic garden discovers a wonderfully beautiful woman. The moment he awakens he falls in love with the miner's daughter Ulla, who responds to his wooing. But he then thinks that she has been unfaithful to him and returns to his mountain queen, who welcomes him with open arms. Now he is in thrall to the goddess of the underworld. On his return to the world above ground, he realizes that Ulla has not been unfaithful after all and that it was simply a misunderstanding. But on the day of their wedding, he disappears back down the mine, where a rockfall buries him alive.

The passage of time between the events outlined above and the discovery of the body and the elderly Ulla's death was difficult to depict on stage and so Wagner ended his draft with the 'terrible crash' of the explosion caused by firedamp. Although this meant the elimination of the love-death, Wagner had none the less discovered a new tragic hero in Elis, in whom the secret discord of his Dutchman, torn between satanic desire and the longing for redemption, becomes an open rift. Elis loves his blonde angel Ulla with all his heart, while all the sinews of his heart simultaneously draw him down into the depths where the queen of night yearns and waits for him. He succumbs to her blandishments all the more willingly in that, as Wagner explicitly states, he believes that he has been 'betrayed, abandoned and deceived' by Ulla.

Hoffmann had made it plain that the mountain queen is the classical goddess of love. She is the mistress of 'evil desire', in whose enchanted grotto wondrous flowers are transformed into dancing nymphs. Here, for the first time in his life, the young Elis feels a 'burning desire', the devilish mixture of 'anguish and lust' that all Wagner's heroes will savour. When the temptress addresses him with the voice of his mother, she seems utterly irresistible. Torn between two worlds and also between two irreconcilable identities, the hero is bound to perish, with Wagner deferring the time of his redemption to some unspecified date in the future.

The image of a mine in whose tunnels the coveted treasures and the beloved 'treasure' may be rediscovered is one that had exercised Wagner even before he began work on the draft. In 1840, when brooding on the nature of the true artist in the columns of Schlesinger's *Gazette musicale*, he had compared this artist to a miner digging for the 'magic jewel' of art. While virtuosos seek only the veins of gold that they can mint as ducats, true creative artists such as Mozart and Beethoven are allowed to glimpse the lustre of the wondrous gemstone whose fire pervades their senses like a sea of light and fills their hearts with 'a feeling of utter voluptuousness'.[3]

Like the artists of genius discovering the work of art in the mine shafts of the past, Elis – driven from the present by his sense of betrayal – encounters the love he has lost. But instead of heavenly beauty, he finds the hell of insatiable desire that has already driven the Dutchman to distraction. Once he has descended into Venus's night-time realm, Elis finds the death through immortality from which only an angel can redeem him.

Wagner was entirely at home in the mine whose inexhaustible veins he tapped for his various subjects. He also knew that it was ruled over by a dangerous goddess who would turn his head with a devilish drink of pain and voluptuousness, the desire for possession and the fear of loss, and, finally, jealousy and compulsive betrayal. In later life, too, he continued to be fascinated by Hoffmann's short story, the poetic conception of which struck him as 'wholly admirable'. He told Cosima that he thought it must have been influenced by Ludwig Tieck's *Der Runenberg*, 'which had made a tremendous impression on him in his youth'.[4]

The erotically obsessive nature of this subterranean realm emerges even more clearly from Tieck's fairytale narrative than it does from Hoffmann's. Here the hero, who is likewise lured underground by a messenger from hell, discovers a tall female figure in a crystalline hall who undresses before his eyes. A profusion of black hair falls over her bosom and as far as her thighs, forming a darkly billowing sea of dangling locks against which the dazzling outlines of her white body stand out like marble. Although he later marries a blonde-haired Elisabeth, the single sight of this Venus is enough for him to remain in thrall to her for ever. Whether or not Wagner discovered this soft-core pornography on the shelves of his Uncle Adolf, who, as we know, was friendly with Tieck, it is clear that he wanted to breathe new life into it in reworking *Die Bergwerke zu Falun*.

Although the project was never realized, the idea of a divided hero continued to obsess Wagner, whose new hero differs from the protagonists of traditional operas on one decisive point: unlike the heroes of the operas of Weber, Marschner and Meyerbeer, he does not simply live between two contradictory worlds but bears those two worlds within him. Two irreconcilable elements clash within his consciousness, their life-and-death struggle reflected in the action of the drama.

The actual tragedy remains invisible, taking place, as it does, within him. It is not the stage that is the scene of conflict but the hero himself. Only in this way – Wagner sensed – does the hero enter the world of reality that he experiences within him. Just as the Dutchman was both a demonic seducer and the seducer's victim and, as such, in need of redemption, so Wagner could discover in himself not only the wounds that had been dealt by Geyer but also Geyer's own features.

Wagner's life in Dresden – a city to which he was returning after a five-year absence – took place on two different levels, each of which ran counter to the other. He re-established a harmonious relationship with his family in Leipzig, although, as usual, they were required to lend him a helping hand financially. He also visited his brother Albert in Halle and warmed to the gifts of the latter's adopted daughter Johanna, who had recently embarked on a career as a singer. And he even renewed contact with some of the Dresden friends of his late step-father, generally carrying on as though he had never been away. During the rehearsals for *Rienzi*, he helped as he had done in his distant days as a Kapellmeister, preparing his singers for their roles, while at the same time thinking about his drama of the future, of which no one else had the slightest inkling as yet.

His old flame Wilhelmine Schröder-Devrient likewise re-entered his life. Now thirty-seven years old and no longer the sylphlike figure of her youth, she had declared her willingness to take on the trouser role of Adriano in *Rienzi*. For the title role, the metallic-voiced tenor Joseph Tichatschek offered his services, his chief interest in the part being the silver armour that he had specially made at his own expense. It cost four hundred thalers – more than a quarter of the annual income of Dresden's assistant conductor.

Wagner rehearsed *Rienzi* with the chorus master Wilhelm Fischer on an old piano in the rehearsal room at the Court Theatre. Fischer, who was the only member of the company to believe in the opera's future, spent most of the time keeping an anxious eye on his watch: the tale of the last of the Roman tribunes was proving worryingly time-consuming. Once the rehearsals were over, Wagner and Minna would repair arm in arm to 'Papa' Fischer's house where they demonstrated the truth of Heine's prophecy, generally fortifying themselves on potatoes and pickled herring.

The opera opened on 20 October 1842 and lasted a legendary six hours. Wagner watched in 'total perplexity' as the audience remained in their seats until midnight, then accorded him a thunderous final ovation. The next morning he modestly offered to cut the opera to a more reasonable length, but his offer was indignantly rejected by all concerned: the music was simply 'too heavenly'.

In the presence of his family, who had come to Dresden by train, the composer enjoyed the first operatic triumph of his life. A friend reported that he spent the intervals wandering round the theatre like some lost shade, half weeping and half laughing, and throwing himself into the arms of everyone he encountered, while 'cold sweat' dripped from his brow.[5] 'Success! Success!' Wagner exulted in a letter to Paris. 'The whole city was in uproar, there was a veritable revolution.' He had been 'tumultuously' called out four times in front of the curtain and had been assured that 'there was no comparison between my own *Rienzi* and Meyerbeer's success with the local production of *Les Huguenots*'.[6]

Not yet thirty, Wagner had finally made a name for himself. Unfortunately, the opera belonged to a period in his life that was no longer of any real interest to him as a composer. And there was no sign of any of the fortune that regularly overwhelmed Meyerbeer after each of *his* successes. Lüttichau offered him three hundred thalers by way of a fee, but his debts in Magdeburg alone, of which he was now reminded as a result of legal action, amounted to more than twice that figure.

The success of *Rienzi* remained very much the exception in Wagner's career as a composer, and it was to be decades before he enjoyed another one like it. By the same token, the idea that there was money to be made in grand opera was shown to be an illusion. Yet besides consolidating his burgeoning fame, the work proved to have another, wholly unexpected consequence: instead of proclaiming a musical revolution, the declared enemy of traditional theatrical practices accepted a permanent appointment as Kapellmeister to the Royal Court of Saxony and agreed to conduct a familiar repertory at the ultraconservative Dresden Court Theatre.

His salary was a modest fifteen hundred thalers a year, a sum that pales into insignificance beside the massive debts of twenty thousand thalers that he had amassed by the time he fled from his post and the city in 1849. For a composer like Meyerbeer, Wagner was all too well aware, such a sum was no more than a trifle: thanks to *Robert le diable* and *Les Huguenots*, his rival was able to pocket three times that amount each year. On the other hand, the Dresden Court offered its new conductor a contract for life, and there was always the chance that his salary would be increased.

Meanwhile, Wagner's art went its own way. He had descended into the mine and was now exploring all the old tunnels. While his examination of the past was not without its pleasures, he also felt drawn to the place where his mother had once sought Geyer's protection shortly after his birth: he must have known about the mysterious episode that had occurred in Teplitz almost thirty years earlier. Now he met his mother in the Bohemian resort where she was in the habit of taking the waters each year. This time he took Minna and her sister with him and reforged the family ties that had long since begun to loosen.

For five weeks they lived alongside each other, the younger generation some-what outside the town, above a stables, while Johanna Rosine herself was 'frightfully elegantly' lodged at the Blue Angel overlooking the main road. It was no doubt here that her son told her one evening about a subject that was now exercising him. On Johanna Rosine, too, it clearly left its mark, as she com-plained the next morning that she had been 'too agitated to sleep a wink all night'.

The story in question was the legend of the minnesinger Tannhäuser who disappears into the Venusberg, never to be seen again. With this story in his rucksack, Wagner set off to climb the various peaks in the area, recovering his strength at night on a bed of straw. At full moon he could be seen at Burg Schreckenstein, wrapped in a white sheet, like some ghostly apparition, instill-ing fear in all who saw him there. In the castle ruins overlooking the Elbe – famously captured by Adrian Ludwig Richter in one of his canvases – Wagner also jotted down the prose draft for a three-act opera.

Although it told the story of the singer, its title was that of the sinister moun-tain to which he owed his fame. While the piece continued to grow in Wagner's notebook, the surrounding area provided him with all the ideas he needed. On hearing a shepherd's lively tune, he saw in his mind's eye a chorus of pilgrims passing through the valley, and in the sensually saccharine painting of the Madonna in the local parish church he recognized his own Elisabeth in the glimmer of the votive candles. By the time he returned to his family, *Der Venusberg* was fully drafted.

In the wake of his summer break, to which he owed an important creative impulse, Wagner allowed himself to be provoked into a curious outburst against his mother: in a letter to Cäcilie Avenarius written shortly before their mother's sixty-fourth birthday, he described her as a stranger against whom he evidently felt he had to warn his sister. 'You have to admit that within our family', he wrote, 'she creates nothing but trouble because of her remarkable predilection for misrepresenting and distorting everything and for indulging in endless gossip, with the result that all our other brothers and sisters avoid her like the plague.' He was 'revolted' by her 'deeply offensive avarice and egoism', and as for her 'utter lack of principle' and 'want of cleanliness', he simply pre-ferred not to go into detail. In short, 'our dear mama is utter hell for everyone around her'. If Cäcilie found this too 'harsh', she should ask herself 'whether there is any point in continuing to delude ourselves any longer'.[7]

But what was the point of this litany of complaints, which reads like an act of blind revenge? Was Wagner envious that during their weeks together in Teplitz his elderly mother had more money than he did and that, unlike him, she was leading an 'extremely comfortable' existence? Did he take it amiss that she had argued with Minna because the latter was no longer prepared to be treated as a servant girl? Or perhaps his lapse had less to do with these typical family squabbles than with the subject on which he was currently working, for the road to the Venusberg of which he dreamt in the neighbourhood of Teplitz also led to the remote fastnesses of maternal love from which he had been excluded in the distant past. He recalled the forbidden joys of childhood and also their hideous end, an end followed by lifelong exile.

Had Johanna Rosine made common cause with the usurper, just as Gertrude had done with Hamlet's uncle? Wagner had once loved her, but by betraying her son she had not only become the wicked mother, she had also assumed all the characteristics that distinguished her accomplice, his enemy. Only now, as he worked feverishly on the creation of a myth from which his Tannhäuser was to emerge as a betrayed betrayer, was the maternal archetype so distorted as to assume a recognizable identity as the woman who created the chaos in which love was stifled. Like the lord of lies, she misrepresented and distorted everything. She hoarded money that she refused to share with anyone else. And when her son tried to show her kindness, she had nothing but egoism to offer in return.

Is it surprising, then, that she is said to have revealed the 'very real dirtiness' that Wagner normally imputed to the Jews and to the Nibelungs who lived underground?[8] Even the fact that she made life 'utter hell' for everyone around her fitted in with the mythical archetype, for, as Tannhäuser was to be told by the pope in person, the 'fires of hell' were to be found in the maternal warmth of the Venusberg. Even if Wagner was not aware of this connection, he none the less obeyed the logic of myth in behaving as he did, a logic that he had discovered deep down within himself. And just as his theory of art demanded, he now depicted that logic in the work of art.

Evidently logic also demanded that, in order to begin work on the composition of his opera, he would have to return to this same place a year later. And once again he took his gout-ridden mother with him, carrying on for all the world as though he had not written his hateful letter of ten months previously. On this occasion, he was also accompanied by his sister Klara. As before, he and Minna stayed in their rustic guest house, where he tried out the seductive sounds of the Venusberg on the piano that he had hired for the purpose, while drinking large quantities of the local spa water in an attempt to alleviate the abdominal complaints from which he was suffering. Soon he was able to return to the mine of the past in which he once again discovered his own story among the folk myths that he found there.

His holiday reading this year included Jacob Grimm's *Deutsche Mythologie*, in which he found a fragmentary account of the legend of his hero Tannhäuser. The pagan goddess Holda, who was equated with the figure of Venus only at a later date, is said to have dwelt in the Hörselberg near Eisenach, together with her court, where they all led 'lives as grand and magnificent as dwarf kings'. Only a few mortals such as the 'noble Tanhäuser' were allowed to live with her 'in joy', but the Church had called him to account in consequence. This tale, Wagner could have read in Grimm, was 'one of the most attractive legends of the Middle Ages, with its moving account of the yearning for ancient paganism and the strictness of the Christian clergy'.

Alongside Tannhäuser, a whole army of mythological creatures of heroic, ghostly and godlike provenance now began to make themselves at home in the mansion of his imagination. Writing in *My Life*, he recalled that during this second visit to Teplitz he discovered in the 'most pitiful fragments of a lost world, as conserved by Jacob Grimm', the clear outlines of the figures for whom his febrile imagination longed. The legendary past was a quarry in whose labyrinthine fissures he was 'held in thrall by a wonderful spell', much as his hero Elis had been.

It was a mine of hidden jewels, a wondrous world cut off from the daylight. Here he felt at home: here, it seemed, was his true habitat. Everything, including even the most fragmentary tradition, spoke to him 'in a profoundly familiar tongue and soon my entire sensibility was captivated by ideas that led me increasingly to sense a way of regaining possession of a consciousness which, long lost, I had always been seeking to rediscover'.

This encounter with the world of Germanic legends became a voyage of self-discovery. Here he rediscovered that part of himself that had gone missing and that now miraculously reappeared like some lost heirloom. Now that he had recovered possession of this lost world through what seemed to him to be a process of ecstatic self-revelation, he was able to gain access to the archetypal kingdom of his future dramas. It was his own kingdom. The figures who set foot on stage as independent creatures were the products of his own inner world.

And yet, as he discovered to his astonishment, this world was part of a historical tradition stretching back into the distant past. 'Before my mind's eye there rose up a whole world of figures that proved so unexpectedly vivid and so intimately related on their most basic level that, seeing them clearly before me and hearing their language within me, I could not understand why they seemed almost tangibly familiar and why they appeared so self-assured in the way in which they behaved.'

During the weeks that Wagner spent seeing his family on a daily basis and coming to the sad realization that the local spring water would not help his intestinal complaint, he discovered the source of his own creative powers, and what is more he knew that he had done so. As though by a miracle he had glimpsed in crystalline clarity a world whose figures seemed to him to be 'intimately related on their most basic level', a world, moreover, 'in which I had until now moved blindly and merely presciently, like a child in its mother's womb'. In *My Life*, Wagner described this epiphany as a 'complete rebirth'.[9]

Tannhäuser

It had been purely by chance – Wagner reported in *My Life* – that he had come across 'the chapbook about the "Venusberg"' towards the end of his stay in Paris. Here he had stumbled upon the legendary character of Tannhäuser. The vagueness of his description suggests he had something to hide. There is, after all, no 'chapbook' of this title, but rather a detailed reworking of the subject by Heinrich Heine that Wagner had discovered in *Der Salon*, the journal that had already provided him with the idea of *Der fliegende Holländer*. Here, in his disquisition on 'elemental spirits', Heine not only quotes the sources on which his own view of Tannhäuser was based, he even adds his own poetic account of the subject, striking a wilfully anachronistic note by incorporating a number of autobiographical elements.

Heine, too, had recognized himself in his hapless hero. When the folktale collector Ludwig Bechstein had asked him in 1835 whether he would ever return to Germany from his exile in France, Heine had responded with a wistful smile: 'I am the Tannhäuser who is held prisoner in the Venusberg; the magic spell won't let me go.'[10] It was the magic of the city that held him captive, but also the spell woven by his lover Mathilde Mirat, who was later to become his wife.

If in his poem Heine/Tannhäuser abandons his beautiful Venus of the Montparnasse in keeping with the legend, it is in part because he is jealous of the many 'gods and heroes' who have worshipped her lily-white body. As a result, his desperate attempt to persuade the pope to free him from her magic power is bound to fail. Venus, after all, is more powerful than any pope. Condemned to the eternal torments of hell, Heine's Tannhäuser returns ruefully to the Venusberg, where the goddess revives him with a bowl of nourishing soup.

Wagner seems to have interpreted this tale in a somewhat different fashion. If he too felt that he was held captive in the Paris Venusberg, it was not because of love but as a result of material need, a state from which he sought to break free with all the means in his power. On reading the tale, he later reported, he felt the 'liveliest' desire to return to Germany as soon as he was able. Thanks to the legendary subject matter, he now became aware of the German Middle Ages, that deadly earnest age in which art and humanity were still believed to flourish. 'A new world had opened up to me here', he wrote, imagining the Germany from which he had fled on account of his debts and painting a portrait of it in the boldest conceivable colours. It was curiously apt that on his subsequent return to the country, he saw the Wartburg rising up in front of him and alongside it the mountain in which Frau Venus herself had held court.

In this Wagner went further than Heine, for neither in the latter's version of the legend nor in the old ballad on which he had relied is the Wartburg mentioned by name. But the Wartburg suited Wagner's concept admirably. Just as Tannhäuser struck him as a pre-eminently German hero fleeing from the hotbed of vice of the modern world, so the Wartburg was regarded as the epitome of unadulterated German history. From Landgrave Hermann's election of the Hohenstaufen Friedrich II as king of Germany and Saint Elizabeth's working of miracles with her self-sacrifices to Martin Luther's translation of the New Testament, the Wartburg embodied a sublime strand in the country's history, a tradition to which an emotional tribute had been paid as recently as the Wartburg Festival of 1817.

For Wagner, the castle meant even more than this. Hard though it was for him to believe, his own mother had named a Weimar prince as her 'high-born fatherly friend', suggesting that in some indefinable way her son was related to the house of Saxe-Weimar, and as the successors of the legendary landgrave and his thaumaturgic niece, this dynasty had now come into possession of the Wartburg. Indeed, Johanna Rosine's lovesick prince, Constantin, had once spent a memorable night there with Goethe in 1778. When Wagner returned home to Germany and discovered his historical self, he saw in the minnesingers' castle what was effectively the country's holy of holies – and in a certain sense he could even regard it as his rightful inheritance.

As for the Wartburg Song Contest, to which Landgrave Hermann invited the leading minnesingers of his day, including Walther von der Vogelweide, Wolfram von Eschenbach and Heinrich von Ofterdingen, Wagner was fully in the picture. Of the various versions familiar to him, the best known was undoubtedly that of E. T. A. Hoffmann, whose *Serapionsbrüder* tells how the lovelorn troubadour, his songs inspired by the demon Klingsohr, descends into hell, while his rival Wolfframb wins the fair Mathilde with his God-fearing songs. Wagner claims to have found the story 'thoroughly garbled' in this version, preferring the hypothesis advanced in a scholarly study by Christian Theodor Ludwig Lucas of Königsberg, according to which Heinrich von Ofterdingen, in league with the devil, was none other than the minnesinger Heinrich Tannhäuser. Unsuspected perspectives were opened up in this way.

The first steps in this direction had been taken by Ludwig Bechstein. The first volume of his collection of Thuringian legends – published in 1835, the same year as his meeting with Heine in which the latter had compared himself with Tannhäuser – includes an account of the well-known story of the noble knight who visits Frau Venus in the 'Hörseelenberg'. Driven by feelings of remorse, he abandons her after a year and repairs to Rome in order to obtain absolution from Pope Urban IV. But as Bechstein stresses, the latter was himself not free from carnal desire, quite apart from the fact that he was an enemy of the Hohenstaufens, and so he condemned his German supplicant to eternal damnation: Tannhäuser would not find mercy in God's eyes until the lifeless stick in his hand put forth green leaves. Scarcely had the despairing hero departed when the papal crozier began to sprout leaves. But by now Tannhäuser had already descended into the Venusberg through 'the gates of hell'.

In Bechstein's collection this tale was immediately followed by one that he titled 'Der Sängerkrieg auf Wartburg' – 'The Wartburg Song Contest': criticized by the other singers, Heinrich von Ofterdingen is defeated in the contest, but the landgravine defends him against his enemies. Bechstein does not suggest that the landgravine is identical with Saint Elizabeth, but the tale of the minnesinger's troubles is followed by his account of the legend of the auxiliary saint who, prior to her premature death, devotes herself to good works, thereby allowing the mythical connection to be forged as though of its own accord.

For Wagner, everything depended on this link, as his new opera would hardly have filled a whole evening if it had involved no more than the tragicomic love story of Tannhäuser and Venus. Although it combines the life's puzzle of the Dutchman, who is tormented by his insatiable desire for love, with that of Elis, for whom this torment is revealed in the horribly fascinating world underground, it fails to account for the heroes' misfortune. Why are they spirited away from the world? Who robs them of all 'rest and peace'? What exactly is the true nature of the curse that brands them as outlaws and outsiders? The 'sins of the flesh' are in themselves insufficient to explain this. Wagner was convinced that 'only by merging the Tannhäuser legend with that of the Wartburg Song Contest' could he provide an answer to this problem.[11]

The festival of song that took place at Hermann's court in the early thirteenth century may have been merely one of many such festivals, but in the poetic versions of Hoffmann, Bechstein and the Brothers Grimm the stakes are increased in no uncertain manner. What is involved here is not simply art but, as in Meyerbeer's *Robert le diable*, the hand of a woman in marriage, with the winner in the song contest claiming a wife as first prize, while the loser is put to the sword. The musical trial of strength has thus become a battle of life and death. The contestants are no longer concerned with finding the right tune but with love, inheritance and the propagation of the species. Only the fittest will survive, while the rest will perish without trace.

According to tradition, Heinrich von Ofterdingen – in whom Wagner saw his own Tannhäuser – stood alone against the world. He had been isolated because of his refusal to sing according to certain prescribed rules: instead, his singing was unconventional and prompted by the exuberance of his emotions, transgressing the rules to such an extent that he was even suspected of sorcery. According to Bechstein, Heinrich had also written the *Nibelungenlied* (thereby underlining his superiority), while according to another source he had taken part in one of Friedrich II's crusades. But society was against him.

Moreover, if we may believe the tradition that Heinrich von Ofterdingen hailed from Eisenach, then it is impossible to avoid a comparison with the 'Ghibelline' Rienzi. As a simple Roman citizen, Rienzi, too, had to face the superior might of the aristocrats who deceived, betrayed and finally destroyed him. Tannhäuser, in whom Wagner saw 'the spirit of the whole Ghibelline race for all time',[12] presents himself at the Wartburg in order to lay claim to his Hohenstaufen legacy, but instead he is treacherously destroyed by the powers that be.

This leads ineluctably to the Venusberg, for this struggle, which sounds like an abridged version of the second act of *Tannhäuser*, is in fact an integral part of its prehistory. The fatal conflict whose outcome is decided by an act of betrayal is the actual reason for the sufferings not only of the Dutchman but of Elis and Tannhäuser, too. It is the brutal loss of both lover and legacy and hence exile from Eden that condemns the individual to a life of endless wandering. And this life acquires such desperate features because every attempt to regain the lost Paradise is bound to revive the old trauma.

In each case, the hero hopes to discover the love that he longs for, only to find himself deceived and betrayed. Or else he himself is guilty of an act of deceit and betrayal each time the gates of an even more tempting Garden of Eden seem to open. This garden of delights offers the brief illusion of happiness and is discovered every seven years by the Dutchman on the coasts of the world's oceans, while Elis finds it in the glittering depths of the mine. For his part, Tannhäuser – likewise for a period of seven years – enters the enchanted realm of the goddess of love herself. Thanks to Wagner's music, the public is able to follow him there, ignorant of the story's sad prehistory and immediately held captive by the overture's gently enticing music, which then strikes a note of greater yearning, before finally inflaming our senses as it whips itself up to a climax.

Just as the hero breaks free from the confining constraints of the world, so the music that conjures him into existence breaks down the rules that usually govern composition. Here the music becomes a medium for the ideas that it expresses. Music was now to be a language, no more and no less, with Wagner even wanting the winds to play the opening theme 'as though they have words to express to it'.[13] And he left a detailed account of the inner vision that is meant to accompany the music. At the start of the overture, he wrote in 1852, the orchestra plays the Pilgrims' Chorus, but this is soon swept away by 'sounds of sensual jubilation' that rise up from the rosy mists. The hero appears at the centre of a 'horribly voluptuous dance', a slim, manly figure who sings his proudly jubilant love song.

Tannhäuser's invocation is answered by maenads with cries of wild exultation. Entrancing perfumes – these too depicted in sounds – envelop him, until finally the naked form of Venus appears in a particularly seductive pose. With her siren call, she bids him sit on a downy pillow, where – as Wagner's music makes plain – she offers to 'satisy the bold knight's wildest desires'. He has barely completed a single strophe of his 'jubilant love song' when the wondrous world of the Venusberg opens up before him in its entirety.

The goddess invites the doughty champion to sink down into 'the realm of non-being'. Already the Wild Hunt races through the mist-enshrouded grotto, and now only a 'horribly wanton whir' still pulses in the air 'like the breath of unblessed desire'. There is a sound of groaning and sighing in the Venusberg, as though the horrors of the Wolf's Glen have returned, albeit in different circumstances. After a brief eternity of sinful self-oblivion, the chorus of worthy pilgrims again becomes audible with the first light of dawn.

The 'eerie sounds of souls condemned in the Venusberg' now assume a more joyful note, as the sun at last rises in all its splendour and, in Wagner's words, the billowing waves of sound become 'the joyful frenzy of hearts inflamed by a feeling of the sublime'. This jubilation unfolds alongside the pilgrims' pious chorus, expressing the joy of 'the Venusberg itself, redeemed from the curse of impiousness', and even the infamous underworld, the composer insisted, is redeemed by the morning sun. Normally sharply divided, the two elements of 'spirit and senses, God and nature' fervently embrace and 'unite in love's hallowed kiss'.[14]

Although Wagner had revealed the plot's inner logic from the very beginning, it remained lost on his audience, only his mistress Mathilde Wesendonck later realizing that in the overture the composer had appeared as an impassioned preacher 'inveighing against the sin of hypocrisy'.[15] But the majority of spectators saw only that the sorrowful hero was redeemed. His release from the jaws of this hell of wanton delights was ascribed to Saint Elizabeth's assiduous prayers and even to the might of the Catholic Church.

No one noticed that at the end of the opera this hell of wanton delights was redeemed at the same time as the poor sinner. Wagner's aim of appealing to his audience not only through their feelings but through their thoughts as well had not been achieved. He repeatedly subjected the work to substantial revision, each time bringing it into line with the latest developments in his compositional technique and appearing to spend his whole life labouring away at the piece. Shortly before his death he told Cosima that he 'still owed the world *Tannhäuser*'.[16]

But he had provided the world with an inside view of the legendary Venusberg from the moment the curtain rises. This was a challenge that had attracted poets from classical antiquity onwards: just as the nymph Calypso had held Tannhäuser's predecessor Odysseus captive for seven long years in a secluded, sea-girt grotto, so Grimm, in his *Deutsche Mythologie*, describes the Venusberg as an underground cavern where folk could live at length and 'in joy'. Seductive witches would appear here, 'leaping and dancing'.

In his Baroque book on witchcraft, *Blockes-Berges Verrichtung*, Johannes Praetorius ventured the view that Venus dwelt in 'large and admirable vaults and caverns' and that she used a carriage drawn by swans and doves to move from place to place. As soon as she alighted from the vehicle and showed herself, 'her movement appeared like the fairest and brightest star'. But the author was unwilling to commit himself: after all, he wondered, who could know 'what a devilish cave' the place might ultimately be.

Among the plays that the young Wagner had seen on stage, enchanted caves of vice gaped open in awesome profusion, with E. T. A. Hoffmann's musical sprite Undine, for example, dwelling in the crimson glow of crystalline vaults through whose golden trees the stars twinkle down, while not far away we find Marschner's subterranean palace ruled over by the queen of the earth spirits, its vaulted rooms flashing with red. From here her pallid son, Hans Heiling, sets out in search of a mortal lover.

In his play *Sappho*, Franz Grillparzer describes a rose-clad grotto, with an altar dedicated to Venus and an inviting grassy bank. The young Wagner had once been allowed to set foot on this bank when, under Geyer's tutelage, he had been harnessed to the triumphal chariot by Sappho's lover Phaon when the latter is impelled to return home and quit the embrace of his singing Circe. Just as Sappho tunes her harp to songs of love and bids her lover attend 'love's celebration', so Tieck's Tannenhäuser is lured into the 'mine' of delights by the strains of lovely music. Here, banished from the world of day, the gods rule in a hall adorned with flowers, Frau Venus at their head. As soon as she rouses her visitors to wild and lascivious desire, the flowers become young women whose naked bodies breathe the enchantment of springtime blossoms.

Nothing escaped Wagner's attention, just as nothing escapes Tannhäuser's. All the charms of the underworld, from the celestial sounds of the crystalline vaults to the assembly of classical gods and the beautiful dance of the nymphs, have been taken over into his Venusberg, a stage vision of superlatives which, over the years and in the course of many productions, was to become a universal depiction of eroticism at its most sensual.

In the prose draft prepared in the castle grounds at Burg Schreckenstein, the grotto was filled with 'half-naked young women',[17] whereas in the 'Dresden version' of the score, a procession of Dionysus's ecstatic acolytes disrupts the idyllic scene. In the 'Paris version' these bloodthirsty bacchantes drive a black ram before them, which a priest of Satan butchers 'to the accompaniment of dreadful gestures'. Following the orgiastic climax of this Witches' Sabbath, in which the couples unite 'in the liveliest contrasts, wildly, with no distinction',[18] the gods of Olympus appear in a roseate glow accompanied by the gentle susurration of the singing of distant sirens.

There follows a series of scenes from Zeus's secret love life. In the guise of a bull he abducts the virginal Europa who, entrusting herself to fate, holds fast to his brandished horn. Then, disguised as a swan, he forces himself on the recumbent Leda, stretching his neck, which the naked woman bends towards her to caress, then coupling with her mortal form before Tannhäuser's astonished gaze.[19]

As in the dumb show in *Rienzi*, with its depiction of the rape of Lucretia, so here too Wagner portrays the nub of the action in silent images interpreted only by the music in the pit. For the world into which Tannhäuser descends is obscene: the mysteries of these couplings have no place in the light of day, while the excesses to which the hero abandons himself obey no law save that of pleasure, a pleasure which, like the Bacchanal itself, indulges in ever greater excesses. Although this pursuit of pleasure frees him from his hated self, it can offer him nothing in its place. The hero is lost in a whirl of desire. From the frenzy of self-oblivion there arise only phantasms of his insatiable longing. What Tannhäuser has lost cannot be found in the entrails of the earth.

But Hans Mayer was doubly wrong to compare the Venusberg with a *paradis artificiel*. In first describing this phenomenon, Charles Baudelaire had meant not sexuality but the imaginary worlds of a drug-induced intoxication produced by opium and hashish. Within Venus's realm, only the visions conjured up by Tannhäuser's lust are artificial, but their nucleus – sexuality – is entirely real, making the actuality of the Wartburg seem a *réalité artificielle* in comparison.

This home of God-given order had been the hero's abode before his descent into the realm of very real desire. In the traditional contest between rival poets, we discover in retrospect, he had fared much as the composer himself had done: he had proved to be a better singer and had inflamed the young Elisabeth with his love song, yet victory and lover had been snatched from his grasp. The breakdown of her relationship with Tannhäuser may well have been due to her paternal uncle, the Landgrave.

Robbed of his prize and his bride, Tannhäuser leaves the castle. Although the Landgrave later describes him as 'arrogantly proud', his heart is in fact broken. The behaviour of these aristocratic rulers strikes him as an act of betrayal, driving him out into the world and a life of restless wanderings. Like his predecessors, he soon enters an accursed world, hoping to find his lost happiness in the mine shafts of the past in which Elis has already discovered the consolation of the disinherited.

It is at this point that the actual drama begins: Tannhäuser wakes up from the timeless state into which the Venusberg's spiral of desire has led him, and, figuratively speaking, he looks at his watch. He is lying with a woman whose love – it transpires – he won with his irresistible singing, just as he had once won Elisabeth's love. But enough is enough, he now finds, and without further ado he tells Venus that he has to leave her.

The reasons that he gives are no worse than those of any other Don Juan when abandoning a woman. He feels homesick, he says, he longs for change. Venus sees through his excuses and, not inappropriately, calls him a 'traitor' and a 'hypocrite'. When her spoilt guest further reproaches her for condemning him to slavery, she curses him, and in prophesying that he will return to her 'crushed' she proves an accurate judge of men. But like her hounded lover, she too will be reduced to a state of despair by her lovelorn desire.

At first glance, Tannhäuser's decision to leave seems morally motivated – the result of his resolve to abandon the Venusberg's world of vice. But the truth of the matter is that he merely perpetuates this world in reality. At the very moment that he repudiates his lover, he is already calling out the name of another: 'My salvation lies in Mary.' Following the first performance of the opera, the waggish reviewer of Schumann's *Neue Zeitschrift* noted that members of the audience had involuntarily glanced at their programmes at this point 'to find out who this Mary' was.

The joke was spot on. 'The fact that the Blessed Virgin is meant', the reviewer went on, 'we can only surmise from the following scene. The name of Elisabeth, as that of his lover, is the more obvious one for him to remember.'[20] Wagner, too, had conceded that his hero 'turned from Venus to Mary without having been inspired to do so by any great sense of piety'. In the Mother of God, Tannhäuser had in fact seen the virginal Elisabeth. And here, it later emerges, he finds the change of scene that he is looking for.

This act of betrayal on the part of the minnesinger who seeks to justify his need for a change of partner is mirrored in fact by his lover's infidelity, an infidelity of which he has been conscious from the very outset, inasmuch as the goddess Venus is polygamous by nature, her relationship with a mortal representing an exception in the life of a woman famous as the playgirl of the gods. In his song in praise of her, Tannhäuser admits that she has allowed him to taste 'the ardour of the gods'. Her supreme lover, Zeus, occasionally looks in on her grotto.

The lurking threat posed by the father of the gods has already been made clear to Tannhäuser in the prelude, where we see Zeus assuming animal shapes in order to ravish virgins. To impregnate Leda, he plumes himself in foreign feathers, seeking out his defenceless prey in the form of a vulture-like bird. Tannhäuser flees from the arms of Venus just as he flees the man whom she had embraced before him.

Scarcely has the name 'Mary' rung out when the world of Venus collapses 'with a terrible crash', just as the mines at Falun had once done and as Klingsor's magic garden will do later. Accompanied by the sounds of a shawm, Tannhäuser finds himself in a pleasantly wooded valley overlooked – by no means fortuitously – by the distant Wartburg, and it is not long before the minnesingers who had driven him away from there appear in hunting pink. The Landgrave rebukes him for his 'hostile' absence, after which the others ask him what he has been up to.

Tannhäuser can scarcely tell them about his intimate adventures, and so the trap is already laid in which he will later be caught. The knights reluctantly admit that he has won Elisabeth's heart with his singing, the Landgrave even speaking of a 'magic spell' that he has cast on her and that he, the Landgrave, now means to break with God's help. In short, the pale virgin is lovesick and only the man whom she worships can cure her. The Landgrave now seems to scent his chance, for there is no doubt that the dark secret that allows Tannhäuser to exercise power over his niece is bound up with the mystery of his long absence. He now hopes to wrest that secret from him.

When Tannhäuser's rival Wolfram von Eschenbach takes him to see Elisabeth in Act Two, happiness seems to beckon. In a scene that looks forward to

Götterdämmerung, one woman effortlessly replaces another in the hero's affections. Tannhäuser has now achieved all that he set out to achieve. Venus has been dealt with and forgotten, just as will later happen to Brünnhilde. With her outburst of 'Sei mir gegrüßt', Elisabeth reveals herself as Rosalie's true successor.

He sinks to his knees and, in the prose draft, the virginal Elisabeth, overwhelmed, recognizes him as the true ruler: 'In these rooms you are king.' But of course her uncle is the true king, and once again inevitable conflict ensues. The other singers are no threat to Tannhäuser – on this point they differ from the Landgrave, whose authority has been challenged and who, in his cunning, now threatens to destroy the unsuspecting singer whose tongue is loosened by his happiness in love.

Hermann calls for a song contest in which the competitors, naturally enough, are to define the nature of love. Its judge is to be Elisabeth, who simultaneously finds herself on offer as first prize. Since she has already confessed her love for Tannhäuser, this seems a mere formality that has the additional advantage of allowing the other singers to show off their splendid voices. But the truth of the matter is that the Landgrave is keen to find out more about Tannhäuser's secret past.

'Whatever may have brought him back,' the Landgrave says quite openly, 'it seems to me a wondrous mystery; to us you shall reveal it through the art of song.' In this way, he imperceptibly manoeuvres the hero onto the horns of a tragic dilemma, forcing him, for his lover's sake, to reveal the secret of the love with which he has cast his spell on her. That this secret is not fit for another's ears does not occur to the ebullient Tannhäuser. By forcing the singer to betray the true nature of his love, the Landgrave simultaneously betrays that love, which is exactly what he wants to do. Like Hagen in *Götterdämmerung*, he calls out: 'Sing then, hero.' And like Siegfried in years to come, Tannhäuser forfeits both life and love.

Encouraged by Elisabeth's applause and by the amateurishness of his rivals, Tannhäuser begins by offering the odd hint on the art of seduction, then, provoked by their violent resistance, he reveals the mystery of the art of sensual love, his revelation culminating ineluctably in his song in praise of the goddess Venus, whom he invites his 'wretched' rivals to visit with all despatch: 'Be gone, be gone to the Mount of Venus!'

Faster than Tannhäuser can think, the trap has closed around him. It is as though he has been asked what it is that he finds so lovable about his lover and has answered: 'Women in general'. In his ardour, his song, which should have been no more than a private confession of his love of Elisabeth, has become a song in praise of love in its most general terms.

But love in general is sex, and any song in praise of such love must inevitably be directed at the goddess Venus. In rising to the challenge, the minnesinger has given himself away, exposing himself as a Don Juan for whom every woman, be she Venus or Elisabeth, holds out exactly the same charms. At the same time he betrays not only the virginal Elisabeth, against whom he was playing off her rival in the Venusberg, but also, and in the same breath, Venus herself, whom he commends to all the menfolk present as an object that they can use. The same tragic misfortune will later befall the hero Siegfried, when he exchanges his wife Brünnhilde for another woman and, moments later, places her in a new suitor's marriage bed. On this later occasion, it is a potion that is to blame.

Tannhäuser is unmasked, and the result is a public outcry. Unimpressed by the dialectical niceties of universality and individuality, the minnesingers bare their swords, planning to kill the miscreant there and then. This, after all, is the Middle Ages. The Landgrave, whose plan has turned out exactly as he had wanted, adds to the tension of the situation by angrily reproaching the curse-laden sinner for the 'mask of hypocrisy' with which he has infiltrated the virtuous world of the Wartburg. The truth of the matter is that it is Hermann himself who has been wearing this mask. Behind his indignation lies the satisfied knowledge that he has disposed of the upstart pretender with a clear conscience. Meanwhile, Tannhäuser finds himself back in the nightmare world from which he had once fled to Venus. This time there is no way out.

And it is because of Elisabeth that the way out is barred. Trampled underfoot, she shows herself steadfast. Like all the heroines cast in Rosalie's mould, she stakes her life on saving the lover to whom she feels bound by sibling bonds. First she fearlessly throws herself in front of the drawn swords and then she shields Tannhäuser 'with her body' as though providing a silent commentary on his earlier remarks.

Finally she adopts the tone of the age and begs that Tannhäuser may be allowed to prove himself and seek his salvation through Christian exercises. A party of pilgrims is just setting out for Rome, and so he is advised to seek out the pope and ascertain God's view of his sinful status. If this turns out not to be what they want to hear, their swords will do the rest. 'To Rome!' Tannhäuser exclaims, staggering from one world to another as though in a dream. 'To Rome!' call out the Landgrave and the supporters of the song contest, thus washing their hands of the whole problematical affair.

By the start of the final act, the situation has resolved itself for the world of Wartburg society, whereas for the three main characters it has deteriorated markedly: the betrayed goddess Venus longs insatiably for her human lover; Tannhäuser suffers, as before, because his life has been destroyed by betrayal, a feeling compounded by the certainty that he has destroyed another's life through his betrayal. But as Wagner indicates, it is Elisabeth who suffers most of all. It is not her lover's immorality that drives her to despair, as this is something between him and God, but her suppressed jealousy of another woman, coupled with a feeling that causes her the most intense distress. Once it has been stirred by Tannhäuser's voice, her sensuality can no longer be satisfied. The love that was praised by Tannhäuser she now feels for herself but is not allowed to express it.

The situation seems hopeless. The overture had promised redemption, but how can all three characters achieve it? Certainly not in Rome, where Tannhäuser, begging forgiveness from the Guelph pope, encounters the same hostile reaction as has already destroyed other members of the Hohenstaufen dynasty, including Rienzi. But Tannhäuser had expected as much: after all, he no longer needs the Church's blessing.

Even before he leaves on his pilgrimage, a decisive transformation has already taken place in him, placing the tragedy of his life in a new and wholly unclerical light. The 'whole significance of the catastrophe that befalls Tannhäuser', wrote Wagner, 'nay, the whole of his nature', lay in a single idea, an idea that strikes the contrite hero only when he realizes that he has betrayed Elisabeth and, indirectly, Venus, too. Wagner described this moment as 'the nub of the entire drama'.

Until now, Tannhäuser has viewed women only from the perspective of the seducer, but he now discovers for the first time in his life that he is loved for his own sake. Even though, in his own words, he has dealt Elisabeth a 'mortal blow', she continues to stand by him. Suddenly he realizes that she has always loved him. His mating call was a shameful error that merely served to humiliate her. It was not his infringement of any taboo that had broken her heart but his own heartlessness.

'To guide the sinner to salvation,' Tannhäuser perceptively explains, 'the God-sent woman came to me.' From his loveless existence as a Don Juan and a betrayed betrayer she could have redeemed him as his 'angel': 'But, ah! impiously to touch her, / I raised my blasphemous eyes to her!' His brazen praise of Venus debased her from the level of a loving woman to a dumb female with conditioned reflexes. As Wagner wrote to Liszt in 1852, it was in this insight that 'the whole significance of the catastrophe that befalls Tannhäuser lies, nay, the whole of his nature'.[21]

If Tannhäuser undertakes a pilgrimage to Rome, it is not for the sake of his soul's salvation, still less on account of the Landgrave or the Church. To quote his own poetical explanation, he hopes to 'sweeten the tears' that his lost lover has wept for him. This too constitutes his contribution to their joint redemption. He abandons his wonted existence as an artist and seducer in the hope of becoming more like the woman of whom he can really expect nothing more. For her sake he denies his true nature and allows himself to be humiliated by the pope – a figure who means nothing to him. Only in this way does he finally abandon the Venusberg and 'women in general' in order to unite with one woman alone, a woman whom he hails as his 'angel'.

At the same time, completely unnoticed by everyone, a similar miracle takes place on the Wartburg. Elisabeth, too, has changed. Out of her love for Tannhäuser, she becomes Venus. Ever since his first appearance as a singer, she has been enthralled by him, but at the moment of his greatest fall from grace, when she too is dragged down into the depths, her infatuation turns to passion, a passion that increases as her body – like that of the saint that she is – begins to die. Day and night she prays for him, Wolfram tells us, stretched out on the ground in 'ardent anguish': here Wagner prefers the adjective 'brünstig' – 'on heat' in a sexual sense – to the more usual 'inbrünstig'. Consumed with yearning desire, she waits for Tannhäuser to return, ostensibly for the sake of his 'salvation' but in fact for the sake of their joint love, which alone can bring him true healing.

But she seeks Tannhäuser in vain among the returning pilgrims and in her despair confesses her sins to the Virgin Mary – the same Virgin Mary whom her lover had once invoked in his hope of salvation: within her chaste body, 'sinful longing' and 'worldly yearning' have sprung up, emotions that she has sought to deaden 'by a thousand pains'. But to no avail, she indicates. Her love is now greater than herself, and so she abandons the struggle and longs to die in order to obtain forgiveness 'for his guilt'. But in truth it is in order not to have to be anything other than the woman who is united with him in love. Like the goddess Venus, she can merge with him only in death.

The virgin sacrifices herself to her lover by committing an apparent error similar to his own, just as Senta does with the Dutchman and Isolde does with Tristan. Wagner repeatedly stressed this surprising turn of events. In his instructions for staging the opera, he countered the usual 'pious' interpretation of Elisabeth by describing her 'marvellously anguished situation' as a woman: the first 'violently awakening seed' of her affection is followed by 'all the phases in the growth' of her love, culminating in the 'final efflorescence of the death-perfumed bloom'. Only a sympathetic performer, Wagner argued, could feel this 'with the subtlest organs of a genuinely feminine sensibility'.[22] Wagner describes the secret love of the saint – in other words, her transformation into Venus – as though it were a pregnancy: she should not mature into a fruit but into the 'death-perfumed bloom' that blossoms only in the night of the Venusberg and in the dark and 'wondrous realm' of *Tristan und Isolde*.

But it is the opera itself that expresses this most clearly. Once Elisabeth has taken her decision to die in the hope of being united with Tannhäuser, Wolfram sings his famous 'Ode to the Evening Star'. For all its melodiousness, this is a deeply serious piece, dealing as it does with the death of the lovers. Darkness descends, enveloping not only the valley of the Wartburg but also the sad tale of the thwarted couple. With its fearful foreboding of death, it shrouds the world 'with sable-black wings'.[23] It was, then, as a distant memory of the 'vulture' that this night of death first appeared before Wagner's inner eye. Only subsequently did he exchange these ill-starred pinions with the 'sable-black raiment' with which the gathering gloom covers the countryside in the published version of the score.

Freed from the body, the soul now has to set out on its journey through 'night and its terrors'. The 'lovely evening star' appears to it like an angel, a heavenly messenger high above earth's vale of sorrow. Accompanied by the gentle sounds of a harp, Wolfram sings his melancholy serenade. For Wagner, however, the evening star symbolized Elisabeth transfigured in death, pointing out to her lover the way to their ultimate union. The star's other name is Venus.

And with this the promised reconciliation between the two worlds comes about. The goddess of love is freed from her semblance of life below ground, Elisabeth from her unfulfillable love, the hero from his impossible existence as the Flying Dutchman. Just as Tannhäuser – a brief relapse notwithstanding – abandons all self-interest in order to be united with the woman he loves in true humility, so Elisabeth sacrifices her life in an act of boundless self-abandon. And with her last breath, she breathes human life into the powerless goddess of self-abandonment, a figure who exists solely as the object of her suitors' desires. Thus the poet allows his three hapless characters to die almost simultaneously. The heavenly joy at the end leaves us in no doubt that they have all found 'the peace of the blessed'.

So why did Wagner believe that he still owed the world *Tannhäuser*? The answer is that the 'idea' of the drama, as expressed in his various statements on the subject, is lost in the stage versions of the work that are familiar to us. Perhaps out of consideration for the feelings of his audiences at the time and certainly for those of the Catholic royal family in Dresden, he avoided the confrontation between court and individual that was suggested by his sources. In keeping with the Biedermeier spirit of the age, he transferred this clash to a moral plane, having precious little interest in the struggle between sin and salvation.

Wagner relocated the conflict within his hero. The Landgrave's trickery is clear only on a close reading of the text, and so the opera lacks a real antagonist. Unlike all Wagner's later dramas, there is no villain purposefully driving the hero to his destruction. There are no eerie sounds reminiscent of Caspar providing a sombre background for Tannhäuser's meteorlike trajectory.

The Young German playwright Karl Gutzkow was struck by this absence and asked the composer why he had let slip the opportunity to introduce the character of Hoffmann's Klingsohr, who played the part of the seducer in Wagner's sources. In Klingsohr, Gutzkow argued, Wagner would have had a character corresponding to Bertram in *Robert le diable*, a Mephistophelean trickster who could 'represent the demonic element' and 'work on Tannhäuser in dramatic form'.[24] Wagner forbore to inform his colleague that he was saving the enigmatic figure of Klingsohr for a very much later date.

As in the catechism, it is vice that is forced to take over this role in *Tannhäuser*. If the Landgrave and his minnesingers are portrayed as worthy individuals just to please the audience, Venus and her retinue are required to wear the devil's horns. But this failed to clarify the drama. Happily, Wagner himself undermined this arrangement, ennobling the pilloried Venusberg with the most thrilling music that he had written until then. Fifteen years later he revised the Venusberg scene, allowing the anguished goddess of love and her rose-coloured grotto to profit from the new musical language that he had developed with *Tristan und Isolde*. But no new life was breathed into Landgrave Hermann and his sterile courtly society.

Weber's Heir

In February 1843 one of Wagner's life's dreams came true when he was appointed to the permanent staff of the Dresden Court Theatre. It was in Dresden that he had grown up in the theatre world of the court actor Ludwig Geyer, and here too that he had been frightened by the ghostly fifths of an invisible fiddler and, at the same time, hoped that one day he would 'stand there' like the court Kapellmeister Carl Maria von Weber and conduct Dresden's legendary orchestra. Twenty years later, the world of the theatre lay at the little man's feet.

Like his great predecessor, he even owned a silver-embroidered blue uniform with a lyre on the collar patch. Needless to say, he had to pay for it himself. He wore it whenever he conducted services at the Catholic Court Church or, baton raised, marched in front of the Court Orchestra during the Corpus Christi procession or performed his own choral compositions, including one that he wrote as a 'loyal tribute' to King Friedrich August II.

But ordinary working dress was sufficient for rehearsals. Here he could draw on his manifold experiences of preparing operas both at home and abroad. Whether it was Marschner or Mozart, Adam or Auber, the perennially popular *Zampa*, *Robert le diable* or the hundredth Dresden performance of *Der Freischütz*, the work would have been familiar to him from his days in Magdeburg, Königsberg and Riga. Equally familiar were the faces of his creditors from these places, with even the helpful Abraham Möller – now described by Wagner as 'the Königsberg Jew'[25] – travelling to Dresden in person to round up his debts. Everything pursued its well-worn course, except that it was all now on a higher level, guaranteed by Wagner's salary for life and his entitlement to a pension. By October he had even moved into rooms in the elegant Ostraallee opposite the Zwinger art gallery, an apartment splendidly furnished with a grand piano and a private library. On credit, as usual.

But at least Minna liked to believe that her life's dream had come true. Writing from the vantage point of 1852, Wagner claimed that 'I think back on Dresden only with feelings of abhorrence: no one ever sacrificed his entire soul more selflessly than I did there – and what walls of indifference the sound always echoed against!'[26] If he regarded himself as a singer pouring out his inmost feelings, the people around him, especially his employer, saw him simply as a cog in a machine whose function was to run smoothly. He was not expected to perform miracles, only to carry out his duties, including all manner of ceremonial obligations, to plan the Court Theatre's programme in as entertaining a way as possible and to follow his superior's instructions.

Baron Wolf August von Lüttichau was the first wall of indifference with which Wagner collided. If there was any quality that distinguished this former forestry commissioner, who had moved to his present position on health grounds, it was his love of his king Friedrich August II. He had already demonstrated his loyalty to Friedrich August I when the latter had been held captive in the wake of Napoleon's defeat. Perhaps the fact that Friedrich Wagner had died while serving the king in 1813 had contributed to Lüttichau's surprising decision to appoint his son in 1843. A whole generation older than his new conductor, Lüttichau supported him as best he could, but only within the context of his court appointment. At the same time, he regarded Wagner's supremely high opinion of himself as whimsical and presumptuous and did what he could to counter it. In the end, the two men were united only by their mutual hatred.

Wagner's real sphere of activity was the orchestra, but this too initially seemed to be an impenetrable wall, with the players seeking to undermine his euphoric self-assurance on the podium by all manner of carping criticisms. And while Wagner himself tried to please everyone all the time, his enemies implicated him in personal intrigues that even reached the ears of his intendant. His colleague Carl Gottlieb Reißiger, who insisted on his own seniority, became a tenacious and envious rival, while other members of the company who had originally been well disposed to him 'suddenly lost all need to show any human consideration whatsoever'.

Envy, he complained, was rampant not only within the theatre itself but in every newspaper in Germany. He saw himself 'belittled, disparaged and reviled', turning him into 'the most vacillating and insecure of men'. Only by sheer pretence was he able to find any outward calm, but he was incapable of expressing all that seethed within him, and still less could he translate it into action.[27] But this was no different from the fate of all employees, a fate that he had brought down on himself and confirmed with a solemn oath of allegiance. In real life, the visionary of the Venusberg was no better than any royal servant.

Nor were the two main occasional works with which he enriched Dresden's cultural life during these years undertaken on his own initiative, being written at the instigation of the guiding spirit of the local Liedertafel, Maximilian Leopold Löwe. This strange individual had persuaded Wagner to sit on the Liedertafel's committee as its 'Liedermeister', an appointment that involved the obliging composer in only wasted effort, as the organization's members were interested solely in social entertainment, calling each other 'citizen' and existing in the main to serve the ambitions of its secretary, Professor Löwe. The latter's followers – whom Wagner dismissed as 'completely worthless from a musical point of view' – were marshalled by Löwe with 'furious zeal', their performances designed to spread his Liedertafel's lustre far and wide.

One such project of Löwe's devising was a great festival of Saxony's male-voice choirs that was held in Dresden in June 1843 and for which Löwe felt that only superlatives were good enough. The organization's Liedermeister naturally found himself faced with the task of writing an effective piece for this massed choir on condition that it did not last more than thirty minutes. In order to avoid what he called the 'wearisome monotony of male-voice singing', Wagner decided to strike a dramatic note in his 'Pentecostal Feast of the Apostles with the Outpouring of the Holy Ghost', as he termed *Das Liebesmahl der Apostel*. He made no attempt to avoid (pre-)echoes of the Pilgrims' Chorus in *Tannhäuser*, a work that was not to be staged for another two years.

The first draft of the words of *Das Liebesmahl der Apostel* was jotted down on the back of his review of the oratorio *Saint Paul* by his mentor and rival Mendelssohn, a review remarkable for its hyperbole.[28] *Saint Paul* had been performed at Dresden's annual Palm Sunday concert in 1843 and it seems that Wagner felt challenged to produce a related work of his own. Like Mendelssohn, he took his cue from the Acts of the Apostles.

What he discovered while leafing through his old copy of the Bible in Martin Luther's translation seems to have filled him with the same sense of divine inspiration as that vouchsafed to the Apostles by the Holy Ghost. Certainly, the miracle that befell the first Christian congregation was worthy of taking its place in any heroic drama. Even in his very first sketch, Wagner had already singled out the decisive parallel: following the loss of their beloved Saviour, the Apostles find themselves in a 'state of dejection' again. They have lost everything thanks to an act of betrayal and murder, their despondency made worse by 'ill tidings' of imminent persecution. In their despair they implore heaven's help, a plea that is followed by a period of anxious uncertainty before their prayer is finally heard and the miracle duly takes place. With the flames of the Holy Ghost, the lost inspiration of love returns to their hearts: 'Grand communion of souls and goods.'[29]

Wagner wrote this confessional work within the space of only two weeks and, according to his letter to his sister Cäcilie, 'would often sit here for fifteen minutes at a time and weep'.[30] His health was affected by his excessive workload, but no doubt also because he rediscovered himself within this latest subject of his. Without divine assistance and despised by an alien environment, the Apostles – like Wagner himself – begin to lose faith in themselves. Threatened by 'the hatred of the mighty', which weighs upon them like a storm cloud, they are forced to stand by as 'the hatred of the envious' – thus the wording of the first version of the text – continues to grow. Soon 'the mighty' start to 'spy' on them, and cruel 'persecution' rains down 'on their heads'. Anyone who dares to accuse the mighty of a 'crime' against Christ is himself put to death.

This fervent lament by the male-voice choir does not remain unanswered: consoling voices are heard from the heights, and the sudden entry of the orchestra reveals that the miracle has happened. With a *pianissimo* drumroll, redemption steals softly in, soon swelling to a powerful display of symphonic might. Divine inspiration burns anew in the Apostles' anxious hearts. 'What rustling fills the air?' they ask in their joyful terror.

Wagner's music provides the answer. The effect, he told Cäcilie, 'enthralled everyone who was there'. A choir of twelve hundred men, skilfully positioned throughout the Frauenkirche, where they occupied even the dome, was fired by a one-hundred-strong orchestra. The Pentecostal miracle proved to be a musical event of the first importance, a foretaste of both the magic of *Lohengrin* and the mystery of *Parsifal*. 'Nothing like it', Wagner assured his sister, 'has ever taken place in any church.'[31]

Although Wagner later distanced himself from the 'folly' of all undertakings involving massed choirs, *Das Liebesmahl der Apostel* none the less points beyond the immediate circumstances that produced it, Wagner expressing his philosophy of art by means of a biblical parable. Ever since he had read E. T. A. Hoffmann's *Serapionsbrüder*, which had already provided the inspiration for both *Die Bergwerke zu Falun* and the song contest in *Tannhäuser*, art had been elevated to the status of a religion in Wagner's life.

Whenever Wagner reworked a religious theme, we can be fairly certain that his concern was less with religion than art. In the present case it was symphonic music to which he ascribed the messianic power of redemption, a point on which he followed E. T. A. Hoffmann. No sooner has the choir appealed to the Holy Ghost for help in *Das Liebesmahl der Apostel* than the Romantic orchestra fills the space with its triumphant gestures. This alone, Hoffmann had rhapsodized, embodies our 'presentiment of the highest and most supreme being, the spiritual power that ignites the spark of life in the whole of nature'. This is the 'divine spark' that pours its flames over the whole congregation in the form of the Pentecostal visitation. Thus music became a 'religious cult'.

The liberating power once invested in Christianity was now attributed to Wagner's music, which entered his listeners' hearts with the rushing of the Holy Ghost. But there was also a modern equivalent of the power that resists redemption. The antagonist who was missing from *Tannhäuser* now propels the drama forward, allowing it to build to a climax, where it is swept away by the storm that is unleashed in the orchestra. Anyone familiar with the Acts of the Apostles in Luther's translation knew, of course, that the powerful enemies of the Holy Ghost could only be the Jewish priests. It was they who persecuted the Apostles, throwing them into prison and forbidding them to mention the name of their Messiah. When Peter accused the rabbis of crucifying Christ, they decided to have him killed.

In the user's guide with which he prefaced his translation of the Acts of the Apostles, Luther spoke for simplicity's sake of 'the Jews': they would find out soon enough where their 'ranting and raving' against the Holy Ghost had got them. Wagner knew this text: Luther's translation formed part of his private library in Dresden. One wonders whether he was reminded of his hated patron Meyerbeer, who that very same year had championed the Berlin première of *Der fliegende Holländer*. Or was he perhaps thinking of Felix Mendelssohn, whom he secretly emulated and to whom he had issued a vocal challenge on the occasion of the unveiling of a monument to the late King Friedrich August I? In order to avoid any misunderstandings, he included in the piece the modern-sounding question 'Is Jerusalem the world?', providing his own consoling answer: 'Behold Rome! It is there that the word is invested with the power needed to penetrate the whole of the world like a ray of light!' With this, Wagner paid his respects to his employer, the Catholic king of Saxony.

But Professor Löwe's energies were not limited to organizing large-scale festivals: with the untiring efforts of the fanatic, he had for years been pursuing a plan to bring back to their native soil Carl Maria von Weber's mortal remains, which had been languishing in London since 1826. Even while Wagner was still in Paris, the *Gazette musicale* had drawn its readers' attention to the regrettable fact that a whole pile of more recent coffins had been placed on top of Weber's, the older ones having to make way for the newer ones.[32] Löwe had no difficulty persuading his Liedermeister to throw his weight behind his plans for the transferral of Weber's remains.

After all, it was Weber's legacy that Wagner had taken up by becoming Kapellmeister in Dresden. Wagner regarded the composer of *Der Freischütz* as his 'spiritual father', and so the latter was virtually a member of his family. Weber's death in a remote land in 1826 had 'filled' his 'childish heart with horror', and was it not the opportune death of Weber's great enemy, Francesco Morlacchi, that, as if by the workings of some beneficent fate, had opened up a vacancy for Wagner? And in setting *Tannhäuser* to music, had the younger composer not proved himself to be the legitimate successor and executor of Weber, who had planned a similarly entitled opera in 1814?[33]

Wagner was left with no choice in the matter, and so he impetuously leapt astride Löwe's hobby horse, allowing himself to be elected to Löwe's committee and planning the campaign with military precision. Collections were made at various theatres, and even Meyerbeer donated the proceeds of a Berlin performance of *Euryanthe* to the fighting fund, with the result that by October 1844 the composer's remains, released from the pile of other coffins, could finally be shipped to Hamburg, where they were transferred to a smaller vessel for their journey up the Elbe. But at Wittenberge the river froze and so the coffin was transferred to a train, reaching Dresden on 14 December, where it was ferried across the river. Darkness had already descended by the time the torchlit procession, accompanied by a large crowd, set off for the Catholic cemetery, where the reinterment was due to take place the next morning.

Wagner had mustered eighty wind instruments and twenty muffled drums for the solemn transfer. Based on motifs from *Euryanthe*, his funeral music left 'an indescribably sublime' impression on its listeners. Not only was the immortalized composer himself present in spirit in the music, so too, it seems, was Berlioz, who was still very much alive and whose influence evidently escaped Wagner's attention when he was drawing up his report on the reinternment: Berlioz's *Grande symphonie funèbre* for the victims of the July Revolution had clearly impressed its German admirer when he heard it in Paris during the summer of 1840.

Decades later, Wagner still recalled the transfer of Weber's remains as one of the most beautiful experiences of his life. Among his memories was the sudden appearance of Wilhelmine Schröder-Devrient as she emerged from the mortuary chapel carrying a laurel wreath. The two of them 'exchanged a curious look', Wagner later told Cosima.[34]

Wagner had written a funeral oration for the next day's service, but although he had committed it to memory, he found this no help. According to his later account in *My Life*, when he reached the end of the opening paragraph he fell into a cataleptic state and, lost in reverie, felt as though he had stepped outside himself and was listening to his own speech and watching himself objectively. To the embarrassment of the mourners, his silence lasted several minutes, with no one knowing 'what to think' of him. It required the total silence to rouse him and induce him to continue his speech.

Wagner attributed his mysterious interruption to a trance, but there may have been a simpler explanation for it: the eulogist was unable to stop himself from introducing a polemical sideswipe into the second paragraph of his speech, in which he directed his envenomed barb at 'those cold-hearted souls who are addicted to fame but who have no fatherland' because 'their favourite spot on earth is where their ambition finds the rankest soil in which to thrive'.[35] If any of Wagner's listeners had failed to realize that he was referring to his absent friend Meyerbeer, his silence will have given them pause for thought.

At the same time, it should come as no surprise to find Wagner sometimes acting out of character: after all, he was regularly required to change out of his court uniform and into his rehearsal clothes. These, in turn, would be laid aside when he was composing, when he would slip on a silk dressing gown with matching headgear. In short, he lived on several levels at once. He conducted fashionable operas that he despised and was rubbed up the wrong way by bureaucrats who questioned his right to certain privileges. When not carrying out the special wishes of the court, which were communicated to him by Lüttichau, he worked away at home, under considerable pressure, on *Tannhäuser*, while at the same time seeking to impose some sense of systematic order on his philosophical ideas, for this highly strung and endlessly loquacious man, now cared for by the matronly Minna, yapped at by his little dog Peps and addressed by name by his parrot Papo, was busily constructing a veritable edifice of ideas. Onlookers who saw in him only a court Kapellmeister or the opera composer of the day failed to notice this new dimension, which only a few years later was to become central to his world of creative endeavour.

At Wagner's instigation, the much-travelled August Röckel was appointed director of music in Dresden, where he was instantly struck by his colleague's philosophical bent. As early as 1843, Röckel was convinced that Wagner's intellectual gifts surpassed everything he had encountered in Europe until then: 'You cannot imagine how the daily intercourse with him develops my admiration for his genius. His earnestness in art is religious; he looks upon the drama as the pulpit from which the people should be taught.' All this, Röckel concluded, conspired to convince him that here was someone 'whose greatness overshadows that of all other men I have met'.[36]

In the company of friends, he would hold forth for hours on end not only on his librettos but on his music and writings, too, commenting on them and bringing out their hidden logic. He was one of that rare type of artist who creates nothing without immediately offering an appropriate interpretation. 'Wagner is a man of genius,' wrote the music journalist Johann Peter Lyser at this time, 'but he always knows what he wants. He can do something that very few other men of genius can do, and there is perhaps no one who can do it to this extent: he can explain clearly both to himself and to others what he is composing and why he has to compose in this way and no other.'[37]

What mattered to Wagner was not the feelings that his art inspired but the ideas it communicated. He expected nothing less from this message than that it would radically change the world, just as the Gospels had done.

Wagner's years in Dresden also enjoyed their fair share of happy coincidences. The woman who more than any other had influenced his theory of dramatic art was engaged at the very theatre where he was now employed as a conductor. The idol of his schooldays, the Romeo for whom he had conceived his first infatuated passion, Wilhelmine Schröder-Devrient was now in daily contact with him. Eclipsing the girlishness of his sister Rosalie with her self-assured and almost tomboyish nature, she was now *prima donna assoluta* at the Dresden Court Theatre.

It was Carl Maria von Weber himself who had discovered her in Vienna in 1822 and who had entrusted to her the roles of his heroines Agathe and Euryanthe. Now she was able to leave her mark on the characters of Adriano, Senta and Venus in the first performances of *Rienzi, Der fliegende Holländer* and

Tannhäuser, while leaving a no less lasting mark on Wagner himself, who soon fell under her energetically direct influence.

They had been acquainted for nearly ten years, and their relationship was now compounded by both an artistic and an erotic charge. Indeed, both of them agreed that the artistic embraced the erotic and vice versa. If Wagner could hear in music an expression of creative love and if he had given that love its world-redeeming due in *Der fliegende Holländer* and *Tannhäuser*, so he discovered in Wilhelmine Schröder-Devrient the matchless incarnation of that idea.

Everything about her, whether in her private life or on stage, tended to extremes of self-expression, a quality reflected both in her commitment to the roles she played in the opera house and in her relationships with her real-life lovers. So numerous were her affairs that she was even honoured with the authorship of the pornographic *Memoirs of a Singer*. When Wagner was reintroduced to her in Dresden, he found her in the throes of various relationships whose impassioned nature, as her admirer observed, was graphically reflected in her roles on stage.

Having won Wagner's trust and extolled his 'genius' wherever she went, she initiated him into the intimate secrets of her relationships with men. At the present time, she was resolved to end her long-standing affair with a tall young lieutenant in the Royal Saxon Guards, Hermann Müller, and to start a new one with an 'equally young, tall and slim' Herr von Münchhausen, a decision that was causing her 'extreme agitation'. As Wagner was forced to realize, she had 'betrayed' her earlier lover 'in the most faithless manner, with empty pretexts', but when she then ruefully returned to Hermann Müller, she proceeded to treat his temporary successor in exactly the same way. At this juncture 'the star that she had really been waiting for' appeared on the horizon of her love life in the form of another lieutenant in the Guards, a Herr von Döring, and it proved 'horribly easy' for her to betray Hermann Müller all over again. Döring lost little time in robbing her of her savings and pension entitlement, after which she found peace for a time with a Livonian landowner, Baron Heinrich von Bock, whom she married in 1850.

Wagner experienced these affairs of the heart at first hand, no doubt remarking on their vague similarity to the subject matter of his own operas, and in 1843 he wrote to his friend in Paris Ernst Benedikt Kietz to report on his remarkable experiences in this regard. He had been 'initiated into the curious secrets of this extraordinary woman' and had got to know the tempestuous violence of her 'inner demon'.[38] Later he found it inappropriate to reveal his true relationship with a woman who had broken so many hearts, and in this his biographers have followed his lead. 'She never became Wagner's mistress', Gregor-Dellin states with total confidence. 'According to Cosima's diaries, he considered her too "played out," even in his Dresden kapellmeister years.'³⁹ But younger men certainly found the forty-year-old soprano attractive, and the jealous Cosima may not be the most impartial of witnesses.

Wagner left a number of pointers of his own. That his relationship with the soprano was one of the most stimulating of his life he openly admits in *My Life*. That this may have been due not only to her 'fearsome talent' but also to her 'sensuality' may be inferred from an entry in Cosima's diary.⁴⁰ In his hymn to Schröder-Devrient in *A Communication to My Friends*, he uses the words 'Berührung' and 'berühren' half a dozen times within the first half page, generally in the sense of physical contact but also in that of emotional impact. Above all, he insisted, she felt 'impelled to have contact with, and to merge with, the whole'.

But did Wagner himself ever want anything different? He too, after all, felt a 'yearning for love – for real love, a love sprung from the soil of the fullest sensuality'. How could he fail to recognize a 'longing similar to my own' in the woman he so admired? Unfortunately, he told his friends, she felt that she could satisfy her desires only 'in the most trivial encounters', whereas he himself felt drawn to a 'higher, nobler element'.

It was for this reason, he went on, that the score of *Tannhäuser* was written in a state of 'all-consumingly sensuous agitation' that held his 'blood and every nerve in feverish excitement'. According to his own account, his 'supreme desire in love' culminated not in the bed of the goddess of love whom he worshipped but in the 'violent and ardent embrace' of his operatic characters.⁴¹ Should we believe him? On 11 February 1883, two days before his death, he saw the soprano again in a dream. 'In telling me about it,' Cosima noted in her diary, 'he says, "All my women are now passing before my eyes."'⁴²

It would undoubtedly be going too far to see in the characters of Senta and Venus a direct portrait of Schröder-Devrient, but it is equally certain that in conceiving all his heroines, Wagner was guided by the quality that this singer represented. This was her gift for ecstatic self-expression – Wagner himself called it a loving 'self-giving', in which he also discovered the highest potential of the spoken language.

When taken to its furthest extreme in drama, this gift entailed the willingness for self-sacrifice through which the individual is subsumed by the work of art. It was to the 'consciousness that is lost in the moment of supreme self-realization' that Schröder-Devrient owed the spell that struck Wagner like an electric charge. In 1851, long after their relationship was over, 'I saw, heard and felt her whenever I was inspired by the urge to work creatively.'⁴³

Her one tragedy in life was that she was already a little too old for the role of Venus that seems to have been written with her in mind. Moreover, she now had a dangerous rival in the barely eighteen-year-old Elisabeth. And it must have been particularly annoying for her that this singer was Wagner's niece. For years, the composer had had his eye on his brother's adopted daughter as Schröder-Devrient's successor. She had been appearing on stage from a very early age and was already familiar with a repertory ranging from *Der Freischütz* to *Rienzi*.

At her uncle's instigation, Johanna was engaged by the Dresden Court Theatre in 1844 and made her début in Spontini's *La vestale*, 'overshadowing' Schröder-Devrient, who was a whole generation older. She delighted audiences with her outstanding mezzo-soprano voice, with Wagner himself declaring that he had 'never heard a finer one'. Alongside her tall slim figure the portly diva seemed positively matronly. 'For God's sake,' the latter asked the composer with a despairing smile, 'what do you expect me to wear as Venus? A belt on its own won't do!'

Like Geyer before him, Albert Wagner had trained his stepdaughter for the stage from a very early age. By now his own career had gone into a state of terminal decline, and so he was able to devote himself wholeheartedly to hers. Nor was it only her precocious maturity that enabled Wagner's niece to take her place in the family myth: she too was the illegitimate daughter of an aristocrat, in her case a Guards lieutenant by the name of Bock von Wülfingen. Her mother, Elise Gollmann, married Albert Wagner when the child was not yet two. Her Uncle Richard was impressed by the girl's talents and lost no time in commandeering her for his own works and in commending her to Wilhelmine Schröder-Devrient, with the result that Johanna sank down in gratitude at the feet of the admired and bosomy Romeo and in memory thereof wore a torn-off finger from the singer's glove as part of her necklace.

Johanna lived relatively close to her uncle in the Ostraallee, and so the two were soon in regular contact, with Schröder-Devrient viewing with a suspicious eye the attentions that Wagner lavished on his pretty niece. When the two women appeared together in *Tannhäuser*, vying not only for the hero's affections but also for those of the audience, she was forced to admit defeat. Her Venus sank from sight, while a new star rose in Dresden's operatic firmament in the person of the transfigured Johanna. Schröder-Devrient's contract with the Court Theatre expired in 1847 and was not renewed.

The singing actress never forgave her erstwhile admirer for this act of 'treachery' and openly declared that Wagner had helped to have her hounded from the theatre. 'It was out of jealousy of my niece', Wagner fumed in *My Life*, that she instructed her lawyer to reclaim the sum of one thousand thalers that she had lent him in the ardour of their first approchement. The fact that the avaricious Lieutenant Döring was behind this move did not make it any more palatable in Wagner's eyes, as he simply lacked the money to repay her.

In the event, his niece's newfound fame failed to improve his lot, and it seems as though her stepfather, whose relations with his younger brother were still extremely strained, merely used Wagner to advance Johanna's career. All that the court Kapellmeister had taught her in many hours of singing and acting lessons she now made use of in other operas, and thanks to her uncle's enthusiastic encouragement the young singer was soon able to break free from him. Like his hero Tannhäuser, Wagner could see himself as a traitor betrayed in turn.

Although Wagner had long been making contemptuous remarks about Meyerbeer, he turned to him in 1846 to initiate him into his plan to help his niece continue her vocal studies in Paris. In order to induce him to write a letter of recommendation, he stressed her merits and the great success that she had scored in *Tannhäuser*. An outstanding teacher was duly found, and, predictably, they worked together not on her Wagner roles but on the Italian repertory. By the time she returned to Dresden six months later, all she could think of was grand opera. Soon she was no longer impressing her audiences as Saint Elizabeth but as Norma, a role she had studied in Paris, and, to Wagner's horror, as Valentine in *Les Huguenots*. 'I've never been so angry,' he wrote to a friend, 'but there's nothing I can do about it. I find this whole business an absolute abomination.'[44]

Instead of inheriting Schröder-Devrient's Wagnerian mantle, as the composer had intended, Johanna wilfully rejected the part of Senta in favour of Donizetti's *La favorite*, a work all too familiar to Wagner from his arrangements for Schlesinger in Paris and one that he dismissed as 'repulsive' in the extreme. Needless to say, the new prima donna got her way in the face of opposition from the company's second conductor, a victory that left him 'extraordinarily embittered'.

Soon she had abandoned Wagner altogether and gone over to the enemy camp. In 1850 she scored a tremendous personal triumph as Fidès in Meyerbeer's *Le prophète* and two years later was offered a contract with the Paris Opéra to sing only Meyerbeer roles. This was too much for her Uncle Richard, who, even before this latest turn of events, had broken with her family, dismissing her stepfather as a spineless opportunist, his sister-in-law Elise as a typical actress's mother and a Gorgon to boot, and the whole family as 'out-and-out riffraff'.[45]

In another letter to her stepsister Franziska, Wagner extended his venom to the diva herself: how painful it was for him to discover that Johanna, for whom he had created the role of Elsa in *Lohengrin*, had 'had to sell herself to that rapacious Jew; she might easily have found a nobler object for her youthful powers than to lay them on the altar of that rotting bag of bones!'[46]

Quick though he was to forgive his niece her infidelity, his resentment at his rival continued to gnaw away at him. Once again he saw confirmation of the archetypal image of the adversary who seizes the throne by disposing of the legitimate heir and robbing the latter of both life and lover. If the beguiling Johanna had followed in Wilhelmine Schröder-Devrient's footsteps in assuming the role of Wagner's sister Johanna Rosalie, he now found himself separated from her for good. Although she had shown little inclination to sacrifice herself to her uncle in the way that Elisabeth had done for Tannhäuser, the blame for this could be laid at the door of her parents, who were no better than a pair of degenerate actors. But in the case of Meyerbeer, who had again robbed him of the fruits of his labours, there were no extenuating circumstances at all.

This experience may perhaps provide an explanation for one of the perplexing mysteries of Wagner's life – his defamatory article on 'Jews in Music'. For a long time, writers have speculated on how such apparently unjustified hatred could spring seemingly from nowhere and take root in Wagner. Some commentators have argued that it was Wagner's envy at his more successful rival, while others have claimed that his rabid outburst was provoked by his annoyance at Meyerbeer's refusal to lend him yet more money. But Meyerbeer's refusal dates from November 1846,[47] whereas it was not until September 1850 that Wagner's article appeared in print.

There is much to be said in favour of the view that it was the return of his old trauma, involving the loss of a woman he loved, that goaded him into this frontal assault. Meyerbeer's latest operatic crowd-puller, *Le prophète*, arrived in Berlin in April 1850, and all the newspapers were full of reports of the 'extraordinarily enthusiastic acclaim' with which Johanna Wagner was fêted as the true star of the evening.

In an onrush of 'patriotic gratitude', the *Vossische Zeitung* even noted that, thanks to Johanna's art, Germany, too, could now boast a worthy Fidès. In Wagner's eyes, then, his own kinswoman had allowed herself to be misused as a prophetess of that 'rotting bag of bones' Giacomo Meyerbeer. He had no hesitation in dealing him his death blow before the year was out.

Headed 'Jews in Music', Wagner's article appeared a little over six months later in the *Neue Zeitschrift für Musik* and was aimed not only at Meyerbeer but at a second rival who had contested his 'inheritance', Felix Mendelssohn, whom Wagner included under this heading even though he must have known that Mendelssohn had been baptized and was a fully practising Protestant. Moreover, Mendelssohn shared Wagner's dislike of the successful Meyerbeer, whom he criticized for exactly the same weaknesses, albeit using more temperate terms.

Mendelssohn came from a well-to-do family and, at an age when Wagner was still picking out the notes of the Bridesmaids' Chorus on his family's cottage piano, was already giving concerts as a 'child prodigy', gaining even Goethe's acclaim. But Mendelssohn also had a number of points in common with Wagner, who was his junior by only four years. His concert overture *Fingal's Cave* left a powerful mark on Wagner's compositional style. Even in old age Wagner was still describing it as 'one of the most beautiful pieces of music that we possess'. 'There is a magnificent intellectual vision throughout, a fine sensibility, and the observations of both are reproduced with the greatest art.'[48]

Just as those passages in Wagner's early operas that already sound distinctively 'Wagnerian' in fact constitute a tribute to Mendelssohn's concert overtures and symphonies, so the latter's tone-painterly mastery fired Wagner's imagination even as late as the time of *Parsifal*. In Bayreuth he would sing Mendelssohnian themes to himself, playing his colleague's overtures at the piano and telling Cosima that 'such an enormous talent as Mendelssohn's is alarming'.[49] The fact that, in spite of all this, Wagner numbered Mendelssohn among the adversaries with whom he was involved in a lifelong struggle defies rational explanation – as, indeed, does everything else bound up with his childhood trauma.

By the time Wagner took up his post in Dresden in 1843, Mendelssohn was Germany's most famous living composer. As conductor of the Leipzig Gewandhaus concerts, he not only welcomed Wagner's appointment, he had already offered to conduct the *Rienzi* Overture, an offer that Wagner gratefully declined, while describing himself as Mendelssohn's 'most ardent admirer'.[50] When earlier that same year the two men had met in Berlin, where the older composer had just been appointed general music director, they had, in Wagner's words, developed 'extremely friendly relations', Mendelssohn even inviting his colleague to visit him in his 'luxurious domestic surroundings'. Presumably he knew that his guest had described him in a newspaper article as the leading representative of 'genuinely German art'. But Mendelssohn was far less susceptible to flattery than Wagner.

Mendelssohn was in fact temperamentally disposed to react with marked reserve, a reaction that Wagner interpreted as coldness. That he did not wear his heart on his sleeve, as Wagner did, was something the younger composer held against him. When the two men met again in November 1842, this time in the company of Wilhelmine Schröder-Devrient, Wagner even thought that Mendelssohn was 'spying' on him. Mendelssohn was even more puzzled by the demonstrative affection that the soprano showed Wagner. While they were walking home together after the rehearsal, Mendelssohn had admitted 'with sudden agitation' that one of the drawbacks about music was its particular tendency to stir up negative qualities such as envy. Wagner thought this a surprising admission on Mendelssohn's part, evidently failing to realize that his elder colleague had already seen straight through him.

A calculating streak now crept into Wagner's dealings with Mendelssohn. In 1843 he praised the latter's oratorio *Saint Paul* in the most extravagant terms, describing it as an example of art at its greatest and recommending that it become 'a part of the Protestant liturgy'.[51] Adopting the sort of tone that he had earlier used when singing Meyerbeer's praises, he announced that he was proud to belong to the nation that 'has produced you and your *Saint Paul*'.[52] When he took another look at the work in Bayreuth in 1879, Cosima noted that it filled him with 'utter disgust': it was 'Jewish through and through, facile in form, shallow in content'. The next day he returned to the attack, observing that in nature the most heroic are bound to perish, 'and what remains are the rats and mice – the Jews'.[53]

Over the years, Wagner's gnawing resentment towards Mendelssohn developed into a veritable complex, and there seems little doubt that a contributory factor in this process was the fate of the younger composer's C major Symphony. Wagner had first met the Gewandhaus conductor in 1836 – the year of the first performance of *Saint Paul* – and shortly afterwards he had sent his colleague his backward-looking journeyman's piece in the hope that Mendelssohn would perform it. In the event, Mendelssohn did not do so and could not even remember receiving the score, prompting Wagner to speculate in *My Life* that Mendelssohn had 'presumably destroyed it'.

According to Wagner, his jealous rival had discovered things in it that he did not like. His stepdaughter Natalie even asserted that Mendelssohn had 'done away' with the score in a spirit of 'ugly envy' in order to 'discourage him' and 'break the wings of his spirit'. Presumably parroting Wagner's own comments, she described Mendelssohn as a 'slippery, subtle, sly Jew' who had 'deliberately disfigured and mutilated' the *Tannhäuser* Overture when he conducted it in 1846.[54]

Prior to this fiasco, which, like Mendelssohn's alleged envy, had sprung from Wagner's imagination, the two men had again met when in January 1844

Wagner travelled to Berlin to conduct *Der fliegende Holländer* at the Theater am Gendarmenmarkt in the presence of King Friedrich Wilhelm IV. The performance was attended by Mendelssohn who, at the final curtain, had hurried backstage to congratulate the acclaimed composer, hugging him warmly in a rare show of emotion. Wagner's reaction seems to have been no less genuine when, in his letter of thanks, he described his colleague as 'my dear, dear Mendelssohn', adding 'it gave me great pleasure to learn how well-disposed you are towards me. If I have come a little closer to *you* in the process, then that is the most welcome gain of my entire expedition to Berlin.'[55]

Even this state of apparently perfect harmony was soured for Wagner by his old suspicion: writing much later in *My Life*, he recalled that Mendelssohn had followed the tempestuous applause 'with a wan face', as though he could see the Dutchman himself before his eyes, after which he had 'lisped' to him: 'Now you can be satisfied!' Wagner's malicious reference to Mendelssohn's speech impediment (a defect from which Cosima also suffered) makes it clear that Mendelssohn's understatement was lost on him. The older composer avoided the sort of effusive praise that Wagner had earlier lavished on his Overture to *A Midsummer Night's Dream*, with the result that Wagner thought that Mendelssohn envied him. Equally at home in the worlds of the sublime and the demonic, Wagner proved a failure where a simple knowledge of human nature was concerned.

Like Meyerbeer before him, the mild-mannered Mendelssohn was likewise transformed into a demon. The composer who in his incidental music to *A Midsummer Night's Dream* had conjured up a world of earth spirits and goblins with proto-Wagnerian immediacy was now said to have a 'demonic goblinlike character rendered all the more sinister by its taciturnity.'[56] In Mendelssohn's Dance of the Elves Wagner could hear only the disagreeable sound of gnats. Where Liszt had discerned the 'rainbow air and nacreous shimmer of these little goblins', Wagner felt overcome with disgust at the thought of the insects that Mephistopheles knocks from Faust's old fur coat.

During the 1870s Wagner thought of writing some funeral music for the German war dead and, as a joke, announced that he planned to end it 'with the buzzings of *A Midsummer Night's Dream*', which would represent 'the chuckling Jews'.[57] The image of gnats was even transferred to the composer himself. In the history of music, Wagner believed, Mozart represented the creation of nature and Beethoven the world of humankind, while he himself embodied the revealed religion of the divine. Mendelssohn by contrast was no better than a 'gnat'.[58]

If the voluble Wagner was unsettled by Mendelssohn's reserve and 'furtive taciturnity', he may also have felt cowed by a direct comparison between their respective appearances. Unlike Wagner, Mendelssohn commanded the elegant manners and self-assurance of a man on whom Goethe's eye had once lovingly rested. Wagner, by contrast, gesticulated wildly when speaking, his rushed and restless movements reflecting the fact that, whereas his rival had already arrived, he himself still had a long way to go. Two years before his death, he recalled how 'handsome' Mendelssohn had been before 'becoming so Jewish when he turned thirty'. It was 'terrible', he added, that 'we have this foreign Jewish element in our midst'.[59]

Since Wagner was well aware that Mendelssohn regarded himself as a Protestant, his emphasis on his rival's Jewish origins probably goes back to a remark made by Gaspare Spontini in 1844. Long since out of fashion, Spontini had described his two successful rivals Meyerbeer and Mendelssohn as 'deux juifs errants' who ensured that German music was now a hopeless cause.[60] Wagner was present when Spontini said this, with the result that from then on he too lumped together these two fundamentally dissimilar composers: both, he argued, were interested only in musical effects and dazzled their audiences with their apparent charm and selflessness, which on closer examination turned out to be no more than cunning deception.

As an example of this, Wagner refers to Mendelssohn's decision to renounce his well-paid position in Berlin in favour of the simpler post of music director of the Gewandhaus in Leipzig on artisitic grounds. Instead of a salary of three thousand thalers, he would receive only a third of this amount. As a result, Wagner went on, Mendelssohn allowed himself to be acclaimed as a 'fine example of a man prepared to sacrifice his personal interests'. But this was less than the truth, for in addition to his basic salary Mendelssohn received a secret supplement from the king to the tune of two thousand thalers, thus allowing him to draw exactly the same salary as in Berlin. As Mendelssohn scholars have pointed out, this 'revelation' on Wagner's part is 'untrue from beginning to end'.[61]

Mendelssohn died suddenly in 1847, apparently as the result of a broken heart caused by the death of his sister Fanny. Wagner seems to have regarded this as the workings of fate. He was now rid of his most dangerous rival and hence need no longer fear the threat that Mendelssohn might have posed in the field of the music drama. He organized two memorial concerts, one of which, by a curious slip, he described as a 'Todesfeier', a celebration of death, as though he were celebrating not the dead man but his passing. Later he commented sarcastically that Mendelssohn's 'guardian angel' had sealed the death of opera 'when he closed his protégé's eyes at an opportune moment'.[62]

Not until 1881 did Wagner reveal his true thoughts on what he regarded as the cause of Mendelssohn's death. Evidently no one had suspected the extent to which the older composer had repined against Wagner's superiority as an opera composer. In the end it was *Tannhäuser* that 'might have had a strangulating effect on him, for he died not long afterwards'.[63]

Lohengrin

The extent to which Wagner was plagued by the pressures of his professional appointment – pressures from which Meyerbeer and Mendelssohn were both spared – is clear from the sudden bursts of creativity that characterized his periods of annual leave. During the summer of 1845 he travelled to Marienbad to be cured of what he described as a build-up of 'hypochondria'. He was accompanied by his wife Minna, his dog Peps and his parrot Papo, but not on this occasion by his mother Johanna Rosine. Once again the mythological mine shaft opened up and led him back to the Middle Ages that so closely resembled his own past.

He spent five weeks immersed in the books that he had brought with him from his impressive private library in Dresden, reading them not only at the Pension Kleeblatt where he was staying with his *ménagerie à trois* but also beside a stream in the seclusion of the forest, on the Brunnenpromenade and in the bath tub that the local doctor had prescribed by way of a water cure for his various abdominal ailments. He read until the mines of the past had revealed all the subjects he still lacked to complete his life's work. They were tales about the impossibility of love and the struggle to win a bride, about the inheritance that is lost through betrayal and about heartbreaking decline and fall. And all of them led to the miracle of redemption with which the drama revealed its true metaphysical significance.

Thanks to his sudden release from theatrical routine, with its trammelling rules and regulations, the archetypal tragedy of his own existence abruptly appeared before him in a new and unfamiliar light, just as it had done in Teplitz. The complications of everyday life were replaced by a clarity of ideas that could freely unfold within a historical space. Again he felt reborn, and his 'exuberantly carefree mood' continued even after his return to Dresden. 'It was as though I had grown wings,' he wrote later.

In the 'strange and yet intimately familiar' poems of Wolfram von Eschenbach – a historical figure he had already brought to life in *Tannhäuser* – he discovered the archetypal figure of the questing fool, young Parzival (as Wolfram spelt the name). And in the literary history of Georg Gottfried Gervinus he found much of the bachground of *Die Meistersinger* and, tangentially, his Nibelung hero Siegfried. And it was also in Wolfram's *Parzival*, he wrote, that he re-encountered that other Grail knight who had haunted his imagination since he first read Lucas's *Ueber den Krieg von Wartburg* towards the end of his years in Paris.

A messenger from a better world had appeared before him, bringing salvation and, like some statue of a smiling god, standing apart from the demonic inner turmoil of his earlier characters. As though seeing himself as an actual miner, Wagner wrote to his brother Albert in August 1845 that he had had to free the tale of his figure of light from the 'rubble and decay' of the traditional accounts of the story. It was practically his own invention, he concluded. The urge to set it down on paper had been so great that, in spite of his doctor's orders in Marienbad, he had leapt from his bath tub and, barely taking the time to dress properly, rushed back to his room at the Pension Kleeblatt in order to write down what was 'tormenting' him.

It was Lohengrin who 'suddenly stood before me, fully armed, in the most detailed dramatic conception of the whole subject'.[64] With a 'golden horn at his side and leaning on his sword', this was exactly how he later appeared before the heroine in the opera, arriving to rescue his ideal sister as she grieved for her lost brother. For the poet, the sorrowing Elsa already bore the features of his niece Johanna.

If Wagner offered his unloved brother such a detailed account of the genesis of this 'highly poetical legend', he did so simply because Albert's stepdaughter was already part of his plan. 'Johanna's role', he told his brother, 'is very important and in point of fact is the principal role in the work.' It was 'bound to turn out the most attractive and moving in the world'.[65] But events proved otherwise: in keeping with the logic of the myth, Johanna betrayed her uncle just as surely as Elsa betrayed her Swan Knight.

When *Lohengrin* finally received its first performance in Weimar in 1850, Wagner was living in exile in Switzerland and reduced to following the performance, watch in hand, from his hotel room in Lucerne (the hotel, fortuitously, was called the Swan), while his niece was triumphing as Fidès in Berlin. Not until 1861 did Wagner hear the work for the first time on stage, but without his ideal Elsa. He also had to make do without Wilhelmine Schröder-Devrient, whom he had imagined as the wild Ortrud but who had died in 1860 at the age of only fifty-five.

In both *Der fliegende Holländer* and *Tannhäuser*, Wagner had depicted the sombre phenomenon of the curse that dogs the hero from an early date and that can be lifted only through love. In *Lohengrin* he brought the counterpart of this phenomenon vividly to life: the curse that had led to the abyss is here followed by the miracle that opens up the way to heaven. In fact even the two 'curse' operas culminate in a miracle in the form of 'redemption', but in both cases the composer had left it to his audience to think through this metaphysical process to its logical conclusion. The accursed individual cannot be helped on earth, but by merging with the object of his love he can be raised to a higher plane, which of course means shuffling off this mortal coil.

What had previously been left to the audience's powers of reasoning and hence to chance was now to be staged: on this occasion, the miracle was to take place not in people's minds but on stage, ascending, miraculously, from the orchestra pit even before the curtain rises. For the first time in his career, Wagner eschewed the usual overture that announces what is to come and instead provided a prelude that represents the opera's whole premises. In his own words, it depicts 'the descent of the Grail'. Even before its tale has been told, the miracle already takes place in the darkened theatre before the audience's mind's eye.

This is no music in the traditional sense of the term, but an act of conjuration, evoking a particular mood or atmosphere with the help of musical instruments. The floating sonorities of the violins, flowing along with no rhythmic divisions, carry the audience with them. Raised above the laws of gravity, the listener allows himself to be lifted aloft to those realms embodied by the violins' highest register. These instruments normally speak with a single voice, but here they are divided into eight different parts, suggesting the miracle of angelic choirs. As the expression of a universal ethereality, a melody now emerges that the listener, buoyed up by his newfound weightlessness, follows through countless repeats entrusted to the gentle sonorities of the winds. With the radiant entry of trumpets and trombones, we reach the point of greatest intensity before the tension gradually dies away to a gentle ebbing, with the divided violins welcoming the listener back in a transfigured recollection of the opening.

In short, it is music about ideas, music whose only purpose is to raise its subject to the level of our conscious awareness and to do so, moreover, with the greatest possible clarity. In *Der fliegende Holländer* and *Tannhäuser* it was the notion of the individual's hounded existence and his release from it that was depicted in the music, whereas here it is the idea of art itself that Wagner presents, together with the way in which art is revealed to humankind. As soon as art appears in our lives, it transforms us and raises us to a higher plane. By revealing its immutable beauty to us, it allows us to partake of infinity for one brief moment. It then gently withdraws again, leaving the mortal listener with a final nostalgic glimpse of reality. Art: a miracle.

This musical self-revelation with which Wagner prefaced his miracle opera was soon followed by the most fantastical interpretations. On first hearing the prelude, the French Wagnerian Charles Baudelaire claimed to feel, 'as it were, lifted from the earth': 'I felt myself released from the bonds of gravity, and I rediscovered in memory that extraordinary thrill of pleasure which dwells in high places.' From one such peak he sensed that he could see an immense horizon bathed in a diffuse light, while above it was 'infinity itself'. A sense of increasing brightness then made itself felt, seeming to generate an ever more gleaming light. His soul then appeared 'to move about in a luminous medium', experiencing 'an ecstasy composed of knowledge and joy'. Baudelaire was familiar with drug-induced states of higher consciousness and presumably rediscovered in this musical vision 'the dizzy perceptions of an opium dream'.

Liszt, who gave the world's first performance of *Lohengrin* in Weimar, similarly found the prelude a heady experience, but he concentrated not on the experience of the self when released from itself but, adopting the tone of a Christian mystic, glimpsed before him a heavenly vision: before his inner eye he saw the Temple of the Grail initially reflected 'in the mirror of azure waves, beamed back by iris-coloured clouds'. These suddenly shrink away in order to allow 'the sacred edifice to appear before our dazzled eyes in all its bright and radiant splendour'. But then, like some sinking comet, the otherworldly radiance abruptly fades. The translucent haze of the clouds grows dense again and 'the vision disappears in the same multicoloured mists' at whose heart it had first been revealed. For the God-fearing Liszt, this prelude seemed to come straight from those 'mystic heights' in whose paradisal beauty the Blessed Souls make their home in Dante's *Divine Comedy*.

Needless to say, Wagner, too, provided his own interpretation of the prelude, a reading that seems to combine Liszt's rapt and unworldly vision with Baudelaire's delighted ecstasy. But instead of the temple that Liszt saw reflected in the clouds, Wagner's gaze falls at once on the Holy of Holies that has been established for its worship. Normally hidden from mortal eyes, the mystery of the divine is revealed with the very first notes of the prelude.

Embodied in the cantilena of the *divisi* violins, a host of angels bears the Grail through the blue ethereal vault and offers it 'to the rapturous gaze of those whose hearts are fired by the greatest yearning for otherworldly love'. The heavenly host sweeps down from the empyrean heights, holding out the vessel containing Christ's Blood to the waiting congregation as though it is a monstrance. At this point the miracle takes place that is conjured up by the music: the Grail comes to life, the blood within it is renewed, and 'perfumes of ravishing sweetness well forth from its womb'.

It is as though the Venusberg has been transformed into a Fata Morgana. 'Entrancing perfumes waft down like clouds of gold', filling the onlooker's breast now with 'blissful pain', now with 'trembling delight', and causing to blossom within it 'those stifled seeds of a love that is woken to marvellous growth by the vision's life-giving spell'. We feel a powerful longing, 'an urge for self-surrender and an instinctive wish to dissolve away such as no human heart has ever felt before'.

At the moment of ultimate ecstasy, 'the holy vessel finally stands revealed in all its wondrously naked glory' and the onlookers' senses desert them as they sink to the ground in worship and annihilation, while the Grail pours forth its blessing on their prostrate forms. Already the fiery flames have begun to die down to a gentler glow, as the smiling host of angels soars aloft 'in chaste delight', melting away into heaven's ethereal blue. But the Grail remains below, a vessel that Wagner describes with good reason – as his readers were bound to notice – as 'the wellspring of love'.[66]

What the reverent public failed to notice, however, is that Wagner's 'Romantic opera' thus begins with a musical evocation of the miracle of sexuality as so often depicted in the visual arts, not least by Bernini in his *Ecstasy of Saint Teresa*. Likewise, Wagner's exegetical text may be effortlessly decoded as a description of a sexually ecstatic experience. Whatever the legend may say, the bleeding Holy of Holies is not, therefore, a Christian symbol of the Holy Sacrament but a biological phenomenon that similarly shies away from public disclosure.

Lohengrin, wrote Wagner, is an 'ancient *human* poem', for it is 'a fundamental error to regard the specifically Christian outlook as capable of creating anything original'. The idea revealed by the miracle painted in the silvery blue empyrean by the divided violins has very little to do with ecclesiastical faith and very much with the redemption that love alone can offer.

What Wagner has in mind here is not the pious view of love as promoted by the Bible but, as in *Tannhäuser*, love experienced both physically and sensually. Only in love do human beings abandon their divided nature and merge as a new unity in much the same way as the reverent host of listeners merges with the prelude of *Lohengrin*. In the Grail man's buried nature is revealed by Wagner.

'But what is the innermost essence of this human nature,' Wagner asks in his account of the work in *A Communication to My Friends*, 'a nature to which the yearning for the remotest distances turns back because only here can it find satisfaction?' His answer reads like a sober extract from his own highly poetical interpretation of the work: 'It is the necessity of love, and the essence of this love, in its truest expression, is the longing for the utmost physical reality, for the enjoyment of an object that must be grasped with all the senses and held fast, firmly and inwardly, with all the force of actual being.'

This Holy of Holies of sensual ecstasy is bound to remain a mystery, and so it is symbolized by the Grail that is revealed only in the ecstasies of art. In this way, the fictitious God whom mankind creates in his imagination dissolves in 'the finite, physically certain embrace' of the act of love.[67] Thus begins the drama of the hero Lohengrin, central to which – as in *Der fliegende Holländer* and *Tannhäuser* – is the bloody mystery of love. In order for the tragedy to begin, this mystery has to leave behind it the dream world of the prelude and enter into real life.

All of this is at odds, of course, with the fairytale notion that audiences have formed of Wagner's 'Romantic opera'. Indeed, not even the sources he used give any obvious pointers to his own erotico-philosophical reading. A glance at the sources he mentions suggests that his inspiration was less Wolfram's medieval romances than the modern compilation of German legends by Jacob and Wilhelm Grimm. While this anthology may not have provided him with the initial idea, it none the less furnished a plot capable of sustaining a full-length opera.

For Wagner, the mythographer Jacob Grimm was 'a kind of mother' to him.[68] (For a time, he even used Grimm's orthographical system, with lower-case initials for nouns.) In the world of Grimms' legends he felt he had entered the secret cellars of his own past. It was here that he found the story of 'Lohengrin in Brabant', the tale of a Grail knight who comes to Brabant in a small boat drawn by a swan in order to liberate persecuted innocence in the form of Elsam, as she is called here.

But having married her, he has to leave her again: in spite of his specific injunction, she asks him who he is and whence he has come. An evil woman persuades her to commit this heinous act, which robs her of her love as surely as it brings the tale to an end. This woman, too, appears in the Grimms' anthology. If Wagner had leafed backwards and forwards a few pages, he would have found other episodes from the life of the Swan Knight, including not only the true identity of the aquatic bird but also the remaining details of his opera.

The argument between the two women outside the minster, on the other hand, is taken from the *Nibelungenlied*, while Wagner's decision, on dramaturgical grounds, to turn the evil woman into a pair of intriguers was inspired by Weber's *Euryanthe*. If Wagner claimed that he had first had to excavate the Lohengrin legend and free it from the 'rubble and decay' in which it had become embedded, this is scarcely true of the sources that were freely available to him. Yet it may well be true of the story itself, whose legendary surface conceals the hidden meaning that he first had to lay bare. Here Wagner discovered the idea that lies behind his hero and the taboo surrounding his origins, and here too he found the notion of the miracle of love that is fatally threatened by its own past.

From the dream of the prelude, Wagner rouses his audience by martial horns that rudely confront us with actual reality: a threat hangs over the empire. On its eastern border are assembled the serried ranks of the Hungarians, and it is against them that King Henry has come to call the Brabantines to arms. But the country's internal peace has also been disturbed: 'God Himself is angry with the country', we read in Wagner's Marienbad draft. Scourges and famine are rife in the land, just as they once afflicted the Thebes of King Oedipus. Here too, on the banks of the Scheldt, a crime has been committed, and Count Telramund now bids King Henry act and, as the country's highest judge, ensure that that wrong is righted.

In the finest Wagnerian tradition, the hereditary succession is at stake and hence the question of who is to marry the bride. Telramund reports that, on the death of his brother the duke, he took the latter's children into his care as a surrogate father, ruling the country in place of the underage Gottfried, while seeing in Elsa – thus Wagner's variant of her name – his future wife. But, Telramund continues his litany of recriminations, Elsa had been fired by a secret love for another man and had murdered her brother in order to seize his inheritance. Having seen through her deceit, he has married Ortrud. That Ortrud is the 'wicked woman' of the sources is clear from the very first notes with which Wagner characterizes her. But as the late duke's next of kin, Telramund now demands the country of Brabant for himself and Ortrud, and for Elsa a condign punishment. 'Solemn horror' seizes hold of the assembled warriors.

The details of Telramund's account are not in fact true: he has simply been repeating what Ortrud has told him, for it ultimately emerges that it was she who committed the crime. And if on this occasion it is not the stepfather alone who represents evil, all that mattered for Wagner, as he pored over Grimm, was that here he had found the archetypal relationship that underpinned his own life: on the father's death, the uncle – in this case misled by the mother – replaces his brother and lays claim to the throne by unlawfully disposing of the legitimate heir.

In Ortrud – it is no accident that her name recalls that of Hamlet's mother – Wagner found an embittered antagonist for the daughter Elsa and at the same time her rival for throne and power, now that the real heir is out of the way. In his prose draft, Wagner even claims that Ortrud hails 'from an ancient princely

Saxon house',[69] suggesting, no doubt unconsciously, that she resembles his own mother, whom he believed to be mysteriously linked to the Saxon royal family. Ultimately, it was she who, together with the usurping Geyer, had robbed her son of the dead duke's inheritance. Now the deed is laid at the sister's door.

Like all his heroines, Elsa is one of the family. According to the prose draft, she appears before the tribunal 'poorly dressed', yet she reveals the mixture of virginal charm and authoritative composure that Wagner found embodied in his saintly sister Rosalie. If in terms of her appearance she seems as pale and dejected as the penitent Gretchen, this conceals the impassioned emotion of Auber's Fenella. Like the latter, Elsa initially answers the questions that are put to her merely by timid gestures that are more eloquent than any words. And when she makes her way to the altar in Act Two, Wagner allots to her 'an uncommonly important silent role' that should 'command our entire attention'.[70]

The visionary Senta, too, is reborn in the Brabantine virgin. Instead of answering the charges levelled against her, Elsa falls into a trance, and with the open eyes of the somnambulist she sees a dreamlike image of the hero who brought heavenly solace to her suffering in days long past. Just as her Norwegian sister saw the sombre Dutchman in her hallucinatory vision, so Elsa sees a knight 'bearing radiantly bright arms' and offering her 'consolation with his well-bred demeanour'. This man, crows Telramund, is her clandestine paramour. In order not to waste any more time, he insists on a trial by ordeal intended to prove that she is guilty of murdering her brother. And again we hear the military horns that Wagner modelled on trombones and that he recalled having seen on altarpieces 'played by the Angels of the Resurrection'.

And this is exactly what we see on stage, with the music undergoing a veritable resurrection as it swells from the softest beginnings to an unprecedented sense of ecstatic jubilation, followed by the resurrection of the hero who, a product of Elsa's imagination, is transformed by dint of a miracle into a living human being. Just as this miracle had once been enacted in the darkened auditorium, so it now takes place on the brightly lit stage. The spell that was cast by the divided violins in the prelude is now repeated with the human beings themselves.

Shaken to the very depths of their being by the events that have been unfolding before them, the choir breaks down into individual voices, before merging together again with their increasingly rapid invocations of the hero and their shouts of joy that form a single hymn of triumph. The miracle that had manifested itself in the prelude as a vision of love both sacred and profane now comes to earth in the form of a real human being drawn by a swan from another world. Differently from the audience, however, no one on stage knows who this unexpected visitor can be nor whence his journey has brought him.

He has come from afar – further, in fact, than even the audience suspects. His true origins may be found in Loschwitz just outside Dresden, where Johanna Rosine liked to send her son during the summer months and where, pining for her and for his sisters, Wagner hit upon an idea. Two years before his death, he could still recall his plan to build a boat and sail back home along the Ziegenbach and the Elbe. He imagined the surprise and astonishment of his loved ones when their lost son and brother suddenly turned up in his boat before their startled eyes.[71]

This plan was never realized, of course, but the idea of this apparently miraculous riparian epiphany continued to haunt him. Drawing up instructions for the first performance in Weimar, it was as though he was remembering this early fantasy when he wrote that, 'in order to create the necessary illusion', the figure of Lohengrin should be played on his arrival 'by a child standing in a boat proportionately reduced in size'.[72]

The poetic swan that pulls the hero's boat in the legend was likewise familiar to Wagner from his beginnings as a poet. His first ballad, he told Cosima, had dealt with the fate of a young man whom he describes variously as a boy, a youth and a huntsman.[73] This hero is so weary of life that he wants to drown himself but is rescued by a swan. Having regained his love of life, he finds that as his punishment he is 'constantly aware of the swan summoning him to death'. But when Wagner read this morbid swansong to his artistic conscience, Rosalie, she thought that 'there was something not quite right about it'.

Like everything that failed to survive her scrutiny, the ballad vanished into thin air, yet it remained lodged in Wagner's memory, together with the hero's acclaimed arrival on the Elbe. Perhaps he retained such a lively memory of it because his own love of life was soured by the man who had 'rescued' him on Friederich Wagner's death. As with the boy and the swan, so Wagner's stepfather, who bore the name of a bird, was bound up in his imagination with the unsettling thought of death and destruction.

In *Lohengrin*, however, sheer delight reigns on stage with the arrival of the Swan Knight. 'A miracle has come', sings the chorus, and in the outburst of general rejoicing no one dares doubt that 'a God-sent hero' – a Messiah and Saviour – has arrived on the banks of the Scheldt. Only the sombre figure of Ortrud suffers 'a near-fatal shock at the sight of Lohengrin and the swan'. But no one suspects anything. Her petrified dismay attracts no more attention than the fact that the subservient swan evidently understands what its master is saying. When Lohengrin sends it home with a few well-chosen words of thanks, the bird turns obediently to the boat. All feel a sense of 'blissfully sweet dread'.

And now, as if the world exists in a state of prestabilized harmony, events come thick and fast. The nameless hero has barely offered to protect the damsel in distress, linking it to the express demand that she trust him 'without fear and dread', when all of Elsa's floodgates open. Without having the first idea whom she is addressing, she offers herself to him, together with all that she owns: 'May my heart, my soul and my body be dedicated to you!' she exclaims in the prose draft with a total lack of inhibition. Coming as it does from the lips of a virgin, this too amounts to little less than a miracle.

At the same time, she must know very well to whom she is giving herself. It is none other than the man of her dreams, the heavenly comforter whom she had recognized at once. In this she is like Senta, who on first seeing the Dutchman had similarly been struck by a thunderbolt. In much the same way Sieglinde recognizes herself in a fleeing stranger, greeting him as her lost twin brother and at the same time taking him as her husband.

In none of these encounters is it a question of people meeting by chance and being united in love. Rather, the opposite is the case: forcibly torn apart and robbed of their earlier unity, they have been brought back together by fate. Their union is not something that lies in the future; rather, it took place long ago. The very act of getting to know each other is an act of recognition, allowing them to take possession of each other at once.

On this occasion, however, the opposite seems to be the case. After Elsa has sunk down at the Swan Knight's feet and is effectively already united with him, he places a condition on her that seems to fly in the face of their earlier union. This is the famous forbidden question: 'Never', he peremptorily orders her, 'shall you ask or care to know whence I came or what my name and nature may be!' Or, as the original version more prosaically puts it: 'Never shall you ask or seek to know who I am and whence I came here!'

This results in a dilemma that dictates the subsequent course of the opera. Love that is bound up with conditions of any kind cannot, of course, be true love. And the man who seeks a union with his lover under the cloak of anonymity presumably has something to hide. But Elsa, in the heady intoxication of young love, does not hesitate and promises Lohengrin all that he wants, whereupon he presses her to his manly breast and, 'moved and delighted', confesses: 'Elsa, I love you!'

This too seems out of place in the light of the forthcoming ordeal. Yet at the same time it recalls the violence with which Tannhäuser and the Dutchman insist on a spontaneous union. In spite of the chilling effect of the forbidden question, it appears that Elsa and her unknown knight are already as intimate as brother and sister. It is no accident that the stranger agrees to fight a duel occasioned by her brother's death. Once again we hear the trumpets of the Last Judgement, this time calling the contestants into the ring, but the tussle has barely begun before Telramund finds himself stretched out on the ground. The messenger of the Grail whom even swans obey is invincible in battle. On a great wave of enthusiasm, Elsa and Lohengrin sink into each other's arms and allow themselves to be carried away on the shields of the jubilant crowd, who bear them off to their wedding feast and their marriage bed. This would be a welcome ending, were it not for two questions that remain unanswered: who exactly is Elsa's bridegroom, and where is her brother hiding?

The most elegant solution would undoubtedly be to answer one question with the other. But what exactly constitutes the tragedy of the opera? Wagner himself regarded Lohengrin as a tragic figure, claiming that the hero is 'typical of what is really the only tragic subject, the real tragedy of life in the modern age'.[74] This reference is in itself sufficient to make it clear that with Wagner's *Lohengrin* we are not dealing with the fairytale of the Middle Ages that was to lead to Neuschwanstein but with an unresolved conflict in the life of a man who regarded himself as spearheading the arts in the modern world.

In his *Communication to My Friends*, Wagner lays this conflict bare. Lohengrin, he writes, is in fact himself, with the opera depicting the outcome of his own intellectual development. In *Tannhäuser* he had yearned to escape from the 'repugnant sensuality' of the present and find refuge in a world of nobler 'but essentially still sensuous longing'. But after this he had ascended to the heights in whose clear and sacred ether he had enjoyed his loneliness with 'a thrill of voluptuous delight'.

Into this icy contentment on the part of the artist – a state whose description recalls Baudelaire's vision of *Lohengrin* – there suddenly fall the warming rays of love. The lonely individual longs for company. Seized by an irresistible 'longing to descend from the heights into the depths', he is drawn to the woman who, instead of the happiness of the sun-drenched peak, greets him with the 'familiar shadow of the most human loving embrace'.

It was, then, as a reflection of this psychological process that Wagner invented the figure of Lohengrin. Like the Dutchman in the oceanic depths of his misery and like Tannhäuser in the 'voluptuous caves' of the Venusberg, he too seeks redemption at the hands of the woman who 'points him upwards' and simultaneously 'draws him down to the earth's warming breast'.

In portraying himself in this way, Wagner was guided by a single 'urge': 'To communicate to the perception of others what I had seen myself and to do so, moreover, as clearly and intelligibly as possible.' If, following the breakdown of his relationship with Minna, which he ascribed to a false sensuality, he had withdrawn into creative isolation, he now longed to return from the spirit's ersatz delights and enjoy the experience of love once again.

On this occasion, however, he hoped for a successful relationship in which the 'highs' of his spirituality did not have to be sacrificed to the 'lows' of the cave of wanton desire. He dreamt of a mixture of chastity and sensuality in which the contrast between mind and body would be superseded as the lovers themselves were united. This longing, he noted, had already fired his earlier heroes and, now that he himself had reached a new level of insight, was embodied 'with supreme clarity' in the figure of Lohengrin, the knight of the Grail.

In this act of self-analysis, Wagner reveals the roots of his own creativity. The longed-for woman, represented by the sisterly Elsa, struck him as his hero's ideal complement. She offers an answer to his urge to descend from the blinding brightness of the spirit into the darkness not only of the body but of instinct and the unconscious. In short, the heroine epitomizes that aspect of Lohengrin that is turned away from the light.

'Elsa', Wagner explained, 'is the unconscious, the instinctive, in which Lohengrin's conscious, wilful nature longs to be redeemed.' As we can see for ourselves on stage, Elsa feels drawn to Lohengrin, body and soul, and evidently hopes to discover in real life the oneness desired in her dreams, and so it seems that nothing lies in the way of their mutual happiness.

But Wagner's own interpretation also emphasizes a feature of his hero that is not immediately apparent from the events that unfold on stage. If Lohengrin had appeared like some Messiah safeguarding Elsa's threatened innocence and, with it, saving the whole country, it now becomes clear that he too is suffering and therefore in urgent need of saving. He brings the hoped-for deliverance, but he also seeks salvation for himself. Yet this completely subverts the familiar picture of the Grail knight.

What can a man lack who partakes of the joys of the Grail and of the miraculous strength of a father who is worshipped as the God of love? At the end of the opera, when everything has gone wrong, Lohengrin returns to the point from which he set out, a point that is both real, inasmuch as his obligations recall him to the Castle of the Grail, and conceptual, as he has failed to find the love he hoped for. This failure of his life's dream seems to be followed by a defiant reaffirmation of the role that he had wanted to give up.

'In a distant land, inaccessible to your steps,' he begins his confession, and picking up the melody from the now distant prelude, he tells us all that happened before the events that we have just watched unfolding took place. In a distant land, then, remote from common mortals, lies the Castle of the Grail and, at its heart, the temple in whose inner sanctum the Grail is preserved as the Holy of Holies. Once brought to earth by angels, this mystic vessel, which had caught Our Saviour's blood as He hung on the Cross, is visited once a year by the dove of the Holy Ghost, which renews its miraculous powers. Thus strengthened, the temple brethren can perform miraculous deeds on their travels to distant lands. The result is a picture of the most perfect knighthood, although it is not entirely clear why the actions of these knights have to be cloaked in a veil of secrecy in the form of a forbidden question.

Generally described as the 'Grail Narration', Lohengrin's official account originally included further details that may help to answer these questions. Wagner cut them as he was afraid they would have an 'anticlimactic effect' on his audience. But the longer version of events reveals what happened at the Castle of the Grail when Elsa's ardent lament reached the knights' supersensitive ears. Their initial reaction was to ask the oracle where the damsel was to be found, but this proved unnecessary when a swan turned up on the riverbank, together with a boat. Lohengrin's father immediately recognized in it a bewitched soul that would be redeemed only if it spent a year providing a ferry service for the Grail. It was to help both the bird and the damsel in distress that Lohengrin set out on his vicissitudinous journey 'along rivers and over the sea's wild waves'. His Brabantine listeners knew the rest.

Yet even this explanation of the origins of his mission reveals less than the whole truth, and it is only when we turn to the prose draft prepared by Wagner while he was taking the waters in Marienbad that a fuller picture emerges. All who are allowed to serve the Grail, we read here, are relieved of earthly cares. His needs miraculously met, the knight is spared the ageing process and does not even know death. But eternal youth has its price: the Grail knight is not allowed 'to cultivate a woman's love', a voluntary asceticism made worse by the fact that it is limited to the brethren themselves, while the 'king of the host of Templers is allowed a pure wife in order that his sublime line may be perpetuated unadulterated'.[75] In short, the true delights of the Grail that are so seductively depicted in the prelude are the father's exclusive prerogative.

Lohengrin's progenitor Parzival was thus granted an entitlement denied to Lohengrin himself, who is allowed to serve but never to love. To perform God-fearing deeds, he is sent out on long journeys that take him away from his mother for incalculable periods. The knights of the Grail are lonely wanderers scouring the earth in search of salvation. It was for this reason that Karl Simrock, whose translation of *Parzival* Wagner read in Marienbad, called Lohengrin a 'German Ulysses'. And like Ulysses Lohengrin pines perpetually for his Penelope. Condemned to wander the earth, the hero is allowed to work miracles but is denied the miracle of love.

If we lift the transfiguring fairytale veil from the Grail community, we find a patriarchal family, with the father dominating the sons by enjoying the right to take them into service and send them away whenever he likes. The mother provides the food and, like the Temple containing the Grail, bears within her a bleeding vessel. Once a year the miracle of new life takes place when she is impregnated by the paternal dove and the knights' next little brother is born.

On one occasion Wagner suggested that Lohengrin, too, issued from this maternal vessel: with evident surprise, Cosima noted his comparison between his hero and the 'mandrake pulled out of the bottle (the Grail the bottle)'.[76] Wagner uses the old German word 'Galgenmännchen',[77] literally 'the little man of the gallows', a reference to the popular belief that the mandrake was produced by the semen of hanged men, implying that the Grail's role is that of the 'bottle' or uterus from which Lohengrin is 'drawn'.

Even while carrying out his godly missions, then, the son sees himself as a prisoner of this hierarchical family structure comprising the father who begets the children, the mother who gives birth to them and the progeny who are reduced to a state of servitude. As long as he fails to free himself from this situation, the son remains immortal – in other words, a permanent child. It is for this reason that the castle of this dynasty seems 'inaccessible to your steps' as it lies in the past. Like the young Wagner dreaming of the rejoicing that would greet him when he arrived home by boat, Lohengrin comes from a distant past from which he attempts desperately to free himself. If, as in Wagner's stage directions, he appears at the outset to be a child, he has to return at the end, defeated, to the land of children who are not sprung from his own seed.

For Lohengrin, this return is a painful punishment, being less of a journey home than a relapse. What he tries to pass off as a sublime sanctuary blessed with divine healing powers merely holds out the promise of yet more family problems, and it can appear godlike only because it is the actual source of his art and of his sublime isolation on the mountain summit of his music. And so Lohengrin returns to the Grail Castle of his past with the same degree of compulsiveness that Tannhäuser shows in returning to the Venusberg and the Dutchman to his ghost ship.

He has no choice but to do so as he has violated the patriarchal law of purity. As soon as he set eyes on Elsa – he reveals in his farewell speech – he was 'so inflamed by love' that he wanted to lay his miraculous powers at her feet. This is rather more clearly expressed in the passage that was cut: as a result of the desire aroused in his heart by Elsa, his 'heart' has turned away 'from the chaste service of the Grail': 'But having turned from God to you, / Atonement and remorse I must endure.'[78]

This is a severe penalty that makes no sense when judged by Christian standards. Since when has God felt offended by people falling in love? It makes sense only if Lohengrin regards his whole existence as a punishment, an existence in which he is forced to forswear love for his father's sake. This results in the paradoxical situation that he is banished from Elsa's presence for the very reason that brought him to her in the first place. Just as the swan brought him to Brabant, so it now returns to collect him and take him back to the place from which he has come.

The other reason for Lohengrin's forced return is provided by Elsa. In order for her to be helped, she has to swear a curious oath and refrain from asking her saviour about his homeland, name and family. This might work if he were merely offering her the help she requires. But as soon as love raises its head, which it does here on both sides at once, the condition becomes illusory.

Love means becoming one with another person not because of some universal category, be it his humanity or his divinity, but because of his individuality. Love is always personal, it always asks after origins, name and nature. For all that it is dictated by the Good Lord Himself, the hero's demand alone makes it abundantly plain that we are not dealing with a particularly humane institution.

At the same time, Lohengrin appears from the outset to be surrounded by a quasi-divine aura. He seems to hail from another world, and so we find Wagner himself explaining the forbidden question by reference to the legend of Zeus and Semele: the human Semele, finally wanting to see her hidden lover with her own eyes, is burnt to a crisp by the melting bolt of his divine presence. When transferred to Elsa and Lohengrin, this means that the earthly lover is simply not equal to the celestial goodness of her husband. According to Wagner, the 'story' is intended to show that 'all contact between a supernatural phenomenon and human nature' is doomed to fail. Although Elsa is not burnt to a cinder, she none the less reacts by revealing worrying signs of weakness. Nature in her is bound to 'seek revenge and destroy the revelation', thereby snuffing out her own life.[79]

This might explain why, as an artist who has come down from the mountain peaks of his intuition and walked among men, Wagner remained misunderstood and exposed to the barbs of mediocrity. Yet not even this can account for Lohengrin's tragedy. The fact that divine actions are not appreciated as such but are ascribed by carping critics to the all too human conditions of their genesis is not in itself sufficient to constitute a tragedy. If, on the other hand, the alpine peaks are such an attractive abode, why is he drawn down to nestle at earth's warming breast? Or why does the hero fall head over heels in love if he is satisfied with his celestial office of serving the Grail?

He cannot be satisfied with it as it prevents him from being a human being, for all that it invests him with godlike powers. In order to be a human being, he must love and couple with another human being. His tragedy, then, consists in the fact that, in order to be able to love, he has to deny his origins, while being confronted with those origins by virtue of his love. As a human being, Lohengrin becomes as vulnerable as any human. Just as he is starting a new life, his old one catches up with him. His rebirth on earth is thwarted by the return of the past.

And the past has a name: Ortrud. With the very first sounds that usher in the second act, we are aware of a much darker alternative world to offset the rapt and radiant realm of the Grail. And this alternative world is represented by Telramund's wife. The celestially floating violins are now replaced by the menacingly muffled drumroll of fear that seems to well up from the abyss, and by the dark and eerie string sonorities of the Wolf's Glen. What had been merely hinted at in *Der fliegende Holländer* and *Tannhäuser* now makes its ghastly début: Wagner's embodiment of evil, seeking to destroy the hero, to undermine love and seize power for itself. In *Euryanthe*, the enemy couple were called Lysiart and Eglantine, while in the *Ring* they are represented by Alberich and Hagen. Here they are Telramund and Ortrud.

Ortrud is a 'wild woman' who embodies the past that the hero wants to cut out of his life. There are two reasons for this: first, as Telramund's wife Ortrud lays claim to Elsa's inheritance, which falls to Lohengrin as a result of the ordeal; and secondly, she strives for the return of a long-lost world in which her own dynasty had reigned thanks to the pagan gods. As Wagner told Liszt in a letter of 1852, she is a woman who does not know love and whose fanatical desire for power is turned into a hatred of all living things. In the hope of breathing new life into her 'decaying gods', she wants 'to destroy the world and nature', and if her goal can be attained in no other way, she is even prepared to countenance 'her own annihilation'.[80]

The young couple thus finds itself confronted by evil, an evil which, in this satanic guise, seeks to assert the claims of the past. The pagan sorceress insinuates herself into the vacillating Elsa's confidence and convinces the latter that it is best for her love if she asks the forbidden question of the mysterious knight. But this question relates to the past, and so Elsa falls under Ortrud's spell. As a trained witch, Ortrud knows who or rather what lies behind the strange knight. His origins make him unable to love. The boy who performs miracles is forced to yield to the miracle of manhood.

The demonic Ortrud knows Lohengrin's weak spot so well not least because she hails from a world not so very far removed from his own and perhaps even identical with it. According to Wagner's prose draft, the Castle of the Grail is located in mountains surrounded by forests and a wilderness, while Ortrud, as 'the sinister denizen of the darkling forest', lives in a 'wild forest castle'. Nor is it mere accident that, like the Temple of the Grail, it lies beside a lake. She too has mastered the magic arts, representing the claims of her gods on earth and, like the Grail, possessed of the gift of prophecy so that Telramund can describe her, respectfully, as a 'wild seeress'. To underline her ancient Germanic roots, she appeals to 'Wodan' as the god of vengeance.

The Christian knight is no stranger to her, and so she also knows an antidote to the miracle that he embodies. Her double intrigue is designed to destroy him. Before the lovers are united, Elsa has to ask the forbidden question on their wedding night, a question designed to remind him of his suppressed origins. At the same time and in order to be on the safe side, Telramund will 'tear a member, a finger, nay, even a tiny piece of flesh' from him in order to reveal him in all his 'naked impotence'.

'Anyone who knew how to counter him', Ortrud prophesies in the prose draft, 'would find him weaker than a child.' Only a mother could know this. By delivering Lohengrin up to his murderer, she repeats the initial act of betrayal and reveals herself as the 'wicked mother'. At the moment of truth, when Lohengrin and Elsa approach each other naked as man and wife, the witch recalls the trauma of his past, and at a single stroke he loses his bride, his love and his inheritance.

It is clear that central to his trauma is his fear of castration: the question of his origins is one whose dark 'secret must remain hidden from the whole world', and it invariably includes the question of 'Geschlecht', a word which in German has a wide semantic field, ranging from lineage and generation to sex, gender and genitalia. A crime has been committed against this, calling into question the hero's future viability and turning the son variously into a lonely alpine artist, a Tannhäuser incapable of love and a knight travelling incognito on Grail business.

This explains why, at the very moment that Elsa asks the forbidden question on their bridal night and thus reminds him of his origins, his enemies attack him with drawn swords, thereby repeating the crime of physical disinheritance. Wolfram von Eschenbach's hero was able to enjoy Elsa's love 'with his body', but in Wagner's version, Elsa can only press her body against Lohengrin's in an attempt to protect him. Thanks to her presence of mind, he is able to strike down his enemies and kill Telramund, but what has been done cannot be undone: their marriage is over even before it has been consummated. In both cases, their longing for love has ended in their old despair.

Ortrud has triumphed, at least for the present. Nor is this her only triumph. The starting point of the whole drama – a point overlooked in the sudden rush of events at the end – is also her doing. Did not Elsa's little brother have to disappear in order for the tragedy to run its course? Only when the Grail knight, who is not allowed to love, has taken his leave does the wicked mother allow her mask to drop. The way in which she uses her skills to drive Lohengrin from the world of humans is presumably related to the way in which she spirited Gottfried away. The only son of the ruling dynasty, she exults, has been turned into a swan so that she might rob him of his inheritance.

But why did Wagner use a swan as a symbol of enchantment? In the first ballad he ever wrote, a swan had saved his life, but by constantly reminding him of death it had also reduced him to a state of tormenting dependency. This already recalls the role of Wagner's stepfather, who, it will be remembered, bore the name of a bird. And the swan also appears in an identical form in Tannhäuser's Venusberg, where, as the secret lord of the goddess of love and as a rival of the hero, it stalks its female prey in feathered form.

Alongside the parallel between Wagner's vulturine father and the swan we find another between his mother and Ortrud. It is no accident that Lohengrin's antagonist worships Wodan and that she therefore has at her disposal the magic skills of a swan maiden. This allows her to turn the country's heir, Gottfried, into a swan, much as Johanna Rosine had earlier turned her youngest son into a bird by changing his name from Wagner to Geyer. Robbed of his identity, this son – like the bewitched Gottfried – lost everything. Just as Lohengrin was brought to Brabant by a swan, so Wagner was brought up by Geyer and at the same time deprived of both his inheritance and his mother's love, a love for which he felt an insatiable desire. It was a desire which, as Lohengrin was forced to realize, could not be fulfilled on earth.

And so only his sister remained. There is no doubt that in Elsa we rediscover Wagner's beloved Rosalie. His sympathy with his tender creature, who in *Lohengrin* is forced to die of a broken heart, even inspired him to draft a song in which the enchanted swan sings tenderly: 'On the bank there waits my little sister who must be consoled by me.' Condemned twice over to victimhood, Elsa is a tragic figure. Made to suffer shame and distress as a result of hatred, as she complains in the prose draft, she finds death through love. Wagner never lost faith with her: even as late as 1880 he declared that in *Lohengrin* 'all the scenic splendour and the majesty of the music' existed 'only to throw light on the unique merits of this one heart'.[81]

Conversely, Lohengrin's own tragedy remains hidden as it takes place not so much on stage as in our minds. Unlike his lover, he seems to leave the battlefield alive, but he disappears as the dream figure that he was when he first appeared to Elsa. As his boat drifts away on the Scheldt, the real Lohengrin remains behind on the riverbank, invisible, with no one noticing that the two unhappy lovers, faithfully following in their predecessors' footsteps, are allowed to die a Wagnerian love-death together.

Just as Elsa continues to love Lohengrin, even though she has betrayed him, so Lohengrin remains true to his wife even though he has repudiated her. And he asks God for 'balm' for her wound. In his *Lohengrin* letter of 1846, Wagner even has his two lovers swearing eternal fidelity to one another. 'But death alone remains when reft of thee,' Elsa was originally to have sung, prompting Lohengrin to reply: 'The Grail's own knight must live in godly fane, / Thy husband, ah! is prey to parting's pain!' A vision as nebulous as the Grail in the prelude, he disappears into the sunset, as Elsa raises her eyes 'in ultimate transfiguration'.

For Gottfried has returned. Lohengrin has freed him from the spell that had been cast on him, allowing him to lay aside his swan's plumage and become human once again. Yet this miracle is achieved not by the hero's prayer, which is no more than a makeshift solution demanded by the need to stage the scene, but by the deaths of the lovers. The tragedy of the loss of love that had begun with Gottfried's transformation into a bird can end only when the love that has been lost is regained. This is something that cannot take place in life but only in the union effected by 'transfiguration' in death.

Only when brother and sister are no longer divided but united as lovers can this tragedy about humanity's failure find its resolution. Only then can the hero, who has been alienated from himself and destroyed, be reborn. That he owes this rebirth to the union of the male and female is clear from Wagner's stage directions, according to which the redeemed Gottfried in his glistening white armour should be 'played by a young actress'.[82]

In *A Communication to My Friends*, Wagner speaks of the 'genuine, deep sadness, often welling up in me in the form of hot tears', which he felt when he realized the tragic necessity of the lovers' separation and hence their 'annihilation'. Here too he explains why he felt so close not to his own self-portrait as Lohengrin but to Lohengrin's sisterly lover.

It was Elsa who first set him 'on the trail of the genuinely womanly that shall bring redemption not only to me but to the whole world'. This surprising idea, which once again reveals Wagner's tendency to confuse stage and reality, is explained by his theory of love: something that the 'male egoism' of the knight errant could never achieve on its own is accomplished by the loving wife, as she is not satisfied with the mere Idea, the radiant phenomenon, the celestial façade, all of which demand blind faith. Elsa wants to experience the Idea in all its reality.

As a loving woman, she demands that her anxious lover reveal himself in his entirety and expose his most hidden self, in other words, his 'sex'. She demands this not out of mere curiosity but because love is not satisfied with incompleteness. She wants everything. She wants to hold the dream in her arms. Instead of worshipping the past, she wants to beget and give birth to the future. She wants art to cease being no more than a delightful mirage and to descend into living reality and become fruitful.

It was as a 'woman', wrote Wagner the political refugee, that Elsa 'made a complete revolutionary of me'.[83]

The Tinpot King

Throughout his life, Wagner was fortunate in being able to experience in real life the ideas that exercised his mind. In part, he himself ensured that this was so, and in part fate came to his rescue. At the time of his early enthusiasm for *Der Freischütz*, for example, Weber was a regular visitor to the family home in Dresden. He was introduced to the world of E. T. A. Hoffmann by the writer's friend, his Hoffmannesque Uncle Adolf. His envied model, the composer Giacomo Meyerbeer, became his patron, as did the poet Heinrich Heine, who provided him with the legends on which he was to base many of his later operas. In his adolescent infatuation, Wilhelmine Schröder-Devrient, he found the incarnation of his early heroines, and even Mendelssohn, from whom he borrowed the sounds of a maritime storm and the harmonies of the spheres, left traces on Wagner's life that far outlasted the brevity of their personal encounters.

Yet the most surprising of all these coincidences is one that Wagner owed not to any of his contemporaries but to the age itself: the conflict that was looming throughout his years as Kapellmeister in Dresden was identical to the one that brought about a crisis in his life in general. The social disaster that occurred in

1849 had already taken place in his head, and its outcome was far closer to that of his dramas than he had hoped.

The city that offered him a job for life, together with a pension entitlement, was governed by a conservative ruling house. When compared with the regime of Friedrich August II of Saxony, even the Bavarian monarchy, which could afford the luxury of a Lola Montez, gave the impression of being positively progressive. Saxony had already been on the wrong side in the Wars of Liberation against Napoleon and had resisted attempts at German unification, becoming a centre of reactionary government during the years that followed. Both the court and public life in general gave the impression that the wars of 1813 had never happened. At the time of the People's Uprising in 1830 – an event triggered by the July Revolution in Paris – Wagner was a pupil at the Thomasschule in Leipzig and, in his own words, 'became a revolutionary overnight'. In his enthusiasm, he dedicated a hymn of liberty to the new co-regent Friedrich August II, who was regarded as a liberal.

But the monarchy was quick to recover from this temporary lapse, and when the acclaimed regent ascended the throne in 1836, the country slowly reverted to its old reactionary ways, while keeping a watchful eye on its subjects. By the 1840s, the call for a united Germany and for civil rights was growing increasingly vocal at the very time that Wagner entered the service of a king who had just dismissed a moderately liberal government and replaced it with a deeply conservative ministry. The former revolutionary in his silver-embroidered court uniform was on the wrong side of the political divide.

The outbreak of the February Revolution in Paris in 1848 led to further popular uprisings in Germany, in the wake of which Friedrich August II appointed a liberal ministry that granted press freedom and acknowledged the right of assembly. Wagner, too, joined in the celebrations. But the partying proved premature. When the German National Assembly met in Frankfurt a year later and drew up a democratic 'imperial constitution' for the whole of Germany, their plans encountered resistance on the part of both Friedrich Wilhelm IV of Prussia and Friedrich August II of Saxony.

In spite of the fact that twenty-eight German Länder had already agreed to the new progressive constitution, Friedrich August II dissolved the elected parliament in April following its acceptance of the Paulskirche laws and in May 1849 he replaced the liberal 'March ministry' with a strictly royalist government under Friedrich Ferdinand von Beust. In doing so, Friedrich August II violated his country's constitution in order to secure his own power and thereby destroyed the dream of a united democratic Germany in favour of an antiquated particularist state. The wheels of history seemed to have been turned back and the present definitively overtaken by the hated past.

And this was very much a recurrent theme in Wagner's life. When he returned to Germany from Paris in 1842, he thought that a glorious future lay ahead of him, one in which a liberal state would provide him with a stage for his new art. He saw in the Wartburg a symbol of both a mythical and a democratic Germany, an emblem of the medieval song contest and the Wartburg Festival of 1817. With *Rienzi* he sparked a theatrical revolution in the sleepy city of Dresden. Its hero called for 'freedom', and the town responded with a rousing cheer.

But the future had barely begun before it was over. The spectre of theatrical routine returned to haunt Wagner. His superior carried on like minor royalty and never lost an opportunity to remind him that he was subject to directives from on high. Old promissory notes came through the letter box of his newly furnished apartment. Even in the matter of love, the prospects were less than rosy, his marriage to Minna finally settling into the bourgeois framework for which she had yearned for so long and ultimately degenerating into a Biedermeier idyll complete with parrot and crochet antimacassars.

Here, cut off from the world, Wagner could indulge in his dreams, but in real life he had to submit to the wishes of a monarch and his bemedalled general administrator. His contempt for both men found expression in an anonymous newspaper article that he published in 1849, in which he described Friedrich August II awaiting the revolution 'with anxiously beating heart' and 'bated breath', while Lüttichau responded to the impending disaster 'with the assiduous industry of all the little tricks that have already earned him so many petty titles and medals'.

And there was a third enemy of progress whom Wagner depicts in the form of a spiteful caricature. 'Speculating' on the outcome of the revolution, this individual runs off to the stock exchange and calculates the 'rise and fall of the bonds', haggling over the 'least fraction of one percent'. Wagner's picture of his enemies is thus completed by his portrait of the 'stock-exchange Jew'. Where the monarch, civil servant and stock-exchange Jew hold sway, 'no ray of light breaks in'. Here 'eternal night and darkness reign', and 'into night and darkness', Wagner prophesies, 'everything will sink without trace'.[84]

These lines were published in the *Volksblätter* in April 1849, less than a month before fighting broke out on the barricades in Dresden. By now Wagner had lost his trench war with the powers of the past and had done so, moreover, on every front. Just as the trauma of his origins refused to leave him in peace, so in real life he came up against the obstacle that created not just a mental but a physical block. Whenever he tried to share his enthusiasms with others, he encountered only 'walls of indifference' ranging from outright rejection to cunning reserve. Dresden could boast a lively social life that basked, self-regardingly, in the reflected splendour of the court, but there was no sign of the humanity and love for which he himself yearned.

Wagner knew that this inner conflict could be resolved only on the battlefield of reality, for both the inner and the outer conflicts were concerned with the question of power. Unnoticed by Lüttichau, he stopped kowtowing to the court and adopted a more belligerent attitude. By 1846 he had already started to publish a whole series of memoranda and directives suggesting concrete reforms, all of them aimed ultimately at removing his superior from office. Once his proposals had been rejected, he had no hesitation in calling on the whole of humanity to rise up in armed revolt.

He began by levelling his sights at the object closest to hand, the Dresden Court Orchestra, which he described as notoriously undermanned and over-taxed and whose 'arbitrary chaos' he contrasted with the orchestra of the future in his memorandum *Concerning the Royal Orchestra*. The reforms that he proposed and the reorganization that he suggested, going into the minutest detail in terms of resources and budgets, would have cost very little extra, but his comprehensive plans, submitted to Lüttichau in March 1846, were not deemed worthy of a response for over a year. Predictably, they were rejected.

Far more radical was Wagner's next submission, which dealt not just with the orchestra but with the entire theatre. His *Plan for the Organization of a German National Theatre for the Kingdom of Saxony* was submitted to the minister of the interior in May 1848 and was intended to bring a new spirit of enterprise to a company in which routine and inefficiency were now endemic. In order to avoid cuts in its subsidy and avert the threat that it would be taken over by a leaseholder,[85] the Royal Court Theatre was to be turned into a National Theatre based on democratic principles. The company would be run collectively and, freed from the control of people who knew nothing about opera, could be handed over to the overall supervision of a conductor of their choice, a post for which Wagner tacitly recommended himself. Lovingly worked out to the very last detail, this submission, too, found its way on to Lüttichau's desk. Having already rejected the earlier one, the baron lost no time in declaring it unneces-sary, while at the same time seeing in it 'a new cause for hostility' towards his assistant conductor.

Just as his ambitions had moved from the orchestra to the theatre, so Wagner now raised his sights still further and took in the entire state, writing a private letter in May 1848 to the Saxon delegate in the German National Assembly, Franz Jacob Wigard, and setting forth the assembly's future priorities, which, in Wagner's view, included a strengthening of the role of parliament, territorial reform and the arming of the populace. In June he initiated the good people of Dresden into his plans for a radical reorganization of the state: 'How Do Republican Aspirations Stand in Relation to the Monarchy?' he asked in an inflammatory speech to the radical Vaterlandsverein, a speech published the next day in the *Dresdner Anzeiger*.

Wagner's answer to this question was nothing if not radical itself. For the sake of the common good, the aristocracy would have to go, otherwise the 'shirt of Nessus' represented by its privileges would go up in flames 'one scorching hot day'. This would have to be followed by universal suffrage for men and women and also by a reinforced democratic militia. At the same time, money would be abolished, so that humanity would no longer languish in 'servile dependency' on it.

Having dealt with the aristocracy and the civil service, Wagner was left only with the Jews, whom he held responsible for the sins of the money economy, although as yet he does not name names. Only when the earth had been freed of this 'evil nightmare', to quote Wagner's sibylline prophecy, would the 'human race achieve full emancipation'. In order to ensure that his audience was in no doubt about the exact nature of this nightmare, Wagner equated its removal with 'the fulfilment of Christ's pure teachings'.

Having dealt with the removal of these obstacles, the author could devote himself to the real answer to his own question: how, then, do republican aspirations stand in relation to the monarchy, aspirations aimed at freeing his readers from the tyranny of a money economy and investing them with the right to vote? Wagner's answer is simple: they stand in the same relationship to the monarchy as the monarchy does to them.

As soon as the monarch agreed to abolish the old feudal system, this order would be replaced by the new republic. The 'emancipation of the human race' would be followed by the 'emancipation of the monarchy'. Friedrich August II merely had to make the necessary effort. As soon as he declared the country a free state, the latter would proclaim him 'the freest of the free' and grant his family 'the right of primogeniture' for all time.

When Wagner, 'with vigorous emphasis', declaimed this speech to three thousand enthusiastic listeners, the applause turned into something of a political demonstration. But it soon turned out to have 'appalling' consequences for him, when Lüttichau, representing the aristocracy whom Wagner had playfully threatened with death by fire, lost no time in cancelling a planned performance of *Rienzi*. At the same time, court officials and theatre staff inundated the king with demands that his muddle-headed Kapellmeister be dismissed on the spot.

The newspapers printed squibs aimed at the 'tinpot king' who now wielded his baton not over a brass band but over world history.[86] 'How can such a dreamer destroy his life like this?' sighed his colleague Eduard Devrient. Wagner's head was again 'bursting with big ideas on socialism', the director and actor complained: 'A united Germany is no longer enough for him, what he wants now is a united Europe, united humanity.'[87]

This was no exaggeration. In his emancipatory mood, Wagner was now thinking in universalist terms. Whether it was the individual he had in mind or the orchestra, theatre, state or the whole of the earth's population, radical emancipation was now his watchword. Once this 'rebirth' had been achieved in Germany, he promised his listeners at the Vaterlandsverein, the Germans would 'sail across the seas in ships and found a young Germany', where they would 'father and educate the noblest, most godlike children'. 'We shall do things', he concluded, 'in a glorious and German fashion: from its rising to its setting the sun shall look down upon a beautiful free Germany.'[88]

Although this may sound like a pre-echo of Emanuel Geibel's notorious dictum about the German character providing a solution to all the world's problems, Wagner was in fact merely obeying the logic of his subconscious. As soon as the people had broken the diabolical power of the usurper and restored the throne to the rightful king, thereby assuring the propagation of the true – in other words, the German – ruling dynasty, not only would the composer gain his own personal freedom, the whole world would become free. Once he himself was out of debt, the whole of the money economy would end.

Just as the features of the hard-hearted aristocrat were merged with those of the demonic, money-grubbing Jew in Wagner's picture of the usurper, so the legitimate people's ruler could appear as King Friedrich August II of Saxony. Once the false father had been disposed of, the king would be appointed 'the genuine, free father of his people'. Only then would the power of the past be definitively broken – hence Wagner's appeal to his listeners, whether aristocratic or otherwise, to 'strike all memory of our ancestors from our thoughts, so that henceforth we may be the children of one father, brothers of one family!'

This dream of a popular king in whose realm all men would be brothers is one that Wagner took very seriously, as is clear from an oddly obsequious letter that he wrote to Friedrich August II in person only a week later. Here he not only distanced himself from the 'brutal and violent measures' of the revolution but in effusive tones confirmed the 'most sublime and highest sanctity of the monarchy', a sanctity that consisted in the fact that the king united within himself the freedom of all. Signing himself his sovereign's 'most humble servant', Wagner begged his 'gracious forgiveness' for any misunderstandings that might have been caused by his 'great lapse'.[89]

In many respects, this letter of 1848 resembles the subservient missives that Wagner wrote to the king of grand opera, Giacomo Meyerbeer, in Paris. They too strike a note of wily hypocrisy in seeking to engage the sympathies of a man who was altogether alien to him and who had unsuspectingly slipped into the role of a father figure for Wagner.

As with Meyerbeer, so with Friedrich August II Wagner found the rejection correspondingly hurtful. It was a rejection that came to him in stages over a period of time, beginning with the Court Orchestra's tercentenary celebrations in September 1848, when he was passed over and his colleague Carl Gottlieb Reißiger – who was 'normally treated very dismissively' – was made a Knight of the Order of the Saxon Civil Service. That same evening a worthless composition by Reißiger was received with unusually enthusiastic applause, while the radiant finale to Act One of *Lohengrin*, which Wagner offered as a sample of his new opera, met with a demonstratively 'lukewarm response'.

The next wound was inflicted the following month and proved even more painful, when Lüttichau cancelled the planned première of *Lohengrin* on which Wagner had pinned all his remaining hopes. Not only was the opera a perfect reflection of Wagner's own view of the world, it was admirably in tune with even the most conservative tastes of the time. It also offered him one last chance to escape from his present financial difficulties. But this dream, too, now appeared to be over.

With a single stroke of Lüttichau's pen, all Wagner's work of the preceding three years was destroyed. At the same time, he was informed that the court was 'deeply dissatisfied' with his skills as a conductor. In Meyerbeer's *Robert le diable*, in particular, he had 'beaten time incorrectly'. Wagner struck back under the cloak of anonymity, and in an article published in the *Volksblätter* in October under the title 'Germany and Its Princes', he attacked the aristocracy head-on, demanding their abolition and even their 'self-destruction'. This time not even the king was spared: he could no longer appeal to his ostensible 'rights as a prince'. For Friedrich August II, 'the hour has struck', his Kapellmeister wrote threateningly.[90]

The Spark Ignites

Like Daniel, Wagner began by writing prophecies of doom on the palace walls and, in an essay on the political situation, worked himself up into the role of a dithyrambic poet, singing a hymn to 'the sublime goddess Revolution', rather than calmly discussing the question of suffrage and the arming of the people. Published anonymously as a leading article in the *Volksblätter* in April 1849, this last of Wagner's appeals strikes a note of Schillerian effusiveness that creates the same sort of parodistic impression as his fawning letter to the king. Yet in both cases he was perfectly serious. Although his allegory could add nothing substantially new to existing arguments, it none the less makes clear exactly how Wagner himself interpreted the term.

For Wagner, revolution was a highly dramatic turn of events, when the appearance of some divine power would rescue and redeem a desperate situation. If, in a political context, redemption was synonymous with 'freedom', the power that would achieve that end was 'the goddess of revolution'. But surprisingly, the starting point – the 'world of misery' from which the divine liberator would save mankind – is defined as 'the dominion of the dead over the living'.

It is a fatal force that the past exerts over the present, and one that Wagner conjures up in more and more new variants, binding the living with 'the fetters of the dead' and even having young people stifled 'within the embrace of death'. 'I mean to destroy this order of things', the 'eternally self-rejuvenating mother of humanity' exclaims as she 'consumes the strengths of human beings in the service of the dominion of the dead'.[91]

This has little in common with the usual justification for revolt, a revolt which in the present case was designed to end repression and exploitation and, more concretely, a breach of the constitution and particularism, but it provides a link between the historical situation in Dresden in the late 1840s and the crisis in Wagner's own private life: for Wagner, the 'dead' numbered among their ranks not only the monarchy and a money economy but also the sinister power of his own individual origins.

As though the old Wolf's Glen has returned to haunt his imagination, he begins his hymn to the revolution by evoking the sound of a 'constantly growing and frightening roar'. From the abyss, 'dark clouds, heavy with a storm', arise, covering the whole land with night. Soon the depths begin to stir. Where seething horror had once reigned, a 'tremendous volcano' now rises up. Its hard crust starts to break, streams of lava force their way to the surface before surging down into the valley, 'fiery messengers' of what is to follow, destroying everything in their path. Now the volcano erupts. The forces that have been building up inside it shatter the solid surface that has lain on life like a tombstone. And so the old world is 'smashed to pieces', and a new one, lit by flashes of lightning, raises its godlike head.

To recognize in this poetical allegory the political situation in Dresden during the early months of 1849 requires a certain theatrical imagination, but this is something that Wagner could expect from his readers as he himself had prepared them for it. A week before his article 'Revolution' appeared in the pages of the *Volksblätter*, he had already offered them a musical demonstration of it at the head of the Court Orchestra, performing Beethoven's Ninth Symphony at the annual Palm Sunday concert in the old opera house. With its setting of Schiller's ode about the 'divine spark', the work had been enthusiastically acclaimed by its audience, who interpreted it as a tribute to the murdered revolutionary Robert Blum.

Blum had represented Saxony in the National Assembly in Frankfurt. His unlawful execution in Vienna in October 1848 had provoked outrage throughout Germany, and according to Wagner, even government ministers turned out to show their support at a funeral march in Dresden. For the audience, Blum and Beethoven's Ninth Symphony went together inasmuch as the republican groups that he had founded went under the name of 'Schiller Societies', so that the Ode 'To Joy' that Beethoven had set became the password by which would-be participants in the planned rebellion recognized one another.[92] The key concept, on which the revolutionaries laid special emphasis, was the 'divine spark' of inspiration. It was this that served as the fuse leading to the powder keg of society. Following the explosion, humanity – 'drunk with ardour' – could enter the celestial sanctuary of joy.

The violent death of the freedom fighter, which seemed an all too potent symbol of the failed revolution of 1848, was not the only memory bound up with the Ninth Symphony in the minds of Dresden's audiences. Ever since Wagner had first conducted the work at the city's popular Palm Sunday concert in 1846, it had become what he himself termed a 'point of honour' for him. In 1846, the performance had gone ahead against the wishes of the orchestra, whose members had even complained to Lüttichau, but in the event it turned out to be one of his greatest triumphs thanks to endless rehearsals and a massed choir whom he raised to a 'veritable ecstasy' of delight. A significant part of the concert's success was due to the fact that prior to the performance Wagner had organized an information campaign in the form of anonymous newspaper advertisements and detailed programme notes revealing the work's hidden import.

Drawing on quotations from *Faust*, Wagner showed that the work was based on a clearly recognizable idea: Beethoven starts by depicting the way in which humanity is forced to suffer from 'the pressure of a hostile power'. People rebel against this 'demon that robs them of their joy' and which, like a bird of prey, overshadows them with its 'mighty pinions', but their revolt proves futile. The 'sombre mood' that prevails at the end of the opening movement affects the whole of the universe, but in the final movement liberation draws nigh with a 'wild and chaotic cry'. Divine light illumines the chaos, 'spirited, warlike strains' ring forth, while young men rush enthusiastically into battle. Soon the 'insidiously powerful foe' of the opening has been routed, and liberated humanity joins in the final hymn 'with the most sublime enthusiasm': 'Welcome, all ye million creatures! / Brethren, take this kiss of love!'[93]

Anyone who had read Wagner's exegesis of the Ninth Symphony in 1846 was bound to recognize its style and ideas in the anonymous article 'Revolution' of 1849, with even the imagined 'millions', who in 1846 had prostrated themselves before the God of the world, returning in the run-up to the May Uprising and expressing the same frenzy of emotion. 'Inspiration shines from their ennobled faces', the prophet Wagner waxes lyrical, 'a radiant light streams from their eyes', and 'the millions, the living Revolution, the God become Man, rush down to the valleys and plains and proclaim to all the world the new gospel of happiness'. This was Wagner's theatrical view of the revolution. Whether anyone shared this view or had even the vaguest notion of what the conductor was trying to say with his effusions about the 'divine spark' was another question.

But there were at least a few people who believed him. As early as 1846 he had confided in the writer Alfred Meißner, telling him that the political situation was ripe for radical change.[94] And the following year he wrote to the music journalist Ernst Kossak to announce that 'preaching to audiences' was not enough: 'There is a dam that must be broken here, and the means we must use is revolution!' But he would be satisfied if the king of Prussia were at least to reform his opera house.[95] And in 1848 the music critic Eduard Hanslick noted that Wagner was 'all politics: with the victory of the revolution, he was convinced, would come a total rebirth of art, society and religion'.[96]

Wagner's Dresden colleague Eduard Devrient had already tried to reform the theatre and left a record in his diary of his despair at the hopeless state in which it found itself, a state that soon spread to the whole of society. Wagner's 'hobby horse' was 'the destruction of capital', as capital alone stood in the way of any amelioration of the human race. At the same time, Wagner had been seized by a sense of 'sublime enthusiasm for world dominion', which he felt would be within striking distance once victory was assured. But before the world could be rebuilt, Wagner argued, the old order first had to be destroyed. Without destruction there could be no rebirth.

There were some who thought they had an even clearer idea of Wagner's revolutionary goddess, a figure who by no means fortuitously holds a burning torch in her hand. At the final rehearsal for the 1849 Palm Sunday concert, onlookers noticed a tall bearded man in a black coat. At the end, he came over to the orchestra and, speaking in a Slav accent, assured the conductor that even if all other music were to be lost in the coming world conflagration, this symphony at least must be preserved. For all his self-assurance and public joking, the speaker was deadly serious. Here was a man with a price on his head, and even his assumed name, Dr Schwarz (consciously borrowed from the inventor of gunpowder), was known to the police. Mikhail Alexeevich Bakunin was already under police surveillance.

This larger-than-life figure was afraid neither of God nor the devil. Russian by birth and cosmopolitan by upbringing, Bakunin had studied Hegel in Berlin and espoused the causes of Communism and the liberation of the Slavs. He had arrived in Dresden with the aim of tossing the divine spark into the waiting powder keg. In his hiding place not far from Wagner's rooms and on the long walks they took together, the oversized anarchist and the undersized court musician exchanged their radical views, Wagner being especially impressed by Bakunin's 'childlike and demonic delight' in playing with matches.

In *My Life*, Bakunin is depicted as a merry incendiary who recommended a global conflagration as the only remedy for the ills of civilization. To Wagner's approving amazement, he predicted that the 'whole European world, from Saint Petersburg to Paris and London, would be turned into a heap of rubble'. But a start now had to be made, and in the sleepy royal residence of Dresden, Bakunin took on the 'task of chief pyrotechnician'.[97]

Assisting him was August Röckel, an unsuccessful composer and socialist who owed his appointment as music director to Wagner. With a large family to support, Röckel earned less than half the conductor's wages and was as out of place in a court appointment as Wagner himself. Röckel believed implicitly in violent revolution and openly championed the arming of the populace, a position that led to his instant dismissal. From August 1848 he edited the *Volksblätter* as a public platform agitating for the violent overthrow of the existing regime, something to which he looked forward with the same impatience as his co-editor and fellow contributor.

The notion advanced by earlier writers on Wagner that the Austrian Röckel was a Mephistophelean figure who lured the naïvely Faustian Wagner from the straight and narrow is one of Minna's attempts to exculpate her husband.[98] The truth of the matter is that Röckel looked up to Wagner with reverential awe and willingly allowed himself to be 'used as a loyal standard-bearer'.[99] It was never Wagner's practice to waste time listening to others. He was an eloquent and interminable speaker who, not without good reason, felt called upon to be the philosopher of emancipation, so that it is simply not possible to accept Gregor-Dellin's claim that Wagner owed everything to Röckel.

Although Röckel introduced the Russian Bakunin to his idol in March 1849, he was by no means their equal. While the two others discussed the world's future behind closed doors, their assistant stood at the printing presses of the *Volksblätter* or wrote exhortations to the Prussian military that resulted in a brief spell in prison. It was no accident that the good socialist spent thirteen years behind bars in the wake of the revolution, while his mentor escaped with typically Wagnerian elegance.

Wagner's step from poetic to active revolutionary presumably coincided with Bakunin's arrival in Dresden, but it did not require him to be untrue to himself. For him, art was merely a higher form of reality, while reality, at best, was an inferior form of art, and so it needed no great awakening for him to involve himself in the planning of the May Uprising. He bore within himself the contradictions that demanded a violent resolution.

The works with which he had revolutionized the art of staging opera had left no impression on the traditional world of art. His attempt to rid himself of an intolerable burden of debt by publishing his works at his own risk had proved a failure, thanks to a public lack of interest in them. His commitment as court conductor bordered on self-denial, but it had left him exposed to institutionalized bodies who held views completely at odds with his own. Even with Minna, who had progressed from the role of lover to that of the wife of a court conductor, he felt trapped. The time seemed ripe for upheaval both in his own private life and within the country in general.

But revolution meant far more to him than simply an opportunity to remedy a deplorable situation. His expectations were totally different from those of Bakunin, Röckel and the Vaterlandsverein. Inasmuch as he saw himself in the vanguard of modernism, the solution to the problems that beset him in his own private life seemed to be synonymous with a resolution of the problems associated with the whole of his age, an age in which an arrogant aristocracy, a Jewish-dominated money economy and a moribund culture, all of which cast their shadows on his own personal circumstances, were holding back society at large. As soon as the nightmare that was haunting him had been lifted, he felt that the country as a whole would be able to breathe freely again. The freedom for which people yearned was offered by his art, in which they could see themselves as though in a transfiguring mirror and thus become conscious of their own drama and also of their divinity.

They could do so, except that they did not yet know this. As long as his works were garbled, mutilated or simply ignored, people could never discover this for themselves. What was of use to him, Wagner believed, was of use to everyone else. His own emancipation from the evils of the past would bring freedom to the whole of Germany. What possible comparison could there be between, on the one hand, the right to vote, the arming of the populace and even democracy and, on the other, the perfect work of art in which the whole nation would recognize itself again? Beethoven's Ninth Symphony was merely a foretaste of what was to come. The true miracle of art, Wagner was convinced, would reveal itself in the future, much as the Grail appeared in the ethereal vault. Assuming that the 'divine spark' ignited.

Wagner had the unusual gift of being able to devote himself entirely to his dreams and at the same time, with no less commitment, to attend to their implementation. As a result, the part that he played in the drama that unfolded in Dresden in May 1849 reveals him as a dreamer apparently standing to one side of events that he had in fact organized and that he himself was now guiding. He threw himself into these events body and soul, while simultaneously observing them from a distance. Whenever anything happened, Wagner was generally there. If he passed unnoticed, we cannot say for certain that he was not implicated in the incident in question. Like his god Wotan, whose slouch hat he himself wore, Wagner was invariably one step ahead of events. When the revolution failed, he had already made good his escape.

The Opera House On Fire

Wagner's eyewitness account of the Dresden revolution was written twenty years after the event for the benefit of Ludwig II and is one of the most successful episodes not only in *My Life* but perhaps in the whole of his output as a writer. Like Goethe in his famous description of the Cannonade of Valmy, Wagner, adoping a superior standpoint, allows his reader to join in the drama of history through the eyes of an inspired observer.

The particular appeal of Wagner's lively and, in spite of the seriousness of the subject matter, entertaining account is that it is simply not true. Here he claims that he stumbled into the revolution by chance and that, after wandering around for a few days that were as turbulent as they were aesthetically delightful, he stumbled out of it again. Like Gulliver among the Lilliputians, he registered everything that he saw and heard with exactly the same astonishment and the same smile of lofty superiority.

The opposing faction, represented by eyewitnesses and the royal investigating commission, was unable to follow him down this particular road. They clearly saw Wagner as a criminal, guilty of 'substantial involvement' in the uprising,[100] which he had planned as 'one of the most prominent supporters of the insurgents' and helped to carry through to its bloody conclusion. Even long-standing friends such as Ferdinand Heine privately admitted that he had been 'undeniably involved in leading the uprising'.[101] The statement by the Saxon foreign minister Friedrich Ferdinand von Beust that Wagner was sentenced to death in his absence for treason thus seems entirely plausible.[102] Beust knew the court conductor very well, making it unlikely that he was capable of confusing him with a baker's apprentice of the same name, a hypothesis advanced by early biographers such as William Ashton Ellis.[103]

If we pause for a moment to examine the activities of the rebellious Kapellmeister as they emerge from behind the protecting veil of his own later reminiscences, we shall see that they appear to be motivated not by poetic exuberance but by sober pragmatism. Wagner knew exactly what he wanted and how he could best achieve it. It was no dreamer at work here but an out-and-out strategist. Where necessary he joined in the action, only then to create the distance he needed to pull the strings – or, in this particular instance, the ropes of the bells that were rung to sound the alarm.

The very first day of the uprising reveals the unbridgeable gulf between a historically accurate account of the situation and the novelistic rewriting of his life that Wagner was presumably already penning as the Prussian bullets whizzed round his ears. According to *My Life* he had just left a meeting of the Vaterlandsverein on Wednesday 3 May 1849 (the third was in fact a Thursday) when suddenly he heard the tocsin being rung from the tower of Saint Anne's Church. The excited pealing of the bells, combined with the knowledge that the revolution had broken out, inspired in Wagner a feeling that reminded him of Goethe's Valmy. Like Goethe, he saw the world bathed in a yellow light as though during an eclipse of the sun and felt a 'great, nay, extravagant sense of well-being'. What could have been more natural, then, than to call in at the nearby home of the tenor Joseph Tichatschek and, purely as a precautionary measure, to ask to take charge of the singer's collection of rifles? He was anxious, he told Tichatschek's wife, that these dangerous firearms should not fall into the hands of the 'rabble'.

Once this 'eccentric whim' had been gratified, Wagner returned 'to the streets to see what was going on in the town, apart from the clangour of the tocsin and the yellowish solar eclipse'. To his agreeable surprise, the first person he bumped into was Wilhelmine Schröder-Devrient, who proved much agitated by the news that troops had fired on the local townspeople. She now proceeded to harangue the 'dull-witted masses', but the latter remained unmoved by her eloquence.

Later he discovered that a 'reckless' mob had tried to storm the armoury but had been met with cannon fire and driven back. He had 'mechanically' followed the crowd that was calling out 'To the barricades!' and, before he knew where he was, had found himself in the council chambers at the Town Hall, where the prevailing mood was one of total helplessness. By now night was falling, and so he hurried back to his rooms, before continuing to 'participate as an observer' the next morning.

Although Wagner's whimsical account occasionally degenerates into sarcasm, its wealth of detail and narrative realism left earlier readers in no doubt as to its credibility, but it has to be offset by the following facts, all of which were known to the legal authorities in Dresden. Conspiratorial meetings had been held over a period of several weeks both in Wagner's summerhouse and in the nearby apartment of one of the editors of the *Dresdner Zeitung*, with whom he was on friendly terms. Here they had discussed arming the populace and had presumably also planned the impending onslaught. These meetings were attended not only by Wagner, Bakunin and Röckel but also by officers of the Dresden Communal Guard.

In total, there were some 'twenty to thirty male persons' whose names later appeared in police files. In short, Wagner had long been aware that there was to be a revolution. The day before the uprising, Wagner had summoned his friend August Röckel back from Prague. It had been agreed to ring the tocsin as a signal, and according to the testimony of the daughter of Wagner's old friend Alexander Müller, it was Wagner himself who rang it.[104] The speech that Wagner then claims to have heard delivered by Wilhelmine Schröder-Devrient in the Altmarkt was addressed to a vast crowd that passed with a cart bearing the body of a townsman killed by Saxon soldiers.

As Wagner was well aware, the soprano was calling for vengeance for the army massacre at the armoury. Once the tocsin had been rung, the crowd, keen to implement plans to arm the people, tried to storm the arsenal but was met by a hail of bullets from the Saxon infantry that left four of the attackers dead. This was followed by case-shot fired from a cannon, a brutal rejoinder on the part of an overzealous artillery carpenter acting without the orders of his superior officer. The case-shot was filled with lead bullets and exploded in the middle of the crowd of rioters and members of the Communal Guard, leaving 'more than twenty dead and fatally wounded'.[105] According to Clara Schumann, fourteen 'terribly mutilated' victims of the uprising were laid out the next day in the courtyard of the Dresden Clinic. Following the massacre, the crowd stormed the armouries and helped itself to rifles.

The uprising had thus acquired its martyrs right from the outset. The king fled the city the very next day, taking the whole of his court with him. In order to gain time, the military, which, now very unsure of itself, saw itself confronted by manned barricades, agreed to a truce. By midday on 4 May – not the fifth, as Wagner claims in *My Life* – a provisional government had been formed in the Town Hall. To the sounds of jubilation and tolling bells, its members appeared before the people, swore on oath to uphold the imperial constitution and demanded loyalty on the part of the Saxon troops.

'I recall', wrote Wagner, 'that this all had a far from edifying impact on me.' Others remembered things differently: it was Wagner himself, they recalled, who led the cheers for the new government and who offered his services as 'secretary'. He even addressed the crowd directly from the Town Hall balcony. From now on he was often seen at the Town Hall, where Bakunin had established his headquarters. Wagner evidently functioned as a link between the command centre and the 'front'.

On 4 May – the second day of the uprising – the picture changed decisively. Beust had asked for Prussian troops to assist his own army, and these were now approaching. In order to counter their military superiority, which threatened to bring a rapid end to the revolution, there were only two possibilities: first, the Saxon soldiers would have to be persuaded to change sides and join the popular government, and second, auxiliary troops would have to be brought in from the surrounding area.

These were the two tasks to which Wagner devoted his energies. The graphic account of his activities in *My Life* omits to mention only their strategic importance for the subsequent course of the fighting. According to Wagner's own account, he had hoped to force the king himself to oppose this 'Prussian occupation' and thereby achieve an 'honourable peace' in the midst of the overall chaos.

In his Annals, by contrast, Wagner not only recalls the oath taken by the provisional government and the midday 'market parade' (entered under the correct date), he also mentions his activities during the afternoon, 'agitating against the arrival of the expected Prussian troops'.[106] Wagner had issued instructions for posters to be printed with the words 'Are you with us against the foreign troops?' and for these to be posted on the barricades where a Saxon assault was expected.

Events that in *My Life* read like a schoolboy prank were in fact part of a strategy decided on by the provisional government. Wagner himself had instructed the printer of the *Volksblätter* to produce several hundred posters that were not only displayed on the barricades and on house fronts but personally handed to the Saxon soldiers by Wagner himself. It is something of a miracle that he was not shot on the spot for such a brazen act that was effectively an invitation to the troops to commit high treason.

It may have been this heroic but useless action that inspired him to meditate on Homer's Achilles,[107] a curious episode recorded in *My Life*, where he recalls 'good-humouredly' walking home on this glorious spring evening and finding time between the barricades to conceive of a 'drama' based on the old tale. It seems from the surviving fragments that Wagner saw a clear parallel between himself and the demigod.

For Achilles, only vengeance matters. Even the immortality offered him by his mother Thetis he 'contemptuously' rejects in order to devote himself wholeheartedly to the 'gratification of his thirst for vengeance'. When the Greek commanders ask him to join in the destruction of Troy following his 'disposal of Hector', he gives them to understand that the only thing that counts for him is to savour the fruits of retribution. In Wagner's eyes, this obstinacy, by placing personal will over fame in battle and eternal life, allows Achilles to rise above the gods themselves. It was in contemplation of such flattering ideas that the poet ended the second day of the uprising, while the secretary of the revolution considered the next steps to be taken in pursuit of revenge.

Perhaps a role in this revenge was played by the hand grenades he had ordered before Easter from the brass founder Carl Wilhelm Oehme. These were temporarily stored in the offices of the *Dresdner Zeitung* prior to Wagner's reminding his comrades of their existence on 3 May – his Annals for this date include a reference to 'shrapnel-shells'. The insurgents evidently intended to use these one hundred and fifty or so pineapple hand grenades, as Oehme later recalled under oath that on 4 May Wagner had instructed him to fill them with gunpowder. The effect produced by Wagner's hand grenades was much the same as that produced by case-shot, the only difference being that they were of a smaller calibre.

The fifth of May again found Wagner at the Town Hall, which served both as the seat of the provisional government and as the headquarters of the defenders. Their hold over the inner city could be maintained only by means of barricades extending to first-floor level and decorated with black, red and gold flags and with portraits of the martyr to the revolution, Robert Blum.[108]

Wagner's description of the arrival of Gottfried Semper introduces a note of rib-tickling humour into his narrative. As a gunner in the Communal Guard, Semper raised a Wagnerian smile by turning up in full regalia, including his militiaman's hat. The architect of the new opera house advised the provisional government secretary that the improvised bulwarks were 'extremely faulty in their construction', so Wagner duly sent him to the offices of the commission entrusted with the defence of the inner city, and the commission in turn invited him to help in the construction of new barricades, a task which, according to Wagner's report, Semper carried out 'with the artistic dedication of a Leonardo da Vinci or Michelangelo'. The opposite was in fact the case: it was Wagner who hit upon the idea of calling on the services of the experienced court architect, and Semper was all the more willing to help in that he had already attended the conspiratorial meetings in Wagner's garden. His 'minor fortifications' even commanded the respect of the besieging troops. The losses on both sides were correspondingly high.

Towards six o'clock on the afternoon of 5 May, Wagner is said to have approached members of the Communal Guard stationed in the Zwinger and acted as spokesman of a group of insurgents intent on setting fire to the castle and palace with the help of inflammable liquids. The militia resisted this drastic measure, but the arsonists refused to be discouraged. Once again, it was Oehme, a confidant of Wagner's, who provided the fireworks.

Oehme later swore on oath that it had been a group of unknown miners who had tried to set fire to the palace using turpentine and spirit. In order to prevent this from happening, he had watered down the turpentine before it could be sprayed on the roof using a fireman's hose, with the result that the fire could not spread.[109] Needless to say, the court did not believe a word of all this. As Beust recalled, the court had in front of it a document in which Wagner personally boasted of 'setting fire to the Royal Palace', an act that happily had no serious repercussions.[110]

By late on the Saturday evening, Wagner was beginning to feel the need to rise above the situation. According to his much later account in *My Life*, he found it difficult to hear the shooting while 'being unable to see what was going on'. And so he hit on the idea of climbing to the top of the Kreuzkirche tower, at ninety-six metres the city's highest landmark. As he himself emphasized, it commanded a splendid view over the roofs of Dresden. Whenever the rattling of the guns fell silent, he could even hear nightingales from his airy lookout. But even the confused sounds of the tolling of bells and the roar of cannon fire struck him as 'intoxicating'.

Wagner fails to mention that the tower was used by the insurgents as an observation platform, a command centre and a signalling post. He himself was presumably occupied in all these capacities. While up to seventy irregulars opened fire on the surrounding area from here, Wagner and others followed enemy troop movements, tying their messages to stones and throwing them down to the waiting guards below. He could also attract attention acoustically, using an agreed code and, as the commander of the Prussian forces later reported, giving 'the cue for the tocsin and other signals'. When orders were given to withdraw from the town, 'the great bell in the tower of the Kreuzkirche gave out a ninefold boom' at eight o'clock.[111]

Wagner remained at his post throughout the whole of the Saturday night, and while enemy bullets buried themselves in the mattresses set up to protect him, he engaged in long philosophical discussions, debating the difference between the classical and the Christian views of the world and between absolute and dramatic music and also holding forth on the subject of Hegel's famous dialectic of master and servant. When questioned about the threat posed by the enemy sharpshooters, he is reported to have answered light-heartedly that the bullet that would strike him down had not yet been cast.

Extraordinary scenes greeted Wagner the next morning. While the Prussian army took up their positions in the newer part of the town, columns of insurgents came marching in from the opposite direction, as Wagner was the first to notice. And 'the guns glittered brightly in the blood-red rays of the rising sun'. Wagner was particularly pleased to see that they were bringing with them four small cannon taken from the estates of Baron Thade von Burgk, whom he knew very well as a member of the Dresden Liedertafel. They were normally positioned in the baronial vineyards but were now 'fired on the enemy from the barricades', a redeployment that Wagner found 'particularly ironic' as the baron had apparently once made an unspeakably boring speech at the Liedertafel.

Thade's cannon inflicted injuries no less terrible than those caused by the case-shot at the armoury: the insurgents lacked munitions, and so, at Bakunin's bidding,[112] they filled them with iron cylinders, pieces of broken lead and nails, which, whistling through the air like humming tops, caused appalling injuries to their victims, including a major general by the name of Homilius. Thade knew the effect his cannon would have, with their illegal projectiles, and had protested against their confiscation, whereupon a scrap of paper was pressed into his hand, bearing the seal of the provisional government and the signature of Adjutant Leo von Zychlinsky.

Wagner knew Zychlinsky very well. He mentions him several times in his Annals and was still in contact with him many years later. The former law student had also attended the conspirators' meetings in Wagner's garden and now served as the commander's adjutant in the Communal Guard. It is clear from entries in Wagner's Annals that it was in this capacity that Zychlinsky had dealings with the composer. Zychlinsky was also responsible not only for the manning of the Kreuzturm, where he occasionally kept Wagner company, but also for bringing in auxiliary troops from the surrounding area. Other 'revolutionary activities' were later laid at his door.

Among these incidents is one that was to go down in the annals of the uprising as a particularly senseless but symbolic act. At seven o'clock on the morning of Sunday 6 May (or at half past three if we are to believe the account of Richard von Friesen, who occupied various political and administrative posts in the Saxon government), fire broke out in the old opera house on the Zwinger next to the Royal Palace. From his observation post on the Kreuzturm, Wagner was able to watch the fire spread to the Zwinger itself.

It is all the more curious, then, that in spite of all the noise of the various bells and alarms, Wagner claims not to have noticed the fire until eleven o'clock, a fire he describes as 'turning into a tremendous sea of flames within the shortest possible time'. He then watched, fascinated, as the flames spread to the copper roofs of the Zwinger, on which 'strange bluish tongues of fire began to dance', just as they would later do on his Valkyrie Rock. Only now did he and the other onlookers feel any 'regret' at the incident, whereas the destruction of the opera house, which was completely gutted, seems not to have worried them at all, Wagner even noting in his Annals: 'Opera house now burnt down: strange sense of contentment.'[113]

In *My Life*, Wagner was evidently at pains to play down the significance of the damage. In the first place, he claims, such a disaster had long been feared, as the building was full of 'extremely combustible material' such as wood and canvas. Moeover, it was a 'hideous' provisional structure whose removal had long been demanded.

Wagner, as we know, was writing this for the benefit of Ludwig II, who was presumably unaware of something that every inhabitant of Dresden knew, namely, that the charred building had been a Baroque masterpiece by the Zwinger architect Matthäus Daniel Pöppelmann. It was here that Wagner's Palm Sunday concert had taken place exactly a month earlier. In the presence of his friend Gustav Adolph Kietz, Wagner had repeatedly expressed his 'delight and wonderment' at the old opera house's 'wonderful acoustics'.[114]

But the damage done to the Court Opera, too, was irreparable, because, as Wagner knew very well, Pöppelmann's building was used as a store for productions at Gottfried Semper's new opera house. Sets and costumes for the repertory pieces that Wagner conducted all went up in flames. 'Our great opera house in which our magnificent sets and costumes were stored', Reißiger lamented on 16 May 1849, 'is in ruins'. As a result all contracts had to be cancelled and all performances, including two new productions, abandoned.

Wagner himself must have been aware of at least one of these new productions as it replaced his own *Lohengrin*: it was Meyerbeer's *Le prophète*.[115] As a result of the fire, the work could not be given until January 1850, when King Friedrich August II took the opportunity to appoint Meyerbeer a Knight of the Saxon Order of Merit.

In Wagner's eyes, the loss of the old opera house meant the end of a hated world: a symbol not only of the monarchy but of the forced labour of his life as a court conductor and of a moribund operatic tradition that had now disappeared for good. Shortly before, in a poem entitled 'Need', he had called on the 'sacred fire' to reduce to ashes 'all the places devoted to the service of Mammon'.[116] This had now happened, and Wagner had every reason to feel a 'strange sense of contentment'. His claim that the building had had to be destroyed for tactical reasons – namely, in order to protect Semper's barricade from 'a surprise attack' – is unconvincing, as the shell remained intact while only the magnificent interior was gutted.

No convincing reason can be found for the destruction of this architectural masterpiece and the resultant threat to the Zwinger. So why did it have to be burnt down? According to Richard von Friesen, enquiries revealed that the provisional government had ordered this 'completely pointless outrage'. But the provisional government, having no military know-how, was thrown back on the recommendations of its advisers, the most likely contender for this title being the trained officer Mikhail Bakunin, who had set up his card table in the government's conference room. Within days of the end of the uprising, a local journalist was already reporting that the Russian had issued 'the most terrible orders', including 'permission to set fire to houses to make the fighting easier'. One of these buildings was said to be 'the old opera house'.[117] There had been plentiful supplies of miner's blasting powder, oil of turpentine and 'pitch-rings'.

Clearly, there were plenty of potential suspects, including Wagner's friend August Röckel, who had helped in ordering the hand grenades and who was also said to have 'prepared the pitch-rings intended to set fire to the Royal Palace'.[118] Wagner had summoned Röckel back from Prague on the Wednesday, but it was later claimed that he had not returned to Dresden by mailcoach until the Sunday morning, by which time the old opera house was already a charred ruin. His alibi would have remained unassailable had it not been for the fact that eighteen years later, in January 1867, Wagner had reminded him of 'various incendiary attacks on the Royal Saxon Court'.[119]

Possibly Röckel had returned to Dresden in secret the previous evening. After the failed assault on the Royal Palace, he could have joined forces with Oehme, a turpentine specialist with whom he was on friendly terms, and turned his attentions to a building whose interior was intimately familiar to him. All that was missing was an intermediary to pass on Bakunin's incendiary instructions. And according to the files drawn up by the investigating commission, this go-between was their mutual friend Leo von Zychlinsky, who was involved in 'conveying the orders for setting fire to the opera house'.[120]

The insurgents themselves seem to have had a good idea who was behind this wanton act. The following day, Wagner noted not without pride in his Annals that he had been crossing one of the barricades when a voice called out: 'Herr Kapellmeister, well, the beautiful spark of divine joy has ignited.' In *My Life*, Wagner adds that the speaker – a member of the Communal Guard – had gone on to explain: 'The rotten building has been razed to the ground.' Evidently, Wagner surmises, 'this was an enthusiastic member of the audience at the recent performance of the Ninth Symphony'.

The Dresden Revolution came to a sticky end. In spite of further reinforcements, some of which were organized by Wagner himself,[121] the military gained the upper hand, reasserting its supremacy in house-to-house fighting that lasted until the Tuesday and resulted in heavy losses. The Tuesday night saw the start of a general flight in which the leaders of the uprising, including Bakunin himself, defiantly clung together.

Wagner initially travelled in the government coach, venting his feelings in 'inflammatory tirades', but then decided that it would be preferable not to be found in the company of the ringleaders of the revolution if, as seemed likely, they were to be arrested. Thanks to his presence of mind, he was spared many years' imprisonment that might well have spelt the end of his career as a composer.

Four days later, on 14 May 1849, he also took his official leave of the failed uprising: in a letter to Minna clearly intended for public consumption, he announced that he was attracted by the idea not of destroying things but of refashioning them. 'Look! In this way I cut myself off from the revolution!'[122]

Wagner's account makes no mention of any injuries or fatalities but treats the uprising like a coup de théâtre. Yet from his vantage point on the Kreuzturm, he must have seen the damage inflicted by the guns, by the hand grenades and Prussian percussion needle firelocks. As a confidant of the provisional government, he was presumably also aware of the losses, but although he refers to the 'most terrible disaster' in his letter to Minna, he preferred to say nothing about the number of fatalities.

According to official estimates, the military lost forty-four soldiers and officers, while some two hundred and fifty insurgents of both sexes perished in the uprising. This second figure is almost certainly an underestimate, as it is known that, following the end of the fighting, an unspecified number of captured rebels were thrown to their deaths from windows, drowned in the Elbe, shot in the street or bayoneted. The victors exacted 'the most terrible' vengeance. Wagner, who was extremely lucky to have escaped alive and who, as a serenely Olympian autobiographer, refused to acknowledge these facts, none the less took note of them for future reference.

For the benefit of the outside world, he laid claim to a state of 'dreamy otherworldliness' which, notwithstanding the purposefulness of his destructive energies, presumably never left him. He was completely absorbed by his revolutionary role, while regarding everything that happened as symbolical. If in his initial euphoria the world had seemed to be bathed in an artificial Goethean light, the drumbeat that he heard at the end of the uprising reminded him of the 'spectral rattle of the skeletons' bones in their nocturnal dance round the gallows that Berlioz had depicted with such frightening verisimilitude in the final movement of his *Symphonie fantastique* when I heard it in Paris'. In this way, even the idea of his own execution – an idea that is by no means far-fetched – produced a musically vivid picture. What happened was part of a politically necessary process and at the same time part of his own private drama in life.

Just as he later – perhaps quite rightly – saw his performance of Beethoven's Ninth, with its reference to the 'divine spark', as an overture to the uprising, so he brought his account of the débâcle to an end with the symphony's sounds of joy, as though there had been no bloodbath in between. When at the beginning of June 1849 he set off for Paris by mailcoach, armed with a Swiss travel permit, he found himself struck by a 'strange phenomenon'. The noise of the cannons and rifles that had continued to echo in his inner ear was suddenly driven out by a different sound. 'Now', he wrote in *My Life*, 'the humming of the wheels as we rolled rapidly along the highway cast such a spell on me that throughout the whole journey I thought I could hear in this sound, as though played by deep bass instruments, the melody of "Freude, schöner Götterfunken" from the Ninth Symphony.'

4   World View

Jessie

Three days after Wagner wrote to Minna to announce that he had 'cut himself off' from the failed revolution, he informed his Dresden colleague Eduard Devrient that he was keen to return to his post as court Kapellmeister. He was ready, he went on, to take six months' leave of absence and 'with all his heart held out his hand in the expectation of a subsequent return to Dresden'.[1] Devrient could not believe his eyes: Wagner, after all, was a traitor who faced the death penalty if caught, yet he was carrying on as if nothing had happened.

The truth of the matter, Wagner told Devrient, was that he had been impli-cated in the fighting only as an observer who had adopted 'the most objective position in the world'. But he wondered idly whether he had 'now been stupidly condemned as a traitor or the like'. It was 'stupid' because no sensible person could believe that 'the revolution was the result of a conspiracy'. There had been no plan, he assured Devrient, everything had happened spontaneously. Even the assault on the armoury had been no more than an 'act of impetuosity'. Shaking his head in dismay, Devrient replied to the effect that Wagner could not expect him to share his attitude and gloss over the situation in this way, as 'your extreme political opinion was invariably the subject of our violent argu-ments'. Any form of self-justification seemed illusory. At best Wagner could hope for an amnesty.

In short, the situation was hopeless. If the revolution had not produced the result that Wagner had wanted, at least he now knew where he stood. Although the strains of the Ninth Symphony may have consoled him on his way to Paris, this journey, too, proved to be a futile undertaking. The city that he had heaped with imprecations only seven years earlier was now expected to offer him the financial salvation that he needed. True, he had left his mountain of debt behind him in Germany, which was a source of some relief to him. But his finances remained depleted.

In Paris there had been an outbreak of cholera, and funeral processions passed beneath his window to the sound of muffled drums. The risk of infection meant that the city's water supply was undrinkable. And the heat was oppressive. Wagner was involuntarily drawn back to the offices of Maurice Schlesinger, who had commissioned so much hackwork from him in the past. As fate would have it, Meyerbeer was in the shop when Wagner arrived and was introduced by an assistant as 'votre maître'. The older composer pointedly asked him whether he would be 'writing scores for the barricades' in future. No, Wagner retorted, he was no longer thinking of writing anything at all. Yet this was precisely why he had come to Paris – at Liszt's suggestion, he was planning to write a new work for the Opéra.

It was clearly a futile project. The Paris Opéra had no more need than before for unknown artists and their unknown works. Wagner remained in France for a little over a month, spending all the money that Liszt had given him, before returning to Zurich, his mission unaccomplished. Once again it was all Meyerbeer's fault: as he wrote to tell Ferdinand Heine in Dresden, 'the operatic situation in Paris' had become so 'appallingly bad' as a result of Meyerbeer's 'financial influence' that 'no honest person can put up with it'.[2] His only recollection was of 'repugnant contacts' with this plague spot that called itself a world capital.

From the 'morass' of Paris he returned to the confines of Zurich. He may have lacked possessions, but at least he had a certain standing and in a provincial town like Zurich was gaped at like some exotic creature, some of the locals seeing in him an eccentric opera composer while others regarded him as a heroic revolutionary who had fought on the barricades. This twofold aura helped him. A friend from his distant days in Würzburg, Alexander Müller, took him in. Émigrés such as Leo von Zychlinsky turned up, and local worthies like the cantonal secretaries Jakob Sulzer and Franz Hagenbuch and the zealous editor of the *Eidgenössische Zeitung*, the lawyer Bernhard Spyri, sought out his company, discussed the international situation with him, gave him money and generally made themselves useful. Without exception, Wagner's biographers have claimed that 'he was happy that summer in Switzerland'.[3] He himself later claimed that on his arrival Zurich had been 'wholly devoid of public art'. Its 'simple' citizens took 'an amiable liking' to his 'unadorned person', without having the least idea about his art.

With Minna, too, there was no longer any hope. She seemed to have written him off and had replied neither to his prompt recantation of the revolution nor to the letters that he had subsequently written to her in his attempt to lure her to the Limmat. Once again, he felt abandoned, begged for forgiveness and appealed to a love that had long since died. As he later wrote in *My Life*, their relationship had cooled 'since the first tempestuous and passionate year of our marriage' – in other words, since 1836. If Minna's feelings had been briefly rekindled by Wagner's post as court Kapellmeister, his breach with society had caused those feelings to grow cold again. His marriage had begun to fall apart just as his position in Dresden had done.

For two months Minna sulked, then proposed a reunion, but only under certain conditions. It was clear from the moment that she arrived in Zurich, with Papo, Peps and Natalie, that Wagner could not forgive her this latest act of 'betrayal'. 'I was particularly won over, I must admit,' Wagner wrote maliciously in *My Life*, 'by the little dog and bird.' By contrast, Minna, who struck him as having aged considerably, threatened to leave straightaway unless he found some suitable way of supporting her. The plight from which he had escaped as a result of the revolution had now caught up with him in the guise of his wife. It was with horror, he wrote in *My Life*, that he recognized in her 'an unconscious ally of the inimical circumstances that beset me'.[4] Even his parrot, which in Dresden had squawked, 'Richard! Freedom!', had been retrained and now screeched, 'The wicked man! Poor Minna!'[5]

This was one side of the story. If the picture of a cold and selfish Minna was calculated to appeal to Cosima, to whom Wagner later dictated his memoirs, the surviving correspondence between husband and wife reveals a different story. Wagner clung to the wife he hated much as a child clings to its mother. However 'curt and wounding' he may have found her in his daily dealings with her, he longed for her whenever they were apart. As a good mother she hurried to be with him and to comfort him in September 1849, but by the following February she was again the wicked mother, packing him off to Paris to earn some money, in spite of an attack of bronchitis. In March 1850, he wrote to tell her that he knew of no greater happiness than to live with her, whereas only a month later he was assuring her that if he spent another year in her company he would 'die the most shameful of deaths'.[6] His emotional ambivalence was beyond his control, with the result that Minna, well versed in the ways of strife and intimately familiar with her 'Richel' (as she called Wagner), now had a dangerous weapon at her disposal.

Wagner had long wanted to break out of this prison. Wilhelmine Schröder-Devrient had once described him as a 'casualty of married life', and the term had stuck. While he had managed to escape from the professional cul-de-sac in which he had found himself in Dresden, he was still trapped in a loveless marriage. If he was to find the love of which his heroes dreamt, he would first have to break free from Minna. Only by leaving her, he thought, would he find true happiness.

Yet as soon as he left, he was overwhelmed by a fear of loss that even after Minna's death repeatedly turned into his old familiar fear of punishment. He was suffering from a 'life-long illness', he told her after their separation, a separation that filled him with perpetual disquiet. This increased to the point where it became an 'all-destructive fear of a kind that I unfortunately always feel whenever a letter arrives from you'.[7]

If ever he forgot the power that Minna had over him, he was reminded of it by his nightmares. It now became imperative to destroy that power. True, the first revolution that he fought against the enemies who filled him with fear had proved a failure, but at least he had broken free from their toils and, in spite of the defeat he had suffered, had found freedom. And so he now prepared to make a second attempt. 'Only love can cure me', he wrote from Paris in April 1850, 'and that is something I cannot find in my own home.'[8]

He had returned to Paris with 'feelings of unspeakable bitterness'. Egged on by Minna, who longed to escape from Zurich's civilizational diaspora, and by Liszt, who provided him with advice and his fare, he spent his time in Paris desultorily working away on his draft for a new opera, *Wieland der Schmied*. The doors that had previously been closed to him were now to be opened by Liszt's private secretary, Gaetano Belloni. But as ill luck would have it, Belloni had just returned to be with his master in Weimar, and Wagner spent a whole six weeks waiting for him in Paris, while Liszt's money evaporated.

Time seemed to have stood still: the debts that he had left behind him in 1842, including even his tailor's bills, remained unpaid, and the Opéra continued to be dominated by Meyerbeer, this time with *Le prophète*. Goaded by curiosity, Wagner attended a performance and reported feeling 'physically sick'. In order to make some money, he pinned all his hopes on a performance of the *Tannhäuser* Overture, but the performance was unexpectedly postponed after it had already been announced by the Saint Cecilia Society. 'This turn of events', Wagner reported, 'was enough to make me realize the wretchedness of my situation.' The idea of remaining a moment longer in the city filled him with the same degree of 'horror' as the thought of returning to Zurich.

At this point a miracle occurred in the form of a perfumed letter. The billet-doux arrived from Bordeaux and was written by Jessie Taylor, a name that had only pleasant memories for Wagner. The daughter of a well-to-do English advocate, Jessie had been a frequent visitor to Dresden since 1842, invariably staying with the Ritters, who were among Wagner's staunchest supporters. It was not long before the aspirant pianist was bitten by the Wagner bug, her definitive conversion coming with the première of *Tannhäuser* in 1845. Three years later, the young Karl Ritter introduced her to her idol. By now she had changed her name from Taylor to Laussot, having married a wine dealer in Bordeaux and become even wealthier in consequence.

When his revolutionary proclivities led her Dresden idol to his ruin, she assumed the mantle of a patron of the arts. Julie Ritter had already declared her willingness to assist the composer with a generous annuity, and Jessie was keen not to be outdone. She duly wrote to him, announcing that her own contribution was waiting for him in Bordeaux. The offer, which Wagner described as a 'real tonic', was in fact made before he set off for Paris and seems to have struck a chord with him.

If Minna, in her role as the wicked mother, had left Wagner in the lurch, Jessie now hastened to help him, much as Rosalie had done. He wrote to Liszt, no doubt causing much bemusement with his exhortation: 'Acknowledge this woman as your sister and as someone who thinks as you do!'[9] And he even told Minna about Jessie's 'most sisterly communication assuring our future'.[10] It was while he was feeling at his most miserable in Paris that he received Jessie's invitation to visit her in Bordeaux. He set off without delay in order to take possession of his sister and her money.

The main characters and the setting of the episode that followed corresponded in every detail with the archetypal constellation that underpins all Wagner's dramas. It was almost as though he had stage-managed the whole affair, casting himself in the role of the hero who, in his search for redemption, sought refuge on the distant banks of the Gironde, where he gazed into the eyes of a heroine in need of redemption herself. Needless to say, this became clear to him only when he looked at the matter more closely.

The facts of the matter are as follows. He first set foot in the Laussots' lavishly furnished town house in Bordeaux in mid-March 1850. The family consisted of the young couple, together with Jessie's mother, Ann Taylor. Wagner was presumably wearing his best clothes from Zurich when they welcomed him over the threshold: snow-white trousers, a bright blue frock coat with gilt buttons, sulphurous yellow gloves, a narrow-brimmed top hat and, beneath his arm, a gold-handled walking stick.[11] In order to ensure that his stay was not clouded by material cares, Ann Taylor explained that she and her friend Julie Ritter were granting the indigent artist an annuity of three thousand francs, an arrangement that would continue 'until his fortunes revived', which from Wagner's point of view was bound to mean for ever. The miracle had finally happened.

In his single room in Paris, Wagner had had to make to do with home-made sandwiches, but in Bordeaux he was waited on hand and foot. As Laussot was generally away on business and Ann Taylor was hard of hearing, he spent most of the day, in his own words, in conversation with his 'young and sympathetic friend'. He thought that she was 'then around twenty-two years old', although other estimates make her two years older.

It cannot have taken long for them to recognize their mutual bond. Jessie was pretty, blonde, sentimental and completely besotted with Wagner's music. Just as Rosalie had done, she played Beethoven to him on the piano and enchanted him with the Grimms' fairytales, which her father had translated into English. 'Whenever she reads to me', Wagner wrote delightedly to Julie Ritter's daughter Emilie, 'I sit there like a child and often sob like one, too.'[12]

He repaid the favour by playing her his still unknown *Lohengrin*, taking all the parts himself. Any similiarities to living persons were purely coincidental. But when Wagner went on to initiate her into his draft for *Wieland der Schmied*, the parallels could no longer be ignored. Here was an artist who, lamed by the powers that be, made wings for himself in order to escape to a life of freedom. Here too was Schwanhilde, whom Wieland had once rescued and who now flew away with him in order that they might embrace their common future over the ruins of the past. Jessie admitted that she had rediscovered 'her own private fate' in the swan-maiden. It was impossible to overlook the fact, Wagner later wrote to Minna, that he had 'kindled a violent affection in the young woman's heart'.[13]

Given the situation in which he found himself, Wagner was bound to feel the same. Like a sister, Jessie had helped him in his hour of need, contributed to his prosperity and opened her heart to him. She too wanted to live only for art, for *his* art, and declared her willingness to make any sacrifice that was necessary to achieve that aim. With astonishment the young married woman and the thirty-six-year-old married man acknowledged the spiritual bond between them. 'I barely needed to touch on something', he later recalled, 'for it to be immediately and, it seemed, equally familiar to her.'

At this point, Jessie, perhaps at story time, revealed that not everything in the Laussot household was as it seemed. Their marital happiness served as a cover for a clandestine arrangement: following her father's death, she explained, her mother had helped the handsome but almost bankrupt wine merchant to get back on an even keel, and he had repaid her with his passionate affection. But instead of marrying the widow, he had proceeded to walk down the aisle with her sixteen-year-old (or, according to other estimates, eighteen-year-old) daughter, towards whom he nurtured a true 'aversion', as Wagner soon claimed to notice for himself. He was witness to ugly scenes, all of which fitted in with this picture.

In short, Jessie had been sold. Since then, she had lived far from her Dresden friends under the thumb of a man who had been forced on her. The latter shared his love with a mother who had surrendered her own daughter to him. The happiness that seemed to beckon had turned into the deepest suffering. The tragedy of the defenceless young woman required a hero, and, as Lohengrin now understood, the invitation to Bordeaux was in reality Elsa's desperate cry for help.

Her saviour had scarcely set foot inside the door when the female prisoner broke the chains that bound her to this 'nest of repugnant horse traders'.[14] If we may believe the confessional letter that Wagner later sent to Julie Ritter, Jessie gave herself to him. 'If only you could have seen this triumph of love!' he wrote to her, striking a note of conscious indiscretion. 'It issued from every sinew of this rich and happy woman, who did not admit that she was mine but who revealed it through herself, through the involuntary, bright and naked phenomenon of her love!'

The most glorious wonders had now been revealed to him in his enemy's house, he went on to inform Julie Ritter, 'and how privileged I was to enjoy them and taste the most blissful intoxication of love!'[15] The scene in which Jessie emerged from the darkness, while her loose-fitting nightdress slipped slowly from her shoulders, was to recur in Wagner's poetry and dreams. By contrast, this confidence must have had a most curious effect on Julie Ritter, who was herself in love with Wagner.

They devoted themselves, in Wagner's words, 'to the god of love', and Jessie's kiss brought him 'the greatest enjoyment of my life'. In order to prolong the pleasure, they planned a future together on the model of Wieland and Schwanhilde, a future that would start with their common flight. While in his single-room lodgings in Paris, Wagner had already been seized by a desire to visit the Orient, which, as the land of the *Arabian Nights*, seemed to him to hold out the promise of oblivion and even of 'death'. He had been preceded to the East by Frederick Barbarossa, whose Aryan ancestors had once emerged from its mythical fastnesses. As Greece lay on their itinerary, the eloping couple also thought of stopping off for a few days on the Isles of the Blessed. Jessie, too, seemed keen. Arabia was then all the rage.

Wagner's decision to turn his back on 'modern Europe' once and for all was presumably bound up with his recent past. In Bordeaux he read a false report in the newspapers to the effect that the king of Saxony had confirmed the death sentence on two of his fellow revolutionaries, Mikhail Bakunin and August

Röckel. He immediately wrote to them in their prison cell at Königstein, hailing them as heroes who had sacrificed themselves to their love of humanity and congratulating them on their fate. He ended with a cheery 'Die happy'.[16] As he himself was in no particular hurry to share their fate, his travel plans, by removing him from the reach of the long arm of the law, acquired a new topicality. The lovers soon found a suitable ship that was due to sail from Marseilles via Malta to the land of the Olympians, and from there the ship would continue its journey to Asia Minor, with Wagner and his fairytale-telling lover on board.

It was only later that Wagner discovered that his fond farewell to his two friends on death row had never reached its destination, having been destroyed by August von Lüttichau.[17] But it was in any case rendered redundant by the fact that the king had commuted their sentences to life imprisonment. Meanwhile Minna had started to interfere in Wagner's new relationship, an eventuality for which he himself had prepared the way when he had encouraged the two women to correspond with each other in the hope of removing any mutual mistrust.

In March, it was the loving husband who wrote to inform his wife of his arrival in Bordeaux, but by April he was already declaring that their marriage was over. 'Heart and soul, you cling to possessions, hearth and house, implements and homeland', he told her, adopting his philosopher's stern mien. 'I abandon all this in order to become a human being.' That he was not alone in this, he did not for the present reveal. In order to sweeten the pill of separation, he generously offered his wife half the annuity that Jessie had made over to him.

The swan-maiden's flight, too, was to be made easier: no doubt in order to lull her family into a false sense of security, Wagner left them after three weeks, with the excuse that he had to return to his wife in Zurich.[18] Instead, he stopped off in Paris, where he intended to wait for his lover. But Jessie appears to have insisted that he should first put his affairs in order and so he had promised to end his marriage with Minna, a marriage that existed only on paper and possibly not even there. Their wedding ceremony, he suggested, had not been performed by a properly ordained priest, and so an official divorce was superfluous. Now that he was separated from Minna, nothing seemed to lie in the way of their liaison. As soon as Jessie was informed of this, she signalled her unconditional readiness to flee with him.

There remained the question of how they would pay for their journey. Although Wagner had already received 625 francs from Ann Taylor as an advance on the first quarter's instalment of his annuity (a sum he was 'supposed to hand over' to Minna), this was not enough for a trip to the Orient. And so, as he later told Ernst Benedikt Kietz, he lingered in Paris, 'waiting for the money' for his 'planned journey to Greece'.[19] Problems began when Jessie tried to obtain the funds from her mother. Questioned closely on the matter, she was forced to admit to her plan to elope. When it was objected that, as a married woman, she would be living in sin with a married man, she appears to have assured her mother that Wagner was already separated from Minna and, indeed, had never really been married to her at all.

Thus Minna's hour had finally come after weeks of uncertainty. 'Shocked beyond belief' by Wagner's letter of farewell, she hurried to Paris to discuss the matter with him, but when he got wind of her impending arrival he pretended not to be at home and sought refuge at the Hotel Byron on Lake Geneva – so called after the poet who had likewise broken his journey here while travelling across Europe. Meanwhile Minna, who already had an inkling of the true reason for Wagner's letter, scoured the streets of Paris in search of the man she still loved. On her return to Zurich, she was surprised to receive a letter from Ann Taylor, who – as Wagner later surmised – was 'anxious to find out at first hand whether I was really divorced in the eyes of the Church and the law'.[20] Utterly humiliated, Minna lost no time in providing her English correspondent with the evidence she required.

But Wagner's plan to elope had been thwarted even before Minna made her move, as Jessie had written to inform him that she had told her mother everything, whereupon her husband, consulted by his mother-in-law, had promised to put a bullet through the craven abductor's head. Feeling his honour impugned, Wagner wrote Eugène Laussot a note, making a duel inevitable. He could not understand, he told Laussot, how 'a man could bring himself forcibly to detain a woman who wanted nothing to do with him'. By the time that Wagner, bent on a violent confrontation, returned to Bordeaux, the Laussots had left, and the police, tipped off by the husband, made it clear to Wagner that his presence in the town was unwanted. Wagner had not only made himself look ridiculous, he had lost both his lover and his allowance at one fell swoop.

Nor was it long before he had forfeited his honour, too. In order to clarify the situation, Minna sent Ann Taylor what she called a 'document' – presumably her marriage certificate – together with two letters that Wagner had written, including the one he had sent from Bordeaux. From this it was clear beyond a shadow of a doubt that his marriage was far from having broken down irretrievably. Quite the opposite, in fact: Wagner seemed tormented by his desire to be reunited with his wife. 'Believe me', he had written, like some adolescent lover, 'I now know no happiness, save that of being able to live with you calmly and contentedly in our little home.' Their reunion was 'the happiest moment I can long for'.[21] It is unclear whether Wagner was merely trying to help her come to terms with the fact that from now on he was planning to be kept by a pretty young admirer, still less do we know whether Minna took these lines at face value. Their true meaning must have become clear to her only when she received Ann Taylor's enquiry.

Once Minna's little bundle of documents had arrived in Bordeaux, apparently exposing her husband as a seducer and a cheat, Jessie broke with him completely. If he wrote to her again, she told Karl Ritter, she would burn his letters unread. The heroic play about love and redemption that he had scheduled for performance had turned into a common tragedy on the subject of mutual betrayal. In the wake of the failure of the revolution, Wagner now suffered a second débâcle in his attempt to break free from his past, a setback that plunged him into 'boundless misery'. To Julie Ritter, he described it as a 'disaster'.

Even so, he got off lightly. The Ritters travelled posthaste to the Hotel Byron to help the suffering genius celebrate his thirty-seventh birthday. Julie, who was almost twenty years older and whom he called 'mother', was inclined to forgive him, such was her affection for him, which she revealed 'in a flood of tears'. Even the spurned Minna took him back, and together they returned to the Abendstern, which their friends had renamed, somewhat inappropriately, the 'Villa Rienzi'. It was in a suburb of Zurich known as Enge – ironically, the word can also mean cramping confines and narrow-mindedness. 'Like Minna, I regard what has happened as salutary', Wagner wrote to Kietz on his return, 'as it has shown us both what we are to each other and what we can be to each other from now on.'[22]

Wagner's ability to recover so quickly was due in part to the changing perspective from which he viewed what had happened, which he regarded not just as a passing infatuation: from the outset, he saw it bathed in the light of myth. Familiar archetypes had reappeared in an equally familiar relationship, their unfolding development hampered – according to the drama's eternal rules – by hostile forces that had finally destroyed the couple. There was nothing new in this for the old tragedian.

Wagner's life as an émigré had begun with his forcible expulsion from Dresden, and this was now followed by his betrayal of Minna. As a homeless refugee, he discovered first in Zurich, then in Paris, that the doors that had once been locked to him were still closed. It was his old nightmare all over again. When Jessie entered his life as a miracle promising affluence, love and hence total redemption, his dream of an ideal sister seemed to have come true. 'What made Jessie so unutterably attractive in my eyes', he wrote later, 'was the fact that she understood me in everything, quickly, clearly and certainly.' They felt like brother and sister in an alliance that offered the homeless hero the rest for which he longed.

The transfiguration of Jessie went hand in hand with the demonization of her rival: unable to compete with the youthful radiance of the wealthy daughter, Minna shrivelled away to become a woman who 'cannot love'.[23] Even before she was exposed by her husband as an intriguer, Minna had been equated with Ortrud. Through her lovelessness and obsession with worldly goods she cast herself in the role of a witch who had no choice but to destroy the happiness of Elsa and Lohengrin.

As soon as Wagner found out that Jessie was unhappy in marriage, a new perspective opened up for him, too. Just as he himself had sought redemption and had even found it for a time, so Jessie now proved to be in need of redemption. In this way she was just like the heroine of the opera whose music lay open on the Laussot piano. In Jessie's case, the antagonists consisted of a wicked mother who had married her off against her will and a usurper who held her in his power. In his letter to Julie Ritter, Wagner called them 'the mortal enemies' of love.[24]

It was with 'terrible force' that they had subjected his helpless lover to their repressive measures and shackled her by means of 'education, marriage, decency and business'. And in typically satanic fashion, they had hidden behind the mask of their hypocritical love. 'Mercilessly and murderously' they had ridden into battle against the helpless bride, 'but always with the smile of loving concern'. Just as Wagner himself had been impelled by need to become a revolutionary through the force of circumstances, so Jessie now rebelled against her oppressors.

Her decision could be carried out 'only with the boldest revolutionary resolve'. She too had to find the courage to rebel. 'He who rebels out of love', wrote Wagner, 'even though he were to perish while rebelling, is mine, and inasmuch as this love was directed at me in person, it could have brought me happiness only if I too had perished in the process.' The result would have been a love-death as the final refuge of a forbidden passion.

But things turned out differently. As in *Lohengrin*, the hero was betrayed. Urged on by his enemies who, 'according to plan, tore the love from her heart', Jessie lost her strength of purpose, and the lover with whom he wanted to flee and find freedom – even if it were the freedom of death – became what Wagner called 'a beautiful corpse'. Like Elsa, she should have sunk lifeless to the ground. Without the lover whom she had betrayed, her life must surely have lost its meaning. Although Jessie and her mother left the wine dealer some years later, it was not to return to her old love. For Wagner, Jessie was dead, at least for the present. Even the diary-like jottings that he entered in his 'Red Pocketbook' at this time were destroyed when he began to dictate his autobiography in 1865.

If Jessie and Minna betrayed Wagner, it is no less true that he betrayed them. The hero had been faithless from the outset. In keeping with the familiar model, he had abused his position as a guest and, although tied by the bonds of marriage, forced his way into another marriage. He had turned to a new lover without first having broken free from his previous one. When the latter provided proof of this, she destroyed his happiness.

The hero who was caught between two women had finally been exposed and destroyed. But Wagner, who was not only the hero but also a private individual, refused to be divided in this way. In the end, he confirmed the claims of the older woman and declared that the younger one was not responsible for her actions. 'The woman who wanted to bring me redemption', he coldly concluded, 'has proved to be a child.'

Yet the fact remains that Wagner had once again failed. He had lost everything that seemed so easily won, as though his curse was at work once again. 'I am almost afraid of each new contact', he wrote; 'it is just like a curse – whatever I seize in my need for love breaks into a thousand pieces as soon as I touch it'.

He had arrived as a man in search of redemption only to find himself cast in the role of a Lohengrin bringing salvation, but the metamorphosis now took a more sombre turn. 'I must entrust my ship to the winds,' he told Julie Ritter, 'I cannot make a home for myself or knock together a new sailing ship from the timbers of my own shipwrecks.' As the Dutchman, he returned defeated from another failed attempt to find redemption.

Together with his assistant and treasurer Karl Ritter, he withdrew to 'the wildest imaginable mountain fastness' in the Valais, where he read the *Odyssey*, a work which, he assured readers of his autobiography, a kindly fate had placed in his hands. He made himself at home in the world of myth. In *My Life*, he recalled that 'Homer's long-suffering hero, yearning for his homeland, condemned to incessant wanderings and stoutly triumphing over every obstacle, was an image uncommonly appealing to my soul.' From Circe's arms, the cunning hero was drawn back home to Penelope. Wieland had hoped to soar aloft on wings of his own making and gain his freedom, but Wieland, he told Julie Ritter, 'is dead: he will not fly'.[25]

In the Ancestral Realm

Just as Wagner rewrote his life in order to make it fit the relevant myths, so he tinkered with the myths in order to be able to rediscover himself in them. His

creative attention was drawn in particular to the Hohenstaufens, who embodied the Germans' longing to return to the Middle Ages and re-establish the
Empire and who had been the historical guarantors of German superiority
since the time of the Wars of Liberation. They were also able to meet the
demand for national heroes, a need fuelled by the dream of a united Germany.
The cycle of legends that included the Emperor Frederick Barbarossa, Friedrich
II of Sicily and their many hapless descendants became a popular source
of subjects for playwrights. With the Hohenstaufens, German tragedy finally
became fully stageworthy.

Wagner's sister Rosalie had appeared in one such piece in 1832, a play in
which she had not only sacrificed her life to the Hohenstaufen Enzio but
obtained a commission for her needy brother. Raupach's *König Enzio* deals with
only one episode in a catastrophic train of events in the course of which the
jewel of German culture was destroyed by its enemies. The Catholic Church
and France jointly drove the Hohenstaufens from their ancestral throne, disin-
heriting and killing their descendants. The entire dynasty was wiped out, living
on only in the popular imagination in the form of a potent myth. One day, the
legend promised, they would return and restore the Holy Roman Empire of the
German nation to all its erstwhile brilliance.

This revival was re-enacted in countless German theatres from the early
years of the nineteenth century: in prose, verse and incidental music, the
Emperor Barbarossa rode valiantly to Palestine, while the head of the last of the
Hohenstaufen emperors fell bloodstained upon the sands of Naples. The battle
between the virtuous Ghibellines and the evil Guelphs was in the repertory of
every German playhouse. Raupach wrote a whole series of dramas on the subject, each of them dealing with a different generation of the Hohenstaufen
emperors from Barbarossa to Konradin, following up *König Enzio* with a play
about Enzio's brother Manfred, the son of Friedrich II. Barely ten years after
Wagner had written his incidental music for *König Enzio*, he stumbled upon
Enzio's successor in Paris.

Seized by a desire to return to his mythic homeland, Wagner had begun to
read Friedrich von Raumer's history of the Hohenstaufen emperors in 1841, and
it was here, among the figures who 'sprang to life' beneath his inquisitive gaze,
that he discovered Manfred, who was excommunicated by the Church and
betrayed by his friends. Like the self-exiled Wagner, Manfred despaired of the
present and dreamt of bygone greatness.

In Wagner's imagination, Manfred followed on naturally from Rienzi, who
had in fact lived a century later. Whereas Rienzi regarded himself as the natural son of the Emperor Heinrich VII, whose battle with the Guelphs he took up

and continued, Manfred was the illegitimate son of Friedrich II. Like Rienzi, he had tried to re-establish German imperial rule in Italy before succumbing to the power of the rival Guelphs. The fact that he was briefly successful inspired the unsuccessful Wagner to plan a grand historical opera in five acts that was intended to stand alongside *Rienzi*. Perhaps he knew that in Vienna and other German-speaking towns and cities censors had insisted on presenting Meyerbeer's *Les Huguenots* as *Ghibellinen und Guelfen*. There was a demand for Hohenstaufen operas.

As retold by Wagner, Manfred's story began in an oriental banqueting hall where veiled beauties dance their 'voluptuous national dance'. A vassal of the pope, Manfred has devoted himself to a life of affluence and ease since the death of his father and has forgotten his family's great past. Like Tannhäuser in the Venusberg, Manfred finds that his belly-dancing beauties fill him with a sense of satiety at his inactive existence. As though on cue, a foreign singer emerges from the group of bayadères and introduces herself as a messenger from his dead father. In point of fact, the Saracen woman informs him, Friedrich is not dead at all but lives on as a glorious memory in the hearts of all Muslims. 'He was a god', she sings, to Manfred's mounting excitement, 'and, revered as a god, he lives on in the Orient.'[26]

Scarcely has the mysterious stranger revealed this and acclaimed Manfred as the son of a god when the Guelphs seek to overthrow him. He is robbed of the rest of his inheritance, evicted from his oriental palace and, 'accursed by God', driven away into the mountains. Here, in the depths of his despair, he is visited by an eerily sublime vision. One moonlit night following a storm he sees between the mountain peaks a regiment of soldiers flying through the air, with the Emperor Friedrich II at their head.

Just as Wagner, stranded in Paris, had dreamt of the Hohenstaufens, so his despairing hero now sees the past rise up before him like the Wild Hunt, with his father assuming the role of Wotan as god of the tempest. Scarcely has the deified emperor given his son a sign when Manfred wakes up. Before him stands the beautiful Saracen woman. As an oneiric emissary, she predicts that his shame will end and that he will regain his empire. Lit by the rays of a new dawn, Manfred is overcome by the greatest enthusiasm. 'Awake,' he calls, anticipating *Die Meistersinger*, 'greet the day that has allowed the Hohenstaufen Empire to be subject to me once again!'

Although this grand historical opera tells of the hero's victory over his enemies, Wagner called it *Die Sarazenin* – 'The Saracen Maid'. It was not Manfred whom he saw embodying the spirit of the Hohenstaufen emperor but the oriental beauty. It was she who was the motivating force, alerting him to his

destiny, persuading the people to side with him and leading his victory procession. Whereas Rienzi had been inspired by an idealized 'mother Rome', Manfred's passion was directed at a real person, albeit one of a supremely idealistic
nature. Wagner had found her not in Raumer's study of the Hohenstaufens but,
as he proudly admitted, in the world of his own imagination.

The Saracen maid is in fact a composite figure drawing on the characteristics
that distinguish all Wagner's other heroic sisters. Like Rosalie, she is a singer;
and like the somnambulist Senta, she has clairvoyant powers. When Manfred
calls on 'the angel of God', she appears before him in order to save him. Like the
maid of Orléans, whom the angelic Rosalie had once played, she leads the hero
into battle and ultimately to victory.

But as a woman she remains unapproachable. Although Manfred's love is
inflamed, she is not allowed to return it. Only after she has become his victim
by receiving the fatal blow that is aimed at his breast does she reveal her secret.
'Dying, she confesses that she is Manfred's sister', wrote the poet, 'and she
reveals the full extent of her love for him.'[27]

Wagner never completed this 'nostalgic fantasy'. Instead, his colourless hero
Manfred was replaced by the minnesinger Tannhäuser. Like Manfred,
Tannhäuser is dispossessed and shown the road to redemption by his sisterly
lover, representing in Wagner's eyes 'the spirit of the whole Ghibelline race for
all time'. But, if Friedrich's son had thus been subsumed by the tragic hero,
Friedrich himself continued to exercise Wagner's thoughts. In him the composer saw 'the most intelligent of all the emperors', a man through whom the
dying flower of the Hohenstaufen dynasty imbued the world 'with the heady
perfumes of a fairytale'. Did he perhaps know that a forebear of the Saxon
dukes, Frederick the Undaunted, was a grandson of Friedrich II, thereby
making the Hohenstaufens part of the same ancestral line as the house of Saxe-
Weimar?

In 1846, five years after making the first sketches for *Die Sarazenin*, in which
he had in the meantime tried to interest Wilhelmine Schröder-Devrient,
Wagner drafted a new piece on the Hohenstaufens. Although he later claimed
that he had intended it as a popular verse drama, it was probably another grand
historical opera. Central to its plot was to have been the most famous member
of the Hohenstaufen dynasty, Frederick Barbarossa himself. Wagner had thus
worked his way backwards from Barbarossa's great-grandson Manfred and the
comet's tail of Hohenstaufen rule to its central galaxy.

Following his death on a crusade, Barbarossa – a key figure in the revival of
the Holy Roman Empire and the leader of western Christianity – became the
great white hope of the Germans. His line had been robbed of its right to rule,

but one day he would return from his underground exile and win back his lost empire at the head of an army of ghosts. The empire would then be restored to all its former glory. The Wild Hunt that Wagner's Manfred had seen riding over the peaks of the Abruzzi belonged in reality to his great-grandfather.

But it was not the mythical figure that Wagner wanted to glorify in his opera. Rather, he was fascinated by the hero as a historical ruler in his 'most powerful and tremendous significance'. The brief sketch traces the stages of his battle against the Guelphs and the pope, the victorious outcome of which is marked by a glittering court celebration in Mainz. This illustrated broadsheet in five acts ends with Barbarossa's 'departure for the East'.

Wagner's dry-as-dust jottings, which read like excerpts from a history book, were supplemented in 1848, when he added a speech on the part of the emperor that surprisingly breaks through the historical framework by placing in the medieval ruler's mouth sentiments lifted from the composer's own revolutionary speech to the Vaterlandsverein. Barbarossa speaks as Wagner thought. If in his speech 'How Do Republican Aspirations Stand in Relation to the Monarchy?' Wagner had described the ruler as 'the true free father of his nation', the Hohenstaufen emperor now reveals himself as the just father of all. If in Wagner's inflammatory speech the cares of the modern prince are directed at 'one thing alone, the whole',[28] so Barbarossa announces that his 'only concern is for you all!'[29]

Wagner's apparent attempt to cite the crusading emperor as the authority for a monarchy enlightened by republican ideals was in fact aimed at achieving exactly the opposite: rather than seeing Barbarossa as a precursor of the revolution, Wagner interpreted the leadership ideal of the Hohenstaufen emperor as the real aim of the revolution. It was not revolutionary ideas that provided Wagner with his model for a future state but the universal kingship of the Hohenstaufens. When he described Friedrich August II as the republican people's king, he was really thinking of the revenant Barbarossa. 'The cyclical development of the historical kingship', Wagner proclaimed in the presence of the Vaterlandsverein, 'will have reached its goal when it has returned to the point from which it set out.'

At the time of the 1848 revolution, Wagner hoped that the folk would be freed from their plight at the same time that his own existential sufferings ended. While he himself repined at the humiliations to which he was exposed as an artist and at his lack of material wealth, the common people groaned beneath the tyrannical yoke of the aristocracy and a money economy. In his address to the Vaterlandsverein he proposed a solution to help everyone: while the revolutionary folk put an end to the power of capital and the stock exchange, the king would abolish the rule of the aristocracy that was based on inherited wealth. A people united by the common bond of fraternity would then recognize its father in the king and rediscover its transfigured image in art. In this way, the hostile forces of folk and dominion, worldly power and creative spirit would be reconciled. Wagner found a model for this world-redeeming act in Barbarossa's return.

But this mythical ruler's importance for Wagner could not be depicted in an opera in the style of *Rienzi*. And even the sketch for *Friedrich I* covered too brief a span of the emperor's life to portray an idea associated not only with Frederick himself but with the history of his whole line. In order to gain an insight into the conditions under which that dynasty had come into being, Wagner needed to take a broader view of the subject, and it was with increasing boldness that he raised his sights from the crusades to Charlemagne and thence to Julius Caesar. Since Caesar himself believed in his own Trojan ancestry, it was not long before Wagner had delved into the Homeric age. And from here it was but a stone's throw to Adam and Eve. Ultimately, he discovered Barbarossa's earliest ancestors in the forebears of the human race, whom he located in the Himalayas.

The essay in which Wagner expressed his view of the world in the autumn of 1848 has always been regarded as a puzzle, even its title – *The Wibelungs* – suggesting a typographical error. But a glance at the text shows that, however strange, the word is correct and that it reflects Wagner's belief that behind the historical Ghibellines lay the legendary Nibelungs as a result of the alliterative assimilation of their name with that of their enemies, the Welfs.[30] In Wagner's eyes, the treasure that was owned by the Nibelungs became a symbol of Hohenstaufen world rule. Encapsulating, as it did, all the splendours of the world, this mythic gold hoard had a history of its own, a history that Wagner proceeded to trace back in time from the Trojan Palladium to archaic prehistory. In his search for the good father and his lost legacy, Wagner had finally stumbled upon the source of all true humanity, the origin of all history.

But no one bought it. Published in 1850, Wagner's pamphlet alienated his opera audiences and left his fellow revolutionaries scratching their heads in incomprehension. Scholars have given a wide berth to this drolly fanciful tract, which Wagner subtitled 'World History from Legend', while his biographers have complained about its 'endlessly rambling colour supplement journalism' and 'confused historical vision'.[31] But Wagner never intended *The Wibelungs* to be subjected to a 'historico-juridical critique'.[32] Rather, it was a kind of esoteric pointer for those of his friends who shared its premises. As its opening sentence makes plain, the essay was Wagner's response to 'the reawakening of Frederick Barbarossa that so many people long for'.[33] Readers who did not feel this for themselves had no right to set foot in this mythic realm of Wagner's.

One person, at least, showed himself impressed. When Wagner read the text to his colleague in Dresden Eduard Devrient in February 1849, the latter found much to praise in this 'historico-philosophical study'. With an extraordinary mixture of wit and poetry, the composer had summoned up a sense of 'sublime enthusiasm for world rule' based upon sources in legend. Above all, Barbarossa, as 'the most powerful representative of the whole import of this idea', had appeared before Devrient 'in all his vast and wondrous beauty'.[34] Wagner could be well pleased that his hero had been successfully 'reawakened', at least at a local level.

Of course, he secretly hoped that the whole nation would find inspiration here: after all, he was presenting the Germans with a view of their own history that was as flattering as it was surprising. It was a history that began not with the Merovingians or Charlemagne but with the very first ray of light that pierced the darkness of the world at the dawn of history. In the sun that wrung from night the wealth of figures that constitute creation, their ancestors worshipped their divine father, while living in fear of the darkness which, to quote Wagner's metaphorical language, 'unfolded its dark dragon's wings over the rich treasures of the world, filling them with ghostly terror'.

For Wagner's primeval man, life itself seemed to be a struggle between day and night, between the principles of light and darkness. In primeval myth, the creative power that appeared to them as a radiant hero of light wrested the treasures of the material world from the dark dragon of night. But as the course of the sun suggests, the hero is struck down at the height of his power and dragged by the dragon into the underworld, with the result that the treasure, too, disappears into the night. His murder does not go unpunished. A new solar hero appears and avenges his predecessor's death, winning back man's stolen inheritance from the winged monster. Joy at the marvels of the world is mingled, therefore, with grief at their loss, worship of the bounteous god with the desire to avenge his death.

Wagner conceived of the origins of humanity along lines derived from his own private myth. In the beginning was the family. In it the father wielded absolute power, revered as the supreme being on account of his wisdom and goodness, and combining within himself authority and spirit, worldly and spiritual might. His rule was the family hoard. But he suffered the same fate as the solar hero with whom he was later equated.

He was murdered by his enemy, who destroyed his city and stole the hoard from his heirs. Revered as a superhuman being during his lifetime, the father now rose to the rank of a god who was worshipped in a sanctuary. His heirs' only aim in life was to avenge his death and win back the hoard. Wagner had translated his own life into the language of world history.

In *The Wibelungs*, the sun-worshipping ancestors of the Hohenstaufens lived on the roof of the world. Once the crime had been committed, they were exiled from the Himalayas and driven into the depths of existence. Throughout their earthly wanderings, they retained a memory of their divine ancestral king and of the holy city and its hoard. This hoard was their rightful inheritance and symbolized world rule. They settled in Troy, where they built a sanctuary and worshipped the solar hero as they had once done in the mountains. The power that had been vested in a single hand was now divided. Royal Priam held secular sway, while spiritual power was vested in god-fearing Aeneas.

Yet this newly founded city suffered the same fate as the first divine kingdom. According to Homer, the Trojans were stripped of their power, their sanctuary razed to the ground, and the populace scattered abroad. Aeneas escaped from burning Ilium, taking the sacred Palladium with him and seeking refuge in Italy, where he became the progenitor of the ancient Roman race of the *gens Julia* and hence of the world-conquering Caesar.

Meanwhile, Aeneas's Trojan colleague Priam took a more northerly route, appearing under the name of Pharamund as one of the tribal kings of the Franks. The long march from the Himalayas thus ended in Germany. Thanks to an economic migrant from Troy, the right to world dominion passed into German hands. While Rome represented the priesthood's universalist claims, the Franks demanded power over the world as their own legitimate inheritance.

They derived their right to this power from their religion. Their god, the solar hero Siegfried, had slain the winged dragon of chaos and in that way had won the hoard and, with it, sovereignty over creation. In Scandinavian myth, this treasure had been forged by subterranean dwarfs, the Nibelungs, and so when Siegfried won the hoard, he also acquired power over these 'children of night and death'. In this way, the hero, like all future owners of the treasure, became a Nibelung in turn.

Like all his predecessors, the German Siegfried suffered the same fate as the god and fell victim to the insidious treachery of the powers of darkness that sought to regain the hoard for themselves. The gift that he had entrusted to his people was lost. 'Thus the god became man', Wagner explained his own myth, 'and as a victim of the deed that brings us joy' he roused in the Franks 'the desire to punish his murderer for his death'.

If they themselves had become Nibelungs or, since their confrontation with the Welfs, Wibelungs, they had also changed the name of their tribal god, the light-bringing Siegfried being replaced by the Christian Saviour. Yet their ancient religion had only apparently yielded to the faith of Rome. The truth of the matter is that they had remained loyal to old Siegfried and hence to their claim to world dominion. In Christ, Wagner argued, the Frankish Nibelungs discovered 'a decisive similarity with Siegfried in that he too had died and was lamented and avenged, just as we still avenge Christ on the Jews'.[35]

But the main battle was between Rome and Germania. If Charlemagne briefly succeeded in reconciling the power of the state with that of the Church, the old antagonisms soon reasserted themselves with the advent of the Hohenstaufens. As a descendant of the dragon killer, now known as Christ, Barbarossa claimed world dominion, including the power exercised by the priesthood. While the Church adopted an increasingly worldly manner, basing its authority on possessions pure and simple, Barbarossa came to embody the ideal search for God-given rule.

The battle between Ghibellines and Guelphs – or, translated into Wagner's German, between Wibelungs and Welfs – became a confrontation between ancient kingship and modern power politics. Barbarossa's line flourished again briefly in the person of Friedrich II in Italy, but thereafter his descendants were destroyed by the pope and the French Capetians. In keeping with heroic myth, the hoard's heirs succumbed to the old dragon's acquisitive greed. The loss for the whole of world culture was irreparable. 'With the downfall of the Wibelungs,' wrote Wagner, 'humanity was torn from the last fibre by which it still hung, as it were, to its tribal and natural origins.'

Barbarossa seems to have foreseen this. Although he had no choice but to relinquish his power over the world, he continued to believe in the idea of an ancient kingship. Like Wagner, who, having been destroyed by the present, reconstructed the family myth of his past, Barbarossa turned away from unedifying reality and returned to the roots of his tribe. 'He felt powerfully drawn to Asia,' wrote Wagner, 'to the primeval home of all nations.' He knew from ancient legends that in distant India there lived a 'primevally godlike priest king' who had been granted immortality by a wonder-working relic called the 'Grail'. But scarcely had Barbarossa set out eastwards in search of the lost talisman when he was drowned while crossing the River Calycadnus.

Since then, the myth of the hoard had been transformed into the myth of the Grail.[36] The Germans no longer strove for world dominion, which had passed into inherited possessions and a money economy. Rather, they sought the spiritual comfort of the Grail in which the living blood of Christ was preserved.

From the standpoint of the Wibelungs, this meant that this 'first relic of humanity' contained within it the immortal legacy of the slain solar hero. Instead of earthly power, Siegfried's hero's blood would henceforth vouch for the continuation of ancient kingship. The divine power of the beginning lived on, not in the possessions of secular rulers, but in the hearts of the German people.

But one day, according to legend, Siegfried would return and reclaim the world's inheritance. He would then appear not as a sun god but in the form of the emperor who had embodied him in the days of the Wibelungs. Like the mythic hero, Barbarossa was only apparently dead, having merely disappeared into the darkness of the underworld. Since then he had waited with the maternal deity Venus in the mine shaft of the past. According to legend, he sat in the Kyffhäuser or Untersberg, 'around him the treasures of the Nibelungs, beside him the keen-edged sword that once slew the fearsome dragon'. The first king lived on, and one day he would rise like a radiant sun and destroy the dragon of night in an apocalyptic final battle.

For the author of *The Wibelungs*, this time now seemed to be at hand. The people were rebelling against all who had usurped their power and were breaking the chains with which they had been bound by the false rule of possessions and gold. All that was missing for the final victory was the hero who would restore not only freedom to humankind, but also ancient kingship and world dominion. 'When will you return, Frederick, O glorious Siegfried!' Wagner calls out to the hero in his mountain retreat. 'When will you slay the evil gnawing worm of humanity?'

'Two ravens are flying round my mountain,' comes the old emperor's oracular response, 'they are glutted on the spoils of the empire!' Only when the Germans have driven away these birds of prey can they reclaim the hoard. 'But leave me in peace in my mountain of the gods!' Barbarossa concludes his oracle.[37]

This ghostly conversation between the author and his forefather went unheard. The Germans of 1848 were no more willing to let Wagner raise them to godlike status than to assume their documented claim to world dominion. Still less did they understand that the winged dragon of night had in the meantime been transformed into little black-feathered crows that could be variously interpreted as Prussians and Habsburgs or, on a figurative level, as aristocratic rule and Jewish acquisitiveness.

How could they know that for Wagner the adversary of the good father Frederick was symbolized by a bird of prey? How could anyone suspect that for the poet of this new mythology the beginning of all things lay in the happy nuclear family that was fated to perish through betrayal and the theft of its inheritance? Wagner saw that he was not understood, and when he included *The Wibelungs* in his collected writings in 1871 he suppressed his supernatural conversation with Barbarossa in the underworld.

The World Spirit

The sources from which Wagner's ideas sprang are mostly shrouded in a veil of obscurity not unlike the one surrounding his origins. The uncertainty concerning his background is mirrored by the secrecy with which he cloaked his models. It is as though he was afraid that he would be numbered among the copyists whom he branded as the grave-diggers of art and so refused to divulge the names of those of his contemporaries who had provided him with ideas, instead claiming for himself the inspiration of the natural genius. In order to prove himself a classic composer, he preferred to name the classics as his models, tolerating only such great minds as Aeschylus, Shakespeare and Beethoven as the wellspring of his art and, with feelings of shame, concealing his next of kin, be they Heine, Mendelssohn or Berlioz.

Few writers provided Wagner with as many ideas as Georg Wilhelm Friedrich Hegel – and there were few towards whom he maintained such an obdurate silence. If he mentions Hegel at all, it is as an irrelevance in terms of the history of ideas, a writer whose thinking has long been superseded or as a curiosity whose unintelligibility persuaded him to embark on an unfortunately futile search for the 'absolute'. And he gives the impression that, while he occasionally read Hegel's writings, he never took any serious interest in them. Since he later professed his impassioned allegiance to Schopenhauer, who notoriously dismissed Hegel as a 'charlatan' and a 'windbag', Wagner's biographers have followed suit and struck the older philosopher from their subject's list of precursors, thereby overlooking the fact that on one decisive point Wagner corrected his idol by appealing specifically to Hegel.

Writers who are not blinded by Wagner's own account of himself will surely see what the dramatist owed to the philosopher. For Nietzsche, who got to know Wagner at the very pinnacle of his success, the composer was first and foremost a thinker, a man capable of conceptualizing all that he created. And whereas the two men had learnt to respect each other through their common admiration for Schopenhauer, it was not long before the disciple realized that Wagner's thought patterns were borrowed not from Schopenhauer but from his diametrical opposite. His verse and music were conceived according to Hegel's dialectical method. For Nietzsche, the *Ring* represented a 'tremendous system of ideas' built up on Hegelian lines. Hegel's philosophy of contradictions had been 'set to music' in the cycle, and in that way Wagner had 'immortalized' Hegel. He was 'Hegel's heir'. Wagner's art demonstrated 'music as "Idea"'.[38]

This is exactly what Wagner had claimed in one of his earliest essays, 'Pasticcio' of 1834, when he had declared that the 'Idea' was central to dramatic art. This Idea, he went on, derived not from the subject matter, however interesting, or from any other points of view, however surprising they may be, but simply from the ability to present on stage the innermost nature of things. As late as 1870 Wagner was still telling Cosima that music was 'not the delineation of an idea, but the Idea itself'.[39] Although he later passed himself off as a philosophical pessimist, Wagner was always an idealist as an artist.

This idealism he owed as much to the aesthetics of E. T. A. Hoffmann as to the philosophy of Hegel. And thanks to his Uncle Adolf, Wagner was familiar with both. While the Leipzig scholar had introduced him to idealism's world of ideas in the course of their walks round the city, it was Adolf's friend Christian Hermann Weiße who familiarized him with its system. A pupil of Hegel, Weiße had published his *System der Ästhetik* in 1830, interpreting art along dialectical lines and acclaiming love as its supreme expression. Hegel died in 1831, the same year as that in which Wagner sporadically attended Weiße's lectures on aesthetics and listened in on the latter's conversations with his uncle. In this way he heard 'things about philosophy and philosophers that left a great and exciting impression on me'.[40]

In short, Wagner assimilated Hegel's world view long before he studied the philosopher's main works during his final years in Dresden. Without having understood or even read them, he had grasped the unique features of Hegel's system, features that may even have seemed familiar to him, for, as he once said of himself, 'the state of inner contradiction in which, to my great regret, I find myself and shall probably always find myself' reflected Hegel's view of the dynamics of world events. The negative element by which Wagner saw himself called into question from the outset was the most basic force in history. In Hegel's thinking, the 'I' whose puniness was under constant threat turned out to reflect the self-consciousness of the whole.

Man was able to see himself not only as the centre of all creation but at the same time as its creator, a creator who simultaneously raised it to its highest pitch of perfection. Wagner's delusions of grandeur, which already struck his contemporaries, merely reflected Hegel's own understanding of the self. His conviction that he represented the ne plus ultra of a vast process of human evolution was his unacknowledged prototype's most fundamental idea. With typically grand self-importance, Wagner saw himself as the instrument of the Hegelian world spirit, while failing to display the greatness of spirit needed to acknowledge his dependence.

Wagner was aware of the central ideas of Hegelian thinking without study-ing the philosopher's complex writings, for they reflected his basic experiences in life. The past was not past but was present at every moment. The obstacles that lay in the way of his development were part of that development. Only through negation could man learn to understand himself. As human history had to evolve in exactly the same way as any individual, the whole was at stake at every phase of that process. If people did not want to be destroyed by the obstacles against which they stumbled, they had to learn to remove them.

Hegel's man was no tiny cog in an existing machine but the actual centre and goal of the world process, the different periods in history representing stages in his acquisition of self-knowledge. The position once occupied by God was now taken by man, who was responsible for the whole. It was in man's self-awareness that the whole of creation recognized itself, in his spirit that the world spirit manifested itself. His deeds did God's work for him. On his freedom or lack of freedom depended the success or failure of the universe. But as soon as man understood evolution in its entirety, this process would come to an end. When the final resistance was overcome, redemption would surely follow. Then the whole would know itself. Time, the great destroyer, would have destroyed itself.

'Time is absolute nothingness,' Wagner wrote to his friend Theodor Uhlig in 1850, 'only that which allows us to forget time, only that which destroys it, is something.'[41] Wagner knew his Hegel, even though he rarely mentioned him by name. He knew that the resistance he encountered could be overcome only from within and that the curse that seemed to annihilate him in fact helped to define him as a person. With Hegel, the negative acquired the force of some-thing positive. 'All painful experience', wrote Wagner in 1859 at the height of his admiration for Schopenhauer, 'must be offered up as a sacrifice to the higher aims of the world spirit that creates from within itself experiences for us to suffer and that through those sufferings raises itself still higher.'[42] For Schopenhauer, conversely, there was no world spirit leading mankind onwards through suffering to fulfil its own higher aims.

The world spirit was part of Hegel's world of ideas, and the great minds among whom Wagner was so keen to number himself were for the philosopher the 'managing directors of the world spirit'. It was their task to bring progress, for the spirit of humankind – and here Wagner could recognize his own predicament – consisted in a constant and generally violent struggle to over-come the obstacles that lay in its way. Every epoch was thrust aside by its suc-cessor, every historical figure was obliged to yield to the following one. For the sake of the new, the old had to perish. And it was in this, in destruction as in the act of rebuilding, that the task of the world's great men lay.

It was from this perspective, too, that Wagner saw his own artistic mission. The art in which human progress was revealed could not tolerate any rival art. Once humanity had found its rightful expression, all other forms of expression must necessarily disappear. Just as Hegel saw the task of the human spirit as understanding both the world and itself through its forms, so Wagner con-ceived of art as a form of universal self-knowledge that spoke not in concepts but in ideas that could be grasped through the senses. In this way the Idea became a dramatic event that demanded to be perceived as a whole.

'In order to be perfectly understood', Wagner wrote to Liszt in November 1851, 'I must communicate my entire myth, in its deepest and widest signifi-cance, with total artistic clarity; no part of it should have to be supplied by the audience's having to think about it or reflect on it; every unbiased human feel-ing must be able to grasp *the whole* through its organs of artistic perception, because only then can it properly absorb the *least detail*.'[43] From the time of Hegel, it was 'the whole' that mattered above all else: it was no longer the indi-vidual and his fate but the future of the whole of humanity that was decisive in philosophy and art. They were the point at which the living universe became conscious of itself.

'If we may describe the whole of nature as an evolutionary march from unconsciousness to consciousness,' the Schopenhauerian Wagner wrote in 1860 in the finest Hegelian tradition, 'we may undoubtedly regard our observation of it within the life of the artist as one of its most interesting forms because in him and in his creations the world reveals itself and assumes conscious expres-sion.'[44] It was not he himself, he once told Wendelin Weißheimer, but 'time' that 'produced' his works 'through him'. In mid-century, Wagner saw himself as the authorized representative of the world spirit. When he became a father in 1869, he offered Cosima – who was still married to Hans von Bülow – the extraordi-nary explanation that 'the world spirit wanted me to have a son by you'.[45]

It was during his years as Kapellmeister in Dresden that Wagner read Hegel's *Phenomenology of Spirit*. It is here that the idea of the world spirit is set forth, and here too that Hegel insists that the time has now come for a 'rebirth' of soci-ety. But this radical upheaval would not be a gradual process. Rather, it would resemble a 'bolt of lightning that suddenly illuminates the features of the new world'. The existing world would first be dismissed in spirit and 'relegated' to the past. The spirit, thought itself, exercised the 'tremendous power of the negative'. Sacrifices must be made if there was to be any progress. It would be risible to judge Alexander, Caesar or Napoleon by moral criteria, for 'the life of the spirit is not the life that is afraid of death and that keeps itself free from the ravages of time but the life that tolerates death and maintains itself in death'.

As Wagner's friend Friedrich Pecht reports, Wagner was immensely enthusiastic about Hegel's notoriously difficult text, praising it effusively as 'the best book ever published'.[46] But if it is true, as Pecht claims, that he read out a passage that Pecht found incomprehensible and that the two men began to laugh 'uproariously', this does not necessarily mean that Wagner, too, failed to understand the passage in question. Some time later he started on Hegel's *Lectures on the Philosophy of History*, a text that deals with the necessary and violent upheavals in human evolution, but as he ironically notes in *My Life*, his attempt to penetrate this 'inner sanctum' of Hegel's thought was 'thwarted' by the revolution.

If this seems to indicate that his interest in the *Philosophy of History* dates from the revolutionary year of 1849, his Annals make it plain that it was in fact during the summer of 1847 that he read this particular text. Inasmuch as Wagner's essay *The Wibelungs*, written in 1848, reveals a number of points in common with Hegel's study, the discrepancy is of some significance. If it was not until 1849 that Wagner discovered Hegel's book, then the similarities would be a mere coincidence. If, on the other hand, he had studied the volume two years previously, then we are dealing with actual borrowings. And Hegel's work does indeed appear to have provided Wagner with the foundations on which to erect his fantastical hypotheses. Like his great model, Wagner, too, abandoned himself to all-encompassing speculations that his then admirer Eduard Hanslick summed up in 1847 when he accused Wagner of 'the original sin of all Germans: speculative philosophy'.

In Hegel's vision, world history was a realm ruled in turn by the father, the son and the spirit. The world's origins led to a sense of alienation that ended in reconciliation. Whole nations came to embody the world spirit, destroying each other in their bitter struggle for supremacy. Only one nation could profess to world dominion at any one time, while the others were forced to submit to it. But however powerful these empires might be, the world spirit continued to trample over them in order that the idea of freedom that had already been glimpsed at the outset could achieve its realization.

For Hegel, too, the human race began to evolve in Asia, passing via intermediate stages in the Greek and Roman empires (the former devoted to art, the latter based on power) and culminating in the German empire. Only here was the 'spirit of the new world' realized, a spirit that mediated between the inner world of the heart and the outer world of existence. 'The pure inwardness of the German nation', wrote Hegel, 'was the actual soil for the liberation of the spirit.' Germany alone could reconcile the world spirit with itself. Only over Germania would the flag of humankind's ultimate liberation one day flutter.

In Hegel's view, the struggle fought by the Hohenstaufens represented a single stage in this process. In his *Philosophy of History*, he describes how the antagonism between emperor and pope was intensified in the factionalism of the Ghibellines and Guelphs and how this centuries-old struggle for world dominion ended tragically for the Germans. 'In the brilliant period of the Hohenstaufen dynasty', he goes on, 'individuals of commanding stature sustained the dignity of the throne, sovereigns like Frederick Barbarossa, in whom the imperial power manifested itself in its greatest majesty.' But however great the impression that this dynasty may have made on history, it was none the less destroyed by its great adversary, the Church of Rome. The struggle and defeat of the Hohenstaufens, which Wagner felt embodied the fate of the German Siegfried, struck Hegel as 'the tragedy of the family of this house and of Germany, too'.

It was Hegel's fate to be branded a 'charlatan' by Wagner and to be dismissed as irrelevant.[47] The same fate was shared by Hegel's pupil Ludwig Feuerbach. If Wagner's sense of spiritual kinship had once persuaded him to write to the influential philosopher and invite him to join him in Zurich, it was not long before he was dismissing him as a dry-as-dust academic who was a matter of total indifference to him. The enthusiastic tribute with which he dedicated *The Artwork of the Future* to him was removed when this study was republished within the context of Wagner's collected works: the dedication, he explained, had been the result of an 'impassioned aberration'.[48]

According to *My Life*, Wagner was guilty of this aberration at precisely the moment that his study of Hegel was interrupted by the revolution. An insurgent ex-theologian in Dresden had converted him to his 'lone philosopher of the modern age', but it was not until he reached Zurich that he first set eyes on a copy of Feuerbach's essay on death and immortality. But Wagner refused to rule out the possibility that he had taken an interest in Feuerbach's theories during his first visit to Paris, even if at that date he knew nothing about their author. This would explain why Feuerbach's idea that the dead are elevated to the status of cultically revered gods occurs at such a prominent point in *The Wibelungs*.

With its detailed theological speculations, Wagner's operatic draft on the subject of Jesus of Nazareth likewise betrays a certain familiarity with the world of Feuerbach's ideas. Indeed the latter's curious doctrine that death is the conciliatory sacrifice that man offers up to the community out of love recurs almost word for word in Wagner's Nazarene meditations. Death, we read here, is 'the self-sacrifice of every creature' in favour of humanity, a sacrifice whose essence is 'conditioned by love'.[49] Wagner's dramatico-theological study dates from the early months of 1849 – in other words, from a period prior to his official initiation into Feuerbach's work on the subject.

It was very much by contradicting his mentor Hegel that Feuerbach confirmed the validity of Hegel's principles. Even if the Young Hegelians, including Feuerbach, wanted to turn their model 'upside down', the ideas were still Hegel's: from the dialectical clash of opposites sprang a history of the world that moved through conflict towards its final state; where there had once been a state of being, there was now progress; man was no longer created by God but was the creator of his own destiny; his god was his own achievement, existing within him as the still unconceived essence of himself; the end of this painful process of self-alienation seemed to be at hand; world history was proving to be a Last Judgement that would finally release mankind and set us free.

It was the poet Georg Herwegh who first noticed how close Wagner the revolutionary was to Feuerbach as a thinker. In 1851 he wrote to Feuerbach, saying that he knew of no one who 'possessed a truly revolutionary nature, both emotionally and rationally, save you and Wagner'.[50] As early as 1842 Feuerbach had urged a reform of philosophy that would lead to a radical change on the part of society. As soon as man thought of himself as a social being, politics would replace religion. Where men had previously been content to think, they would now feel an 'urge to become actively involved in the affairs of state', and this was tantamount to an 'urge to end the existing political hierarchy'. In the case of the monarchy, this was to culminate in the demand that Wagner spelt out in his speech to the Dresden Vaterlandsverein in 1848: 'The king is not above the state.'

When in 1848 Wagner declared the need for destruction as the precondition for a fresh start, he was merely repeating Feuerbach's thesis that only the man who feels the courage 'to be absolutely negative' can find within him 'the strength to create something new'. As a result, the new philosophy swept away all the ghosts from the past that stood in the way of progress. At the same time, it offered mankind 'the realized idea', the fulfilment of dreams that had once been projected on the afterlife. But this meant that people had to abandon pure thought and take action. The new truth in the world was 'a new, autonomous deed on the part of humankind'.

Published in Leipzig in 1843, Feuerbach's *Principles of the Philosophy of the Future* finds the philosopher exploring a new way of 'thinking, speaking and acting in a purely and truthfully human manner': it is as if Feuerbach's hard-edged theses have acquired an almost Wagnerian soft focus. What for Wagner was to be the ideal of the 'purely human' was defined by Feuerbach as an aspect of living corporeality, sensuality and fusion. Only in love, claimed Feuerbach, did the other person acquire his or her absolute value. Only when man reclaimed the infinite for the finite would he discover in the object of his love 'the depth, divinity and truth of love'. Only on the basis of this love could the new and true art arise, art that would discover the divine in the human and true immortality in the most profound grief at our own mortality.

This was Wagner's most Wagnerian theme. Yet it is one that Feuerbach had already treated. It was in 1830, the year in which Wagner first dipped his toe in the waters of revolution, that Feuerbach's groundbreaking *Thoughts on Death and Immortality* had first seen the light of day. Here Feuerbach declares that the only immortality is that which is granted us through death. But we first need to understand that dying represents the abandonment of the self and our merger with the community. This in turn is made manifest to the individual only through love, which is itself synonymous with this act of self-abandonment and merger with the object of our love. The lover rediscovers himself in his beloved, but in doing so he becomes dead to himself. 'I' becomes 'you', the individual becomes the loving whole. Death is 'the revelation of love'.

In no other work in the whole history of philosophy is the identification of love and death, joyous union and annihilation, celebrated in such ecstatic terms. Yet only in Wagner's music dramas does Feuerbach's mystical treatment of death find artistic expression. Even in *Der fliegende Holländer* we already find Feuerbach's striking belief that in death 'the world fragments into nothingness', while Tristan and Isolde, although said to be Schopenhauerian in spirit, live and die as if they are idealized figures from *Thoughts on Death and Immortality*. Even their famous disquisition on night, with all its puzzling dialectics, sounds like a continuation of Feuerbach by other means.

In a visionary hymn appended to his theoretical musings, Feuerbach broaches a further theme to which Wagner no doubt felt personally drawn. Here the poet-philosopher draws a contrast between the earthly existence that finds its joyous confirmation in death and a life based on falsehood, a wearisome loveless life that seems like a slow and protracted death. In the midst of sublime dreams of transience that lighten 'death's dark house' with the 'fiery splendour' of love, there rise up the grimacing features of the pale and calculating individual, whose weakly self-seeking existence in life's daily round Feuerbach compares to 'unsalted Jewish matzos'.

This anti-Semitic sideswipe was no momentary aberration. In his later works, too, Feuerbach allotted to the Jews the thankless role of monsters for whom there was no place in his future society. Although Feuerbach turned his back on traditional Christianity on rational grounds, he clung to its most irrational prejudice. In his *Essence of Christianity*, which appeared in Leipzig in 1846, he contrasts the omnipotence of love that is embodied in God and Jesus with the 'egoism' of the Jews, whose God is nothing more nor less than 'the personified self-interest of the tribe of Israel', its supreme principle being not to ennoble reality but to exploit it to the hilt. This egoistical religion declared 'Israel's needs' to be 'the fate of the world'. Everything had to be 'sacrificed' to its salvation, prompting the imaginative Feuerbach to write of the 'destructive fires of anger in the vengeful eye of an Israel obsessed with extermination'.

Wagner's deep-seated hatred had already transferred all the qualities of the 'enemy' to the Jews, and now this hatred found its philosophical justification. All that he had dimly felt and figuratively expressed in his works could now be justified before the tribunal of reason. The glad tidings of the New Testament's damnation of the Jews retained their validity even in a demythologized Christianity, and Wagner lost no time in taking over Feuerbach's concepts in his systematic attempt to deal with the vague threat he felt that he faced. Where Feuerbach spoke of Jewish 'utilitarianism' that 'tasted nature only through the taste buds', Wagner writes in *The Artwork of the Future* of 'modern Jewish utilitarianism appropriating nature only as the object of crudely sensual enjoyment'.[51] On the strength of an unfortunate choice of words on the part of the philosopher, who drew a perhaps unintended analogy between the Jewish attitude to nature ('obsessed with extirpation') and the attitude of vermin to carrion, Wagner may later have felt entitled to draw a comparison between the Jews and vermin.

Barely had he set foot in Zurich when Wagner cast himself in the role of the dialecticians Hegel and Feuerbach in order to raise the failed revolution to a new conceptual level. In August 1849 he sent his historico-philosophical treatise *Art and Revolution* to Feuerbach's publisher Otto Wigand in the hope of 'appealing to, and finding refuge beneath, the protection of this great thinker'.[52] This appeal to his patron helped, and Wigand duly published the pamphlet, even paying Wagner the sum of five louis d'or for doing so. Writing much later in *My Life*, Wagner was reduced to claiming that Wigand had issued it only in the 'hope of provoking a money-spinning scandal'.

Apollo and Jesus

Although the world of ideas of *Art and Revolution* picks up the historical speculations of *The Wibelungs*, it lacks the glorification of all things Germanic found in the earlier essay. As Wagner never questioned Germany's leading role in the liberation of humankind, its omission may well be due to its intended readership, inasmuch as the pamphlet was originally written for Paris. Wagner was nothing if not obstinate in believing that his salvation would come from the city that more than any other had caused him to doubt his own vocation. He consciously chose a 'major French journal' that he hoped would publish his disquisition in six instalments, but the article was sent back to him by return of post as unsuitable. Only then did he turn to his German readers, and this time he was successful. It was not long before Wigand was able to reprint the pamphlet.

Whereas the main emphasis in *The Wibelungs* had lain on world dominion, the new essay dealt with the world's redemption. In both cases, the starting point was Asia. In *The Wibelungs*, Wagner had traced the spirit of ancient kingship from the Himalayas to Troy and thence to the Wibelungs, following whose downfall the idea lived on in the Grail and in legend. Now he drew a line of development that led directly from man's Asiatic origins to Greece. But the myth remained the same. Both tribes retained a lively memory of early kingship in the form of the solar hero. Whereas the German Siegfried slew the dragon, Apollo killed Python. The victory of light over the chaos of night became central to both religions.

There was, however, a difference. Whereas the Germanic branch concentrated on world dominion as symbolized by Siegfried's treasure, Greek consciousness was shaped by the figure of the hero himself, Apollo becoming the idealized incarnation of a 'handsome, strong and free human being' and Greek manhood attempting to emulate its godlike model by training their bodies through gymnastics, dance and contests.

But only through art could Apollo be depicted in all his perfection. All the different forms of expression of the Greek spirit, from poetry, song and dance to painting and architecture, conspired together to give physical form to the revered object, and thanks to inspired tragedians such as Aeschylus, the Greek people witnessed the resurrection of the god and hence the rebirth of their own essential nature. This miracle was enacted not in any temple but on the stage of the nation's amphitheatres.

Wagner had already studied the tragedies of Aeschylus during the summer of 1847, while he was working on *Lohengrin*. So clear was the 'intoxicating image of performances of Athenian tragedies' and so great the 'state of ecstasy' to which he felt transported that he could 'never again be fully reconciled with modern literature'.[53] Two years later, when he set down his ideas on art and revolution, he was still obsessed with the notion of a day-long performance of tragedies in Athens as an idealized 'celebration of the god'. Here the people were confronted by their own selves raised to their highest potential. 'Here the god expressed himself clearly and intelligibly.'

But the tale that Wagner recounted in the changing masks of his tragic heroes remained familiar. Fate willed that it should lead from radiant beginnings to a state of tragic entanglement that spelt the hero's downfall. The hero then bled to death, and, to the awestruck dismay of the nation, the night of the gods descended. The worshipped god perished, but his death was a 'loving sacrifice'[54] that united his people. In comprehending its own essential nature, it knew that it was subsumed by the god. In Wagner's view, it was the Greek nation itself 'that faced itself at a performance of the work of art, learning to understand itself and, as it were, consuming itself in the course of a few brief hours in its own most ennobling enjoyment'. In the theatre the whole nation died a communal love-death.

It was not long, however, before this celebration of the god's demise died in turn. Greek tragedy ended with the downfall of the Greek state. Just as the nation was fragmented and its collective spirit broken down into a vast number of egoistical wills, so the arts that drama had united fell apart. The 'total artwork', as Wagner called Greek drama, died like its heroes, and from now on there were only individual arts. As these were no longer concerned with the whole, they all pursued their own selfish interests. It was no longer the hero but market forces that dictated the action. The art that had once expressed the world spirit now took its cue from the world's currency, money.

The state fared no better. Once world dominion had passed from Athens to Rome, it was no longer the beauty of Apollo that reigned supreme but the rules of gladiatorial games. Men who had once been like gods degenerated to the level of slaves, their only comfort the otherworldly consolation offered by Christianity. There was no longer any room for art and for the ecstatic celebration of life in the here and now, a life transfigured in the god. In their hostility to nature, the ensuing centuries of Christianity became a breeding ground for hypocrisy and despotism, and in the end world dominion passed to money, which the arts, adept at providing mere entertainment, served like so many court jesters. Once the sacred scene of godlike epiphanies, the theatre now appeared 'like the rotting fruit of a hollow, soulless, unnatural order'.

Once art had taken this course, the need for revolution followed as surely as day follows night. But as long as world dominion lay in foreign hands, art, as understood by the Greeks, was incapable of flourishing, for its true content was the fate of the solar hero embodied by the folk's first king. If they were to become one with this tribal ancestor, as they had once been able to do in the cultic celebration of the total work of art, they would first have to reclaim their world inheritance. Only when men recalled their common origins, which most emphatically did not lie in the Jewish God, would they again feel any desire to rediscover the lost work of art. Once this work of art was reborn they could take up the legacy that had been stolen from them. This was what Wagner under-stood by revolution.

'From the dishonouring yoke of universal artisanship with its sickly monied soul,' he wrote in *Art and Revolution*, 'let us soar aloft to liberated artistic humanity and its radiant universal soul.' To attain this goal, 'the most tremen-dous revolution' was needed. Only over the sequence of events was Wagner still unclear. Was it first necessary to have a revolution, so that the total artwork could reveal the true meaning of the overthrow of the status quo? Or should art remind people of their true nature so that, carried away by the sight of their res-urrected national god, they might now take the steps necessary to liberate themselves? History itself would have to decide this question.

Wagner provided his own models for the planned rebirth of art from the spirit of Greek antiquity, his pamphlet culminating in an impassioned appeal to two divinities who until then had been regarded as opposites: 'Let us then set up the altar of the future, in life as in living art, to the two most sublime teach-ers of humankind', Wagner called out to his astonished readers: 'To Jesus, who suffered for all mankind, and to Apollo, who raised them to their joyous dig-nity!' This final exhortation is all the more surprising in that only a few pages earlier Wagner had described Christianity as an enslaving ideology that seduced mankind into leading a life of hypocrisy and self-denial.

Wagner's synthesis of the Python-slaying Apollo and the crucified Christ can have made sense only to readers already familiar with his essay *The Wibelungs*. Here he had shown that in both the national god of the Greeks and in the Saviour of the West lay the solar hero of the world's first religion. Apollo and Jesus were not isolated figures but merely different aspects of one and the same primeval myth. Whereas the Greek god represented the deity's radiant origins shedding his light on the beauty of men and the treasures of the world, so the carpenter's son from Galilee embodied the god who had to suffer and die in order that men might recognize their divine origins through his loving sacri-fice. Only the artwork of the future would reveal the hero in whom both Apollo and Jesus would merge as a single entity. His name was Siegfried.

By the early months of 1849, Wagner had relocated the Christian Jesus within the Germanic tradition: in his draft for *Jesus of Nazareth*, love's gentle messenger has become a tragic hero, with the Saviour transferred from the act of divine worship in church to the theatre. Jesus' stage début begins with a spectacular awakening of the dead and ends with his death on the Cross. The miracle achieved by his appearance on earth is transferred to the mystery of his death, when the earth's very foundations tremble. The operatic stage is transformed into a place of cultic celebration on the model of the Greeks, but the message that the composer associates with the death of his hero could hardly have been more modern.

For all that the various episodes remain close to their biblical source, even quoting literally from the Gospels, Wagner was not seeking to establish a second Oberammergau. Rather, he evokes the biblical story in order to free Jesus from it: no longer was Christ to be of the line of David – the line that made him the Messiah. Instead, his eyes are opened to the wretched egoism of his age, but also to the impossibility of destroying that egoism by force. In his *Philosophy of History*, Hegel had claimed that 'nowhere is language more revolutionary than in the Gospels', and Wagner now planned to have this language spoken on stage.

Wagner understood the dilemma that paralyzed Jesus. He knew that 'the modern world of today is filled with the same sort of worthlessness as that which beset Jesus', and so he could also sense Jesus' despair. The carpenter's son from Galilee could not change society, and so only 'self-annihilation' remained to him as a means of redemption. In denying himself, Jesus sought to 'deny the loveless multitude'. In this way, the Christian Saviour was transformed into an individual who acts out of a sense of political conviction. If Jesus allowed himself to be killed, it was not out of obedience to God but in order to register his protest at a humanity that had forgotten its godlike roots.

The image of the 'sacred head sore wounded' had impressed itself on Wagner's imagination from a very early date. As a schoolboy, he had even been struck by certain similarities with himself. 'With anguished longing', he later recalled, he had gazed up at the altarpiece in the Kreuzkirche in Dresden and, 'ecstatically inspired, wanted to replace the Saviour on the Cross'.[55] *Jesus of Nazareth*, too, contains passing allusions to Wagner's own life, with his hero setting great store, for example, by his 'premarital birth'. Jesus tells his brethren that whereas they were 'born of the flesh', he himself was 'born of love'. He even goes so far as to ask his mother quite candidly: 'Mother, why did you conceive these men?'

Among Wagner's additions to the New Testament is the hero's intimate relationship with the adultress Mary Magdalene. When Jesus is told that she has 'lived in a sinful relationship with a great man from Herod's court', he does not hesitate to 'acquit' her. At this point Wagner says only that she had at once been overcome by a 'blissful love' of Jesus, but elsewhere he paints a detailed picture of his redeemed heroine's grand passion.

In 1852, he told Eliza Wille 'with fiery animation' that Jesus 'was loved with earthly love by the sinful Magdalene' and that this 'must be presented on stage with touching beauty',[56] at which point the piqued Frau Wille left the room. The God-fearing Liszt and his even more God-fearing mistress Carolyne Sayn-Wittgenstein likewise gave Wagner to understand that Jesus as a singing and loving freedom fighter was de trop.

Wagner sacrificed this work about his hero's sacrificial death to the spirit of the times. In a theoretical appendix to the draft, in which he sought to compete with his dialectical models, he explained Christ's death on the Cross in terms of Feuerbach. Every individual, he wrote, must be absorbed into the communal life of the species when he dies. This is the natural limitation of all egoism. He who achieves this union with the whole in the form of an act of conscious sacrifice rises above humanity and becomes 'co-creator and, by dint of the fact that he applies his free will to the greatest possible moral import of the sacrifice, God himself'.[57] In short, Wagner's Jesus did not come into the world as the son of God but attained to divinity as a result of his actions, becoming a hero who, in helping others, triumphs over his natural egoism. It is love that gives him the strength to do so.

In *Jesus of Nazareth*, this human dimension, as embodied by the hero, is contrasted with the cold world of egoism. The world is no longer ruled by the love that the sun god had taught human beings to offer each other, but by the law, by the world of oaths and contracts, punishment and atonement. Only apparently do laws place restrictions on egoism, whereas in fact they perpetuate it and fetter human beings, whose dealings with each other are no longer governed by mutual sympathy but by prescribed rules. The isolation that egoism brings with it also leads to the world's fragmentation.

Instead of the splendours of the universe that the sun god granted his children, the world is now ruled by possessions. Enshrined in laws, these possessions regulate all human relationships. The God of love has become a judge, with nature degraded to private ownership, love to marriage. It is not men and women who violate the law, but the law that violates them. Wagner's Jesus comes to put an end to egoism. Unable to achieve this aim, he puts an end to his own ego. But death is not to be his last word, as he leaves behind a message to the effect that he 'will return to set man free'.

This allowed Wagner to posit a link with the present. For the hero who had succumbed to the forces of darkness a surprising resurrection lay in store, and the hour now seemed to be approaching. In *A Communication to My Friends*, Wagner writes that the time has come to turn the loving hero's desire for self-destruction into revolutionary resolve. Only the 'actual destruction of the outer, visible bonds of that dishonourable sensuality' would bring with it the liberation of which Jesus could only dream.[58] The tragic love-death of the hero, who in his protest at the country's rulers voluntarily offers himself up to them, is merely the prelude to this. Only when the hero who has succumbed to the dragon of egoism is reborn as the hero who kills that dragon will the curtain rise on the artwork of the future.

Threatening Gestures

The books and articles that Wagner wrote during his Zurich diaspora have generally been seen as a kind of stocktaking, a pause to draw breath before he embarked on his large-scale project for the *Ring*. Deprived of his job and robbed of his hopes, the composer is said to have abandoned himself, in the absence of any musical ideas, to theorizing between 1849 and 1851. The fruits of his meditations are regularly described as his 'aesthetic writings', 'reform essays' and even as his 'revolutionary tracts'.

Only one essay emerges like an erratic block from the quarry of his reflections: 'Jews in Music'. As this ghastly treatise lacks all aesthetic, reformative or revolutionary justification, writers have preferred to dismiss it as an expression of Wagner's own 'personal' opinion: in penning it, the composer had merely wanted to 'ridicule' his old rivals Meyerbeer and Mendelssohn and with them 'the whole of contemporary music'.[59]

No one, writes Jürgen Kühnel in the *Wagner Handbook*, should take too seriously Wagner's thoughts on annihilation and destruction: 'Self-destruction is meant here in the Hegelian sense', Kühnel insists,[60] which is as much as to say that Hegel did not take it seriously either. In his apologetic enthusiasm, one writer has even gone so far as to claim that Wagner's insistence on destruction and annihilation 'harks back to the imaginative world and the symbolism of a type of poetry, which flourished in Europe in the early decades of the nineteenth century, whose theme was weltschmerz, or world-weariness'.[61]

But Wagner had no need for the poetry of an earlier generation here: he owed his tragic view of the world to sources other than those found in libraries.

As long as the philosophical views that he espoused in Zurich are seen merely as the fruits of his reading during his revolutionary period, the significance of these writings for their author's own life is bound to remain obscure. Before they were exposed to aesthetic, reformative or revolutionary interpretations, they were part of Wagner's own life. Ideas that were distilled to form a written message began life as part of an experimental conversation with himself, a conversation in which he had first made sure of his own position.

In Wagner's inner monologue, his own private existence was at stake. Both entailed the archetypes of family, betrayal, decisive encounter and an act of reconciliation that coincided with death. In his search for salvation, Wagner had always had to assert himself in the face of an implacable foe who conjured up disaster. This returns again and again as a basic motif of his Zurich essays. In this regard, even the town where he had settled acquired a symbolic significance: driven from home, banished from his family and inheritance, Wagner gradually reclaimed lost ground in these reflections, naming names and asserting claims that he bolstered with historical arguments, demonstrating with dialectical acuity that redemption was bound to follow. With or without Hegel, his enemy had no choice but to be annihilated. The fact that, at the end of this process, 'reconciliation' beckoned will have been little comfort to those affected by it.

Wagner's train of thought, beginning in Dresden with *The Wibelungs*, was picked up seamlessly once the revolution had been put down. The appeal to Siegfried to return and slay the evil gnawing blight on humanity became a hymn to Greek tragedy celebrating the hero's sacrificial death. The success of *Art and Revolution* encouraged Wagner to adopt a yet more radical tone.

He now staked out the field of battle, describing the causes that had led to the decline of pure humanity and classical art and at the same time setting out the conditions that would have to exist before a 'total artwork' could be reborn. In a word, these conditions consisted in the destruction and annihilation of the aforementioned causes. What Wagner suggested in 1850 in 'Jews in Music' had already been philosophically justified only a few months earlier in his essay *The Artwork of the Future*.

Wagner's overzealous use of Hegel's three-part model has always tended to obscure the fact that his Zurich essays draw on his own private mythology. He peered through Hegel's and Feuerbach's telescope, but what he discovered was his old tragedy about his family origins. As in *The Wibelungs*, so in *The Artwork of the Future* the first patriarchal family formed the starting point. Man, seen as a child of nature, was part of a racial community descended from a single progenitor. The legend surrounding the origins of this first king provided the mythic bond that held his descendants together. The cultic act of commemoration in which the congregation recalled its common ancestor developed in ancient Greece into a tragedy about the god who died and who was reborn in art.

If family history, mythically transformed, became a part of the heroic history that was brought to life in the drama, the artistic medium that enables it to be staged replicates family structures. Just as the children were one heart and soul in a blissful primeval state, so the sister arts were combined in the drama to form a harmonious whole. As though recalling his own childhood, Wagner saw music, dance and poetry as three sisters who danced their 'enchanting measures' upon the Attic stage.

Only the living union of the arts could guarantee the unity of the community that celebrated its origins in them. Another word for this living union was 'love'. Only when all three sisters, Wagner wrote rhapsodically in *The Artwork of the Future*, 'held each other in tight embrace, breast to breast, limb to limb, in love's ardent kiss' and merged together 'to form a single, blissfully living figure',[62] would the ideal of an art intended for the whole of humanity finally be achieved.

But this love could scarcely exist between sisters, and even 'love's ardent kiss' hardly suited the picture of a delightful dance among members of the same family, at least as long as the reader was unfamiliar with Wagner's model. At Zurich's Café Littéraire, where he regularly repaired for coffee after his midday meal, the idealized classical landscapes on the wallpaper reminded him of a watercolour that he had first encountered as a young man. It showed the sisterly band of Muses gathered harmoniously around a naked youth whom a raised bowl of wine reveals as Dionysus. Is it possible that the young Wagner saw in this watercolour an idealized image of his own life? With himself as cock of the walk, surrounded by his artistic sisters, who, if the truth be told, rarely paid him the attention that the much-loved god received from the admiring Muses?

Dionysus certainly seems to have enjoyed to the full the admiration of the Graces, who brought him up as their brother. 'It was here', Wagner wrote in *My Life*, 'that I conceived the ideas for my *Artwork of the Future*.' One of these ideas, the loving embrace of the sisterly Muses, could have been directly inspired by his memory of Genelli's watercolour. As though Dionysus, the god of ecstasy, were to couple orgiastically with one of the Muses, so Wagner saw the artwork of the future emerging from a 'complete embrace' on the part of the sisters. As with Siegmund and Sieglinde, this 'complete subsumption within the sister' meant that all the barriers that were arbitrarily erected by society fell down 'in their entirety'. This union between the separated lovers, Wagner continued in this hymnic vein, 'is the love and life, the joy and courtship of art'.

Its sad end was like that of the family. The drama, which Wagner likened to the 'all-loving father', died, and the bond that was provided by the religion of art and that held the family together fell apart. Just as, following the death of the father 'in whose love they were all united', each child arrogates its inheritance to itself, so the sisters who until then had been held together in their loving embrace were broken down into their constituent parts as individual arts. Without the religious content that united them in commemoration of their god, they were reduced to a form of sophisticated handiwork that prostituted itself in return for money.

The horror that the young Wagner had felt when faced by the theatre's imitation of life now seems to have transferred itself to all the arts, and it is with the same disgust once triggered in him by painted actors that he reacts to the decadent art forms that chased after every fashion in their attempt to make life more agreeable for a narrow luxury-loving stratum of society. This general decline in the quality of the arts had turned them into caricatures of the egoism to which they owed their frivolous semblance of life and to which the community at large owed its current enslavement. Kotzebue was everywhere.

With the death of Greek tragedy, the community lost its principal focus. Egoism was now rampant. In place of the sun god in whom the people had once recognized themselves, there were now possessions and money. No archetypal king reigned supreme any more, only naked greed. Where gods had once ordered our lives, calculating reason dictated our actions. But in the common folk, in whom all memory of their mythic origins had long been exorcized, there emerged a growing feeling that they had been disinherited.

The splendours of the world that had once been entrusted to the folk to enjoy in common had been arrogated by others. No less bitter than the loss of the world's inheritance was that of the sense of belonging together as a nation. According to Wagner, the fragmented people were at least agreed on one point: 'The folk is the epitome of all who feel a common need.' And who, Wagner asks, are the enemies of the people? 'All those who feel no sense of need?'[63]

The intellectual barrier that divided the world into a handful of egoists and the rest of suffering humanity is one that had been erected by Feuerbach. Just as Wagner took over the title of *The Principles of the Philosophy of the Future* for the title of his own pamphlet *The Artwork of the Future*, so he took over its basic thesis from Feuerbach's *Provisional Theses for the Reformation of Philosophy*. Here the philosopher declares suffering to be one of the fundamental conditions of human existence. Where there is no deprivation, there is 'no resolve, no fire, no love'. Only the 'suffering creature', Feuerbach proclaimed in 1843, is 'the necessary creature'. As long as man felt that his isolation was a shortcoming, so he continued to maintain a vestigial awareness of a unified humanity. 'Only the creature that knows suffering is godlike.'

Feuerbach drew the grim conclusion that a 'needless existence' is an 'useless existence': those men and women who are not part of suffering humanity cannot be human beings. Those who have no needs 'have no need of existence'. A 'creature devoid of suffering' is a 'creature devoid of essence'. Strictly speaking, such people do not exist. If they fail to recognize their own superfluity, Feuerbach tacitly concludes, they should be made to see it by force.

This was exactly the idea that Wagner had been looking for. It offered a common denominator to the people who had lost their sense of a mythical community, while at the same time depriving their enemies of their right to exist. He who is not painfully aware of the fragmentation of the human race and of his separation from its true basis in life can have no reason for living. By elevating himself above the people, the rich man cuts himself off from his own essential nature and becomes insubstantial. His single need in life – that of adding to what already exists in excess – derives from no natural need. Such a need is 'imagined, untrue, heartless, inhuman'. This 'devil' of luxury, a figure by no means unknown to Wagner personally, rules the world and has turned God's creation into a hell of senseless greed. The 'murderous lust of the despot' is reflected in 'wanton modern operatic music'. But a solution is at hand, it seems. 'Need', Wagner declares, 'will end the hell of luxury.'[64]

Earlier writers have claimed that it was in 'Jews in Music' that Wagner took the decisive step, but he had in fact already taken it in *The Artwork of the Future*. Lacking the means to put his ideas into practice, he was reduced to mere threatening gestures. But there is no mistaking his intention of calling for action or at least of intimidating the people towards whom his threats were directed. It was against the oppressive 'ruling world spirit' that had proved 'fatal to all communal existence' that he issued his death threat. 'Only when the ruling religion of egoism, which has split the whole world of art into crippled, self-seeking types and tendencies', he proclaimed in the strains of an Old Testament prophet, 'only when this religion has been mercilessly driven from every aspect of our lives and torn up root and branch can the new religion come into being of its own accord.'

For Wagner, this 'religion of egoism' was synonymous in its widest sense with the ideology of increasing possessions and capital, while in its narrower sense it can be equated with the Jews, an equation already made by Feuerbach. Their God, the philosopher had written in *The Essence of Christianity*, was nothing but 'the personified selfishness of the Israelite people'. Wagner drew from this the radical conclusion that the suffering caused by egoism could be ended only if that egoism were destroyed. This was justified by the suffering that made that step appear 'needful'. And annihilation, too, followed logically. If annihilation ultimately brought with it the triumph of humanity, all egoists would at least join in the act of general redemption at the moment of their destruction.

'The folk', Wagner predicts in *The Artwork of the Future*, 'will achieve redemption by becoming self-sufficient' – in other words, by following inner necessity – 'and at the same time redeeming their own enemies.' What sounds like cynicism merely reflects Wagner's dialectical thinking according to which all that is currently invalid can triumph only by being completely invalidated and destroyed. 'The folk', Wagner continues with razor-sharp logic, 'have only to deny by their deeds the thing that is indeed nothing – in other words, unnecessary, superfluous and invalid; they need only to know what they do not want, and this they are taught by their instinctive desire for life; by dint of their own need, they need only to turn what they do not want into what does not exist and to annihilate what deserves to be annihilated, and the reality of a future that is no longer a riddle to them will appear before them as though of its own accord.'[65]

In uttering this sibylline prophecy, Wagner was referring to the new society of the synthesis of the arts. Following the 'great annihilating blow of fate' that would also put an end to all the prevailing 'musical nonsense', the artwork of the future would come into being of its own accord. And Wagner ends his declaration of war by offering his readers a foretaste of his new folk drama. Just as at the end of his previous essays he had conjured up the mythological heroes of Siegfried, Apollo and Jesus of Nazareth, so on this occasion he resurrects the early Germanic hero Wieland. The community had once invented this hero 'out of inner necessity'. Now he returns to the world stage as a necessary expression of man's universal fate. As soon as the folk recognize themselves in the hero's sufferings, they will not shy away from repeating the hero's actions, actions that bring Wieland both redemption and release.

The myth that Wagner retells for his readers' benefit begins at the dawn of history, when men still consorted with the gods. A hero by the name of Wieland, who is capable of making dainty trinkets with the same perfection as sharp-edged weapons, has taken a swan-maiden as his wife and lives with her 'in blissful union'. But the idyll of their liaison is destroyed by King Neiding, who burns down Wieland's home and claims his treasure as his own. Wieland is reduced to servitude and his tendons are severed, leaving him 'limping, crippled and ugly'. Whereas he has previously practised his trade in order to give pleasure to all, he is now forced to work 'in order to increase his lord's wealth'.

1. Hopes of the Paris Opéra: Wagner in Paris. Pencil drawing by Ernst Benedikt Kietz, 1842

2. Wagner's stepfather Ludwig Geyer. Self-portrait, ca. 1813

3. Wagner's legendary 'grandfather' Prince Constantin of Saxe-Weimar

4. Wagner's mother, Johanna Rosine, in the year of Wagner's birth, 1813. Oil painting by Ludwig Geyer

5. Wagner's model: his Leipzig uncle, Adolf Wagner, ca. 1813

6. Wagner's favourite sister Rosalie at the piano. Drawn by Ludwig Geyer, ca. 1820

7. The ideal artist: Wilhelmine Schröder-Devrient. Oil painting by Carl Joseph Begas

8. The highly gifted Hans von Bülow, 1850s

9. Mephistophelean profile: Court Kapellmeister Wagner. Pencil drawing by Joseph Tichatschek, 1840s

10. The Dresden Uprising: insurgents in front of the Town Hall, with one of Baron von Burgk's cannons to the left, May 1849

11. The ideal Wagner heroine: the composer's step-niece Johanna Wagner after her apostasy. Oil painting, 1864

12. Wagner's unloved brother: Albert Wagner acted as agent for his adopted daughter Johanna

13. A friend with a fortune: Franz Liszt in the mid-1850s

14. 'Sieglinde': Jessie Laussot, later Hildebrand, in old age

15. The abandoned wife: Minna in Zurich, mid-1850s

16. Grand passion: Mathilde Wesendonck. An idealized sketch by Ernst Benedikt Kietz, 1856

17. Wagner in Paris in March 1860. Clearly visible on his cheek is the rash caused by erysipelas that is generally airbrushed out in reproductions of this photograph

18. Wagner as couturier: silk items of indoor clothing made to Wagner's designs by Bertha Goldwag

19. The daughter of a notary, the notoriously well-behaved Mathilde Maier almost became Wagner's wife in 1864

20. Well known for her wild manner, the actress Friederike Meyer accompanied Wagner to Vienna in 1862

21. The Stork: Cosima Liszt, now of marriageable age, with a relief of her father, 1850s

22. Wagner's flame in Paris: Blandine was the first of Liszt's daughters to catch Wagner's eye, ca. 1860

23. Trio Infernal: Wagner and his private secretary Cosima, followed by her husband Hans von Bülow, with the score of *Tristan und Isolde* under his arm. Munich caricature, 1864

24. 'Vreneli': Wagner's favourite servant Verena Weidmann. This photograph was taken in 1882, when she was fifty

Orchester-Probe.

25. On the brink of the 'mystic abyss' in Bayreuth: the Master giving instructions to the orchestra, 1876

26. Wagner's children: his son and heir Siegfried, with Eva and Isolde, 1880s

27. The 'Hurricane': Judith Gautier. Photograph by Nadar, 1875

28. Demons of the night: the Nibelungs Alberich and Mime as Wagner saw them

29. Bayreuth trompe l'oeil: the interior of the Festspielhaus seems to pass imperceptibly into the interior of the Temple of the Grail

30. Group portrait with dogs: Wagner standing one step higher than Cosima, surrounded by Blandine, Isolde, Heinrich von Stein, Daniela, Eva, Siegfried and Joukowsky, 1881

31. Fatal love: Carrie Pringle (left) among the solo Flowermaidens, suing for the favours of the pure fool Parsifal in 1882

32. Wagner's death mask: 'His delicate mouth', wrote Joukowsky, 'remained half open, as though he were gasping for breath.'

Longingly he gazes up through the chimney stack at the blue sky into which his valkyrie had once disappeared.

Like the humiliated hero in the mythic past, Wagner explains, the Germans of the present day have been reduced to servitude by envious masters and robbed of their inheritance. All that they have created has been for the use not of themselves but of the usurpers whose wealth they have had to increase. 'O unique and glorious race!' Wagner exclaims at the end of his broadsheet, 'you have created this for yourselves, you yourselves are this Wieland! Forge your wings and soar aloft!' It is this that the hero succeeds in doing, after he has been kept alive by his longing for his lost lover and by his hope that his wrongs will be righted: 'Vengeance, vengeance on this Neiding who out of base self-interest had reduced him to such infinite misery! If only he might annihilate this wretch, together with his whole brood!'

It is not lameness but need that inspires him to act. 'Terrible all-powerful need', writes Wagner, encourages Wieland to forge a pair of wings for himself and to use them to escape from his prison. But before he soars away to a better future on 'his wife's blessed isle', he first wants to sate his desire for vengeance. 'Borne aloft on his own work of art, he flies up to the heights from where he strikes Neiding's heart with his fatal bolt.' This is Wagner's unmistakable message to his 'unique and glorious folk'. The tragedy, he makes clear, does not have to end with the death of the hero: the example of Wieland teaches us that destruction may yet catch up with our enemies, too.

Wagner rarely had any luck with dramas that had a happy ending. His grand heroic opera *Wieland der Schmied*, a sketch of which he prepared on completing *The Artwork of the Future*, remained unwritten. He completed the draft in Paris and planned to have it translated into French in order to offer it to the Opéra, but lack of interest meant that he did not even get as far as a translation. Wagner resigned himself to the inevitable. Even in its initial stages, the artwork already had its future behind it. During the years that followed, he repeatedly offered the draft to friends such as Liszt, suggesting that if Liszt himself did not like it he might recommend it to Berlioz. Later he even tried to interest less talented composers such as August Röckel and Wendelin Weißheimer in the crippled Wieland, but in vain.[66]

It is entirely possible that the reason why Wagner failed to elaborate the draft was that its main motifs had already found their way into his next work, *Der Ring des Nibelungen*. The butterfly had spread its wings, and only the dead larva remained. Yet even its cocoon, in the form of the draft, makes its overall structure clear. Elements missing from the summary of the work that Wagner appended to *The Artwork of the Future* are supplied by the draft.

Even the hero's ancestry follows a familiar Wagnerian tradition: Wieland's grandfather was the first king, Wiking, who, like Wotan, drew no distinction between mortal women and mythical creatures when propagating his line, fathering the race of Wieland on a water sprite by the name of Wachilde, while Wieland's wife Schwanhilde is a granddaughter of an 'elfish prince' who had assumed the form of a swan and who was presumably the same mythic ruler. As a result, Wieland shares the mysterious origins of all Wagner's heroes and apparently loves his own sister. As both a loving wife and a winged valkyrie, she thus reveals the dual nature of her origins. The fact that Wieland loses her is entirely in keeping with the fate of all his predecessors.

And it also anticipates the fate of his successor, Siegfried. In Jacob Grimm's *Deutsche Mythologie*, Wagner could have read that both Wieland and Siegfried were apprenticed to a dwarf by the name of Mimir and that both heroes learnt smithying from him, discovering both freedom and death in the process: whereas the tools they made for themselves allowed them to triumph over their oppressors, a metalwork ring results in their downfall. The magic trinket that was soon to be central to Wagner's creative endeavours was something he had found in Karl Simrock's *Amelungenlied*, from which he also took the story of Wieland. But as a symbol of omnipotence and the magical power of love, the golden ring also casts a spell that causes the heroes to be untrue to themselves. Having tamed the elements, they are destroyed by themselves.

Wieland receives the ring from Schwanhilde as a token of her love, but it is then stolen by King Neiding's daughter Bathilde. In this way Wieland not only loses his freedom and his inheritance, but, blinded by Bathilde's ring, he also forgets his own bride. In addition to being enslaved by his enemy, he is tormented by his own betrayal of his love. Whereas Siegfried succumbs to the curse on the ring, the trinket rekindles Wieland's spirit of resistance when finally restored to his hands.

The impetuous song that Siegfried sings when forging his sword is already heard on Wieland's lips as the latter conjures up his own artwork of the future 'to the soughing of the bellows, the flash of sparks and the beat of the hammer'. The inspired contraption that enables him to fly turns him from a 'lame and limping cripple' to the proto-king's rightful heir. His crutches fall to the ground, and his false bride Bathilde utters a rapt cry: 'One of the gods stands before me!' Wieland corrects her: 'A human being in his greatest need!' He then torches the building and, with it, the world, and brother and sister are united in love, soaring above their enemy's corpse in the radiant dawn sky of the revolution that will free the whole of humanity.

Wagner saw himself in his folk hero Wieland as he did in so many of his other heroes, writing to Liszt in 1853 to announce that, 'as nature has everywhere been bent and broken', he has been left with only one choice: 'I must forge for myself a pair of artificial wings.'[67]

Ahasuerus's Downfall

Wagner's Zurich essays were completely ineffectual. For all his hopes to the contrary, aesthetics did not enter a new era, nor did any of his readers draw the revolutionary consequences that he had commended to them. The philosophers to whose keen minds these treatises might have appealed took no notice, and the artists whose Germanic consciences he eagerly importuned continued on their benighted way.

Only one of the texts that the exiled Wagner wrote in his Villa Rienzi in the Enge district of Zurich had any impact – and not in the way he wanted. The area on which it left its mark can be described as neither aesthetic nor revolutionary but concerns the internal politics of the German empire. Although the reaction was remarkably slow in coming, Wagner was to survive long enough to derive great pleasure from his actions.

By 1879, anti-Semitism had become a popular movement. At its head was the Berlin court chaplain, Adolf Stoecker, in whose theories the now elderly Wagner took an approving interest. After reading a 'very good speech' that the good pastor had delivered against the Jews, Wagner told Cosima that he was fully in favour of their 'total expulsion' and, with a laugh, noted that his 'article on the Jews really seems to have marked the beginning of this struggle'.[68]

There were presumably several reasons why he laughed. On the one hand, he must have been pleased that an organized movement against the Jews was now being formed and that it was influenced by his own ideas. But he must also have been amused by the fact that these ideas had appeared in print almost thirty years earlier under the title 'Jews in Music'. And finally, he will have been gratified that one of his Zurich essays, far from having vanished without trace, had finally had the political influence he had hoped for.

In fact, his essay had first appeared anonymously in the *Neue Zeitschrift für Musik* in September 1850, when it had had a spectacularly explosive impact – not, however, on those readers against whom it was aimed but on the author himself. From the moment Wagner published the fatal text and admitted to its authorship, he felt he was the victim of a Jewish conspiracy. Of course it was not the Jews he had attacked in his article who were to blame for this, but Wagner himself. The sinister picture of them that he had drawn with his febrile pen proved to be a self-fulfilling prophecy.

Following the publication of 'Jews in Music', every critical reaction that Wagner provoked seemed to him to be a direct consequence of his essay. All who attacked him were acting at the behest of the Jews. All who broke faith with him were guilty of betraying him to the Jews. Every action that he interpreted as directed against himself was an act of vengeance inspired by his article. As the only person who believed in the picture he had painted, he served as living proof of the validity of his assertions. With 'Jews in Music', the archetypal enemy became a concrete threat, and from then on his life was to be overshadowed by his fear of Jewish persecution. Between that time and his death, he was tormented by his fear of a ghost that he himself had created.

'The fuss that this article caused,' Wagner wrote in his autobiography in the late 1860s, 'nay, the actual terror that it spread can be compared to that of no other publication.'[69] Since the autumn of 1850, he went on, he had experienced 'unprecedented hostility' on the part of the European press, which – he hardly needed to remind his readers – was in the hands of his enemies. From then on he had been subjected to an 'unceasing and vicious campaign of persecution' that eventually took the form of a 'sense of European outrage' directed against his music. The seething anger of early responses to the article soon 'assumed the character of malice and wilful slander'.

And it was an old acquaintance who lay behind this campaign of extermination. 'The movement', Wagner went on, convinced as he was that all criticism against him was part of a concerted campaign, 'was systematically organized by a man intimately familiar with such matters, Herr Meyerbeer.' Needless to say, there could be no question of any such action on Herr Meyerbeer's part, still less of an orchestrated campaign, but Wagner believed in it implicitly, just as he was afraid of the image of the adversary that he bore within himself.

Ten years before realizing that this essay had triggered the anti-Semitic movement in Germany, Wagner decided to republish the piece. Embroidered with a few additional passages designed to hone his arguments, the article now appeared under his own name, a name, it may be added, that had in the meantime acquired a certain notoriety. Believing that the hatred of every Jew was now focused upon him, by 1869 he no longer saw any reason to hide his light under a bushel, quite apart from the fact that he was angered by parliament's decision to grant equal rights to Jews living in Prussia and northern Germany. For the present, however, the republication failed to achieve its intended effect, and Jewish emancipation continued apace, while the claims he made in the pamphlet served merely to add to his own sense of isolation within the society of his time.

While bringing the text up to date, Wagner also took the opportunity to add a foreword in the form of an open letter in which he informed one of his female supporters about the true nature of the scandal confronting Germany. It was not he who, with his theses, was persecuting the Jews; rather, the revelation that he was the article's author had ushered in an 'inverse Jewish persecution' against him, and this had grown 'like ripples in a pond'.[70] In the course of a hate campaign directed not only at his person but also at his works, the ideas that he had presented had been ignored. These ideas had 'merely provided a pretext for the war of persecution' that was aimed at destroying his art and that of his friends. 'That is why I assure you', he informed his patron Marie Muchanoff, 'that the fate that Liszt, too, has suffered is due to the effects of that article on "Jews in Music".'

As a suitable image for this 'total victory of the Jews' over true art, Wagner could think only of 'the wrangling over the Saviour's garments at the foot of the Cross'. Elsewhere, he wrote in a similar vein that his enemies 'may care to play with my garments at the foot of my Cross',[71] once again drawing an analogy between his own life and the story of the Passion. As a child, Wagner had wanted to be nailed to the crucifix in the Kreuzkirche, and it almost looks as though as an adult he still hoped that this childhood wish would come true. Right up to the end of his life he saw himself 'nailed, as it were, to the Cross of the German ideal'.[72] Like his solar hero Jesus, he had to suffer persecution and a painful death in return for the godlike gift that he offered humanity. It never seems to have struck him that this idea, which caused him abiding fear in life and led to the depression that afflicted him in old age, may have gone back to his childhood. The antagonist who plotted against his life with such terrible obstinacy had merely donned a new mask.

This too was part of the conspiracy theory that he developed for Marie Muchanoff's benefit. The Jews were persecuting his art but in fact were thinking of his article. While insulting him in person, they were aiming their barbs at the champion of Germanic myth. It was for this reason that even critics such as Eduard Hanslick, who had 'initially declared their support for me with a fondness bordering on enthusiasm', now fell away from him. Hanslick's 'conversion', Wagner went on, 'took place so suddenly and with such violence that I was deeply shocked by it'. From now on, Hanslick attacked Wagner's works 'in the most daintily dialectical manner'. 'About that article on "Jews in Music", however, there never appeared another word.' Instead, Wagner's essay 'produced its effect all the more successfully in secret, becoming the Medusa's head that was promptly held up before everyone who evinced so much as a scintilla of unthinking concern for me'.

Wagner's metaphor reveals the active role that he seems to have concealed not only from Marie Muchanoff but even from himself. In his article, he portrays the Jews as a childhood ghost that is bound to fill the observer with a sense of mortal dread. Like some latterday Perseus, then, he himself had struck off the hideous head that the Jews were said to be presenting to his friends. Evidently he too had stared at this Medusa's head, the very sight of which paralyzed him from the moment it was held up in his presence.

Wagner's reproach can also be interpreted as a sign that the campaign directed at his music was in fact intended to punish him for his hostility towards the Jews, for, as he was no doubt aware, he himself had used the Jews' alleged unmusicality as a pretext for his attempts to get even with the whole 'Jewish business'.[73] He explicitly rejected the notion that his essay was aimed solely at rival composers, and there is no doubt that 'Jews in Music' takes its place within the series of essays that he wrote in Zurich, continuing their theses and taking a current conflict as its starting point. Music served merely as a symptom of a life-threatening illness that affected the whole of the nation's health.

Wagner's diagnosis of the malaise affecting modern music was already familiar to readers of his *Artwork of the Future*. It was here, rather than in the polemical 'Jews in Music' as writers on Wagner have claimed, that the composer first complained about the 'repugnant, indescribably nauseating deformation and distortion' of popular music for which he blamed Mendelssohn's 'saccharine haggling' among others. The final section of 'Jews in Music' has regularly been regarded as a mystifying aberration peculiar to that article, but Wagner had already appealed to his fellow Germans in *The Artwork of the Future* to undertake 'a great, annihilating blow of fate'. In turn, its predecessor, *Art and Revolution*, had recommended 'the destruction of all that deserves to be destroyed'.

Exactly who Wagner meant by this became clear with 'Jews in Music', its attack triggered by Meyerbeer's latest success, *Le prophète*, which reached Berlin in April 1850, with Wagner's own niece Johanna playing a not inconsiderable part in Meyerbeer's triumph. While his own works were universally ignored, Johanna, who had once seemed destined to become a Wagnerian singer, had sold herself to his arch-enemy in return for filthy lucre. His 'long-repressed fury' was further fuelled by an argument over *Le prophète* in the pages of various music journals in which his friend Theodor Uhlig was implicated.

Writing in the *Neue Zeitschrift für Musik*, Uhlig had claimed that as a Jewish composer Meyerbeer showed a 'Hebraic taste in art' from whose cunning sophistries 'good Christians' could only turn away in disgust. When the *Rheinische Musikzeitung* leapt to Meyerbeer's defence, Uhlig returned to the attack, appealing to Robert Schumann, no less, who in 1837 had accused Meyerbeer of 'vulgarity, distortion, unnaturalness and immorality' in a notorious assault on *Les Huguenots*, which he dismissed as 'non-music'. Schumann ended by darkly prophesying that only when the stage was turned into a gallows and the deliquent had uttered a 'scream of utter terror' was there 'any hope that things might improve'.[74] Just as Wagner was to do thirteen years later in his own essay on 'Jews in Music', Schumann left the interpretation of this passage to his reader's imagination.

Wagner had already claimed that Jewishness and art were irreconcilable opposites in his other Zurich essays. As the true work of art owed its existence to the loving union of the folk and the reunion of all the arts, the religion of egoism – for this is how Wagner defined Judaism – was bound to result in its fragmentation and destruction. This radical point of view is one that Wagner could have found adumbrated in an anonymous pamphlet issued by his Leipzig publisher Otto Wigand in 1841. In *Die Posaune des jüngsten Gerichts über Hegel den Atheisten und Antichristen* ('The Trumpet of the Last Judgement on Hegel the Atheist and Antichrist'), Hegel's pupil Bruno Bauer regaled his readers with a parodistic account of his mentor's teachings, branding the stern political philosopher an outright revolutionary, while repeatedly referring to the 'genius' of the Leipzig thinker Christian Hermann Weiße, whom Wagner already admired as a friend of his Uncle Adolf.

With almost religious zeal, Bauer, casting himself in the role of Hegel's mouthpiece, expresses the irrefutable view that in its present state the world invited wholesale destruction. It was time for the older forms of consciousness to disappear in the sacrificial fire of the Absolute. The destruction of an outmoded world would usher in the rule of the philosophers who would henceforth determine the course of the world spirit and provide the resolve necessary to ensure that the 'fanaticism of thought' became the 'fanaticism of action'. Liberated humanity would then recognize its true destiny in art. Art alone allowed man to produce 'the divine' from within himself, as it had done in ancient Greece. The classical beauty that raised man to heaven would spell the end of monotheism. 'Away with this fruit of the Orient and Galilee,' wrote Bauer, putting words into Hegel's mouth, 'let us become Greeks, let us become human beings once again!'

But artistically liberated society still had to contend with the dark forces of ancient religion. There was nothing that Hegel hated more than Jewry, claimed Bauer, for there was no place for the free individual within its religion's harsh laws. The Jewish God was 'pure terrible egoism', the 'content of the religion of egoism' none other than 'ownership'. There could be no more glaring contrast than that between the slavish irrationality of the Hebrews and the rapt vision of beauty of the Greeks. 'When man exults in art as the creator of the universe and sings a paean to himself', Bauer rhapsodized, 'then Hegel must of course hate the Jews and their harsh religion.' This consciousness consisted solely of subservience and covetousness, but as soon as it disappeared, the new world would come into being of its own accord. Once 'finite consciousness and the slavery bound up with it are killed, then freedom will emerge. Man will become free, and God will become the God of free human beings.'[75]

It is not only in the tone it strikes that Wagner's 'Jews in Music' recalls Bauer's *Die Posaune des jüngsten Gerichts*. For the composer, too, the day of reckoning seemed to have arrived, and in the best dialectical tradition his outspoken language reflects the importance of the world-historical moment. At the very beginning of his article, Wagner insists that his concern is by no means limited to the sort of music mentioned in his title. It is, he announces, 'emancipation from the spirit of Jewry' that strikes him as the 'most necessary' step of all. In the 1869 version of his article, he clarified this by insisting that he meant 'emancipation from the *pressure* of Jewry'. In order to ensure that his readers had the 'strength for this struggle for liberation', he needed to provide them with a detailed description of the enemy. Perhaps, he speculated, the 'naked exposure' of the foe would suffice to 'drive the demon from the field in which he has been able to maintain his presence only beneath the shelter of a sombre semi-darkness'.[76]

It is clear from this formulation that we are dealing not with ordinary men and women but with an archetypal figure invested with superhuman powers and embodied in the individuals in his line of fire. Wagner called this figure 'the Jewish being'. The fact that in the original version of the text it concealed itself beneath the mantle of a 'greyish semi-darkness' was due not only to its proverbial fear of the light or its consciously averting its eyes 'in order to make the sight of it less repugnant to us': the demon of 'Jewry' that seemed to seek out the dark sprang in fact from the darkness of Wagner's own subconscious. Whatever the image may suggest to the contrary, it does not evaporate when examined more closely, but as a mythological conglomerate it does not stand up to rational enquiry either. The darkness of this monster reflects the lack of clarity surrounding its origins, just as the term 'demon' suggests that it derives not from the world of adult understanding but from that of childhood's incomprehensible fears.

Wagner makes no attempt to deny that his violent reaction stems from his subconscious, but instead of seeking out the personal reasons for his 'involuntary sense of revulsion', he declares his idiosyncrasy an 'instinctive dislike'. By twisting the facts in this way, he is able to justify his vague feeling as though it is something entirely normal; indeed, he even ennobles it to the point where it becomes an 'involuntary loathing' on the part of the popular spirit. The physical appearance of the Jew, he claims, is so repulsive as to be unsuited to artistic representation, while the Jew's speech is said to offend the ear with its 'hissing, shrill, buzzing, grunting sounds'. When the Jew prays, it sounds like a 'gurgling, yodelling and babbling', and when he tries to speak a foreign language, he succeeds only in mimicking it like a parrot, 'without expression and with no real emotion'.

Abundant and detailed as Wagner's observations may seem, they can be reduced to two basic emotions: horror and loathing. The feelings that left their mark on his picture of Jews are thus the very ones that were inextricably linked to his childhood fears. His loathing of the masks that so accurately mimicked reality mirrored the terror he felt at the painted portraits that awoke to eerie life. From the demonic depths of the theatre there rose up the old enemy who, thanks to his skills as an actor, had insidiously wormed his way into his father's position. Behind Wagner's 'instinctive aversion' lay his fear of the usurper.

Wagner's violent attacks on the Jews ultimately boil down to this. From the outset, he refuses to show any tolerance on the grounds that tolerance is an airy concept, whereas 'actual reality' has long been 'usurped' by a demon that has acquired a position of power as a result of the money to which 'the blood of countless families' clings. Thanks to his ability to imitate others, the Jew has found it easy to adopt the language and manners of the Germans. At the same time, the Jew attempts 'to wipe away all traces of his origins', an attempt that is generally futile.

But the Jew has gone on to seize control of music. As Wagner has previously explained in *The Artwork of the Future*, music has already been cut off from its sister arts and hopelessly emasculated, making it easy for the Jew to take possession of it. In actual fact, he is making use of a corpse whose flesh, Wagner explains in nauseous detail, 'teems with a swarming mass of worms'. What Wagner means by this is not that the Jews are worms but that their nature consists in rousing dead matter to a semblance of life.

As a result, a 'Jewish composer' – whom we may suppose to be Meyerbeer – believed that his 'life's work as an artist' consisted in 'deceiving' his public, while Mendelssohn, whom Wagner mentions by name, was able to produce something which, if not art, at least consisted in 'vague, fantastic and shadowy shapes'. It is in song, however, that the 'repulsive peculiarity of the Jewish character finds its most extreme expression', with the result that Wagner hopes that the imitative demon will be prevented from setting foot in that field of artistic endeavour 'whose basis is song'. In 1850 he simply states that the Jew should not be regarded as 'artistically competent', whereas in 1869 he insists that, as far as music is concerned, the Jew 'has no artistic justification'. The grotesque professional ban that Wagner demands here was to be given legal status in the course of the following century.

Wagner was able to justify his dictatorial directive by equating his own emotions with the popular instinct. Without mentioning it specifically, he harks back to the category of the 'necessary' that he had posited in *The Artwork of the Future*. Just as the folk is defined by its common need, so all that it feels to be necessary reveals the true conditions of its existence. According to this thesis, the real history of the people's origins – a history that goes back to its mythic beginnings in the first family – is manifested in its instincts.

Even in his essay *The Wibelungs*, Wagner had projected his own private mythology onto German history. The Hohenstaufen tradition had been destroyed, and so memory of the country's great past survived only in the form of legends. While his essay on 'Jews in Music' reminded the Germans of their necessary instincts in life, Wagner also took the opportunity to take the demon who merely mimicked life and cast him in the role of the adversary and usurper.

Just as the first king of the Franks became the solar hero Siegfried and just as the latter became the Saviour Jesus, so the usurpers of the empire appeared as its enemies and murderers. But at this point myth became reality. In *The Wibelungs*, Wagner had reminded the Germans that 'even today we continue to avenge Christ on the Jews'. In 'Jews in Music', he showed that the mythical Jews were indeed the same as those who continued to hold in their hands the power they had seized.

Wagner's one concern was to prove this point. After all, it was already abundantly plain to him that the Jews were incapable of producing true art. Everyone who had a pair of ears knew this. Not even their repulsive appearance could be hidden from anyone in possession of his natural instincts. Only the fact that this demon had insidiously seized power and arrogated to itself the Germans' rightful inheritance had passed unnoticed, as this was clear only on an epistemological and not on an emotional level. And it was the Jews themselves who ensured that this truth remained hidden, as it was well known that they had extended their power to encompass the press and science.

Having found the Jews guilty of usurpation, Wagner proceeded to pass sentence on them in the second part of his article. His surprising conclusion takes up only twenty lines, whereas he had needed nearly twenty pages to present his evidence, with the result that readers failed to appreciate the form that the proceedings took. At best, writers puzzled over the reasons why Wagner, after so much finicking and colourful detail, should suddenly lapse into the language of the writer of the Apocalypse, following up his references to the absurd hissing, babbling and buzzing of the Jews' mode of speech with his dark prophecy of self-extermination and destruction.

Writers on Wagner have been reluctant to accept that the composer meant this to be taken seriously. Why should the inability of the Jews to live up to his artistic standards entail their death and destruction? 'It goes without saying', claims one recent apologist, that Wagner meant an act that was 'of a symbolic nature, intended to bring about a mystic transformation of the whole of humankind. Only as a result of this process of transformation will the Jew become a true human being.'[77]

That the Jew had never been a true human being is one of Wagner's premises. As a demon, he merely mimics humanity – as everyone realizes instinctively. This is why, in passing sentence on Jewry, Wagner insists that they must first become human, in other words, 'cease to be Jews'. But they can become 'true human beings' only by means of revolution. When Wagner prescribes a 'self-destructive, bloody battle' as a way of 'redeeming' Jews from their Jewishness, he is repeating Hegel, Feuerbach and Bruno Bauer, all of whom believed in the need to overthrow the old consciousness – a consciousness that would end with the revolution – in order to be reborn on the funeral pyre of the past.

But this was only the first part of Wagner's punishment, a part that speaks the conciliatory language of the age, offering freedom to the whole of humanity, including the Jews. In order to become human beings, the latter have to take part in the revolutionary process, abandon their claims to power, hand over their possessions to the workers and eke out their lives in 'sweat, need and an abundance of suffering'. This period of probation is followed by a second punishment, however, one that is demanded not merely by Wagner the human being and freedom fighter but, he was convinced, by the international tribunal itself.

'But consider', Wagner enjoins the Jews, 'that there is only one thing that can redeem you from the curse that weighs upon you: the redemption of Ahasuerus – destruction!' This harsh sentence stems not from the world of politics but from that of myth. Although the revolution may succeed in investing the Jews with a certain human dignity, they are still afflicted by the curse that the deity once placed upon them, for it was the Jews who murdered the loving solar hero and seized possession of his universal inheritance. That is why Jesus cursed Ahasuerus – the stand-in for a whole nation of deicides – and condemned him to a life of eternal wandering. Nothing can wash away the blood of the hero or the Jew's sin of betraying the Saviour. Only destruction can redeem him from his fate.

For Wagner, this prophecy obeyed a basic mythic law. Greek tragedy, too, was all about curses and death, their bitter inevitability constituting the very essence of the hero's fate. Whole families of rulers had fallen prey to this implacable logic. The 'curse that is uttered in myth as the divine punishment for a primordial crime', Wagner was to declare in his following study *Opera and Drama*, 'attached itself to a particular family until such time as that family was destroyed'.[78]

For the present, Wagner's curse seemed to have attached itself to him alone. He had cut himself off and was now surprised that people avoided him. He had promised to create the artwork of the future and instead was rehashing yesterday's prejudices. The indignation triggered by his essay was an expression not of the wrath of Jehovah but of the bewilderment of those who had admired his art. The writer on music Johann Christian Lobe, for example, had made the pilgrimage to Weimar for the first performance of *Lohengrin* and had been carried away by his 'effusive enthusiasm' for the work, an enthusiasm that found expression in a euphoric review. At that point he stumbled upon the composer's newly printed essay 'Jews in Music'. He could scarcely believe his eyes and in a review he wrote for the Leipzig *Illustrirte Zeitung* provided a parody of its contents for the benefit of those readers who were equally baffled by the essay: '*I* hate the Jews; *I* hate and envy Mendelssohn and Meyerbeer; and so *I* advise you to annihilate all Jews.'[79]

Genesis

The ghosts that Wagner had conjured up would not leave him in peace. During the late autumn of 1850, in the midst of the stir caused by 'Jews in Music', a new scandal erupted, when Wagner found himself referred to in the same breath as his diametrical opposites Meyerbeer and Mendelssohn in an article that appeared in *Die Gegenwart*, a lexicon published by the firm of Brockhaus – the very publishing house into which two of his own sisters had married. As a result of his early death, claimed the author of the article 'Modern Opera',

Mendelssohn had been prevented from giving the Germans a national opera, whereas Wagner, in spite of his clear weaknesses, had the merit of 'having sought to appropriate for the German spirit the full extent of Meyerbeer's great achievements'.[80]

Against the background of his essay 'Jews in Music', this must have sounded like a death sentence, prompting Wagner to return to his desk, which he had barely left, and to dispose of a calumny that was now being repeated the length and breadth of Germany. For a period of several months he remained in a state of breathless excitement, but his 'exhausting zeal' was 'cruelly requited' when his parrot, neglected by its master, became ill and, the day after Wagner completed his manuscript, fell off its perch, stone-dead. Wagner's almost hysterical grief at Papo's loss and the tormenting feeling that he was somehow to blame for the bird's death suggest that behind his reaction lay his repressed sympathy for those he had just condemned to death for their skill at parroting others.

It is striking, certainly, that in his new essay *Opera and Drama* Wagner attempts to play down his earlier desire to settle old scores with the Jews and at the same time seeks to give an objective air to his hostility towards Meyerbeer. 'It would be terrible', he confided in Uhlig, 'if this book were to be seen as merely an attack on Meyerbeer.'[81] As a result, he removed 'a whole number of polemical sallies' against him.[82] In spite of the loathing that Wagner continued to harbour towards his former patron, he even brought himself to concede that this 'most corrupted of fabricators of art' was occasionally capable of 'the richest, noblest and most moving expression'. There were, he went on, 'very few instances of works of music – and certainly only the most perfect instances of such works – that can stand comparison' with Meyerbeer at his best.[83]

As though wanting to counter the charges of both personal resentment and aesthetic imbalance, Wagner now reduced all his Zurich ideas to a single rigorous system that took longer to expound than any of his other essays, its impressive length encouraging writers to assume that *Opera and Drama* is his 'principal theoretical work'.[84] The truth of the matter is that its 641 pages merely summarize the views that Wagner had already expressed with various shifts of emphasis in all his essays from *The Wibelungs* to *The Artwork of the Future*.

What seems to be new is the excessive dialecticism with which each and every phenomenon is subjected to the same mechanical treatment. Once a single entity, the whole had been broken down into its egoistical components which, when the present alienating life form ended, would regain their lost unity. The consequentiality with which Wagner applies this three-step procedure to every aspect of world history, including even human hearing, leaves one suspecting that he modelled his study on Hegel's *Philosophy of History*. As he later recalled, *Opera and Drama* sprang in part from a real conversation that he had with a Zurich friend, an eloquent Hegelian by the name of Jakob Sulzer, and in part from an imaginary continuation of that dialogue in which 'I wanted to make everything clear to Sulzer by first making it clear to myself.' But, as he explained to Cosima, it was all really only 'a single thought'.[85]

Although this thought followed the current Hegelian model, it ultimately derived from Wagner's own remote past. No longer a mere variant of a subsidiary motif as it had been in his earlier writings, it now became his central theme. In 'Jews in Music', the emphasis had been placed on the second stage in the dialectical process – negation – whereas it was now the turn of the synthesis, the res ipsa, the genuinely creative element. This element was to be found in love, and herein lay the work's 'single thought'. But it was not the love that the solar hero Jesus had held up as an antidote to the egoistic world spirit, nor was it the love with which the Muses' divided arts would unite through their sisterly kiss and dance: central to *Opera and Drama* is the question of sexual love, which symbolizes the mystery of art, just as art reveals the mystery of love in the drama. The two belong together and are, in fact, a single entity. Humanity, torn apart by the difference between the sexes, is reconciled in love. Dying in the act of love, it reproduces and creates new life. Thus sexuality proves to be the great redeemer that unites all that has been put asunder, healing the wound of mortality through the birth of new life.

And as Wagner had already shown in *The Artwork of the Future*, this is precisely what happens in true art. Its unity, which for Wagner was embodied in Greek drama, had been broken down into the sister arts of dance, music and poetry, all of which were slowly destroyed by dint of their isolated existence. An awareness of their lost unity was preserved in the sense of loving desire with which they yearned to touch each other, when each art would be 'completely subsumed by its sister art'. Propriety, too, persuaded Wagner to move on from the same-sex triunity of the three sister arts to the heterosexual couple of *Opera and Drama*. Following the decline of classical tragedy, music and poetry were now like an alienated husband and wife who longed to be reunited.

While working on *Opera and Drama*, Wagner wrote to Liszt, cheerfully informing him that he had put the whole of his past life behind him and was now clearly conscious of 'all that had been slumbering' within him. As a result of his introspection he had now found a suitable metaphor for his artwork of the future. As a woman, music needed to be 'fertilized by the poet', just as her male counterpart felt 'the need to marry music in its fullness and entirety'. Cut off from each other, they were condemned to die. Only through the 'true, irresistible love' that the poet feels when sleeping with his wife, music, could the new work of art be created.[86]

It was not long after this that Wagner used the same biological language to initiate his friend Theodor Uhlig into the structure of his new book. Here too he adopted a dialectical interpretation, whereby the two unhappy antitheses came together to produce a redemptive synthesis. 'Music', Wagner summed up the first part of his book, is 'an organism that gives birth' and hence is feminine in gender. According to the second, antithetical section of the work, 'the poetic understanding' represents 'the generative organism' whose 'poetic intent' resembles the 'fertilizing seed' that is produced 'only in the ardour of love'. The 'urge to fertilize a female organism' makes itself felt in the poet's 'procreative organism', with the result that the female organism has no choice but to give birth to the male heir embodied in 'the seed received in love'. The third section of the book is then given over to 'an account of the act of giving birth to the poetic intent by the consummate language of music'.[87]

The arid title of this section, 'The Art of Poetry and Music in the Drama of the Future', reflects the rigour of the volume as a whole, a rigour that seeks forcibly to deduce even the most trivial ideas from superordinate categories. This has confirmed writers in their conviction that, in spite of its puzzling sexual metaphor, *Opera and Drama* is a scholarly treatise. But the scientific aspect is a masquerade: Wagner uses logical argumentation only to be able to prove beyond doubt that a revolution culminating in the artwork of the future is inevitable.

Both here and in his earlier pamphlets, Wagner saw Greek drama as the beginning of this development. But now he added an aspect that had been kept in the background from the time of *The Wibelungs*. World domination, symbolized by the hoard and Grail, is bound up with sexual reproduction. Whenever power and possessions are contested, it is really love that is at stake. The survival of a race depends on sex above all else. Tragic history is always family history, too.

Wagner discovered that the secret essence of all artistic creativity, as described in the three-stage biological process depicted in *Opera and Drama*, was a reflection of the nucleus of the archetypal myth as realized in the Greek Gesamtkunstwerk. This myth shows how the chaos of nature is tamed and ordered by the loving hero, only for the dragon to reclaim him for the darkness. From the gloomy wilderness of the primeval world, the solar hero creates a garden of Eden that is reduced to rubble by his envious adversary. The object created by love is destroyed by hatred as surely as night follows day. The birth of the radiant universe gives way to the death of that world's creator.

Behind this mortal god lies a memory of the progenitor to whom the human race owes its whole existence. The light that he brought was the seed that produced the family and, with it, the glories of the first kingship. In the beginning was love, the union of opposites. It is not possessions that the family holds sacrosanct but propagation. Love ends when the enemy arrives on the scene and kills the first king, lovelessly propagating himself in his predecessor's stead. Representing the murdered god, the tragic hero experiences this loss of love that leads to loss of the self. By reuniting music and poetry, tragedy brings the first family back together on a symbolic level. The sexual act of artistic union mirrors the initial act of procreation to which the human family owes its very existence. Only through this work of art will the wound inflicted by its fragmentation be healed.

Wagner uses the example of Oedipus to prove that Greek drama was indeed concerned with the same process as the one to which the true work of art owes its existence. In *Opera and Drama*, the Theban prince is the tragic hero tout court. As a result of his father's orders to have his newborn successor killed in the wilderness, Oedipus is robbed of his kingdom, just as the first king had been. But this 'basest of crimes', against which Wagner fulminates with peculiar indignation, rebounds against the miscreant, and Oedipus survives an attack that sprang from 'the most unfatherly self-interest', unwittingly avenging himself when he slays a stranger whom he does not know to be Laius, his father. Although this murder is condemned by society, it has Wagner's complete understanding.

The hero then marries his own mother, an act which, as a symbol of Oedipus's regained royal power, strikes Wagner as a further example of 'natural necessity'. 'Did Oedipus violate human nature when he married his mother?' Wagner asks, answering his own question with the words 'most emphatically not'. Although it was condemned by the state as a terrible crime, nature showed herself, in Wagner's words, 'entirely willing' and blessed the incestuous pair with four children.

This successful reconquest of the hoard was further expressed, in Wagner's view, in the fact that Oedipus solved the riddle of the Sphinx. Like Hegel, Wagner interpreted this as a decisive stage in man's self-realization: just as Oedipus triumphs over the murderous mythological beast, so man rises above nature through the agency of thought. For Wagner, Oedipus was a precursor of his hero Siegfried, who likewise breaks free from an 'unfatherly father', slaying the man-eating dragon and, desperately calling on his dead mother, marrying the woman to whom he owes his birth. As an incarnation of the solar hero who is condemned to die, Siegfried none the less seems ultimately to succumb to the 'curse' that is bound up – as it was in Oedipus's case, too – with all loss of memory of his own identity.

It is clear from the story of Oedipus's victory over the Sphinx, then, that the usurper is again the 'wicked father' who has attempted to deprive his son of love, legacy and life. In much the same way, Wagner uses the figure of Antigone to show that the ideal woman and redemptress can be found only in the hero's own sister. As Oedipus's daughter she replicates his own heroic feat, but on another plane. Hegel too had seen Antigone as 'the most glorious figure ever to appear on earth', as she places 'the most hallowed love of her brother' above the state and even above her own life. Like Wagner's solar hero Jesus, she defies the laws of inhuman reality and 'destroys herself out of sympathy'. As a result of her revolutionary action, Wagner's Antigone – who is invested with the features of his late sister Rosalie – destroys the rule of the usurpatorial Creon just as Brünnhilde puts an end to the power wielded by Wotan.

The state, Wagner demonstrates by reference to the fate of these two Sophoclean figures, came into being through a primordial act of betrayal. The rule that destroys love for the sake of 'undiminished ownership' strikes him as being the 'nucleus of all crimes'. 'All the crimes of myth and history' derive from ownership, which despises humanity and which – 'wonder of wonders', as Wagner sarcastically remarks – is 'regarded as the basis of all proper order'.[88] This tale of man's self-alienation culminates in the decline and fall of the state. 'The need for this decline', Wagner stresses in the context of Antigone and her triumph in death, 'is sensed in advance in the myth.' Provocatively he adds that it is now the task of history 'to carry out' this necessary act.

Wagner's own contribution to this process consisted in his revival of the archetypal myth that had crystallized round the figure of the solar hero Siegfried. At the same time he proposed an art form that would do justice to the universalist claims of this myth. In *Opera and Drama*, he forged a link between the forgotten early history of the Germans and the no less forgotten tragedy of the Greeks. In turn, these two elements were to emerge into the broad light of day as a unified work of art.

Curiously enough, this link or bond is a family bond. Wagner had discovered that the history of his own origins was fully congruent with the three-stage dialectical process familiar to him from Hegel. The hero's origins led to exile and to a life of wandering from which he could be redeemed only by love, ideally the love of his sister. The same process was also to be found in art. Drama, once unified, had been fragmented, resulting in uprooted sister arts that could reproduce themselves and acquire a new life only in their loving reunion.

Wagner devotes much of his new book to laboriously proving that true art is ruled by the laws of kinship, leaving no stone unturned in discovering brilliant and even comic ideas in support of his thesis and taking the occasional sideswipe at Meyerbeer and Mendelssohn, while never losing sight of his goal: the genealogy of the music drama. It is as though the fate of the whole artwork of the future depended upon his ability to demonstrate an unbroken line of descent.

Above all, however, it is a question of finding the right progenitor. Although music and language were created by the same primordial organ of the human voice, they have lost touch with their roots. Just as the voice has been broken down into individual instruments and as a result lost its power of expression, so the primordial melody has been fragmented into the language of music and the language of concepts. The male word, suffocating in the 'grey confusion of prose', longs for its twin sister music, from which it has become separated and in which their common mother lies concealed. This explains why Wagner now recalls his hero Oedipus, 'who was born of Jocasta and who fathered the redemptress Antigone on her'.

In colourfully biological language, Wagner sees the 'fertilizing seed' of the yearning poet implanting into 'the gloriously loving woman, music, the material that she requires to give birth'. And in an even more graphic image, he describes this act of penetration as 'the outpouring of direct emotion' that results when 'the poet dissolves the vowel of the accented and alliterative root word in its maternal element, the musical sound'. A precondition of the 'rapid conception of feeling' is the 'primordial relationship' between the two partners.

Inasmuch as the conditions governing the origins of the human race coincide with those of his work of art, in which words and music consort together, Wagner is also able to use genealogical imagery to explain the structure of his drama of the future: from the original key of a melody, the individual notes arise 'like youthful members of the same family', before leaving their familiar surroundings and leading a life of their own. In its search for 'contact' and depending on the mood of the poem, each note of the melody feels attracted to a different harmonic family as though to a 'young woman'. The youth falls in love with her, before 'pouring himself' into her 'according to the necessary law of love', as Wagner soberly notes. Marital fidelity, it may be added, was not on the agenda in this world of musical modulations. The melody would unfold depending on the dictates of the poem, each animated note changing its harmonic surroundings before finally – 'after the most manifold climaxes and couplings' – returning to the key of its ancient homeland, much as Odysseus returned to Penelope.

Wagner uses the term 'poetico-musical period' to describe the fate of the melodious youth from the moment he leaves his primordial harmony to his safe return home. The artwork of the future was to be made up of several such periods, each conditioning the other and ultimately producing 'a rich overall statement'. In this way, the actual story of the drama – namely, the life and death of the hero – is ideally mirrored within the music in the development and harmonic transformation of the melody.

Not only the hero, but every aspect of the poem, obeys the same rules, and so the distinction between words and music is ultimately superseded. Every poetic phenomenon can just as easily be defined by a musical term that sums up its whole development from past to future. Wagner uses the term 'motif' to describe these 'melodic elements' in which the 'profoundest secrets of the poetic intent' are revealed.[89]

Whereas Hegel had devised a system for explaining the world through the dialectical development of concepts, this same goal is achieved in the music drama (Wagner uses the term 'word-tone drama') through the development of the 'poetico-musical periods' and motifs. Self-knowledge on the part of the reflective world spirit is followed by self-discovery on the part of humanity, which learns to understand itself through art.

Until now, the consummation of Hegel's world spirit had taken place only in thought, but Wagner's artwork of the future was designed to help it come true in a way that could be perceived by the senses. In doing so, it would constitute the musical culmination of the whole history of humankind.

Schelling

Wagner's musings in Zurich revolved around the question of origins. How had the world begun? In what way was the work of art created? Why did reality emerge from nothing? When did the first note awaken from silence? Why did the primordial harmony that had reigned at the outset have to turn into a dissonance of betrayal and despair? Whence came the blind hatred that led creation astray after it had only just opened its godlike eye? As Wagner had demonstrated in *Opera and Drama*, the real world obeyed the same laws as the drama, with the result that an answer to the question of the origins of art would also throw light on the conditions under which existence itself first arose.

In the beginning – according to *Opera and Drama* – was the darkness of night, nature and the maternal womb. The dully lightless primordial ocean produced no forms as 'the generative power lay outside it'. Until it was 'fertilized' by some antithetical element it could not 'bring anything forth'. Characterized as a woman, primordial existence consisted only of a desire for the seed that generates life. Only when light penetrates the chaos of night, as described in the myth of the solar hero, can the world grow light. Only when – to quote the metaphorical langage of *Opera and Drama* – the poetic word encounters the sea of sound's 'desire to bring forth music' does the infinite melody of life arise from the depths. Yearning love merges with giving love. The work of art of creation is born from darkness and light, from the divine word and the musical ground.

Wagner's ecstatic vision must have struck him as a kind of universal formula, and he now tried to encapsulate it in a whole series of different images, with even the familiar fairytale of Undine resurfacing in the sea of his ideas. This 'child of the waves', he now realized, symbolized the primordial state of musical nature, part of whose being still clung to the dark river-bed, while the other part yearned to become human and speak the language of men. This hybrid creature lives 'soullessly' in the 'waves of its native element until it receives a soul through a man's love'. In turn, her lover discovers himself in this encounter, seeing in the woman's eye an 'infinitely pellucid mirror' in which he is able to 'discern his own image'.

The spirit of poetry now plunges down into the 'unfathomable sea of harmony' in which it has delightedly recognized itself, discovering the primordial source of all being in the deepest part of the sea. Whereas the God of the Bible had tamed chaos by means of his logos, the poet uses language to order 'the columns of waves that rise up to the light of the sun in order to surge along in blissful billows in its rays'. The old god is replaced by the artist as the 'lord of nature' who summons up the radiant life forms from the bottomless depths of the sea.[90]

The darkly flooding primordial wellspring, encircled by female water sprites, was also to be the starting point for Wagner's creation of the world in the *Ring*. But this source sprang not from his own imagination but from the philosophy of Friedrich Wilhelm Joseph Schelling, in whose writings it had first appeared almost half a century earlier in answer to the question as to the origin of all existence. Here Schelling uses the same images as those found in *Opera and Drama* to conjure up the coming age of art.

For Schelling, who was a friend of the young Hegel, all existence consisted of the clash between light and darkness, and this opposition could be resolved only in God. This God was not to be found in the eternal stasis of the Absolute but was an active will yearning for creative deployment. 'Will is original being,'

Schelling recognized long before Schopenhauer, and ensured that his God acted accordingly. The active primal spirit was not content to live in the 'pure light' but wanted to raise its own darkness into the light in order to 'give birth to itself'.[91] Creation was an act of divine self-realization.

God's dark aspect lay in the depths like a 'seething, surging sea' that longed to be lit by his light. Creation began when the night of the sea-bed was lit by the godlike sun. The ray of light, which Schelling compares to the spoken word, created nature. But instead of merging with God's love, nature shut itself off from his gaze. The word assumed an independent existence. Nature became concentrated as matter and darkly resisted the light that sought to illumine it. Gravity, not the lightness of heavenly being, became the law of nature. Wherever the light of our origins attempted to shed its beams, the obduracy of dull matter began to prevail instead.

The word that God uttered when creating the world had woken nature from the sleep of non-being, but nature failed to show any love in return, reacting merely with egoism. God had barely glanced in the mirror of nature before evil came into the world. The light that was intended to illumine the night had merely made the darkness visible. Instead of a single divine will giving birth to the whole, there now reigned countless individual wills, each concerned only with itself. Made up of egoism and desire, the blind will filled the whole universe. The power of darkness triumphed. Creation broke free from its creator.

Only in human beings was it hoped that nature could be won back for the divine light in a second attempt at creation. Like God, man was made of both spirit and nature, both the word of reason and the yearning depths of the ground of all creation. He could lighten the darkness of earthly existence with the light of his spirit and 'give birth' to himself by depicting that spirit. But he did not have to do so. For this divine self-realization was countered and resisted by the reverse possibility that man would place his intellectual powers in the service of his natural egoism and work not for the whole but for himself alone.

In this way, man was invested with the power to do both good and evil. He had to decide between these two extremes. He alone could help creation, which risked being destroyed by evil, and ensure that it was brought to a satisfactory conclusion. The freedom with which God had created the world had now passed to man. In his hands lay the fate of all creation. He could choose the path of love or egoism, the path of all-embracing light or of the darkness that divides the world. He could defeat the dragon of night and liberate nature through love, or he could allow himself to be drawn back by the egoism of nature into the chaos with which the world had begun. His will would decide. The fate of the whole depended on the freedom of the individual.

The essay in which Schelling expounds his mystical theory on the origin of the world is called *On the Essence of Human Freedom* and was published in 1809. According to the literature on Wagner, the composer did not know of its existence. Its title appears neither in his own accounts of his life nor in any of the scholarly writings on him. At best, Schelling's name features only peripherally in handbooks on Wagner and in accounts of his life. In *My Life*, Wagner mentions Schelling's *System of Transcendental Idealism* only in passing, with the result that the philosopher has effectively been excluded from Wagner's world. That he may have played a part in its genesis has never been considered, an omission for which Wagner himself must bear full responsibility. After all, he once told Cosima that both Schelling and Hegel – to whom he also owed so many of his ideas – were nothing but charlatans. In both cases he took care to erase all trace of the lines of thought that had made him the thinker that he was.

In fact, Wagner knew Schelling's speculative philosophy through his erudite uncle, who had attended Schelling's lectures in Jena. And one of Adolf Wagner's best friends was the philosopher Johann Arnold Canne, whose work was influenced by Schelling's ideas on myth. Adolf Wagner even wrote an 'Overview' of Canne's 'Mythological System' as a supplement to one of his books.⁹² Christian Hermann Weiße, the writer on aesthetics whom we have already encountered and whose conversations had a 'great impact' on Wagner, was another of Schelling's followers. Wagner attended Weiße's lectures on art and can scarcely have remained in ignorance of his aesthetic model. We know for a fact that Wagner was familiar with Schelling's *Philosophy of Mythology* and his later *Philosophy of Revelation*, even if, when dictating his autobiography, he could recall only Schelling's writings on transcendental philosophy. Glasenapp even thought that the young Wagner had 'become hopelessly bogged down in the densest Schellingianism',⁹³ whatever that may mean.

In his study *On the Essence of Human Freedom*, Schelling compares world history to the drama that Wagner was to stage with his *Ring*. Once the flooding ground of existence has been lit by the first rays of light, creation can enjoy itself in the water sprites' playful sport. Then disaster strikes. The ground egoistically seizes the divine light for itself and matter becomes concentrated in space, bringing back the darkness that seemed to have been banished. Evil appears and reclaims the world for itself.

In order to win back the light that has been ravished, God produces an antagonist in a second act of creation. But like evil this new creature issues from nature and, being vulnerable, can fall victim to the temptation of evil. In Schelling's view, this led to the decisive confrontation between light and darkness. World history began, and the earth became a battleground on which the contending parties fought desperately for world dominion.

According to Schelling, good and evil did not exist in primeval times. The world then lived 'in blissful indecision'. This 'golden age' was followed by the age of gods and men, when the principle of light successfully asserted itself in battle with the omnipotence of nature. At this date, nature had still to reveal itself as a force for evil. Dragons and monsters threatened the peace of the world, but the wisdom of the ground that was ultimately a part of God also rose up from 'oracles that welled up from the earth'.

By the following age, however, the beauty of the gods was threatened by the powers of the deep that set themselves up as the 'world-conquering principle'. World kingdoms were founded that flouted and hounded the divine principle of love. With their collapse, the world relapsed into its former state of chaos in which the last vestiges of God's light were extinguished. The whole history of the creation was threatened with failure.

Thus the hour of the redeemer struck. The son of God appeared on earth and took up the final battle with the serpent. With his advent, the good revealed itself in all its majesty, but evil, too, then showed its true colours. The insidious enemy challenged the hero, with both of them laying claim to creation. Unable to assert himself in the face of divine might, the enemy had recourse to 'mirrored representations' with which to tempt humanity into committing acts of treachery. Evil 'lured men from being into non-being, from the truth into lying, from light into darkness' in order 'to rule over all things'.

The son of God appeared to fall victim to the fatal wiles of the serpent, but in fact the voluntary death of the solar hero restored love to the world – love that had been banished on the emergence of egoism. Only with the death of the Saviour was creation complete and God's redeeming light rose on the world. 'But love is supreme', wrote Schelling in his apocalyptic vein. 'It is that which was there before the ground existed', it is all that existed before light and its opposite, darkness, existed. It had returned to the world with the Saviour. In this way, the loving human being brought history to an end. In Schelling's words, man 'redeemed nature'.[94]

Schelling also explored the redeemer's dark counterpart, examining the mythic origins of the world in his essay 'On the Gods of Samothrace' of 1815. The ancient nations, he showed, had expressed the mysteries of their origins in their ideas on religion. The stages of creation were represented by gods whose relationships reflected the laws of nature. Since the dawn of history there had existed a secret cult on the Greek island of Samothrace, where mysterious gods were worshipped in the form of dwarfs. According to Schelling, they embodied the dark ground of nature in which godhead and underworld were as one.

Schelling draws surprising parallels with these archaic gods. The Cabeiri reminded him not only of the Nordic dwarfs who, together with the 'Nibelung warriors', guarded treasures in the depths of the earth, but also of the early Jewish nephilim, who had once walked the earth as giants, before continuing their existence in the underworld as dwarfs. Schelling argues that there was a connection between the Hebrew nephilim and the Germanic term 'Niflungen', just as their underground home resembled the 'Niffelheim of Old Norse mythology'.[95]

Schelling also offers a surprising answer to the question why these gods of darkness were worshipped only in the guise of a secret cult. For him, the 'form of a mystery' was designed to exclude non-initiates and resembled Jewish life in general. 'What else was the strict segregation of the Jewish nation', he asked, 'if not an institution similar to a mystery, except that in this case it placed a barrier not between members of the same nation but between one nation and all others.' The advent of the Saviour put an end to this egoistical isolation. 'It was Christianity', wrote Schelling, 'that was to remove all barriers.'

In his bold analogy between the dwarfs of Samothrace, with their magical powers, and the subterranean Nibelungs in whom the Jewish nation could be recognized, Schelling was following up the implications of one of the central ideas of his study on human freedom. There was, he believed, a direct link between the god of light and the dark power of the ground. This power was both a part of the god and at the same time cut off from him. It was the dull longing for the bright day, hunger for love and union.

The dwarfs who dwelt in the depths of subterranean night longed for the light. But when God's sun rose and lit the darkness, the darkness egoistically shut itself off from it. At the very moment that the underworld refused to accept God's love it was transformed into evil, becoming the creator's insidious antagonist and disputing control of the world with him in the person of his sons.

Schelling claimed that this dark ground was embodied in one of the dwarfish gods of Samothrace. One of the Cabeiri, Axieros, represented night, 'the most ancient object in the whole of nature'. Night, however, was nothing but lack and need. In Axieros, the mystery cult venerated 'the longing for the beginning as the first cause of creation'. Even his name showed that he represented only desire and a longing for satisfaction. The Hebrew root of the name, Schelling explains, means 'ownership (especially as a result of inheritance)'. But it can just as well mean 'to be consumed by lack'. The concept of lack is followed in turn by 'that of appropriating, holding on to and taking possession of' the missing object. In Hebrew, Schelling goes on, the word would be pronounced 'Achsieros', suggesting that 'ultimately it was in fact the name Achas-Weros'.[96]

But Ahasuerus was the mythical name of the Jews who had been cursed for their refusal to accept the love of God's son. Having cut themselves off from redemption, they were left to suffer the torments of the ground that was consumed by unfulfilled desire. In his essay 'Jews in Music', Wagner himself had held out to Ahasuerus the promise of redemption from this curse. Destruction alone would bring it.

Schelling's underworld powers of darkness reappear in Wagner's *Ring*. Like the Cabeiri of Samothrace, they are dwarfish of stature. As Nibelungs, they collect the treasures of the earth. Like the Jews, they languish, unredeemed, beneath their self-imposed yoke. And they are ruled by a demonic creature that resembles Schelling's Axieros alias Ahasuerus. Wagner's new name for the covetous spirit of the underworld who sets himself up as the eternal foe of divine love and seizes the gold of creation was Alberich.

Nostrums

Wagner, meanwhile, was suffering a fate similar to that of Schelling's God. All willpower and delight in his own creativity, he cast his ray of light into the darkness of the auditorium. If he encountered love in return, he felt heaven on earth. But there was no question of any dialogue with his audience. Wagner was always the giver who hoped that the public would long to take what he offered them. If humanity received his ideas and works as though they were the divine seed, the common artwork of the whole of humanity could come into being.

Unfortunately the opposite was generally the case, just as it had been in Schelling's account of prehistory. Wagner encountered indifference. The light that he gave in abundance was swallowed up by the darkness. Instead of the total self-sacrifice that his gift of love deserved, he found only self-love. People shut themselves off from him, grimacing in their hatred. But Wagner without an audience was like God without his creation. Denied the mirror in which he could recognize himself again, he felt that his life was a failure.

Wagner's early years in Zurich seemed to him to be a tormenting continuation of the sense of failure that the revolution had instilled in him. There was no substitute for Germany, where he was threatened with imprisonment. Paris was plague-ridden, Zurich a provincial backwater. His works were performed in neither place. In Germany they had been taken out of the repertory, their creator declared politically incorrect. Now he had donned the mantle of a philosopher of art and was gathering around him a circle of friends and admirers who in turn attracted others. From Germany came disciples such as Karl Ritter and Hans von Bülow in search of an idol. It was not long before he was venerated as the centre of a cult, with the city of Zurich acquiring not only a local attraction but also the material for all the usual gossip.

Almost forty, Wagner had neither an income nor a private fortune of his own, and so he was permanently reduced to begging favours from others. The only beneficiary of his stay in Zurich was Zurich, the Saxon composer bringing it cultural flair, conducting subscription concerts and even staging operas as in his days as a Kapellmeister. The Wolf's Glen was now relocated on the banks of the Limmat. By contrast, a draft plan for reorganizing the Zurich Theatre went unheeded, much as his earlier plans had been comprehensively ignored in Dresden.

Meanwhile, he did what he could to deserve his reputation as a rare bird. The gap between his lack of means and his lavish lifestyle gave pause for thought even to the secret police, who continued to keep him under surveillance as a known terrorist. Striking a note of irony, he spoke of the 'criminal luxury' in which he indulged in his 'doll's house' in his attempt to realize certain self-indulgent 'fantasies from the *Arabian Nights*'.[97]

A local woman who ventured into his boudoir reported on the riot of green silks and satins with which he had swathed his refuge. Even a miniature statue of Venus was dressed in a green silk kimono. The Master had been 'declaiming at the piano in an emotional tone of voice, setting down the intervals by picking out notes on the instrument', but he now entered the room, wearing a 'long velvet gown', while a dog yapped furiously round his ankles. His genius, his visitor later declared, clearly needed the colour green 'in order to find inspiration'.[98]

She was not far off the mark. Wagner himself wrote to Liszt at about this time to say that, if his imagination was to be fired, he could not 'live like a dog, sleep on straw and drink common gin: mine is an intensely irritable, refined, and hugely voracious yet uncommonly tender and delicate sensuality which, one way or another, must be flattered if I am to accomplish the cruelly difficult task of creating in my mind a non-existent world'.[99]

For more than five years, this world had remained obstinately non-existent. Since completing *Lohengrin* in April 1848, Wagner had composed nothing of substance. The sea of sound seemed to have run dry, and only words flowed from his pen: instead of operatic scores, he produced only new variations on his artwork of the future. Not until the end of 1853 did the waves of *Das Rheingold* begin to well forth. The intervening years were occupied by revolution and philosophizing. The dreariness of his life as a pure thinker was at one with his patched-up marriage with Minna and the cultural amateurishness of Zurich, to which he offered his foreign-aid package.

'As for myself', he complained to Liszt, 'things are going from bad to worse with each passing day: I am leading an indescribably worthless existence.' This was due, in part, to 'the surroundings in which I now find myself as an "artist"!! Do you know Zurich?? I am bound to go mad here, I cannot do otherwise.'[100] It was with real impatience, he told Liszt, that he longed to be 'released from the mortifying state in which I find myself here in Zurich'.[101] For years he toyed with the idea of suicide in both a metaphysical and a practical sense. His clique of admirers noticed none of this and lived in astonished awe of the Faustian genius driven by forces beyond both his ken and his control. While his self-esteem swelled 'to the size of the Swiss mountains', as he told Liszt, he longed only to sleep, 'a sleep so deep that all feeling of life's anguish ceases. I should be able to achieve this: it's not so hard.'[102]

He suffered a physical reaction. Problems that had troubled him sporadically during his youth now returned with a vengeance. His digestion, ruined by medical quackery and poor diet, now began to get its own back in the form of flatulence and constipation. He suffered from constant abdominal pains, to which haemorrhoids added their burden and from which he deduced that his nerves were shattered, a state that found expression in breathless activity and hypersensitivity. He was always excitable and prone to fits of anger or would burst into tears or sweat profusely. When he was not suffering from insomnia, he was plagued by nightmares from the past. Soon he was convinced that the sufferings of the whole human race were the result of 'ruined abdomens'. 'Improve your digestion, you good people', he exclaimed with a saviour's fervour, 'and life will be completely transformed for you.'[103]

Wagner himself was certainly completely transformed as a result of the physical ailment that he feared most: at least since his early twenties he had suffered from erysipelas that caused his nose and cheeks to become swollen. According to Glasenapp, this infectious rash was generally prefigured by feelings of melancholy and irritability. Wagner would then withdraw to his room. Long latent, the ailment returned in 1850, and in the letter he wrote to Minna announcing his intention of starting a new life with Jessie Laussot, he mentions that his 'old nervous complaint' had returned. 'It haunts me like a ghost.'[104]

This time the ghost came to stay. By the spring of 1851 his whole body was affected by it, with the result that he had recourse to sulphur baths, which at least brought him poetic inspiration and helped him to 'conceive' the poem of *Der junge Siegfried*, as he initially titled the third part of the *Ring*.[105] Convinced that underactivity of the intestines was to blame, he swallowed laxatives and drank spa water designed to aid his digestion. And as he knew from Dresden, champagne could also work miracles. Often his attacks were preceded by a chill. On one occasion, he was visiting Karl Ritter's unheated apartment and reading E. T. A. Hoffmann's short story *Der goldene Topf*, in which the magician Lindhorst turns into a mighty vulture, when 'to the horror of all present' he found himself 'sitting there with a swollen red nose'. In some pain he 'dragged' himself back home.

This neuralgic inflammation, which also affected his vanity, might strike as many as thirteen times a year. In describing the affliction to Julie Ritter, he assumed an ironical tone, punning on the German name for the ailment ('*Gesichtsrose*' means 'facial rose') and claiming that the thorns of his existence had produced 'a rose that often withers but just as frequently breaks into bud again; as a good gardener, I have had to devote myself to tending it almost continuously for nearly three months'.[106] In vain he sought some relief from his 'appalling sufferings', which he felt were 'bound up in demonic fashion with the locality of Zurich'.[107] He never forgot that Zurich was a place of exile for him. He had been driven from his homeland. The principal ill, about which he said nothing, seemed to ooze from every pore.

He sought relief in the maternal element of water. As he knew very well, Feuerbach had already advocated the healing powers of 'holy' water, claiming that it could restore the lost clarity of mind and body. Only in 'the depths of nature', he promised his readers in *The Essence of Christianity*, would man rediscover his own image. 'Water is the likeness of self-awareness', he wrote in a passage that recalls Schelling's mystical approach to nature and that looks forward to Wagner's *Ring*. 'In Baptism we bow to the power of a pure nature-force; water is the element of natural equality and freedom, the mirror of the golden age.'

At the suggestion of Theodor Uhlig, who was an enthusiastic advocate of hydrotherapy, Wagner resumed the regimen familiar from Teplitz and Marienbad and in September 1851 began a course of hydropathic treatment at Albisbrunn to the south-west of Zurich. His companions were Hermann Müller – Wilhelmine Schröder-Devrient's former lover and, following his revolutionary activities, a former Guards lieutenant – and his youthful admirer Karl Ritter. Their company helped Wagner to overlook the presence of the sanitorium's chief physician, Dr Christoph Zacharias Brunner, whom he dubbed 'the water Jew'.

An additional source of pleasure not only for his disciple but for the Master himself was the death of Karl Ritter's rich uncle, which placed Julie Ritter in the position of being able to make over a stipend of eight hundred thalers a year to the indigent composer, a sum that she continued to pay until 1859. As a result, Wagner not only joined what he called 'the cooperative of the Ritter family' but was finally able to devote himself to the completion of the *Ring*. Even before finishing his course of treatment at Albisbrunn, he had written to Liszt to initiate him into the secrets of his plan and to assure him in the best of spirits that he was now on his way to becoming 'a perfectly healthy human being'.

His announcement was premature. Although he lost weight, his principal ailments – neurasthenia, constipation and shingles – could not simply be washed away. Since the summer of 1851 Wagner had been in correspondence with his old friend in Paris, Ernst Benedikt Kietz, who, apprised of his complaints, sang the praises of an apparently miraculous cure that he had already tried himself. From his surgery in Paris Karl Lindemann informed his Zurich patient that his problems lay neither in his intestines nor his skin but in his 'cerebral nerves'. Wagner wrote back enthusiastically to report that Lindemann had 'correctly identified' his condition. As his illness was 'transcendental' rather than physical, dietary measures were of little use. He first had to be 'cured at the top'. In order to make it easier for Lindemann to prescribe the right treatment, Wagner described his pitiful condition: he was suffering from 'feverish excitement and tiredness' and felt an 'unpleasantly worrying befuddlement of the brain', as well as 'melancholy' and 'fear of work'. A cure, he supposed, was out of the question, and so he asked Lindemann for 'some palliative to enable me to lead my life as an artist'.[108]

Hermann Müller evidently shared Wagner's confidence in Lindemann, whom the composer hailed as a 'genius' but who was hardly needed to recommend tranquillizers. As was usual in the nineteenth century, the obvious solution was laudanum. Ever since the *Confessions* of Thomas de Quincey, which Alfred de Musset had translated into French in 1828, opium had enjoyed cult status. Wagner's model, Berlioz, had been inspired by De Quincey to experiment with it, experiments which, as Wagner noted in *Opera and Drama*, found expression in his *Symphonie fantastique*. Liszt was introduced to Berlioz's world of dreams by George Sand, and Baudelaire – soon to declare himself France's most committed Wagnerian – likewise drew much of his inspiration from the wonder drug.

At the same time, laudanum was regarded as an effective psychopharmatological cure for precisely the sort of anxieties, neuralgias and psychosomatic ailments of which Wagner had complained. And drops of laudanum were a cure for insomnia. Although Wagner had first turned to Lindemann for help in September 1851, it is not until 1853 that his Annals first mention the drug. According to Glasenapp, his doctor had until then advised merely a 'moderate use of water' with a suitable diet. Not until Wagner visited the wonder doctor's practice in Paris in October 1853 was laudanum prescribed. 'Dr Lindemann: laudanum; metals. Poor health', we read in the Annals.[109]

And so Wagner finally found the sleep for which he had longed, sleep 'so deep that all feeling of life's anguish ceases'. For years he kept faith with Lindemann and continued to use the doctor's miracle cure until the end of his life. On his return from Paris he even seems to have recommended it to Minna for her 'overwrought nerves and sleeplessness'. It was then, he later explained to her doctor in Dresden, Anton Pusinelli, that she had 'started on laudanum, which she was imprudently advised to take in small doses to counteract sleeplessness'. Unfortunately, she had exceeded the prescribed dosage, often taking 'several times the specified amount of twenty drops'.[110] It remains unclear whether she heeded Pusinelli's advice to take the laudunum, advice behind which Wagner, too, threw his whole weight.

No less shrouded in mystery is Wagner's own drug habit. Although his works contain magic potions that cause amnesia and ecstasy and alleviate chronic complaints, all we learn about their origins is that they come from Arabia or at least 'from further away than you can conceive'. If Wagner himself occasionally gives the impression of being under the influence of drugs, then writers have ascribed this to his effusively eccentric nature. Excitability – Wagner used the German word 'Exaltation', with its associations of hysteria and excess – was his natural state, he declared in 1854: 'In fact I feel well only when I am "beside myself", only then am I entirely at one with myself.'[111] If some means such as champagne allowed him to intensify this state, he regularly took advantage of it.

A comparison between the typical symptoms of opium use and Wagner's descriptions of himself reveals striking similarities. On one occasion, during a visit to Paris, he ate something that was not on his diet and fell ill. But then he 'suddenly felt divinely well', he told Mathilde Wesendonck. 'Gone was all the annoyance, every worry, every care, every wish and obligation: the most perfect accord between my innermost mood and my physical state; silence of all life's passions: rest, allowing the reins of life that I had been gripping convulsively to slip from my hand. For two hours I enjoyed this great sense of happiness.'[112] What sounds like the effect of prolonged exposure to Schopenhauer points rather to the suggestion that Wagner was high on Lindemann's laudanum.

Once Wagner had opened his heart to Lindemann in 1851, these experiences increased in frequency. The mental block from which he had been suffering as a composer began to lift. In the course of a visit to Italy in September 1853, he reports 'being in a state of veritable intoxication for several days', a condition that culminated in La Spezia in the 'somnambulistic state' in which, like the poet in *Opera and Drama,* he plunged into the depths of the musical ocean and discovered the source of all creation, whence rose the mystic triad from which his world drama of the *Ring* was to issue in the boiling waters of the Rhine. After taking the famous drops, writers such as De Quincey had already been reduced to speechless amazement at such experiences.

Scarcely had Wagner met the miracle doctor in person and returned to Zurich from Paris when the definitive breakthrough came. 'Since the end of March 1848', he recalled in his autobiography, 'five and a half years had passed during which I had completely avoided all musical creativity,' with the result that he now felt this new beginning to be a 'total rebirth following a state of metempsychosis'. In December 1853, he told his benefactress Julie Ritter that thanks to Lindemann's 'method' he not only felt 'far better' but was writing music 'with the greatest and most consequential delight'.[113]

By January 1854 he had finished drafting *Das Rheingold,* 'and thus the plan for the musical structure of the entire four-part work was prefigured in its most important thematic relationships'.[114] When he told his friend Kietz in June 1854 that he had completed the full score, he remembered to mention that he had been busily taking 'Lindemann's powders'. What the twentieth century was to describe as a psychedelic experience seems to have been the catalyst for Wagner's creativity in 1853.

'Papa Liszt'

It was with some astonishment that Liszt registered this change in Wagner's character when he visited him in his Zurich exile in July 1853. 'When he saw me again,' Liszt wrote to the strait-laced Princess Carolyne Sayn-Wittgenstein, 'he wept and laughed and romped for joy for at least a quarter of an hour.' Twenty times a day Wagner threw his arms round Liszt and even rolled on the ground in his high spirits. For the decorous Liszt, who set store by dignified manners, this was something of an ordeal. By the very next day, however, he was forced to correct his impression of Wagner as a genius 'strewing bunches of lilac: it is customary for him to look down on people, even on those who show him assiduous obsequiousness'.[115]

In spite of his weakness for the aristocracy, Liszt still retained a sense of deep humanity, whereas Wagner, dependent on the gifts of generous contemporaries such as Liszt, insisted on his incommensurable superiority. Notwithstanding their friendly dealings – and on Wagner's side an attitude almost amounting to infatuation – the two men remained strangers, representing the two most extreme views of the image of the artist that the nineteenth century regarded with positively religious veneration.

If Wagner had to work his way up and effortfully extricate himself from the tangle of his origins in order that, with a dictatorial gesture, he might impress on the world his artistic ideas, then Liszt was one of those sons of the Muses to whom all doors were opened with a smile. Wagner had to fight hard to achieve things that came easily to Liszt. While Wagner received his visitors in his second-floor rooms in a Zurich apartment block, Liszt – when in Weimar – resided with the princess and five servants at the Altenburg, a palatial mansion generously placed at his disposal by the Grand Duchess Maria Pawlowna.

Even the very first encounter between the two men had been marked by the crassest of contrasts: in 1841, while Wagner was eking out a living in Paris by preparing opera transcriptions, Liszt was appearing in public as a celebrated piano virtuoso, earning a fortune with a repertory that included Meyerbeer transcriptions. The society that gazed up in idolatry at the magician of the keyboard did not even notice the German immigrant in the audience. Spurned on all sides, Wagner attended the concert in his capacity as a reviewer, concealing his envy behind brilliant prose in the style of Heinrich Heine. Liszt, Wagner recalled in his autobiography, was 'beleaguered by the élite of Parisian female society', basking in the sun's rays, while he himself returned, embittered, to the dark night of the non-entity.

When fame seemed finally to have dawned with the success of *Rienzi*, the envied virtuoso turned up in Dresden with a 'Spanish dancer' by the name of Lola Montez in tow, in order to see for himself Wagner's crowd-puller about the last of the Roman tribunes. He professed to being impressed by the opera, and Wagner realized why it was not just the ladies whom this charismatic figure reduced to a 'state of enchantment'.

In keeping with the psychological mechanism that had already marked his dealings with Meyerbeer, Wagner pinned all his hopes on his successful colleague and, although Liszt was his elder by only two years, cast him in the role of a father figure. Liszt had the fortune, fame, power and even the women that Wagner palpably lacked. In tears, Wagner offered himself as Liszt's son and heir. In 1840 he had advised Meyerbeer – the first candidate for the vacant post of father – to resort to acts of artistic 'terrorism' in order to be of assistance to him. Nine years later he wrote to Liszt in a similar vein, entreating him to indulge in 'a little artistic terrorism' and to direct his actions, moreover, against 'Meierbeer'. In both cases, Wagner misjudged the mentality of his correspondents, neither of whom had any time for acts of Wagnerian violence.

Unlike Meyerbeer, who felt uncomfortable about his petitioner's importuni-
ties, Liszt had no defence mechanism. He had set foot on the world's stage as a
grand seigneur to whom earthly goods were of value only to the extent that
they could be used to give pleasure to others less fortunate than himself. He
would not be put off by an enthusiast like Wagner, whose 'fits of cynicism
towards other people's purses' he had no difficulty in seeing through. After
commenting on Wagner's lack of consideration, he went on in the same letter
to Bülow to confess to a 'subservient and subordinate affection' that in spite of
everything left him feeling in debt to Wagner's 'genius'.[116]

There could be no question of 'debts', of course, and not even their differing
talents justified subservience, even when such subservience seems to have
been coupled with real affection. Yet Liszt's generosity, both material and spiritual, is revealed not least by the fact that he made it so easy for Wagner's
chutzpah to place him in this position. He conformed to the image that the
younger man had prepared for him. While Wagner emerged from the arrangement as the clear beneficiary, the role of fatherly friend brought the older man
only drawbacks, as he saw himself obliged to make every sacrifice demanded
of him but without being able to lay claim to any fatherly authority. When his
former protégé began to take an amatory interest in his daughter Cosima
while she was still married to Bülow, Liszt felt this lack in a particularly painful
way.

The darling of princely houses who early in 1849 encouraged the Dresden
Kapellmeister to 'dispose' of him as he liked could hardly suspect that he would
soon be dealing with a revolutionary guilty of high treason and with a price on
his head. But Liszt refused to be put off. For all his seditious activities, Wagner
remained the greatest living composer in his eyes, and everything else followed
from that. When the Dresden Uprising collapsed in disarray, he concealed
Wagner at the Altenburg, helped him to escape to Switzerland and provided
him with his travelling expenses. When Wagner's hopes of settling in Paris were
dashed, Liszt patiently contributed to his upkeep in Zurich.

At the same time, Liszt was the only conductor who dared to perform the
works of a composer who was outlawed in Germany. Only in Weimar, where
Prince Constantin's family continued to reign, could Wagner's operas be seen
and heard under Liszt's direction. Liszt also performed his works in the concert
hall and prepared bravura transcriptions for the piano, while celebrating
Wagner's genius in newspaper articles that helped to 'pave the way' for him.[117]
Whenever he spoke to influential individuals, he sought discreetly to obtain not
only a pardon but also an income for the refugee. Although he was more
famous than his protégé, he acted as what one Liszt scholar has termed

Wagner's 'plenipotentiary' in Germany.[118] Wagner seems to have interpreted this to mean that Liszt had given him the right to dispose freely of his life.

Even in his *Communication to My Friends* of 1851, Wagner had publicly laid claim to Liszt's patronage by labelling him his 'alter ego'. It was Liszt, he announced, who had saved him from despair and restored him to his art, Liszt alone who had provided him with a home for his music at a time when he was a homeless vagrant. 'Everywhere and always caring for me, invariably prompt and resolute in his help', his friend had evinced 'the most devoted love of my entire being'. In this way Liszt had become something 'that I had never found before'.[119] After naming him his father, Wagner repeatedly reminded Liszt of the obligations bound up with this role: 'I have a right to you', he admonished him, 'just as I have a right to my creator! You are the creator of the man I am now: I now live through you – this is no exaggeration. Take care of your creature: I enjoin you to do this as a duty that you have to perform.'[120]

Liszt never managed to rid himself of his role as Wagner's father. Unable to escape from the composer's powers of suggestion, he also found himself exposed to the darker qualities associated with the image of the father in Wagner's mind. In 1851 – the year of *A Communication to My Friends* – there were already warning signs in this regard. In their 'loving relationship', Wagner waxed lyrical, 'there is no torment, no joy that does not tremble in this love! Today I am plagued by jealousy, fear of what, to me, are alien aspects of your own nature; and here I feel fear, concern – even doubt.' Liszt was a 'wonderful' man and 'wonderful is our love!' Yet 'if we had not loved one another, we could only have felt the most terrible mutual hatred!'[121]

Wagner's words were to prove all too true. Vampirically voracious, he made demands that went far beyond Liszt's private fortune and diplomatic connections. Liszt's daughters, too, were part of his catchment area. Wagner began by flirting extensively with Marie von Wittgenstein, the fifteen-year-old daughter of Princess Carolyne Sayn-Wittgenstein and as such Liszt's own particular favourite. Moving on from the 'child' (as he called her), Wagner then turned his attentions to Blandine, one of three illegitimate children whom Liszt had fathered on Marie d'Agoult. The fact that she was married was of no more concern to Wagner than it was in the case of Blandine's younger sister Cosima, whose turn was next. It looks almost as though Wagner wanted to free the sisters from their father's jurisdiction. When, in the case of Cosima, Liszt resisted the idea, Wagner naturally saw in him the ghost of the wicked father who robs the loving son of his legacy and love.

The image of Liszt the saviour redeeming Wagner from the evil of his insolvency and insignificance then assumed the features of this evil itself. Now Liszt was said to be trying to extricate himself from the relationship as best he could and to be abandoning his destitute friend in his time of need. In this way he was betraying true art and selling his soul and services to his audiences and the aristocracy. He had submitted to the Princess Carolyne, who had reduced him to the level of a hen-pecked husband. But ultimately – and this was the nub of all Wagner's reproaches – Liszt was no more than a virtuoso. He did not create works of art but merely performed them by dint of his technical adroitness. He was not art: he simply played it.

There was little difference between Liszt and an imitator like Meyerbeer. In 1865 Wagner even expressed the conviction that the same theme found expression in countless variations in Liszt's life, as in his music. Like an actor, he appeared before the public, 'but always slightly altered, adorned, ornamented, reclothed, now virtuoso, now diplomat, now martial, now religious'. And 'after every variation, applause – that goes without saying'.[122] In 1882, Liszt's name came up in conversation with Cosima, who noted in her diary that her father was 'a man of such talents' but that his life was 'so miserably squandered, as if in the clutches of an evil witch'. His true gift, 'virtuosity', had condemned him to 'worldliness – and this is no doubt the dismal explanation of the whole phenomenon'.[123]

Wagner had long since fallen prey to the old trauma associated in his mind with Ludwig Geyer. In the nightmares that haunted him in later years, the black-cassocked figure of Liszt took over the role of the dark enemy who had designs on his wife and blood. On one occasion in 1872, Cosima noted in her diary, Wagner woke up screaming loudly: 'He had dreamt that my father was trying to kill him with an instrument of torture' and that she herself had withdrawn into an adjoining room 'with a cold look' in her eyes as her father had 'told her to guard the door'.[124] Once again the 'mother' had turned out to be in league with the 'father' in helping to get rid of the son.

Generous to a fault, Liszt found it difficult to understand Wagner's fits of hostility, but he was soon forced to realize that his younger colleague had no intention of repaying him for his various acts of kindness. In 1851 Liszt published an article on *Lohengrin*, praising the work and thereby laying the foundations for Wagner's subsequent successes in the theatre. Wagner, it is true, responded six years later with a pamphlet on Liszt's own compositions, but with the best will in the world it is impossible for the reader to work out exactly what Wagner thought about them. While admitting that, as a virtuoso, Liszt was not just a performing artist but a creative artist, too, he declined to say what he thought about Liszt's music in general or his symphonic poems in particular.

At best he ascribed to them an important place in the history of modern music, but only as the immediate forerunners of his own compositions, which by implication were more advanced. Writers who spoke of the formlessness of Liszt's music failed to understand that their form was conditioned by their subject matter. Each symphonic poem was based on a 'poetic motif' that found its true significance only in the work itself. Liszt achieved this by 'revealing' the music that was 'latent' in this conceptual motif.[125]

Readers familiar with Wagner's other Zurich essays will have gathered from this that in his friend's tone-paintings he had discovered the very music that awaited the poet's redeeming words. Such music formed the dark primeval sea whose womb was still to be fertilized by language. Before his gaze, the whole of Liszt's musical output extended like the ground before Schelling's God, while the latter rejoiced in creation.

Wagner ended his observations by unequivocally assigning to Liszt the role of precursor, a man whose mission would be over with the advent of the Messiah: 'Do you know a musician who is more musical than Liszt?' he asked his readers in a final rhetorical flourish. 'Do you know anyone who holds within his breast all the powers of music in richer, deeper store than he?' This sentence gives the game away: the infinite wealth of forms contained within the 'ground' of music would remain locked away until such time as it was lit by the celestial light that Wagner's poetry radiated. But as soon as the poetic word helped the billowing harmonies to find physical expression, Liszt's music would be redeemed and at the same time superseded.

Although Wagner does not say so in as many words, his article, which first appeared in Brendel's *Neue Zeitschrift für Musik* on 10 April 1857, leaves the reader in no doubt about the true relationship between his own music and that of his friend. Liszt's tone poems were the rung on the ladder that allowed Wagner to rise to the perfection of his own word-tone drama. In this way, he skilfully sidestepped the question as to which of Liszt's imperfections he had taken over into his own works. Did the virtuoso exert any influence on the creator of the total work of art? Or to put it another way: did Wagner copy any of Liszt's ideas?

Wagner did not like this question. When one of his critic friends once drew attention to Liszt's influence, Wagner reacted with some acerbity, insisting that such questions should remain a secret among initiates. Within his own family, by contrast, he had no such inhibitions and told Cosima that her father's symphonic poems were a 'veritable treasure trove for thieves'. He himself had 'stolen a good deal' from them. At a rehearsal for *Die Walküre*, he even called over to Liszt, 'Papa, here comes a theme that I took from you', to which Liszt drily retorted, 'Then at least someone will get to hear it.'[126]

Yet even the comic insolence with which Wagner admitted to this debt merely serves to distract attention from the fact that we are dealing here not just with vague borrowings but with a very close dependence on Liszt's symphonic poems. Here alone Wagner discovered the orchestra's infinite capacity for language that was to produce his drama of the future. Yet his debt to Liszt – evident to anyone familiar with Liszt's tone poems – has always been treated as a taboo. In point of fact, there is no other composer to whom Wagner owed more, no other influence about which Wagner maintained so highly revealing a silence.

Before he got to know Liszt's orchestral works, Wagner was – in Liszt's eyes, too – a brilliant opera composer who played fast and loose with the rules of the game. If he used its grammar, it was in order to rise above it. But it was Liszt's tone poems that allowed him to discover a new language as a composer. Music no longer followed any prescribed rules but only the inner development of the idea that it communicated to the world. It was expression, nothing more, nothing less. It was not representational, still less did it imitate reality as the term 'programme music' suggests but revealed the hidden essence of reality. What philosophy achieved with concepts, music realized by dynamic means, constituting as it did a veritable relevation of the whole.

It was not until mid-century that Wagner completed his transition from opera to what he termed his word-tone drama, by which time Liszt had already made this move. Liszt had ended his career as a brilliant pianist in 1847 in order to devote himself simultaneously to composing works of his own, carrying out his duties as Kapellmeister to the Weimar court and indulging his great love of the Princess Carolyne Sayn-Wittgenstein. In a veritable explosion of creativity, he drafted no fewer than twelve symphonic poems during the years that followed. All of them, including the contemporaneous *Faust* and *Dante* Symphonies, translated poetic sources into the transparent world of sounds.

Taking as his starting point poems by Victor Hugo, Lamartine and Byron, Liszt treated the fates of tragic heroes such as Tasso, Mazeppa and Hamlet or mythological subjects such as Orpheus and Prometheus. Themes and motifs were assigned to poetic ideas, and like their subject they underwent dramatic metamorphoses in the floodtide of the orchestral melody, not shying away from frequent repetitions. The changing moods were mirrored by magical tone colours that spread out before the listener like a turbulent sea of sound while harp glissandos ran across it like flickering light reflections. All that Wagner attempted in vain to do in his *Faust* Symphony, Liszt had already achieved to perfection. But even Liszt was powerless to deal with the shortcoming that had caused Wagner's experiment to fail, leaving the latter fully convinced that it was up to him to take the final step.

In the same year that Wagner was introduced to Lindemann's palliative remedy, Liszt's world of sound was opened up to him. Following the extended break in Wagner's musical creativity, these two influences proved to be catalysts that set the wellspring of his inspiration flowing. When Liszt visited Wagner in his rented apartment in Zurich in July 1853 and expressed his delight at its 'modest elegance', the week he spent there witnessed not only the tears of joy and embraces already described but also a serious exchange of ideas. Liszt introduced Wagner to his latest works, which he played for him at the piano. In this way, Wagner was able to hear at first hand his colleague's *Faust* Symphony and several other symphonic poems, some of which had yet to be performed in public.

As he explained to his friend years later, it was as though he had dived into 'a deep crystalline river in order to be completely at home' with himself.[127] What he had heard was his own musical language articulated by means of Liszt's living interpretative skills. Not long after this revivalist experience came the *Rheingold* vision in La Spezia, and this in turn was followed by a further meeting with Liszt in Paris, where Wagner read his libretto for the *Ring* to a small group of listeners that included Liszt and the princess, the princess's daughter Marie and Liszt's three illegitimate children, Blandine, Cosima and Daniel. Liszt repaid the favour with further samples of his symphonic poems. It was immediately after his return from this 'feast of the gods celebrating the most loving friendship'[128] that Wagner began work on the score of the *Ring*, with the sounds of his friend's music still ringing in his ears.

These sounds were to continue to reverberate within him. While working on *Das Rheingold*, he wrote to Liszt to confess that he still felt his presence very deeply. 'Whenever I am composing and instrumenting', he announced in May 1854, 'I think only of you and of how you will like this or that detail: you are always in my thoughts.'[129] Liszt's musical language accompanied him into Nibelheim's night-time depths and up to the sunlit heights of Valhalla. Lisztian tone-painting conjured up the grey dawn, gathered the clouds for a thunderstorm and glittered in the colours of a rainbow. Wagner had plunged into the crystal flood, as he had foretold in *Opera and Drama*, and from the swirling depths, into which he had been accompanied by his Virgil, had raised into the light of day the archetypal symbols of his own history of the creation.

Wagner was fully aware of this dependency, but he kept it to himself. What he wrote, he believed, was uniquely his own. Having named Liszt as his father, he proceeded to appropriate his legacy. He was amost literally following in his footsteps, while standing on his own two feet. Rarely did he lift the veil on the secret of his own creativity. Only to Marie von Wittgenstein, the delightful 'child' whose attentions he had diverted from Liszt to himself, did he reveal anything about this fusion. Liszt, he told her in 1858, 'has something about him that involuntarily invites appropriation. I have observed this in the case of myself with the greatest clarity: in my nature, as well as in my behaviour and conduct, changes have taken place that, outwardly too, I often recognize as reproducing the impression that Liszt made upon me.' And he concluded by confessing that 'with a smile I am bound to see myself as a copy of him'. In fact, this was not such a disagreeable discovery for Wagner, 'for I find in it a decisive step on the road to my own perfection'.[130]

5   The Creation of the World

Life's Work

In writing the *Ring*, Wagner realized his dream of a perfect work of art. Unsurprisingly, it occupied him for half his life. His view of the world took shape while the artistic reflection of that view was created in parallel, the erection of a conceptual edifice mirroring what he termed 'the cruelly difficult task of creating a non-existent world'.[1] While German idealism had remained mired in the world of thought and the German revolution had foundered on its material realization, Wagner created a work of art in which the distinction between thought and reality was finally abolished. Here alone both philosophy and revolution found their true meaning: the self-consciousness of the whole.

Between 1841, when the mythical Frankish Emperor Frederick first entered Wagner's field of vision in Paris, and 1876, when he met his fate in Bayreuth as the solar hero Siegfried, Wagner spent thirty-five years planning and working on his drama. He needed the other half of his life to lay the foundations and draw the artistic consequences from it. The *Ring* became Wagner's life's work in every sense of the term. He himself called it 'the poem of my life and all that I am and feel'.[2]

This private connection between, on the one hand, the fate of his hero and the whole drama and, on the other, the drama of his own life demanded a special art form. In parallel with the genesis of the poem, Wagner developed his concept of a music drama in which words and music would be placed in a hitherto unattained synergetic relationship: just as music needed words to achieve intelligible reality, so language would develop as melody, acquiring its semantic context only when embedded in the language of harmony.

Wagner's new art did not merely depict its developing subject, as had been the case in the past, but evolved out of its opposites, with language and poetry enhancing each other, adding to each other's precision and achieving their most apt expression. Until then, there had been no representational art to do justice to this revolutionary linguistic potential. 'With this new conception of mine', wrote Wagner, 'I am moving completely away from our present-day theatre and its audiences.'[3]

This meant not only the abandonment of the traditional operatic stage and its conventional lovers but a break with the genre as a whole. Wagner was no longer concerned with the representation and depiction of ideas but with the Idea itself. Until now, existence as a whole had been the preserve of only religion and idealistic philosophy, but all this was about to change. Did human life have a meaning, perhaps even a teleological aim? How were the origins of history related to its end? In what way did the whole become conscious of itself?

The *Ring* answers these questions, questions normally asked only in metaphysics. It presents its audiences with a visual and oral account of their own history, with Wagner using every bar to make it clear that all who have ears should listen. The *Ring*, he insisted, 'contains the world's beginning and its end'.[4]

Modern theatres were not able to show this. In modern theatres, costumed actors paraded in front of painted sets while an orchestra struggled to accompany the artifice of their singing. The pitiful nature of their acting reflected that of the audience's perception. The singers performed on stage while the members of the audience pursued their own independent thoughts, with nothing on the playbill to suggest that there was anything that they needed to grasp. By contrast, the medium of which Wagner dreamt gave human beings an idea about themselves. It was the mirror in which they recognized themselves in their true essence. It ended the distinction between above and below, between performance and music, work and audience.

The new work of art did not imitate reality. Rather, reality itself became the action, with a presence that was ideally intensified and that might best be compared to today's widescreen cinema. Everything breathed an immediate vitality, with none of the subtleties in the plot being lost. The monumentality of its physical aspect mirrored the detailed nature of its perception. Events unfolded like an inner film. By understanding the course of history, audiences understood themselves. Where once there had been only 'theatre', there was now a film that was, as it were, fully conscious of itself. For want of such a film, Wagner built Bayreuth.

The *Ring* was not always intended as a work for the theatre. The stage for which Wagner designed it was the only means available to him for making intelligible something that transcended that age. Before the 'Stage Festival for Three Days and a Preliminary Evening' (to quote Wagner's subtitle for the cycle) was staged for the first time in Bayreuth in the summer of 1876, it had gone through various phases: grand opera, meditation on world history, mythic narrative and philosophical system.

The *Ring* first found written form as a prose narrative, then as a poem and finally as a word-tone drama. Yet in spite of its numerous variants, it remained the same story, covering the creation of the world, the decline and fall of humanity and the miracle of its rebirth in self-consciousness. Even while working on it, Wagner was convinced of the *Ring*'s uniqueness in terms of cultural history, telling Theodor Uhlig in 1852 that 'the work as a whole will be – out with it: I'm sufficiently ashamed to say so! – the greatest thing ever written!'[5]

Of decisive importance for this lifelong passion of Wagner's was the confluence of his own private myth and the Germans' suppressed national history. The archetypes that had evolved in his life and art he now rediscovered in myth – in such sources as Grimm, the *Nibelungenlied* and the Old Icelandic legends of the Edda. The relationships that had left their mark on him since his childhood turned out to be part of the poetic legacy of the Germans as a nation. The distress that he himself had felt expressed the distress of the people cut off from their source.

In short, Wagner's life reflected his nation's history. While that history strove for its definitive delineation in the *Ring*, it sought a revolutionary decision in the political arena. With the *Ring*, he told Uhlig, 'I shall make clear to the people of the revolution the meaning of that revolution in its noblest sense. That public will understand me: the present-day public cannot.'[6]

The congruity between Wagner's private history and German national history led him to the refashioned myth of the solar hero. All that found expression in his world of eloquent images could be grasped on a conceptual level only in the language of German idealism, where it was no abstract principle but freedom of thought itself that was central to world events. God broke free from religion and came to epitomize a freedom that was itself invested with its own thought processes.

As the source of all being, God obeyed the same law of contradiction as existence itself. And like all forms of discord, that contradiction strove for resolution. In Wagner's thinking, too, the historical alienation of humankind was bound to lead to redemption, a redemption which, he was firmly convinced, was close at hand. 'My whole view of the world', he wrote in 1852 in the context of the *Ring*, 'has found its most perfect artistic expression here.'[7]

This view of the world has two aspects to it. One view sees the world as family history in which the first kingship is destroyed by a usurper before being avenged by the hero's son and restored to its former greatness. Wagner had already seen this for himself in his own family and it now became the key that opened up German history to him. Deprived of their power as heirs of the hoard, the Germans had submitted to an insidious enemy who robbed them of their identity. Only through their forgotten national myth would they be reminded of their origins. Only in the murdered solar hero would they recognize their plight. The *Ring*, Wagner told the king of Bavaria in 1881, is 'undoubtedly the Aryan race's most characteristic work of art: no nation on earth could be so clearly conscious of its origins and predisposition than this one tribe from Upper Asia, which was the last to enter European culture and which until that time had remained the purest of the white races'.[8] Wagner is referring here to the tribe of the first kings that he had baptized Wibelungs in 1848. Thanks to the *Ring*, this tribe would be made conscious of its origins and predisposition and could look forward to its imminent rebirth in Germany.

In short, the racist reading of the *Ring* that was to be determinative during the decades that followed can invoke Wagner's own authority. The idea of an Aryan Siegfried destroyed by the Jewish assassin Hagen was seen as crucial to the confrontation on the world's stage between the 'creative' Teutons and the 'egoistically destructive' Jews. Like Wagner, the two later Wagnerites Wilhelm II and Hitler believed that the decisive encounter was imminent. This would be the final battle between good and evil, a battle in which the roles were already allotted. The hero could look forward to world dominion, while only destruction awaited Ahasuerus, as Wagner had already predicted in his essay 'Jews in Music'.

The other aspect of the world view built into the *Ring* contains elements of the revolution. According to this view of the work, the confrontation is not between races but between estranged social classes. It is not the Aryans who must be freed from their Jewish yoke but the proletariat languishing beneath the all-powerful sway of capital. Here Siegfried is a freedom fighter from 1849, ending the rule of the aristocracy and gold with the sword he has forged for himself. Having freed the downtrodden Nibelung workers, he is betrayed and treacherously murdered, much as the German revolution had been betrayed.

This interpretation became a particular favourite of post-1945 exegetes, and it too can claim Wagner's approval. While working on the *Ring*, he drew attention to the link between revolution and its failure, and thirty years later he could still take pleasure in the fact that in the cycle he had 'given a complete picture of the curse of the lust for gold and the downfall associated with it'.[9] This sounded sufficiently progressive to inspire most of the *Ring* productions of the post-Hitler period.

Writers have referred to the 'Utopia' of Wagner's *Ring*, by which they mean a classless society. They have hailed Wagner as a revolutionary and discovered in the work what one German writer has described as the 'programme for an anti-modernist vote in favour of non-differentiation between industrial societies organized on the basis of a division of labour'.[10] Others have seen in the *Ring* an account of the rape and violation of man and nature, with Wagner held up as a prophet of non-violence and environmental protection. Spurned in his own day, the composer has become a contemporary of the avant-garde.

All these interpretational models can appeal to Wagner for support, yet they find only partial confirmation in the *Ring* itself, even becoming ensnared in irreconcilable contradictions. The nationalistic and apocalyptic interpretation that regards the *Ring* as a symbolic account of the final battle between the sons of Aryan gods and the devil's Jewish offspring overlooks the simple fact that 'evil' is found not only in the sinister Nibelungs but also in the august race of gods and their blond-haired Wälsung line. If the distinction between good and evil is blurred, it is difficult for the work to be put to any moral or political use.

The same applies to the progressive interpretation of the *Ring*. It is true that Wagner depicted our sense of alienation as a consequence of ownership and tyranny, but there is no suggestion that our liberation involves the enactment of human rights. Indeed, it seems clear that the *Ring* does not foresee a future in which equal rights will be established alongside popular rule. Nor is it possible to identify in the work any unequivocal representatives of either social reform or wholesale oppression.

Although he is the *Ring*'s real expert on violent overthrow, even Siegfried reveals characteristics that are hard to square with our modern understanding of democracy. The good regularly acquires features of the diabolical, just as the diabolical assumes a semblance of law-abiding conventionality. It is simply not possible to draw the sort of clear dividing line between the parties of progress and grim reaction that is desirable if the work is to be subjected to a political interpretation.

Never intended to be merely theatrical, Wagner's great world theatre has always remained a puzzle, reflecting the contradictory interpretations that have been imposed on it. Time and time again it has been interpreted, explained and made to conform to the prevailing spirit of the times. The story of the *Ring* has continued in the history of its interpretations, but the contradictions that it contains have proved impossible to remove.

Neither the conservative Bayreuth performing tradition under Cosima and Siegfried Wagner nor the post-war 'clear-out' undertaken by Wieland and Wolfgang Wagner (an attempt to free the work from its ideological past that was in turn to be swept aside in the 1970s) produced results that were free from contradictions. If a solution was found that seemed to overshadow all its predecessors, this too was soon forced to make way for an even bolder hypothesis. Like the Dutchman, Wagner's life's work seems to wander the world, aimlessly, in its futile hope of redemption.

It is almost as though Wagner created the *Ring* merely to prove his theory that art needs to be interpreted in order to be understood. Bayreuth became the centre of the art of exegesis, proudly calling itself a 'workshop', with the *Ring* being treated as a 'work in progress' that is open to every contemporary trend, its meaning dependent on whichever director is entrusted with the task of staging it. Given the range of increasingly 'daring' interpretations designed to surpass all that has gone before them, it is perhaps inevitable that the question has been asked whether Wagner's *Ring* has any meaning at all. If so, that meaning appears to have eluded all attempts to pin it down. But if the *Ring* makes no coherent sense, does this not mean that all attempts to impose a post hoc meaning upon it are themselves meaningless? Does this sort of meaning make any sense at all?

In the absence of an interpretation that has proved satisfactory in the longer term, the contradictions have been transferred to Wagner himself. Cracks have been discovered in the fabric of the work and inconsistencies between the different versions noted, inconsistencies excusable and excused on the grounds of the drama's lengthy genesis, with writers pointing out that not even Wagner himself could make up his mind about its ending – in other words, its overall logic. And if the work is illogical and riven by internal contradictions, the effortful search for a meaning is futile. Moreover, if there is no threat of any deeper meaning, directors and interpreters can adopt an even more carefree approach to the piece and illustrate the undeniably highly effective scenes with the music that Wagner, to our eternal gratitude, wrote for them. In this way, we have returned to the theatre of 'effects without causes' that Wagner thought he had left behind him for good when writing the *Ring*.

Yet the *Ring* has a meaning no less than the world view that finds its 'most perfect artistic expression' in it. The contradictions that writers have discovered in it are part and parcel of this view. Strictly speaking, it is they that produce this meaning, always assuming that they are read as reciprocally interdependent. Elements that cancel each other out have no permanence, but precisely because of that they are raised to a higher plane. Wagner reduces the apparent senselessness of human history to its inner contradictions, just as he recognized in those contradictions the fissures in his own life. He describes the stages of this development in all their logical inevitability and shows the implacability and inhumanity of world events that fail to provide satisfaction on any level and for which progress is synonymous with destruction. And he also demonstrates the ineluctability of our deaths, both individually and collectively. His apocalypse takes place in the here and now.

But destruction is not the telos of the *Ring*. Rather, Wagner paints a picture of what he terms the 'true human being' who occupies the position once held by God. In his self-made freedom and self-sacrificing love, he is more godlike than God. Sometimes this miracle is glimpsed in the turmoil of the world, briefly allowing us a presentiment of a new dimension to existence before being swallowed up again by the darkness.

Only at the end of all four dramas – *Das Rheingold, Die Walküre, Siegfried* and *Götterdämmerung* – does this miracle achieve any degree of clarity as the outcome of a tale of infinite suffering. Above the smoking ruins of world history – Hegel's 'Golgotha of the absolute Spirit' – there rises up the self-consciousness that leaves behind it all contradictions and even its own destruction.

'The life of Spirit', wrote Hegel, 'is not the life that shrinks from death and keeps itself free from the ravages of time but the life that endures death and maintains itself in death. It acquires its truth only when it rediscovers itself in absolute disunity.' Wagner came to see the truth of this claim in the *Ring*. In Siegfried he created the living human being of the future triumphing over death. Siegfried finds perfection only in his union with his lover, Brünnhilde. His sufferings, which epitomize the whole history of human suffering, are necessary 'in order that a woman may grow wise'. The work's meaning lies in this wisdom, which is drawn from the *Ring*'s contradictions.

The Rhinegold

The beginning of *Das Rheingold* is the most astonishing opening of any work in the whole history of music. The music does not actually start but enters like a natural phenomenon, not as music but as sound, a sound that arises out of nothing. At the same time, a space opens up imperceptibly, and it is this space that reverberates. New sounds emerge from it and, without encountering any resistance, grow like plants. Whole groups of notes rise up in this way from the darkness, like stops being drawn on an organ. A musical Garden of Eden is born.

The harmonies of these first beginnings remain unchanged for 136 bars, while more and more new shapes break away from them and unfold in space. Yearningly, they strive upwards towards a brightness that seems to exist only in their imagination. While the blackest darkness still reigns in the depths, a light glimmers promisingly above. Anyone who, as Wagner demanded, can see with their ears can watch as nature is born before their inner eye.

For the theatre, Wagner located this origin of all things 'on the bed of the Rhine', where the water flows along in a greenish half-light. But the real miracle unfolds in the music. In its gentle welling, which soon passes into a rocking motion, Wagner heard 'the world's lullaby'.[11] This is the world that the idealistic philosopher Friedrich Schelling had described in his essay *On the Essence of Human Freedom*, where Wagner could have read that God himself has a ground in the form of nature which, in contrast to the brightness of his mind, lies in eternal darkness. Wagner's description of the deep sound of silence corresponds to Schelling's account of nature before creation.

Creation began when God shone his light into the depths. The beam of light of his mind lit up the darkness that yearned for it. As is clear from the increasingly violent wavelike movement of the prelude, the ground strives energetically towards the light that it recognizes as its own kind. This is exactly how Wagner describes the act of artistic creation in *Opera and Drama*: as a nocturnal ground, music needs to be redeemed, an act of redemption that can come only from the word. As the 'word of God', it raises the object to which it gives a name into the bright sounding light of existence. Like the creator himself, the poet plunges 'fearlessly into the full flood of the sea of music' from which a finished world rises up to greet him.[12]

Just as the 'woman' awaits her 'lover', so music awaits the poet. Her yearning grows as the light, falling down from the heights, increases. Wave upon wave, nature wells up, ecstatically foaming as though wedding the light that floods towards it. Like Schelling, Wagner uses the word 'love' to describe this union that leads to the emergence of a new world. Schelling's God, too, had bent down lovingly towards his own darkness before the majesty of his being flared up before his own eyes. Wagner captures creation's delight in its own achievement in the strains of *Das Rheingold*, describing how it emerges from itself, unopposed and unresisted, and strives towards the god that it loves and that strikes it like the sun. Wagner's lullaby for the world also conjures up the music of a Garden of Eden in which the union of light and darkness is celebrated.

The music describes nothing more nor less than its own creation. As the world was initially pure harmony, so the music offers the purest expression of this. It begins in the depths of barely audible sound, then slowly rises and fans out towards its own heights, becoming ever clearer as it does so. The brighter the space becomes, the clearer the shapes appear. All that we have heard in the form of musical sounds appears before our mind's eye. The ground, struck by the ray of light, rings out and creates the space in which the brightness unfolds, revealing an infinite number of animated figures. Creation begins with Wagner's low E flat, and the world begins to sing.

But it is already clear from Wagner's stage picture that not everything here is harmonious. The bed of the Rhine, for example, is still shrouded in night. As though Wagner has relocated the Wolf's Glen underwater, rocks tower up on all sides, the space between them 'broken up by a wild confusion of reefs', while the 'densest darkness' reigns in the gullies that are lost from sight. As the stage sets already make plain, creation is split from top to bottom, only the music has yet to notice this.

The same is true of the Rhinedaughters who emerge all at once from the waves. As natural beings, they live in a state of harmony with their watery element and express in words what they hear in the surging river. In the melodious singing of these three Undine-like water sprites the primordial harmony of the beginning continues to resound, while the wordless lullaby passes into a syllabic melody that Wagner described as a kind of 'hush-a-bye familiar from our children's nursery songs'.[13]

Three decorously veiled sisters, the gratifying sight of whom is revealed to our inner eye, breast the waves of the world's origins and at the same time reveal that we are in the nursery of existence here. Their task is to guard the sleep of their charge as he slumbers gently in his bed. As long as darkness reigns, he remains asleep. Only when the sun's eye falls on him does he open his eye. In song they call out his name. Their darling is called 'Gold'.

Following the account of the first creation contained in the prelude, the first creatures appear in the form of the Rhinedaughters. They were created by God, but they have no human soul. Just as the dark ground longs for the light, so these water sprites yearn for human love to redeem them from their twilight existence. But they are quickly drawn into a momentous encounter, and so this particular aspect of their nature remains concealed. Wagner recalled it thirty years after preparing his initial draft when he played this opening scene from *Das Rheingold* at the piano, commenting on it with the words 'I am well disposed towards them, these subservient creatures of the deep, these creatures of longing.'[14] They were the last words that his wife recorded in her diary. The very next day Wagner died.

This longing for love proves to be the water sprites' undoing. Motivated by the desire that is felt by the whole of nature, they offer themselves to other creatures, but precisely because of that, the being they are supposed to guard can be stolen from them. But this being is nature itself, nature in its primordial state of disinterested delight as awakened by God's divine light. The child that they protect with sisterly affection symbolizes the splendour of creation as it rises from the dark river-bed to greet the sun. The gold embodies the magnificence of created life, a state that Schelling describes as 'molten light'.

But as with the young Wagner, the song-loving sisters perform their duties badly. Playfully gliding through their watery element, the nixies are unaffected by gravity and are no less aware of the darkness that dwells in the depths. From here there emerges a sinister messenger. A dwarf forces his way into this burbling idyll, a figure who, like Schelling's Axieros or Ahasuerus, is driven by dark desire. Alberich comes and sees, and what he sees stokes the fires of his lust. 'How gladly my arm would unfold one of these sleek creatures', he sings with mounting longing. But he misses his mark.

Alberich, this monstrosity from hell, is not the first man to woo them. Another has already come from the opposite direction, from on high, to gaze approvingly on their slender limbs. In his earliest sketch for *Das Rheingold*, Wotan is discovered 'bathing' with the Rhinedaughters.[15] Like the Greek Zeus consorting with maritime nymphs, the god of the Teutons also feels drawn to the beauty of natural beings. He is already closely related to them, a relationship that he is obviously keen to deepen. But he is not their creator.

As with Zeus, Wotan's desire can be fired by all living creatures, which suggests that he is not the loving god of the world's origins: his love, after all, is lustful, acquisitive and not very fussy. Jacob Grimm had already noted that he delights in the sight of virgins and is fond of doing 'what humans do', and it is in this spirit that his wife Fricka reproaches him that 'there are no heights or depths where your lustful desire has not roved, seeking out sources of pleasure and ways of humiliating me'.[16]

It is unclear whether Wotan's divine desire was gratified in the depths of the Rhine, as Wagner cut this scene. But we may infer from it that this god is as much a stranger to the flowing harmonies of the world's beginning as is the dwarf Alberich. If the God of creation turned to his ground out of love in order to illumine it with his light, his successor Wotan was driven to enter the world of nature for completely different reasons. His lust is no different from that of his sinister antagonist who approaches the beauties of nature from the opposite direction.

His head turned by the sight of the nixies, Alberich freely admits that he hails from the underworld: he has clambered up 'from Nibelheim's night' and asks them to respond in kind. The hideous dwarf belongs to the race of the Nibelungs that is 'sprung from the womb of death and night'. In other words, the world drama unfolds between Wotan's realm of light above and the Hades-like night that teems with dwarfs below. Between them lies nature, in blissful contentment but the object of the acquisitive attentions of both these parties.

The primordial state of nature admitted to no such topographical layout. The initial act of creation whose emergence from nothingness is depicted in the prelude had come to an abrupt end. And it had done so, it seems, as the result of an act of violence. Alberich knows very well that, as Wagner writes in one of his prose drafts, Nibelheim's night was once devoured by 'the giant's body of the primeval world'.[17] The light that God had shed on nature fell victim to the rebellious darkness of the beginning. An alternative to creation then came into being, and when God's sun rose on a new creation, this world resisted its loving glance, just as concentrated matter resisted the light.

This decisive disaster, which was to turn the Garden of Eden into a vale of sorrow, took place before the beginning of history. But Wagner wanted to show the beginning and end of the world, and so he could not leave the turning point in the drama – the 'Fall' – in the darkness of prehistory. Instead, he incorporated it into *Das Rheingold* as a symbolic process. An event that actually precedes the creation of the world now takes place belatedly.

As an emissary of doom, Alberich sets foot on stage, and with the same ungainliness that typifies the raw matter from which he springs, he tries to grasp the light that the state of Paradise grants the water sprites. He is driven not by malice but by a yearning for the light, a yearning that fills him just as it fills all things in nature. That is why Wagner felt 'total sympathy' for Alberich, as he admitted at the time of *Parsifal*, for Alberich embodies 'the yearning of the ugly for the beautiful'.[18] But just as the young Wagner once discovered with the Pachta girls in Prague, the beautiful may be alluring and teasing, yet it remains beyond the suitor's grasp. For Alberich, pursuing the nixies in vain, the game becomes merely humiliating and, as Wagner later remarked, the Rhinedaughters unleash 'the whole childlike cruelty of nature' on a creature who is foreign to their species.[19]

Harmonically speaking, Alberich adds significantly to the musical argument: the refractory sounds with which Wagner characterizes him enliven the idyll by introducing its opposite. Only with the addition of darkness does a living picture emerge. Alberich's piercing gaze and stubbly beard, his spiky hair and 'screeching voice' are in striking contrast to the sleek-limbed girls with their pealing voices. But their playful games give rise to impotent rage on the part of their enemy. It is not disinterested delight that motivates him but the desire to possess them.

The darkness desires the light, not in order to merge with it in a state of musical harmony, but in order to seize control of it. Although the girls long for a suitor and want to be 'possessed', they have no wish to be wooed by a shady character like Alberich, whose 'toadlike shape' revolts them. The light that the ground greedily strives to grasp eludes it, causing the 'rutting ardour' of desire – the light concealed in the depths – to rebel against their playful delight in the light and to elude their grasp in turn.

In the midst of their games, the burlesque comedy about the duped suitor becomes a matter of deadly earnest, as the flirting on the bed of the Rhine comes to a sudden end. The drama has begun. From the heights, an increasingly bright light shines down, the sun breaks through the green waters and ignites a 'blindingly bright and beaming gold gleam' in the depths, the reflection from which casts its spell on the entire scene. This replicates the beginning of the world, when God's light fell on the ground and nature rose up from the depths to meet his gaze. The miracle of creation, only inadequately realizable on stage, takes place in the music. The liquid light of the gold that delights the world gleams not in the glow of the theatre lights but in the flashing and flickering strains of the music of *Das Rheingold*.

Hailed by the Rhinedaughters as the 'sun goddess' who offers them sustenance, the light wakens the golden-eyed boy in his cradle, and the world's child responds with a smile. Just as a mother recognizes herself in her child and the lover in his bride, so the deity recognizes itself in nature. Their eyes meet and they exchange glances: this conscious unity of the creator and his world – a world that sees itself reflected in the mirror of his eyes – is for Wagner the epitome of love both divine and human. Wherever such love is found in the drama, eyes flash, enraptured by the unity which, long lost, is suddenly rediscovered. Lost in itself, their glance lights up only briefly before being forcibly closed once again. Only at the end is it to remain 'open for ever'.

Just as thunder follows lightning, so genesis is followed by the Fall. In order to make this decisive moment intelligible, Wagner has his guilelessly garrulous Rhinedaughters explain it to us. Only he who offers himself to the light and returns God's love, they tell Alberich, can share the delights of the world's beginning. Together with all other creatures, he may then live 'blissfully in the gleam' of the gold. But he who shuts himself off from love and seizes the gold will win 'the world's inheritance'. Refashioned as a ring, it invests its owner with 'measureless might'. The girls reveal that this secret was entrusted to them by their father at the same time as the gold.

This was the secret of creation itself. As creation was dependent on his love being returned, God staked his own existence on it. Success or failure depended not on the father but on his creatures. If they refused to give themselves to him, they could still claim 'the world's inheritance'. In using this expression, Wagner was alluding to the religion of the Old Testament, according to which Yahweh promised the tribe of Israel dominion over the earth. If we accept the account of creation, as revealed to the Rhinedaughters by their 'father', this mystery presupposes a fall from the world of celestial light. All who exercise power or who promise it to others have already abandoned the realm of love.

The Rhinedaughters have scarcely blabbed their father's secret when the primordial world is shaken to its very foundations. Just as Schelling had predicted, the ground shuts itself off from the divine light that falls into it and selfishly takes it for itself. 'Your light I'll put out', screams the furious dwarf, and then, as a representative of darkness, he leaps up with 'blood-chilling haste' and snatches the gold from its cradle. 'So hear me, you waters,' he defiantly proclaims to the world, 'thus I lay a curse on love.' To the horror of the Rhinedaughters, the divine light disappears in his grasp, the spark of creation now subject to gravity. Instead of the all-encompassing love that had lit the world, the law of egoism now rules, an egoism in whose endless night the light smoulders as lustful passion.

Just as matter originates by shutting itself off from the light, so he who curses love will rule the world. The gravity of darkness reflects the egoism of the world ruler. He who steals the light shall own the world, but only in his insatiable lust. For he who denies his love to God transforms the splendour of the world into ownership, which in turn transforms all living things into dead matter. Where the sun had once shone, the old darkness now reigns. The dwarf has barely stolen the gold when, according to Wagner's stage direction, the light disappears. 'Dense night suddenly breaks in on all sides.' Only the thief's mocking laughter continues to echo shrilly through the gullies.

For Wagner, this archetypal scene provided a key to understanding not only the history of the human race but also his own experience of the world. Schelling's primordial harmony mirrored the ideal family in which the golden-eyed child, protected by his brothers and sisters, slumbers in his cradle until woken by his mother's loving gaze. Just as the sun is reflected in the light of the Rhinegold, so glances meet, and burgeoning love is fired in their eyes. He lives as a young god, surrounded at all times by his artistic siblings, carefree, cared for and spoilt.

Then the usurper came. Just as Alberich steals the gold, so Wagner's mythological self was snatched from his cradle by Geyer, separated from his family and carried off into the darkness. Through the desire for power and lovelessness, he was deprived of his inheritance. And whereas the dwarf took his booty to the Nibelung smithy in order to craft a ring from it, young Richard saw himself banished to the workshop of Geyer the goldsmith. Here, in the cavernous smithy of Alberich's brother, whom Wagner named Mime, the main figure of the *Ring* – the solar hero Siegfried – will one day be rediscovered. As the Nibelungs' vassal, he is meant to win back the lost ring for them.

Wagner was always convinced that with Alberich's fall the fate of the world was sealed. The curse on love brought with it an insatiable desire to rule the world, a desire that had formerly found expression in nature's innocent longing for love. Light had turned into a hellish glow, love to insatiable lust. But the world on which the splendour of the dawn of creation had once shone belonged to the forces of darkness. 'Let us treat the world only with contempt, for it deserves no better,' Wagner wrote in 1854 after completing *Das Rheingold*, 'but let no hopes be placed in it, that our hearts be not deluded! It is evil, *evil, fundamentally evil.* . . . It belongs to *Alberich*: no one else!! Away with it!'[20]

The world belongs to Alberich from the moment he seizes control of its treasures and becomes the sole owner of the splendours that had once been bestowed on all. As a result of his theft, he has plunged nature into the dark world of lovelessness from which he himself had emerged. But high above him sits enthroned a god who disputes his right to world rule. Like the creator who once raised the world from his ground into the light, he too appears on the scene to assert his claim to omnipotence and omniscience. When he is angry, lightning flashes, and whatever he wants comes true.

As the Norse equivalent of the Olympian Zeus, Wotan holds sway in the midst of his band of jovial gods on cloud-girt mountain summits. Although he did not create the sunlit world, he rules it with sovereign authority. Perhaps he even thinks that he made it and that with the brilliance of his mind he can dispel Nibelheim's underworld darkness. In his godlike sublimity, does he not create exactly the opposite impression to that of the toadlike night-dwelling Alberich? But Wotan is no more the god of creation than he is competent to judge the dwarf who stole the Rhinegold. For Wotan resembles him more than he would like. That is why he is known as Light-Alberich.

The decisive difference between Wotan and Alberich lies not in their characters, for both are equally covetous, lustful and devious. In matters of hubris, too, each gives as good as he gets. While one is able to assert himself through the beauty he has inherited from the Greek gods, the other shines in the light of the hoard that has been laid at his feet by the treasures of nature. And they seem like brothers in their obstinate striving for world dominion. A single feature distinguishes them: Wotan has only one eye.

Wagner appears to have thought this lack so important that he returns to it several times in the course of the *Ring*. For a god, to have only one eye was something of an inconvenience. It recalls the cannibalistic Polyphemus as well as Siegfried's legendary murderer Hagen. Does it mean that Wotan has been cheating? Or that he has only a one-sided view of his world? And then there is the question as to how an all-powerful god could lose the sight of one eye. As Siegfried insolently suggests, someone must have knocked it out for him.

Wagner offers an alternative answer or rather – and this has added to the confusion – more than one answer. According to the Norns, who as the voice of destiny ought to know what they are talking about, Wotan drank from the well of eternal wisdom and paid for that privilege with his eye, although his later conduct invites the thought that this was too high a price. In turn, the dwarf Mime claims to have seen one of Wotan's eyes shining into his cave – presumably the eye which, according to another observation, 'gleams like the sun' in the sky. Wotan, too, has something to say about his embarrassing handicap, for all that his comments are contradictory. After reminding his wife Fricka that he staked his eye in 'wooing' her, he darkly hints to the solar hero: 'With the eye which, as my second self, is missing, you yourself can observe the one that is left for me to see with.'

Wotan's missing eye has become something of a missing link in interpretations of the *Ring*, although its exegetes have fared no better than Siegfried on whom, as Newman comments, Wotan's 'subtlety' is lost. But what lies behind this subtlety? Writers have looked for an answer in Scandinavian mythology, in which Wotan either lost an eye in a primordial well or hid it or left it behind as a pledge. But what does this have to say about the *Ring*? One psychoanalyst has suggested that 'Siegfried is in fact the doubly reborn Wotan', while another commentator has rightly noted that Wotan's missing eye represents the sun but that 'the sun is not, after all, Siegfried's visual organ'.

Under the heading 'Myths and Legends', the recent *Wagner Compendium* states that there is no contradiction at all. Wotan demonstrably sacrificed one of his eyes at the Well of Wisdom, and so he could not offer up the remaining one as a gift to his wife, otherwise he would be totally blind. This can only mean that 'having already sacrificed one eye at the Well of Wisdom, he pledged the remaining one for Fricka but was not, in the event, called upon to forfeit it'. This is fine for Wotan, but it has no bearing on the underlying problem. Only Peter Wapnewski, the wittiest of exegetes, admits that there is a difficulty here. He has failed, he writes, 'to understand this passage and make any sense of it'.[21]

We can make sense of it only if we go back to a point before the beginning of the action, a point described in both Schelling's metaphysics of light and Wagner's prelude to *Das Rheingold*. God, who has been divided into his light essence and his dark ground, allows his creative glance to fall on this ground. His eyes see himself in the mirror of nature as something entirely different from himself. This is how Wagner himself explained this passage to Cosima, who had written to tell Nietzsche that the mysterious eye was 'the sun that is reflected in the sea'. Or to put it another way, it is 'the will that strives to see itself as something different'.[22]

In the darkling depths of the river the golden eye of creation opens to the eye of the sun. But this attempt on God's part to acquire self-knowledge and transform the whole of existence into love proves a failure. Nature seizes possession of the divine spark in order to begin a life of its own away from God. The longing that God awakens in nature turns to gravity, a force that seeks to take control of everything. Love is forced to yield to egoism. Just as the original deities in Greek mythology were destroyed by Zeus and his thunderbolts, so the first God gives ground in the *Ring* and makes way for his successor.

This successor resembles failed creation to a tee or, to use his own puzzling image, is like an eye that resembles its twin. Whereas the loving glance of the first God had recognized itself in the eye that met it in nature, causing both to merge like bride and bridegroom, they are now forced apart when the world is cut off from God. Wotan's eye sees the world without recognizing himself in it, just as the world, which has retained its godlike sight, can see the whole of nature but no longer the god in nature.

The god who gazes into the primordial spring loses his eye in it. From this spring – an aspect of nature – it stares back at him only as something alien. God's sun still shines on nature, but the ground that Wagner located in the depths of the Rhine has sunk back into night. Not only the god himself but his creation, too, has become one-eyed. The egoism of the earth is imperiously countered by that of the god. Only in human beings who recognize each other in their partner's glance and merge 'eye in eye' will the light of our earliest beginnings arise once again.

The musical flight that leads from the bed of the Rhine to the heights, from night to the sunlit heavens, does not last long, the journey being shorter than we think. Heralded by majestic strains, the one-eyed god makes his entrance. He lords it over the earth, which trembles at his thunderous voice. But he is asleep when we first meet him on stage. Like Zeus, he rests on a flowery meadow, a resplendent image of a god. But as with other rulers, his head is filled with empty dreams of honour, power and 'endless fame', ambitions epitomized in the towering turrets of Valhalla, which, like the first royal citadel on the roof of the world, is designed to secure his rule. Since sunrise it has been ready and waiting for its new owner.

Just as in the opening scene of *Das Rheingold* the golden-eyed child in his cradle of waves is woken by his mother's loving gaze, so the slumbering god is roused from his sleep by his wife. Wotan is married, and Fricka, who like Zeus's wife Hera has an unpleasant streak to her, now engages him in an embarrassing argument, in spite of the beautiful weather. Wagner was all too familiar with a spoilsport like Fricka, which explains his decision to invest her with Minna's features. It is clear from her peremptory opening words that the first love of the world's beginnings is nothing to write home about. Alberich is not alone in betraying love: so too has the new race of gods. The 'seed of disaster', wrote Wagner, drawing on personal experience, lay in marriage. 'The fixed bond that binds them both', he informed the incarcerated August Röckel, plunges the former lovers into the 'reciprocal torment of lovelessness'.[23] The *Ring* provides textbook examples of this.

But why did Wagner declare that marriage – the basis of human society – contains within it the 'seed of disaster'? Alberich's curse on love is wholly convincing as an example of the Fall, whereas there seems to be no reason to condemn the loving union between man and woman. Yet it is clear from the *Ring* that it is very much this bond that constitutes the true curse on love and that is directly bound up with the Fall – not, however, with the crime committed by Alberich in the swirling floodwaters of the Rhine but with a parallel process at a higher level. And for this, Wotan himself is to blame.

Like the musical shapes of the prelude, nature, when wakened by God's gaze, strives towards the light and develops in the plant world. In Norse mythology, the World Ash serves as a symbol of this light-dependent vegetable kingdom. Watered by the primordial well of existence, it rises from the dark ground of creation and reaches up to the heavens themselves. But with its pointless beauty it strikes Wotan simply as an eyesore. He breaks off its 'most sacred branch', whereupon the tree begins to wither. Just as the Nibelung robs nature of its radiant equality with God, so the new god despoils it of its eternally burgeoning vitality. 'Fallow fell the leaves, barren, the tree grew rotten,' report the normally well-informed Norns, 'sadly the wellspring's drink ran dry.'

If Alberich replaced light with gravity, which greedily draws everything into its sway, so Wotan imposes laws on nature, laws that it is blindly forced to follow. Where love had once reigned supreme, strict order now obtains. In Greek mythology, too, the Titanic power of the elements waging their chaotic wars was broken by the law-giving god who created the perpetual order that henceforth held sway over nature. Divine law prevailed on Olympus, while the forces of nature lay captive as Titans in the underworld depths of Tartarus.

In the *Ring*, this reversal proves to be a twofold Fall and is transferred to a historical plane: Alberich invents ownership, covetously seeking to take over the whole of nature and subjecting nature's blind forces to it. And in much the same way, Wotan sets up a rule of law in which love, as God's natural union with his creation, no longer has a place. Like the World Ash, the freedom in which nature evolves is cut back. Events are now entirely dependent on his orders.

He decrees, for example, that the world is now private property and uses the timelessness of his treaties to resist the flow of time. The living branch of the World Ash is carved into a spear in whose dead wood he immortalizes the 'runes of his treaties'. And love, too, now becomes an object of contract law. Once the force to which creation owed its existence, it no longer ensures the bond that unites man and wife as it had once united God and his ground. Instead, it is governed by laws that impose permanence on living sympathy. Marriage is placed above naturally burgeoning love, turning it into dead wood.

As a result, both Night-Alberich and Light-Alberich are condemned to perish. In creating their own spheres of influence, they have robbed themselves of their own foundations. The light that Night-Alberich extinguished and replaced with the inextinguishable ardour of desire was the divine spark that had summoned him into life, while Wotan subjected natural freedom to the necessity of his laws, literally breaking from the World Ash the branch on which he had been sitting.

For the divine principle had existed only through love. Nature was God's ground: without its living force, his existence was groundless. God was love, and only in love was the divine conscious of itself. Everything else, as arranged by the princes of the earth, leads to the rule of death. This is the thrust of the story that Wagner relates in *Das Rheingold*. Even this 'preliminary evening' embraces 'the world's beginning and its end', as it already exposes the inner contradiction of the rule of law and possessions that means that from the very outset both contain within them the seeds of their own destruction. The matinal love conjured up in the music is spurned before the day is over. The resigned conclusion of the Rhinedaughters – 'false and fated to die is all that rejoices above' – provided Wagner with the very last music he played on the piano on the eve of his death.

The one-eyed Wotan is roused from his dream of omnipotence and has to be reminded at once that a god who owes his power to the laws is himself subject to those laws. In his one-sided view of the world, he has failed to take account of this. And so Fricka calls her spouse to account. In order to persuade the giants to build his castle, he has promised them her sister Freia, the goddess of love, as their reward. On the level of a fairytale parable, this is as much as to say that only by betraying divine love is it possible to subjugate the Titanic forces of nature that represent the elements.

But in reproaching her husband for his shabby behaviour towards her sister, Fricka is exposed as a hypocrite. Appealing to her marital claims on her husband in the face of his natural amatory impulses, she presents herself as the advocate of a goddess notorious for her aphrodisian promiscuity. Indeed, it is clear from Grimm that even the strait-laced Fricka is said to have committed such lapses 'in order to acquire gold for her personal adornment'.

Wotan, too, is caught in the dubious light that falls on the sisters when we start to examine them more closely. When the giants demand their promised payment, the god turns out to be a hypocrite. He forces the elements to undertake slave labour, while having no intention of keeping his word and rewarding them with the goddess of love, who has served merely as a bait. Love is one of his possessions, and he does not plan to share the divine power to which he owes his being. Unlike the father who bequeathed his light to the world, Wotan maintains a convulsive grasp on it. The 'son of light', as one of the giants calls him, proves to be a son of darkness. Only his own laws prevent him from descending to the level of the rapacious Nibelung.

Wotan is caught on the horns of a dilemma. If he swindles the giants, he will forfeit his identity as a guardian of the law, whereas if he gives them their reward, he will lose his identity as a god, for 'Freia's golden apples' create a link with living nature, and without them the gods are no more than lifeless concepts. He is helped out of his predicament by the demigod Loge, who, unlike the one-eyed Wotan, sees through the true nature of the world: above and below, the two realms are identical, only they fail to understand this. Like the creator himself, Loge sees the oneness of opposites but he lacks God's loving power to reconcile them. He is the spirit whose cold eyes understand all creatures and thereby deny their existence. All that comes into being acquires a natural right to destruction. God's light has become an all-consuming fire in Loge.

He is just the person that Wotan is looking for. As a master of dialectics, the demigod sees the contradiction into which the god threatens to fall: Wotan owes his power to the elements but does not want to share it with them; he has raised himself above nature while being dependent upon it. Loge's solution consists in cancelling out the opposites and playing off the threatening natural forces, one against the other. The reward that the giants are promised shall be paid by the dwarfs. The fiery demigod knows that gold and love are exchangeable, and so, instead of the unavailable Freia, he proposes Alberich's golden hoard, which is not, of course, his to offer. In return for renouncing love, the giants will be fobbed off with the very thing that the dwarf has acquired by cursing love.

Needless to say, the ruse succeeds, as the free spirit is superior to the bound elements. Together with Wotan, Loge journeys to hell, steals the Nibelung prince's stolen gold – a theft that seems right and proper – and uses it to redeem the goddess of love who has been given as a pledge to the giants, though not before Wotan, growing more like his apparent antithesis Alberich with each passing moment, has likewise cast a covetous eye at the glittering hoard.

But the wisdom of God has continued to sleep in the depths of nature, and it is nature herself who now appears in order to warn Wotan to beware of this death-dealing legacy. The primeval goddess Erda, known to the Greeks as Gaia, rises up from the depths as an oracle in order to instil 'care and fear' in the self-satisfied son of light's heart. Erda foretells the death of the deathless immortal in the form of the twilight of the gods. Wotan realizes that, for him, salvation lies only with her, in the dark ground of creation. A new start must be made, but how?

The somnambulant goddess returns to her underground realm, Alberich disappears into a world of shadows and the one remaining Titan, having murdered his brother out of greed, gathers up the dwarfish treasure. Only now can Wotan turn to his latest acquisition. Lit by 'the sun's eye', Valhalla shines in the evening light, while the Rhinedaughters in the river below bewail the gods' falsehood, and in his disgust Loge takes his leave of them, briefly toying with the 'delightful temptation' to consume the supercrogatory gods with his fire.

The god of thunder conjures up a spectacular storm, demonstrating the power that the gods still have at their disposal, after which Wotan is finally allowed to take possession of his ostentatious castle, but while he is on his way to it, he is struck, as Wagner notes, by a 'great thought'. In order to underline his historic decision, the consequences of which are described in the rest of the *Ring*, he picks up a sword left over from the hoard and thrusts it triumphantly into the air. And for the first time we hear the Sword motif. To the pompous strains of the march of the gods, Wotan then sets foot on the rainbow bridge that leads to his home in the clouds.

With the end of *Das Rheingold* we bid farewell to the Olympian world of the gods. Their claim to rule the world without loving it condemns them to the nullity of tyranny and banality. The fact that behind their lovelessness, which is masked by the rigours of the law, lies a self-destructive desire will soon become clear.

Elsewhere this desire already reigns supreme: in Wagner's own expression, a 'demonic delight in destruction' already obtains in Nibelheim, the restless Hades of the *Ring*.[24] And the sounds of it assail Wotan's and Loge's ears as they descend through a sulphur-filled cleft. The deafening hammering of anvils, endlessly booming and echoing throughout the mine shafts, rises up to greet them from the gaping depths, as the pounding rhythm of beaten metal, familiar as the Nibelungs motif, proclaims the end of nature, which has disappeared down the jaws of a machine.

Nibelheim is dominated by the law that greedily demands endless self-reproduction. The divinely radiant element has been beaten into coins of the realm, burying all life beneath its accumulated mass. Scarcely have they emerged from the womb of night and death before the Nibelungs are reduced to a state of living death by Alberich, whirring cogs in the machine of world dominion. Their lives consist of adding the living metal to the sealed hoard, in the course of which they turn themselves into lifeless possessions. The last vestiges of life that remain to them find expression in their endless cries of anguish. Their total powerlessness is in powerful contrast to Alberich's omnipotent rule, a state symbolized by the ring. In reality an object of no importance, a glittering gem on Alberich's finger, it embodies the spell of self-deception by dint of which its owner confuses creative omnipotence with the futility of seeking to impose his control on nature.

For Wagner, Nibelheim was a place of horror, just as the Wolf's Glen had been. The smithying of the enslaved Nibelungs struck him as 'dreadful',[25] the gold that is mined here an 'evil nightmare'.[26] Against the bitter seriousness of this underworld realm, Valhalla is exposed as a mere façade. Wotan's mountain summit is not an alternative world to the Nibelungs' night but a self-satisfied variant of it, lit by borrowed light. But Nibelheim came into being because it had shut itself off from God's love, usurping the radiant day of the world's beginnings, robbing creation – this son of God – of the inheritance of equality with God and subjecting it to the law. Where there had once been Paradise, a tyrant had set up his throne. God's free creatures were now no more than his 'tamed host'.

In this mine of horror, Wagner rediscovered his past. This past had largely been concerned with gold and ways of acquiring it. In Geyer's *Der bethlehemitische Kindermord*, the autobiographical hero had turned his hand to the same trade as Geyer's own brother Karl. According to one scholar, the family had 'great hopes of goldsmithery as a way of earning money'.[27] Wagner's brother

Julius was apprenticed to Karl Geyer, and the young composer, too, was intended for a time to learn smithery. While he clearly failed, his later rivals had more success. Mendelssohn and Meyerbeer both struck him as the purest 'makers of gold', and Schlesinger, who forced him to undertake 'slave labour' in Paris, was even nicknamed 'Goldsmith'.

In this curse-laden world, human relationships are reduced to the level of that between master and slave. The gold that the former owns allows him to force the latter to create yet more wealth for him. But the victim then seeks to cheat his master of his reward, much as Wotan does with the giants. In his *Phenomenology of Spirit*, Hegel had shown that the master is in fact the slave of the slave as he is dependent on him, whereas the slave is his master's slave only because he fails to understand this. Wagner, who certainly understood this, turns the two Nibelungs, Alberich and Mime, into brothers because, although they may appear to be opposites, they both fantasize about becoming all-powerful. In their outward appearance, they both bear the same features of repulsive filthiness that filled their creator with horror and loathing throughout his whole life. And in terms of their character, they combine all the egoistical characteristics that typify the archetypal enemy. With Alberich and Mime, Wagner's evil found its definitive form.

The first scene between the two Nibelungs reveals their natures in all their rankness. They torment, rob and curse each other, rivals in their ability to outwit and deceive one another. Consumed by envy, each wishes the other dead. Whereas Alberich, as master, is characterized by 'haste, greed, hatred and rage',[28] his little brother is notable for his slavish obsequiousness and malice. The hostility between the two brothers reflects their hatred of all that is natural and, as such, was ascribed by Wagner to his chosen enemies.

'The interdependence of the Jews', Wagner wrote in his 'Explanations Concerning "Jews in Music"', creates a 'slavish misery of the most extreme severity'.[29] In his hideous world ruler Alberich, therefore, Wagner might also have intended to immortalize Meyerbeer, Heine's 'Wanzerich' (if Alberich may be translated as 'king of the elves', then Wanzerich may be glossed as 'king of the bugs'), just as Mime's cries of pain are prefigured in the C major Overture by the 'goblinlike' Mendelssohn. If so, the two musically mimetic brothers, each of whom seeks to steal from the other the gold that comes from success, would both be exposed as the monstrous products of night and death.

But the Nibelung prince Alberich also resembles the God of the Old Testament as depicted by the German idealists, for Yahweh represented not the love of the first creation but the law that brands nature a sin. When humanity refused to submit to his yoke, he had recourse to what Hegel calls the 'savagery of vengeance and hatred'. Instead of loving the world, he reduced it to a state of fear and terror and, far from showing paternal leniency, pursued his creatures with vengeful vindictiveness. It was not love that shone in his eye but the delight in destruction. Feuerbach, too, in his *Essence of Christianity* (a text Wagner studied in detail), claimed to have detected his 'destructive fire of anger in the vengefully flashing eye of an Israel bent on extermination'.

The same is true of Alberich. Apart from his anger, which is vented in terrible curses and punishments, the magic helmet that allows him to hide also recalls the God of Moses. Unlike the gods of light, who delight in beautiful human bodies, Yahweh keeps himself hidden from sight. He is the first amorphous creator. Alberich can similarly make his dwarf's misshapen body invisible. As a hidden ruler, he can impart painful blows like a bad conscience, or else he can help himself to any shape that is of use to him. But someone who can be anyone is in fact no one. Alberich derives his essence only from the power that his slaves accord him. His rule rests on deception – the deception that passes off as actual existence the nothingness that feeds his desire.

As a logician, Loge is conscious of this. He has seen through the dwarf's existential deception just as he has seen through Valhalla's façade. The sleight of hand with which he plays off Alberich's omnipotence against itself reveals him descending to the level of the thief in the *Ring*. Wagner had discovered this motif in Tieck's version of Puss-in-Boots, in which the eponymous animal flatters the vanity of a powerful magician until the latter turns himself into a bite-sized mouse. Loge, too, flatters Alberich with his ability to be everything, allowing him to reduce the dwarf to the nothingness from which he is sprung. The dwarf begins by using his magic helmet to puff himself up into a 'giant serpent', then, in order to demonstrate his universal abilities, he shrinks to the size of a toad, the creature which, according to the Rhinedaughters, he most resembles. In this way he is captured by Loge's cunning, at which the cruel demon, having held the world in a state of terror, crumples to the ground, with nothing to hold on to any longer.

Only when defeated and robbed of his two instruments of power, the ring and the magic helmet, does Alberich reveal any human features. The curse that he places on the ring merely encapsulates all that spontaneously occurs to him: the gold that grants measureless might brings its owner not the life of the gods that he longs for but suffering and death. 'May he who owns it be wracked by care, and he who does not be ravaged by greed! Each man shall covet its acquisition, but none shall enjoy it to lasting gain!' As Alberich now realizes, the ring contains, unseen, all the negative qualities by which it has been gained. The curse on love is not the price that has to be paid for it but its abiding effect. Like

Hegel, the overthrown prince of darkness sees that in a world of law there can only be slaves. 'The lord of the ring' is also its 'slave'.

At the moment of truth, the prince of Hades and the ruler of heaven are at their closest. Just as Alberich, clearly aware of his own situation, describes himself as 'the saddest of all sad slaves', so Wotan in the next chapter of the *Ring* vents his feelings in a clear-sighted cry of despair: 'The saddest am I of all living things!'

Wagner often admitted to feeling some sympathy with the suffering dwarf, this 'hapless, fear-stricken' figure who in his search for heaven creates his own hell. Indeed, perhaps he felt even more than that. In triumphantly telling Uhlig that the *Ring* was 'the greatest thing I've ever written', Wagner signed himself 'Your Nibelung prince, Alberich'.[30]

The Valkyrie

When, after years in the musical wilderness, Wagner began work on the score of *Das Rheingold* in 1853, he felt that he had arrived at the wellspring of creation. 'My friend,' he wrote to Liszt, striking a note of jubilation, 'I am in a state of wonderment! A new world lies open before me. The great scene in the Rhine is finished: I see before me riches such as I had never dared suspect. I now consider my powers immeasurable: everything seethes and makes music inside me.'[31]

The new world that he felt he had created was the world of ideas. Alberich's feelings of omnipotence inspired in him the ability to express these ideas. And the language that helped this world of ideas to become living and real was music. Just as every language is made up of terms that acquire their meaning through their contextualizing sentence structures, so the expressive world of the *Ring* consists of musical shapes that acquire their meaning by dint of their melodic context. As the poet speaks with words, so the musician in Wagner spoke with motifs.

Every phenomenon that impinges on our consciousness, from the most powerful natural event to the subtlest emotion, is given its own graphic theme, just as each theme, to quote Wagner himself, is 'the seed corn from which the whole plant must necessarily develop'.[32] The unfolding patterns of nature are reflected in the themes that emerge from each other, developing from the simplest interval to the most complex musical structure and invariably remaining intelligible to all who are familiar with the concepts in question.

In this way, the whole work became 'a tightly interwoven unity'. There was 'scarcely a bar', Wagner insisted, 'that does not evolve out of earlier motifs'.[33] Thanks to their 'increasingly individual treatment', the 'graphic nature motifs' of *Das Rheingold* became 'vehicles' for the performers' 'underlying passions'.[34] In this way Wagner created a universe of sound that overwhelms every impartial listener like a spectacle of nature.

But mere sensory perception was not enough for Wagner. He wanted to be an object not of amazement but of 'total understanding'. Audiences had to be 'able to grasp the whole, as only then can they really assimilate the tiniest detail'.[35] This could not be achieved merely by listening to the work. In order to understand the *Ring*, audiences first had to learn Wagner's universal language. His musical concepts do not illustrate the intended object in the manner of labels but allow audiences to perceive their very essence, with the result that their meaning generally becomes clear from seeing *and* listening. The flickering of the fire is then just as intelligible as the rocking motion of the waves or Nibelheim's booming hammering. Whether it shoots upwards or comes crashing down, the musical figure unmistakably expresses both outward movement and inner emotion. That the giants are no more that gigantic dwarfs is as clear from their motifs as the fact that the earth goddess Erda is synonymous with the nature from which she ascends or that Wotan's home of the gods is no different from Alberich's avenging ring.

Just as the lack of freedom in nature is followed by the freedom of human beings in the story of the creation, so the song of self-aware creatures emerges from the ordered world of motifs. The world's stage opens up to humans, whose voices do not obey the rules of the themes but reflect the free development of the personality that lends meaning to the pre-existent world of sound. Where there had once been only notional expression, reality, fully understood, now prevails. As the music shows, the story of this reality is not substantially different from nature but merely reveals the gradual process of the dawning of consciousness. The actions of the characters decide the fate of nature, just as nature's motifs acquire their historical and hence their decisive significance through the characters' vocal lines.

The singer expresses what nature means, and the stage action shows how the two belong together. In other words, the action on stage is not illustrated by the music, as theatrical tradition claims, for this would lead to an embarrassing duplication. Rather, the opposite is the case: the visible action provides a running commentary on world history as told through music and poetry. In the face of its infinite complexity, the acting, which can bring out only the most essential features, creates the impression of a process of simplification verging on coarseness. The profound conceptual fabric of the motifs that can evoke a whole world of semantic possibilities is at odds, as it were, with a baritone draped in a bearskin. All that takes place behind the footlights remains no more than an illusionistic attempt to reproduce what the drama actually means.

Even before the curtain rises, the theatre has already lost the battle, for the reality of this drama takes place not on stage but in the music, whose widescreen film is projected onto the listener's consciousness. As Wagner realized when the *Ring* was first staged in Bayreuth in 1876, the work is not suited to a proscenium stage.

With the very first bar of *Die Walküre* a veritable storm breaks loose, the intimidating violence of which had not hitherto been known in art. Dark clouds scud across the sky, while the horizon disappears behind a wall of rain, and sheet lightning rends the air. An especially violent gust of wind shakes the whole forest as though with a giant's fists, while a flash of lightning crackles, to be answered by a roll of thunder. The impression is so vivid that the listener may think that it is not the music that is imitating a storm but that the tempest has swept through the orchestra pit in order to express what it has always wanted to say.

In this short prelude Wagner allows Valhalla's world of gods to exercise its sway. The raging elements are merely obeying Wotan's orders. This whole primordial spectacle is staged to ensure his dominion over the new age, too, for the world of the gods and dwarfs has long been replaced by that of human beings who have established their own empire in nature just as they found it. With *Die Walküre* history begins in the *Ring*, the world drama seems to start all over again, yet it is already pursuing the downhill course that had proved the undoing of the previous world. Abandoned by the gods and bereft of their senses, human beings grope their way about and fall unsuspectingly into all the old traps.

It is this that the prelude depicts. Against the background of the storm unleashed by Wotan, a man is seen running for his life. Breathlessly he hurries through the forest, heeding neither rain nor stormwind. Dogs are on his trail, pursuers at his heels. Can we not hear the barking and the steerhorns echoing through the trees? But suddenly they seem to have lost his scent. The storm whose lightning flashes had filled the fleeing hero with dismay has proved to be his salvation. And the tempest now abates as though by magic. A miracle has taken place: Wotan, the god of anger, has stood up for a mortal who does not even know of his existence.

But even if he had known that there was such a god, it would never have occurred to him in his wildest dreams that he was the god's son. And yet, as so often in the *Ring*, it is the inconceivable that is true. The storm to which he owes his salvation conceals his father, the god. But the latter's help in rescuing his son from his enemies is due less to a father's instinct to protect his offspring than to a political stratagem, for Wotan's son has been set a task. This is why Wotan, assuming the name of Wälse, has fathered him and brought him up. This too is why he has abandoned him and exposed him to a hostile world in which his very life is threatened. For need alone can turn him into the hero that the god so desperately needs. These are strange times in which the gods are dependent on the help of mortals.

Nibelheim similarly has known few times as strange as these. Ever since man raised his head above nature, the world of gods and dwarfs has retreated into thought and been destroyed by its inner contradictions. Gods and dwarfs exist only on a notional level, but the real world belongs, it seems, to man and his practical reason, even if he continues to pray to the gods and to fear the underworld. But on earth there is no longer any place for supernatural forces. Instead, the laws have revived the old divisions, with world dominion as the prize for the man who seizes control of the earth.

The majesty of nature, turned into hard cash and symbolized by the ring's rounded elegance, still lies in the giant's grasp. As a natural element he is bound by higher laws, preventing him from freely converting it. And so the gold treasure lies uselessly in a cave, watched over by the monstrous dragon – the giant Fafner disguised by means of the magic helmet. But reality can be found only in the real world and power over it gained only through the hoard, so Wotan and Alberich both plan their comeback by reappropriating the ring. That they have failed because of their own lovelessness does not worry them as long as they can again anchor their power principle in the real world.

Just as Zeus fathered his snake-killing heroes and Yahweh his only-begotten son, so Wotan and Alberich both father progeny intended to place their seal on the world of history. A start had been made by the thunderbolt-hurling Wotan when, as the god of beginnings, he descended into the ground of nature and fathered a band of demigoddesses on Erda. Although human in form, they blindly obey his will, fulfilling their mission of collecting up the men who have fallen in battle and who, by dying as heroes, have qualified to serve in Wotan's spectral army. This Wild Hunt will one day sally forth from Valhalla's ancient citadel and in a final battle free the world from evil, although, as Wotan knows very well, this evil is entirely dependent on the way in which it is defined.

For all that Wotan has long been plagued by self-doubt, human beings still believe that the gods are essentially good. These humans have assimilated the ideas of possessions and laws, thanks to which they have been able to subject the external world of nature to their control. But the aspect of nature that stirs within them in the form of a longing for love has been tamed by marriage. Like everything else, love is governed by legally binding contracts. Wherever it has created any freedoms for itself, it has fallen foul of the law. Like Zeus, Wotan alone has enjoyed a bit on the side and escaped the fatal verdict.

Having forced himself on the earth goddess and fathered the complaisant valkyries, Wotan now feels attracted to mortal women. In his identity as Wälse he sleeps with Sieglinde, a primeval forest beauty who bears human progeny with golden blond hair and eyes that flash like a god's. They are called Wälsungs or Volsungs. Even before the start of *Die Walküre*, the twins Siegmund and Sieglinde – the latter takes her name from her mother – have already known tragedy, a tragedy that is to climax in the drama. As everywhere else in the *Ring*, the present age compulsively repeats the contradictions that have remained unresolved in the past. One name for this mechanism is 'fate'.

Just as Siegmund resembles his sister Sieglinde, so the fate of the Wälsungs, as described by Wagner in his prose drafts,[36] resembles the composer's own. Like the sun, a god descends to earth to found a race of noble offspring intended to spread the seed of his own divinity. Like the first king, Wälse establishes a court from which he rules his land and where he raises his children with his lover, Sieglinde. Symbolically, he has built his home around the family tree, the withered World Ash that has received a fresh infusion of the sap of life as a result of the god's new act of creation. The ash tree begins to grow again, the race of Wälsungs thrives, and Siegmund grows up to become a solar hero. In the midst of the chaos of nature, divine love once again asserts its radiant sway.

But only for a brief moment in history, barely long enough to draw breath. Almost at once the enemy appears on the scene, just as he had done in the case of the Wagners and the Wibelungs. Envious of Wälse's good fortune, he and his vassals attack the first citadel while father and son are out hunting. The Neidings, who had already destroyed Wieland's happiness, torch his home and family tree, butchering his wife Sieglinde and raping his daughter. On their return, Wälse and Siegmund are driven away by the superior force of the intruders. They live in the forest as lupine outlaws, robbed of their legacy and love, while Wotan's daughter is forced to serve the usurper, first as a servant girl, then as a wife who bears him 'faint-hearted sons'.

Her brother, too, is dogged by ill fortune. While fleeing the Neidings, he becomes separated from his father Wälse, who leaves him as his only legacy his wolf's skin, much as a dead bear was left to the young Richard in *Männerlist größer als Frauenlist*. Siegmund is outlawed and mocked, cut off from society, with neither a home nor possessions to call his own. As though hounded by a curse, he wanders through the world in his endless search for the love that he seems to have lost for ever.

When he finally meets a woman who does not reject his advances, her family promises her to another man. She flees to Siegmund, who kills her brothers, but instead of following him, she falls in despair on their bodies. Siegmund barely manages to escape with his life from the Neidings, who have hurried up to help their kinsmen. Defencelessly abandoned to his attackers, the woman is killed by the group's leader as a punishment for her infidelity.

It is the same man who once attacked Wälse's court, killing his wife and forcing his daughter, Sieglinde, to marry him. He is called Hunding – a derivative of the German word for hound or cur – and his faith involves a doglike submission to Wotan's laws. He does not, of course, suspect that he has subjugated Wotan's earthly family, still less that the intruder he has been pursuing in order to avenge his kinsmen's murder is none other than Wotan's son.

When Hunding planted his own line on that of the Wälsungs, the god gave way to him, as Siegmund is meant to develop into a hero through his own strength alone. Now Wotan returns invisibly. The plan to subject the world to his new order seems to be working out. With the help of the tempest he has manoeuvred his son back into the very place from where he had once been driven. Hunding is about to return home, and so the drama depicting the plight of the Wälsungs can begin all over again, this time of course with a different conclusion.

Just as Odysseus returns home from his lengthy wanderings under an assumed name, so the refugee who, all unsuspecting, seeks shelter in Hunding's home passes himself off as a certain Wehwalt. 'Whosoever's hearth this may be,' he exclaims, too exhausted to recognize his surroundings, 'here I shall have to rest.' He no more recognizes his parental hearth than his sister, who, likewise declining to divulge her true name, appears before him as a stranger. 'This house and wife are Hunding's own,' she replies to his question. He has escaped from the frying pan of natural forces into the fire of the world of laws and contracts, a world in which only ownership and power count for anything. Having nothing to offer in this regard, Siegmund is fully prepared to set out on his journey again.

But it is already too late for that. Anyone familiar with Wagner's language of myth will be able to hear in Sieglinde's opening words about a 'stranger' the voices of her sisters Ada and Senta, both of whom are unexpectedly visited by their lost lovers, who also turn out to be their brothers. The music, too, is unable to restrain itself in the face of the twins' reunion: barely have they begun the hesitant process of mutual recognition when both their motifs are intimately merged. Siegmund's eyes revel in 'the blissful delight of seeing', and he is the first to realize that he has reached the end of his odyssey. Sieglinde's gaze answers his, first questioningly, then increasingly resolutely, until they look at each other silently 'with mounting emotion'.

Never before had Wagner written anything like it. Even before the eyes of his performers have met and their voices have merged, the whole of their prehistory, with its suppressed sorrow and insatiable longing, has already been heard in the music, music which, as in Greek drama, expresses the truth of the whole like some all-knowing chorus that sees and hears everything. But the drama as a whole goes beyond the limitations of the particular situation and invites self-knowledge. Just as brother and sister, long separated, recognize each other in one another's eyes, so the world rediscovers its lost identity in this drama of sounds. The voice of the music answers its own call, just as the gaze of one character rediscovers itself in the other as though it were its own. The world of ossified concepts and intractable laws yields to the magic of a universal language that reduces everything to a state of flux and thereby restores it to its lost unity. Where there was dead being, life once again unfolds, a life as radiant as on the very first morning of creation.

This, in brief, is the plot of the opening act of *Die Walküre*. The beginning that takes place before all other beginnings and that Wagner had hinted at, first in the prelude to *Das Rheingold* and then in the effulgence of the gold, is now transferred to an alienated world and developed to its full extent in the relationship between man and wife, brother and sister. Just as the first God cast his light into the darkness of nature, causing nature to rise up in its yearning towards him, so the son of light, in the middle of the night of existence and in the face of his own impending death, encounters a stranger coming to meet him. She hands him a drink – Wagner uses the word 'Quell', meaning 'wellspring' or 'source' – and he recognizes himself in it. She responds to his voice and he thinks he can hear his own. When they look into each other's eyes, the divine love that had long seemed extinguished is kindled anew.

The first person to notice is Hunding. With a rhythmically pounding motif in which the elemental forces of dwarfs and giants still stir, he comes to meet the stranger, noting in his eyes the 'glittering serpent' with which only his wife had previously managed to unsettle him. Siegmund, too, knows that all is not well with this sinister individual who insists on the 'sanctity' of hearth and home. The fact that only disaster awaits him here has already been hinted at by Sieglinde's furtive glance.

Siegmund is not yet aware of Hunding's true identity, although in one of the drafts for this scene Wagner planned to put at least his audience in the picture.

Wotan was to appear incognito and discreetly draw the attention of this uncouth guardian of house and hearth to the fact that he himself would not have been quite so particular about such sanctity: after all, he is all too well aware of the close connection between respect for the law and hypocrisy.

What a stroke of good fortune it is for the usurper to discover the true heir as a prisoner within his own four walls after the latter has twice escaped from him. Siegmund had freely recounted his most recent adventure, in part, no doubt, as a prelude to offering his protection as a gentleman to the beauty of the night who finds herself in a similar position. Now Hunding has good reason to crow. The law is on his side and he will not hesitate to enforce it the following morning. His motto is vengeance. What Siegmund interprets as freedom is regarded by Hunding as a breach of the law. The love that Siegmund defended is a sin to Hunding. And so the new life that has only just been fired in an exchange of glances already seems over.

But Wotan will not allow this to happen. Having stage-managed events right down to the very last detail, the god is just as fond of his children as he is of the new life that they meant to give him. He had betrayed the first act of creation but now makes a new attempt to restore its godlike nature to a degenerate world. A hero has appeared who stands out from the gloom of history like the radiant sun. Wotan brings him to his sister who has been kept alive only by the glimmer of a hope that she may one day re-encounter her 'sacred friend' and brother. Regardless of the 'sanctity' of hearth and home, she has long been ready to take him in both arms. And as soon as a chance presents itself, she tells him as much.

Wotan has ensured that this chance arises. He has kept the sword that was left over from the Nibelung treasure, intending it for the hero who would free the world from the Nibelungs. Evidently recalling Wagner's early short story *Die Hochzeit*, he had turned up as a surprise guest at the hapless Sieglinde's wedding to Hunding, his eye instilling in the bride a sense of 'sweetly yearning sorrow', after which he had marched straight over to the ash tree in the living room, a tree known to the compiler of the Old Icelandic *Saga of the Volsungs* as 'Barnstock' – 'child-trunk'.

In taking possession of the usurped family tree, Wotan prepares the way for a new creation and to this end he uses the 'magically quivering' sword that cannot deny its similarity to the 'Völsi' from which the Volsungs derive their name. 'Völsi' – or 'Wälse' in Wagner's German – was the 'male member of the domestic stallion'.[37] Wotan thrusts it into the trunk, which, flouting the laws of nature, it penetrates as far as its hilt.

Needless to say, one man alone can draw the sword from the tree: the one who is answerable for propagating the Wälsung line. Having just been sentenced to death, Siegmund surprisingly finds things looking up. Waiting in the darkened room, he has glimpsed a glimmer of light from the ash. The 'blind man's eye' is lit by a divine flash of light that sears his heart and holds out a promise similar to that afforded by 'the glorious woman's glance'. She has meanwhile used an opiate to put her dim-witted husband out of action in order to be able to show the like-eyed stranger the Wälsung sword stuck fast in the tree.

They can now mate. Just as they are embracing for the first time in 'sacred delight', the door flies open, as though by itself, and the full moon of the spring night shines into the room. Nature, which had lain as though dead in the bonds of winter, wakes to new life. 'Wide open', the eye of the new world ruler laughs, and the love felt by the whole of nature smiles back, 'blissfully greeting the light'.

The undertow of the action invests the music with a previously unknown intensity of expression that affects not only the couple themselves but the audience, too. Siegmund's aria-like crowd-pleaser about 'winter's storms yielding at May's command' describes precisely the moment at which the solar hero frees the ravished Persephone from Hades. This is the endless moment in creation when Wagner's god creates the world.

But the sun and the Rhinegold rising luminously to greet it have now been replaced by human beings who recognize each other's eyes and voices and faces and even their most private thoughts. Only in this way is the love of the beginning raised to a conscious level. Knowledge of the whole – the aim of creation – is now vouchsafed in humankind. Only when individuals are consumed by each other in love, Wagner claims in *Die Walküre*, does the god cease to be alienated from himself in history.

'The whole', Wagner wrote to his friend August Röckel, explaining the philosophy of the *Ring*, 'reveals itself to us only in the individual manifestation, for this alone is capable of being apprehended in the true sense of the word; we can really "grasp" a phenomenon only if we can allow ourselves to be fully absorbed by it, just as we must in turn be able to assimilate it fully within us. How is this marvellous process most fully achieved? Ask nature! Only through *love*! . . . But the full reality of love is possible only between the sexes: only as *man* and *woman* can we *human beings* really love. . . . Only in the union of man and woman does the true human being exist.'

Sieglinde has barely shown Siegmund the sword when he draws it from Barnstock with a 'tremendous tug', naming it 'Nothung' and running off into the spring night with his 'sister-bride'. Following his famous exclamation 'Now may the blood of the Wälsungs blossom!', the two throw themselves into each other's arms 'in raging passion', and with a genuinely divine finale Wagner celebrates the success of his creation of a new world. 'The curtain falls quickly', Wagner comments with a nudge and a wink, prompting Schopenhauer to add: 'If it doesn't fall quickly, we'll see something unpleasant.'[38]

One person does in fact see this. The door that opens onto the spring night as it rejoices in creation does not fly open of its own accord. According to an earlier draft for this scene, Wotan himself has cunningly opened it while the tempestuous love scene was unfolding between his children: he has been spying on them from the hayloft. What he sees seems to have been a novel experience even for the god. 'Did you witness their love?' he later asks the prudish Fricka. 'What do you know if you didn't see and hear them?'[39]

In this way, Wotan restores to nature the love that had once been ousted by the laws. But the old world has no intention of giving up without a struggle, least of all Hunding, who now awakes from his deathlike sleep.

When Hunding discovers that his wife has run off with his mortal enemy, he fires off a quick prayer to heaven. Even before rounding up a search party, he begs Fricka, the guardian of wedlock, to help him in his quest for vengeance. The eternal law has been violated, and it must be in the goddess's interest to ensure that it is strictly observed.

But the individuals who have broken the law have been brought up to do so by Wotan himself. His son was intended to rebel against 'the council of the gods' and, unmindful of the laws of ownership and marriage, to help free love to replace them. Siegmund has been conceived by the supreme legislator as a lawbreaker. The scandal in Hunding's house that is intended to establish a future humanity has been planned right down to the very last detail. During his offsprings' night of love, Wotan left nothing to chance, and in the same spirit he now summons his chief valkyrie to provide an escort for the fugitive couple. Siegmund is supposed to be able to fend for himself, of course, with the god's weapon clasped in his hand, but Wotan must have anticipated certain complications that his plenipotentiary Brünnhilde may be in a better position to deal with than the blond upstart.

Wotan knows his whole approach has been problematical from the outset. But no one has noticed. The gods have been disposed of behind their backs, but Hunding's religious scruples have alerted Fricka to the creeping subversion, and so both women – Brünnhilde and Fricka – now present themselves to Wotan, the former to receive orders, the latter to issue them.

While the valkyrie's martial *galop* suggests nothing so much as the coldly glittering splendour of a world power, Fricka rides up in a chariot drawn by rams that seems to have come straight from Nibelheim. To the strains of dwarfish complaints, the goddess marks her entrance, brandishing a golden whip like Alberich's and angrily striking the groaning animals. Once again the god is given a lesson in the two aspects of the legalistic world that he is keen to overthrow. He must surely suspect that he cannot confide his secret desire to abdicate in either of them.

And so, on the morning after the Wälsungs' wedding night, when the whole of nature is aglow with the radiance of early spring, a series of decisive encounters takes place. No fewer than three confrontations occur, the first between god and goddess, the second between god and valkyrie and the third between valkyrie and human being. All three are concerned with nothing less than the future of the world, a future which in Wotan's view depends entirely on man. But man differs from nature and the gods only in respect of his freedom, and so all three encounters hinge on a single topic, the participants arguing, with a perceptiveness worthy of Schelling, about 'the essence of human freedom'.

The contradiction that the god has fostered within himself confronts him initially in the guise of his wife. Fricka reproaches him for the fact that, as the lord of earthly order, he has violated this order and voluntarily relaxed 'heaven's grip' on the world. The products of his extra-marital affairs are merely the blind agents of his will, in addition to making him guilty of adultery and incest: 'You alone provoked them,' Fricka informs her husband and with implacable logic demands that he rid the world of this nuisance, while at the same time putting an end to his own absurd contradictions.

But Fricka's seething indignation stems less from her feeling that the law has been violated than from jealousy. She has long followed her husband's escapades, watching him fall upon the distaff side of humanity with the voracious appetite of a Zeus and suffering not only from wounded amour propre but from a contradiction of her own. Like the god, she secretly longs for power and pleasure, attributes offered only by natural reality. But she is the guardian of virtue and so, unlike the roving god, she has to deny her desires, making up for this denial by seeking to take revenge on Wotan. As the latter now discovers for himself, the suppressed desire for love turns into hatred and a delight in extermination that disguise themselves behind the hypocritical mask of morality.

Fricka's secret contradiction is revealed by a blatant misunderstanding: in Wotan's actions she can see only the depravity that she denies in herself. That her husband has additionally allowed the fruits of his adultery to break eternal laws strikes her as the acme of divine wrong-doing. She can see no other explanation. In her eyes, the Wälsung twins act merely as agents of Wotan's caprice, with the god celebrating his own omnipotence in their brazen revolt.

Fricka is incapable of understanding Wotan's aim of putting an end to his own world in order to rehabilitate the love that had initially ruled on earth. For her, the world of laws and contracts is not a failure: quite the opposite, it guarantees the gods' rule. As products of the divine will, all the earth's creatures obey the gods' laws. Wotan contrasts this state of affairs with his own concept of freedom: only a human being who, 'lacking godly protection, might break loose from the law of the gods' can restore the world's lost integrity. Only a free man can free the world from the toils of power and ownership. Only when selfishness ends can love reawaken. And Siegmund is this free man, not a puppet like other creatures, but a creature in his own right: 'In grievous distress he grew up by himself.'

In Fricka's eyes, this seems merely to be Wotan's attempt to make his own downfall more palatable to her: 'You seek to deceive me with deep-set meaning', she seethes indignantly. But the case is plain for all to see. A being created by God cannot be free. If Wotan claims the opposite, he is lying. Nothing could be simpler than to accuse him of this. If Siegmund is his weak-willed creature, then Wotan has sinned against himself through his crimes, and for his honour's sake he must expunge his guilt and kill his son. If, on the other hand, Siegmund is free, as the god claims, he cannot enjoy his protection. After all, freedom consists in never being dependent on anyone's protection. But anyone who does wrong, freely and on his own initiative, must atone by losing his freedom.

Wotan is trapped. After all, Fricka demands from him only what he has already claimed. In short, the god has to withdraw his protection from Siegmund. Brünnhilde, too, is instructed not to intervene. There remains only Nothung. But the sword that the hero won 'in his need' falls victim to Wotan's own definition of the term, for as Fricka perceptively counters, 'You fostered that need no less than you fashioned the fearsome sword.' If Wotan wants to remain true to himself, he must also deprive Siegmund of his inheritance. 'Withdraw its magic,' Fricka demands, triumphantly anticipating her revenge. Wotan, disenchanted, gives her his word.

It is clear from this first disputation that in an inhuman world the essence of human freedom leads to violent death. The man who wants to break free from natural law falls victim to that law because he owes his whole existence to it. Siegmund has freed himself, with God's help, from the law of the gods but is now to be destroyed by that law because it was the god of the law who created him.

There is no freedom outside God unless this God could exist outside himself, emerging from the womb of nature and history. Then there would no longer be any need for gods who exist outside nature and history. But at the very moment that the new god appears, Wotan, having fathered him and brought him up as his son, must personally destroy him. Siegmund, the son of man, must, as it were, die on the cross that his father has erected for him.

Wotan's bitter realization leads to a second discussion that follows straight on from Siegmund's sentence of death. His favourite daughter Brünnhilde appears in shining armour and a winged helm, a spear-brandishing Amazon whose superhuman perfection is tarnished only by the fact that she is a puppet. This glorious woman, the cynosure of all *Ring* productions, can do only what Wotan wants, encouraging Fricka to describe her, contemptuously, as the 'bride of his wishes'. But jealousy also plays a part here inasmuch as Wotan, like Pygmalion, has fallen in love with his own creation. Mindful of her lack of freedom, however, he declines to make the thought the agent of the deed: she remains a bride in name alone.

Following his argument with Fricka, Wotan knows himself to be the 'least free of all things living'. Caught in his 'own fetters', he is forced to stifle his feelings of love for his son and to maintain his position as an omnipotent ruler, a position he has long since ceased to want. The ageing god has come up against his own limitations. He is permitted to love his creatures only as long as he subjects them to his laws. One such creature is Brünnhilde, who has just followed in disbelief the outbursts of his impotent rage. If, conversely, Wotan were to act out of love and raise his son above both the world and his own omnipotence, he too would inevitably perish, even while he loved him.

The law that he embodies demands Siegmund's death. 'What I love, I must relinquish,' he realizes, 'I must murder him whom I cherish.' In stifling the love within him, the god dies with it. The essence of human freedom contains within it not only the end of the individual but also the end of the god. This is the 'plight of the gods' that destroys him, the 'endless fury' and 'eternal grief' that oblige him to suffer death on the cross of history in the person of his own creature.

Brünnhilde does not understand a word of all this. She is programmed to seek out heroes on the battlefield, not to experience love. How can she understand a dilemma about freedom when she herself is merely Wotan's instrument? 'Who am I', she asks in all innocence, 'if not your will alone?' And so her father confides in her the secret of his will in a form intelligible both to herself and to the audience. Once, he explains, he betrayed love in order to seize control of the world, but the laws with which he shackled his creatures bound him in turn. Hegel's doctrine is no less true of Wotan. 'I who am lord of treaties', he complains, 'am now the slave of those treaties.' Events that have already taken place in the brightness of the gods' day are repeated, mirror-like, at night. Alberich has also forsworn love, winning 'measureless might' by refashioning the gold as the ring and enjoying unlimited power just as Wotan does at the opposite end of the earth.

After losing the ring, the night-elf stakes all on winning back world dominion. He seduces a mortal woman in the hope that the 'fruit of his hatred' may regain the ring that is buried beneath Fafner's bulk. It is no accident that he pursues the same course of action as his antagonist. Wotan, too, has returned to nature to defend his threatened omnipotence by means of his natural progeny and to save the ring from Alberich's grasp. If he fails, he knows that 'love's dark foe' will turn the world into a lightless Nibelung cave for ever. This apocalyptic threat has long worried Wotan and now seems about to come true.

At least this is what the god tells his closest confidante, focusing on the question of simple power, while saying nothing about the essence of human freedom, something that his agent understands no better than she understands the mystery of love that threatens to destroy him. The valkyrie, after all, is not free but a dependent being, and the love she knows has been limited to her own 'Walvater' – literally, the 'father of the battle-slain' – and to the propagation of the flying valkyrie steeds. For the sake of her limited understanding, he restricts his 'plight as a god' to the dilemma surrounding the ring: having paid off the giants with the gold, he cannot reclaim it from Fafner without breaking his own law. This – he explains to Brünnhilde – is why he has fathered the Wälsung: Siegmund is the hero 'who, of himself, achieves what I alone desire'. As a result, Siegmund may be able to steal the ring on his behalf. But unfortunately Fricka has caught him out: his cunning plan has been exposed, and Siegmund appears to be lost.

To judge by this simplified version of events, Wotan's despair and subsequent death wish seem to make little sense. What, after all, would prevent him from attempting a further experiment along the lines of his failed attempt with Siegmund? Why does he tremble at Erda's prophecy that the 'end of the blessed immortals' will dawn with the birth of Alberich's black-browed son when their bliss has been of no interest to him? Does he really believe that by regaining the ring he can make good all the wrongs he has caused through his own lovelessness? And would 'godhood's empty glitter', which so disgusts him, once again bask in the light of eternity if he regained his former power?

In offering this detailed account of his actions, Wotan portrays himself as a calculating, if unsuccessful, politician, but his account is in stark contrast to his unbridled despair. The truth of the matter is that he collapses beneath the weight of the guilt that he has brought down on himself. As Wagner later explained, Wotan is the 'most tragic' of all the characters in the *Ring*: 'he has recognized the guilt of existence and is atoning for the error of creation'.[40] His son's death takes away the final glint of the empty glitter with which he has otherwise dazzled the world. For a moment he no longer plays the part of the immortal god but becomes a mortal capable of losing his composure and of being crushed by his own existence. It is almost as though he is vicariously suffering the mortal torments that he has been forced to inflict on his innocent son.

In his dismay, Wotan seems to realize that the world is being destroyed not by desire on the part of apostate nature, as represented by Alberich, but by himself, the god who has subjected nature to his laws. For it is these laws, not the prince of the Nibelungs, that prevent love from getting the world back on an even keel, just as it is these same laws that call the Wälsung lovers to account for following their natural desires. Wotan himself will cause the death of his loving son by depriving him of his divine inheritance – the sword – at Fricka's bidding. In this way the deity repudiates itself: by lording it over creation, it thrusts its origins, love, down into the abyss. All that is left – the desanctified and dehumanized universe – is bequeathed by Wotan to the Nibelungs, so that the world can finally disappear in the womb of night and death and do so, moreover, with the god's blessing.

Wagner saw this as a 'disaster' that was a cause of great suffering for him personally. While working on the score, he admitted to Carolyne Sayn-Wittgenstein that he was 'all too painfully' affected by the subject: 'There is really no suffering in the world that does not find its most anguished expression here; but this playful game with this anguish is taking its revenge on me: I've repeatedly fallen quite ill because of it and have had to lay off completely'.[41] If this act was ever to be performed as he imagined it, he told Liszt, it was 'bound to produce a degree of emotion unlike anything previously known, at least if all my intentions are fully understood'. In the same letter he admitted that he was 'most afraid of the great scene with Wodan [*sic*] and especially the moment when he reveals his fate to Brünnhilde'. This, he insisted, was 'the most important scene in the whole of the great four-part drama'.[42]

Wotan lacks the strength to murder his son, and so he delegates the deed to his daughter. 'Siegmund you must kill and fight for victory for Hunding!' At this, a decisive change takes place in Brünnhilde, too. Having listened credulously to his puzzling explanations, she suddenly catches an 'ambiguous word': whereas Wotan had previously enjoined her to ensure that Siegmund was victorious, he now withdraws his support. Worse still, he orders her to murder his own son. 'Never have I seen Father of Victories like this', she muses to herself, as though dazed. A spark of freedom has been kindled in the puppet.

By contrast, the fires of passion that Siegmund has kindled in his sister seem to be dying down again. Infected by the civilization that her brother knows only from the outside, she is tormented by fear and by the pangs of a guilty conscience. The breach that has divided the world is one that she feels all too clearly herself. She 'starts up' from the 'rapture' of Siegmund's embrace, seeking to flee with precipitate speed, such is her fear of her cuckolded husband who will wreak bloody vengeance upon her. But she is no less motivated by horror at a deed to which she is not equal. To her lover, who can scarcely keep up with her, she seems to be hounded by the Furies, much as her thoughts are harried from extreme to extreme. The freedom that Siegmund brought her has now been turned into panic and so she has lost her bearings.

When she looks back on her married life, which is now over, she feels defiled and dishonoured, for she 'obeyed the man who held her without any feelings of love'. As a result, she feels unworthy of her 'radiant brother' and of a solar hero who woke her with his 'star-bright eye'. But she also sees the situation from the standpoint of a wife who has 'broken wedlock's oath', a sin that weighs heavily upon her and cries out to be atoned.

The portrait that Wagner paints of Sieglinde here seems heavily influenced by his experiences with Jessie Laussot. She too suffered at having been married against her will and gave herself to a kindred soul who offered her the love she longed for, only to shy away from taking the definitive step and regaining her freedom when unsettled by the world on which she was planning to turn her back. Their joint flight to the Orient had come to an end even before it had begun.

Sieglinde's flight, by contrast, leads her back into her past. During a brief rest in the forest during which Hunding's horn calls can be heard in the distance, she is assailed by all the old ghosts. The trauma of usurpation returns. The act of violence that had once destroyed her freedom is now repeated, robbing her of that freedom all over again. Hallucinating, she relives the moment when the Neidings invaded her home, recalling the vain hope that her father and brother would come to her aid and remembering her mother's grief and the fire whose billowing smoke prevented her from seeing. 'The ash tree topples – the trunk is riven!' On that occasion, it was her parents who fell victim to this attack by the rapacious world of the law. Now history seems to turn back its wheel and inflict a similar fate on the children who had escaped on that earlier occasion.

But fate is only one aspect, enshrining the laws of creation to which even the gods are subjected. That there may be another aspect is inconceivable to the gods and to the Norns who predict the world's destiny. But such an aspect does indeed exist. It is represented by the human beings who flout the laws, mock the gods and oppose fate with their own willpower. This is the aspect of freedom, something for which no provision had been made in the book of fate.

But the love that existed before all the laws and that woke the ground in which fate slumbered yearns for this freedom. A free god could not recognize himself in serfs but only in human beings as free as himself. But as Wotan is forced to learn in a particularly painful lesson, the god cannot create this freedom for human beings, and so they are wholly dependent on themselves. Only as the result of a miracle does this divine light dawn on them. In the third of the dialogues on the nature of human freedom this miracle takes place twice over.

The two participants encounter one another in extreme circumstances of a kind that neither has previously known: Brünnhilde is to kill the son of the father she idolizes and do so in the face not only of his own conviction but of hers as well. In other words, she is forced to submit to an authority that has undermined itself precisely because it has issued these instructions. In turn, it looks as though Siegmund will have to abandon the supreme happiness in life that he has only just discovered for himself. As a result his sister-bride goes out of her mind just as he himself loses his life. And so they meet, Wotan's son and daughter, in circumstances that fate had not foreseen.

Half-brother and half-sister discuss the situation calmly, even solemnly, as though dimly aware that they hold the fate of the world in their hands. The unshakeable composure with which they face up to the horror of their situation restores the sense of dignity that Wotan had lost only moments earlier. The divine element has passed to those of his creatures who are marked out to die, and Wagner, who had to express the inexpressible in words and music, complained at having to work on a 'scene in which Brünnhilde comes to Siegmund in order to announce his death: you can hardly call this composing any longer!'[43]

Brünnhilde comes to Siegmund to announce his death: 'Look on me!' But her eyes, which normally inspire dread in those who are destined to die, strike him as 'beautiful and earnest'. He gazes at them at length, as though reading something in them. And Brünnhilde, having come to kill him, returns his gaze. Presumably they recognize one another, as brother and sister in Wotan. But Wotan has forfeited Brünnhilde's love. Consumed by her terrible task, she attempts to portray Siegmund's death as a step towards a better future. All eyes and ears, Siegmund gives further proof of his freedom: instead of agreeing, as all other heroes would, he asks her a series of questions, calling into question the divine authority that Brünnhilde embodies to such impressive effect. Representing nothing but himself, he is superior to all such authority.

With great self-assurance, he takes note of all that she says: the heaven that she promises him; the host of fallen heroes who are ready to bid him welcome; his father, Wälse, who awaits him; and the wish-maidens who will look into his eyes and read his every desire up there in Valhalla, in the better world of the gods. He thanks her kindly for her offer, then makes so bold as to ask whether Sieglinde will be allowed to accompany him there. When Brünnhilde naturally says no, as there is no room for mortals in heaven, Siegmund politely but firmly declines her offer. She may pass on his good wishes to gods, heroes and wish-maidens, but 'I'll not follow you there.'

Brünnhilde cannot believe her ears: is Siegmund really prepared to forgo the joys of life in heaven for the sake of the poor creature 'who, tired and sorrowful, lies there, faint, in your lap'? What has come over him that he renounces immortality for the love of a frail mortal woman? Evidently it is the spirit of Achilles, as invoked by Wagner in his 1849 plan for a revolutionary drama. When the Greek hero is told of his imminent death, he rejects the immortality that is offered him, preferring to avenge the death of his lover, Patroclus, than be accepted into the world of the gods. As long as he gets his way, he would not even be afraid of descending into Hades. As a result, he is 'greater than the elements (the gods)', Wagner noted at this time. Man, he went on, is 'the perfection of God. The eternal gods are the elements that father man. It is in man, therefore, that creation culminates.'[44]

This is something that the valkyrie seems vaguely to realize during her encounter with Siegmund. He is sufficiently superior to reject the god's gift because his love of his mortal bride means far more to him. If he is to fall in battle, he will renounce Valhalla's all-male company and go voluntarily to hell with Sieglinde, whom he will kill before turning his sword on himself. Brünnhilde dutifully points out the madness of his resolve, prompting him to turn the tables on her. She does not know that love is not something that can be bartered. How 'cold and hard' her heart must be if she does not understand this. 'Can you but scoff, then be on your way, you false, unfeeling maid!'

This miracle, whereby a mortal breaks free from the gods for the sake of his freedom, is followed by a second miracle, when Brünnhilde breaks away from Wotan for the sake of her love of this mortal. The light of the first creation begins to shine. Siegmund's unconditional love opens her eyes: his dignity in the face of death induces a change of heart, and Wotan's puppet is transformed into a living woman who determines her own destiny herself. Brünnhilde has become Antigone. Wotan has condemned the innocent couple to death, but Brünnhilde now overturns this miscarriage of justice. 'Sieglinde shall live – and Siegmund with her!' she proclaims, inspired as she is by a new spirit that she had known neither in Wotan's Valhalla nor in his equestrian Praetorian Guard.

But it is not to be. Even during the Annunciation of Death scene there had already been an ominous reminiscence of *Der Freischütz*, and the scene in the forest quickly becomes a veritable Wolf's Glen, as the stage darkens and storm clouds gather over the forest, while the sound of Hunding's steerhorns mingles with that of the rolling thunder. A storm blows up, as though the Wild Hunt is approaching. A flash of blinding lightning lights up the mountain ridge on which Siegmund and Hunding attack one another with their swords. Suddenly Brünnhilde appears in the clouds, like a guardian angel 'in a blaze of dazzling white light', protecting Siegmund with her shield in order for him to deal the fatal blow.

But at that very moment a 'bright red glow' appears in the sky,[45] as though the prince of hell is appearing in person. It is not Samiel, however, who emerges from the night to claim a new soul, but Wotan, the god of anger. He raises his spear, the symbol of laws and contracts, against Siegmund, who is fighting for his life, and Nothung falls jangling and shattered to the ground, allowing Hunding to thrust his sword deep in the defenceless hero's breast. In the dense darkness that descends on a grieving world, Brünnhilde, with great presence of mind, draws Siegmund's widow onto her horse and escapes with her.

Wotan remains behind, swearing to exact terrible vengeance on the valkyrie. Light-Alberich has finally revealed himself as a destructive demon.

Towards the end of his life, Wagner likened Wotan, enamoured of the idea of his own destruction, to the Flying Dutchman.[46] He too wanders through a world from which love has vanished, yearning for the clap of doom that will spell the end of creation, even though he has no hope of release. Wagner's other name for him was Ahasuerus, a ghostlike figure driven through history by the curse of his own lovelessness. This ghost brings death to the solar hero Siegmund with the 'destructive fires of anger in the vengeful eye' of a god 'obsessed with extermination', to quote Feuerbach's sketch of the God of the Jews.

Wotan had set foot on the stage of the *Ring* in the proud awareness that 'the everlasting work is ended', but he takes leave of his own creation with the words 'Vengeance is mine.' The god of light is merged with his shadow Alberich. With her newfound sense of humanity, his daughter realizes to her horror that the

Father of the Battle-Slain has become the Wild Huntsman. The place where Valhalla once stood is now dominated by the Wolf's Glen.

With the opening of the third act, the cold brilliance of the world of power – in reality, a world of death – is paraded one last time. In the fly-past of the exulting, corpse-gathering valkyries, the age of iron flashes before our eyes, intimidating the world with the aggressive force of a phalanx of Amazons and drawing it into the wake of a violent order that passes itself off as nature. Its bois- terous savagery is vented in screams of delight on the part of the horsewomen but is tamed by a powerful rhythm that tramples everything underfoot, sub- jected as it is to a single will that has set the seal of its law on nature. Pleasure in the Wild Hunt of the Ride of the Valkyries is pleasure in our own destruction.

But when Brünnhilde returns to this horde of triumphing barbarians, every- thing has changed. She has become a human being who has sacrificed her life out of pity, while her sisters, faced with the crime that affects them all, break into cries of lamentation all too reminiscent of the Nibelungs. Tomboyish arro- gance turns to howls and the chattering of eight sets of teeth. The law has been infringed, and a terrible punishment threatens. But this is far from true of Brünnhilde, who is no longer concerned with divine omnipotence but with the helplessness of a mortal woman. She heeds only her own inner voice, not the alienating authority obeyed by the others. Her sisters merely receive orders, while she confronts them as a free woman. Among soldiers in uniform, she is the only heroine.

A change has also taken place in Sieglinde, who has spent her whole life as a victim. After being liberated by Siegmund, she had relapsed into her intellec- tual and spiritual dependency on the old order, but Brünnhilde now opens her eyes to the new one. 'Live, O woman, for the sake of love!' she enjoins Sieglinde. 'A Wälsung stirs in your womb!' Brünnhilde has saved not only Sieglinde but also the offspring of her love for Siegmund. It is to this offspring, not to Wotan and his henchwomen, that the future is to belong.

In the face of the approaching weather front in which Wotan comes thun- dering along, Sieglinde breaks into an unprecedented cry of jubilation and for a moment the perpetually downtrodden woman rises above herself in order to thank Brünnhilde for rising above *herself*. Her hymn in praise of the 'sublimest wonder' of love, as manifest in the valkyrie, is not to be heard again until the end of the drama. Wagner consciously 'saved' this motif as his final word on the *Ring*. When Sieglinde sings it from the depths of a heart overflowing with emo- tion, it seems for a moment as though love has finally triumphed.

Not even the callous valkyries can escape entirely from this new force, and when Wotan comes storming in, snorting with 'terrible fury and agitation', they burst into tears and plead with him to show mercy to Brünnhilde. It is almost as though Wagner recalled his sisters weeping outside the door while Geyer chastised him. Certainly, Wotan is like a father scolding them for 'weeping and wailing'. Only when Sieglinde is out of harm's way does the delinquent Brünnhilde emerge to meet her executioner. As calmly composed as she was when announcing Siegmund's death, she now awaits her own death sentence. 'Here I am, father: dictate my punishment!'

But instead of organizing a drumhead court martial to punish the 'miscreant', Wotan – no longer sure of himself – becomes embroiled in an argument with her. And so, for the fourth time on this spring day in world history, the characters debate the essence of human freedom and do so, moreover, with a dialectic astuteness entirely worthy of Wagner's Zurich essays.

The debate is launched by Wotan, who reduces his former agent Brünnhilde to a series of contradictions. She who existed only by virtue of his will has wilfully rebelled against him. And she has contrasted his own freedom, to which she was subjected, with hers. As a result, he is relieved of the need to punish her. She has turned her back on her own true nature, and so Wotan gives her the freedom that she has already claimed for herself. 'Your punishment you yourself ordained.'

From the standpoint of the world of laws and contracts, this means that Brünnhilde is now an outlaw, no longer a demigoddess but a mortal woman who, like her charge Sieglinde, must submit to the brute force of a man. For Wotan, freedom can mean only abandonment. She will be put to sleep as a valkyrie in order to wake up as a married woman who 'sits by the hearth and spins'. This is not merely an act of perfidious cunning, it reflects the role of women in a society ruled not by love but by the law.

This is a crucial point, and Brünnhilde seizes on it at once. The discord that Wotan implacably exposes is in fact his own. He himself broke the law that he himself had created, turning his own nature, which Brünnhilde had loved, into its opposite. She knows that he loved his son and that in deciding to kill him he was untrue to himself. By admitting to the emotion that he suppressed and by doing what he was forced to forbid, she was more loyal to his true nature than he was himself. It is not she who betrayed him, but he himself.

Brünnhilde begins to feel love not through flouting the god's wishes but though acting as the agent of his own secret desire. She describes this light flaring up as she gazes deeply into his eye. All that she describes to Wotan on the strength of her memory – the sound of Siegmund's voice, the expression in his eyes and, finally, the indescribable feeling which 'deep in my breast caused my heart to tremble in holy awe', in other words, the feeling of recognizing herself in the other person – all this now seems to take place between her and the god. The feeling that people call love takes possession of Wotan, too. In short, a further miracle turns the demon bent on revenge and with thoughts only for the apocalyptic end of the world into a loving father sad and bereft of hope.

The pacified god, shaken by Brünnhilde's plea, submits to her entreaty without a struggle, even admitting with surprising candour that 'for the sake of a world' – the world of the eternal laws – he staunched 'the wellspring of love' in his 'harrowed heart'. He acted out of a love of lovelessness, as it were, but this is now over and done with. A new Wotan stands before his daughter, able to abandon himself to love for the first time – love that as a god he was not allowed to feel for her. Their eyes meet and their contradictory thoughts are reconciled. In this long exchange of glances, god and valkyrie slip out of their traditional roles and discover each other in their kiss and embrace. As the day draws to a close, the murderer and his willing accomplice are turned into the incestuous lovers whose death they encompassed that morning. The day on which love died ends with its rebirth.

This, at least, is how Wagner interpreted the legend that he knew from Grimm's *Deutsche Mythologie*. Here, Wotan punishes the valkyrie by robbing her of her virginity when he pricks her with a 'sleep thorn', also called a 'wish thorn': like Sleeping Beauty, she falls into a deep sleep from which she will be woken by her earthly bridegroom. In Wagner's case there could no longer be any question of a punishment. The spark that Brünnhilde has ignited flares up 'in Wotan's heart in the fullness of his love for his favourite child'.[47]

But a change has occurred in the virginal valkyrie, too. In the past, only dead men have been of any use to the cold-hearted Amazon, but she now becomes a woman. Compassion for Siegmund, growing into tender affection, has sparked a hitherto unknown desire in her, and the prospect of being woken by a man – something that had previously seemed the worst of all punishments – now loses its terrors. But it must, of course, be 'the fearlessly freest of heroes', not just the first passer-by.

Only a man as free as herself will be able to bear her love when it becomes an all-consuming fire. Since meeting Siegmund, she knows that love is synonymous with self-sacrifice. Only the man who is prepared to perish in her fiery ardour is worthy of being reborn in her arms. Only the man who is not afraid of death merits the sacrifice of her immortal being that she is now prepared to offer him.

Symbolized by the blazing fire, the awakening of the woman in Brünnhilde is depicted in several stages. She begins by entreating Wotan to kindle a 'raging fire' around her rock, prompting him to admit his love for the 'laughing delight' of his eye, a passionate avowal that is at the same time a sorrowing lament at the fact that he has no choice but to lose 'you whom I love'. In keeping with his promise, he causes a 'bridal fire' to break out, before taking 'her head in both hands' and kissing her, first on one eye, then on the other. 'So', he explains his actions in the third person, 'he kisses your godhead away!'

The two remained locked in a lengthy embrace in the 1876 world-première production in Bayreuth, while the orchestra, as Camille Saint-Saëns recalled, 'produced such strains that many spectators could not hold back their tears'.[48] Brünnhilde's 'strength gently ebbs away' and, having become a woman, she sinks down on the mossy bank, just as the dying Adelaide had done.

The god, by contrast, is denied this ultimate act of self-abandonment. The moment at which human love between man and woman is woken in him also spells the end of that love. Man alone has been given the freedom to love, and so he has no choice but to abandon the bride to the man 'who is freer than I, the god'. The desire for love that he has woken in Brünnhilde burns for another man. The fire that his kiss has kindled is not one that he himself is allowed to extinguish.

But he can at least use his spear to cause it to blaze up. He strikes its point three times against Brünnhilde's rock, and all at once a 'stream of fire' springs from the ground, soon becoming a 'sea of flames'. It is the god of fire whom he has summoned, and thanks to Loge a cheerfully blazing fire is soon licking around the sleeping Brünnhilde, its 'flickering flames' growing before the mind's eye until they acquire a universal dimension.

On the Bayreuth stage, by contrast, Wagner wanted the magic fire to be no more than 'gently hinted at'. The pyrotechnical displays already favoured by stage directors in his own day struck him as 'gross exaggerations'.[49]

Siegfried

The title of the tetralogy is misleading, as it is not the ring that is central to the work but Siegfried. Whereas the gold serves only as a symbol, the hero around whom not only the drama but the whole of creation revolves appears as a real human being. The fact that he also embodies the solar hero of myth does not detract from his naturalness. Just as the myth assumes human features in the child of nature, so Siegfried acquires a mythic identity by virtue of his super-human actions.

As an art form that does justice to both these aspects, the fairytale seemed the most suitable to Wagner. In the tales of the Brothers Grimm, he had already encountered the fluid interface between ancient mythic lore and the modern children's fairy story. In these vivid and memorable tales he rediscovered archetypal relationships in ludic form. The comic adventures in which their heroes have to prove themselves transmitted in passing the store of knowledge of all the earth's nations.

Siegfried is the tetralogy's scherzo, a work in which Wagner found 'the most carefree, engaging and heart-warming aspects' of the world tragedy. For one last time, history pauses to catch its breath before plunging into the abyss. Unlike *Die Walküre*, which is a drama of ideas, Wagner wanted to allow reflection a brief respite in this 'heroic comedy' of his. Here, he declared, there was 'no need for brooding or for logical thought'. Rather, the audience would experience myth in its 'most popular aspects' and would understand it 'in a playful way, as it were, much as children get to know it through fairytales'.[50]

And Wagner was certainly thinking of fairytales in the case of Siegfried. Indeed, several of the Grimms' tales have contributed to the characterization of a figure who differs substantially from his prototype in the *Nibelungenlied*.[51] In 1851, while working on the first prose sketch, Wagner wrote to tell Uhlig that behind Siegfried lay the 'lad who leaves home to learn fear', but as he later explained to Röckel, this lad would 'never succeed in doing so because, with his healthy natural instincts, he always sees everything exactly as it is'.[52] As a result, he refuses to allow either ghosts or a threatening father figure to prevent him from winning the bride who, to his immense surprise, will then teach him the meaning of fear after all.

But Wagner was also reminded of Till Eulenspiegel while working on *Der junge Siegfried*. The chapbook about the enfant terrible had cheered him up on his depressing journey to Riga in 1837. In the eyes of the Brothers Grimm, the keen-eyed joker and the dragon-killing Siegfried belonged together: they even described the latter as the 'nobler giant Eulenspiegel'. And according to the Grimms, both characters were related to the 'young giant' known to the world of fairytales as Tom Thumb. Tom Thumb's father, too, tries to teach him fear, but in vain, for the tiny figure grows up to become a giant who disposes of everyone in authority either by disarming them with his humour or by kicking them out of his way. For Wagner, there was no difference between the two. 'The man who genuinely lives for his own destiny alone', he told Cosima in 1869, 'has nothing to fear. The common people have perpetuated this prototype of the utterly self-assured human being in the Siegfried legend and in the fairytale of Tom Thumb.'[53]

In Siegfried, the fairytale hero, Wagner encountered this human being 'in the most natural and carefree fullness' of his nature. Freed from the 'historical garb' of tradition, he struck Wagner as the epitome of the 'purely human'. No outward force inhibits Siegfried in his freedom, for he draws his vital strength 'only from the innermost wellspring of his love of life'. And he succeeds in doing so because he remains untouched by the fear that intimidates human beings in the world of laws and contracts.

'Even in the face of death', Wagner wrote in his *Communication to My Friends*, Siegfried does not abandon his fearless nature, which consists in the 'necessary expression of the incessantly bubbling wellspring of inner life'. What Siegfried is, he gives entirely to others. The gravitational pull of egoism, drawing everything into its sway, is contrasted with Siegfried's delight in self-sacrifice, a willingness to give away everything and retain nothing for himself. In this 'fullness of the highest and most immediate strength and the most indubitable amiability', love too develops in him, 'physically alive, swelling every vein and stirring every muscle of the carefree human being so that its very essence finds all-enthralling expression'.[54]

With his love of life and love, Siegfried gained legendary status in *The Wibelungs* before moving centre-stage in the *Ring*. As a solar hero, he smiled down benevolently in the earliest Frankish tradition before assuming new guises in a whole series of idealized human figures. Like him, Jesus of Nazareth and Frederick Barbarossa opposed the powers of darkness in order to help the divine light break through into reality. Like him, they sacrificed themselves to the ancient dragon out of their love of humanity. In this way, the most varied traditions came together in Wagner's imagination in the form of the German national myth whose 'genuine Aryanism' he never ceased to stress.[55]

But the emphasis on the dragon killer who frees Germany from the 'evil gnawing dragon of humanity' obscured Siegfried's origins in fairytale. The lad who left home to learn fear had little in common with the Teutonic Messiah, and the subversive wit of Till Eulenspiegel rebelling against power consorted ill with a sword-wielding hero who represents that power. His crude triumphalism overshadows Tom Thumb's sufferings, while his grim victory over his oppressor obscures the playful light-heartedness of the world child who derives happiness only from bestowing that happiness on others.

Siegfried represents freedom as such, and so no earthly order can claim him for itself. All unheeding, he has shaken off the world of laws and gold, the world of power and dominion, in order to live for love alone. As the possessor of the Nibelung treasure he remains an ordinary hero. Only as the man who is not afraid of Brünnhilde's fire does he become the human being in whom the god of the beginning returns to earth: a smiling, love-drunk god from the radiant dawn of the world.

As Brünnhilde will shortly realize, it is not the Nibelung treasure but Siegfried who is now 'the hoard of the world'.

For all that the fairytale seeks to avoid the need for reflection, this is in fact how it begins. The dwarf sits, helplessly, in his dark cave, brooding to himself. As the darkly pensive music makes plain, he is thinking of the Nibelung world that he has left behind and of the pain that continues to haunt him. His thoughts revolve compulsively within his head, constantly returning to the same point: the hoard and its dazzling embodiment. Only in his burning desire for the ring does the perpetual anguish of his existence grow momentarily brighter and lighter. World dominion alone seems sufficient to still his infinite thirst.

His pause for thought over, he returns to his interminable slave labour. His cave has been converted into a forge, and in a state of mechanical bustle the dwarf fulfils his Nibelung destiny, which he himself feels to be 'shameful'. He hammers and welds away, day in, day out, knowing all too well that he is driven only by 'appalling avarice, accursed greed for the circlet's gold'.[56] The weapons that he forges are intended to slay the giant that guards the hoard in a cave. It is only a short distance to Fafner's lair, and the hero who is to make this journey and kill the giant serpent has already been born. A kindly fate has even arranged for this young and innocent warrior to fall into the dwarf's hands. He is now his foster son, his weak-willed instrument.

But the lad is not allowed to know this. In order that the dragon killer designate may remain clueless, the dwarf wears a mask that conceals his true intentions, playing the loving father, while bringing him up to be no more than a useful idiot. As soon as he has served his purpose, he will be disposed of. In 1849 Wagner had reproached 'existing society' for exercising a 'terrible power' over humanity by intentionally inhibiting our development and purposefully preventing us from 'achieving our destiny, rights and happiness',[57] and there is no doubt that this is true of the Nibelung dwarf. He exploits his victim while merely mimicking the solicitous father. In Wagner's sources the dwarf is called Reigin but the composer changed this to suit his nature and called him Mime instead.

By the same token, the foster father's false and insidious nature is based not on the Old Norse sources but on one of more recent provenance. In the book from which he took his ideas on the mines at Falun, the Wartburg Song Contest and the Mastersingers, Wagner stumbled across the prototype of this Hoffmannesque monster. In *Signor Formica*, one of the *Serapionsbrüder* cycle of tales, E. T. A. Hoffmann tells of a deceitful dwarf who, out of greed, tries to poison the artist Salvator Rosa. In order to steal his paintings, he brews some foul-smelling potions, from which Rosa would have died if he had not hurled the medicine bottles at the head of the perfidious thief. But the dwarf is not the only person to have designs on the artist's life. In a poem that treats his name allegorically, Salvator complains that 'the faithlessly black-hearted band of the Jews' – this 'brood woven from hatred and envy' – would like to have crucified him 'because I'm called Saviour'.

The saviour in *Siegfried* is called Siegfried. He bears within him the light of the beginning, and in his eye there glints the 'glittering serpent' of the Wälsungs. Yet the hero who is to rid nature of the law has been fathered in the face of the law. His parents were sired by the god of the law and so they had to pay for their love with their lives. Their father cheated them out of their lives and love, just as his grandson, Siegfried, is brought up by a loveless foster father who threatens his life in turn.

Like the composer, the young hero grows up in straitened circumstances. He has discovered nothing about his true origins and does not suspect that Mime snatched him from the arms of the dying Sieglinde. He does not even know that he had a mother. He knows only the smithying dwarf who, wearisomely, has taken him on as an apprentice Nibelung, while at the same time impressing on him the extent to which he loves him. But for reasons he cannot explain, Siegfried is unable to return that love.

If he is Mime's son, as the dwarf insists, why does everything in him rebel against the art of smithying that he is supposed to learn? Why does he seize every opportunity to escape from the smoke-filled cave in which he grew up? Why does the creature to whom he is supposed to owe everything weigh on his soul like an incubus? How can he feel such hatred for the dwarf when Mime speaks only of love? 'Love', the dwarf explains to his charge, is the desire that young animals feel 'for their parents' nest: so you, too, pined for me; so you, too, love your Mime – so you *have* to love him'.

Wagner had similarly found himself, all unsuspecting, in a strange 'nest', that of Ludwig Geyer, an actor – in German, 'Mime' – by profession. He had been brought up in the belief that Geyer was his true father. After various futile attempts to teach his foster son a trade, the actor had washed his hands of him and allowed him to run wild. Geyer became a nightmarish figure for Wagner, haunting the whole of his life, yet the composer was obliged to feel grateful to him for 'rescuing' him after the death of his true father.

Mime, too, insists on his foster son's debt of gratitude to him, hammering it into him that he brought him up only out of pity, feeding the little mite out of sheer compassion and tending him like a second self. 'Suffering torment for you alone, for you alone I suffer affliction and wear myself out,' he complains, but 'the only reward for the burdens I've borne is that the quick-tempered boy torments and abhors me.' Needless to say, moral pressure is another of Mime's stratagems to bend the fool to his will. It is no accident that Wagner set Mime's litany of complaints at Siegfried's ingratitude to a melody from *Die erste Walpurgisnacht* by his Jewish rival Mendelssohn, whom he had already dismissed as a maliciously calculating 'goblin'.

If Mime is as false and as cunning as the composer's enemies, the hero emerges as the artist as a young man, loving animals above all else, hating 'schoolmasters' (as he calls the dwarf),[58] and proving incapable of the sort of self-discipline that is needed to study. From the cave of compulsory schooling he escapes into the world of nature, where he educates himself in a state of 'total anarchy'. The young Richard, too, was a wild and undisciplined child abandoned by his family. Even as late as 1849 – the year of revolutions – Wagner was still attributing his misfortune to his 'wildness',[59] a quality that Mime also blames for his charge's intractability. 'For that, you must blame your wildness, which you ought to curb, you wicked boy.'

None of Wagner's characters comes as close to caricature as Mime, even if the composer refused to acknowledge this. 'He is small and bent, somewhat deformed and lame,' he describes him in the stage directions to *Der junge Siegfried*. 'His head is abnormally large, his face a dark ashen colour and wrinkled, his eyes small and piercing, with red rims, his grey beard long and unkempt, his head bald and covered with a red cap.' But, Wagner insisted, 'there must be nothing approaching caricature in all this'. Rather, the character should appear credible and drawn from real life. 'His aspect, when he is quiet, must be merely sinister.' Only at moments of excitement should be appear 'ridiculous'. 'His voice is harsh and husky, but in itself this too should never provoke the listener to laughter.'[60]

In rehearsing his works on stage, Wagner always showed his singers how he wanted their parts interpreted. None of his demonstrations was as masterly as that of the false foster father. According to Glasenapp, he 'truly excelled in the role, bending and twisting, and developing such an outrageous falsetto that even the hardest heart would have melted. At the same time, he was able to pull such a face that you could see the hideous dwarf with his runny eyes standing in front of you, plain to see.' As Glasenapp stressed, Wagner's grotesque impersonation brought out his 'mimetic' gifts.[61] It was above all the dwarf's repulsive characteristics that the composer highlighted and that provoke the most violent antipathy in Siegfried. 'Your invincible loathing of Mime', Wagner demanded of his first Bayreuth Siegfried, 'should be expressed by irritable annoyance and the clearest possible articulation of a lively speech-song!'[62]

One of the reasons for Siegfried's loathing may be sought in Mime's attempts to teach him fear. Like Geyer with his iron doll, Mime leaves no stone unturned in his efforts to instil a sense of fear in his foster son, a fear that would allow an external force to take root inside the person dominated by such an emotion. Just as man, inspired by greed, grasps at the whole, so in the case of fear the whole seems to grasp the individual. Both go together, like law and punishment and like the dwarf Mime and the giant Fafner. Only Siegfried belongs with neither, hence his foster father's desperate attempts to get him onside.

As the hero explains in the prose draft, Mime begins his attempts by telling him horror stories about 'storms, blows raining down, noise and violent overthrow, and you ask me whether I feel fear?'[63] Mime paints a scene of 'one horror after another' waiting for him in the world outside, even claiming that Sieglinde had asked him to teach her son to fear the false and insidious world. Otherwise, he will be oblivious to danger, for 'he whose senses are not newly stirred by fear will blink in the blinding light of the world'. But unlike his creator, in whom fear was so thoroughly instilled that he was never to forget it, Siegfried remains impervious to all Mime's attempts to teach him the meaning of fear. 'I wanted to trap him with fear, but with fear he now entraps me!'[64] With this paradox Mime sums up his failure.

The fearless hero now bursts 'with sudden impetuousness' into the brooding dwarf's cave, and it is immediately clear that their relationship has been turned on its head. Now it is Siegfried's turn to instil fear in the 'so-called smith' by setting a bear on him. But it is not only with the bear that he reduces the dwarf to a state of trembling. A sword strong enough for his pupil is beyond his skill as a smith, and however much Siegfried may threaten him, calling him names and 'seizing him by the neck', it makes no difference. Whatever Mime makes shatters in the 'rascally lad's' hands. The whole art of the Nibelungs ends at the point where human freedom begins.

As Mime is well aware, there is one sword that Siegfried would be unable to break: only the weapon that his father received from Wotan and that was inopportunely snatched away again could withstand his impetuous strength. Although it too comes from Alberich's hoard, it embodied Siegmund's urge for freedom, a desire coterminous with his love of Sieglinde. This sword belongs to Siegfried as his rightful inheritance, yet he knows as little about it as he does about the dead Wälsung. When it shattered on Wotan's spear, Brünnhilde picked up the pieces and gave them to Sieglinde, but they were then taken from her by Mime. Now the dwarf sits brooding on their fragments, unable to piece them together again. And as long as he is unable to do so, Siegfried will be unable to kill the gold-guarding dragon.

At his wits' end, Mime finally reveals Siegfried's true identity and tells him not only about his hapless parents but also about the sword that his father wielded 'when he fell in his final battle'. Until now, Siegfried has expressed only his instinctive loathing of the 'scurvy fellow' in terms that suggest that he has been studying 'Jews in Music', but now he is suddenly filled with a real sense of hope.

Liberated from the nightmare of a mendacious past, he can set out into the world as one of the Grimm Brothers' fairytale heroes, 'never to see you, Mime, again'. With a laugh he rushes out of the hated cave and into the forest, planning to return only long enough to collect the repaired sword from Mime.

But before he can do so, Wotan looks in on Mime, incognito of course. Long-bearded and with a patch over what we assume is his missing eye, he wears the sort of slouch hat associated with the failed revolutionaries of 1849. It is drawn down over his brow, and he is wrapped in a voluminous cloak like a brigand. Resting on his spear, he bids his host a friendly good evening.

'Wanderer' is his name, he explains, though it could just as well be the Flying Dutchman or Ahasuerus. But there is one thing that he no longer is: a god. A radical change has taken place in him, just as it has in his creatures. Ever since the cold-hearted god kissed his daughter and awakened the fires of love in her, he has become disenchanted with his godhood, and life in Valhalla has become a torment. He has tasted human love and freedom, yet he was unable to partake of them fully. In his immortality he yearns in vain for reality as he remains eternally committed to the idea and the law that he himself created.

'Once he has taken his leave of Brünnhilde', Wagner wrote to Röckel in prison, Wotan is 'in truth no more than a departed spirit' who has abandoned all hope of seeing his ideas come true. Freedom can no more be prescribed than love. Either they blaze a trail for themselves unaided or they perish. True to his resolve, Wotan 'must now allow events to take their course, leave things as they are and nowhere interfere in any decisive way; that is why he has now become the "Wanderer": observe him closely! He resembles *us* to a tee; he is the sum total of the intelligentsia of the present day.'[65]

If ever Wagner's comrade in revolutionary arms doubted that behind the tale of the lad who leaves home to learn fear lay the composer's revolutionary philosophy, then the present letter will have served to disabuse him. As representatives of the present-day intelligentsia, Wagner and his incarcerated colleague had realized that nature was being destroyed by the laws that thought had established over it.

Created from love, the world yearned for love but was forced into a state of lovelessness by the laws of property and marriage. It was not evil but the law that had brought sin into the world – Wagner knew this from Paul's Letter to the Romans, which he had taken over into *Jesus of Nazareth*. 'In the law, therefore, was sin,' Jesus proclaimed to his disciples, 'and now I destroy this law and thereby eradicate sin: I free you from sin by giving you love.'[66]

But this love cannot simply be given to people. It has to be reawoken in them. Yet the very consciousness that seeks to replace the world of thought with living reality is itself still part of the world of thought. It thinks in terms of love but cannot communicate that love to others. It wants to make love real, but reality shuts itself off from it. Like the Dutchman, this consciousness yearns for a love that eludes our grasp because it is a product of the crime against love.

This 'consciousness of life, of its existence and activity,' is only an agonizing over this existence and activity,' Hegel wrote in his *Phenomenology of Spirit*, 'for therein it is conscious that its essence is only its opposite, is conscious only of its own nothingness'. Hence Hegel's use of the term 'unhappy consciousness' to describe this sensation. For Wagner, it embodied 'the sum total of the intelligentsia of the present day'.

From a delighted awareness of his omnipotence, Wotan has sunk to the unhappy consciousness that he is incapable of willing what he can do and is not allowed to do what he wants to do. He now becomes involved in a conversation with Mime, who is unable to do what he wants to do and who has therefore brought Siegfried up to do his bidding for him. It is a conversation, therefore, in which the wishes and abilities of both characters are at stake. In keeping with the antithetical nature of their different worlds, the conversation leads to a life-and-death struggle fought not with weapons but in the form of a quiz. In a game of question and answer, they go back over the history of creation and its failure, culminating in Wotan's attempt to avert the inevitable.

The two show that they are a match for each other in terms of their general knowledge. Only on one particular point does the Wanderer demonstrate his superiority. Unlike Mime, who thinks himself omniscient, the disempowered god realises that he no longer knows anything, as the age is now past when fate was knowable. If the dwarf thinks he can rule the world through the power of gold, the former world ruler has realized that power is powerless to prevent the onset of doom. The Wanderer's riddle – who can forge the world-liberating sword? – is one that Mime cannot solve: he has no concept of freedom and love, which alone can bring redemption. But the end of knowledge and the law spell the end of the life of the dwarf who has clung to them for support.

Mime and the Wanderer belong to the same world, a world destroyed by its own lovelessness. The only difference between them is that the Wanderer knows it. Even so, he cannot avert the end and does not even want to. Now that he is aware of the existence of a new world, his only concern is to bring about the end of the old one. The new age must then take care of itself. Siegfried is 'the man of the future, the man we long for and want', Wagner explained in his letter to Röckel, but he 'cannot be made by us'. He has to 'create himself' and, as Wagner significantly added, he must do so 'through our extermination'.

The old god means to help this process along. Only apparently is he a 'subtle intriguer', lending Siegfried his support. If he were really to meddle in the action, Wagner insisted, this would be 'an act of deceit worthy of our political heroes, but not of my jovial god who stands in need of self-annihilation'.[67] In point of fact, he merely offers Siegfried's enemies an opportunity to destroy each other through their own contradictions. Likewise he allows the dwarf who has incautiously wagered his head to become caught in toils of his own making: Mime covets world dominion, but for this he needs the sword that he is unable to forge. And he is unable to do so because only the man who does not know fear can forge it.

But Mime lives in a state of constant fear, a fear that reveals his consciousness of his own nothingness. What he fears is his own end. But this 'fear of the end', Wagner told Röckel, was 'the source of all lovelessness'. If the fearful, loveless dwarf were to find someone who, innocent of fear, were to relieve him of the task, he could gain the hoard, as he wants, but at the same time he would forfeit his life.

The end of fear will also mark the end of the Nibelungs. And so the Wanderer has the covetous dwarf pronounce his own death sentence, thus marking the onset of a general annihilation.

The end of fear has a name, and it is Siegfried. He has barely returned from the forest when Mime attempts to teach him fear. But his extremely vivid evocation of the terrors of the Wolf's Glen and the loss of self seems to arouse only a presentiment of sexual pleasure in Siegfried. Mime is in any case beyond help. If he teaches his foster son fear, the latter is unlikely to prevail against Fafner. But if Siegfried fails to learn fear, then Mime will suffer the consequences. The best solution, he thinks, would be for Siegfried and Fafner to kill one another. But if only the dragon falls by the wayside, he does at least have an answer: as a child of night and death he knows how to brew poisoned potions.

Siegfried is not Siegfried until the moment he appropriates his father's inheritance. Until then he represents merely a counterreaction to Mime's nature. Mime's characteristics inspire disgust, his appearance loathing, his educational methods defiance. Siegfried thus consists only of defence mechanisms and flight reflexes. The education that he has managed to acquire he has picked up in the forest, nature seeming closer to him than his alleged father. Nature reflects his own essence, and all attempts to tame him for the world of the law having failed, he remains in the state that typified nature prior to the Fall.

Love has been driven from nature by the law and cannot be restored on prescription. Thought has alienated nature from itself and cannot reinstate its lost integrity. As the sum total of the present-day intelligentsia, Wotan has come to see this for himself. But Siegfried does not need to understand this because, thanks to the miracle of his birth, he already embodies the integrity of nature. He knows as little about the law as he does about the divisive power of thought. Greed and fear are as alien to him as his foster father's divided self.

For Wagner, Siegfried was 'the most perfect human being conceivable', a man whose consciousness was expressed not through reflection 'but only in the most immediate life and actions'. In this way he fulfils the conditions associated with the new man. Natural freedom must emerge from nature. The love with which everything began must grow from nature itself. Only in this way can creation begin anew.

As yet, however, Siegfried has only the vaguest ideas about love, and even his sense of freedom is nothing to write home about. He has found it, not won it. He has defended it against Mime's encroachments but not made any use of it. Only when he learns about his origins and his inheritance does he become conscious of his identity. The line from which he is descended is twisted, the weapon that his father left for him shattered. He discovers for himself the ruins of the real world of which he had been wholly innocent. This world has robbed him of his family and his inheritance and so, as if by proxy, he destroys its remains. Nature attempts to make a new start with him. He senses that he will find it only in these fragments.

But annihilation leads to a fresh start. Siegfried begins by felling a tree that grew 'wild in the forest', much as the family tree of the Wälsungs had done. In *Der junge Siegfried*, Wagner described it as a pine tree, but in the definitive version of the text it becomes the tree that appears in *Das Rheingold* as the violated World Ash and that is destroyed in *Die Walküre* as Siegmund's Barnstock. In 1863 Wagner told Mathilde Maier that it was 'the mightiest ash' that Siegfried selected. Although 'he is showered by sparks from the angry tree, it is of no avail: the tree must burn and smelt the steel for him'.[68] Thus the old world goes up in flames, but the conflagration proves to be what Wagner called 'a fire cure'. A new passion for life emerges from its shavings and, as Siegfried jubilantly exclaims, melts 'the chaff of the steel'.

The broken sword is now subjected to the same treatment by Siegfried. Instead of listening to Mime, who is all for soldering the pieces together, he prefers a more radical solution, destroying its form and reducing it to fine metal filings which he then smelts in the ash tree's embers. In this way his inheritance is reduced to the matter from which it was once fashioned. During the smelting process he uses a vast pair of bellows that he feeds with his wild singing, as though his very life were at stake.

'One morning, while I was playing and singing the Forging Song in a loud, ringing voice at my open window,' Wagner goes on in his letter to Mathilde Maier, 'my neighbour heard me and asked me what terribly majestic music it was. I told him that Siegfried was feeding the flames with a large pair of blacksmith's bellows that are intended to melt to a paste the steel filings of the sword of victory that he has filed down.'

Siegfried pours the molten steel into a mould and then cools it in a bath of water, appearing in the process to resurrect his own life from the furnace. Wagner depicts this technical process in lifelike detail, suggesting a symbolic recasting of Siegfried's own identity. But this revolutionary rebirth had to be preceded by the end of history. For Siegfried, who lost his parents at the very moment that he found them again, it is a heartbreaking experience. 'What you see here', Wagner explained to his neighbour, who had expressed his surprise at the strangely emotional Forging Song, 'is a terrible kind of artist, that is why his singing sounds almost like a majestic lament.'

What he meant by this 'terrible kind of artist' was not only Siegfried, of course, but himself as well. Just as Siegfried destroys the broken sword, so Wagner had destroyed traditional music. Only when it was broken down into the tiniest elements of expression which then fused together in a volatile sea of sound could he create from it a homogeneous whole that would allow the whole world of ideas to appear in its infinite flow of words. The technique adopted by his false foster father, by contrast, consists in soldering together new swords from old fragments, and as such it resembled the compositional process favoured, according to Wagner, by his enemies Meyerbeer and Mendelssohn.

Once Nothung has been forged and its blade sharpened, Siegfried greets it as though it is a living being. It had lain dead in ruins, but 'I waken you to life again.' Like the first creation, this newborn sword is perfect in every way, and so without further ado, Siegfried uses it to shatter the anvil on which it has just been forged.

The parallel with Wagner's own art is unmistakable. Just as no more weapons need to be made after Nothung, this sword of all swords, so no further works were necessary after Wagner's dramas. The *Ring* had reached the furthest limit of artistic expression, thus bringing to an end the whole history of music.

Siegfried may be the man of the future, but the world around him still clings to the past. Nibelheim's army of night lies in wait, ready to seize control of the world, a rule enshrined in the ring now locked away in a safe-deposit box deep in the giant's cave. With the forging of the magic sword, a new age has dawned, but the old one has yet to notice. Greed and avarice hold nature in their grip of iron, and the shrine at which they worship is Fafner's cave, also known as Neidhöhle. But it is very much the apparent strength of this world of laws, its timelessness and immutability, that will lead to its destruction. The grimace of death with which it terrifies nature will soon become its own death mask.

From the Olympian vantage point that the Wanderer occupies, this is not without its comic aspect. The potential for threat that maintains the world in a state of downtrodden fear turns out to be a sleight of hand no different from Geyer's iron doll outside the Wagners' larder in Dresden. With jovial acuity, the Wanderer, who has already bid farewell to Valhalla's empty splendour, reveals the nullity of the age of money and can only laugh at the gloomy, pounding strains of the Wolf's Glen with which the second act begins. Alberich's blind will to power, which holds him riveted to the spot outside Neidhöhle, strikes the humanized god as just as risible as Fafner's get-up as a dragon, a disguise that Fafner thinks will protect his property.

Both are so preoccupied with themselves that they have long lost sight of the living world and neither takes seriously Wotan's warning that the young hero is already approaching. The Wanderer even goads Alberich by way of a joke, encouraging the dwarf to think – absurdly – that he may still regain his gold with the Wanderer's help. Fafner, meanwhile, looks forward to his breakfast. As the Wanderer is pleased to note, the old world is ripe for destruction. It is not only the gods whose twilight is at hand.

Everything now depends on Siegfried. Once the sword has been forged, Mime is determined not to waste a further moment but sets off with his foster son without delay for the goal of his desire. All night long they tramp through the forest in order to lure the fearsome dragon from the depths of its cave. Mime's final attempt to teach Siegfried fear by means of a detailed description of the terrors in store proves no less futile than his earlier ones. The only thing to fill the hero with horror is Mime himself. It is not mortal danger posed by the dragon's jaws and tail that gets under his skin but the 'loathsome nodding and blinking' that unnerves him. 'When shall I see it no longer? When shall I be free of the fool?'

And now, for the first time in his life, Siegfried finds himself alone. He sits down in the middle of the forest, free from all his old torments in life and still untroubled by those to come, a lonely child of the world with no past and no future. From the rustling of the trees and the light falling down from the canopy of leaves an ancient melody rises. Dancing up and down in mid-air, the forest murmurs well forth like a distant memory of *Der Freischütz*, spinning their web around him and enchanting him with their hypnotizing sounds. Nature returns in its former radiance, whispering a lullaby in which the glittering waves of the Rhine appear to be reflected.

Siegfried now seems to have returned to the womb of nature, and as he does so he first becomes conscious of himself, an awareness that he expresses not with a triumphant 'I' but in the simple sentence: 'How happy I am that he's not my father!' It is not the sword, but this insight that leads to the new beginning not just of his own life but of the world that he has yet to topple. But for this he needs the sword. For his worthless father and the latter's false world of greed and fear have to be destroyed before new life can flourish.

But at this point something unexpected happened: Wagner could not go on. Even before the dragon comes out of its cave and Mime tries to poison the hero, Wagner broke off work on the score. It is as though some subliminal fear held him back from taking the decisive step, with the result that on 27 June 1857 he added a note after Siegfried's words 'How happy I am that he's not my father!': 'When shall we see each other again??'[69] Two weeks earlier there had already been signs of an initial crisis, when 'my desire to continue and complete my Nibelungs' had sunk 'to vanishing point'.[70] The enterprise now ground to a halt with Siegfried's solitary meditation on his father.

Although Wagner went on to finish the orchestral sketch of this second act, the project came to a complete standstill in August 1857, and another seven years were to pass before he overcame his resistance and completed the first two acts in 1865. Another break followed – this time it lasted more than three years – and it was not until 1869 that Wagner was able to start work on the third act. The full score of this final act was completed in February 1871: work on the score of his fairytale scherzo had occupied Wagner for a total of fourteen and a half years.

Of course, there were external factors, too, that forced him to keep interrupting his work on the score, but it remains unclear why Wagner allowed them to get in his way. This, after all, was his life's work, the culmination of his view of the world. When he wrote to Liszt shortly after breaking off work for the first time, he explained that his main reasons for doing so were difficulties with his publishers, problems in realizing the whole of this 'obstinate venture' and his work on a different project. He hoped that this other project – *Tristan und Isolde* – would 'soon' provide him with a 'decent income' when it was translated into Italian and performed in Rio de Janeiro, where he had been invited to stage the new work by the Emperor Dom Pedro II.

But behind the note of cold calculation lay violent emotions, and even the manner in which Wagner informed Liszt of this abrupt hiatus suggests his inner turmoil. 'I have led my young Siegfried into the forest's beautiful solitude,' he wrote. 'There I have left him under the linden tree and taken my leave with heartfelt tears: – he's better off there than anywhere else.' If this suggests that he was merely anxious to spare his hero an unpleasant fate in the world, he speaks elsewhere in the same letter of a positively violent process. He is even uncertain whether he will ever complete the drama. 'This depends on moods over which I have no control. On this occasion, I have had to use force; while feeling in the best of moods, I had to tear Siegfried from my heart and place him under lock and key as though I were burying him alive. . . . It has cost me a hard and bitter battle to reach this point!'[71]

By delaying work on the score, Wagner spared his hero this hard and bitter battle: for in the drama Siegfried has to raise his sword first against the fearsome dragon, then against his foster father Mime and finally against the father of the gods himself. The extermination of his enemies was all part of his plan. But Wagner himself had not yet reached this point. The freedom that he wanted to grant his hero was still denied to the composer himself. The revolution had ended in failure, while his marriage to Minna had survived, in spite of his unsuccessful attempts to break out of it. The power of money and possessions still had him – eternally in need as he was – in its grip of iron. For this reason, too, he was bound to feel like a man buried alive in his exile in Zurich, and whenever he crossed the border to his homeland, he soon found himself back at the point where he had left his hero. If the *Ring* was 'the poem of my life and of all that I am and feel', as he had admitted in 1853, then Wagner the loser could not continue to work on setting to music the fate of his hero in *Siegfried*.

Later Wagner spoke openly about the inner conflicts that were responsible for the creative block that he suffered in 1857. 'You will understand', he admitted to Cosima in 1870, 'that, after writing these sections of the Nibelungs, I felt the need to abandon this terrible element and write *Tristan und Isolde*, which was just a single love scene, as it were.'[72] The following year, while referring again to this 'terrible element' in a work intended as a scherzo, he described an emotion that recalled his childish terror of objects suddenly coming to life. When he began *Siegfried*, he told Ludwig II, 'I finally felt myself overcome by a deep unease: I heard nothing, everything around me remained silent; none of the new sounds came to life; I felt terror at my work as though at some dead-alive being. I threw the rolls of paper aside and told myself I'd taken on something superhuman, not to say inhuman. – And so I conceived *Tristan*.'[73]

But as Wagner explained elsewhere in 1871, *Tristan und Isolde* was merely a continuation of *Siegfried* by other means. On the strength of the same basic conflict in which both heroes become involved, Wagner saw his new work as 'complementing the great Nibelung myth that encapsulates an entire world'.

As Wagner knew very well, all fears derive from our childhood, and so he makes Siegfried become a child again immediately before his decisive encounter with the dragon. Exposed in the wilderness, he longs for his distant parents. Just as he is dreaming of his mother, a 'beautiful bird' appears in the treetops. He has never seen such a creature before. Convinced that he would be able to understand its message if only he could imitate its song, he carves a flute for himself and attempts to mimic the sound, but in vain. His hope of discovering something about his mother from the 'dear little bird' proves futile.

But his instinct has not misled him. In the prose draft, he had exclaimed, 'I think I can hear my mother singing', an interpretation later confirmed by Wagner when he admitted that within the Woodbird lay 'Sieglinde's maternal soul'.[74] In response to Siegfried's appeal to his mother, nature itself replies. At the same time, however, the monster appears. Woken by the sound of the horn that Siegfried begins to play in an attempt to make up for his musical setback, Fafner heaves himself into view 'in the form of an immense, lizardlike serpent' and yawns unattractively. Childish experience had shown that calling for mother invariably brought the enemy onto the scene. The latter calls the hero a 'boastful child' and 'valiant boy', but Siegfried will have none of this and loses little time in showing that he has already outgrown his infancy. Unimpressed by the grown-up's frightening behaviour, which he sees through at once, he plunges Nothung into the dragon's heart.

The giant has scarcely been despatched when Siegfried's ears are opened. 'Until now, the forest murmurs had been a delightful fascination for him,' Wagner explained, 'but now they weave their magic spell.'[75] Siegfried finally understands the voice of nature and, with it, the message that the Woodbird is chirping at him. With his victory over his enemy, his mother's soul tells him, he has won back his lost inheritance. Now that he has broken the hegemony of fear and lovelessness, the splendours of nature lie at his feet. The 'rosy-cheeked hero', who has just been carving a willow flute for himself, now finds world dominion beckoning. Understandable though his mother's jubilation may be, she seems to have forgotten that he does not even know where the world is, let alone what he should do with it as 'ruler of the world'.

The Nibelungs, by contrast, are in no such uncertainty. When Siegfried, acting on the Woodbird's advice, goes off into the cave, Alberich and Mime emerge from its shadow and confront one another. A bitter dispute breaks out between them such as Wagner could have read about in E. T. A. Hoffmann's *Serapionsbrüder*. Here, in *Die Brautwahl*, a Jewish 'Ahasuerus' quarrels with his nephew over a gold file, the two of them roundly cursing each other. In Alberich and Mime's breathless squabble we also find an example of the speech patterns so offensively described by Wagner in 'Jews in Music'.

To a torrent of insults that the Nibelung brothers heap on each other's heads, we witness a veritable explosion of the egoistical world spirit whose end is heralded by Siegfried's appearance. By contrast, these two restless demons, in whom Wagner sought to give graphic expression to the state of corruption into which nature has sunk, interpret it differently. The hero's arrival has finally brought the end of Fafner. It will be child's play, they think, to wrest the treasure from his hands, and the only bone of contention is which of them will ascend the vacant throne of the universe.

Needless to say, things work out differently. When the hero emerges from the cave, he seems a changed man. He has seen the heaped-up treasure. Not radiantly, but pensively, he returns to the light of day. Wagner described this scene at some length in a letter to Ludwig II: 'Siegfried, sunk in thoughtful contemplation of the ring, then re-emerges from the cave onto the high ground in front of it: the Nibelungs notice with horror that he has picked out the ring from the hoard, and they withdraw, each to strive after his own fashion to gain the ring for himself. Siegfried, contemplating the ring and the tarnhelm: "What use you are to me, I do not know." As he emerges, we hear the motif of the ring winding its way eerily through the accompaniment (during the speeches of the two Nibelungs): now it passes, with supreme and ghostly pliancy, into the theme of the Rhinedaughters from the end of *Das Rheingold*.' To 'the accompaniment of a gentle tremolando on the strings', the theme of the radiant gold of the beginning is now heard 'on six horns, as though from some distant natural dream world'. As a whole, Wagner explained to his benefactor, this was 'no scene from family life: the fate of the world hangs on the boy's godlike simplicity and on the uniqueness of a fearless individual!'[76]

Events now follow hard on each other's heels. On a specious pretext, Mime approaches Siegfried, hoping to talk him into drinking his poisoned cordial. Having failed to note the change that has taken place in his foster son, he thinks he can allay his suspicions with his usual babblings. But Siegfried has been warned by the maternal Woodbird and sees through him, divining the true meaning behind his deceitful words. When Mime says, 'Here, drink, you'll find this refreshing', Siegfried hears, 'Drink this and choke to death.' And when Mime, with 'repulsive importunacy', tries to raise the poisoned vessel to his lips, Siegfried lashes out with a reflexive gesture.

'As though in a paroxysm of violent loathing,' to quote the composer's stage direction, Siegfried kills the dwarf with his sword. As early as 1850, Wagner had written in the context of his unsuccessful visit to Paris, that 'there is a force in us that irresistibly repels us from all that is alien and intolerable to our nature: it is – loathing'. This sentence relates to Wagner's break with the Meyerbeerian operatic tradition and occurs in his planned preface to his drama *Siegfried's Tod*.[77]

After despatching his foster father, Siegfried drags his body into the cave containing the Nibelung gold, where, as the hero ironically remarks, 'the wondrous hoard is now yours to command'. With his cruel joke, this scene from family life is finally over. The tale of the lad who left home to learn fear, on the other hand, can now move on, unhindered, to its climax. Now that these false father figures have been disposed of, Siegfried feels an unusual longing. He is free, but something is missing that would make his happiness complete. How often has he looked around in the forest in vain for a 'companion'. Now nature itself offers to speed up his search for him.

At the very moment that Siegfried sees the sun's eye gazing down on him and the forest murmurs begin to cast their spell again, the Woodbird returns, and the maternal song rings out, bright-toned, commending a suitable wife to her lonely son: 'High on a fell she sleeps, fire burns round her hall.' The 'sweet breath' of her voice is enough to reduce the youth to a state of violent agitation. 'Its meaning burns my breast with searing heat! How it thrills my heart with kindling desire!'

If Brünnhilde had been inflamed by her father's kiss, her husband-to-be receives his initiation from his mother's voice. Will he be able to waken the bride, he asks. 'He who wins the bride and awakens Brünnhilde', replies the voice, 'shall never be a coward: only he who knows not fear!' And that man is Siegfried. And how will he find the way? The Woodbird replies by fluttering up and, after hovering teasingly above the boy's head, flies off ahead of him.

Even before Siegfried sees the wall of bridal flames, its fires have already inflamed him. He burns to see Brünnhilde and unite with her, although he does not even know what a woman looks like. It is the same desire that drove the first God to cast his light into his own dark ground.

According to *Opera and Drama*, this is the creative moment at which the poet plunges into the yearning sea of harmony in order to be initiated by love into 'the profound and infinite secrets of feminine nature'.

Like Siegfried, the abdicated god in turn now turns to the depths of nature. It is not love, however, that drives him but uncertainty. Once abused by him in his lust for power, Erda lies in a deathly slumber. His call awakens her, but it is not longing that responds, as it had been at the beginning of the world, only resignation. The two begin a conversation, the time for which has already passed, and they know it. They need nature as their foundation and are now overtaken by the end that the world of the law imposes on natural freedom. It was for this reason that Erda, as the lore of this eternal ground, had withdrawn into the darkness. Forcibly awoken, she can only confirm that there is no longer anything that can be changed.

The Wanderer has consciously sought out the goddess as it is only from her that he could acquire certainty about the future. She is a storehouse of lore about creation, knowledge that has lain in God's ground from the outset. All that can ever happen is enclosed there, and the earth goddess sees in a dream what happens in the world of reality. 'All things, it is said, are known to you', the Wanderer calls out to her, optimistically. He once considered himself all-knowing, but now he seems to rely on hearsay. The former son of light has himself stumbled upon the dark side of the earth.

A sense of 'dark, sublime and awesome dread' overwhelmed Wagner when he entered the world of Act Three of *Siegfried*. Here, he told King Ludwig, 'we come, like the Hellenes at the reeking crevice in Delphi, to the nub of the great world tragedy'. Here everything is 'sublime terror and can be spoken of only in riddles'.[78] Once the sanctity of the beginning has been buried, the world's wisdom forces its way up through the ground in the form of mists and vapours. Nature no longer speaks openly. Where the ground once shone in golden radiance, the oracle now utters only the darkest sayings.

This is not enough for the Wanderer. He wants to know 'how to hold back a rolling wheel'. But as Erda makes plain to him, it was Wotan himself who set this world wheel in motion, and it no longer obeys the laws of fate as spun by the Norns. 'I've grown confused since I was wakened,' Erda groans; 'wild and awry the world revolves.' It circles and revolves around itself, evidently with increasing speed. Is it returning to its original state of chaos? Wotan himself is to blame, she says, as he plunged the goad of contradiction into nature, and it is on this goad of contradiction that the two of them will perish.

In truth, she tells him, he is no god but a dark force that brings annihilation. 'You are not what you say you are!' she throws at him, and with equal justification he says to her, his former partner: 'You are not what you think you are!' The age of the world of the law has passed, but so too has that of natural wisdom. The old gods are moving away from the centre of things and fading into the twilight. 'And so, sleep on,' the Wanderer calls out to the earth goddess before he too steps aside from history, 'close your eyes and, dreaming, behold my end!'

Light and darkness have now been replaced by the antithesis of freedom and lack of freedom. But freedom was not on fate's agenda and so it transcends Erda's wisdom. The Wanderer, by contrast, knows all about it, as this was another of the developments that he had set in train. A boy is waiting to enter upon his inheritance. Siegfried knows nothing of the world and its laws, he lives a life free from greed and from the desire for power, and he has just disposed of those of his enemies who wanted to bend him to their will by dint of fear and cunning. 'Rejoicing in love, while free from greed,' the Wanderer announces, full of a father's pride in his offspring, 'the noble youth is untouched by Alberlich's curse, for fear remains unknown to him.' This hero, he tells the goddess, has already set off to waken Brünnhilde so that, in the Wanderer's cryptic phrase, she may 'work the deed that will redeem the world'.

At this, Erda sinks down in a bluish shimmer of frost, and her cave is plunged into darkness for all time. Outside is night, but grey streaks of light portend the dawn and light up the stage a little. Bizarre rock formations cast their eerie shadows. In one of them lurks the Wanderer's sombre form. When the Woodbird flutters past, it stops in mid-flight before 'disappearing quickly upstage'. Siegfried's spiritual guide flees from the lord of the ravens. Here Wotan awaits the hero just as the devil Samiel had waited for Wilhelm the bridegroom in Apel's *Der Freischütz*.

Wotan's metamorphosis is not yet complete. In the Wolf's Glen atmosphere outside Erda's vault he casts aside the itinerant Wanderer's mask and reveals himself in one final disguise, becoming the solar hero's dark enemy, a foe resolved to take up the struggle one last time. As with Siegmund, it does not trouble him at all that, having initiated human freedom, he has now become its destroyer.

In spite of this, Wagner felt a certain sympathy for Wotan. 'See how he confronts Siegfried in the third act,' he wrote to Röckel. 'Faced with the prospect of his own annihilation, he finally becomes so instinctively human that – in spite of his supreme resolve – his ancient pride is once more stirred, provoked moreover (mark this well!) by his jealousy of Brünnhilde; for this has become his most vulnerable spot.' In a 'sudden burst of passion', Wagner goes on in his letter to Röckel, 'he even aspires to victory, a victory which – as he says – can only make him more wretched than ever'.[79] Through his love of his daughter, Wotan has become a human being who seems to suffer more from his separation from her than from the certainty of his downfall. It is not the end of his omnipotence that angers the god but the irreversible loss of his love. Exactly the same had happened to his night-black counter-image, Alberich.

There follows the all-decisive encounter between father and son. The old man had been prepared to abdicate power, but not love. But love has been at stake from the very beginning. It was out of lovelessness that Wotan subjected nature to his will, out of jealousy that he now wants to stop the rolling wheel of history. Consumed by love, Siegfried approaches the flame-girt rock on which his bride awaits him, and no one will be allowed to prevent him from taking possession of this citadel of the first king, together with the woman who lies asleep there and, with her, dominion over the world.

No one, that is, except Wotan. As the archetypal enemy who keeps his son from his lover, he represents a conflation of Samiel the prince of darkness, the demonic Torbern from *Die Bergwerke zu Falun* and the sinister old man from the Grimms' tale of the lad who left home to learn fear. All of them have only one goal: to destroy the lad's urge for freedom and hence to stamp out the fires of love that represent such a danger to them.

Like the fairytale hero, Siegfried makes short work of it. When the stranger, to his annoyance, addresses him as 'boy', he quickly loses his temper. 'As long as I've lived, an old man has always stood in my way', he tells the Wanderer – and it is almost as though Wagner were speaking through him. When he notices that Wotan has only one eye, he offers to knock out the other one for him, proving wholly unimpressed by the old man's irritable response that he should not rouse his 'wrath' as 'it could ruin both you and me'. Siegfried refuses to be told what to do and especially to be told what *not* to do. Least of all will he be deterred from his aim of waking the 'sleeping woman'.

Wotan holds out his spear to bar the 'foolish child's' way, adding by way of a threat that Nothung has already been shattered by it before. Siegfried exults: 'What a glorious chance for vengeance is this!' And without further ado he strikes the spear and breaks it. A 'terrible clap of thunder' suggests that a god of thunder and lightning has been given his marching orders. Had he not disappeared from the face of the earth like Rumpelstiltskin, there is no doubt that Siegfried would have dealt with him as he has dealt with everyone else who has tried to bar his way.

After its long and unhappy digression into human history, nature has finally returned to the point from which it started out. In the heroic figure of Siegfried, it has rediscovered itself, no longer sicklied o'er by the pale cast of thought or by the rigours of the law, but consumed by the desire to recognize itself in the other. Having triumphed over the dragon of night and various demons, the solar hero now stands at the high point of his existence, radiant with his love of life and in search of a being in which his light can be reflected. 'The whole world', Wagner said of the third act of *Siegfried*, 'exists just to ensure that two such beings may gaze at each other!'[80]

If the first creation had been conjured up musically in *Das Rheingold* and acted out on a human level in *Die Walküre*, it is raised in *Siegfried* to the level of a universal occurrence. Just as Schelling's God approaches the ground of nature and Wagner's poet plunges into the ocean of planetary harmonies, so Siegfried draws closer to the unknown Other that has been promised to him as a 'sleeping woman'. He feels his love with every fibre of his being, but he has no idea at whom it is directed. If true understanding is possible 'only through love', as Wagner told Röckel, and if love exists 'only in the union of man and woman', then Siegfried is on the road to absolute knowledge. But this knowledge will become a 'complete reality' only 'when the "I" is subsumed by the "you"'.[81]

Siegfried's initiation into supreme knowledge resembles God's rapprochement with nature. Just as nature existed only as a possibility within the depths of existence, so Brünnhilde has been sunk in the deep sleep of non-existence. She has been reduced to a state of rigor mortis like Persephone, and like Sleeping Beauty she lies behind an impenetrable protective wall. Love alone can break through the wall of death, a wall which to the man who fearlessly overcomes it reveals itself as the consuming fire of pleasure.

And herein lies the essence of creation, namely, that the lover stakes his very existence upon it and risks leaping into the unknown. In his letter to Röckel, Wagner called this 'the most deeply tragic situation of the present', which he claimed to have depicted in *Lohengrin*: 'the desire to descend from the most spiritual heights and plunge into the depths of love, the yearning to be grasped by feeling'. But the tragedy lay in the fact that, as the revolution had shown, the descent into real life led inevitably to disaster. The spirit did not recognize itself in nature, just as nature shut itself off from the spirit.

But with Siegfried there begins a new creation. Inflamed by his love for his unknown bride, he passes through Wotan's old magic fire as though it were his very own element. To the magic shimmering of the violins, with their distant echo of Meyerbeer's Cemetery of Saint Rosalie, the hero approaches the creature that he already bears within him and that he now discovers in real life.

No sooner has he removed the sleeping figure's helmet than he sees the radiant sun reflected as a 'laughing likeness' in the 'shining celestial lake' of its eyes.

But on lifting up the breastplate he discovers that this creature is not a man. The discovery makes him uneasy. The fearless hero now has to deal with a feeling of anxiety. Everything starts to reel and spin, causing him to call out in despair to his mother who, after all, had sent him the well-informed Woodbird.

Once again nature comes to his rescue. This calling into question of his whole existence not only teaches him fear, it also provides the basis for his loving surrender. The 'burning enchantment' that robs him of his senses triggers the 'searing desire' that impels him towards the 'maid'. True love, wrote Wagner, is revealed only through total self-surrender. At risk of 'perishing and dying', Siegfried places his lips on Brünnhilde's 'burgeoning mouth' and sinks, 'as though dying', on her sleeping form. The 'kiss of love', Wagner explained this scene to Cosima, 'is the first intimation of death, the cessation of individuality, that is why a person is so terrified of it'.[82] Thus the solar hero disappears into the night of death in order to rise again at once in all his glory. For the eye of love shines on him through the darkness.

The dawn of the world now breaks in the music, as the light that falls into the depths is answered by a radiant glow from the abyss. This mystic and momentary glance trembles in the sound of the harps in which Wagner heard the 'musical equivalent of light'.[83] Brünnhilde awakes from her deathlike slumber, her first words apostrophizing what had woken the whole of nature at the time of the first creation: 'Hail to you, sun! Hail to you, light! Hail to you, light-bringing day!'

It is Siegfried who has kindled this light. Enraptured, he too bursts into cries of jubilation, praising his mother and the earth but above all Brünnhilde's eye, which 'laughs on me now in my bliss'. This frenzy of recognition, which includes a sense of jubilation at the characters' own origins, seemed to Wagner to be an archetypal expression of religious feeling: Siegfried's wooing of Brünnhilde, including his outburst 'Hail to you, mother!', was an example of 'religion, when a person forgets himself and transfers his happiness to the whole universe'.[84]

And so, once more, the gold in the depths is woken by the sun's rays, but this time no Alberich appears to rob the world of its treasure. Like Siegmund and Sieglinde, the two lovers not only recognize themselves in each other, they see themselves as the other. 'Your own self am I if you but love me in my bliss', Brünnhilde sings. Siegfried responds by giving her to understand that union should take place not just in their heads. In this way their duet, which repeats the first dialogue between God and nature, moves inexorably towards the problematical moment when the ground, fearing the loss of its self, had shut itself off from the light.

The closer Siegfried gets to taking possession of her, the more the bride recoils, and when he asks her to extinguish the terrible fire that she has kindled within him, she thrusts him aside. Virgin that she is, she even speaks of her shame at giving herself to him. 'He who woke me has wounded me, too!' she complains. But the young god sees in her only the natural being in whom he has recognized himself and who, as his property, has no choice but to open herself up to him. On seeing her drawing away, he entreats her a second time: 'Awaken, and be a woman for me!' The astonishment of the creator at nature as it acquires an independent form as matter and confronts him as a stranger seems to overcome Siegfried, too.

At the same time, Brünnhilde senses the nub of this egoism which, like gravity, shuts itself off from the light. It is the fear felt by Chaos that she now experiences in turn. 'Grieving darkness clouds my gaze; my eye grows dim, its light dies out: night enfolds me; from mist and dread a confusion of fear now writhes in its rage!' But Siegfried refuses to give up and explains to her that, with the fetters that he has loosed, her 'gloomy dread' will fade: 'Rise from the darkness and see – bright as the sun shines the day!'

The drama of the world's origins, fought out in the battle between light and darkness, now comes to a temporary rest, for the all-wise Brünnhilde recalls that it is by no means as a stranger that Siegfried now approaches her: he has been destined for her from the outset. When she launches into her solemn reflection 'Eternal was I, eternal am I', she is only apparently contradicting the fact that she was conceived by Wotan and Erda. She was not eternal as a valkyrie but is so as the solar hero's bride, belonging to him as a sister to her brother, as darkness to the light and as nature to God. With Siegfried's arrival, creation is complete. 'O Siegfried! Glorious hero!' she exclaims in mystic ecstasy. 'Hoard of the world! Life of the earth!'

Even without possessing her, she suggests, he may recognize his perfection in her as in the clear mirror of a stream. 'Trouble me not: ever bright in your bliss you will smile a smile that passes from me to you.' But Siegfried is not one of the contemplative gods. He wants to plunge into the waters that seethe all around him like some 'glorious floodtide', filling his senses with 'scorching passion'. He feels a raging desire to cool his inner fire in its waves, so he embraces the aloof valkyrie, calling her his 'sweetest delight' and pressing her body to his until they stand holding each other, 'eye to eye, and mouth on mouth'.

This miracle of the darkness becoming light is followed by a second miracle of creation when the lightning sets off a fire in the depths. An emotion once triggered by Wotan's kiss now bursts tempestuously forth. 'Godly composure rages in billows,' groans Brünnhilde; 'the chastest light flares up with passion.'

The virginal world bursts into flames, an annihilating fire of the kind that had previously burned round her rock. Her gaze begins to consume him, but he is not blinded by it. Her arm squeezes him, but he does not feel it. Even when her blood streams in torrents towards him and its furious fire envelops him, he shows no sign of fear.

'Do you not fear the wildly raging woman?' she shouts at Siegfried, and he laughs in her face with a defiantly triumphant 'Ha!' As the result of her transformation into a fire-breathing dragon (a change signalled by the appearance of the Dragon motif in the orchestra), he loses the final vestige of fear that was still holding him back. A duel has been sparked between them, a duel from which he has already emerged victorious on a previous occasion. The bizarre struggle that presumably awaits him can no longer inspire him with fear.

Brünnhilde understands this and grows less tense. To the sound of their 'supreme jubilation in love', the light can finally penetrate the dark ground. The act of love that removes the distinction between man and woman replicates the act of creation in which God was merged with his ground. Through the union of Siegfried and Brünnhilde, nature is finally redeemed.

The twilight of lovelessness yields to love's radiant sun. The sufferings of nature in a world of laws are over. The gods who had been caught up in the maelstrom of general decline can go to their doom in peace. 'Light-bringing love, laughing death!' exults the couple in whom the first creation becomes conscious of itself. The new era of freedom dawns while the old world ends up on the Golgotha of the absolute spirit.

'Be gone, Valhalla's light-bringing world!' exclaims Brünnhilde in the frenzy of her love. 'Rend, you Norns, the rope of runes! Dusk of the gods, let your darkness arise! Night of destruction, let your mists roll in!' Fate is to take her at her word.

Twilight of the Gods

It was not until 1852, when the poem was almost finished, that Wagner hit on the title for his four-part drama on 'the beginning and end of the world'. After toying with Der Reif ('The Circlet') and Das Gold des Nibelungen ('The Nibelung's Gold'), he settled on Der Ring des Nibelungen ('The Nibelung's Ring'), yet however striking this title may be, it does not reflect his real aim. Just as the ring serves merely as the symbol of a form of world rule that is rendered redundant by the appearance of the solar hero, so the Nibelung

Alberich, who became the titular hero only by an indirect route, functions as a catalyst rather than playing a formative part in the action. It was never his intention that his hatred should pave the way for redemptive love. Rather, he provides the pitch-black background against which the hero's effulgent trail of light stands out.

The love that Alberich and Wotan betrayed returns to the world with Siegfried. It is for this reason that the nub of the drama, to which Wagner belatedly prefaced the other three parts of the cycle, was devoted from the outset to the story of Siegfried. This central part of the work was ultimately given the not entirely appropriate title of *Götterdämmerung* when it was incorporated into the *Ring*, whereas it had originally been called *Siegfried's Tod* ('Siegfried's Death'). A heroic drama, it was written in 1848 – the year of revolutions – and owes its existence to the same spirit of world redemption as the following year's plan for a drama on the life of Jesus of Nazareth.

Immediately before starting work on *Siegfried's Tod*, Wagner had reconstructed the whole of the Nibelung myth. 'Die Nibelungensage (Mythus)' – 'The Nibelung Legend (Myth)'[85] – constitutes the first sketch for the later libretto, and in it the drama of Siegfried's death takes up almost two thirds of the epic as a whole. Not until three years later did Wagner decide on a four-part structure, when he announced to Theodor Uhlig that he had 'big ideas for Siegfried'.[86]

Even in Wagner's most explicit statement on the *Ring*, which he sent to his erstwhile revolutionary colleague August Röckel in 1854, it was not the ring – which 'really poisons love' – that was central to his account but Siegfried and Brünnhilde as a couple. 'Love in its fullest reality', he declared here, is possible 'only as man and woman'. The new man would come into being, metaphysically and biologically, only through their union. But genuine union between opposites can occur only when both parties are prepared to give themselves utterly and, as it were, to perish in the other. As a solar hero, Siegfried illustrates to perfection this ability to squander one's life completely and disappear in a riot of blazing colours. But for love to arise, an equally willing partner is needed. 'Not even Siegfried alone (man alone) is the complete "human being"', Wagner told Röckel: 'he is merely the half, only with Brünnhilde does he become the redeemer; one man alone cannot do everything; many are needed, and a suffering, self-immolating woman finally becomes the true, conscious redeemer'.[87] The *Ring*, which had begun with the failure of creation, only to discover its salvation in the essence of human freedom, culminates in the birth of this new human being through love. The godly union of opposites, which had proved unsuccessful in the history of the world, is now achieved through the loving union of two human beings. The ring that gods and Nibelungs had pursued like men possessed has done its duty.

Only against this historical background can we make sense of what happens in the final part of the *Ring*, with its culminating twilight of the gods. Siegfried and Brünnhilde have merged to create the new man in whom man and woman, consciousness and nature, god and ground are reconciled through the bond of love. Although this leads to an awareness of the whole and although such awareness had flared up between the light and the radiant gold at the time of the first creation and in the eyes of infatuated lovers at the time of human history, it has remained profoundly unknowing in its ecstatic self-referentiality.

Neither Brünnhilde nor Siegfried is familiar with the history of the alienated world to which they are to bring redemption. Like her mother Erda, the valkyrie knows only about fate as enshrined in nature, with the result that day-to-day politics pass her by. As the divine spark of freedom, Siegfried is so bound up with his own wild nature, which he blindly trusts, that he has never been placed in the embarrassing position of analyzing and reflecting on his sense impressions. As a child of the forest who has had to spend his life defending his skin, he has remained unfamiliar with the finer points of human coexistence. But as a dim-witted human being – which, in spite of his amiability, is ultimately what he is – he is not much use at redeeming the world. The couple that has just scaled the world's highest peak together could hardly be less suited to its depths.

Even if the title *Götterdämmerung* suggests otherwise, this final part of the *Ring* is concerned solely with politics. But in order to avoid too sudden a slide into current affairs, Wagner decided at an early stage to preface his poem with a mythological prologue in which three Norns struggle to explain destiny and reality, fate and politics. Writing at this time in *Opera and Drama*, Wagner had pondered on this antithesis, over which bloody battles are fought in the drama. 'Politics', he notes here, 'are the secret of our history and of the conditions that have arisen from them. Napoleon said as much. He told Goethe that the role of fate in the ancient world has been taken by politics since the days of the Roman Empire.'[88]

The remark by Napoleon to which Wagner is alluding here dates from the time of the Congress of Erfurt in 1808, although the Corsican general was referring not to the fate of the world but to the sort of French plays that dealt with fate and that were popular at this period. 'What do people nowadays want with fate? Politics is fate.' It was Hegel who, in his *Philosophy of History*, turned Napoleon's comment on the theatre of his day into a sententious assessment of world history when he claimed that the Corsican leader had said that 'fate has been replaced by politics'. Wagner took over not only this interpretation but also Hegel's reading of it, with politics as 'the irresisitble force of circumstances to which the individual has to yield. Such a force is the Roman world.'

For Hegel, Rome represented the moment in world history when men's only concern was power and world rule. All 'sense of vitality' was then stifled and the world's 'heart' was literally 'broken' as the individual was prevented from freely developing and was sacrificed to the state. Instead of personal freedom, there was only the master–slave relationship, while people were interested solely in property, which was safeguarded by means of laws, contracts and oaths. Even love was treated 'in the manner of a material relationship'. 'The wife was part of the husband's property', while marriage assumed the sort of form 'that might have been adopted on the occasion of any other purchase'. Into this world of utter heartlessness, a world entirely 'sunk in grief', stepped the Redeemer Jesus of Nazareth, as a result of whose death 'the reconciliation of the world' was enacted in human consciousness. The 'suffering' of the world, Hegel argued, 'is henceforth recognized as an instrument necessary for producing the unity of man with God'.

Wagner, as we know, had studied Hegel's *Philosophy of History*, and there is no doubt that it left extensive traces on *Siegfried's Tod*. For Wagner, Hegel's Rome lay on the banks of the Rhine. Jesus gave way to Siegfried. And the fate of ancient Greek memory was now proclaimed by the Norns. Wagner's goddesses of fate have draped themselves in Hellenic garments and taken up their positions on the Valkyrie Rock in order to predict the heroic couple's future. But their efforts get no further than a historical excursus. They foretell the end of Wotan and his gods but fail to realize that this also spells the end of all predictability. They themselves, as the mouthpieces of fate, are now past history, but they have failed to notice this. Only when their rope breaks do they realize that their wisdom is at an end. Fate is replaced by politics.

Wagner suffered another of his writer's blocks just before starting work on this scene, too, a scene that looks forward to more than just the destruction of the patriarchal world. 'I stood before this scene in a state of veritable terror, and for a long time I did not think that I would be able to bring myself to make a start on it. . . . But there was no alternative, and in the end I too wove away at the rope in terror and fear.'[89] In the midst of this terror of primeval times, Wagner was again reminded of his own distant past, including the Wolf's Glen scene: 'It sounds like the fluttering of night birds,' he told Cosima while working on the score; 'here in the Norns' scene I can see the tall fir tree near the rock and hear the nocturnal rustling.'[90] In the wind that heralds the storm and in the beating of the wings of the ravens that serve their master as messengers of death, we hear a disaster looming that is not in the book of destiny. The terror that now walks abroad issues from the irresistible force of circumstances that Wagner also called 'politics'.

Before politics can raise its head, Wagner added a further prologue, this too embedded in myth. Following their night of love in the world of nature, Siegfried and Brünnhilde appear in the very place that has just been vacated by the Norns. The morning light drives away the last remaining shadows of the Wolf's Glen, and the stage is set for the world's redemption.

Yet this represents not the solution, but the problem: although the lovers have created the new God-man through their union, they do not understand what this means. Their self-awareness has experienced the self in the union of 'I' and 'you' but does not know the history that has led to this point. Yet they need to experience this history before they can reconcile it within themselves. And experience always means experience of the other – that is, the splitting and tearing apart of the self. History that is experienced is the history of suffering. It was not his knowledge that made Jesus the Son of God but his passion.

Brünnhilde's very first words express this transition from empty self-awareness to experience: 'To new adventures, beloved hero, what would my love be worth if I did not let you go forth?' Relying on her knowledge, Siegfried should prove himself in the real world and conquer his empire. But she does not know that her godlike primordial wisdom, into which she seeks to ordain the hero, has lost its validity following the Norns' supersession.

Her bridegroom is entirely fixated on material reality and has not understood a word of what she says. She in turn takes as her dowry the Nibelung's ring, which she treats as a glittering token of Siegfried's love. Neither of them realizes that it embodies the curse on love and hence the history of creation's suffering. Inspired by love, they fail to see the truth and talk at cross-purposes. To shouts of 'Hail', they conjure up their oneness, yet even before Siegfried has high-spiritedly bade farewell to his lover, they are already separate entities.

Yet this separation signifies the onset of experience. The lovers have rediscovered the origins of creation in their ecstasy, and the lightning flash of divinity from the beginning of time has returned in them. They have merged as a knowing entity. But just as God was alienated from himself through the emergence of nature, so Siegfried and Brünnhilde move apart. And just as the law and nature had been antithetical opposites in the history of the world, so the lovers will be enemies when they next meet.

There is, however, a decisive difference between the first occasion when creation was forced asunder and the alienation felt by these human lovers. God's infinite anguish consisted in the fact that he and creation confronted each other as irreconcilable opposites. Although God's sorrow was reflected in the infinite suffering of human history, neither recognized itself in the other. This breach affected the whole of existence. Nor was there any cure for it.

With the appearance of Siegfried and Brünnhilde, this breach affects human beings, too. The suffering felt by the world at being cut off from its loving origins is no outward experience for them, but an inner one. The two aspects, facing each other as enemies, are part of a single being formed by their love. The suffering that was experienced in history and that was felt to come from outside and hence to be random now comes from within and appears, therefore, to be necessary. This is precisely what Hegel had said about Jesus in his *Philosophy of History*: 'In this Idea of God, then, is to be found also the Reconciliation that heals the pain and inward suffering of man. For Suffering itself is henceforth recognized as an instrument necessary for producing the unity of man with God.'

Without this philosophical and theological background, it is impossible to make sense of the terrible events that follow on from Siegfried's departure from Brünnhilde. At a superficial level, the child of nature allows himself to become caught up in a political intrigue whose first victim, unknown to him, is his lover. If both had been separate individuals, the incident would have been no different from any other political affair whereby even the most impassioned liaison can turn to betrayal as soon as power and possessions are involved. But they had become one through love, and so they experience for themselves this breakdown into hostile forces. Just as God's absolute knowledge is at odds with a history of nature and of the world that develops on an unwitting level, so Brünnhilde, all-wise but powerless, finds herself at the mercy of the unknowing Siegfried, who merely obeys his own powerful nature. Siegfried was not really a tragic figure, Wagner declared, 'because he is never conscious of his situation, there is a veil over him'.[91] Everything about him is 'unconscious, just driven on'.[92] All unsuspecting, he is guilty of betraying Brünnhilde, thus repeating nature's original sin against God. All that he does is natural, but in history nature itself becomes unnnatural.

Thus Siegfried learns for himself the tragedy of humanity, a humanity previously alien to him. He endures this tragedy to the bitter end, whereas the experience achieves conscious expression only in Brünnhilde. Precisely because, having been one with her, he brings the suffering of history into her life, he acquires in her the self-knowledge that he himself had lacked. At the same time, his passion makes her conscious of all that is involved in this experience of suffering. Everything that has happened, from the opening in the

Rhine to the ending on the burning funeral pyre, has happened 'in order that a woman may become wise'. Only in this way, Wagner explained to Cosima, could 'the world be destroyed and redeemed by Brünnhilde'.[93]

But with this reconciliation of history comes Wotan's release. As the god of laws and contracts, he had subjected the world to his loveless rule, but his godly guilt is 'expunged' by Siegfried, the free human being who 'is capable of bringing down all guilt on himself and atoning for it'.[94] Although this eschatological aspect of the drama does not emerge until the end of the work, it ultimately overshadows not only the Nibelung's titular ring but also the magic helmet, the enchanted sword and Hagen's fatal potion, reducing them to mere fairytale symbols.

The fatal intrigue that has been hatched even before Siegfried arrives on the Rhine has a history. The Burgundian tribe of the Gibichungs, at whose heart this intrigue is fomented, resides on the Rhine 'in splendour' and is now considering ways of ensuring its future. Jacob Grimm – Wagner's Virgilian guide through the circles of myth – traced this family's origins back to Wotan or at least to a related god, allowing the Gibichungs to lay certain claims to world rule. Although this close relationship between the Gibichungs and the gods of Valhalla is not explicitly addressed in the *Ring*, Wagner alludes to it in his set designs: behind the Gibichung stronghold, altars to Wotan, Fricka and Donner have been raised.

As a result, Wotan's 'chosen race' of the Wälsungs is in a strained relationship with that of the Gibichungs: thanks to their common ancestry, they are related but at the same time they are competing for power. When the Wälsung Siegfried, riding out in search of adventure, turns up on the doorstep of his Rhenish relatives, an ambivalent welcome is only to be expected. 'Through Siegfried', Grimm wrote forebodingly in his *Deutsche Mythologie*, 'the Franconian Welisungs [*sic*] are linked to the Burgundian Gibichungs, and so both are called Nibelungs.'

It is very much this link that is now at stake and that Hagen's intrigue sets out to encompass. The Gibichung court cultivates the habits that Hegel, in his *Philosophy of History*, ascribed to the Roman world, and so the plot inevitably centres on power and possessions – which in the case of the family's plans for its future prosperity are bound to be concentrated on the possession of women. Where marriage has become a political concern, love stands no chance. Fully occupied in redrawing the boundaries of their empire, neither the incumbent tribal chieftain nor his sister has looked round for a suitable partner. Gunther and Gutrune think themselves self-sufficient.

Politically speaking, this is highly imprudent. An adviser offers to help them, a man who, as the half-brother of the ruling couple, credibly represents their dynastic interests. The result, as Wagner jokingly described it, is a 'family council'.[95] As the éminence grise, Hagen draws the others' attention to the evident problem of the succession and offers his immediate help. He has already found ideal partners for his half-brother and half-sister. Both have excellent references, and as love is not involved, his suggestion is promptly accepted, sight unseen.

The proposed partners are Siegfried and Brünnhilde, whose recent liaison has yet to become public knowledge. But what is truly inspired about Hagen's suggestion is that, like Wotan, he can play his two main enemies off against one another. The Gibichungs do not even have to worry about obtaining their future spouses: Siegfried will be entrusted with the task of bringing back Brünnhilde, whose wall of fire needs breaching, with the hand of Gutrune as his reward.

A specialist as a marriage broker, Hagen is himself the product of an extramarital affair. His mother, the queen of the Gibichungs, had been rendered compliant by the Nibelung prince with the help of a gold gift that she found irresistible. Needless to say, outsiders have no idea about the ambitious plans that Alberich has for his natural son: Hagen is to win back the ring of world dominion for him. It is currently on Brünnhilde's finger, waiting to be collected. But only her bridegroom, from whom she received it, is able to remove it. A cunning intriguer like Hagen will have no difficulty in persuading him to undertake such an act of madness.

Hagen is driven not only by Alberich's desire for power but also by his own unquestioning faith in the world of laws and contracts on which the Gibichungs' rule is based. Mingled in his veins with the black blood of the Nibelungs is the blood of the god who created these laws. As Grimhild's son, Hagen can point to his divine descent, a descent suggested in the mythological tradition by the fact that he has only one eye and by his alternative name as Hagedorn, a name used by Wotan himself.

As the son of Alberich, he strives to regain the ring, but as a son of Wotan he must also be anxious to dispose of its owner. Siegfried is not only his rival for world power, he has also humiliated the lord of the ravens and abrogated his laws. Like all good intrigues, this one, too, is intended to produce a twofold benefit: without lifting a finger, Hagen will have seized control of the world and at the same time taken revenge for the god from whom it had been wrested – and everything strictly within the framework of the law.

Siegfried duly puts in to land on the bank of the Rhine and is instantly drawn into the intrigue by which he is to bring about his own downfall. The young lad from the forest cave has no means of resisting it. He is delighted to be accepted as brother of the Gibichung ruler and takes a deep draught from the drinking horn offered to him by the lady of the house. He cannot, of course, know that for his parents this same harmlessly hospitable gesture had had unforeseeable consequences. Scarcely has he looked into the vessel, then into Gutrune's eyes, when his fate is sealed, just as it had been for Siegmund.

This is the sort of potion which, to quote Goethe's *Faust*, causes the man who drinks it to see Helen in every woman. Hagen, who proffers it, has already claimed two properties for it: it makes the man who drinks it both forget the woman he loves and at the same time fall in love with the person who serves it to him. Tannhäuser had had a similar experience, forgetting Venus as soon as he was introduced to Elisabeth. Although we are dealing in both instances with the divine gift of love for which the whole of nature longs, in Hagen's case it turns out to be a gift of the devil.

This is a love that destroys love. Instead of leading to the union of man and woman in which creation finds redemption, it turns back into the egoism from which it sprang. Far from leading to the new man, this love results in an unquenchable desire for love for which there is no cure in nature. All who are robbed of love's unity, whether they be the itinerant Ahasuerus, the Wanderer or the mortally wounded Tristan, will be drawn into a desperate search for it. And Siegfried, the hoard of the world, has just been robbed of it.

With Gutrune locked in his heart and Brünnhilde put from his mind, he allows himself to be recruited for an undertaking that demands total self-denial. By donning the magic helmet, whose properties Hagen explains to him, he will slip into Gunther's shape and bring Brünnhilde down from her mountain summit. The awful irony consists in the fact that he willingly takes part in an intrigue that robs him of his will. This loss of self that results from a change of identity and that he cheerfully accepts blinds him to the true loss of self that he has suffered by quaffing from Gutrune's drinking horn.

When in keeping with his nature he falls head over heels in love, he has already become that interchangeable sexual being, 'man', who is to rape his own bride. Thus Siegfried is lost in history, just as nature had been, unsuspectingly and self-sacrificingly bringing about his own downfall. The hero who is meant to become the new man repeats his forerunner's bitter fate and, like his brother Jesus of Nazareth, shoulders his cross – in his case, unwittingly.

The story of Siegfried's Passion begins with the sacred oaths that seal the bond between Wälsungs and Gibichungs. As blood-brothers, he and Gunther sail off on their predatory wooing expedition, while Hagen remains behind to keep watch over the hall. With his spear, enshrining the law, in his hand, he stares mutely ahead of him.

For a moment history holds its breath. Sinister sounds rise up from the depths. As Cosima noted, it is as though 'the strings of the instruments are spun from ravens' feathers'.[96] To a demonic tritone in the tubas and double basses, 'annihilatory syncopations' pound away,[97] while ghostly sighs fill the air. A miasma seems to lie on the world, and even the sound of the instruments acquires a bilious hue. Wagner called it his 'concert for toads, crows and ravens'.[98] It is as though he has once more allowed the frightening world of the Wolf's Glen to gain entry to the piece.

Hagen does not waste his words. If creation was God's word, evil answers with silence. And evil does not act, but allows others to act for it. While the hero thinks he is undertaking an adventure for his newfound friend, he is in fact bringing home his own bride as booty for him, whereas for the patiently waiting Hagen he is bringing the ring. 'Though you think him lowly,' he sums up the situation, 'you'll serve him yet – the Nibelung's son.' Evil has not committed evil but has merely offered human beings the chance to do wrong and to become caught in their own trap. In this way he helps dark nature finally to come into its own. The hour of Hagen's triumph seems to be at hand, and in the flickering, wailing sounds of this concert of ravens that hour is already beginning to strike.

Twice within the course of this single day Brünnhilde believes she has reason to be pleased, and on each occasion she is mistaken. She sits alone in her rocky eyrie, a part of that perfect human being whose other half has returned to the old world and its loveless inhabitants. And here she waits. He whose love is whole has abandoned himself wholly. If he does not win himself back, he is lost. Suddenly dependent on human contact, Brünnhilde finally receives a visitor. It is not, however, the man she longs for but her sister Waltraute, who rides in on her air-borne steed, bringing the latest news from Valhalla.

The gods, having failed, have surrounded themselves with the piled-up logs from the World Ash, which has been felled on Wotan's instructions, and here they await their auto-da-fé. Only Brünnhilde could still change all this, Waltraute explains, if she were to return the ring to the Rhinedaughters. In plain English, this means that nature can be restored to its original state only if world dominion is renounced. In this way, the guilt of the gods who have destroyed that state will be expunged.

The hapless denizens of Valhalla have evidently failed to notice that world dominion has passed to the new man who has brought a spirit of reconciliation to the world through his love. The symbol of this age, which has begun with the union of Brünnhilde and Siegfried, is the ring. To abandon it would be tantamount to betraying love. 'One glance at its bright-shining gold, one flash of its noble fire,' Brünnhilde tells her sister, fully aware of her superiority, 'is worth far more to me than all the gods' eternal joy. For Siegfried's love shines blissfully forth from it!' As she knows very well, it is not in the depths of the Rhine but on her finger that the gold has finally dissolved into love. It is not the unconscious Rhinedaughters but the conscious woman who offers an answer to the riddle of history. Waltraute, Wotan's emissary, is sent packing.

But Brünnhilde has no answer to the riddle that is posed by her second visitor of the day. It seems to be Siegfried who is returning, seems to be his horn that she hears, while the flames appear to flare up more brightly than ever. In 'the utmost joy' and with the words 'into the arms of my god' on her lips, she rushes to meet the lover whom she so misses. Without him, she is 'no human being', whereas with him she is a goddess.

But the man who announces himself with Siegfried's horn call is not Siegfried. A stranger stands before her, leaning on an unknown shield and speaking in an eerily disguised voice. 'Betrayal!' she cries, but her cry sounds more like a despairing question. For who, apart from Siegfried, is meant to hear it? And against whom is this act of betrayal committed? Against her who sees herself defencelessly abandoned to a man even though she has long since bonded with another man to create a single entity? Or against Siegfried, who may have lost his hunting horn and, with it, his life, although she knows that he is unvanquishable?

And who – this is the most harrowing question – has shown the stranger the way to her rock, a path that she thought no mortal would find? As Wagner told Röckel, herein lies 'the terrible, demonic nature of this whole scene: . . . a "stranger" passes – effortlessly – through the fire which, in accord with his destiny and her own experience, none but Siegfried should or could traverse: everything collapses at Br.'s feet, everything is out of joint.' But who could have given this 'stranger' the power to pass through her celestial fire?

Not even her visitor could have answered these questions. For Siegfried is no longer Siegfried. Although he knows that the magic helmet has helped to turn him into his blood-brother in order to tame a shrew in his stead and although he is conscious, therefore, of this outward sense of alienation, there is an inner alienation that escapes his notice. What Siegfried has forgotten is not some other object, such as the woman he once loved, but himself. Only through Brünnhilde had he acquired this awareness, which he has now lost. The wrong body conceals the wrong heart. The man who has mutilated his outward appearance has long been inwardly deformed.

The former valkyrie, with her instinct for heroes, senses this. It is no man who stands before her but a ghost. Even before he has drawn any closer to her, she has seen through him as a 'demon', a wicked magician who, like an eagle, has come to tear her to pieces. The bird of prey – Wagner's archetypal image of the usurper – has supplanted the true lover, except that in this traumatic situation the lover, regarding himself as another's stand-in, is in fact usurping himself. The violence that he inflicts on the woman is committed against himself.

Like a sleepwalker mistakenly thinking himself awake, he declares Brünnhilde his property, a possession whose ownership must be sealed through physical union. He subjects her to another – the man he himself is playing – and forgets that he has already submitted to the rules of the other man's game. Within this game, he and the lover with whom he had merged as a single entity have been given roles to play that will mean their permanent separation. Driven from the Eden of divine love, they lose their dignity as human beings and become pawns on a stranger's chessboard. This reflects man's experience of himself in history: the atrocities committed against him are carried out by himself – and, like Siegfried, he remains unaware of this fact.

Brünnhilde has one last card she can play. By way of a deterrent, she holds out Siegfried's ring, which embodies the love that has left a whole world behind it. Would a usurper from that outdated age not be forced to yield to its power? Would the darkness of history not fade away before the bright light of liberated humanity? But if, as the glance in his eye suggests, it is Siegfried who stands before her, albeit a Siegfried alienated from himself and his bride by a magic spell, would the flash of the gold not wake him? The ring represents his love for Brünnhilde, and so it should restore his memory of her and hence of himself. In fact, as Hagen has already explained, the drink that was served to Siegfried would make him forget only the living woman. It would have no power over lifeless objects.

It remains a puzzle why Siegfried is not roused to his senses by the sight of his ring, as he must recognize it. But he says nothing to the unknown woman who incomprehensibly is wearing it. In much the same way he suppresses the knowledge because it consorts ill with the role he has now taken on. Instead of asking himself how his own property has gone missing, he immediately sets about winning it back. The result – the unbearable climax of their encounter – is an act of rape.

This painful event recurs on a generally subliminal level in most of Wagner's poems from *Leubald* onwards. In the case of *Rienzi* it had been depicted in obscenely graphic detail in the mimed account of the rape of Lucretia. But what now takes place achieves a new level of horror. It is as though the Roman Collatinus, dressed as the usurping Tarquinius, had returned to his waiting wife

Lucretia in order to subject her to his lubricious desires. In much the same way, Siegfried, mimicking Gunther, assaults his own bride.

Following the example of *Rienzi*, he wrestles with Brünnhilde, a struggle that the weaker of the two is bound to lose, in spite of her desperate resistance. 'In a terrible struggle', Wagner explained in his letter to Röckel, 'she is overpowered, she is "God-forsaken".' Just as Wotan once tore the ring from Alberich's finger, so Siegfried now tears it from his bride. But according to Wagner, her whole strength was preserved in this token of her love, and so she now collapses and 'complies'. In the twinkling of an eye the Paradise of new love has turned into a hell of betrayal and rape.

Although the Norse tradition describes the act of possession, symbolized by the wrested ring, Wagner's Siegfried consciously holds back. True, he lies with his booty in the 'rocky chamber' that was once his bedroom, but his oath of loyalty to Gunther and his tender regard for Gutrune prevent him from having his way with Brünnhilde. Ultimately, he prefers to play by the rules of the game.

'There is no doubt', Wagner wrote to Röckel after describing this appalling scene to him, 'that you feel that something "unspeakable" is taking place here.' It is unspeakable not least because we are dealing not with anything objective but with a process that takes place within the self-consciousness of the two participants. In fact, it is they alone who are affected, as these unfathomable events follow hard on the heels of their union, with the result that the torment for anyone aware of this is bound to be utterly unbearable.

And Brünnhilde is aware of it. She recognizes Siegfried from his radiant eye and at the same time is bound to despair in their radiance. For the godlike eye that awoke her from her valkyrie slumber only a short time previously now flashes with a rapaciousness reminiscent of a bird of prey. The youth who had sacrificed himself to her now sacrifices her to his own caprice. The supreme self-consciousness of love is transformed into the deepest humiliation of unawareness.

Neither the somnambulistic Siegfried nor Brünnhilde, who has woken up to the most terrible nightmare, is conscious of his or her true situation. The divine element has been lost in the darkness of matter, just as it had been following the first creation, and the memory of their former love survives only in the suffering caused by their dislocation. The world is once again shrouded in night.

With the following act of the tragedy, the day of consciousness dawns. As we might expect, this consciousness stems from a contradiction and – no less predictably – this is bound up with the ring. The ring entered Brünnhilde's life as a token of Siegfried's love, and since this love coincided with their indissoluble unity, it was also the embodiment of a freedom that no longer needed the gods for its own happiness. With the catastrophe of the rape perpetrated by a demon looking like Siegfried, the ring changed its whole nature, and the symbol of love became a token of the power that it had represented once before. The thief himself had defiantly proclaimed: 'Let it give Gunther a husband's rights; be wedded to him with the ring.'

When Brünnhilde is dragged down from her Valkyrie Rock into the depths of the Rhine valley, she is inevitably struck by inconsistencies. The man who, on board their ship, introduces himself as her abductor is undoubtedly not Siegfried but an ordinary mortal by the name of Gunther, who lacks not only the glittering serpent's eye that all the Wälsungs are said to possess but, more particularly, the little souvenir of a night of love from long ago. Since the time of her rape, the trinket has officially been designated the wedding ring with which Gunther married her. But he is not wearing it. Brünnhilde starts to suspect.

It is still night on stage. Hagen is sitting outside the Gibichung castle, silently watching the hall, while the River Rhine flows past. Has he fallen asleep? The old, bloodcurdling sounds of the Wolf's Glen stir, the rustling of ravens' feathers, cries of anguish from the underworld. He is caught in the lurid light of the moon that falls down through scraps of scudding clouds and that also lights a dwarflike figure crouching before him, its arms resting confidentially on his knees. It is his father.

Hagen is indeed asleep, and Alberich is the nightmare that haunts him incessantly. Betrayed, like Ahasuerus, by 'rest and sleep', he will not even allow his son to rest. The result is what Wagner described as an 'eerily dreamlike dialogue'[99] that he wrote down at a single sitting and that he later described as the high point of the first production of the *Ring*.[100] 'Can you hear me, Hagen, my son?' Alberich hisses. 'I hear you, evil elf,' his sleeping son replies, his eyes now open. He knows what his visitor wants to tell him as it was he who brought it about. Siegfried is again wearing the ring, the Nibelung prince reports, but 'even my curse grows feeble in the face of the fearless hero'.

A more cunning approach is called for. This will not be difficult, of course, as Siegfried 'burns his life away, laughing, in loving desire'. The flames of his desire are currently directed at Gutrune, and the fire is already spreading. Hagen simply needs to sit back and wait, and the problem of Siegfried will resolve itself. 'To his own undoing, he serves me even now,' he tells his tormentor. The self-consciousness that the lovers have lost has now passed to the side of evil. Evil has gained control, and its victims are already twitching convulsively in their death throes. Reassured, Alberich can return to the underworld.

Siegfried is soon back at the Gibichung court, once again the very image of a hero. He informs his fellow conspirators, Hagen and Gurtune, of the success of his mission. Hagen blows his horn, much as Siegmund's murderer, Hunding, had once done, and 'with curiously good-natured contentment', as Wagner describes it,[101] prepares the stage for the fatal confrontation.

The vassals, alarmed by Hagen's horn call, rush in, resolved to ward off what they assume is an imminent danger, only for Hagen to put them in the picture and tell them that he has been amusing himself at their expense. It is not war but a marriage that is on the agenda, so they should begin by slaughtering some steers. 'On the altar-stone let their blood flow for Wotan.' Needless to say, his announcement of his revenge is lost on these bearskin-clad vassals, who are used only to obeying orders. Still less do they understand his allusion to the fact that the bride has been won with the help of the 'dragon killer'. They simply do as they are bidden, and without turning a hair the master of manipulation ends by having them burst into raucous laughter at their own inveterate stupidity.

Brünnhilde can now be seen approaching on Gunther's arm. Her head bowed and her face drained of colour, as befits a new bride, she stands before the horde of vassals. The 'happy Gibichung' presents his latest acquisition, the happy mother of future generations. Shouts of 'hail' ring out. Brünnhilde has landed up in the world of laws and contracts over which her father Wotan had once held sway. Here all that counts is power, possessions and marriage. Once the god's right hand, she now plays a more modest role, passing into the possession of her husband like some lifeless object. Wotan's punishment for her disobedience seems to have come true after all. What she had earlier not even dared to imagine is now a terrifying reality.

Somewhat inhibitedly, Gunther now introduces her to her future brother-in-law and bashful sister-in-law, for he has plans for a double wedding: 'Brünnhilde – and Gunther, Gutrune – and Siegfried!' The valkyrie wakes up for a second time and sees Siegfried standing in front of her, the hoard of the world, grinning at her in his embarrassment. Just as Wotan's daughter has sunk to the level of sleeping with a coward, so the scion of Wotan has degenerated to the level of a courtier.

The laws of the old god are thus carved into the flesh of his children. In a flash, Brünnhilde seems to see through the shameful deception. Clearly aware of her situation, she still does not suspect, however, that she understands only as much as Hagen has allowed her to grasp. If Siegfried has, of necessity, been initiated into one aspect of the intrigue, Brünnhilde is now party to the other.

She openly looks the hero in the eyes, and he returns her gaze, shocked by the intensity of her stare. Naturally he feels that he has been seen through, and she reads this in his eyes. But they are thinking of different things. He thinks that the stranger has seen through the change of masks, whereas she thinks that the change of masks was merely the result of a change of mind and that, as his ex-lover, she is the price that he has paid for a new one. In the world of laws and contracts it matters little that one woman is exchanged for another, as long as the transaction is sealed by a marriage contract.

But the same world of laws is insistent on clear property conditions. As Wotan's daughter, Brünnhilde knows that Siegfried cannot be indicted for betraying his love, however flagrant that betrayal may be. But the situation takes on a different complexion if recent events can be seen as a crime against property. The perspective abruptly changes. She faints in Siegfried's arms and quite by chance discovers the missing ring on his finger, pointing to the corpus delicti and, according to the stage directions, shouting 'with terrible violence'. In his role as director, Hagen invites his esteemed audience to pay close attention: 'Mark closely now what the woman discloses.'

Brünnhilde's indictment sounds plausible. The wedding breakfast becomes a tribunal. The ring glittering on Siegfried's finger, she states, belongs not to him but to Gunther, who took it from her while staking his claim to her as one of his possessions. In wearing the ring, the hero is laying claim to another man's property. 'If you took from me the ring by which I was wed to you,' she tells Gunther, who is so embarrassed that he wishes the ground would open and swallow him up, 'then tell him of your right to it, demand the token back!' Brünnhilde now knows for certain that it was Siegfried who visited her on her rock, and so this becomes a move in a game of chess that allows her to check-mate both men at once. If they had played for her with the trick of a cheap dis-guise, she will now play the two fools off against one another. As yet she does not suspect that she is merely aping Hagen the grandmaster, much as Gunther and Siegfried had done.

Now that she understands her situation, her despair turns to the sort of aggression that befits a valkyrie. Dealing with death is all in a day's work for her. Her attack, launched by an apparently half-conscious woman, takes both trai-tors by surprise. Gunther stutteringly suggests that she may have mixed up the rings, while Siegfried, with a clear conscience but an unpleasant aftertaste, assures his listeners that he won it honestly by killing a dragon. None of this helps to resolve the dilemma. Hagen needs to stoke the fires of passion only a little more and the whole of the Gibichung court will go up in flames.

Buoyed up by her old belligerence, the valkyrie now appears in as unfavourable a light as her lost bridegroom. He had taken the first step on the road to destroying their love, and now she follows this up with a second, no less radical step. Her grandstanding naïvety is a sham, for she now knows all too well what has happened. For the present, however, she is so blinded by her fury that she cannot conceive of the idea that she is not the only victim of the intrigue. She literally throws herself into a state of frenzied jealousy, so that her former lover is turned into a hideous caricature. She has only one desire, to slake her thirst for vengeance. 'Deceit!' she cries, forgetting all the wisdom that normally distinguishes her. 'Most shameful deceit! Betrayal! Betrayal – as never before avenged!' Now that she thinks she knows the truth, thought is replaced by desire. And she desires Siegfried's death.

What this proves, however, is that their loving unity persists. For what the young god has done to her she now repays in kind. It is no longer a question of 'eye to eye' but of 'an eye for an eye' and of inflicting on Siegfried the same sort of harm that he has caused her. If the emotion of love has misled him into forgetting his lover, she now allows the emotion of anger to provoke her into committing a like atrocity. Had she remained true to her love, she would never have been able to doubt him.

Like Siegfried, Brünnhilde now strips away the new identity that she had acquired through her love and reverts to her former self. Just as her bridegroom has once again become the ruthlessly thoughtless wild man of the woods, so she falls prey to the valkyrie's callous cold-heartedness. Having relapsed into their former ways, they both indulge in equally dirty tricks, Siegfried in order to hand over his lover to Gunther, Brünnhilde in order to hand over her lover for Gunther to kill.

In her fury, she betrays the mystery of their erstwhile love. Siegfried, she declares, forced 'pleasure and love' from her, revealing him not just as a liar but as a criminal who has sinned against his blood-brother's property. Siegfried naturally denies this, saying that he took the ring but not her virginity – he has forgotten, of course, that he had indeed taken her maidenhead only a few days earlier, albeit in very different circumstances. But Brünnhilde cleverly refers to that sacred night of love that no one could know about save herself and the accused, and in this way she denounces their godlike union as a violation, thereby more than making up for Siegfried's betrayal of her.

Each has betrayed the other. And both believe that they understand everything, while suspecting virtually nothing. They bandy oaths, each of them swearing 'by the point of their spear' that the other is a liar. Siegfried will forfeit his life if he is found guilty of an untruth, and Brünnhilde confirms this by claiming that his guilt is already proven. Hagen selflessly places his spear at their disposal. As the guardian of the law, he assures them that it will 'honour their oath'. The two lovers have turned into mortal enemies. 'Recall the oaths that unite us', Brünnhilde had entreated her lover on the morning after their night of love. Now they are united in swearing oaths on Hagen's spear.

During their violent exchange, Brünnhilde is clearly struck by a thought that is not part of Hagen's plan. Although Siegfried thinks he knows exactly why the 'wild mountain woman' is consumed by anger, he still asks her the hypocritical question 'what demon's cunning craft' can be responsible. The idea takes root, and, pensively, she later repeats his words: 'What demon's art lies hidden here? What store of magic stirred this up?'

She begins to suspect that none of this bears the hallmarks of the guileless Siegfried, and with this suspicion comes her old feeling of love. As before, he continues to hold sway over her, binding her to him with bonds that she cannot understand but which she is unable to break. 'Who'll offer me now the sword with which to sever those bonds?' Even while she desires Siegfried's death, she cannot forget their first encounter when his sword severed the bonds that constrained her.

Fate wills it that she recounts the riddle of the demon to the demon in person and seeks deliverance from her 'sorrow' from the sorcerer who caused it. Hagen, who had earlier offered himself as an honest broker, willing to represent both their interests, wastes no more time but counsels Siegfried's death. His crimes are obvious: he has betrayed not only his blood-brother Gunther but also the latter's wife-to-be, so the sentence is demanded not least by reasons of state. Nor does it take long to find the official version of his death: he will be killed in a hunting accident.

The world of laws and contracts that seemed to have been written off is still fully operational, and the Nibelungs, still grieving for their hoard, can draw new hope from this. In a darkly demonic act of consecration Wotan's three descendants unite in a common chorale on the subject of death. While Gunther and Brünnhilde appeal to Wotan as an 'avenging god' and as the 'guardian of vows', entreating his help in murdering Siegfried, Hagen beseeches the help of Alberich, a 'fallen prince' and the 'father of elves'.

With this dissonant discord, the final doubts have been swept aside: both Light-Alberich and Night-Alberich are rendering outstanding service to the destruction of the world.

Empirically, however, the destruction of the world precedes the dawning of self-consciousness. Unless he understands his own history, the new man will gain no self-understanding. Strictly speaking, he would then not exist at all. The human couple of the future has been wrenched from its dreamlike state in order to experience for itself the alienation of creation. When they meet again,